To: Don
From: Al Mar'ers & Jan
In Christmas Love!

Truth for Today
Commentary

EDDIE CLOER, D.MIN.
GENERAL EDITOR

DAVID STEWART, M.A.R.
ASSISTANT EDITOR

DON SHACKELFORD, TH.D.
ASSOCIATE OLD TESTAMENT EDITOR

DUANE WARDEN, PH.D.
ASSOCIATE NEW TESTAMENT EDITOR

Truth for Today
Commentary

An Exegesis & Application of the Holy Scriptures

Jeremiah 26–52
and
Lamentations

Dayton Keesee

Resource □
Publications

2205 Benton
Searcy, AR 72143

Truth for Today Commentary
Jeremiah 26—52 and Lamentations
Copyright © 2011 by Resource Publications
2205 Benton, Searcy, AR 72143

All rights reserved. No portion of the text of this book may be reproduced in any form without the written permission of the publisher.

ISBN: 978-0-9837098-0-0

Scripture taken from the NEW AMERICAN STANDARD BIBLE®, © Copyright 1960, 1962, 1963, 1968, 1971, 1972, 1973, 1975, 1977, 1995 by The Lockman Foundation. Used by permission. (www.Lockman.org)

Contents

Editor's Preface	vii
Abbreviations	ix
Hebrew Transliteration	xi

Jeremiah

Jeremiah 26—52 — 1

The Expanded Outline	3
Chapter 26: God's Prophet on Trial	9
Chapter 27: The Years of the Yoke of Babylon	23
Chapter 28: False and True Prophets	35
Chapter 29: A Message to the Captives	45
Chapter 30: Restoring the Fortunes of God's People	61
Chapter 31: Restoration and Redemption	78
Chapter 32: A Deed Declaring Hope in Troubled Times	108
Chapter 33: God's Visit of His Prophet in Prison	129
Chapter 34: Disobedience Leading to Defeat	144
Chapter 35: The Rechabites Versus Judah	157
Chapter 36: The Power and Impact of God's Message	170
Chapter 37: Payment for Prophesying: Imprisonment	187
Chapter 38: Zedekiah: A Weak and Wavering King	199
Chapter 39: Jerusalem's Fall to Babylon	216
Chapter 40: The Follow-up After Jerusalem's Fall	230
Chapter 41: The Assassination of Gedaliah	242
Chapter 42: The Remnant's Course	254
Chapter 43: Migrating to Egypt	267
Chapter 44: A Final Glimpse of Jeremiah	280
Chapter 45: God's Message to Baruch	301
Chapter 46: The Judgment of Egypt	310
Chapter 47: The Judgment of Philistia	329
Chapter 48: The Judgment of Moab	337
Chapter 49: The Judgment of Other Nations	360
Chapter 50: The Judgment of Babylon, 1	382

Chapter 51:	The Judgment of Babylon, 2	406
Chapter 52:	A Review of Judah's Ruin	431

LAMENTATIONS

Introduction		453
The Expanded Outline		467
Chapter 1:	A City Suffering from Sin	471
Chapter 2:	The City and Its Creator	491
Chapter 3:	The Cry of the Distressed Prophet	508
Chapter 4:	The Cost of Sin	535
Chapter 5:	A Penitent Plea	550

Appendix: Maps and Charts	565
Selected Bibliography	583
Have You Heard . . . About Truth for Today?	589

Editor's Preface

This volume called *Jeremiah 26—52 and Lamentations* is a continuation of the series of commentaries on the Holy Scriptures that aspire to cover, the Lord willing, every book in God's divine revelation to us. With this commentary, twenty-one volumes in this series have now been completed: *Exodus*; *Job*; *Psalms 1—50*; *Psalms 51—89*; *Isaiah*; *Jeremiah 1—25*; *Jeremiah 26—52 and Lamentations*; *Ezekiel*; *The Life of Christ, 1*; *The Life of Christ, 2*; *Matthew 1—13*; *Matthew 14—28*; *Acts 1—14*; *Acts 15—28*; *Ephesians and Philippians*; *Colossians and Philemon*; *1 & 2 Thessalonians*; *Hebrews*; *1 & 2 Peter and Jude*; *Revelation 1—11*; and *Revelation 12—22*.

A comprehensive undertaking of this kind is quite ambitious, but it is of great value. We hope to publish three or four commentaries each year until the set is finished. May the Lord in His gracious providence allow us to reach the goal we have envisioned. More important, let us pray that each commentary will be a faithful servant in the proclaiming of God's truth on earth.

Any study of the Scriptures should be predicated upon the understanding that the Word of God—and the Word of God alone—is our guide to truth. A commentary must never be seen as taking the place of God's Word; it must be viewed as a printed teacher that seeks to guide the reader to a better understanding of the Word that God has given.

The author of this volume does not intend for his comments on the Scriptures to be regarded as infallible; he knows that he is subject to mistakes, as is every scholar. In writing a commentary such as this one, the author only wishes to share with others the fruits of his lifelong study of the Scriptures.

Dayton Keesee, the author of this two-volume set, holds a B.A. degree from Abilene Christian University and an M.A. from Butler University in Indianapolis, Indiana. He has also done special studies in language and counseling.

One of brother Keesee's great loves has been local preaching and teaching. He has served as a full-time preacher in Indiana, Texas, and Louisiana. His pulpit preaching has led local churches to grow in the Word of God.

In scholarship and diligence he has made a tremendous contribution to spirituality in the land by teaching young men in the classroom. For twenty-one years he taught at the Sunset School of Preaching in Lubbock, Texas. As an author, brother Keesee has written works on *Restoration Revival: The Way (Back) to God*; *Hebrews: A Heavenly Homily*; *A Re-Evaluation of the Eldership*; *Teacher Training Tools*; *A Chronological Survey of the Old Testament*; and *The Churches of Christ during the Civil War*. He has especially enjoyed teaching the Book of Jeremiah through his life as a preacher and teacher. This two-volume work on Jeremiah and Lamentations will take its place among the most valuable commentaries that have been written on these two books.

Good commentaries are not easily written. They actually require a team that is made up of the author, the editors, the stylists, and the proofreaders. Suggestions and helpful comments have come from many sources and people.

So far as we know, the churches of Christ have never completed a multi-authored commentary series on the entire Bible. We hope, by God's grace, that we may provide such a set. We trust that this will be one of the finest legacies that we can leave the generations who follow us. May each volume that we produce result from diligent scholarship and a faithful handling of the Scriptures.

Let us join together, as brothers and sisters bought by Christ's blood, and work together until the task of this commentary set is completed.

Eddie Cloer
General Editor

Abbreviations

OLD TESTAMENT

Genesis	Gen.	Ecclesiastes	Eccles.
Exodus	Ex.	Song of Solomon	Song
Leviticus	Lev.	Isaiah	Is.
Numbers	Num.	Jeremiah	Jer.
Deuteronomy	Deut.	Lamentations	Lam.
Joshua	Josh.	Ezekiel	Ezek.
Judges	Judg.	Daniel	Dan.
Ruth	Ruth	Hosea	Hos.
1 Samuel	1 Sam.	Joel	Joel
2 Samuel	2 Sam.	Amos	Amos
1 Kings	1 Kings	Obadiah	Obad.
2 Kings	2 Kings	Jonah	Jon.
1 Chronicles	1 Chron.	Micah	Mic.
2 Chronicles	2 Chron.	Nahum	Nahum
Ezra	Ezra	Habakkuk	Hab.
Nehemiah	Neh.	Zephaniah	Zeph.
Esther	Esther	Haggai	Hag.
Job	Job	Zechariah	Zech.
Psalms	Ps.	Malachi	Mal.
Proverbs	Prov.		

NEW TESTAMENT

Matthew	Mt.	1 Timothy	1 Tim.
Mark	Mk.	2 Timothy	2 Tim.
Luke	Lk.	Titus	Tit.
John	Jn.	Philemon	Philem.
Acts	Acts	Hebrews	Heb.
Romans	Rom.	James	Jas.
1 Corinthians	1 Cor.	1 Peter	1 Pet.
2 Corinthians	2 Cor.	2 Peter	2 Pet.
Galatians	Gal.	1 John	1 Jn.
Ephesians	Eph.	2 John	2 Jn.
Philippians	Phil.	3 John	3 Jn.
Colossians	Col.	Jude	Jude
1 Thessalonians	1 Thess.	Revelation	Rev.
2 Thessalonians	2 Thess.		

AB	Amplified Bible
ASV	American Standard Version
CEV	Contemporary English Version
KJV	King James Version
NASB	New American Standard Bible
NCV	New Century Version
NEB	New English Bible
NIV	New International Version
NJB	New Jerusalem Bible
NJPSV	New Jewish Publication Society Version (*Tanakh*)
NKJV	New King James Version
NLT	New Living Translation
NRSV	New Revised Standard Version
REB	Revised English Bible
RSV	Revised Standard Version
TEV	Today's English Version

HEBREW TRANSLITERATION

Studying the Word of God in the original languages brings out more fully the richness of the biblical texts. This series attempts to incorporate a healthy number of Greek and Hebrew words that help clarify the passages under investigation. Although translating and transliterating are difficult tasks with any language, Hebrew poses a particular challenge. First, it is an old language, and spelling and pronunciation have evolved over time. Second, there are multiple methods for transliterating Hebrew words into English. Therefore, the editorial committee has discussed how we will transliterate Hebrew, and we have adapted our own method for the series. It is assumed that not all of our readers will have a working knowledge of Hebrew. Our system attempts to present a transliteration that will simplify pronunciation and assist in word studies. In order to accomplish this, we have applied the following rules throughout the commentary.

Rule 1. No difference is indicated by the hard/soft pronunciation of "Begad Kapath" letters: תתפפככ דדגגבב. The meaning of a word is not affected by whether or not these letters are hard or soft.

Rule 2. When the *Daghesh Forte* indicates a doubling of consonants, the letter is doubled in the transliteration.

Rule 3. The Tetragrammaton (יְהוָה) is transliterated *YHWH* and written "Yahweh" in the text. Since the original vowel pointings are unknown for this word, they have been left out when it appears in the commentary, thus forming יהוה.

Rule 4. The transliteration distinguishes between ה when used as a consonant and ה when used as a vowel letter to lengthen the vowel *Qamets*.

Rule 5. The vocalized *sheva* is indicated by ᵉ.

Rule 6. Since the word "torah" (law) is a commonly known word, the ת that begins this word is transliterated as *t* rather than *th*.

Examples of transliterated words:

לְדָוִד, *lᵉdawid*; חַטָּאִים, *chatta'im*; תּוֹרָה, *torah*; אַשְׁרֵי, *'ashrey*; and אִישׁ, *'ish*

Consonants

There are twenty-three consonants in the Hebrew text. They are listed below by name, Hebrew symbol, and transliteration.

Name	Hebrew	Transliteration
Aleph	א	'
Beth	ב	b
Gimel	ג	g
Daleth	ד	d
He	ה	h
Vav	ו	w
Zayin	ז	z
Heth	ח	ch
Teth	ט	t
Yodh	י	y
Kaph	ך כ	k
Lamedh	ל	l
Mem	ם מ	m
Nun	ן נ	n
Samekh	ס	s
Ayin	ע	'
Pe	ף פ	p
Tsadhe	ץ צ	ts
Qoph	ק	q
Resh	ר	r
Sin	שׂ	ś
Shin	שׁ	sh
Tav	ת	th

Vowels

The vowels in Hebrew are used more for determining the form of a word rather than the root meaning. We have tried to differentiate between these vowels to help guide their pronunciation and grammatical function. They are listed here by name, Hebrew symbol, and transliteration.

Name	Hebrew	Transliteration
Qamets	ָ	*a* (long)
Patach	ַ	*a* (short)
Tsere	ֵ	*e* (long)
Segol	ֶ	*e* (short)
Hireq Yodh	יִ	*i* (long)
Hireq	ִ	*i* (short)
Qamets Yodh	יָ	*ay*
Segol Yodh	יֶ	*ey*
Tsere Yodh	יֵ	*ey*
Holem	וֹ	*o* (long)
Qamets-Hatuph	ָ	*o* (short)
Shureq	וּ	*u* (long)
Qibbuts	ֻ	*u* (short)
Hatep-Patach	ֲ	*a*
Hatep-Segol	ֱ	*e*
Hatep-Qamets	ֳ	*o*

Suggested Hebrew Grammar Books

For further study of the Hebrew language, we recommend the following books:

Kelly, Page H. *Biblical Hebrew: An Introduction Grammar*. Grand Rapids, Mich.: Wm. B. Eerdmans Publishing Co., 1992.

Pratico, Gary D. and Miles Van Pelt. *Basics of Biblical Hebrew Grammar*. Grand Rapids, Mich.: Zondervan, 2001. This book includes an interactive CD-ROM.

Seow, Choon Leong. *A Grammar for Biblical Hebrew*. Nashville: Abingdon Press, 1987.

Weingreen, J. *A Practical Grammar for Classical Hebrew*, 2d ed. New York: Oxford University Press, 1959.

The Expanded Outline
Jeremiah 26—52

II. JEREMIAH'S PROPHECIES AGAINST JUDAH AND JERUSALEM (2—45) (continued)
- Y. God's Prophet on Trial (26:1–24)
  1. The sermon in the temple courts (26:1–7)
  2. The sentence proposed for God's prophet (26:8–11)
  3. The statement in rebuttal by God's prophet (26:12–15)
  4. The suit against Jeremiah appealed (26:16–19)
  5. The sentence of death illustrated (26:20–23)
  6. The saving influence of a friend (26:24)
- Z. The Years of the Yoke of Babylon (27:1–22)
  1. Warnings to the nations (27:1–11)
  2. Warnings to Zedekiah, king of Judah (27:12–15)
  3. Warnings to the priests and to all the people (27:16–22)
- AA. False and True Prophets (28:1–17)
  1. The report by a false prophet, Hananiah (28:1–4)
  2. The response by Jeremiah (28:5–9)
  3. The reaction by Hananiah (28:10, 11)
  4. The results of a false prophet and the people's rebellion (28:12–17)
- BB. A Message to the Captives (29:1–32)
  1. A plea with plans for the present (29:1–7)
  2. Present problems and promises for the future (29:8–14)
  3. Perils the people would face (29:15–20)
  4. Perils the false prophets would undergo among the captives (29:21–32)

CC. Restoring the Fortunes of God's People (30:1–24)
  1. God's promise that their problems would pass (30:1–11)
  2. God's view of the problem and His solution to it (30:12–17)
  3. God's promises of glory restored (30:18–22)
  4. God's pattern and plan made clear (30:23, 24)
DD. Restoration and Redemption (31:1–40)
  1. The past reviewed and a loving promise made (31:1–9)
  2. A preview of pleasantness (31:10–14)
  3. The return to be made possible by penitence (31:15–22)
  4. The sweet perception of the promise (31:23–30)
  5. The prophetic promise of the new covenant (31:31–34)
  6. Proof for these promises (31:35–40)
EE. A Deed Declaring Hope in Troubled Times (32:1–44)
  1. Prophecy of a return backed by the purchase of a field (32:1–15)
  2. The prophet's prayer—a tribute to God (32:16–25)
  3. The polluted people and God's future plans (32:26–44)
FF. God's Visit of His Prophet in Prison (33:1–26)
  1. A prediction of restoration (33:1–13)
  2. A promise of a reign of righteousness (33:14–26)
GG. Disobedience Leading to Defeat (34:1–22)
  1. The decree of death for Zedekiah (34:1–7)
  2. Their disobedience to God's command to release slaves (34:8–16)
  3. The desolation resulting from their departure (34:17–22)
HH. The Rechabites Versus Judah (35:1–19)
  1. The Rechabites' example of faithfulness (35:1–11)
  2. Judah's refusal to listen (35:12–16)
  3. The Lord's reward and punishment (35:17–19)
II. The Power and Impact of God's Message (36:1–32)
  1. The message transcribed (36:1–7)

THE EXPANDED OUTLINE

      2. The message's impact on various people (36:8–20)
      3. The message's impact on the king (36:21–26)
      4. The message rewritten and punishment for the king (36:27–32)
  JJ. Payment for Prophesying: Imprisonment (37:1–21)
      1. God's message sought but not accepted (37:1–5)
      2. God's promise of punishment (37:6–10)
      3. God's prophet incarcerated (37:11–16)
      4. God's providence for His prophet (37:17–21)
KK. Zedekiah: A Weak and Wavering King (38:1–28)
      1. His consent to charges against Jeremiah (38:1–6)
      2. His support of a eunuch's suggestion for Jeremiah (38:7–13)
      3. His request for counsel from Jeremiah (38:14–23)
      4. His demand for Jeremiah's silence (38:24–28)
  LL. Jerusalem's Fall to Babylon (39:1–18)
      1. God's prophecy concerning Jerusalem fulfilled (39:1–10)
      2. God's providence for His prophet (39:11–14)
      3. God's provision for a trusting eunuch (39:15–18)
MM. The Follow-up After Jerusalem's Fall (40:1–16)
      1. Jeremiah set free (40:1–5)
      2. Judah's provincial government set up by Babylon (40:6–12)
      3. Johanan's attempt to protect Gedaliah (40:13–16)
  NN. The Assassination of Gedaliah (41:1–18)
      1. The murder at mealtime (41:1–3)
      2. The murders that followed (41:4–10)
      3. The multiplied tragedy (41:11–18)
  OO. The Remnant's Course (42:1–22)
      1. The people's question: "What should we do?" (42:1–6)
      2. God's answer: "Stay in this land!" (42:7–18)
      3. Jeremiah's word to the disobedient: "You will die!" (42:19–22)
  PP. Migrating to Egypt (43:1–13)
      1. Rejecting the prophet's message (43:1–4)
      2. Entering Egypt (43:5–7)

3. Prophecy uttered in Egypt (43:8–13)
QQ. A Final Glimpse of Jeremiah (44:1–30)
  1. Their past punishment (44:1–6)
  2. Their current condition (44:7–14)
  3. Their persistent rebellion (44:15–19)
  4. The divine perception (44:20–27)
  5. The promise of God's power (44:28–30)
RR. God's Message to Baruch (45:1–5)
  1. His interest in Baruch (45:1, 2)
  2. His insight into Baruch's mood (45:3)
  3. His message for Baruch (45:4)
  4. His mercy to Baruch (45:5)

III. JEREMIAH'S PROPHECIES AGAINST THE NATIONS (46—51)
  A. The Judgment of Egypt (46:1–28)
    1. The fall at Carchemish (46:1–12)
    2. Egypt's ultimate fall (46:13–26)
    3. God's encouragement for His scattered people (46:27, 28)
  B. The Judgment of Philistia (47:1–7)
    1. Authority and destination (47:1)
    2. The power coming "from the north" (47:2, 3)
    3. The complete fall (47:4, 5)
    4. The cry of "Enough!" (47:6, 7)
  C. The Judgment of Moab (48:1–47)
    1. Self-sufficiency (48:1–6)
    2. No escape (48:7–10)
    3. Disturbed (48:11–25)
    4. Shame and reproach (48:26–29)
    5. The lament of God (48:30–39)
    6. The conqueror's arrival (48:40–46)
    7. The hope of restoration (48:47)
  D. The Judgment of Other Nations (49:1–39)
    1. Ammon to the east (49:1–6)
    2. Edom in the heights (49:7–22)
    3. Damascus to the north (49:23–27)
    4. Kedar and Hazor (49:28–33)

           5. Elam, far to the east (49:34–39)
       E. The Judgment of Babylon (50:1—51:64)
           1. Survey of the cause for Babylon's fall (50:1–46)
               a. Babylon's fall (50:1, 2)
               b. The open door (50:3–10)
               c. A heritage of shame (50:11–13)
               d. The vengeance of the Lord (50:14–16)
               e. A scattered flock (50:17–19)
               f. The day has come (50:20–32)
               g. A song of redemption (50:33, 34)
               h. The mighty sword (50:35–37)
               i. The idol (50:38–40)
               j. Forces and sources (50:41–46)
           2. Further description of Babylon's fall (51:1–64)
               a. "The spirit of a destroyer" (51:1–14)
               b. God, the great Judge (51:15–26)
               c. The consecration of nations (51:27–33)
               d. The cause for conquest (51:34–44)
               e. Final instructions (51:45–51)
               f. God's summary (51:52–58)
               g. A unique method (51:59–64)

IV. A REVIEW OF JUDAH'S RUIN (52:1–34)
    A. The Last King's Evil Reign (52:1, 2)
    B. The Long Siege of the City (52:3–6)
    C. The King and His Sons Sentenced (52:7–11)
    D. Jerusalem and the Temple Destroyed (52:12–23)
    E. Judgment Passed (52:24–30)
    F. Jehoiachin Enthroned in Babylon, Offering a Ray of Hope (52:31–34)

CHAPTER 26
GOD'S PROPHET ON TRIAL

In this chapter, Jeremiah delivered a sermon of Jerusalem's doom in the temple courts (26:1–7). The prophets, priests, and the people responded to his message by calling for his death (26:8–11). With great boldness, Jeremiah defended himself by claiming that God had sent him to speak (26:12–15). The elders, the officials, and the people were persuaded by Jeremiah. They cited the prophet Micah as a precedent for pronouncing doom and bringing about deliverance for Jerusalem (26:16–19). A parenthetical section records the death of the prophet Uriah, one of Jeremiah's contemporaries, by King Jehoiakim. This example underscores the fact that Jeremiah could have been killed for proclaiming this message from God (26:20–23). The chapter ends with Jeremiah's life being spared (26:24).

Chronology may again be a question, since these events occurred at the beginning of Jehoiakim's reign (26:1), while those of chapter 25 were in the fourth year of his reign (25:1). Chapter 26 is obviously in the early part of Jehoiakim's reign because he was on good terms with Egypt (26:21, 22). This was not true in the fourth year, for Nebuchadnezzar had invaded and made Jehoiakim his vassal (2 Kings 23:34—24:1). (See comments on chapter 7 concerning the first temple sermon.)

THE SERMON IN THE TEMPLE COURTS (26:1–7)

¹In the beginning of the reign of Jehoiakim the son of Josiah, king of Judah, this word came from the LORD, saying, ²"Thus says the LORD, 'Stand in the court of the LORD's house,

and speak to all the cities of Judah who have come to worship in the LORD's house all the words that I have commanded you to speak to them. Do not omit a word! ³Perhaps they will listen and everyone will turn from his evil way, that I may repent of the calamity which I am planning to do to them because of the evil of their deeds.' ⁴And you will say to them, 'Thus says the LORD, "If you will not listen to Me, to walk in My law which I have set before you, ⁵to listen to the words of My servants the prophets, whom I have been sending to you again and again, but you have not listened; ⁶then I will make this house like Shiloh, and this city I will make a curse to all the nations of the earth."'"

⁷The priests and the prophets and all the people heard Jeremiah speaking these words in the house of the LORD.

Verse 1. On this occasion, Jeremiah's temple sermon is dated to **the beginning of the reign of Jehoiakim the son of Josiah, king of Judah**. Since Jehoiakim reigned over Judah from 609 to 598 B.C., "the beginning" of his reign could refer to the accession year, that is, 609/8 B.C. Another possibility is that it simply means "early" in his reign (see 28:1).

Verse 2. God instructed Jeremiah to **stand in the court of the LORD's house**. Douglas Rawlinson Jones proposed that Jeremiah was to position himself "at the gate between the inner and outer court."[1] The prophet was then called to **speak to all the cities of Judah who** [had] **come to worship**. During the festivals, people from throughout the land gathered at the temple in Jerusalem. If anyone would hear God and respect His prophet, it should have been this group.

God told Jeremiah to convey to the people everything that He had **commanded** him. God's directions to Jeremiah were specific: **"Do not omit a word!"** "Omit" comes from the Hebrew word גָּרַע (*gara'*), meaning "diminish," "restrain," or "withdraw."[2] No doubt Jeremiah knew the possible implications of a hostile

---

[1]Douglas Rawlinson Jones, *Jeremiah*, The New Century Bible Commentary (Grand Rapids, Mich.: Wm. B. Eerdmans Publishing Co., 1992), 341.
[2]Francis Brown, S. R. Driver, and Charles A. Briggs, *A Hebrew and English Lexicon of the Old Testament* (Oxford: Clarendon Press, 1972), 175.

crowd. It would have been tempting to leave out the harsher elements of the message and avoid conflict—especially in light of the prophet Uriah's death (26:20–23).

Verse 3. Besides Jeremiah's need to speak faithfully, Judah had a twofold responsibility. First, they had to **listen** to ensure a positive response to what was right and good (see 7:24, 27; 11:11; 25:3). Second, each person had to **turn from his evil way** to correct his negative conduct.

True to God's longsuffering nature, if only Judah would do these things, then God would **repent of the calamity which** [He was] **planning** to pour out on them (19:15; 25:29). The Hebrew word for "repent" (נָחַם, *nacham*) could also be translated "relent" or "change [His] mind" (4:28; 18:8).

Verses 4–6. God's plan was conditional. If they would **not listen** and obey His **law**, which had been their pattern, then the warning in a previous temple sermon (7:8–15) would stand.

God said that, in the past, the people had failed to **listen** to **My servants the prophets**. This phrase is a common expression in the Old Testament (7:25; 29:19; 35:15; 44:4; 2 Kings 9:7; 17:13; Ezek. 38:17; Zech. 1:6). It emphasizes that these messengers were speaking on behalf of the Lord. God had sent them **again and again**. A more literal translation is "both rising up early, and sending them" (KJV) (see comments on 7:13).

The Lord's warning was clear: **This house** (temple) would be devastated, **like Shiloh**, and **this city** (Jerusalem) would be **a curse to all the nations of the earth**. For the temple to be relegated to a similar fate as Shiloh was a tragedy indeed (see 26:9). Not far away from there, thirty thousand Israelites were slaughtered by the Philistines in battle, and the ark of the covenant was taken as plunder (see comments on 7:12, 14, 15). It may be that Shiloh was also leveled at this time. While the tabernacle at Shiloh was not destroyed (1 Kings 8:4; 2 Chron. 1:3; 5:4, 5), God did abandon it (Ps. 78:60, 61).

Verse 7. Jeremiah faithfully obeyed God, declaring the message he had been commissioned to speak. Due to his prime location at the temple (26:2), **the priests and the prophets and all the people heard** [him] **speaking these words**. Their reaction is recorded in the next section.

THE SENTENCE PROPOSED FOR GOD'S PROPHET (26:8–11)

⁸When Jeremiah finished speaking all that the Lord had commanded him to speak to all the people, the priests and the prophets and all the people seized him, saying, "You must die! ⁹Why have you prophesied in the name of the Lord saying, 'This house will be like Shiloh and this city will be desolate, without inhabitant'?" And all the people gathered about Jeremiah in the house of the Lord.

¹⁰When the officials of Judah heard these things, they came up from the king's house to the house of the Lord and sat in the entrance of the New Gate of the Lord's house. ¹¹Then the priests and the prophets spoke to the officials and to all the people, saying, "A death sentence for this man! For he has prophesied against this city as you have heard in your hearing."

Verses 8, 9. The animosity which had been brewing in this vast audience of **priests, prophets,** and **people** from the cities of Judah did not boil over until **Jeremiah [had] finished speaking all that the Lord had commanded him to speak.** The crowd was greatly offended by the message of Jerusalem's desolation, and their conclusion was clear: **"You must die!"** They surrounded Jeremiah and would not let him escape. Jones called attention to their legal justification:

> Their vendetta against Jeremiah had a legal justification which no doubt gave them a warm feeling of self-righteousness. Once they had persuaded themselves that Jeremiah was a false prophet, they were required by the [Deuteronomic] law (Dt. 13) to put him to death.³

Verse 10. As the turmoil spread to **the king's house, the officials of Judah** came to **the Lord's house.** The title "officials" comes from the Hebrew word שַׂר (śar), which has a broad range of meaning. It can denote a "king," "representative of the king,"

---

³Jones, 342.

"commander," "leader of a group," or "person of note."[4] Here the term probably indicates representatives of the king, since they had come from his palace. Certainly, they had jurisdiction over matters pertaining to Jerusalem.

These officials set up a hearing at **the New Gate** (36:10). Gates often had rooms where business was transacted and legal matters were resolved (Gen. 23:10; Ruth 4:1; Prov. 31:23). The exact location of the New Gate is uncertain.

Verse 11. The priests and the prophets became prosecutors before **the officials** and **all the people**, demanding, **"A death sentence for this man!"** (see Deut. 13:5; 18:20). They were upset because Jeremiah had **prophesied against** the holy city Jerusalem. Declaring that the Lord's house would be treated like Shiloh seemed to be a blasphemous impossibility to these people. In their eyes, God would never allow such a thing to happen when they were innocent (2:35; 18:18).

THE STATEMENT IN REBUTTAL BY GOD'S PROPHET (26:12–15)

[12]Then Jeremiah spoke to all the officials and to all the people, saying, "The Lord sent me to prophesy against this house and against this city all the words that you have heard. [13]Now therefore amend your ways and your deeds and obey the voice of the Lord your God; and the Lord will change His mind about the misfortune which He has pronounced against you. [14]But as for me, behold, I am in your hands; do with me as is good and right in your sight. [15]Only know for certain that if you put me to death, you will bring innocent blood on yourselves, and on this city and on its inhabitants; for truly the Lord has sent me to you to speak all these words in your hearing."

Were God's words in 1:17–19 going through Jeremiah's mind at this pressure-filled moment? Mob action is unpredictable and

---

[4]Ludwig Koehler and Walter Baumgartner, *The Hebrew and Aramaic Lexicon of the Old Testament*, study ed., trans. and ed. M. E. J. Richardson (Boston: Brill, 2001), 2:1350–53.

often irrational. Jeremiah's response indicated that he harbored in his heart the sentiments expressed in 20:11–13.

Verse 12. The prophet was given an opportunity to defend himself. **Jeremiah spoke to all the officials and to all the people** who had gathered at the gate. The prophet's defense included no apology. Instead, he boldly asserted that it was **the LORD** who had **sent** [him] **to prophesy against this house and against this city** (see 26:1, 2). Unlike the false prophets (23:21), God had commissioned Jeremiah, giving him the very **words** to speak.

Verse 13. Jeremiah called the officials and the people to repentance: **"Now therefore amend your ways and your deeds and obey the voice of the LORD your God"** (see 7:3, 5). If they would change their ways, then **the LORD** [would] **change His mind about the misfortune** He had planned for them. The grace and patience of God are evident in Jeremiah's charge.

Verses 14, 15. In verse 14, Jeremiah told the officials and the people, **"I am in your hands; do with me as is good and right in your sight."** At first glance, it appears that the prophet was unconcerned about his life. However, in verse 15, he sternly warned against any injustice: **"Only know for certain that if you put me to death, you will bring innocent blood on yourselves, and on this city and on its inhabitants"** (see comments on 7:5, 6; 19:4, 5). Jeremiah closed his rebuttal in the same way he had opened it in verse 12—by maintaining that God had sent him **to speak all these words in** [their] **hearing.**

THE SUIT AGAINST JEREMIAH APPEALED (26:16–19)

¹⁶Then the officials and all the people said to the priests and to the prophets, "No death sentence for this man! For he has spoken to us in the name of the LORD our God." ¹⁷Then some of the elders of the land rose up and spoke to all the assembly of the people, saying, ¹⁸"Micah of Moresheth prophesied in the days of Hezekiah king of Judah; and he spoke to all the people of Judah, saying, 'Thus the LORD of hosts has said,

"Zion will be plowed as a field,
And Jerusalem will become ruins,
And the mountain of the house as the high places of a forest."'
¹⁹Did Hezekiah king of Judah and all Judah put him to death? Did he not fear the Lord and entreat the favor of the Lord, and the Lord changed His mind about the misfortune which He had pronounced against them? But we are committing a great evil against ourselves."

Verse 16. Jeremiah's defense had a definite impact, dividing this court gathering. On one side, **the priests** and **the prophets** were still insisting on the death penalty. On the other side, **the officials and all the people** changed their earlier response, saying, **"No death sentence for this man! For he has spoken to us in the name of the Lord our God."** For twenty years Jeremiah had been trying to get them to acknowledge this fact (6:16, 17; 11:21; 17:15–18). Though this brief reprieve lacked depth, it must have been refreshing.

Verses 17, 18. Some of the elders urged that Jeremiah be treated as the people had treated **Micah**, who had spoken of the impending destruction of Jerusalem **in the days of Hezekiah king of Judah** (see Mic. 1:1–7).

Micah was from the town of **Moresheth**, located half way between Lachish and Azekah in Judah. It was also known as "Moresheth-gath" because of its proximity to the Philistine city of Gath (Mic. 1:1, 14). The KJV refers to this prophet as "the Morasthite."

Micah had warned the people of his time, saying, **"Zion will be plowed as a field, and Jerusalem will become ruins, and the mountain of the house as the high places of a forest."** This quotation deserves some special scrutiny. The elders both recalled and correctly quoted the words of Micah 3:12. No exact citation from another prophetic source occurs anywhere else in prophetic literature. Even though about one hundred years had elapsed from the days of Micah to this incident, these elders still gave a verbatim quote of the text from Micah that has come down to our time. This is encouraging testimony to the accuracy of the transmission of the Hebrew text.⁵

Micah warned the people of his day that, if they did not repent, the city of Jerusalem and the temple would be destroyed. This was essentially the same message that Jeremiah was proclaiming to his generation.

Verse 19. The argument made from the passage in Micah is to the point. **Hezekiah** did not punish Micah for his negative prophecy. Instead, the king heeded his warning, responding in a manner that led to Jerusalem's deliverance. When Hezekiah **entreat[ed] the favor of the LORD,** God **changed His mind about the misfortune which He had pronounced** against Judah.

The historical records of Hezekiah's reign do not mention Micah or the circumstances surrounding his prophecy. Nevertheless, from the available information, a few possibilities exist. (1) This episode may have been connected to Micah's warning of Jerusalem's destruction during the reforms undertaken by Hezekiah (2 Kings 18:1–6). In this case, the reforms may have taken place as a result of the prophecy.

(2) More specifically, Micah's words may have been directly related to the Assyrian attack on Jerusalem in 701 B.C., when the city was besieged by Sennacherib and his great army. At that time, both Hezekiah and Isaiah fervently prayed to the Lord. As a result, God miraculously delivered Jerusalem, putting 185,000 soldiers to death in one night. Sennacherib abandoned the siege and returned to Nineveh (2 Kings 18:13—19:37; 2 Chron. 32:1–23; Is. 36:1—37:38).

(3) Micah's prophecy may have been given in the context of Hezekiah's illness. God had given the king a sign that he would be healed. However, due to the king's pride and ingratitude, he stirred up the wrath of God (2 Chron. 32:24, 25).⁶ In response to God's wrath, "Hezekiah humbled the pride of his heart, both he and the inhabitants of Jerusalem, so that the wrath of the LORD did not come on them" (2 Chron. 32:26).

---

⁵James E. Smith, *Jeremiah and Lamentations*, Bible Study Textbook Series (Joplin, Mo.: College Press, 1972), 466.

⁶Since 2 Chronicles 32:24 begins with the phrase "in those days," this event may have been connected to the Assyrian invasion already mentioned.

The elders' argument concerning Hezekiah's response to Micah's warning had to make some impact on the people. The implication was that, if they listened to God's prophet Jeremiah, Jerusalem might once again be spared. These men concluded their testimony by declaring that if they killed Jeremiah, they would be **committing a great evil against** themselves (see 5:25; 6:19; 7:19).

THE SENTENCE OF DEATH ILLUSTRATED (26:20–23)

²⁰Indeed, there was also a man who prophesied in the name of the Lord, Uriah the son of Shemaiah from Kiriath-jearim; and he prophesied against this city and against this land words similar to all those of Jeremiah. ²¹When King Jehoiakim and all his mighty men and all the officials heard his words, then the king sought to put him to death; but Uriah heard it, and he was afraid and fled and went to Egypt. ²²Then King Jehoiakim sent men to Egypt: Elnathan the son of Achbor and certain men with him went into Egypt. ²³And they brought Uriah from Egypt and led him to King Jehoiakim, who slew him with a sword and cast his dead body into the burial place of the common people.

The precise relationship of this paragraph to the rest of the chapter is not expressly stated. Perhaps an unnamed person spoke up and proceeded to reason why Jeremiah should die. In fact, an "old Jewish interpretation of the passage" says that "this episode was cited by Jeremiah's accusers as a counter-precedent during the trial."[7]

On the other hand, it could be that the section was added by the author to illustrate the gravity of Jeremiah's situation. These statements reveal the great injustice done to the prophet Uriah, who spoke the same message as Jeremiah did. Like Uriah, he could have also been killed for his prophecies, yet God chose to

---

[7]Smith, 467.

spare his life. This interpretation is adopted by most English translations, since they do not place the paragraph in quotation marks. A few versions even put it in parentheses, demonstrating that it is an additional thought (TEV; NIV; NCV).

Verse 20. The prophet **Uriah** is only mentioned in this passage in the Old Testament. He is further identified as **the son of Shemaiah from Kiriath-jearim**, a town located about nine miles west of Jerusalem. Like **Jeremiah**, Uriah **prophesied in the name of the** LORD, foretelling the doom of Jerusalem and Judah.

Verse 21. When **King Jehoiakim** learned about the prophet's message of destruction, he was offended by it and **sought to put him to death**. Learning of the king's intentions, **Uriah . . . fled and went to Egypt**. His flight should not be calculated to prove him guilty and weak. It is parallel to Christ's instruction to flee persecution in Matthew 10:23. The land of Egypt was sometimes used as a place of refuge from both famine and enemies (Gen. 12:10; 1 Kings 11:17, 40; Mt. 2:13).

Verse 22. In an effort to find Uriah, **King Jehoiakim sent men to Egypt**. The group was led by **Elnathan**, a high official of the king. He was one of the men who later urged the king not to burn Jeremiah's scroll and warned Baruch and Jeremiah to hide (36:12, 19, 25). The emissaries were sent to arrest Uriah and bring him back to Jerusalem. J. A. Thompson concluded that the extradition of political refugees was a part of ancient treaties. Since Judah was subjected to Egypt at this time (2 Kings 23:34, 35), a suzerain-vassal treaty likely existed between the two nations. In this case, "such extradition clauses were reciprocal, becoming a part of international law."[8]

Verse 23. After extraditing **Uriah from Egypt**, the men took him back to Jerusalem and **led him to King Jehoiakim**. Without mercy, the king had Uriah killed **with a sword** and his corpse dumped in **the burial place of the common people**. This area was apparently located in the Kidron Valley east of Jerusalem (2 Kings 23:6).

---

[8]J. A. Thompson, *The Book of Jeremiah*, The New International Commentary on the Old Testament (Grand Rapids, Mich.: Wm. B. Eerdmans Publishing Co., 1980), 527.

If this episode was cited by Jeremiah's accusers, then Jehoiakim's pursuit and persecution of Uriah added weight to their argument. After all, Jeremiah had prophesied against Judah and Jerusalem, just as Uriah had done. If Uriah was killed for his (supposed) treason, then Jeremiah should suffer the same fate.

On the other hand, if this example was added by the author, then it was used to underscore the extreme danger faced by Jeremiah at this time—as well as any true spokesman for God. The justice of God occurred in Jehoiakim's death, when his own burial mirrored similar inhuman treatment (see comments on 22:18, 19). He reaped as he had sown.

THE SAVING INFLUENCE OF A FRIEND (26:24)

24But the hand of Ahikam the son of Shaphan was with Jeremiah, so that he was not given into the hands of the people to put him to death.

Verse 24. Ahikam the son of Shaphan stepped forward to save the day. His argument has not been preserved; the text simply says that his **hand . . . was with Jeremiah**. As a result, God's prophet **was not given into the hands of the people** who wanted the **death** penalty for him.

Some people still obviously wanted to put Jeremiah to death, but the One watching over the prophet had spoken long before this trial, assuring Jeremiah,

> Now behold, I have made you today as a fortified city and as a pillar of iron and as walls of bronze against the whole land, to the kings of Judah, to its princes, to its priests and to the people of the land. They will fight against you, but they will not overcome you, for I am with you to deliver you (1:18, 19).

Thank God for His providential care.

We should be thankful for souls like Ahikam, who fit so willingly into God's caring plan. Ahikam's father, Shaphan, was the scribe who read the Book of the Law that had been found during temple renovations in the days of King Josiah. Both Ahikam and Shaphan were among those sent by Josiah to inquire of Huldah the prophetess (2 Kings 22:8–20). Ahikam's son was Gedaliah, who also befriended Jeremiah and later was appointed by Nebuchadnezzar as governor over the remnant (39:14; 40:5–16; 43:5, 6). At this time of need in a troubled land, Ahikam was a bright spot of moral integrity, an honorable servant of God.

APPLICATION

Misjudging Others (Ch. 26)

Are we the type of people who take a stand in an hour of trial, or do we sit silently in the shadows during conflict? Have we ever misjudged others, especially one among God's people, as some of these people did? Have we grown spiritually, like Jeremiah, to the point that we can courageously respond with a "thus says the Lord"—even if it puts our lives in jeopardy?

The foregoing questions interlace a number of significant individuals and circumstances related to Jeremiah's day in court. The fact that priests, prophets, and all the people united to declare to Jeremiah, "You must die!" (26:8) is a sober warning that a mass majority can be swayed to commit a grave injustice. Whether in the home, school, work force, government, or the church, a democratic majority is no guarantee that right or wrong will be declared. Jeremiah's case reminds us of an equally unfair and foreboding moment, when even Pilate's court found no evil that Jesus had done, only to hear from the unrelenting mob, "Crucify Him!" . . . "Crucify Him!" (Mt. 27:22, 23; Mk. 15:12–14; Lk. 23:20–23; Jn. 19:13–15). One of the common weaknesses of mankind is doing nothing when something needs to be done (Acts 18:12–17). Another tendency is to act with limited insight and misguided motives, being unjust, cruel, and abusive to innocent parties (Lk. 23:34). Before we pass judgment, and certainly before we act, we should be certain we have collected all the facts and that we are worthy to act on those facts (see Deut. 17:1–12; Rom. 15:14). Misjudgments would surely be a sobering record to have when we come into judgment (2 Cor. 5:10).

"Do Not Omit a Word!" (26:2)

When God called Jeremiah to speak at the temple, He solemnly instructed him, "Do not omit a word!" (26:2). This charge raises the question "How many preachers and teachers are guilty in some way of omitting the word?"

We must not leave out important truths that our audiences need to hear. It is tempting to overlook controversial points in order to avoid offending people. However, addressing such topics may lead them to repentance and make a difference in their eternal salvation (2 Tim. 4:1–5). We should imitate Paul, who did not hesitate to proclaim "the whole will of God" (Acts 20:27; NIV).

We must not misinterpret God's Word, taking it out of context. A statement removed from its context can easily be distorted. Some have adopted the method of using prooftexts to support their doctrines or win arguments in debates, without understanding the original meaning of the verses they cite. Peter warned against those who had carelessly treated Paul's letters, ignoring his authorial intentions. They had twisted his words, along with "the rest of the Scriptures, to their own destruction" (2 Pet. 3:15, 16).

We must not mislead or deceive people. Many false teachers existed in the first century (1 Cor. 15:12–19; Gal. 1:6–9; 2 Thess. 2:1, 2; 2 Tim. 3:13; 2 Pet. 2:1–3; 1 Jn. 4:1–3), and many exist today. Paul warned the Ephesian elders that some would arise, even from their own number, "speaking perverse things, to draw away the disciples after them" (Acts 20:30).

Conclusion. We must approach God's Word with humility and sincerity. We should seek to share His Word in its fullness, not diminishing from it.

Jeremiah's Suffering (26:7–11)

Since some wanted to give Jeremiah the death sentence, this chapter is a good place to survey what the prophet endured to serve God. He was rejected by his family (12:6), mocked daily as a laughingstock (15:10; 20:7, 8), and then charged, beaten, and put in stocks as a false prophet (20:1–5). He was declared to be worthy of death (26:8, 11; 38:4) and labeled as a madman (29:26). Later he was charged as a traitor and put in a dungeon (37:11–15) and in a muddy cistern (38:6). He was rebuked for being one who discouraged his own people, while seeking to warn them of their evil ways (38:4). He was forced to go against his own words, being called a liar (43:1–7).

These injustices emphasize Jeremiah's steadfast service under severe and stressful circumstances. His example challenges us to be faithful in our service to God, despite any opposition we may face. If we are doing what is right, we should never dare to give over, give in, or give up.

CHAPTER 27
THE YEARS OF THE YOKE OF BABYLON

In chapter 27, God called on Jeremiah to deliver a message, warning several nations (27:1–11), Zedekiah (27:12–15), and the priests and all the people (27:16–22). The prophet was instructed to wear a yoke as he proclaimed God's truth to these groups.

The central figure in this chapter is "the LORD of hosts, the God of Israel" (27:4, 18, 19, 21). He is referred to as "the LORD" (יהוה, *YHWH*) 16 times. The personal pronouns "I" (found 12 times) and "My" (5 times) further identify His presence in this chapter. His preeminence is also seen in His directives to various nations (27:3) and His reference to Nebuchadnezzar, king of Babylon, as "My servant" (27:6).

Attention should also be given to the prophetic utterances concerning the duration of the Babylonian Empire (27:7) and the vessels from the house of the Lord being taken to Babylon and later returned in the restoration (27:19–22). Time proved the accuracy of these prophecies—divine proof that our God is the one true God of heaven and earth.

WARNINGS TO THE NATIONS (27:1–11)

¹**In the beginning of the reign of Zedekiah the son of Josiah, king of Judah, this word came to Jeremiah from the LORD, saying—**²**thus says the LORD to me—"Make for yourself bonds and yokes and put them on your neck,** ³**and send word to the king of Edom, to the king of Moab, to the king of the sons of Ammon, to the king of Tyre and to the king of Sidon by the messengers**

who come to Jerusalem to Zedekiah king of Judah. ⁴Command them to go to their masters, saying, 'Thus says the LORD of hosts, the God of Israel, thus you shall say to your masters, ⁵"I have made the earth, the men and the beasts which are on the face of the earth by My great power and by My outstretched arm, and I will give it to the one who is pleasing in My sight. ⁶Now I have given all these lands into the hand of Nebuchadnezzar king of Babylon, My servant, and I have given him also the wild animals of the field to serve him. ⁷All the nations shall serve him and his son and his grandson until the time of his own land comes; then many nations and great kings will make him their servant.

⁸"'"It will be, that the nation or the kingdom which will not serve him, Nebuchadnezzar king of Babylon, and which will not put its neck under the yoke of the king of Babylon, I will punish that nation with the sword, with famine and with pestilence," declares the LORD, "until I have destroyed it by his hand. ⁹But as for you, do not listen to your prophets, your diviners, your dreamers, your soothsayers or your sorcerers who speak to you, saying, 'You will not serve the king of Babylon.' ¹⁰For they prophesy a lie to you in order to remove you far from your land; and I will drive you out and you will perish. ¹¹But the nation which will bring its neck under the yoke of the king of Babylon and serve him, I will let remain on its land," declares the LORD, "and they will till it and dwell in it."'"

Verse 1. This message was given **to Jeremiah at the beginning of the reign of Zedekiah.** Instead of "Zedekiah," some Hebrew manuscripts have "Jehoiakim" (see KJV; ASV). C. F. Keil contended that "Jehoiakim" was a copyist error, based on a repetition of 26:1. After all, several verses in chapter 27 clearly indicate that the events occurred in Zedekiah's time (27:3, 12, 20). Therefore, some ancient Hebrew manuscripts and translations have substituted the name "Zedekiah."[1]

---

[1]C. F. Keil and F. Delitzsch, *Commentary on the Old Testament*, vol. 8, *Jeremiah, Lamentations* (Grand Rapids, Mich.: Wm. B. Eerdmans Publishing Co., n.d.), 396.

Verse 2. The message proclaimed by Jeremiah included a visual aid: He wore a yoke throughout the events of this chapter and part of chapter 28. God frequently incorporated visual aids as a part of a prophet's message in order to illustrate and intensify it. At this point, God had already used visual aids several times in Jeremiah's ministry, whether visionary or material: the rod of an almond tree and the boiling pot (ch. 1); the dirty waistband (ch. 13); the potter and the clay (ch. 18); the potter's earthenware jar (ch. 19); and the good and bad figs (ch. 24). These aids added drama and detail to the messages.

A striking touch is found in verse 2 when God told Jeremiah, **"Make for yourself bonds and yokes and put them on your neck."** The "bonds" likely refer to leather straps, whereas the "yokes" were bars of wood. This must have been a yoke that was similar to an ox-yoke, which John Bright described as consisting of "a wooden bar, or bars, held about the animal's neck, or lashed to the horns, by cords or leather thongs."[2] Jeremiah constructed this yoke and placed it on his own neck. The image of a yoke was commonly used as a metaphor for submission (2:20; 5:5; Lev. 26:13; Deut. 28:48; 1 Kings 12:4–14; Is. 9:4; 10:27; 14:25; Ezek. 34:27; Nahum 1:13). For several days the prophet moved about the streets of Jerusalem with this yoke around his neck,[3] proclaiming God's message of submission to Babylon (27:8, 11).

Verse 3. Jeremiah was instructed to **send word** to certain foreign rulers: His message was for the kings of **Edom**, **Moab**, **Ammon**, **Tyre**, and **Sidon** (see comments on 25:21, 22). By sending them a message, he was fulfilling his role as "a prophet to the nations" (1:5).

Jeremiah was able to communicate with these kings because their **messengers** had been dispatched **to Jerusalem to Zedekiah king of Judah**. They may have come to Jerusalem in order to discuss rebelling against Babylon. J. A. Thompson reconstructed the events:

---

[2]John Bright, *Jeremiah*, The Anchor Bible (Garden City, N.Y.: Doubleday & Company, 1965), 199.
[3]For similar demonstrations, see Ex. 4:1–5; 14:13–16; Ezek. 37:16–23.

In the fourth year of Zedekiah's reign (594/3 B.C.), vassal states in the western parts of Nebuchadrezzar's empire began to explore the possibility of a rebellion, probably encouraged by disturbances to the east of Babylon in the previous year. Jerusalem was the center to which representatives from neighboring states came to enlist Zedekiah's support.[4]

Verse 4. Jeremiah instructed the messengers to return **to their masters** with a word from **the LORD of hosts, the God of Israel**. It was not unheard of for foreign kings and other officials to listen to the prophets of Israel (Judg. 3:19, 20; 1 Kings 19:15; 2 Kings 5:9–14; 8:7–15; Jon. 3:3–9).

Verse 5. The message began with a statement of God's sovereignty: **"I have made the earth, the men and the beasts which are on the face of the earth by My great power and by My outstretched arm"** (see Gen. 1; Ps. 33:6–12; Acts 17:24). That universal display of His power justifies the Owner in giving His creation to whomever He pleases (Ps. 37:9, 11, 22, 29, 34; Mt. 5:5).

Verse 6. The Lord then indicated that He had **given all these lands into the hand of Nebuchadnezzar king of Babylon**. Since Nebuchadnezzar's power over the nations was a divine gift, it was futile for them to resist or rebel. Once again, God referred to this powerful king as **My servant** (see comments on 25:8, 9). To emphasize that nothing was beyond Nebuchadnezzar's control, God also said that He had granted the king **the wild animals of the field to serve him** (see 28:14; Dan. 2:38).

Verse 7. God made it clear, however, that Babylon's authority over the nations would not last forever: **"All the nations shall serve him and his son and his grandson until the time of his own land comes; then many nations and great kings will make him their servant."** This prophecy was fulfilled literally in the succession of kings. Nebuchadnezzar reigned forty-four years

---

[4]J. A. Thompson, *The Book of Jeremiah*, The New International Commentary on the Old Testament (Grand Rapids, Mich.: Wm. B. Eerdmans Publishing Co., 1980), 531. Zedekiah made a trip to Babylon during the fourth year of his reign (51:59). Ultimately, he did rebel against Nebuchadnezzar (52:3).

(605–562 B.C.), followed by his son Evil-merodach (see 52:31). After a two-year reign (561–560), he was murdered by Neriglissar, his brother-in-law, who then reigned four years (560–556). Next, Neriglissar's son, Labashi-Marduk, reigned less than a year before being killed in a conspiracy (556). Then Nebuchadnezzar's son-in-law, Nabonidus, reigned seventeen years (556–539).[5] The grandson mentioned in Jeremiah's prophecy was Belshazzar, who was co-regent with his father, Nabonidus, for most of his reign (553–539). Therefore, Jeremiah's prophecy was fulfilled through Nebuchadnezzar, his son Evil-merodach, and his grandson, Belshazzar. Belshazzar's death on the night of a wild party ended the Babylonian Empire (Dan. 5).

Verse 8. God indicated that any **nation** unwilling to subject itself to **Babylon**, placing **its neck under the yoke** of **Nebuchadnezzar**, would greatly suffer. For any who refused to cooperate, He would use the Babylonians to **punish that nation with the sword, with famine and with pestilence** (see comments on 14:12).

Verses 9, 10. A warning was given against five types of leaders who might cause the nations to rebel. (1) **Prophets** comes from the Hebrew term נָבִיא (*nabi'*), which means "spokesman" or "speaker."[6] These were *false* prophets who had not received a genuine message from God (5:31). (2) **Diviners** is from קָסַם (*qasam*), meaning "practice divination."[7] Such methods as drawing lots, inspecting animal livers, and consulting the dead were used by diviners in order to predict the future (see comments on 14:14). (3) **Dreamers** derives from חֲלוֹם (*ch*ᵃ*lom*), a word that literally means "dream."[8] While dreams sometimes had prophetic meanings in Bible times, false prophets either misinterpreted dreams or fabricated them altogether. (4) **Soothsayers** is from עָנַן (*'anan*), a term that could mean "interpret the clouds [or other phenomenon]," "tell fortunes in a quietly droning voice,"

---

[5]While the evidence is sketchy, many believe that Nabonidus was married to Nebuchadnezzar's daughter, Nitocris.

[6]Francis Brown, S. R. Driver, and Charles A. Briggs, *A Hebrew and English Lexicon of the Old Testament* (Oxford: Clarendon Press, 1972), 611–12.

[7]Ibid., 890.

[8]Ibid., 321.

or "recite magic spells."⁹ (5) **Sorcerers** is from כַּשָּׁף (*kashshap*), a word for one who works magic.¹⁰

Centuries before, God had declared through Moses all of these as detestable (Lev. 19:26; Deut. 18:9–12). The passing of time had not altered His views of them or the fruit they produced among men and nations. These leaders all had one common characteristic—they were liars. They would deceive the people by saying, **"You will not serve the king of Babylon."** God promised that the price for listening to these liars meant that the people would be driven from the **land** and they would **perish**.

Verse 11. God has never threatened punishment without mercifully offering a way of escape (see 1 Cor. 10:13; 2 Pet. 3:9). His intention was for each nation to **bring its neck under the yoke of the king of Babylon and serve him**—just as Jeremiah symbolized by the yoke on his neck (27:2). If they respected God's will, they would continue to **till** and **dwell in** their **land**. Indeed, some of the nations assisted in the destruction of God's people under Babylon's command (2 Kings 24:1, 2). They had surrendered to Babylon and had become part of their armies of conquest.

God's willingness to give these wicked nations an opportunity to continue again demonstrated His mercy. His great desire has ever been for men to respect His sovereignty as a Prince of peace rather than One who causes people to perish (Is. 9:6, 7; Ezek. 18:30–32).

WARNINGS TO ZEDEKIAH, KING OF JUDAH (27:12–15)

¹²I spoke words like all these to Zedekiah king of Judah, saying, "Bring your necks under the yoke of the king of Babylon and serve him and his people, and live! ¹³Why will you die, you and your people, by the sword, famine and pestilence, as

---

⁹Ludwig Koehler and Walter Baumgartner, *The Hebrew and Aramaic Lexicon of the Old Testament*, study ed., trans. and ed. M. E. J. Richardson (Boston: Brill, 2001), 1:857.

¹⁰Ibid., 1:503.

the LORD has spoken to that nation which will not serve the king of Babylon? ¹⁴So do not listen to the words of the prophets who speak to you, saying, 'You will not serve the king of Babylon,' for they prophesy a lie to you; ¹⁵for I have not sent them," declares the LORD, "but they prophesy falsely in My name, in order that I may drive you out and that you may perish, you and the prophets who prophesy to you."

Verse 12. The warning to **Zedekiah king of Judah** was next presented as a message of life or death. God spoke through Jeremiah, saying, **"Bring your necks under the yoke of the king of Babylon and serve him and his people, and live!"** The yoke worn by Jeremiah must have vividly reinforced the message he related. The word "live" is an imperative, carrying the force of a promise. Zedekiah and his followers seemed to center their attention on the words "your necks" more than God's promise. How often do people concentrate on negative situations while ignoring God's positive promises? Their assumption of what would happen was worse than the fact.[11] Decisions are often based on assumption and imagination, leading to death rather than life.

Verse 13. God knew that Zedekiah would rebel against the king of Babylon (52:3), in direct disobedience to His command. He asked, **"Why will you die, you and your people, by the sword, famine and pestilence . . . ?"** (See comments on 14:12; 15:2, 3.) This question reveals the foolishness of those deceived by the devil, who only offers death, in contrast to those who heed God, the Author of life.

Verses 14, 15. This choice was too critical for God to leave it unclear. **The prophets** who denied that Judah would **serve the king of Babylon** were liars. God had not sent them. He said, **"They prophesy falsely in My name."** As deceptive as these false prophets were, anyone who wanted to know who was presenting the truth could have known. After all, Judah had technically been under the power of Babylon since the fourth year

---

[11] See Jeremiah's later appeal to them to lead normal lives in captivity (29:4–7).

of Jehoiakim (25:1, 11). They could stay in denial and listen to false prophets; if they continued to do so, they would be driven out by the Lord.

WARNINGS TO THE PRIESTS AND TO ALL THE PEOPLE (27:16–22)

¹⁶Then I spoke to the priests and to all this people, saying, "Thus says the Lord: Do not listen to the words of your prophets who prophesy to you, saying, 'Behold, the vessels of the Lord's house will now shortly be brought again from Babylon'; for they are prophesying a lie to you. ¹⁷Do not listen to them; serve the king of Babylon, and live! Why should this city become a ruin? ¹⁸But if they are prophets, and if the word of the Lord is with them, let them now entreat the Lord of hosts that the vessels which are left in the house of the Lord, in the house of the king of Judah and in Jerusalem may not go to Babylon. ¹⁹For thus says the Lord of hosts concerning the pillars, concerning the sea, concerning the stands and concerning the rest of the vessels that are left in this city, ²⁰which Nebuchadnezzar king of Babylon did not take when he carried into exile Jeconiah the son of Jehoiakim, king of Judah, from Jerusalem to Babylon, and all the nobles of Judah and Jerusalem. ²¹Yes, thus says the Lord of hosts, the God of Israel, concerning the vessels that are left in the house of the Lord and in the house of the king of Judah and in Jerusalem, ²²'They will be carried to Babylon and they will be there until the day I visit them,' declares the Lord. 'Then I will bring them back and restore them to this place.'"

Verse 16. False prophets often excite people with the prospect of a spectacular event that is about to happen. The message being spread throughout Judah at this time was that **the vessels of the Lord's house** would soon be returned **from Babylon** (see 28:1–3). Even though Judah had polluted their worship patterns, they still placed much emphasis on these things. Many of the vessels had been taken in the first two deportations of 605 B.C., when Daniel was taken to Babylon (Dan. 1:1–6), and of 597 B.C., when Jehoiachin was taken captive (2 Kings 24:10–16). God had revealed through Jeremiah that the captivity would last for seventy years (25:12), but these false **prophets** sought to pacify the **people** with prospects that it would end **shortly**.

Verse 17. Jeremiah's response remained the same. He warned that the idea of a quick return was a lie and encouraged the people to **serve the king of Babylon, and live**. If they would heed his warning, Jerusalem would be spared.

Verse 18. The directive of Jeremiah in this verse has an element of irony. He instructed those who claimed to be **prophets** to **entreat** God so that the remaining **vessels** would not be taken from **the house of the LORD** or **the house of the king of Judah**. As Robert P. Carroll paraphrased it, "Never mind the furnishings which were taken away to Babylon, pray for what the Babylonians left behind!"[12]

Verses 19, 20. Knowing their nature of rebellion, God told the people that the **vessels** remaining after the deportation of **Jeconiah** (Jehoiachin) in 597 B.C. would also be taken **to Babylon**, along with **the pillars, the sea**, and **the stands**. The "pillars" refer to the two magnificent bronze columns that stood at the entrance of the temple; these were named Jachin and Boaz (1 Kings 7:15–22). The "sea" was the large bronze basin resting on twelve bulls, three facing in each direction. It was used by the priests for ceremonial cleansing (1 Kings 7:23–26; 2 Chron. 4:2–6). The ten "stands" (basins), decorated with cherubim, lions, and palm trees, were also made of bronze and had wheels and axles. They were used to wash the burnt offerings (1 Kings 7:27–39; 2 Chron. 4:6). God's promise was fulfilled in 586 B.C., when the Babylonians destroyed Jerusalem and the temple, taking its wealth as plunder (52:17–23; 2 Kings 25:13–17; 2 Chron. 36:11–19).

Verses 21, 22. True to His nature, God left a ray of hope that His providence would watch over those **vessels** and return them. He would **visit** His people in exile and restore a remnant in the Promised Land. They would rebuild the temple in Jerusalem, and the vessels would be returned for their sacred use in

---

[12]Robert P. Carroll, *Jeremiah 26—52*, Old Testament Library (London: SCM Press Ltd, 1986), 536.

its services. God's promises do not fail; Ezra reported that all of these things came to pass just as the Lord had said (Ezra 1:1–11; 5:13–17; 7:9–28).

APPLICATION

Bearing the Yoke (Ch. 27)
To reinforce his message, Jeremiah wore a yoke on his neck (27:2) as he instructed the nations (including Judah) to submit to the Babylonians. The promise was that those who would bear the yoke would *live* (27:12, 17). How often some relationships seem like yoke-bearing, when that is the very need for one to live and enjoy living. For young people to be under parents (Eph. 6:1–4); for wives to be in subjection to husbands as unto the Lord (Eph. 5:22–24; 1 Pet. 3:1–6); for employees to be bound by rules from an employer (Eph. 6:5–9; Col. 3:22–25; 1 Tim. 6:1, 2); for members of the church to be under elders as overseers (1 Thess. 5:12, 13; Heb. 13:17)—all of these relationships seem to some to be yoke-bearing, whereas God's Word calls for these arrangements to give us the very best quality of living (Jn. 10:10; Heb. 12:5–11). Let it be quickly added that an abusive parent, a selfish husband, an arrogant, inconsiderate employer, or a domineering overseer (3 Jn. 9–11) are not doing their part in any of the above, ideal relationships. However, when the responsibility of parents, husbands, employers, and elders are adhered to for their part of the relationship, any such yoke-bearing (if one calls it that) is a helpful and viable relationship.

One illustration highlights this point. A man's son was vice-president of a large cooperation in mid-America. He wore a suit and tie to work each day and enjoyed a plush, air-conditioned office. At the back of this huge office-warehouse complex, the man was employed by his son to ship out supplies to various parts of the nation. So the father worked under his more educated son through the week. On the Lord's Day, the son, who taught a Bible class and directed the song services, was under his father, who was one of the elders at that congregation. Week by week they labored under this role-reversal with no complications—only blessings—because they loved one another, and each sought to operate by Christ's principles for the posts they occupied. Truly, they did live and found it to be abundant living! May children, parents, husbands, wives, teachers, students, employers, employees, elders, and brethren respect and respond to these varied relationship roles of the Lord that each one may truly live, enjoying the abundant life in Christ Jesus.

Nebuchadnezzar, "My Servant" (27:6)

Great men of God have always recognized their humble relationship to Him. Abraham was mighty in wealth, and he was told that his seed would bless all nations (Gen. 12:3; 13:2). God declared that Abraham would command his children and his household after him, but his commands were that they should "keep the way of the Lord by doing righteousness and justice" (Gen. 18:19). Solomon served hundreds daily at his table (1 Kings 4:21–24), and rulers of many nations sought his presence and wisdom (1 Kings 10:23, 24), but he spoke of himself to God as "Your servant" (1 Kings 8:28). Because Solomon failed to keep God's statutes, God tore the kingdom away from him (1 Kings 11:1–11). Though the church rests on the foundation of the apostles and the prophets (Eph. 2:19, 20; 3:4, 5), when those apostles had done all that was required of them, they were to view themselves as unworthy servants before God (Lk. 17:10). Therefore, it is no surprise that in civil or governmental matters, Nebuchadnezzar, a world emperor, would hear God refer to him as "My servant." In every area of human achievement, man is a servant before God.

God's Providence (27:16–22)

God's constant guardianship is seen in the fact that He even took note of utensils when they fit into His purposes. The Lord's promise concerning the temple vessels and its fulfillment is an amazing story of His providential protection.

The sacred vessels were taken from the Jerusalem temple on three different occasions spanning nearly twenty years: in 605 B.C. (Dan. 1:1, 2), in 597 B.C. (2 Kings 24:10–13), and finally in 586 B.C., when the temple was destroyed (2 Kings 25:13–17). Since these articles were made of gold, silver, and bronze, they could have been melted down and used for other items as the rulers of Babylon pleased. Nevertheless, God watched over these vessels, ensuring their preservation throughout Babylonian rule—a span of about seventy years! They survived the reigns of Nebuchadnezzar, his son Evil-merodach, and his grandson Belshazzar (see comments on 27:7). Belshazzar was the one who foolishly brought out those vessels for his promiscuous drinking party (Dan. 5:1–31). That same night, the Babylonian Empire was overthrown.

After the Medo-Persians came to power, God moved Cyrus the Great to send a remnant back to Jerusalem to rebuild the temple. Cyrus gave the Jewish people 5,400 articles of gold and silver that Nebuchadnezzar had taken, restoring them to the Lord's service (Ezra 1:7–11).

If God's providence can so perfectly protect *things* in this amazing manner, as He prophetically predicted, then we can be completely confident of His care for His people wherever they may be and whenever they may need Him (see 2 Chron. 16:9; Zech. 4:8–10; Mt. 6:25–34; Jn. 10:27–30; 1 Pet. 3:12).

CHAPTER 28
FALSE AND TRUE PROPHETS

This chapter is a continuation of chapter 27: "Now in the same year, in the beginning of the reign of Zedekiah king of Judah, in the fourth year, in the fifth month . . ." (28:1; see 27:1). Jeremiah was still wearing the yoke he had put on in 27:2 (28:2, 10), and the vessels from the house of the Lord were still being discussed (27:21, 22; 28:3). Chapter 28 is divided into four parts: (1) the report by a false prophet, Hananiah (28:1–4); (2) the response by Jeremiah (28:5–9); (3) the reaction by Hananiah (28:10, 11); and (4) the results of a false prophet and rebellion (28:12–17).

THE REPORT BY A FALSE PROPHET, HANANIAH (28:1–4)

¹Now in the same year, in the beginning of the reign of Zedekiah king of Judah, in the fourth year, in the fifth month, Hananiah the son of Azzur, the prophet, who was from Gibeon, spoke to me in the house of the LORD in the presence of the priests and all the people, saying, ²"Thus says the LORD of hosts, the God of Israel, 'I have broken the yoke of the king of Babylon. ³Within two years I am going to bring back to this place all the vessels of the LORD's house, which Nebuchadnezzar king of Babylon took away from this place and carried to Babylon. ⁴I am also going to bring back to this place Jeconiah the son of Jehoiakim, king of Judah, and all the exiles of Judah who went to Babylon,' declares the LORD, 'for I will break the yoke of the king of Babylon.'"

Verse 1. Chapter 28 begins in a similar way as chapter 27, yet more detail is added: **Now in the same year, in the beginning of the reign of Zedekiah king of Judah, in the fourth year, in the fifth month** (see 27:1). Zedekiah's reign began in 597 B.C., so "the fourth year" would have been 593 B.C.

Next, **Hananiah** is introduced as the antagonist of the chapter. His name means "God is gracious," which coincides with his message of deliverance and restoration (28:2-4). He is referred to as **the prophet**; but, as the story progresses, it becomes evident that he is a *false* prophet. The Hebrew term for "prophet," נָבִיא (*nabi'*), was used for true messengers of God and pretenders alike (28:5, 12). This false prophet came **from Gibeon**, about five miles northwest of Jerusalem (Josh. 9:3, 17; 21:17).

Hananiah chose a special place to react against Jeremiah—**in the house of the LORD**, before **the priests and all the people**. The temple setting, which had been used by Jeremiah on several occasions (7:2; 19:14; 26:2), guaranteed a large audience. There Hananiah boldly proceeded to tell three subtle lies.

Verse 2. First, he exclaimed, **"Thus says the LORD of hosts, the God of Israel, 'I have broken the yoke of the king of Babylon.'"** Supposedly coming from the Lord, this message was sure to get the people's attention. The words "I have broken" were spoken with prophetic confidence, "as if the future deed were so sure of accomplishment that it could be described as past."[1]

Comments about the yoke of Babylon were most timely. Such remarks would easily have been taken as mocking the yoke-wearing prophet, Jeremiah. Nevertheless, the Lord had not broken the yoke of Babylon, and circumstances and inspired prophecy testified that He would not do so in the near future. Judah had been under the yoke of Babylon since the fourth year of Jehoiakim (605 B.C.) and still was when Hananiah spoke these words in the fourth year of Zedekiah (593 B.C.).

Verse 3. Second, the announcement that the temple **vessels** taken by **Nebuchadnezzar** would be returned **within two years** was also a lie (27:16). On the contrary, Jeremiah had just revealed

---

[1]Anthony L. Ash, *Jeremiah and Lamentations*, The Living Word Commentary (Abilene, Tex.: ACU Press, 1987), 206.

that more articles would be removed (27:21, 22). Jeremiah had additional vessels going out, while Hananiah had the confiscated vessels coming back. Hananiah claimed this would take place in two years, compared to Jeremiah's repeated reference to seventy years as the duration of the captivity (25:11, 12; 27:7; 29:10; see Dan. 9:2).

Verse 4. Third, the promised return of **Jeconiah** (Jehoiachin), along with **all the exiles of Judah,** was a direct contradiction of Jeremiah's words that the king would die in Babylon (22:24–30). The conclusion of the Book of Jeremiah confirms that Jehoiachin did remain in Babylon until his death (52:33, 34). Hananiah's false prediction concerning Jehoiachin implies that the people still regarded him as the rightful ruler of Judah and anticipated his return.

THE RESPONSE BY JEREMIAH (28:5–9)

⁵Then the prophet Jeremiah spoke to the prophet Hananiah in the presence of the priests and in the presence of all the people who were standing in the house of the Lord, ⁶and the prophet Jeremiah said, "Amen! May the Lord do so; may the Lord confirm your words which you have prophesied to bring back the vessels of the Lord's house and all the exiles, from Babylon to this place. ⁷Yet hear now this word which I am about to speak in your hearing and in the hearing of all the people! ⁸The prophets who were before me and before you from ancient times prophesied against many lands and against great kingdoms, of war and of calamity and of pestilence. ⁹The prophet who prophesies of peace, when the word of the prophet comes to pass, then that prophet will be known as one whom the Lord has truly sent."

Verse 5. A great difference often exists between what we want to hear and what we need to hear. Hananiah had stated what he knew the people wanted to hear: that Jehoiachin, the vessels from the temple, and those in exile would soon arrive home (28:3, 4).

However, the yoke around Jeremiah's neck delivered a different message.

Here **Jeremiah** and **Hananiah** are both identified by the term **prophet** (נָבִיא, *nabi'*). John Bright described it this way:

> Though repetition of "the prophet" is to our taste redundant and awkward, it may be that the writer wished with the utmost emphasis—and irony—to point up the fact that prophet was contradicting prophet, and in the name of Yahweh.[2]

At this juncture, Jeremiah took the opportunity to respond to Hananiah **in the presence of the priests and in the presence of all the people** gathered at the temple (28:1).

Verse 6. Jeremiah said, "Amen! May the L<small>ORD</small> do so." "Amen" is a transliteration of the Hebrew word אָמֵן (*'amen*), meaning "so be it" (NJB), "surely,"[3] or "truly."[4] At least three interpretations of the overall statement could be considered. First, some think that Jeremiah was being sarcastic, mocking Hananiah. Since we do not know the tone he used, sarcasm is difficult to establish here. Second, others suggest that Jeremiah genuinely believed peace was an option. The third interpretation, however, is the most likely one. While Jeremiah personally longed for a quick return of **the vessels** and **the exiles** and could say, "Amen," wishing that might be the case, he knew it was not the truth.

Verse 7. After Jeremiah reviewed the lying promises about the vessels and exiles returning from Babylon, assuring that there was no mistake as to his hearing, he then bluntly added, **"Yet hear now this word which I am about to speak in your hearing and in the hearing of all the people!"**

Verse 8. Jeremiah was keenly aware that what Hananiah

---

[2]John Bright, *Jeremiah*, The Anchor Bible (Garden City, N.Y.: Doubleday & Company, 1965), 201.

[3]Ludwig Koehler and Walter Baumgartner, *The Hebrew and Aramaic Lexicon of the Old Testament*, study ed., trans. and ed. M. E. J. Richardson (Boston: Brill, 2001), 1:64.

[4]Francis Brown, S. R. Driver, and Charles A. Briggs, *A Hebrew and English Lexicon of the Old Testament* (Oxford: Clarendon Press, 1972), 53.

wanted was not what God had said Judah needed. Therefore, he faced the facts and reminded Hananiah and all who were gathered that he was justified in delivering the message he had spoken: **"The prophets who were before me and before you from ancient times prophesied against many lands and against great kingdoms, of war and of calamity and of pestilence."** In other words, the prophets had historically been messengers of doom who called the people to repentance. As with Jeremiah, they fulfilled their missions at the risk of losing their own lives.

Verse 9. Jeremiah further noted that **the prophet who prophesies of peace** could only be established as genuine **when the word of the prophet comes to pass**. It was false prophets, like Hananiah, who typically spoke of peace in order to please the people (6:14; 8:11; 23:17). Such individuals could not be trusted **as one whom the Lord has truly sent** unless their prophecies were fulfilled. Jeremiah was challenging the people, "Wait and see! If peace comes in two years, then you can believe Hananiah!" Of course, Hananiah had no foundation for his foolish predictions.

Jeremiah had prophesied of pending punishment coming from the north for years before it came, but by this time it had arrived. For more than ten years, Judah had been under Babylon's yoke, and the forces of Babylon had been taking Judah's key people into exile (2 Kings 24:10–16; Dan. 1:1–6). This certainly gave to Jeremiah some growing credibility as a prophet. He had passed the test of a true prophet, and Judah knew it. However, Hananiah was left as an unproven prophet by facts and requirements (see Deut. 18:18–22).

THE REACTION BY HANANIAH (28:10, 11)

[10]Then Hananiah the prophet took the yoke from the neck of Jeremiah the prophet and broke it. [11]Hananiah spoke in the presence of all the people, saying, "Thus says the Lord, 'Even so will I break within two full years the yoke of Nebuchadnezzar king of Babylon from the neck of all the nations.'" Then the prophet Jeremiah went his way.

Verse 10. Hananiah made no further argument or claims. When he could not give an answer, he put on an act. He pressed forward to **Jeremiah,** removed **the yoke from** [his] **neck** and **broke it.** The expression "broke it" comes from the Hebrew term שָׁבַר (*shabar*), meaning "shatter," "smash," or "destroy."[5] This bold, dramatic act no doubt made a striking impression on the people gathered there. However, it was done in defiance to God, who had originally instructed Jeremiah to make the yoke and wear it (27:2).

Verse 11. After smashing Jeremiah's visual aid, Hananiah announced that God would **break within two full years the yoke of Nebuchadnezzar king of Babylon.** The breaking of Jeremiah's yoke served to illustrate Hananiah's message. His prophecy was basically a restatement of what he had already said about Judah in 28:2–4, but this time he added that the yoke would be broken **from the neck of all the nations.**

After this, **Jeremiah went his way.** He did not act until he knew what the Lord wanted him to do. Anthony L. Ash pointed out, "The false prophet had the advantage of speaking whenever he wished. The true *prophet* had to await revelation."[6] In this pressure-packed moment, Jeremiah exhibited great self-control. When God's prophet went his way, it was far more a sign of wisdom than of weakness.

THE RESULTS OF A FALSE PROPHET AND THE PEOPLE'S REBELLION (28:12–17)

The Conditions of Judah and the Nations (28:12–14)

¹²**The word of the Lord came to Jeremiah after Hananiah the prophet had broken the yoke from off the neck of the prophet Jeremiah, saying,** ¹³**"Go and speak to Hananiah, saying, 'Thus says the Lord, "You have broken the yokes of wood, but you have made instead of them yokes of iron."** ¹⁴**For thus**

---

[5]See Koehler and Baumgartner, 2:1402–4. The word *shabar* is used in 19:10, 11 for Jeremiah's breaking of the potter's vessel.
[6]Ash, 207.

says the Lord of hosts, the God of Israel, "I have put a yoke of iron on the neck of all these nations, that they may serve Nebuchadnezzar king of Babylon; and they will serve him. And I have also given him the beasts of the field."'"

Verses 12, 13. Sometime after he left the scene, **the word of the Lord came to Jeremiah.** He was instructed to confront the false prophet **Hananiah** with these words: **"You have broken the yokes of wood, but you have made instead of them yokes of iron."** By his words and actions, Hananiah had deceived the people (28:15), hardening their hearts to God's warnings and causing them to receive a severer punishment.[7] If Judah would have worn the (wooden) yoke of submission to Babylon, they could have remained in the Promised Land (27:11). Instead, they would bear heavier "yokes of iron"—a reference to the devastation of Jerusalem and the Babylonian captivity (see Deut. 28:48). The people's attempts to resist Babylonian domination were destined for failure.

Verse 14. Jeremiah was instructed to repeat and emphasize God's judgment, saying, **"I have put a yoke of iron on the neck of all these nations, that they may serve Nebuchadnezzar king of Babylon; and they will serve him"** (see 27:6, 11). "Serve" comes from the Hebrew term עָבַד (*'abad*), meaning "toil," "work for someone," or "serve someone as a slave."[8] The yoke imagery itself symbolizes servitude. While the language is figurative, evidence does exist for some ancient Near Eastern captives actually wearing yokes and pulling heavy burdens.[9] Nebuchadnezzar's complete domination is further stressed by the statement **"I have also given him the beasts of the field"** (see 27:6).

Jeremiah's prophecy rendered Hananiah's supposed revelation of a speedy return impossible. His words meant that addi-

---

[7]Theo. Laetsch, *Jeremiah*, Bible Commentary (St. Louis: Concordia Publishing House, 1965), 228.

[8]Koehler and Baumgartner, 1:773–74.

[9]See the Assyrian relief (eighth century B.C.) in George A. Van Alstine and Nola J. Opperwall-Galluch, "Yoke; Yoke-bar," in *The International Standard Bible Encyclopedia*, rev. ed., ed. Geoffrey W. Bromiley (Grand Rapids, Mich.: Wm. B. Eerdmans Publishing Co., 1988), 4:1164.

tional people were going into bondage instead of the present captives coming home.

Indictments Against Hananiah
And the Price for Falsifying the Facts (28:15–17)

¹⁵Then Jeremiah the prophet said to Hananiah the prophet, "Listen now, Hananiah, the LORD has not sent you, and you have made this people trust in a lie. ¹⁶Therefore thus says the LORD, 'Behold, I am about to remove you from the face of the earth. This year you are going to die, because you have counseled rebellion against the LORD.'"
¹⁷So Hananiah the prophet died in the same year in the seventh month.

Verse 15. Three indictments against **Hananiah** followed. These were grave charges indeed, any one of which would have brought shame to his reputation. First, **Jeremiah** declared, **"The LORD has not sent you"** (see comments on 14:14; 23:21). Since God had neither commissioned Hananiah nor disclosed a message to him, he was a *false* prophet—an imposter and a fraud.

Second, Jeremiah told him, **"You have made this people trust in a lie."** All of the optimism generated by Hananiah's unfounded prophecy was hope without a foundation. It spurred Judah to generate a policy against Babylon that was destined to fail.

Verse 16. A third indictment came from Jeremiah: **"You have counseled rebellion against the LORD."** God had made it clear that His people were to submit to Nebuchadnezzar (25:8–11; 27:6–8). Therefore, any revolt against Nebuchadnezzar was tantamount to advocating rebellion against God Himself.

Jeremiah revealed to the false prophet the consequences of his rebellion: **"Therefore thus says the LORD, 'Behold, I am about to remove you from the face of the earth. This year you are going to die."** "Remove" comes from the Hebrew word שָׁלַח (*shalach*), which is the same word for "sent" in verse 15. God had not "sent" Hananiah to prophesy to the people. Because this man had deceived them, God would "send" him away to his death. According to the Law, false prophets who "counseled rebellion against the LORD" deserved to die (Deut. 13:5; see 18:20).

Verse 17. Soon the people again saw the confirmation that Jeremiah was a prophet of God: **So Hananiah the prophet died in the same year in the seventh month.** This chapter begins with Hananiah's bold comments "in the fifth month" (28:1) and closes with an announcement of his death "in the seventh month." He had falsely prophesied a restoration within two years (28:3, 11), but he died within two months.

When Hananiah died two months later, surely many recognized that a demonstration of a true prophet had been given to them through Jeremiah's pronouncement. Jeremiah's specific statement of "this year" put his prophetic credentials on a narrow timetable. When Hananiah died as predicted, it surely added a stamp of approval on Jeremiah's prophetic ministry (28:16).

APPLICATION

Seeking Truth (Ch. 28)
Although the masses are often deceived, God's truth stands in sharp contrast to lies. In chapter 28, God spoke through His faithful prophet, Jeremiah, whose words were eventually fulfilled. The false prophet, Hananiah, spoke his own message, which in time was shown to be empty deception. Three important lessons surface as we study this chapter.

For those who are searching for truth, God has given His Word and will provide opportunities to hear it (see Mt. 13:14–16; 23:37, 38; Lk. 8:18). God truly does not want people to perish (2 Pet. 3:9), but He frequently must exercise His patience as people refuse to hear and heed His warnings. In Jeremiah's time, God became more specific as redemptive times arose. Early on with the people of Judah, God warned that a force coming from the north would punish them (1:15, 16; 4:6; 6:1). Later, God specifically named Babylon as the nation (20:4) and Nebuchadnezzar as the king who would make this conquest (25:1–14; 27:6–11). In chapters 28 and 29, with some of His people already in captivity (see 22:24–30; 2 Kings 24:8–16), God began to name false prophets, further clearing the way for any honest, sincere soul to know His will and ways (28:15–17; 29:21–32).

For us today, the danger of deception should be a real concern. Jeremiah's statement to Hananiah, "You have made this people trust in a lie" (28:15), shouts out a dangerous course that masses of people have taken (see Ex. 23:2). Ever since Satan deceived Eve in the garden (Gen. 3:1–8), he has pursued a constant path of deception to ensnare souls into his web of wickedness (1 Pet. 4:3–5; 2 Pet. 2:12–22; 1 Jn. 2:15–17). Too often people have allowed themselves to become instruments in his hands (see 2 Cor. 11:3, 13–15; 1 Jn. 4:1). Many of these are very smooth and crafty communicators, adding to the danger of these divisive ways (Rom. 16:17, 18; 2 Pet. 2:1–11). We must guard against joining hands with a Hananiah and being led astray.

Attitude is all-important in discerning truth. Is there any safeguard against becoming a victim of a false teacher like Hananiah? Yes. Jesus gave two guidelines in seeking truth: (1) "Take care what you listen to" (Mk. 4:24), and (2) "Take care how you listen" (Lk. 8:18). This latter directive points to one's attitude in pursuing truth. Some people want a teacher to tell them what they want to hear (Jer. 5:30, 31; 2 Tim. 4:2–4). Some are caught up in deception and become deceivers themselves (44:16–19; 2 Tim. 3:13). It is dangerous when a way seems right and leads to physical or spiritual death (10:23; Prov. 14:12; Is. 59:1–4). People can go on without suspecting the dangers before them (Mt. 24:37–44; 2 Jn. 9).

The way to find what is right is to hunger for truth and search the Scriptures daily to see if truth is being taught (Mt. 5:6; Acts 17:11). We should hunger to know God's will, for He "desires all men to be saved and to come to the knowledge of the truth" (1 Tim. 2:4). If we know these things, blessed or happy are we, if we do them (Jn. 13:17). It is equally important, therefore, to practice the truth.

Chapter 29
A Message to the Captives

Jeremiah's message to the captives was part of God's plan to restore His people. To this point, the Babylonians had carried away Jews from Jerusalem on at least two occasions: the deportation of 605 B.C. (Dan. 1:1–6) and the deportation of 597 B.C. (2 Kings 24:10–16). Thousands had been taken to Babylon, including rulers, craftsmen, nobles, and skilled young men. The better class of people had been deported, leaving behind the lower class, who took over the houses and positions of those in exile.

Chapter 24 has already identified those who were deported as good figs (24:5), while Zedekiah and those left in Judah are referred to as bad figs (24:8).[1] God allowed some of His people—the good figs—to be taken into captivity because He knew that such a journey was necessary to bring them to repentance. God's people had to experience the chastening of captivity so that they could be restored. In chapter 29, God used a letter from Jeremiah to initiate His plans for reformation and restoration.

In a variety of ways, this letter bore a significant message in Hebrew history. The fact it was sent not long after the second deportation (597 B.C.), which ended the reign of Jeconiah (29:2), indicates God's desire to inaugurate the mindset needed to bring about a return.

---

[1]The prophet Ezekiel described those who remained as men who "devise iniquity and give evil advice" (Ezek. 11:2). After the second deportation, during the sixth year of Jeconiah's captivity (592 B.C.), great abominations were occurring in Jerusalem and in relationship to the Lord's sanctuary (Ezek. 8:1; 11:6–18). The bad figs responsible for these evil deeds were destined for destruction (Jer. 24:10).

Since the days of David, Jerusalem had become the center of Jewish worship and festal assemblies.² After Solomon had finished building the temple in Jerusalem, God promised to meet the people there if they kept His commandments (1 Kings 9:1–5). However, He warned them that they would be cast out of that place if they did not obey Him (1 Kings 9:6–10).

The consequences of Judah's rebellion and disobedience had become a reality as many Jews now found themselves in Babylonian captivity. Jeremiah's letter to Jews scattered from Jerusalem became a "declaration of independence" from the temple as a meeting place with God.³ For nearly four centuries, the deep-seated idea that the temple of the Lord was the throne of His glory (7:4) had been the general thought pattern of the Jews. Jeremiah's letter was the seed thought for them to recognize that God could be found in Babylon as well as in Jerusalem; a relationship with God could be independent of localities and national boundaries (see Jn. 4:19–24; Acts 17:22–31). This was a novel and much-needed concept for the exiles in that difficult hour. The unique and extended web of influences springing from the message in that letter make it one of the greatest letters in all literature for broadening one's views of "the LORD of hosts."

This was God's letter to His people. The message contained a plea with plans for the present (29:1–7), present problems and promises for the future (29:8–14), perils the people would face (29:15–20), and perils the false prophets would undergo among the captives (29:21–32).

A PLEA WITH PLANS FOR THE PRESENT (29:1–7)

¹Now these are the words of the letter which Jeremiah the prophet sent from Jerusalem to the rest of the elders of the exile, the priests, the prophets and all the people whom Nebu-

---

²See Ex. 23:14–17; 2 Sam. 5:4–7; 6:12; 1 Kings 8:1–13, 54–63; 1 Chron. 17:1–10; 28:9–12; 2 Chron. 3:1; 5:1, 2; 6:4–11; 11:13–17; 30:1, 5–12.

³Costen J. Harrell, *The Prophets of Israel* (Nashville: Cokesbury Press, 1933), 138–39.

chadnezzar had taken into exile from Jerusalem to Babylon. ²(This was after King Jeconiah and the queen mother, the court officials, the princes of Judah and Jerusalem, the craftsmen and the smiths had departed from Jerusalem.) ³The letter was sent by the hand of Elasah the son of Shaphan, and Gemariah the son of Hilkiah, whom Zedekiah king of Judah sent to Babylon to Nebuchadnezzar king of Babylon, saying, ⁴"Thus says the LORD of hosts, the God of Israel, to all the exiles whom I have sent into exile from Jerusalem to Babylon, ⁵'Build houses and live in them; and plant gardens and eat their produce. ⁶Take wives and become the fathers of sons and daughters, and take wives for your sons and give your daughters to husbands, that they may bear sons and daughters; and multiply there and do not decrease. ⁷Seek the welfare of the city where I have sent you into exile, and pray to the LORD on its behalf; for in its welfare you will have welfare.'"

Verse 1. The chapter begins by mentioning **the letter which Jeremiah the prophet sent from Jerusalem** to the Jews taken captive into Babylon by **Nebuchadnezzar**. Those addressed by the letter include **the rest of the elders of the exile, the priests, the prophets and all the people**. The meaning of the phrase "the rest of the elders" is uncertain. It could simply distinguish the elders in Babylon from the ones who were still living in Jerusalem. Another possibility is that, in Babylonian exile, some of the elders had been imprisoned or executed.[4] In this case, it would be clearer to translate the Hebrew word for "rest" (יֶתֶר, *yether*) as "remaining" (NRSV) or "surviving" (NIV).

Verse 2. A parenthetical note dates Jeremiah's letter sometime **after King Jeconiah and the queen mother** [Nehushta]**, the court officials, the princes of Judah and Jerusalem, the craftsmen and the smiths had departed from Jerusalem**. This was the second deportation of the Jews in 597 B.C. (see comments on 22:24–26; 24:1).

---

[4]J. A. Thompson, *The Book of Jeremiah*, The New International Commentary on the Old Testament (Grand Rapids, Mich.: Wm. B. Eerdmans Publishing Co., 1980), 545.

Verse 3. The letter was carried by two influential men of Judah. The first was **Elasah the son of Shaphan**, whose family was sympathetic to Jeremiah. Elasah's brother Ahikam was the one who protected Jeremiah when others wanted to kill him (26:8, 24).[5] Another brother, Gemariah, was one of the men who pled with King Jehoiakim not to burn Jeremiah's scroll (36:25; see comments on 36:10). Their father, Shaphan, was the scribe who had taken the discovered copy of God's law to young King Josiah (2 Kings 22:9, 10).

The second postman was **Gemariah the son of Hilkiah**. The Old Testament mentions several men named Hilkiah, including the father of Jeremiah (1:1). The Hilkiah mentioned here may have been the notable high priest from Josiah's reign who "found the book of the law in the house of the LORD" and gave it to Shaphan (2 Kings 22:8). If this is correct, both families of Elasah and Gemariah had exercised great influence in Jerusalem over the course of several generations.

Elasah and Gemariah were already being **sent** as messengers of **Zedekiah king of Judah . . . to Nebuchadnezzar king of Babylon**. These men may have been delivering Judah's annual tribute to their overlord or conducting other official business. Diplomatic correspondence between vassals and their overlords was not uncommon in the ancient world.[6] J. A. Thompson proposed that Jeremiah's letter was carried along with official correspondence in "the diplomatic mail bag."[7]

Verse 4. "The words of the letter" (29:1) begin here by establishing authorship. The letter was ultimately from **the LORD of hosts, the God of Israel**. This complete phrase appears three other times in the chapter (29:8, 21, 25), whereas "the LORD of hosts" appears by itself once (29:17). The expressions "thus says the LORD" and "declares the LORD" are also repeated, stressing

---

[5] Ahikam's son Gedaliah was eventually appointed as governor over the Jews left in Judah. He received this office because of his submission to Nebuchadnezzar, which corresponded with Jeremiah's message (40:1–12).

[6] Thompson, 546. The Amarna letters (fourteenth century B.C.) illustrate frequent correspondence between an overlord (Egypt) and subject peoples (in Palestine and Syria).

[7] Ibid., 545.

the divine origin and authority of the message.

The letter was addressed **to all the exiles** who had been **sent into exile from Jerusalem to Babylon**. These Jews had been taken from their homeland by Nebuchadnezzar and forced to live among strangers. Even though they had been taken by the Babylonian king, God emphasized that He was the One responsible for their exile.

Verse 5. The Lord's purpose for the Babylonian exile was to bring about moral and spiritual transformation in the lives of His people. As Jeremiah had predicted, they would be there for about seventy years (see comments on 25:11). Since their stay was not going to be brief—as the false prophets were predicting (28:3, 4; 29:8, 9)—God instructed His people to settle down, live normal lives, and wait for His deliverance.

God told those in exile, **"Build houses and live in them; and plant gardens and eat their produce."**[8] He urged them to build and plant, to provide living quarters and a livelihood for their families. The Lord did not send His people into captivity to starve or merely survive. He wanted them to thrive through penitence.

Verse 6. Rejoicing over marriage had in recent times been impossible or unwise in Judah (7:34; 16:1–4, 9; 25:10). Moreover, the exiles were grieving because of the loss of former neighbors, friends, and loved ones who had fallen as casualties of war. This experience was indeed painful, but God had a positive purpose for it (see Heb. 12:3–11).

At this juncture, the remnant needed renewal—new hearts and minds. God's rebuilding program revived marriage and parenthood in Babylonia so His people could **multiply** and **not decrease**. The men were instructed to **take wives and become the fathers of sons and daughters**. Although not explicitly stated, it is implied that they were to choose wives from among their own people (Deut. 7:3, 4; see Ezra 9:1, 2). The men were also to **take wives for** [their] **sons and give** [their] **daughters to husbands**. As a result of these marriages, the population would continue to grow, and joy would be restored to their lives.

---

[8]Although the context of verse 5 is different, the language ("build" and "plant") is reminiscent of Jeremiah's call (1:10).

Verse 7. God further instructed the exiles, **"Seek the welfare of the city where I have sent you into exile, and pray to the LORD on its behalf."** "Seek" comes from the Hebrew word דָּרַשׁ (*darash*), a strong term that can mean "seek with care," "study," "investigate," "search," "be intent on," or "make supplication [to God]."[9] The word for "welfare," שָׁלוֹם (*shalom*), is used often in this book and is usually translated "peace" (4:10; 6:14; 8:11, 15; 12:5; 14:13; 16:5; 25:37; 28:9). It can also be defined as "safety," "soundness," "health," or "prosperity."[10] Combining the concepts of seeking and welfare, this message called upon those in captivity to show great concern for their captors. The Lord wanted His people to promote the well-being of the place they were staying. Anthony L. Ash noted that the text does not clarify which "city" is intended. Since there were several settlements of the Jews, the idea may be "in which *city* you dwell."[11]

The command for God's people to pray to Him emphasized their need for reconciliation; they had rebelled against Him for too long. The fact that God wanted them to pray for their enemies must have seemed like a revolutionary idea. However, the Jews' own **welfare** was directly dependent upon the **welfare** of Babylonia.

Time would prove the wisdom and depth of God's guidelines. Portions of the inspired text identify the good favor His people had among their captors. They were scattered in various places, and yet the captivity would achieve God's intent that many would come again to know that He is Lord (see Ezek. 6:8–14; 11:16–20; 28:20–26; 29:13–16).

Specific locations of the exiles are sometimes mentioned. Daniel occupied high positions at Babylon in the governments of Nebuchadnezzar (Dan. 1:1–6, 17–21; 2:48, 49), Belshazzar (5:13–

---

[9]Ludwig Koehler and Walter Baumgartner, *The Hebrew and Aramaic Lexicon of the Old Testament*, study ed., trans. and ed. M. E. J. Richardson (Boston: Brill, 2001), 1:233.

[10]Francis Brown, S. R. Driver, and Charles A. Briggs, *A Hebrew and English Lexicon of the Old Testament* (Oxford: Clarendon Press, 1972), 1022–23.

[11]Anthony L. Ash, *Jeremiah and Lamentations*, The Living Word Commentary (Abilene, Tex.: ACU Press, 1987), 210.

17, 29–30), and Darius the Mede and Cyrus the Persian (6:1–3, 22–28). Ezra indicates that a pocket of the Levites were located in Casiphia (Ezra 8:15–20). He also mentions other settlements along the Chebar River, perhaps between Babylon and Nippur, including: Tel-melah, Tel-harsha, Cherub, Addan, and Immer (Ezra 2:59). Another site was Tel-abib, where Ezekiel visited the exiles (Ezek. 3:15). Later, Esther became the wife of King Xerxes (Ahasuerus) who reigned at Susa, one of the capitals of the Persian Empire (Esther 1:1, 2; 2:17). Nehemiah was cupbearer to King Artaxerxes in that same place (Neh. 1:1; 2:1).

God's people were granted much liberty by the Babylonians; they formed colonies and were granted some civic and religious freedoms (Ezek. 8:1; 14:1; 20:1). Through those circumstances, they would remember God and would return to Him (Zech. 10:6–10). Such was the divine intent through the principles and procedures given in Jeremiah's letter.

PRESENT PROBLEMS AND PROMISES FOR THE FUTURE (29:8–14)

⁸"For thus says the Lord of hosts, the God of Israel, 'Do not let your prophets who are in your midst and your diviners deceive you, and do not listen to the dreams which they dream. ⁹For they prophesy falsely to you in My name; I have not sent them,' declares the Lord.

¹⁰"For thus says the Lord, 'When seventy years have been completed for Babylon, I will visit you and fulfill My good word to you, to bring you back to this place. ¹¹For I know the plans that I have for you,' declares the Lord, 'plans for welfare and not for calamity to give you a future and a hope. ¹²Then you will call upon Me and come and pray to Me, and I will listen to you. ¹³You will seek Me and find Me when you search for Me with all your heart. ¹⁴I will be found by you,' declares the Lord, 'and I will restore your fortunes and will gather you from all the nations and from all the places where I have driven you,' declares the Lord, 'and I will bring you back to the place from where I sent you into exile.'"

Verses 8, 9. Evil influences were active among the captives, diverting their minds from God's instructions. False **prophets** and **diviners** were claiming to speak in the **name** of **the** LORD, receiving inspired messages through **dreams** (see comments on 27:9, 10). God warned His people not to allow these self-appointed spokesmen to **deceive** them (see comments on 23:16, 17; 28:15, 16). He made it clear that He had **not sent** these imposters; they were speaking by their own authority (see comments on 23:21).

Verses 8 and 9 suggest that these deceivers, like Hananiah, were calling for a speedy return to their homeland. They were also denying that Jerusalem would be destroyed (see 28:3, 4). Contradicting God's word concerning a seventy-year captivity (25:12; 27:6–10), they discouraged those in exile from obeying God's directions and His efforts to bring about reformation. Verse 15 shows that the people were listening to these deceivers, who offered promises pleasing to their ears.

Verse 10. God had plans for the captives when the **seventy years** of **Babylon**['s] rule was over. He knew these people, and His objective to foster repentance and reformation would not be accomplished by a speedy return. God looked ahead and beautifully described how He would restore His people: **"I will visit you and fulfill My good word to you, to bring you back to this place"** (see comments on 27:21, 22).

Verse 11. The Lord's ultimate desire was to show favor to His people. Although they had forfeited His past blessings by their rebellion, He would cleanse and restore them. His **plans** were for their **welfare** (see comments on 29:7). Instead of bringing further **calamity** on them, He wanted to **give** [them] **a future and a hope**.

Verse 12. The success of God's people depended upon their relationship with Him. In times to come, they would **call upon** Him in prayer, and He would **listen to** them. God had predicted this inner longing more than twenty years earlier (3:18, 19). However, an additional fifty years would pass before a remnant would return to rebuild Jerusalem, reestablishing God's people in the Promised Land. The Lord's promises would only become reality when the carnal focus (5:7–9; 9:3, 6; 18:11–13) was gone and genuine supplications to God were renewed. This humble approach to God is evident from Daniel's prayer (Dan. 9:1–19).

Verse 13. The Lord longed for His people to be devoted to Him. He said, **"You will seek Me and find Me when you search for Me with all your heart."** The Hebrew word translated "search" is דָּרַשׁ (*darash*), a strong term that is rendered "seek" in verse 7 (see comments on 29:7). In verse 13, the word "seek" comes from a different Hebrew word, בָּקַשׁ (*baqash*). It can mean "seek to find," "seek to secure," or "seek [one's] face."[12] These terms imply that the people would have almost a holy covetousness for the Creator. They would search for Him with all of their being (see Lev. 11:44, 45; 19:2; Deut. 6:4, 5; 10:12, 13; 11:13; 13:3; 26:16).

Verse 14. God assured the people that, when they attained this mindset, they would indeed find Him. He would fulfill His good promises, restoring their **fortunes** and bringing them **back** to the Promised Land. Such promises were originally made when God gave Israel the Law through Moses (Deut. 4:27–31; 30:1–5). Unfortunately, many had to suffer before their hearts truly returned to God and His promises became a reality.

PERILS THE PEOPLE WOULD FACE
(29:15–20)

15"Because you have said, 'The Lord has raised up prophets for us in Babylon'—16for thus says the Lord concerning the king who sits on the throne of David, and concerning all the people who dwell in this city, your brothers who did not go with you into exile—17thus says the Lord of hosts, 'Behold, I am sending upon them the sword, famine and pestilence, and I will make them like split-open figs that cannot be eaten due to rottenness. 18I will pursue them with the sword, with famine and with pestilence; and I will make them a terror to all the kingdoms of the earth, to be a curse and a horror and a hiss-

---

[12]Brown, Driver, and Briggs, 134–35.

ing, and a reproach among all the nations where I have driven them, ¹⁹because they have not listened to My words,' declares the LORD, 'which I sent to them again and again by My servants the prophets; but you did not listen,' declares the LORD. ²⁰You, therefore, hear the word of the LORD, all you exiles, whom I have sent away from Jerusalem to Babylon."

Verses 15–17. Some of the exiles in **Babylon** had been deceived by the false **prophets** who were claiming that Jerusalem would not be destroyed (see comments on 29:8, 9). Nevertheless, God revealed that those who remained in the holy **city**—including **the king who sits on the throne of David** (Zedekiah)—would not remain unscathed. Instead, God would strike **the people** with **the sword, famine and pestilence** (see comments on 14:12). He would **make them like split-open figs that cannot be eaten due to rottenness**. This imagery is also seen in chapter 24, where the exiles are referred to as good figs and those remaining in Jerusalem are portrayed as bad figs (see comments on 24:8).

Verse 18. The siege and destruction of Jerusalem would serve as strong deterrents to a speedy return from Babylonian exile. At this time, the exiles were obviously better off in Babylon than at home. The people living in Jerusalem would ultimately become **a terror to all the kingdoms of the earth . . . a curse and a horror and a hissing, and a reproach among all the nations** (see 15:4; 24:9; 25:9, 11, 18; 26:6).

Verse 19. The reason for the punishment in Judah was no mystery. God explained, **"They have not listened to My words."** Moreover, He said, **"I sent to them again and again by My servants the prophets; but you did not listen."** A sudden shift in this verse from third person ("they") to second person ("you") includes the captives in this accusation. God warned them in verse 8 about listening to false prophets, and He warned them in verse 19 about failing to listen to His words.

Verse 20. God was appealing to the **exiles, whom** [He had] **sent away . . . to Babylon** for a better response than He had received from those in **Jerusalem**. His promises in verses 10 through 14 were for people with dispositions different from the rebellious spirits which had led to Judah's ruin.

JEREMIAH 29

PERILS THE FALSE PROPHETS WOULD UNDERGO AMONG THE CAPTIVES (29:21–32)

Death Promised to Two False Prophets (29:21–23)

²¹"Thus says the LORD of hosts, the God of Israel, concerning Ahab the son of Kolaiah and concerning Zedekiah the son of Maaseiah, who are prophesying to you falsely in My name, 'Behold, I will deliver them into the hand of Nebuchadnezzar king of Babylon, and he will slay them before your eyes. ²²Because of them a curse will be used by all the exiles from Judah who are in Babylon, saying, "May the LORD make you like Zedekiah and like Ahab, whom the king of Babylon roasted in the fire, ²³because they have acted foolishly in Israel, and have committed adultery with their neighbors' wives and have spoken words in My name falsely, which I did not command them; and I am He who knows and am a witness," declares the LORD.'"

Verse 21. Two false prophets in Babylon, **Ahab the son of Kolaiah** and **Zedekiah the son of Maaseiah**,[13] were indicted for their sin. These men claimed to speak in the **name** of the Lord; but, actually, they were only proclaiming their own messages. For this deception, God would give them over to **Nebuchadnezzar king of Babylon**, who would **slay them** in full view of the people. A special level of shame is reserved for those whose sin becomes a public spectacle of disgrace. From a political viewpoint, Nebuchadnezzar may have wanted to silence these two men because their message of a short exile constituted treason against Babylon.

Verse 22. The names of these false prophets would live in infamy. **The exiles** would use their names in **a curse** formula, which included the means of death: "**May the LORD make you like Zedekiah and like Ahab, whom the king of Babylon roasted in the fire.**" Although stoning was the predominant

---

[13]These are not references to the kings by the same names.

method of execution used by the Israelites, burning was not unknown to them (Gen. 38:24; Lev. 21:9). Among the Babylonians, however, burning was more prevalent. The story of Nebuchadnezzar's fiery furnace and Daniel's three friends confirms this truth (Dan. 3:1, 6–8, 19–23).[14]

Verse 23. As is evident in the NIV, the curse formula concludes at the end of verse 22. In verse 23, God summarized the rationale behind the execution of these two ungodly men. (1) **"They have acted foolishly in Israel."** The Hebrew word for "foolishly" is נְבָלָה ($n^e balah$), a term that refers to one's stupidity in transgressing God's laws. It denotes a defiance against that which is holy.[15] (2) **"[They] have committed adultery with their neighbors' wives"** (see 3:2; 5:8; 13:26, 27; Ezek. 22:9–11). In the Law, the punishment for adultery was death (Lev. 20:10; Deut. 22:22). (3) **"[They] have spoken words in My name falsely."** The penalty for the one who spoke presumptuously in the name of the Lord was also death (Deut. 18:20). The omniscient God was fully aware of these evil deeds, and He served as **a witness** to them.

Death Promised to Another False Prophet (29:24–32)

24To Shemaiah the Nehelamite you shall speak, saying, 25"Thus says the LORD of hosts, the God of Israel, 'Because you have sent letters in your own name to all the people who are in Jerusalem, and to Zephaniah the son of Maaseiah, the priest, and to all the priests, saying, 26"The LORD has made you priest instead of Jehoiada the priest, to be the overseer in the house of the LORD over every madman who prophesies, to put him in the stocks and in the iron collar, 27now then, why have you not rebuked Jeremiah of Anathoth who prophesies to you? 28For he has sent to us in Babylon, saying, 'The exile will be long; build houses and live in them and plant gardens and eat their produce.'"'"

29Zephaniah the priest read this letter to Jeremiah the

---

[14]Burning as a mode of execution is attested much earlier in Babylonian history. See *Code of Hammurabi* 25, 110, 157.

[15]Koehler and Baumgartner, 1:664.

prophet. ³⁰Then came the word of the Lord to Jeremiah, saying, ³¹"Send to all the exiles, saying, 'Thus says the Lord concerning Shemaiah the Nehelamite, "Because Shemaiah has prophesied to you, although I did not send him, and he has made you trust in a lie," ³²therefore thus says the Lord, "Behold, I am about to punish Shemaiah the Nehelamite and his descendants; he will not have anyone living among this people, and he will not see the good that I am about to do to My people," declares the Lord, "because he has preached rebellion against the Lord."'"

Verses 24, 25. Here is an interesting exchange of letters related to another false prophet. Not only had God witnessed the sordid deeds of Ahab and Zedekiah (29:21), but He also knew about the sins of **Shemaiah**. From Babylonian exile, this man had **sent letters . . . to all the people . . . in Jerusalem**. The Hebrew word for "letters" (סְפָרִים, s^e*parim*) is plural, but it is sometimes used to refer to a single, important letter (2 Kings 19:14). It may be that Shemaiah had written only one letter that was addressed to many people (29:29). In particular, he mentioned **Zephaniah the son of Maaseiah**, a **priest** (see 21:1) and brother to the false prophet Zedekiah (29:21). Shemaiah's correspondence was written **in** [his] **own name**—that is, it did not have divine authority.

Verse 26. Shemaiah's message to Zephaniah was to take the same bold action **Jehoiada the priest** had taken in executing Athaliah and the idolatrous priests in the ninth century B.C. (2 Kings 11:1–20). In more recent times, Pashhur had filled the role of the temple **overseer**. He himself had ordered Jeremiah to be beaten and placed in the stocks (20:1, 2). Shemaiah wanted such action taken against **every madman who prophesies, to put him in the stocks and in the iron collar**. God's prophets, including Jeremiah, were sometimes considered madmen because of their strong stance against immorality and the unique ways in which they illustrated their messages (see Hos. 9:7).

Verse 27. Since it was the temple overseer's responsibility to punish madmen, Shemaiah wrote, **"Now then, why have you not rebuked Jeremiah of Anathoth who prophesies to you?"** Seeing that the prophet's message had stirred up the exiles,

Shemaiah was demanding that Zephaniah put Jeremiah in the stocks and in an iron collar.

Verse 28. Shemaiah's letter was an obvious counterattack against Jeremiah's letter about the extended time of the captivity (29:4–10). **"The exile will be long"** is a paraphrase of Jeremiah's message that the Babylonian captivity would last seventy years (29:10). The rest of verse 28 is a direct quotation from Jeremiah's letter (29:5): **"Build houses and live in them and plant gardens and eat their produce."**

Verses 29, 30. What ruined Shemaiah's scheme? First, **Zephaniah the priest read this letter to Jeremiah**. He decided to cooperate with God's **prophet** rather than to incarcerate him. Second, God supplied **Jeremiah** with another letter to the captives about Shemaiah.

Verses 31, 32. Shemaiah, along with **his descendants**, received the divine promise of death because he had made the people **trust in a lie** and had **preached rebellion against the Lord** (see 28:15–17). Men may lie to men; but lying is, in reality, also rebellion against the God of truth (see Acts 5:1–11). God's punishment was final.

This chapter exposed error as God destroyed deception and urged the remnant to begin reformation. Three false prophets were exposed, and God's good intentions for His people were emphasized (29:4–7, 10–14, 32). The conditions were right for any listening ear in Judah or Babylon. In a unique way, this message opened the door for the reformation and restoration of God's people at His selected time (29:10). The next chapters give more detail about God's intentions for a better tomorrow.

APPLICATION

Important Characters (Ch. 29)

A surface reading of this unique chapter reveals that ten characters besides Jeremiah are included:

- King Jeconiah (or Jehoiachin) in exile in Babylon (29:2)
- Elasah was one of two carrying Jeremiah's letter to those in exile (29:3)

JEREMIAH 29

- Shaphan, the father of Elasah, being the scribe who had taken the copy of God's law to King Josiah (29:3)
- Gemariah, the other postman carrying Jeremiah's letter (29:3)
- Hilkiah, the father of Gemariah (29:3)
- Ahab, the son Kolaiah, a false prophet in Babylon (29:21)
- Zedekiah, the son of Maaseiah, a false prophet, destined to be roasted in the fire with Ahab by Nebuchadnezzar (29:21)
- Shemaiah, the Nehelamite, another false prophet in Babylon, urging through a letter that Jeremiah be imprisoned (29:24)
- Zephaniah, the son of Maaseiah, a priest and chief temple officer who received Shemaiah's letter (29:25)
- Jehoiada, a priest in Jerusalem in past times (29:26)

While sobering lessons relate to the foolishness and destiny of some of those ten individuals, the key personality of chapter 29 is God. Through a careful reading of the chapter, one will find "the LORD" mentioned 25 times and "the God of Israel" mentioned 4 times. The Lord often refers to Himself by using various personal pronouns: "I" (25 times), "My" (7 times), "Me" (5 times), and "He" (once). A total of sixty-seven references to God appear in only thirty-two verses.

Surely a valuable lesson can be found here. How easy it is for us to get in a crowd, thinking about this or that person, and ignore the very God in whom "we live and move and exist" (Acts 17:28)! It was God's letter through Jeremiah that would set the tone for a reformation in thought and a restoration of people returning to Jerusalem. It was judgments of God that would be visited on the false prophets, Ahab, Zedekiah, and Shemaiah. It was God who offered "a future and a hope" to His people (29:11), as He called them to seek and search for Him with all their heart.

This chapter offers great principles of direction (via the letter), correction (by punishment for the false prophets), and restoration (through penitent hearts returning to God)—all of these influences were dependent on the great God of Israel.

Jeremiah's Letter (29:4–7)

The substance of Jeremiah's letter to the exiles could be summarized by the following instructions: (1) "Resume life" (29:5); (2) "Replenish life" (29:6); (3) "Respect your captors" (29:7); and (4) "Respect your Creator" (29:7). Their obedience to these commands would result in great reward.

Seeking the Welfare of Others (29:7)

God promised that, by seeking peace and welfare for Babylon, those in exile would find peace and gain their own welfare. This statement directly parallels 1 Timothy 4:16, where Paul exhorted Christians, "Pay close attention to yourself and to your teaching; persevere in these things, for as you do this you will ensure salvation both for yourself and for those who hear you." An evangelistic spirit and concern for others must always be near the hearts of God's people. Christ is the Savior, but imbibing His spirit is essential for any who would be saved (Lk. 9:23; 19:10; 1 Jn. 4:14).

"A Future and a Hope" (29:11)

Even though life for those in exile appeared dismal, God could see past that time into the distant future. They would not get to return home immediately, as some false prophets were claiming. Nevertheless, after seventy years had past, He would indeed bring a remnant back to Jerusalem. "'For I know the plans that I have for you,' declares the LORD, 'plans for welfare and not for calamity to give you a future and a hope'" (29:11).

Regardless of the difficulties we may face in life, God has promised us a bright future. Paul stated that our "momentary, light affliction is producing for us an eternal weight of glory far beyond all comparison" (2 Cor. 4:17). He then discussed the resurrection body and being in the presence of the Lord (2 Cor. 5:1–10). Peter said that Christians have been "born again to a living hope." Those who remain faithful to Jesus can anticipate an imperishable inheritance reserved in heaven (1 Pet. 1:3, 4).

Chapter 30
Restoring the Fortunes Of God's People

Chapters 30 through 33, sometimes called the "Book of Consolation," comprise the largest positive portion in the Book of Jeremiah. The only specific biblical time frame for this segment is 32:1, where the tenth year of King Zedekiah is mentioned. It was 587 B.C., just a year before the destruction of Jerusalem. At this time, the city was besieged by the Babylonians, and Jeremiah was "shut up in the court of the guard" (32:2). The messages of chapters 32 and 33 were given to Jeremiah during this confinement (32:1, 2; 33:1). Chapters 30 and 31 mention no confinement, but their events apparently took place in the same general time period, when God charged the prophet to "write all the words which I have spoken to you in a book" (30:2).[1] Chapter 31 obviously followed just after chapter 30 (see 31:1).

Extremely important themes are found in this part of the book: the destruction of Babylon, the return of God's people, the coming of the Messiah and the establishment of His kingdom, and the governing principles of a new covenant. Such positive prospects led F. Cawley to refer to this unit as "a little green oasis in a dry and barren desert."[2] Chapter 30 primarily deals with the promised return of God's people to Palestine and the restoration

---

[1] For other specific assignments for Jeremiah to write down (or to have written down) various portions of his prophecies, see 36:1, 2, 27–32; 45:1; 51:59–64.

[2] F. Cawley, "Jeremiah," in *The New Bible Commentary* (Grand Rapids, Mich.: Wm. B. Eerdmans Publishing Co, 1954), 626.

of their relationship with God.³ This message, and the contents of the next three chapters, present a bold contrast to chapters 27 through 29. In chapters 27 through 29, Jeremiah cleared the table, so to speak, of all the false claims relating to the quick reversal of captivity and the restoration of God's people to their homeland. Assuming the reality of the seventy years of exile (see 25:12–14; 27:1–8; 29:10), chapters 30 through 33 move forward and concentrate on happier topics, offering hope and encouragement.

Chapters 30 and 31 should be studied as a literary unit. The splendor and softness of these chapters no doubt lifted the spirits of Jeremiah's original hearers and readers. Almighty God was opening a door of heavenly hope to His people (30:4), attracting them back to Himself, from whom they had wandered in their wicked ways (14:10; Lam. 4:13–18).

Chapter 30 can be divided into the following sections: God's promise that their problems would pass (30:1–11); His view of the problem and solution to it (30:12–17); His promises of glory restored (30:18–22); and His pattern and plan made clear (30:23, 24).

GOD'S PROMISE THAT THEIR PROBLEMS WOULD PASS (30:1–11)

The Fortunes of God's People Be Restored (30:1–3)

¹The word which came to Jeremiah from the Lord, saying, ²"Thus says the Lord, the God of Israel, 'Write all the words which I have spoken to you in a book. ³For behold, days are coming,' declares the Lord, 'when I will restore the fortunes of My people Israel and Judah.' The Lord says, 'I will also bring them back to the land that I gave to their forefathers and they shall possess it.'"

Verses 1, 2. God spoke to **Jeremiah** and said, **"Write all the**

---

³For shorter passages with a similar theme, see 3:14–18; 16:14, 15; 23:3–8; 24:4–7.

words which I have spoken to you in a book." The Hebrew word translated "book" is סֵפֶר (*seper*), a general term that can mean "letter," "register," "legal document," or "scroll."[4] The book form used at that time was a scroll rather than a codex. The more specific term for a "roll" or a "scroll," מְגִלָּה (*mᵉgillah*), appears later in Jeremiah (36:2, 28, 32). God obviously wanted His plans written down. A written agreement was considered definite. Verbal statements can be easily denied, but a written record can be reread and reaffirmed.

Verse 3. God began, **"For behold, days are coming,"** and then reassured His oppressed people at home and in captivity that His plans would prevail (see comments on 23:5 for the repeated use of the expression "Behold, the days are coming"). He foretold of a future time when He would **restore the fortunes of** [His] **people Israel and Judah**. "Restore the fortunes" translates the difficult phrase שַׁבְתִּי אֶת-שְׁבוּת (*shabᵉththi eth shᵉbuth*). One suggestion is that the rhythmic phrase should be translated "turn a turning," but this rendering is unclear.[5] A second proposal is that it refers to restoring material wealth and prosperity to the people (see comments on 30:18). A third possibility is that the phrase means "bring back from captivity" (NKJV). The Assyrians had taken Israel captive in 722 B.C., and the Babylonians had taken many from Judah into exile in 605 and 597 B.C. More people would be led away to Babylon in 586 B.C., after the destruction of Jerusalem. God's assurance that He would return these captives is clearly stated next: **"I will also bring them back to the land that I gave to their forefathers and they shall possess it."** He would return a remnant of His people to live once again in the Promised Land. A fourth alternative is that the phrase is a figurative reference to the Messianic era. In light of the basic thrust of this chapter and the next, the third and fourth views, perhaps, should be symbolically combined for the best approach.

---

[4]Francis Brown, S. R. Driver, and Charles A. Briggs, *A Hebrew and English Lexicon of the Old Testament* (Oxford: Clarendon Press, 1972), 706–7.

[5]See Ludwig Koehler and Walter Baumgartner, *The Hebrew and Aramaic Lexicon of the Old Testament*, study ed., trans. and ed. M. E. J. Richardson (Boston: Brill, 2001), 2:1385–86.

TRUTH FOR TODAY COMMENTARY

The Days of Distress Be Dissolved (30:4–7)

⁴Now these are the words which the LORD spoke concerning Israel and concerning Judah:
⁵"For thus says the LORD,
'I have heard a sound of terror,
Of dread, and there is no peace.
⁶Ask now, and see
If a male can give birth.
Why do I see every man
With his hands on his loins, as a woman in childbirth?
And why have all faces turned pale?
⁷Alas! for that day is great,
There is none like it;
And it is the time of Jacob's distress,
But he will be saved from it.'"

Verses 4, 5. Prior to the return from captivity, God's people would experience days of distress. They would cry out in fear because of their enemies and the devastation surrounding them. They would look for **peace**, but would be unable to find any.

Verse 6. Using irony, God compared the frightened behavior of men to women during childbirth. He said, **"Ask now, and see if a male can give birth. Why do I see every man with his hands on his loins, as a woman in childbirth?"** The figure of labor pains is a common metaphor in Jeremiah for the distress coming on God's people (4:31; 6:24; 13:21; 22:23). The troubles faced by Israel and Judah would cause grown men to be terrified and their **faces** to turn **pale**.

Verse 7. The time of Jacob's distress could be traced back to Israel, the northern kingdom, being sent into Assyrian captivity. This began in 733 B.C., when Tiglath-pileser III overtook Israelite towns and carried away captives (2 Kings 15:27–30). The defeat of Israel culminated in the destruction of Samaria in 722 B.C. The siege was begun by Shalmaneser V, and it may have been completed by his son Sargon II (2 Kings 17:1–41; 18:9–12).[6] "Jacob's

---

[6]*Annals of Sargon II* 10–18.

JEREMIAH 30

distress" would be extended to the Babylonian attacks on Jerusalem by Nebuchadnezzar in 605 and 597 B.C., culminating in the destruction of the city in 586 B.C. At that point, God's people had ceased to exist as a nation. They had become exiles of their own evil nature.

He will be saved from it points to the future hope of the restoration of God's people (see comments on 30:3). In His providence, the fall of Babylon would open the door to the Medo-Persian Empire in 539 B.C. (Dan. 5:18–31). At that time, the Lord would use Cyrus to send His people home (Ezra 1:1–11; Is. 44:28—45:6). His people would be saved from "the time of Jacob's distress."

"Distress" gives the idea of narrowness and pressure, whereas "saved" implies ample space and freedom (see 30:10, 11). "Saved" comes from the Hebrew word יָשַׁע (*yasha'*), meaning "deliver, save" or "give width and breadth to, liberate."[7] This was quite a thought for frightened captives. Whether near or far, they would be saved.

The Days of Deliverance Be Evident (30:8–11)

**⁸"'It shall come about on that day,' declares the LORD of hosts, 'that I will break his yoke from off their neck and will tear off their bonds; and strangers will no longer make them their slaves. ⁹But they shall serve the LORD their God and David their king, whom I will raise up for them.
¹⁰'Fear not, O Jacob My servant,' declares the LORD,
'And do not be dismayed, O Israel;
For behold, I will save you from afar
And your offspring from the land of their captivity.
And Jacob will return and will be quiet and at ease,
And no one will make him afraid.
¹¹For I am with you,' declares the LORD, 'to save you;
For I will destroy completely all the nations where I have scattered you,
Only I will not destroy you completely.**

---

[7]Brown, Driver, and Briggs, 446.

> But I will chasten you justly
> And will by no means leave you unpunished.'"

Verse 8. In verse 7, the phrase "that day" refers to a time of God's judgment. In verse 8, **that day** is used for a time of His deliverance. Concerning this salvation, God affirmed, **"I will break his yoke from off their neck and will tear off their bonds; and strangers will no longer make them their slaves."** The "yoke" was a symbol of submission. Earlier in the book, the people of Judah were admonished to wear the yoke of Babylon instead of rebelling against Nebuchadnezzar (see comments on 27:2, 8, 11). Here God is portrayed as breaking their yoke and their bonds, setting them free.

Verse 9. Instead of serving the king of Babylon, the people would return to the Promised Land and **serve the Lord their God**. They would also serve **David their king,** whom [God would] **raise up for them** (see 23:5, 6; 33:14–16; Is. 9:6, 7; Ezek. 34:12, 13, 23–25; 37:15–28; Hos. 3:5). This phrasing refers to "the expected Messianic king, the 'second David.'"[8] One day God would offer them spiritual redemption through Jesus Christ (Lk. 1:30–33; Acts 2:25–36; Rev. 3:21).

Verse 10. With tender words, God comforted His people in their distress. He said, **"Do not be dismayed, O Israel; for behold, I will save you from afar."** He would bring their **offspring from the land of their captivity** and **return** them to the Promised Land. Although many of the people would die in exile, some—along with the next generation—would be led back to the land of Israel. In that place, they would find **quiet** (שָׁקַט, *shaqat*) and **ease** (שָׁאַן, *sha'an*). These synonyms point to a peaceful, undisturbed environment in which God's people could thrive. After years of war, calm and security are precious. Calm can reign in the soul only in the absence of fear.

Verse 11. The foundation of this passage is the statement **"For I am with you,"** declares the Lord, **"to save you"** (see 1:8; 15:20). Their relief, return, and rest stood on this comforting

---

[8]John Bright, *Jeremiah*, The Anchor Bible (Garden City, N.Y.: Doubleday & Company, 1965), 279.

comment. God's presence with His people would make the difference in their future.

The Lord would not **destroy** [them] **completely**, treating them *to the full extent* that their evil deeds deserved (4:27; 5:10, 18; 46:28). Nevertheless, they would be punished for their sins. God said, **"I will chasten you justly and will by no means leave you unpunished."** "Justly" comes from the Hebrew term מִשְׁפָּט (*mishpat*), referring in this context to what is "proper" or "fitting."[9] This word is found often in Jeremiah's writings, being translated "justice," "judgment," or "righteousness" (1:16; 4:12; 12:1; 22:13, 15; 23:5; 26:11; 30:18; 32:7; 33:15; 39:5; 46:28; 51:9; 52:9). The environment in which Jeremiah lived caused God's judgments to be pronounced repeatedly on many men and nations. Gross evil called for great punishment. The language of verses 10 and 11 is repeated almost verbatim in 46:27, 28.

GOD'S VIEW OF THE PROBLEM AND HIS SOLUTION TO IT (30:12–17)

> [12]"For thus says the LORD,
> 'Your wound is incurable
> And your injury is serious.
> [13]There is no one to plead your cause;
> No healing for your sore,
> No recovery for you.
> [14]All your lovers have forgotten you,
> They do not seek you;
> For I have wounded you with the wound of an enemy,
> With the punishment of a cruel one,
> Because your iniquity is great
> And your sins are numerous.
> [15]Why do you cry out over your injury?
> Your pain is incurable.
> Because your iniquity is great
> And your sins are numerous,

---

[9]See Brown, Driver, and Briggs, 1048–49.

> I have done these things to you.
> ¹⁶Therefore all who devour you will be devoured;
> And all your adversaries, every one of them, will go into captivity;
> And those who plunder you will be for plunder,
> And all who prey upon you I will give for prey.
> ¹⁷For I will restore you to health
> And I will heal you of your wounds,' declares the LORD,
> 'Because they have called you an outcast, saying:
> "It is Zion; no one cares for her."'"

God's patience was great, but His justice was real. He examined hearts and meted out retribution according to how people's lives reflected His law (5:10–13, 18, 19; 10:24, 25; 17:9–11).

Verse 12. God said to the people, **"Your wound is incurable and your injury is serious."** J. A. Thompson observed that "Yahweh now speaks to the people in the way Jeremiah spoke of himself (15:18) or as the people once spoke (10:19)."[10] The Hebrew term אָנַשׁ (*'anash*), which means "be weak, sick," is used here in the metaphor of an "incurable" wound.[11] Nothing could heal Judah's condition. Tragically, nearly an entire generation of Jews would be lost before they would seek God, the only source of health, hope, and happiness (see 29:10–14).

Verse 13. The Lord further said, **"There is no one to plead your cause."** The word דִּין (*din*) is a legal term that can be translated "plead one's cause" or "execute judgement."[12] Most English versions choose the former reading. For example, the CEV has "You are accused of a crime with no one to defend you." Judah had no one who could intervene, delivering them from God's punishment. On their own, the people were incapable of **healing** or **recovery**. The NLT says, "There is no one . . . to bind up your injury. No medicine can heal you."

Verse 14. No **lovers** or allies helped Judah; their supposed

---

[10]J. A. Thompson, *The Book of Jeremiah*, The New International Commentary on the Old Testament (Grand Rapids, Mich.: Wm. B. Eerdmans Publishing Co., 1980), 558.

[11]Brown, Driver, and Briggs, 60.

[12]Koehler and Baumgartner, 1:220.

friends had **forgotten** them (see comments on 4:30; 22:20, 22). Judah had forgotten God (2:32; 3:21; 13:25; 18:15; 23:27), and now neither their fellowman nor their Maker held them in memory to rescue them.

God had **wounded** [Judah] **with the wound of an enemy**. This imagery suggests a soldier seriously injured in battle.[13] The Lord's attack on His people was just, since their **sins** were indeed **numerous**. He was only repaying them for the evil that they had done.

Verse 15. No assistance was extended toward Judah in their intense **pain**. No anesthetic could ease their agony (see 8:18–22). The language of verse 14 is repeated here to emphasize the cause of their suffering: **"Your iniquity is great and your sins are numerous."** Because of their transgressions, they were being devoured, plundered, and sent into captivity (21:4–14).

Verse 16. This section closes with a positive expression of God's providence. God would ultimately vindicate His justice and rescue His rebellious people from ruin. He gave emphasis to that intent by the word **therefore**. God was, in essence, saying, "Because you have been severely afflicted for your sins, *therefore* I will enact against your tormentors their deserved punishment."[14]

God assured His people that the ones who were imposing pain on them would be punished. Those who were devouring them (2:3; 5:17; 8:16; 10:25) would **be devoured**. The **adversaries** who had taken Judah into captivity would themselves **go into captivity**. The plunderers would **be for plunder**. All who had preyed on God's people would see the day when they would be given **for prey**. This assurance became a vivid reality to Babylon in chapters 50 and 51. Though this message of assurance did not relieve the current agony of God's people, it did reemphasize God's justice.

Verse 17. God as a gracious Physician would **heal** the **wounds** of His people. **I will restore you to health** could literally be trans-

---

[13]Anthony L. Ash, *Jeremiah and Lamentations*, The Living Word Commentary (Abilene, Tex.: ACU Press, 1987), 218.

[14]Adapted from James E. Smith, *Jeremiah and Lamentations*, Bible Study Textbook Series (Joplin, Mo.: College Press, 1972), 512.

lated "I will bring up new flesh for you"—that is, "to cover your wound."[15]

Judah would be **called . . . an outcast**, since God would send the people into exile away from their homeland. Their enemies would mock, saying, **"It is Zion; no one cares for her"** (see comments on 18:16; 19:8). However, by reestablishing His people in the land, God would demonstrate that He still loved them. His plans extended all the way into messianic showers of blessings (Ezek. 34:20–31).

GOD'S PROMISES OF GLORY RESTORED (30:18–22)

[18]"Thus says the LORD,
'Behold, I will restore the fortunes of the tents of Jacob
And have compassion on his dwelling places;
And the city will be rebuilt on its ruin,
And the palace will stand on its rightful place.
[19]From them will proceed thanksgiving
And the voice of those who celebrate;
And I will multiply them and they will not be diminished;
I will also honor them and they will not be insignificant.
[20]Their children also will be as formerly,
And their congregation shall be established before Me;
And I will punish all their oppressors.
[21]Their leader shall be one of them,
And their ruler shall come forth from their midst;
And I will bring him near and he shall approach Me;
For who would dare to risk his life to approach Me?' declares the LORD.
[22]'You shall be My people,
And I will be your God.'"

Beginning with verse 18, a grandeur and glory are introduced for God's people that emanates from the everlasting love

---

[15]Bright, 279; Brown, Driver, and Briggs, 74; Koehler and Baumgartner, 1:85.

of God (see 31:3). This love is expressed with a literary splendor throughout the rest of chapter 30 and in chapter 31. God's love has always been the springboard of affection for Him and the true foundation for obedience to His ordinances (see Jn. 14:15; 1 Jn. 4:19). Therefore, out of the dark thunderclouds of God's judgments on His rebellious people, love and compassion shine through in these dazzling assurances now being considered. No passages among the rhapsodies of Isaiah (Is. 6; 9; 11), or the striking symbols of Ezekiel's restored temple scene (Ezek. 40—44), can surpass the faith-building flow of these predictions written by Jeremiah. Strategically placed at the center of Jeremiah's book is this *gospel*—good news of great days to come.[16] These words must have been a thrill to every captive Jew who eventually heard them.

Verse 18. God said, **"Behold, I will restore the fortunes of the tents of Jacob."** Similar language is used in verse 3, where God said He would "restore the fortunes" of His people. Some suggest that the Hebrew word for "fortunes," שְׁבוּת (sh^ebuth), should be more narrowly translated "captivity." In that case, the statement, if viewed literally, simply indicates that God would bring His people back from the land of exile (see comments on 30:3). However, the broader translation "fortunes" is consistent with Job 42:10, where Job's material blessings and even more were restored to him. In the present case, the Lord would bless His people materially, as He had in the past, and with a major Messianic hope.

God promised to aid them in rebuilding their towns and cities, particularly Jerusalem. He indicated that **the city** [would] **be rebuilt on its ruin**. The word for "ruin" is תֵּל (tel), meaning "ruin heap" or "mound, hill on which [a] city stood."[17] Some cities were originally built on hills, while others became mounds over many centuries. Since ancient cities were repeatedly destroyed and then rebuilt on the same site, the various destruction levels

---

[16]Adapted from J. Sidlow Baxter, *Explore the Book*, vol. 3, *Poetical Books (Job to Song of Solomon), Isaiah, Jeremiah, Lamentations* (Grand Rapids, Mich.: Zondervan Publishing House, 1974), 272.

[17]Brown, Driver, and Briggs, 1068.

stacked up to make a mound. The names of archaeological sites in Israel today are often prefaced by the word "Tel."

After rebuilding the city, **the palace** [would] **stand on its rightful place**. The Hebrew term אַרְמוֹן (*'armon*), translated "palace," could also be rendered "fortress" (NJPSV) or "citadel" (NRSV).

Verse 19. In addition to material blessings, God would restore joy to their hearts. **Thanksgiving** would flow from within them, and they would **celebrate** God's deliverance by their **voice**[s]. The Hebrew word for "thanksgiving" (תּוֹדָה, *thodah*) could be translated "songs of thanksgiving" (NIV),[18] heightening the parallel between the first two lines of the verse. "Celebrate" comes from the term שָׂחַק (*śachaq*), which could include joyous singing and dancing (31:4).[19] The scene portrays souls praising God, expressing their gratitude, devotion, and worship to Him under the old covenant.

The Lord would also bless the people by restoring their numbers (**I will multiply them**). In 16:1–4, God had instructed Jeremiah not to marry and have children as a sign of death overtaking families. Sons, daughters, mothers, and fathers would die as a result of the Babylonian siege of Jerusalem. In the future, however, He would rebuild their families.

God would restore the reputation of His people among the nations (**I will also honor them**). "Honor" is from the word כָּבֵד (*kabed*), which literally means "be heavy" or "weighty."[20] The people would **not be insignificant**. The importance and influence of God's people should not be underestimated (see Mt. 5:13–16; 1 Pet. 2:9, 10).

Verse 20. The Lord said, **"Their children also will be as formerly, and their congregation shall be established before Me."** These words indicated that children would be upright. Both the children and the home would be as God intended. The sad rebellion and idolatry in the homes of the past (7:17–19) would be reversed so that families would share in worship to God with thanksgivings ascending on high. The result would be that the

---

[18]See Brown, Driver, and Briggs, 392.
[19]Ibid., 965–66; Koehler and Baumgartner, 2:1315.
[20]Koehler and Baumgartner, 1:455.

JEREMIAH 30

congregation of Israel would be established before God. It is still true today that godly homes result in strong congregations.

God also said He would **punish all their oppressors**. Harassment from a stronger nation was feared even more than captivity. Keeping people under pressure robbed life of happiness and security. God let the people know that such insecurity would someday be gone. A similar guarantee can be found in Leviticus 26:2–9. Security would be especially treasured by people who were living in captivity.

Verse 21. The restoration of God's people would also involve good government, which relies on the character and righteous conduct of leaders. As captives, surely Judah had longed for a return of good leaders, who could offer them some civil, moral, and spiritual security (see 23:1–8).

Verse 21 has typically been interpreted as a messianic prophecy, even by Jewish rabbis.[21] It says that **their leader**[22] **shall be one of them,**[23] **and their ruler shall come forth from their midst**. The fact that the Messiah would be a Jew conformed to the Law, which stated that God would set a king over the people "from among [their] countrymen." They were not to accept a foreigner as king (Deut. 17:15). God also promised to raise up a prophet like Moses "from among their countrymen" (Deut. 18:18). Jesus Christ came as "the Prophet" (Jn. 6:14; 7:40; Acts 3:20–22).

The Messiah would serve as a mediator between the people and God. The Lord said, **"I will bring him near and he shall approach Me; for who would dare to risk his life to approach Me?"** The implication is that the Messiah would be a priest as well as a king and a prophet. The fact that Jesus serves as our only Mediator and great High Priest today is stressed in the New Testament (1 Tim. 2:5; Heb. 2:14–18; 4:14–16; 5:7–10; 1 Jn. 2:1, 2).

Verse 22. Ultimately, a restoration between God and His people would take place: **You shall be My people, and I will**

---

[21]Smith, 514.

[22]The KJV mistranslates the singular noun as a plural. It has "nobles."

[23]The pronouns in these lines are singular, but are generally translated as plurals, being understood as a reference to Jacob/Israel (see 30:18). The NJPSV literally renders these pronouns: "*His* chieftain shall be one of *his* own, *his* ruler shall come from *his* midst" (emphasis added).

be your God. This was God's great desire (see comments on 7:23; 24:7); it had always been His plan (Ex. 19:5, 6; Lev. 26:11, 12; Deut. 26:16–19).

GOD'S PATTERN AND PLAN MADE CLEAR (30:23, 24)

[23]Behold, the tempest of the LORD!
Wrath has gone forth,
A sweeping tempest;
It will burst on the head of the wicked.
[24]The fierce anger of the LORD will not turn back
Until He has performed and until He has accomplished
The intent of His heart;
In the latter days you will understand this.

Verses 23, 24. Three truths stand out at the conclusion of chapter 30. First, God's **wrath** [went] **forth,** when needed, against any people. The same wrath voiced for the false prophets in 23:19–22 would **burst on the head of the wicked.**[24] It would be true for all wicked people, and specifically for those mentioned in verse 16. God's wrath is described as **a sweeping tempest.**

Second, **the fierce anger of the LORD** [would] **not turn back until He** [had] **performed and until He has accomplished the intent of His heart** (15:6; 25:31–33). "Accomplished" comes from the Hebrew word קוּם (*qum*), which can mean "rise," "come to fruition," or "endure."[25] "Intent" is from מְזִמָּה (*m^ezimmah*), meaning "project, plan."[26] God had a purpose. He never acts thoughtlessly, unfairly, or irresponsibly.

Third, the people would someday **understand** God's actions. **The latter days** envisioned by the prophets related to the coming of Christ. God's ways could be discovered. He wants to reason with us (Is. 1:18), but unchecked rebellion incites God's wrath. Understanding may come only after His intent has been carried

---

[24]The wording of 30:23 is almost identical to 23:19 in the Hebrew text.
[25]Koehler and Baumgartner, 1:1086–87.
[26]Ibid., 1:566.

out. For every person who desires to do God's will, an opportunity will be provided to know and to obey it (see Jn. 7:17; 2 Pet. 3:9).

APPLICATION

Triumph Through Trials (Ch. 30)

Do we desire to know God and His commands? In light of this chapter's message, this desire should be natural. Surely, we all long for God's glory given to His people, as opposed to His wrath against the wicked. This chapter swings from incurable wounds (30:12) to the voices of celebration (30:19). Beneath this strange dichotomy of mood swings is one of the most sobering messages. That message can be summarized in these words: Discipline is required in order to develop the divine nature. Stress is necessary to achieve spiritual success. Trials must precede ultimate triumph. When needed, there must be penitence before there can be spiritual power.

Several passages form the foundation for this biblical principle. Hebrews 12:5–11 informs us that God disciplines every child that He receives, and, because of that discipline, we mature spiritually. After the discipline of God is compared to what we receive from our human fathers, the question is raised: "Shall we not much rather be subject to the Father of our spirits, and live?" (Heb. 12:9; see 2 Pet. 1:2–11).

This same principle is presented by Peter, who said that we may be distressed by various trials—if necessary—so that the proof of our faith may be evident at the revelation of Jesus Christ (1 Pet. 1:6–9). The parenthetical expression, "if necessary," relates to the divine insight of a loving Father, who only places such stress on us when it is needed. He does this not to break us, but to make us.

James presented this principle when he wrote,

> Consider it all joy, my brethren, when you encounter various trials, knowing that *the testing of your faith produces endurance*. And let endurance have its perfect result, so that *you may be perfect and complete*, lacking in nothing (Jas. 1:2–4; emphasis added).

Paul presented the same principle through his own experience with a "thorn in the flesh," for which he sought God's help three times that it would depart from him. As surely as Judah might not have selected captivity and its distresses, so Paul did not want that weakness. God's response was not to remove it, but He assured Paul, "My grace is sufficient for you." Through that undesirable experience, Paul learned the great lesson to glory in weakness "that the power of Christ may dwell in me" (2 Cor. 12:9).

Jesus also taught this principle. He is "the way, . . . the truth, and the life," so that no one can get to the Father but through Him (Jn. 14:6). Those who follow Him must take the path of discipline and self-denial. Jesus said, "If anyone wishes to come after Me, he must deny himself, and take up his cross daily and follow Me" (Lk. 9:23).

The foregoing examples should be sufficient to identify God's plan for maturing His people. We should bask in His greatness and glory as given in Jeremiah 30, drinking deeply of the wonderful ways He planned to restore Judah to Himself as well as to their homeland. However, we should not ignore that His compassion would come only through captivity. They would triumph through their trials. Every passage we noted is laced with the Lord's precious promises. They are reliable, but we must not ignore God's designed course by which to gain His glory (see Col. 1:24–29).

God's Presence (30:11)

The following elements can be found in God's great promise of 30:11:

1. *Creator*   "I am" (Ex. 3:14; Jn. 8:58)
2. *Companionship*   "With you" (Mt. 28:20; Gal. 2:20)
3. *Certainty*   "Declares the LORD" (Mt. 24:35)
4. *Comfort*   "To save" (Heb. 7:25; 1 Jn. 4:14)
5. *Condemned*   "You" (1 Tim. 1:15; 1 Jn. 2:1, 2).

Starting at the bottom of this listing of elements and going up, we can behold the richness of God's grace. His plan given through Jeremiah reached its climax in Christ.

JEREMIAH 30

Judah's Desperate Situation (30:12–17)

Current conditions in Judah called for a threefold punishment. (1) *No medicine could heal their wound* (30:12, 13). The people could not escape the coming calamity. It was a just punishment for the grievous sins they had committed. (2) *No memory of them would be kept by their allies* (30:14). Judah had often relied on alliances with foreign nations, but they were forgotten in their time of need. No one would help to deliver them. (3) *No mercy would be shown by God at that time* (30:15). Their cries for deliverance from the Babylonian forces would not be heard. In justice, God would demonstrate His wrath against their sin.

Judah's story, however, does not end in judgment. Ultimately, God would punish their enemies and restore their fortunes (30:16, 17).

Glory Restored (30:18–22)

The glory of God's people would be restored to them after the Babylonian captivity. They would be blessed in the following ways:

1. Material wealth (30:18)
2. Spiritual joy (30:19)
3. Numerical growth (30:19)
4. Honor (30:19)
5. Strong families (30:20)
6. Providential protection (30:20)
7. Godly leadership (30:21)
8. A relationship with God (30:22).

Lordship (30:22)

There is a great difference between just saying "Lord, Lord," and saying, "My Lord and my God" as a fact and in faith (Mt. 7:21; Jn. 20:26–29; 1 Tim. 6:11–16). Can God say to you, "You are one of My people, and I am your God"? (See Mk. 16:15, 16; Acts 2:37–47; 1 Cor. 12:13–18; Gal. 3:26–29.) We should think of the price Judah paid for following other gods while professing to serve God. How pure and sincere is our loyalty in His eyes?

CHAPTER 31
RESTORATION AND REDEMPTION

The contents of chapter 31 served as a harbinger of hope—one that is scarcely equaled in all the Old Testament. Before this time, Jeremiah had been frequently turned to tears by the negative message he delivered and the manner in which his fellow-countrymen received it (9:1–3; 13:17; 14:17, 18). However, at this point, the prophet's message changed. Instead of ruin, there would be rebuilding (31:4). Instead of sorrow and shame, there would be singing (31:7). Instead of mourning and grief, the people would be satisfied with God's goodness (31:14). The dark and gloomy picture resulting from sin is replaced with a divine scene comparable to a watered garden (31:12).

This chapter begins with God's reference to His past relationship with His people and a promise made out of love (31:1–9). It contains one of the most graphic insights in the Scriptures regarding the nature of God's love. A preview of better days follows (31:10–14) because repentance would make Judah's return to God and their homeland possible (31:15–22). Jeremiah's understanding of the promise was sweet (31:23–30). This led to an announcement concerning a promise of the new covenant (31:31–34), followed by assurance that these promises would be fulfilled (31:35–40).

THE PAST REVIEWED AND A LOVING PROMISE MADE (31:1–9)

Clarifying the Time of His Promise (31:1, 2)

¹"At that time," declares the LORD, "I will be the God of all

the families of Israel, and they shall be My people."
²Thus says the LORD,
"The people who survived the sword
Found grace in the wilderness—
Israel, when it went to find its rest."

Verse 1. The opening words of chapter 31 are connected to the discussion that began in chapter 30. **At that time** points back to the phrase "days are coming" in 30:3. In previous texts, Jeremiah prophesied a Jewish return after seventy years of Babylonian exile (see comments on 25:11; 29:10).

The LORD promised that, in those days, a good relationship would exist between Him and His people: **"I will be the God of all the families of Israel, and they shall be My people"** (see comments on 30:22). The statement is significant because it was delivered during one of the darkest eras of Judah's history. The final downfall of the nation was imminent, but Jeremiah's prophetic eyes penetrated beyond the Babylonian conquest and captivity to the return, restoration, and redemption of God's people. Since the captivity lasted seventy years, many of those taken captive would not live to return, but their children would.

Verse 2. The interpretation of this verse has been disputed. God said, **"The people who survived the sword found grace in the wilderness—Israel, when it went to find its rest."** Theo. Laetsch interpreted the event as specifically referring to Israel's deliverance from Babylon.[1] His view, however, places an unnecessary strain on the phrase "found grace in the wilderness." Moreover, the language points to an event that had already taken place—namely, the exodus from Egypt.

God preserved Israel, rescuing them from the Egyptian army ("the sword"). After His people passed through the Red Sea on dry land, He unleashed the walls of water on either side, causing the Egyptians and their horses to drown. He further extended His "grace" to Israel in the Sinai Desert, protecting them from their enemies and providing them with manna from heaven and water

---

[1]Theo. Laetsch, *Jeremiah*, Bible Commentary (St. Louis: Concordia Publishing House, 1965), 245.

from the rock. God brought them into covenant, giving them the Law at Mount Sinai. It was there that He said, "If you will indeed obey My voice and keep My covenant, then you shall be My own possession among all the peoples" (Ex. 19:5). These events took place on Israel's journey to Canaan, the land of "rest."

If verse 2 describes Israel's exodus from Egypt, how does it relate to the Babylonian captivity in the present text? At least, the description was God's way of reminding the people of His unfailing love. Beyond this, it is likely that Israel's exodus from Egypt served as a type for the future deliverance of God's people from captivity. In both cases, they were forced to stay in a foreign land. They were also separated from the Promised Land by a wilderness—the Sinai Desert and the Arabian Desert respectively. In both scenes, God called Israel to be His special covenant people.

A Glorious Tribute to the Nature of God's Love (31:3–9)

> ³The LORD appeared to him from afar, saying,
> "I have loved you with an everlasting love;
> Therefore I have drawn you with lovingkindness.
> ⁴Again I will build you and you will be rebuilt,
> O virgin of Israel!
> Again you will take up your tambourines,
> And go forth to the dances of the merrymakers.
> ⁵Again you will plant vineyards
> On the hills of Samaria;
> The planters will plant
> And will enjoy them.
> ⁶For there will be a day when watchmen
> On the hills of Ephraim call out,
> 'Arise, and let us go up to Zion,
> To the LORD our God.'"
> ⁷For thus says the LORD,
> "Sing aloud with gladness for Jacob,
> And shout among the chief of the nations;
> Proclaim, give praise and say,
> 'O LORD, save Your people,

The remnant of Israel.'
⁸Behold, I am bringing them from the north country,
And I will gather them from the remote parts of the earth,
Among them the blind and the lame,
The woman with child and she who is in labor with child, together;
A great company, they will return here.
⁹With weeping they will come,
And by supplication I will lead them;
I will make them walk by streams of waters,
On a straight path in which they will not stumble;
For I am a father to Israel,
And Ephraim is My firstborn."

God's future acts of love and grace in behalf of His people are described here. The emphasis in 31:3–9 appears to be on the northern tribes (or perhaps the northern kingdom as a whole). In fact, verses 3 through 22 contain names that are used synonymously for those in the north, who had been taken captive by the Assyrians in 722 B.C. The people are referred to by the names "Israel" (31:4, 7, 9, 10, 21) and "Jacob" (31:7, 11), as well as by the major tribe "Ephraim" (31:6, 9, 18, 20) and the capital city "Samaria" (31:5). Judah comes to the forefront in verses 23 through 26. After this, both "the house of Israel" and "the house of Judah" are considered in the promise of the new covenant (31:27, 31).

Verse 3. The LORD appeared to him from afar may have reference to God's revelation of Himself to Israel at Mount Sinai. He had delivered the Israelites from Egyptian bondage and had called them to be His covenant people. God then descended upon Sinai with thunder, lightning flashes, a thick cloud, and a loud trumpet blast (Ex. 19:16).

God had **drawn** the Israelites to Himself **with lovingkindness**. The Hebrew word for "drawn" (מָשַׁךְ, *mashak*) also appears in Hosea 11:4: "I *led* them with cords of a man, with bonds of love" (emphasis added). In that context, Israel's exodus from Egypt is clearly in view (Hos. 11:1). The term translated "lovingkindness" is חֶסֶד (*chesed*), which indicates God's faithful devotion to His people (see comments on 2:2). The loyalty of God to

His people is also expressed in the statement **"I have loved you with an everlasting love."** In brief, God declared that He loved His people with a love that had no beginning or ending and could know no change.

Verse 4. God promised **Israel** that He would **build** them. "Build," from the Hebrew word בָּנָה (*banah*), can mean "build a family" or "develop buildings."[2] Certainly God would perform both acts of kindness for His people. He would numerically bless their families and provide them with shelter, prosperity, and security. *Banah* is repeated in verse 4 and is translated **rebuilt**. This significant term points back to Jeremiah's original call, when God commissioned him "to build and to plant" (1:10).

Although having been unfaithful, Israel is described here as a **virgin**. Apparently, this language reflected God's intent for His people to be pure and the fact that He would eventually purify them of their sins (see comments on 14:17; 18:13).

God's rebuilding of Israel would result in great rejoicing by the people. They would "be adorned" (KJV) with **tambourines** and join in **the dances of the merrymakers** (see comments on 30:19). Victories in battle were often celebrating with tambourines and dancing (Ex. 15:20; Judg. 11:34). This scene stands in contrast to the sadness experienced due to captivity (7:34; 16:9; 25:10; Ps. 137:1–3).

Verse 5. As a result of sin, Israel had forfeited the fruit of their land (Deut. 28:30, 33, 38, 39, 51; Amos 5:11; see Hab. 3:17, 18). God promised to reverse this situation, allowing His people to **plant vineyards on the hills of Samaria** once **again**. Prior to the Assyrian destruction of 722 B.C. (2 Kings 17:22–24), Samaria had been located on a hill about forty miles north of Jerusalem. Omri had made the site Israel's capital during his reign (1 Kings 16:24).

The rest of this verse is not easy to translate or interpret because of its symbolic nature. According to the NASB, **the planters will plant and will enjoy them**. Most English versions have

---

[2]Ludwig Koehler and Walter Baumgartner, *The Hebrew and Aramaic Lexicon of the Old Testament*, study ed., trans. and ed. M. E. J. Richardson (Boston: Brill, 2001), 1:139.

a similar rendering that probably captures the general meaning of the statement. However, "will enjoy them" translates the Hebrew word חָלַל (*chalal*), which usually relates to profaning things—that is, treating what is holy as common (see KJV; NEB; AB). Perhaps the NKJV best expresses the literal meaning of the Hebrew text: "The planters shall . . . eat them as *ordinary food*" (emphasis added).

The background of the language is likely Leviticus 19:23–25. This passage instructed the Israelites to abstain for three years from the fruit of trees they would plant in the Promised Land. In the fourth year, they were to offer the produce to God. When the fifth year came, they were free to eat of it themselves. Therefore, during the first four years, the fruit was *set apart*, but in the fifth year it was for *ordinary use*. Similar language appears in Deuteronomy 20:6 and 28:30 regarding vineyards.

The point of the verse seems to be that Israel would rest secure in the land. They would plant vineyards and live long enough to enjoy the fruit of their labors.[3]

Verse 6. Israel would return to Jerusalem in order to worship God and offer Him the firstfruits of their labors. **Watchmen** were typically stationed at lookouts in order to warn of an approaching enemy (6:17), but here they have a higher purpose.[4] From **the hills of Ephraim**, they **call out, "Arise, and let us go up to Zion, to the L**ORD** our God."**

After the kingdom of Israel divided, Jeroboam instructed his subjects in the north to worship the calf idols at the shrines he had built at Dan and Bethel. This strategy was intended to prevent his people from returning to Rehoboam (1 Kings 12:25–33). When Israel returned to the Promised Land, however, they would once again worship the Lord in Jerusalem, the place where He had established His name (1 Kings 14:21; 2 Kings 21:7).

Verse 7. Although their redemption was still in the future,

---

[3]John Bright, *Jeremiah*, The Anchor Bible (Garden City, N.Y.: Doubleday & Company, 1965), 281.

[4]J. A. Thompson, *The Book of Jeremiah*, The New International Commentary on the Old Testament (Grand Rapids, Mich.: Wm. B. Eerdmans Publishing Co., 1980), 568.

God's promises would cause His people to rejoice in the present: **Sing aloud with gladness for Jacob, and shout among the chief of the nations.** Here "Jacob" (Israel) is apparently matched by the parallel term "chief of the nations" (see Amos 6:1). Israel was chief among the nations because of God's election, not their inherent goodness (Deut. 7:6–8; 8:16–18; 9:4–6; 2 Sam. 7:23, 24). They would **give praise** to God by saying, **"O LORD, save Your people, the remnant of Israel."**

Verse 8. God promised to lead **a great company** of His people **from the north country** back to the Promised Land. This remnant would include those who were weak: **the blind, the lame,** and **the woman with child** (the pregnant). J. A. Thompson referred to this event as a "New Exodus" and said that the inclusion of the weak was "a further sign of the miraculous nature of the event (cf. Isa. 35:5–10; [42:15, 16])."[5]

Verse 9. Israel's return would be accompanied by **weeping** and **supplication**. Their sorrow and prayers may have been an expression of repentance. Another possibility is that their tears and cries reflected the difficulty of the journey; they needed God's help and strength to arrive safely home. In love, the Lord would deliver His people. They were dependent (10:23), but God would **lead them**. Where they would have fallen, God's power overcame and enabled them to move forward (see Ps. 126).

God promised to **make them walk by streams of waters**. The language here may serve as a contrast to the first exodus, when the people constantly grumbled because they lacked water. On those occasions, God miraculously provided water from a rock (Ex. 17:1–7; Num. 20:1–13). At the time of the people's return from exile, God would abundantly provide for their needs (see Is. 35:6, 7; 41:17–20; 44:3, 4; 48:20, 21; 49:9–13). They would walk **on a straight path in which they** [would] **not stumble** (see Is. 40:3–5).[6]

Explaining His relationship to His people, God said, **"For I am a father to Israel, and Ephraim is My firstborn."** God por-

---

[5]Ibid., 569–70.
[6]For more information, see Sellers S. Crain, Jr., *Matthew 1—13*, Truth for Today Commentary (Searcy, Ark.: Resource Publications, 2010), 88–89.

trayed Himself as a loving Father, willing to lead His firstborn son. Israel was identified as God's "firstborn" as far back as the time of the Egyptian bondage (Ex. 4:22, 23; see Deut. 32:6; Is. 63:16). Concerning the exodus, God later commented, "When Israel was a youth I loved him, and out of Egypt I called My son" (Hos. 11:1).

Ephraim's superiority goes back to the time of the patriarch Jacob. Before his death, he blessed Ephraim and Manasseh, the sons of Joseph. Even though Manasseh was the oldest, Jacob placed his right hand on Ephraim's head, giving him the greater blessing (Gen. 48:8–22).

A PREVIEW OF PLEASANTNESS (31:10–14)

> ¹⁰Hear the word of the Lord, O nations,
> And declare in the coastlands afar off,
> And say, "He who scattered Israel will gather him
> And keep him as a shepherd keeps his flock."
> ¹¹For the Lord has ransomed Jacob
> And redeemed him from the hand of him who was stronger than he.
> ¹²"They will come and shout for joy on the height of Zion,
> And they will be radiant over the bounty of the Lord—
> Over the grain and the new wine and the oil,
> And over the young of the flock and the herd;
> And their life will be like a watered garden,
> And they will never languish again.
> ¹³Then the virgin will rejoice in the dance,
> And the young men and the old, together,
> For I will turn their mourning into joy
> And will comfort them and give them joy for their sorrow.
> ¹⁴I will fill the soul of the priests with abundance,
> And My people will be satisfied with My goodness," declares the Lord.

Verse 10. Vivid expressions of God's care for His people are given in this section. To begin with, **the Lord** promised to **gather**

those **He** [had] **scattered**. While their sins had led God to uproot **Israel**, sending them to strange lands, His everlasting love would bring them back. He would **keep** His people **as a shepherd keeps his flock** (see Ps. 23). The Hebrew term translated "keep," שָׁמַר (*shamar*), can mean "watch over," "take care of," "preserve," "protect," "save," or "retain."[7] The language reveals God's constant and patient efforts, as He determined to transform these people into what He longed for them to be (see Ex. 19:4–8; Lev. 11:44, 45; 19:2; 20:7; Jer. 13:11).

The **nations** surrounding Palestine and the distant **coastlands** (Mediterranean islands; 2:10; 25:22; 47:4) were invited to hear about what God was doing for His people (see Is. 41:1; 49:1). They had likely received the news when Israel and Judah had been taken captive. At this point, they would hear about God's forgiveness and the restoration of His people to their land.

Verse 11. The metaphor changes here from shepherding to commerce: **For the L**ORD **has ransomed Jacob and redeemed him from the hand of him who was stronger than he.** The use of two almost identical terms emphasized God's repeated efforts. "Ransomed," from פָּדָה (*padah*), refers to "the transfer of ownership from one to another through payment of a price or an equivalent substitute."[8] "Redeemed," from גָּאַל (*ga'al*), means "to do the part of a kinsman and thus to redeem [one's] kin from difficulty or danger."[9] This was often done by paying off a debt. These terms appear earlier in Old Testament passages relating to the exodus (Ex. 6:5, 6; 15:13; Deut. 7:8; 9:26). As the Redeemer of His people, God had rescued them from Egypt. He would also rescue them from those who had taken them into captivity. Returning to their homeland and to God was not by their own might, but by His grace and goodness (29:10–14; 2 Chron. 36:22, 23).

Verse 12. Joyful praise on **the height of Zion** would be the natural response of the people to God's goodness (see comments

---

[7]Koehler and Baumgartner, 2:1582–83.

[8]William B. Coker, "פָּדָה (*pādâ*)," in *Theological Wordbook of the Old Testament*, ed. R. Laird Harris, Gleason L. Archer, Jr., and Bruce K. Waltke (Chicago: Moody Press, 1980), 2:716.

[9]R. Laird Harris, "גָּאַל (*gā'al*)," in *Theological Wordbook of the Old Testament*, 1:144.

on 31:6). In the future, He would bless them materially, giving them **grain, new wine, oil,** and **young** additions to **the flock and the herd**. This list—described as **the bounty** ["goodness"; NRSV] **of the** LORD—is reminiscent of Deuteronomy 7:12, 13, where ancient Israel was admonished to keep God's laws and enjoy His covenant blessings. The items listed were staples in the ancient Near East. God would bless the people so much that **their life** [would] **be like a watered garden,** lacking nothing (Is. 27:2–6; 58:11).

Verse 13. These blessings would cause all segments of society to celebrate: **Then the virgin will rejoice in the dance, and the young men and the old, together** (see comments on 31:4). In His mercy, God would **turn their mourning into joy** by restoring their fortunes. Their sorrow may have been an expression of repentance or of the suffering they endured (see comments on 31:9).

Verse 14. God also promised, **"I will fill the soul of the priests with abundance, and My people will be satisfied with My goodness."** Should this verse be interpreted as referring to physical blessings (like verses 12 and 13) or spiritual ones? The Hebrew word which the NASB renders "soul" in verse 14, נֶפֶשׁ (*nepesh*), is rendered "life" in verse 12. While the term *nepesh* has several possible meanings, it should probably be understood as "life" in both verses. In addition, the word for "goodness" in verse 14, טוֹב (*tob*), is the same word translated "bounty" in verse 12. Apparently, both verses are referring to the amazing blessings God would grant to His people.

When the people returned from exile and went to worship in Jerusalem, the priests would receive their portions of the sacrifices and be satisfied (see Lev. 7:32–36). The word for "abundance" (דֶּשֶׁן, *deshen*) literally means "fatness."[10] The NEB has "I will satisfy the priests with the fat of the land." The NCV says that "the priests will have more than enough sacrifices."

---

[10] Koehler and Baumgartner, 1:234.

THE RETURN TO BE MADE POSSIBLE BY PENITENCE (31:15–22)

¹⁵Thus says the Lord,
"A voice is heard in Ramah,
Lamentation and bitter weeping.
Rachel is weeping for her children;
She refuses to be comforted for her children,
Because they are no more."
¹⁶Thus says the Lord,
"Restrain your voice from weeping
And your eyes from tears;
For your work will be rewarded," declares the Lord,
"And they will return from the land of the enemy.
¹⁷There is hope for your future," declares the Lord,
"And your children will return to their own territory.
¹⁸I have surely heard Ephraim grieving,
'You have chastised me, and I was chastised,
Like an untrained calf;
Bring me back that I may be restored,
For You are the Lord my God.
¹⁹For after I turned back, I repented;
And after I was instructed, I smote on my thigh;
I was ashamed and also humiliated
Because I bore the reproach of my youth.'
²⁰Is Ephraim My dear son?
Is he a delightful child?
Indeed, as often as I have spoken against him,
I certainly still remember him;
Therefore My heart yearns for him;
I will surely have mercy on him," declares the Lord.
²¹"Set up for yourself roadmarks,
Place for yourself guideposts;
Direct your mind to the highway,
The way by which you went.
Return, O virgin of Israel,
Return to these your cities.
²²How long will you go here and there,

O faithless daughter?
For the LORD has created a new thing in the earth—
A woman will encompass a man."

Verse 15. The text now returns to the time of captivity. God specified a particular place, **Ramah**, to unfold the extended drama of His dealings with these people. Ramah, located about five miles north of Jerusalem, was allotted to the tribe of Benjamin (Josh. 18:25–28). In 586 B.C., the captives went to this place on their way from Jerusalem to Babylon. In addition, Jeremiah was set free from his chains there (see comments on 40:1).

God also mentioned **Rachel** as a key person in the drama. She was Jacob's favorite wife and the mother of Joseph and Benjamin (Gen. 29:30; 30:22–24; 35:18, 19). The tribes descending from her—Ephraim, Manasseh, and Benjamin—were allotted a significant portion of the land of Israel.

Rachel's tomb was associated with Ramah. She had died giving birth to Benjamin and was buried at Zelzah (near Ramah), in the territory later given to Benjamin's descendants (1 Sam. 10:2, 3). This happened as Jacob and his family were "on the way to Ephrath (that is, Bethlehem)" (Gen. 35:16–20; 48:7).

Rachel is pictured in this scene as **weeping for her children**. The image may be of her weeping from the grave as her descendants pass by on their way to Babylonian captivity.[11] James E. Smith surmised that the meanings of the names mentioned here make the description even more graphic. "Rachel" means "ewe," and "Ramah" means "hilltop" (or "height"). The cries of the ewe on the hilltop are heard, as she bleats for her missing lambs.[12] Timothy M. Willis said, "Rachel is one of the great ancestresses of the people, so she represents their basic identity as a people and their most ancient hopes."[13]

---

[11]After the kingdom of Israel divided, many in Benjamin sided with Judah (see 1 Kings 12:21, 23). Indeed, some of Rachel's literal descendants would have passed by her tomb.

[12]James E. Smith, *Jeremiah and Lamentations*, Bible Study Textbook Series (Joplin, Mo.: College Press, 1972), 522.

[13]Timothy M. Willis, *Jeremiah-Lamentations*, The College Press NIV Commentary (Joplin, Mo.: College Press Publishing Co., 2002), 249.

Verse 15 was borrowed by Matthew to describe an event regarding the coming of the Messiah (Mt. 2:18). The words function either typologically (type/anti-type) or as a dual fulfillment prophecy. The Gospel writer envisioned Rachel weeping over the slaughter of little children in Bethlehem after King Herod's attempt to kill the baby Jesus. These children were like those in Jeremiah's day who were being slaughtered or carried away—**they** [were] **no more**.

Verse 16. The LORD responded to Rachel, saying, **"Restrain your voice from weeping and your eyes from tears; for your work will be rewarded."** God was comforting Rachel, who is representative of all mothers saddened by the tragedies of the exile. The "work" that He would reward refers to the labor of childbearing and rearing. Rachel's descendants would not remain in captivity or come to an end, but would **return from the land of the enemy**. God would bring them back from captivity and reestablish them in the Promised Land.

Verse 17. "There is hope for your future," declares the LORD, **"and your children will return to their own territory."** These words further strengthen and clarify the promise of restoration in verse 16. Judah did return from Babylon, as recorded in Ezra and Nehemiah.

Verse 18. Once again, reference is made to **Ephraim** (see comments on 31:9). This term is used in other prophetic books to designate all ten tribes of the northern kingdom (Ezek. 37:19; Hos. 11:12; 13:1, 12). Ephraim—representing the northern tribes in Assyrian captivity (2 Kings 17)—was **grieving** in penitence.

Ephraim had been **chastised** and now longed to be **restored**. "Chastised" comes from the Hebrew term יָסַר (*yasar*), meaning "admonish," "instruct," or "discipline."[14] In the past, they had behaved **like an untrained calf** (see Hos. 4:16; 10:11). After receiving the Lord's discipline, they came under His control. Ephraim now confessed, **"You are the LORD my God."** God wanted the people to develop this spirit before He began the restoration process and returned them to their homeland.

---

[14]Francis Brown, S. R. Driver, and Charles A. Briggs, *A Hebrew and English Lexicon of the Old Testament* (Oxford: Clarendon Press, 1972), 415–16.

Verse 19. Jeremiah gave an excellent listing of the steps it took to break Israel and bring them to repentance. Repentance is listed first in the verse but occurred last. The following listing identifies these steps and the general order of events needed to bring people back to God.

1. **I was instructed.** "Instructed" comes from the Hebrew word יָדַע (*yada'*), which is usually defined as "know." The intensified form found in this verse means "be instructed . . . in [a] spiritual sense, through chastisement."[15] As previously noted, Ephraim had experienced chastisement from the Lord (31:18).
2. **I was ashamed and also humiliated.** Over time, God's discipline caused the people to become "ashamed" (בּוֹשׁ, *bosh*) and "humiliated" (כָּלַם, *kalam*) because of their sin (see comments on 3:3; 14:3). Many passages in Jeremiah emphasize that they were slow to do this (2:36; 6:15; 8:12; 12:13; 14:3; 15:9; 17:13; 20:11; 22:22).
3. **I bore the reproach of my youth.** Humiliation brought disgrace, but "reproach" (חֶרְפָּה, *cherpah*) left the people unwanted and despised. The mentioning of "youth" was "a way of confessing a lifelong sinfulness" (3:25; 22:21; 32:30).[16] Only God's love reached out to these people so that the next step could be taken.
4. **I turned back, I repented.** "Repented" comes from נָחַם (*nacham*), meaning "regret" or "be sorry."[17] Indeed, godly sorrow was a part of this process (2 Cor. 7:10). This inward sorrow was outwardly manifested by striking one's **thigh**, a gesture of great remorse (Ezek. 21:12).[18]

Verse 20. Regarding His relationship with Israel, God asked, **"Is Ephraim My dear son? Is he a delightful child?"** The answer

---

[15]Ibid., 394.
[16]Anthony L. Ash, *Jeremiah and Lamentations*, The Living Word Commentary (Abilene, Tex.: ACU Press, 1987), 225.
[17]Koehler and Baumgartner, 1:688–89.
[18]Homer *Iliad* 15.397–98; 16.125; *Odyssey* 13.198–99.

to these questions was a resounding "Yes!" As a compassionate Father, God still loved His son (see comments on 31:9). Even though He had **spoken against** Israel, judging the people for their sins, He had not forgotten them. God had a deep desire for His relationship with Israel to be restored. The phrase **My heart yearns for him** could more literally be translated "My bowels rumble for him." Thompson wrote, "The very vivid anthropomorphism depicts God's stomach being churned up with longing for his son."[19] The restoration of their relationship was dependent on Israel's repentance (3:19) and God's **mercy**.

Verse 21. God's yearning and willingness to reach out to His people is evident as He directed them back home. He referred to them by the title **virgin of Israel**, even though they had been unfaithful to Him (see comments on 14:17; 18:13). God was no doubt looking at them through the lens of His grace.

God instructed the people, **"Set up for yourself roadmarks, place for yourself guideposts; direct your mind to the highway, the way by which you went. . . . Return to these your cities."** "Roadmarks" is from צִיּוּן (*tsiyyun*), which can refer to a "gravestone," "stone monument," or "road marker."[20] The last meaning fits the present context. The parallel term "guideposts" is from תַּמְרוּר (*thamrur*), which may refer to "high heaps" of stone (KJV) or wooden "signposts" (CEV). These landmarks would serve to guide the people back to the Promised Land. In addition, Willis suggested a spiritual implication of these markers: They not only pointed the people back to the cities of Israel, "but also to the just and righteous behavior, the wholehearted worship, and the sincere honoring of their relationship with the Lord that a loving husband and father deserves."[21] This interpretation is supported by the language of the next verse, which describes a directionless people.

Verse 22. God asked them, **"How long will you go here and there, O faithless daughter?"** While referring to them as "virgin of Israel" in verse 21, here He emphasized their past sins as a

---

[19]Thompson, 575.
[20]Koehler and Baumgartner, 2:1022–23.
[21]Willis, 251.

"faithless daughter" (see 3:6, 8, 11, 12, 14, 22).

Then God announced, **"The Lord has created a new thing in the earth."** Significantly, the Hebrew word for "created," בָּרָא (*bara'*), is only used in the Old Testament for God's activity.[22] Whatever was going to happen, the Lord would accomplish it.

The phrase "a new thing" is challenging (see Is. 43:19). It could refer to the restoration of God's people that was previously discussed in this chapter. Willis remarked, "That new thing is the restoration of an exiled people to its original homeland. The people of Israel cannot lose heart because such a restoration had never happened before."[23] Another possibility is that the "new thing" refers in some way to the state of God's people after their return to Palestine. A final possibility, and apparently the most likely, is that the "new thing" points to the "new covenant" in verse 31. The same word for "new" (חֲדָשָׁה, *ch^adashah*) is used in both cases.

The statement **a woman will encompass a man** is obscure. The term for "woman" (נְקֵבָה, *n^eqebah*) emphasizes the female gender, not age.[24] "Encompass" is from סָבַב (*sabab*), which can be translated "turn (toward one)," "turn (in a new direction)," "march around," "surround," or "protect."[25] The word for "man" (גֶּבֶר, *geber*) refers to a strong man in contrast to the weaker members of society (women, children, and the elderly) whom he is responsible to defend.[26] In view of this statement and these definitions, five general interpretations can be listed.[27]

(1) Is it a proverbial saying, simply illustrating something new? John Bright wrote, "Quite possibly we have here a proverbial saying indicating something that is surprising and difficult to believe."[28] This interpretation is utilized by the TEV, which

---

[22]Brown, Driver, and Briggs, 135; Koehler and Baumgartner, 1:153–54.
[23]Willis, 252.
[24]Brown, Driver, and Briggs, 666.
[25]Ibid., 686.
[26]Ibid., 150.
[27]For other interpretations, see Ash, 226; Thompson, 575–76; Robert P. Carroll, *Jeremiah 26—52*, Old Testament Library (London: SCM Press Ltd, 1986), 601–3.
[28]Bright, 282.

says, "I have created something new and different, *as different as a woman protecting a man*" (emphasis added).

(2) Is the imagery used to demonstrate a role reversal and to bracket the revelation Jeremiah received on this occasion (30:1—31:26)? Under normal circumstances, "a man protects a woman." However, the Lord would bring about a new situation in which "a woman protects a man" (RSV).[29] This collection begins with men, at the time of God's judgment, being as weak as a woman (30:6). However, it ends with a time of God's favor resting on Israel in which a woman is strong enough to protect a man (31:22). T. K. Cheyne explained, "In the coming age, the country shall be so free from danger that the places of men and women may be safely reversed."[30]

(3) Is the woman a figurative reference to Israel,[31] who affectionately surrounded her divine husband, the Lord?[32] Laetsch argued for this interpretation, taking "encompass" (*sabab*) to mean "loving adherence."[33] In other words, upon returning to the Promised Land, "Israel will embrace her God" (NLT). No longer will she chase after other lovers (see 2:20; 3:1).

(4) Should this passage be viewed as messianic? The language could point to the miraculous conception and virgin birth of Christ—"a woman will encompass a strong man" in her womb.[34] Another possibility is that it refers to Mary protecting Christ, holding Him in her arms. Still another possibility is that, in God's new plan, the seed of woman (Christ) will "lead" or "protect" a man (see Lk. 1:30–35; Gal. 4:4, 5). This certainly was God's new plan, and it opens the way to introduce the new covenant in verses 31 through 34.

---

[29]Douglas Rawlinson Jones, *Jeremiah*, The New Century Bible Commentary (Grand Rapids, Mich.: Wm. B. Eerdmans Publishing Co., 1992), 395.

[30]T. K. Cheyne and W. F. Adeney, *The Pulpit Commentary*, vol. 11, *Jeremiah, Lamentations* (Grand Rapids, Mich.: Wm. B. Eerdmans Publishing Co., 1950), 2:13.

[31]Israel is figuratively referred to as a "virgin" and a "daughter" in the surrounding context.

[32]Brown, Driver, and Briggs, 686.

[33]Laetsch, 253.

[34]See Smith, 527–28.

(5) Could it mean that, after the new covenant arrived, females would be viewed in a different light? In the New Testament, a woman may, under certain conditions, "turn a man in a new direction" by teaching him the way of the Lord more accurately (Acts 18:24–26). Further, male and female are united as one in Christ, joint heirs of God's promises (Gal. 3:26–29).

It seems best to regard this obscure phrase as a veiled, symbolic prophecy of the coming of the Messiah. It is similar in nature to Genesis 3:15.

THE SWEET PERCEPTION OF THE PROMISE (31:23–30)

²³Thus says the LORD of hosts, the God of Israel, "Once again they will speak this word in the land of Judah and in its cities when I restore their fortunes,
'The LORD bless you, O abode of righteousness,
O holy hill!'
²⁴Judah and all its cities will dwell together in it, the farmer and they who go about with flocks. ²⁵For I satisfy the weary ones and refresh everyone who languishes." ²⁶At this I awoke and looked, and my sleep was pleasant to me.

²⁷"Behold, days are coming," declares the LORD, "when I will sow the house of Israel and the house of Judah with the seed of man and with the seed of beast. ²⁸As I have watched over them to pluck up, to break down, to overthrow, to destroy and to bring disaster, so I will watch over them to build and to plant," declares the LORD.

²⁹"In those days they will not say again,
'The fathers have eaten sour grapes,
And the children's teeth are set on edge.'
³⁰But everyone will die for his own iniquity; each man who eats the sour grapes, his teeth will be set on edge."

Verse 23. In this context, **the land of Judah** and **its cities** are specifically mentioned. Whenever **God** would **restore their fortunes** (see comments on 29:14), they would once again recite this blessing at the temple mount in Jerusalem: **"The LORD bless you,**

O abode of righteousness, O holy hill!"

Verses 24, 25. All of **Judah** would come **together** in Jerusalem, including those living in **cities, farmer[s],** and shepherds **(they who go about with flocks).** The image is one of unity among God's people as they gather to worship Him. No disputing exists between these groups, who would typically not get along with each other.[35]

In addition, instead of being ashamed because of drought (14:4), the people have an abundance of grain, sheep, and livestock from which they can select offerings for God. The bounty of the land and the spiritual unity of the people are wonderful gifts from God: **"For I satisfy the weary ones and refresh everyone who languishes."**

Verse 26. The contrast between Judah's dark situation and the bright nature of this hope explains the prophet's pronouncement: **At this I awoke and looked, and my sleep was pleasant to me.** The beautiful image of return came to Jeremiah in a dream (see Dan. 10:9; Zech. 4:1). Some suggest that only 31:23–26 comprised Jeremiah's dream. However, it is possible that the content of 30:1—31:26 was all revealed at this time.

We can imagine Jeremiah seeking to get rest in the midst of darkness, disaster, and depression. The horror of that awful hour had overtones from his own messages given by God that affirmed more misery and mourning. Suddenly these scenes are played before God's prophet, offering delight rather than despondency, pleasantness instead of pain.

Verse 27. The phrase **Behold, days are coming** appears three times in the rest of the chapter—in verses 27, 31, and 38. The purpose of these words is to arrest one's attention in preparation for an important prophecy. In each case, a significant and easily understandable statement follows the phrase.

The message in verse 27 opened the door of prosperity to **Judah** and **Israel** as God would **sow** them **with the seed of man and with the seed of beast.** He had uprooted both people and animals in the Assyrian and Babylonian captivities; in the future He would replant them in the land.

---

[35]Willis, 252.

Verse 28. The imagery of restoration is brought into sharper focus by mirroring the language of Jeremiah's call (1:10–12). God said, **"As I have watched over them to pluck up, to break down, to overthrow, to destroy and to bring disaster, so I will watch over them to build and to plant."** The long ordeal of terror, plunder, and destruction would be replaced with a new plan to re-establish the people in the land.

Verses 29, 30. In addition to the external blessing to beautify the place, a reign of justice and righteousness toward each person would ensue. The Lord promised, **"In those days they will not say again, 'The fathers have eaten sour grapes, and the children's teeth are set on edge.'"** The people would give up the practice of blaming others for the results of their own sin. The saying here was a proverb commonly cited by the people (Ezek. 18:2). They blamed the bitter consequences they experienced on the sins of their parents, instead of taking personal responsibility. Perhaps such passages as Exodus 20:5 and Numbers 14:18—which teach that a person's sins can negatively affect his descendants—served as a catalyst for their misunderstanding.

God clearly revealed the reality to them: **"But everyone will die for his own iniquity; each man who eats the sour grapes, his teeth will be set on edge."** Ezekiel 18 details this new insight God would give to His people as they moved closer to repentance and the return to their homeland (see Deut. 24:16).

THE PROPHETIC PROMISE OF THE NEW COVENANT (31:31–34)

³¹**"Behold, days are coming,"** declares the LORD, **"when I will make a new covenant with the house of Israel and with the house of Judah,** ³²**not like the covenant which I made with their fathers in the day I took them by the hand to bring them out of the land of Egypt, My covenant which they broke, although I was a husband to them,"** declares the LORD. ³³**"But this is the covenant which I will make with the house of Israel after those days,"** declares the LORD, **"I will put My law within them and on their heart I will write it; and I will be their God, and they shall be My people.** ³⁴**They will not teach again, each**

man his neighbor and each man his brother, saying, 'Know the LORD,' for they will all know Me, from the least of them to the greatest of them," declares the LORD, "for I will forgive their iniquity, and their sin I will remember no more."**

This section reaches not only to the Messiah, but also to His blood-ratified covenant that would last throughout the ages (Heb. 13:20, 21). This prophecy of the new covenant is quoted in its entirety in Hebrews 8:8–12.

Verse 31. Once again, the introductory phrase **Behold, days are coming** indicates the significance of the statements that follow (see 31:27, 38). God promised to **make a new covenant with the house of Israel and with the house of Judah**. "Make" is from כָּרַת (*karath*), which could more literally be translated "cut." The use of this language is derived from the ancient practice of "the cutting of a sacrificial animal [in two] as is customary when making a covenant."[36] The practice was illustrated by God's covenant with Abraham in Genesis 15.

The covenant is described here as being "new," setting it in opposition to the "old." While other Old Testament passages hint at the new covenant (Ezek. 16:60; 34:24; 36:26–28), this one is the most explicit. The very language we use today—old covenant and new covenant, Old Testament and New Testament—has its origins in this passage (31:31–34), which is quoted in Hebrews 8:8–12. The phrase "new covenant" also appears in other New Testament texts (Lk. 22:20; 1 Cor. 11:25; 2 Cor. 3:6; Heb. 8:13; 9:15; 12:24).

This new covenant would be made "with the house of Israel and with the house of Judah." The prophets envisioned the exiles of the northern tribes (Israel) and the southern tribes (Judah) as coming back to the Promised Land and becoming one people again under the rule of the Messiah (see Ezek. 37:15–28). The New Testament indicates that the new "Israel" is synonymous with the church (Rom. 11:26; Gal. 6:16; Phil. 3:2, 3; Rev. 7:4–17) and that the Messiah's reign is a spiritual one (Acts 2:36; 1 Cor. 15:20–28; Eph. 1:20–23; Col. 1:13–20).

---

[36]Koehler and Baumgartner, 1:500.

Verse 32. God further revealed that the new covenant would **not** [be] **like the covenant which** [He had] **made with their fathers**. The reference is to the old covenant established by God through Moses at Mount Sinai after He had led them **out of the land of Egypt** (11:3, 4, 7). The need for a new covenant resulted because His people had **broke**[n] the former **covenant**. Failure to recognize God's lordship—repeated rebellion and disobedience—had rendered the old covenant void (Ex. 19:3–8; 20:1–7; Jer. 11:1–11; 16:1–13). The people, like an adulterous wife, had violated their covenant with **the Lord**, even though He had been a faithful **husband**. He had provided for all of their needs, yet they had squandered these gifts through pagan idolatry and foreign alliances (Hos. 2).

Verse 33. The Lord described the new **covenant** as being internal: **"I will put My law within them and on their heart I will write it."** The earlier covenant had been written on tablets of stone (Ex. 31:18; 32:15, 16; 34:28, 29; Deut. 4:13; 5:22; 9:9, 11; 10:4), but the new covenant would be written on human hearts (2 Cor. 3:1–6). Inward motivation was now to be the springboard for obedience rather than outward compulsion. Every individual born in Israel—each male being circumcised—was automatically under the national law God gave through Moses (see Gen. 17:9–14; Ex. 12:48; 19:1–9).[37] In contrast, it is a personal, heart-founded choice if one enters into the new covenant under Christ, becoming a part of the church of Christ, which He purchased with His own blood (see Acts 20:28; Eph. 5:23–27; Heb. 5:8, 9; 13:20, 21).

The repeated expression **I will be their God, and they shall be My people** (see 24:7; 30:22; 32:38) emphasizes the Lord's great desire for a close relationship with His people. It also indicates their great need for Him. People need God because they are incapable of directing their own steps (10:23; Prov. 14:12). Apart from Him, man can do nothing (Is. 40:17; Jn. 5:19, 30; 9:33; 15:5).

---

[37]The Law had called for the whole heart in obedience to God (Deut. 4:29; 6:5; 10:12; 11:13; 13:3; 26:16; 30:2, 10; Jer. 3:10; 4:4; 24:7; 29:13). However, since the Israelites were physically born into the old covenant, they often did not yield their whole hearts to Him (3:17; 5:23; 7:24; 9:14; 11:8; 13:10; 16:12; 18:12).

Verse 34. In the new covenant, God said, **"They will all know Me, from the least of them to the greatest of them."** The people would all be acquainted with God, knowing Him by experience (יָדַע, *yada'*), and they would care deeply for Him. Everyone in the kingdom would know God, regardless of their status (1 Cor. 12:13–31). In contrast to the old system of entering the covenant by physical birth, under the new covenant they would be taught first and led to God by personal choice in a new birth (Mt. 28:18–20; Mk. 16:15, 16; Jn. 3:3–5; 6:44, 45; Rom. 10:17; Gal. 3:26–29; Heb. 11:6; 1 Pet. 1:22, 23).

A person would **not** need to **teach . . . his neighbor** or **his brother** concerning **the Lord** because all would have come to know Him in the process of entering into the new covenant. Everyone needs to know God in order to enter into and maintain a relationship with Him (Jn. 17:3).

As a Father, God thoughtfully added His promise to the new covenant. He never assigns responsibilities or makes requirements without offering rich rewards. Here He stated, **"I will forgive their iniquity, and their sin I will remember no more."** These two lines essentially say the same thing, forming a synonymous parallelism: God would not hold the sins of His people against them.

A fundamental inadequacy of the old covenant was its failure to provide a perfect sacrifice for sin. The oft-repeated animal sacrifices related to the old covenant were but a foreshadowing of the once-for-all, perfect sacrifice of God's Son (Heb. 7:25–28; 10:1–10). Sins are forgiven because "He Himself bore our sins in His body on the cross" (1 Pet. 2:24; see 2 Cor. 5:20, 21), not through any self-acquired holiness or meritorious works on our part. We are redeemed, not with silver, gold, or any personal possession, "but with precious blood, as of a lamb unblemished and spotless, the blood of Christ" (1 Pet. 1:18, 19; see Rom. 5:6–11).

The contrast between the ineffective sacrifices of the Levitical system and the perfect sacrifice of Christ raises this question: Did forgiveness of sins exist under the old covenant? Many passages in the Old Testament teach that people were forgiven in an anticipatory fashion during their lifetimes (Lev. 4:20; 5:10; 6:7; Num. 15:25; Ps. 25:18; 32:1; 51:1, 2; 79:9; 103:12; 130:4; Is. 6:7; 44:22;

Mic. 7:19). God—who is not confined by time or space—forgave their sins *in anticipation of* the sacrifice of His Son. Romans 3:25, which discusses the atoning sacrifice of Christ, says that God, in His forbearance, "passed over the sins previously committed." Hebrews 9:15 also says that Jesus died "for the redemption of the transgressions that were committed under the first covenant." The forgiveness of any person—whether from ancient or modern times—is only possible because of the death of Christ.

What is implied by the statement "their sin I will remember no more" (see Is. 43:25)? Since God knows everything, an overly literal understanding of this statement must be avoided. Even if God could forget our sins, we sometimes recall them—and He knows our every thought. Concerning the language of this text, F. F. Bruce wrote, "For the Hebrew, 'remembering' was more than a mental effort; it carried with it the thought of doing something to the advantage, or disadvantage, of the person remembered."[38] Therefore, the idea of God not remembering our sins is that He will not hold them against us. In other words, He will not punish us as our deeds deserve. For the one who is justified before God, it is "just-as-if-I'd never sinned," according to Romans 5:1 and 1 Corinthians 6:9–11. What divine grace and mercy God offers! His lovingkindness enables people through Christ to become new creatures, having their sins forgiven and not being held against them anymore.

PROOF FOR THESE PROMISES
(31:35–40)

³⁵Thus says the LORD,
Who gives the sun for light by day
And the fixed order of the moon and the stars for light by night,
Who stirs up the sea so that its waves roar;
The LORD of hosts is His name:

---

[38] F. F. Bruce, *The Epistle to the Hebrews*, The New International Commentary on the New Testament (Grand Rapids, Mich.: Wm. B. Eerdmans Publishing Co., 1964), 175.

> ³⁶"If this fixed order departs
> From before Me," declares the Lord,
> "Then the offspring of Israel also will cease
> From being a nation before Me forever."
> ³⁷Thus says the Lord,
> "If the heavens above can be measured
> And the foundations of the earth searched out below,
> Then I will also cast off all the offspring of Israel
> For all that they have done," declares the Lord.
> ³⁸"Behold, days are coming," declares the Lord, "when the city will be rebuilt for the Lord from the Tower of Hananel to the Corner Gate. ³⁹The measuring line will go out farther straight ahead to the hill Gareb; then it will turn to Goah. ⁴⁰And the whole valley of the dead bodies and of the ashes, and all the fields as far as the brook Kidron, to the corner of the Horse Gate toward the east, shall be holy to the Lord; it will not be plucked up or overthrown anymore forever."

To the captives, the precious promises of this chapter were so broad in scope, so deep with delight, and so high in redemptive importance that God seemed to anticipate a "Can it really be true?" response.

Verses 35, 36. God replied that His promises to His people were just as definite as His **fixed order** governing the heavenly bodies (**the sun, the moon,** and **the stars**) and the ocean tides (**the sea** and **its waves**) (see Gen. 1:6–10, 14–19). "Fixed order" is from the Hebrew verb חָקַק (*chaqaq*) in verse 35 and the related noun חֹק (*choq*) in verse 36. The verb *chaqaq* can literally mean "carve," "inscribe" or figuratively "enact," "decree." These corresponding definitions reflect the ancient practice of engraving laws in stone. The noun *choq* refers to a "law" or "regulation."[39]

God stated that the created order He had decreed would have to depart before **the offspring of Israel** [would] **cease from being a nation before** Him. God must have been saying that, although He would chasten His people in the captivity, He would not utterly destroy them or cast them off. Since God would eventu-

---

[39]Koehler and Baumgartner, 1:346–47.

ally establish the new covenant (31:31–34), this promise must have its ultimate fulfillment in "the spiritual Israel of God, the church of Christ."[40]

Verse 37. The message of verses 35 and 36 is repeated here using slightly different imagery. God said, **"If the heavens above can be measured and the foundations of the earth searched out below, then I will also cast off all the offspring of Israel for all that they have done."** Obviously, the vast reaches of space and the depths of the earth are beyond man's reach. The language underscores God's commitment to His covenant people, despite their sin.

Verses 38–40. Once more, the phrase **Behold, days are coming** introduces an important prophecy (see 31:27, 31). God's people would return from exile, and Jerusalem would **be rebuilt**. Specific boundaries of **the city** are given, moving around the city counterclockwise. **The Tower of Hananel** was built into the northern wall of the city (Neh. 3:1; 12:39; Zech. 14:10), toward its eastern end.[41] **The Corner Gate** was located on the western end of the northern wall (2 Kings 14:13; 2 Chron. 26:9), where it adjoined the western wall. The locations of **the hill Gareb** and **Goah** are uncertain, but the movement suggests that these places were to the southwest. **The whole valley of the dead bodies and of the ashes** is a description of the Valley of Hinnom, outside the southern wall of the city (see comments on 7:31, 32; 19:2, 6). **The brook Kidron** ran through the valley outside the eastern wall, where **the Horse Gate** was located (2 Chron. 23:15; Neh. 3:28).

What was rebuilt was to be **holy to the Lord**. This description has at least two implications. First, God had cleansed and sanctified the city after its former corruption that led to the Babylonian captivity. This would especially be true for the temple mount and the Valley of Hinnom, which had both been thoroughly defiled by idolatry. Second, the return depended on the people's repentance. There could be no holy hill of Zion without holy hearts in Israel (29:11–14).

---

[40]Smith, 536–37.
[41]Some specifically place it on the northwest corner of the temple mount, in the general vicinity of where Herod the Great later built Antonia Fortress.

The regions to be rebuilt (see Neh. 3) would **not be plucked up or overthrown anymore forever** (see Zech. 14:10, 11). The terms "plucked up" and "overthrown" recall the language of Jeremiah's call (1:10) and God's use of the Babylonian forces against Judah (31:28). However, the Lord's promise was to firmly establish His people in the Promised Land after their return from exile (24:6; 31:4, 28).

This promise contains another use of the Hebrew term translated "forever," עוֹלָם (*'olam*), which only means "age lasting" in this context.[42] In other words, God's protection of Jerusalem would last throughout the age of His existing covenant with Israel. Under the law of Moses, Jerusalem would continue, and the rebuilt temple would not be overthrown. However, that temple and Jerusalem were later destroyed in A.D. 70, after Christ's covenant with the new Israel (the church) became binding. This occurred because the majority of Jews rejected Jesus as the Messiah and His death on the cross as the means of their salvation (Mt. 23:33–38; 24:15–22; Lk. 21:20–24). Today, the law of Moses is no longer binding; the law and its promises are fulfilled in Jesus Christ (Mt. 5:17, 18).

APPLICATION

Distinguishing the Covenants (Ch. 31)

One great lesson we should glean from chapter 31 is the importance of "rightly dividing the word of truth" (see 2 Tim. 2:15; KJV), recognizing the distinction between the covenants God has made with men. In our day, Christ has ratified the new covenant with His blood as an eternal covenant. We are to do His will (Heb. 13:20, 21), for by His covenant we will be judged (Jn. 12:47, 48; 2 Cor. 5:10; Rev. 20:11–15). Several differences exist between the covenants, which some have not always recognized. A failure to recognize these differences has resulted in religious division and multiple stages of strife. Christ's covenant recognizes these painful influences (Mt. 10:34–37; Lk. 12:51–53), plead-

---

[42]Robert Young, *Young's Analytical Concordance to the Bible*, 22d ed. (Grand Rapids, Mich.: Wm. B. Eerdmans Publishing Co., n.d.), 310.

ing with us to avoid such conflicts (Rom. 16:17–20; Gal. 5:13–15), speaking the same things with no divisions among us (Jn. 17:17–21; 1 Cor. 1:10–13). We should be diligent in understanding the distinctions between the covenants, which the chart below illustrates.

DISTINCTIONS BETWEEN THE TWO COVENANTS

Old Covenant	New Covenant
Given by Moses, son of Amram (Ex. 6:20; Deut. 31:24–26; Jn. 1:17)	Given by Jesus Christ, Son of God (Heb. 1:1–4; 8:6–13; 13:20, 21)
National law to Israel (Ex. 19:3–8; Deut. 5:1–3; Neh. 8:1–3)	International law to every creature (Mt. 28:18–20; Mk. 16:15, 16; Acts 1:8)
Animal sacrifices year by year (Lev. 16:1–34; Heb. 10:1–8)	Christ, the sacrifice, once for all (Heb. 7:26–28; 9:11–15, 24–27; 13:15, 16)
Circumcision was binding (Gen. 17:9–14; Lev. 12:1–3; Jn. 7:22, 23)	Circumcision was not binding (Acts 15:1–11; Gal. 5:1–6).
Sabbath, covenant day to Israel (Ex. 20:8–11; 31:12–18; Deut. 5:12–15; Neh. 9:13, 14)	First day is the special day under Christ (Acts 2:1–47; 20:7; 1 Cor. 16:1, 2; Col. 2:16).
Giving through tithes (Lev. 27:30–32; Num. 18:25–29; Neh. 10:37–39)	Giving as one has prospered and purposed in his heart (Acts 2:42–44; 1 Cor. 16:1, 2; 2 Cor. 9:6–11)
Musical instruments used in worship (2 Chron. 29:25–28; Ps. 150:1–6)	Singing only of psalms, hymns, and spiritual songs in worship (1 Cor. 14:15; Eph. 5:19; Col. 3:16; Jas. 5:13)

Incense a part of worship (Ex. 30:8, 9; 31:11; Lev. 16:12, 13)	Prayers to God in Christ's name in worship (Jn. 16:23; Eph. 5:20; Phil. 4:6, 7; Rev. 5:8)
Looking to the coming of the Messiah (2 Sam. 7:12–16; Is. 7:14; 9:6, 7; Jer. 23:5, 6)	Living under Christ, who is the Messiah, and looking for His second coming (Mt. 1:1–25; 28:18–20; Acts 2:22–47; 3:13–26; 1 Thess. 4:16, 17; Rev. 21)

While this abbreviated summary does not cover all the differences between the covenants, a recognition of these distinctions could solve many problems and increase one's appreciation for God's love, patience, and faithfulness through the centuries in His efforts to redeem mankind.

The Greatness of God's Love (31:1–9)

This passage highlights the love God has for His people. The same love that He lavished on Israel under the old covenant He pours out on Christians today. What does this passage tell us about God's love?

1. It is *everlasting* (31:3). The Lord, who delivered Israel from Egyptian bondage, expressed His undying commitment to them: "I have loved you with an everlasting love."
2. It is *elevating* (31:4). God promised to rebuild Israel and bring joy to their hearts.
3. It is *enriching* (31:5). The people would once again plant vineyards in the land and enjoy the fruit of their labor.
4. His love is *enticing* (31:6). After returning to the land, the people would travel to Jerusalem to worship the Lord. They would be drawn to their God.
5. His love is *enrapturing* (31:7). The people would sing the praises of the Lord, giving glory to His name.
6. His love is *ennobling* (31:8, 9). God would restore a captive people, including the blind, the lame, and those who were pregnant. He would make the weak strong, leading them safely home.

God's everlasting love reaches out and draws us in many ways, and it leads us through trials as well as triumphs (Rom. 8:28–39; 1 Cor. 10:13; Eph. 3:20, 21). Pain and suffering are within the scope of His love, not always to be removed, but always within the realm of His sufficiency (Ps. 94:12–16; 119:67, 71; 2 Cor. 3:4–6). God, knowing how to turn weakness into strength, through a love too strong to falter, leads us onward and upward, by a wisdom from above, to fulfill His great purposes (2 Cor. 9:8–11; Eph. 3:8–13; 2 Tim 1:7–11; Jas. 1:5–7; 3:17, 18).

Who can grasp the dimensions of God's love? Paul extended the challenge when he urged Christians to "comprehend with all the saints what is the breadth and length and height and depth" of God's love (Eph. 3:18).

The New Covenant (31:31–34)

A heavenly, opened door and refreshing ray of redemption shines from this amazing passage. God's everlasting love (31:3) in all the annals of history never communicated more compassionately nor kindly than in the context of 31:31–34. God's people who were in misery were offered a refreshing revelation that presented both restoration and redemption. This new covenant would be written on human hearts and offer a solution for sin, purifying everyone who would submit to God's commands. These glorious possibilities had been indicated in previous passages (see 3:14–19; 16:14, 15; 23:3–8), but nowhere had they been so simply stated as in this context.

CHAPTER 32
A DEED DECLARING HOPE IN TROUBLED TIMES

While chapter 32 speaks of a real estate sale, it actually concerns national ruin and God's plans for restoration. The apparent foolishness of purchasing property that was occupied by an invading army blossomed into a faith-building exercise to show that the prophecies of a return to the land were true (30:10, 11, 18–20; 31:38–40). This chapter can be divided into three sections: prophecy backed by the purchase of a field (32:1–15), the prophet's prayer, which included a tribute to God (32:16–25), and God's future plans for the people (32:26–44).

PROPHECY OF A RETURN BACKED BY THE PURCHASE OF A FIELD (32:1–15)

The Setting: Jerusalem Under Siege And Zedekiah to Be Captured (32:1–5)

¹The word that came to Jeremiah from the LORD in the tenth year of Zedekiah king of Judah, which was the eighteenth year of Nebuchadnezzar. ²Now at that time the army of the king of Babylon was besieging Jerusalem, and Jeremiah the prophet was shut up in the court of the guard, which was in the house of the king of Judah, ³because Zedekiah king of Judah had shut him up, saying, "Why do you prophesy, saying, 'Thus says the LORD, "Behold, I am about to give this city into the hand of the king of Babylon, and he will take it; ⁴and Zedekiah king of Judah will not escape out of the hand of the Chaldeans, but he will surely be given into the hand of the king of Babylon,

and he will speak with him face to face and see him eye to eye; ⁵and he will take Zedekiah to Babylon, and he will be there until I visit him," declares the LORD. "If you fight against the Chaldeans, you will not succeed"'?"

Verse 1. A word ... came from God **to Jeremiah** in confinement. This message is dated by the reigns of the **king of Judah** and the king of Babylonia: The prophet received it **in the tenth year of Zedekiah** and **the eighteenth year of Nebuchadnezzar**. Since Zedekiah began reigning in 597 B.C., his tenth year was 587 B.C. Nebuchadnezzar came to power in 605 B.C., also making his eighteenth year 587 B.C.

Verse 2. The Lord spoke to Jeremiah during this **time** when **the army of the king of Babylon was besieging Jerusalem**. This information corresponds with what is recorded in 39:1, 2 and 52:4, 5, which say that the Babylonian siege began in the tenth month of the ninth year of Zedekiah's reign (January 588 B.C.) and Jerusalem's wall was breached in the fourth month of the eleventh year (July 586 B.C.).[1]

Sometime between these dates (588–586 B.C.), the siege must have been lifted briefly. The Egyptian army was attacking from the south. Nebuchadnezzar believed that he must address that threat before finalizing his destruction of Jerusalem (37:3–5). At some time afterward, the Babylonian army returned, just as Jeremiah had said it would, and finished the conquest of Jerusalem.[2]

When **Jeremiah** received God's message, he **was shut up in the court of the guard, which was in the house of the king**. The similar phrase "the court of the guardhouse" is used in 37:21 and 38:28.

Verse 3. The reason for Jeremiah's confinement in verse 2

---

[1]See the detailed chronological reconstruction in William Sanford LaSor, "Jerusalem," in *The International Standard Bible Encyclopedia*, rev. ed., ed. Geoffrey W. Bromiley (Grand Rapids, Mich.: Wm. B. Eerdmans Publishing Co., 1982), 2:1016. Instead of 586 B.C., some date the breaching of the wall and the destruction of Jerusalem to 587 B.C.

[2]James E. Smith, *Jeremiah and Lamentations*, Bible Study Textbook Series (Joplin, Mo.: College Press, 1972), 541.

was his prediction of the downfall of Jerusalem. He said that God would **give this city into the hand of the king of Babylon**. While this message was true, it sounded like treason to those who did not believe it.

Verse 4. In addition, Jeremiah told **Zedekiah** that he would **not escape**. Rather, **he [would] surely be given into the hand of the king of Babylon**. Eventually, Zedekiah did try to escape from Jerusalem, but he and his soldiers were overtaken by the Babylonian army in the plains of Jericho (39:2–5; 52:7–9; 2 Kings 25:4, 5).

Zedekiah would **speak with** [Nebuchadnezzar] **face to face and see him eye to eye**. J. A. Thompson argued that the Hebrew idiom "see him eye to eye" is different from the English expression "see eye to eye" (which means "agree"). Instead, it describes "an 'eyeball to eyeball' confrontation."[3] The force of these words is intensified by the fact that, when Zedekiah finally encountered Nebuchadnezzar, his sons were slaughtered in his presence and then his eyes were gouged out. The face of the mighty Nebuchadnezzar in all its wrath was among the final sights Zedekiah beheld on earth (39:5–7; 52:9–11; 2 Kings 25:6, 7; Ezek. 12:8–13).

Verse 5. Blinded, **Zedekiah** would be forced to make the trek **to Babylon**, where he would remain in prison until his death (39:7; 52:11; Ezek. 12:13). The Hebrew word for **visit**, פָּקַד (*paqad*), sometimes has the positive meaning "deliver." However, in this context, it has the negative connotation "deal with" (NIV) or "punish" (see NCV). Apparently, God's visiting Zedekiah is a reference to his death.

**God's Real Estate Deal
As Judah Faced Its Fall (32:6–15)**

⁶**And Jeremiah said, "The word of the LORD came to me, saying,** ⁷**'Behold, Hanamel the son of Shallum your uncle is coming to you, saying, "Buy for yourself my field which is at**

---

[3]J. A. Thompson, *The Book of Jeremiah*, The New International Commentary on the Old Testament (Grand Rapids, Mich.: Wm. B. Eerdmans Publishing Co., 1980), 585, n. 1.

JEREMIAH 32

Anathoth, for you have the right of redemption to buy it."' ⁸Then Hanamel my uncle's son came to me in the court of the guard according to the word of the LORD and said to me, 'Buy my field, please, that is at Anathoth, which is in the land of Benjamin; for you have the right of possession and the redemption is yours; buy it for yourself.' Then I knew that this was the word of the LORD.

⁹"I bought the field which was at Anathoth from Hanamel my uncle's son, and I weighed out the silver for him, seventeen shekels of silver. ¹⁰I signed and sealed the deed, and called in witnesses, and weighed out the silver on the scales. ¹¹Then I took the deeds of purchase, both the sealed copy containing the terms and conditions and the open copy; ¹²and I gave the deed of purchase to Baruch the son of Neriah, the son of Mahseiah, in the sight of Hanamel my uncle's son and in the sight of the witnesses who signed the deed of purchase, before all the Jews who were sitting in the court of the guard. ¹³And I commanded Baruch in their presence, saying, ¹⁴"Thus says the LORD of hosts, the God of Israel, "Take these deeds, this sealed deed of purchase and this open deed, and put them in an earthenware jar, that they may last a long time." ¹⁵For thus says the LORD of hosts, the God of Israel, "Houses and fields and vineyards will again be bought in this land."'"

Over the centuries, many people have longed for God's guidance in purchasing a house, a farm, or a business. Ironically, Jeremiah received direct counsel from God for this purchase—a transaction which could have left Jeremiah, Baruch, and all the witnesses bewildered. To human thinking, God's suggestion seemed to involve the wrong time, the wrong property, and the wrong person.

Verses 6, 7. God revealed to **Jeremiah** that his cousin was coming to ask him to **buy** a **field**. This scene is likely related to the prophet's previous attempt to leave the city "to go to the land of Benjamin in order to take possession of some property there among the people" (37:12). Since Jeremiah was now confined in Jerusalem, his cousin was coming to him to make the transaction. God identified the person selling the land as **Hanamel**

the son of Shallum your uncle. He also specified that the land was located nearby at **Anathoth**, which was Jeremiah's hometown (see comments on 1:1).

Perhaps the prophet would never have purchased a field at this time had God not suggested the idea. It may even be that others—who were nearer kinsmen—had been given an opportunity to buy the field, but they refused to do so because of the Babylonian threat (see Ruth 4:1–12). The opportunity to purchase the field is referred to as **the right of redemption**. Through Moses, God had set up in ancient Israel a land-retaining pattern so that any estate would remain within a family (Lev. 25:23–28). If a piece of property had to be sold (due to poverty or some other cause), the nearest of kin had both the duty and the right to purchase it.

Verse 8. God's **word** to Jeremiah was fulfilled just as He had spoken. **Hanamel** came to Jerusalem and was allowed to visit Jeremiah in his confinement **in the court of the guard**. He urged him to **buy** his **field . . . at Anathoth**, since he was next in line to redeem it.

The tribe of Levi, from which Jeremiah and Hanamel came (1:1), did not receive a territorial inheritance like the other tribes following the conquest of Canaan. The priests, who descended from Aaron, were given thirteen cities (Josh. 21:13–19). The remaining Levites were given thirty-five cities (Josh. 21:20–40). Counting these together, a total of "forty-eight cities with their pasture lands" were given to the tribe of Levi (Josh. 21:41, 42; see Num. 35:1–7). According to God's plan, the priests owned property that could be sold only to members of the tribe of Levi (Lev. 25:32–34).

Verses 9, 10. Jeremiah **bought the field**, just as his cousin had requested. The procedure was carried out with careful attention to legal detail. The price was stipulated and accepted—**seventeen shekels of silver**. Though this probably would not have been a good price in normal times (see Gen. 23:15, 16), Hanamel was no doubt happy to get anything for the land while Babylon's army was camping on it. The phrase **weighed out** points to a time before coins were generally used. Anthony L. Ash noted, "It was many years before 'shekel' became the name of a coin.

Coined money was not generally used until after the exile."[4] Since the shekel weighed about 0.4 ounce (11.4 grams),[5] the total weight of Jeremiah's payment was about seven ounces of silver. Jeremiah fulfilled each legal requirement: He **signed and sealed the deed, and called in witnesses, and weighed out the silver on the scales**. Documents were often sealed in order to prevent tampering (Is. 8:16; 29:11; Dan. 12:4, 9; Rev. 5:1–5).

Verses 11, 12. Two **deeds of purchase** actually existed, **the sealed copy (containing the terms and conditions** of the land purchase) and **the open copy**. The "open" copy may have been identical to the "sealed" copy, or it could have been an abstract. These types of documents, written on papyrus, have been found at Elephantine, Egypt.[6] The open copy was used for quick reference. If anyone thought that the open copy had been altered, he could break open the sealed copy and examine its contents.

Jeremiah put these legal documents in the hands of **Baruch**, a trusted friend. This is the first time Baruch has been named in the Book of Jeremiah. He served as the prophet's scribe and is prominent in some of the chapters that follow (36; 43; 45). Baruch is further identified as **the son of Neriah, the son of Mahseiah**. This same phrasing in 51:59 indicates that Baruch had a brother named Seraiah, who was "quartermaster."

All of these things occurred in the presence of many **witnesses**, including Jeremiah's cousin **Hanamel**, those **who signed the deed**, and **the Jews who were sitting in the court of the guard**. It was important not only to have witnesses for the legal act but also to witness it as a symbolic and prophetic act.

Verses 13, 14. With everyone listening and watching, Jeremiah instructed **Baruch** to **take these deeds** and **put them in an earthenware jar, that they may last a long time**. The effective-

---

[4]Anthony L. Ash, *Jeremiah and Lamentations*, The Living Word Commentary (Abilene, Tex.: ACU Press, 1987), 233.

[5]Edward M. Cook, "Weights and Measures," in *The International Standard Bible Encyclopedia*, rev. ed., ed. Geoffrey W. Bromiley (Grand Rapids, Mich.: Wm. B. Eerdmans Publishing Co., 1988), 4:1054.

[6]See the photographs of a house deed and a sealed marriage contract in Roland K. Harrison, "Elephantine Papyri," in *The International Standard Bible Encyclopedia*, 2:60.

ness of preserving ancient documents in pottery jars is well illustrated by the discovery of the Dead Sea Scrolls at Qumran, where manuscripts survived two thousand years.[7] The preservation of these deeds served as a sign to the people of a hopeful future.

Verse 15. On the day Jeremiah carried out this real estate venture, he was dramatically demonstrating his faith in God's word. The prophet boldly declared, **"For thus says the LORD of hosts, the God of Israel, 'Houses and fields and vineyards will again be bought in this land.'"** This prophecy was given despite the fact that the Babylonian army was besieging Jerusalem, and Jeremiah had already predicted the city's downfall. Every indication argued against the idea of Judah's having a future in the Promised Land. It surely would have been interesting to observe the impact this business transaction had on those Jews who were present in the court of the guard.

God would indeed punish His people, but He would also restore them. Nehemiah 11:32 affirms that, upon the Jews' return from captivity, some did reclaim land in Anathoth. However, none of these were Jeremiah's descendants, since he neither married nor had any children (16:1, 2).

THE PROPHET'S PRAYER— A TRIBUTE TO GOD (32:16–25)

Jeremiah's Prayerful Tribute to God (32:16–22)

¹⁶"**After I had given the deed of purchase to Baruch the son of Neriah, then I prayed to the LORD, saying, ¹⁷'Ah Lord GOD! Behold, You have made the heavens and the earth by Your great power and by Your outstretched arm! Nothing is too difficult for You, ¹⁸who shows lovingkindness to thousands, but repays the iniquity of fathers into the bosom of their children after**

---

[7]See the photographs of reconstructed jars from Cave 1 at Qumran in William Sanford LaSor, "Dead Sea Scrolls," in *The International Standard Bible Encyclopedia*, rev. ed., ed. Geoffrey W. Bromiley (Grand Rapids, Mich.: Wm. B. Eerdmans Publishing Co., 1979), 1:888.

them, O great and mighty God. The L ORD of hosts is His name; ¹⁹great in counsel and mighty in deed, whose eyes are open to all the ways of the sons of men, giving to everyone according to his ways and according to the fruit of his deeds; ²⁰who has set signs and wonders in the land of Egypt, and even to this day both in Israel and among mankind; and You have made a name for Yourself, as at this day. ²¹You brought Your people Israel out of the land of Egypt with signs and with wonders, and with a strong hand and with an outstretched arm and with great terror; ²²and gave them this land, which You swore to their forefathers to give them, a land flowing with milk and honey.'"

Jeremiah's first act after the purchase of land was to pray to God. It was basically a prayer of praise, dealing with the God of the people (32:16–22) and the people of God (32:23–25).

Verses 16, 17. Jeremiah **prayed to the** L ORD, praising Him because of His marvelous attributes. He began by recognizing God's power. Addressing the Maker of **the heavens and the earth**, the prophet said, **"Nothing is too difficult for You"** (see 32:27; Gen. 18:14; Job 42:1–6; Ps. 33:6–9; Lk. 1:37). The Hebrew word translated "is too difficult," פָּלָא (*pala'*), means "be beyond one's power" or "be impossible."[8]

In an age when some have avowed there is no God, it is sobering that every extended dimension of scientific and space development unveils a universe requiring plan and power that only the divine mind and energy could operate. Jeremiah's observation is still most valid and accurate.

Verse 18. The prophet referred to God as the One **who shows lovingkindness to thousands** (see 9:24; 16:5; 31:3). This language expresses the outreaching nature of God's love and echoes His description of Himself in the Ten Commandments: "showing lovingkindness to thousands, to those who love Me and keep My commandments" (Ex. 20:6; Deut. 5:10). (For "lovingkindness," see comments on 31:3.)

---

[8]Francis Brown, S. R. Driver, and Charles A. Briggs, *A Hebrew and English Lexicon of the Old Testament* (Oxford: Clarendon Press, 1972), 810; Ludwig Koehler and Walter Baumgartner, *The Hebrew and Aramaic Lexicon of the Old Testament*, study ed., trans. and ed. M. E. J. Richardson (Boston: Brill, 2001), 2:927.

While showing His faithful love to the righteous, God also **repays the iniquity of fathers into the bosom of their children after them**. This language again echoes the Ten Commandments: "visiting the iniquity of the fathers on the children, [and] on the third and the fourth generations of those who hate Me" (Ex. 20:5; Deut. 5:9). Rather than imposing punishment because of a father's sin (31:29, 30; Ezek. 18:4–20), verse 18 warns that the influence of evil parents is too often repeated by evil children, leading to their own downfall (16:11–13; Ezek. 16:44; 18:2–4). The **great**, **mighty**, all-knowing **God** can punish—and He knows whom to punish (17:9, 10). Indeed, the New Testament emphasizes that each person will give an account to God on the day of judgment (Rom. 14:10–12; 2 Cor. 5:10).

Verse 19. Jeremiah highlighted God's knowledge and power: He is **great in counsel and mighty in deed**. "Counsel" comes from the Hebrew word עֵצָה (*'etsah*), meaning "wisdom," "advice," "plan," or "decision."[9] God knows all that happens in His creation; His **eyes are open to all the ways of the sons of men** (see 2 Chron. 16:9). The writer of Hebrews said, "Nothing in all creation is hidden from God's sight. Everything is uncovered and laid bare before the eyes of him to whom we must give account" (Heb. 4:13; NIV). Indeed, God will give **to everyone according to his ways and according to the fruit of his deeds** (see comments on 17:10).

Verse 20. God's powerful miracles had made an indelible impression. The ten plagues and the parting of the Red Sea had left their mark on **the land of Egypt**, on the people of **Israel**, and on **mankind** (Ex. 10:7; Deut. 4:34; 6:22; 11:1–4; 26:8; Josh. 2:9–11; Ps. 78:12, 13, 42–53; 135:8, 9). The influence of these events continued in the days of Jeremiah. God had truly **set signs and wonders**, making **a name** for Himself.

Verse 21. God had rescued **Israel** from bondage in **Egypt** by His **strong hand** and **outstretched arm** (Deut. 26:8). This fact was important for Judah to remember on the eve of their complete fall to Babylon. The eternally powerful God, having saved His people in the past, could do it again.

---

[9]Koehler and Baumgartner, 1:866–67.

Verse 22. Not only had God delivered them from bondage, He had also given them **a land flowing with milk and honey**. This happened in fulfillment of the oath He had made **to their forefathers** (11:5; Ex. 3:8, 17; 13:5; 33:3; Deut. 6:3; 11:9; 26:9, 15; 27:3). The Lord was now taking the Promised Land away from His people due to their repeated disobedience, but He could give it back to them again. Jeremiah's purchase confirmed this very thought.

Jeremiah's Prayer Continued Relative to God's People (32:23–25)

²³"'They came in and took possession of it, but they did not obey Your voice or walk in Your law; they have done nothing of all that You commanded them to do; therefore You have made all this calamity come upon them. ²⁴Behold, the siege ramps have reached the city to take it; and the city is given into the hand of the Chaldeans who fight against it, because of the sword, the famine and the pestilence; and what You have spoken has come to pass; and behold, You see it. ²⁵You have said to me, O Lord GOD, "Buy for yourself the field with money and call in witnesses"—although the city is given into the hand of the Chaldeans."'

Verses 23 through 25 continue Jeremiah's prayer. He emphasized the unfaithfulness of Judah that resulted in God's punishment of Babylonian captivity.

Verse 23. The people's violations of their covenant with God are summarized here. While **they came in and took possession of** the Promised Land, they did not show their gratitude to God. **They did not obey** [His] **voice**, which would have brought blessings (Deut. 28:1–14; Jer. 22:1–4). They failed to **walk in** [His] **law**, which called for punishment like that associated with Shiloh (26:4–9). The people had **done nothing of all that** [God] **commanded them to do**. They were not even keeping the Sabbath (17:19–27). They did not have one leader who would do justice and seek truth (5:1–6). This consistent rebellion and rejection of God's will justified this conclusion: **Therefore You have made**

all this calamity come upon them. Jeremiah had been dealing with this possibility for a long time (11:11, 23; 16:9-13; 18:11, 17; 19:4-15; 23:12; see Dan. 9:8-14).

Verse 24. Though confined, Jeremiah received news of the **Chaldeans** (Babylonians) attacking **the city**, which assured him that the calamity had come. His prophecies from God became a reality as **siege ramps** were erected to breach the fortified walls of Jerusalem (see comments on 6:6).[10] God had given His people repeated warnings with details about what was to come (1:12, 13; 5:10-17; 6:6-8; 14:14-16; 20:4, 5). These warnings had become a reality; the word of the Lord had **come to pass.**

Verse 25. Jeremiah's prayer climaxed with a reference to the strange land purchase: **"You have said to me, O Lord God, 'Buy for yourself the field with money and call in witnesses'— although the city is given into the hand of the Chaldeans."** The prophet's statement may imply His great trust in God despite the certainty of the Babylonian conquest. In this case, Jeremiah placed his full confidence in the Creator and expressed his hope for the future. His faith burned brightly in the midst of this dark hour. Another possibility is that he was seeking an explanation or reassurance from God. The Hebrew text of verse 25 begins with a conjunction that is not translated in the NASB. Several versions take this conjunction as conversive, translating it as "but" (NCV), "though" (NIV), or "yet" (NRSV; NLT; NJB; NJPSV; TEV). If this is correct, Jeremiah was questioning why God told him to purchase the land when the Babylonians were attacking them. The CEV renders the statement as a question: "So why did you tell me to get some witnesses and buy a field with my silver, when Jerusalem is about to be captured by the Babylonians?" This interpretation seems to be correct, for, in the next section, God offered Jeremiah reassurance that the people would return and occupy the land in the future (32:36-44).

---

[10]Siege ramps made of three layers of logs are portrayed in the Assyrian reliefs that commemorate their attack on Lachish in Judah (701 B.C.). See James B. Pritchard, *The Ancient Near East in Pictures: Relating to the Old Testament*, 2d ed. (Princeton, N.J.: Princeton University Press, 1969), 130-31 (nos. 372, 373), 293-94.

JEREMIAH 32

THE POLLUTED PEOPLE AND GOD'S FUTURE PLANS (32:26-44)

Their Pattern in This Place (32:26-35)

²⁶Then the word of the LORD came to Jeremiah, saying, ²⁷"Behold, I am the LORD, the God of all flesh; is anything too difficult for Me?" ²⁸Therefore thus says the LORD, "Behold, I am about to give this city into the hand of the Chaldeans and into the hand of Nebuchadnezzar king of Babylon, and he will take it. ²⁹The Chaldeans who are fighting against this city will enter and set this city on fire and burn it, with the houses where people have offered incense to Baal on their roofs and poured out drink offerings to other gods to provoke Me to anger. ³⁰Indeed the sons of Israel and the sons of Judah have been doing only evil in My sight from their youth; for the sons of Israel have been only provoking Me to anger by the work of their hands," declares the LORD. ³¹"Indeed this city has been to Me a provocation of My anger and My wrath from the day that they built it, even to this day, so that it should be removed from before My face, ³²because of all the evil of the sons of Israel and the sons of Judah which they have done to provoke Me to anger—they, their kings, their leaders, their priests, their prophets, the men of Judah and the inhabitants of Jerusalem. ³³They have turned their back to Me and not their face; though I taught them, teaching again and again, they would not listen and receive instruction. ³⁴But they put their detestable things in the house which is called by My name, to defile it. ³⁵They built the high places of Baal that are in the valley of Ben-hinnom to cause their sons and their daughters to pass through the fire to Molech, which I had not commanded them nor had it entered My mind that they should do this abomination, to cause Judah to sin."

The prophet had finished praying to God (32:16-25), and now it was time for him to listen. In verses 26 through 35, God's initial plans for Judah were given.

Verses 26, 27. Once again, **the word of the LORD came to Jere-**

miah. Emphasizing His power and sovereignty, God described Himself as **the LORD, the God of all flesh**. The Hebrew term for "flesh," בָּשָׂר (*basar*), can relate to both people and animals. In this context, however, it appears to simply mean "mankind."[11] A similar expression is "the LORD, the God of the spirits of all flesh" (Num. 27:16).

After identifying Himself, God asked, **"Is anything too difficult for Me?"** Perhaps He was reminding Jeremiah of the confession he had made at the beginning of his prayer: "Nothing is too difficult for You" (see comments on 32:16, 17). Indeed, the Lord has complete power to punish and to deliver.

Verses 28, 29. At this point, God emphasized His punishment of Jerusalem. He would **give this city . . . into the hand of Nebuchadnezzar king of Babylon**; the Babylonians would conquer and **burn it**. A painful price had to be paid for the sins that God's people had committed. The **houses** that had been used for pagan worship would be destroyed. The inhabitants of Jerusalem had stirred up God's **anger** by burning **incense to Baal on their roofs** as well as pouring out **drink offerings to other gods** (see comments on 19:13).

Verse 30. God further explained His just punishment of the people by stating that they had done **evil in [His] sight from their youth. The work of their hands**, which provoked God **to anger**, is a reference to idolatry. From their beginning as a nation, **Israel** had either attempted to worship God in pagan ways or worshiped false gods altogether. As the Lord was drawing the people into a covenant relationship at Mount Sinai, they fashioned a golden calf and sacrificed to it. They declared, "This is your god, O Israel, who brought you up from the land of Egypt" (Ex. 32:4). After entering Canaan, Israel repeatedly slipped back into idolatry, worshiping Baal and other deities (see comments on 3:24; 7:9; 11:13; 19:4, 5; 23:13, 14).

Verse 31. In addition, the **city** of Jerusalem had also provoked God's **wrath from the day that they built it**. The reference to being "built" is likely to David's conquest and development of the pre-existing city in about 1000 B.C. (2 Sam. 5:6–10). By that

---

[11]Brown, Driver, and Briggs, 142; see Koehler and Baumgartner, 1:164.

time, Jerusalem had been settled for at least a millennium by other people. In the days of Abraham, Melchizedek was the "king of Salem," another name for Jerusalem (Gen. 14:18; see Ps. 76:2). This city was also known as "Jebus," and its inhabitants were the "Jebusites" (Josh. 15:8; Judg. 19:10).

God had chosen Jerusalem for the place to establish His name, and Solomon had built the temple there (Deut. 12:11; 14:23; 1 Kings 6:1, 37, 38; 2 Chron. 6:6, 18–42; 7:11–16). However, the city had been defiled by idolatry and immorality (see comments on 7:4, 9). Influenced by his foreign wives, Solomon was largely responsible for promoting pagan worship in the holy city (1 Kings 11:1–13). Many of the kings after him, extending to the time of Jeremiah, continued on this dangerous course. As a result, Jerusalem had to **be removed from before** [God's] **face** (see 18:17).

Verse 32. God's people had committed much **evil**, from the greatest to the least: **kings, leaders, priests, prophets, the men of Judah**, and **the inhabitants of Jerusalem**. In civil, religious, social, and domestic circles, gross rebellion had prevailed (see comments on 1:18; 6:13–15; 7:9, 10).

Verse 33. God said, **"They have turned their back to Me and not their face"** (see 2:27; 2 Chron. 29:6; Ezek. 8:16–18; 23:35). What is more disrespectful than turning one's back to someone who is speaking to him with concern and conviction? God had repeatedly faced this treatment as He sought to teach Judah. They came to His place of worship, but they refused to hear His prophets (7:25–28). The phrase **teaching again and again** is more literally translated in the KJV as "rising up early and teaching." The idea is one of persistence (see comments on 7:13; 25:2, 3). The people's disregard was evident, for **they would not listen and receive instruction**. Ignoring a warning cry hurts both the spokesperson and the one who does not have ears to hear.

Verses 34, 35. The depth of Judah's idolatry concludes this section, which explains the reasons for the calamity that came upon them. God said, **"They put their detestable things in the house which is called by My name, to defile it."** Even the temple of the Lord had been infested with their folly! This reference likely points back to the wickedness of King Manasseh, who "built altars for all the host of heaven in the two courts of the house of the LORD" (2 Kings 21:5). He also took the Asherah pole he had made and set it up at the temple—even though it was the place that God had reserved for His name (2 Kings 21:7). Later, when King Josiah enacted his reforms, he removed from the temple "all the vessels that were made for Baal, for Asherah, and for all the host of heaven" (2 Kings 23:4).

Beyond desecrating God's house, the people also **built the high places of Baal that are in the valley of Ben-hinnom to cause their sons and their daughters to pass through the fire to Molech**. This description also relates to Manasseh, who "rebuilt the high places which Hezekiah his father had destroyed" and "erected altars for Baal" (2 Kings 21:3). This evil king "made his sons pass through the fire in the valley of Ben-hinnom" (2 Chron. 33:6; see 2 Kings 21:6). Of course, Manasseh was not the first or last among God's people to commit this heinous act (2 Kings 17:17; 23:10). The Lord made it clear that He **had not commanded** child sacrifice; this **abomination** had not even **entered [His] mind**. Nevertheless, Judah did not hesitate to offer such sick, shameful devotion to other gods. Their hands, backs, ears, and minds were all against God (see comments on 7:30, 31; 19:4, 5).

The Plan of God Showing His Goodness (32:36–44)

[36]"Now therefore thus says the LORD God of Israel concerning this city of which you say, 'It is given into the hand of the king of Babylon by sword, by famine and by pestilence.' [37]Behold, I will gather them out of all the lands to which I have driven them in My anger, in My wrath and in great indignation; and I will bring them back to this place and make them dwell in safety. [38]They shall be My people, and I will be their God; [39]and I will give them one heart and one way, that they may fear Me always, for their own good and for the good of their children after them. [40]I will make an everlasting covenant with them that I will not turn away from them, to do them good; and I will put the fear of Me in their hearts so that they will not turn away from Me. [41]I will rejoice over them to do them good and will faithfully plant them in this land with all

My heart and with all My soul. ⁴²For thus says the LORD, 'Just as I brought all this great disaster on this people, so I am going to bring on them all the good that I am promising them. ⁴³Fields will be bought in this land of which you say, "It is a desolation, without man or beast; it is given into the hand of the Chaldeans." ⁴⁴Men will buy fields for money, sign and seal deeds, and call in witnesses in the land of Benjamin, in the environs of Jerusalem, in the cities of Judah, in the cities of the hill country, in the cities of the lowland and in the cities of the Negev; for I will restore their fortunes,' declares the LORD."

Verse 36. Beginning in this verse, God apparently responded to Jeremiah's concerns in 32:23–25. The prophet had realized that calamity was overtaking Jerusalem, but did not understand how the command to purchase the field coincided with God's judgment of His people. References to the **sword, famine,** and **pestilence** mirror Jeremiah's language in verse 24.

Verse 37. The Lord reassured Jeremiah that captivity would not be the end of the story: **"Behold, I will gather them out of all the lands to which I have driven them in My anger, in My wrath and in great indignation."** Like a shepherd gathering his lost sheep, God would assemble His wayward people and return them to the Promised Land. Instead of living in fear, He would **make them dwell in safety**. The rebellion, captivity, repentance, and return of Israel were all anticipated in the law of Moses (Deut. 30:1–5).

Verse 38. The Lord looked forward to the time when their relationship would be restored: **"They shall be My people, and I will be their God"** (see comments on 7:23; 11:4; 24:7; 30:22; 31:1). His great desire was to have close fellowship with those whom He had chosen from the nations of the earth.

Verse 39. God would strengthen His people so they could serve Him. He would **give them one heart and one way**, and then they would revere Him (Ezek. 11:19, 20; 18:31; 36:26–28). Walking in the ways of the Lord would be **for their own good and for the good of their children after them**. Indeed, obedience is the pathway of blessing.

Verse 40. The **everlasting covenant** most likely refers to the "new covenant" described in 31:31–34.[12] In this case, **the fear** of the Lord is substituted for the knowledge of the Lord (31:34). These concepts are closely intertwined, for "the fear of the LORD is the beginning of knowledge" (Prov. 1:7). In the future, God would **not turn away** from His people, nor would **they . . . turn away from** Him.

Verse 41. God promised, **"I will rejoice over them to do them good and will faithfully plant them in this land with all My heart and with all My soul."** The phrase "plant them in this land" points back to Jeremiah's sign of buying the field. Beyond this, it echoes the prophet's call, when he was commissioned "to build and to plant" (1:10). Similar promises of God's planting His people in the land appear throughout the book (18:7–10; 24:6; 31:28; 42:10).

Verse 42. The promises of God concerning Judah's return were just as certain as the Babylonian troops surrounding Jerusalem. God said, **"Just as I brought all this great disaster on this people, so I am going to bring on them all the good that I am promising them."**

Verses 43, 44. Jeremiah's land purchase was truly a demonstration, declaration, and verification of God's promises to His people. Even though the Babylonians were making the land **a desolation**, God would later return the people of Judah. After the exile, they would **buy fields for money, sign and seal deeds, and call in witnesses**—just as Jeremiah had done (32:9, 10). His symbolic actions represented the many land transactions that would take place in the post-exilic period.

Once again, the territory is geographically described in two ways (see 17:26). The first is from a sociopolitical point of view: **the land of Benjamin, the environs of Jerusalem**, and **the cities of Judah**. The second is from a topographical point of view: **the hill country** (central mountains), **the lowland** (western foothills), and **the Negev** (southern desert).

---

[12]The phrase "everlasting covenant" also appears in other prophetic passages (Is. 24:5; 55:3; 61:8; Jer. 50:5; Ezek. 16:60; 37:26).

APPLICATION

God's Guidance and Reassurance (Ch. 32)[13]

God gave His prophet a unique responsibility and the disposition to develop into the spokesman he needed to be. As Judah's darkest hour drew near, God gave Jeremiah the refreshing opportunity to recognize again that nothing is too hard for Him (32:27). It certainly did not mean that Jeremiah could understand all of God's ways (see Is. 55:6–11; 1 Pet. 1:10–12), while the Babylonian army was thundering and charging the gates of Jerusalem. The wickedness of his own people was part of the sad scenario, as he was confined by officials from his homeland (32:2). Nevertheless, God came through with another "Therefore" (32:36), followed by a group of "I wills" and "shall bes" that vibrated with the encouraging confidence that He was in command and would do all that He had declared. Truly, both a literal and spiritual restoration would take place when the people returned to their land. These possibilities were gigantic deeds in comparison with the lone land transaction in this chapter.

Therefore, what seems so unreasonable and hopeless to us with our limitations and moments of trial are routine unfoldings in the hands of a Mighty God, from whose love nothing can separate the faithful servant in Christ Jesus (Rom. 8:31–39). We must continue to live an obedient life despite the struggles we face. We should let our requests and perplexities be made known to God, enabling Him to grant the blessed assurance of a peace that surpasses understanding (Phil. 4:4–7; 1 Pet. 5:6, 7).

A Prayer of Praise (32:16–22)

After Jeremiah entrusted the deed of purchase to Baruch, he offered a heartfelt prayer to God. The first part of the prayer praises God, celebrating His great attributes.

1. *Powerful.* The prophet said, "Behold, You have made the heavens and the earth by Your great power and by Your out-

---

[13]Adapted from S. Conway, in T. K. Cheyne and W. F. Adeney, *The Pulpit Commentary*, vol. 11, *Jeremiah, Lamentations* (Grand Rapids, Mich.: Wm. B. Eerdmans Publishing Co., 1950), 2:58.

stretched arm! Nothing is too difficult for You" (32:17). God is the Creator of all things; He is omnipotent.

2. *Passionate.* Jeremiah acknowledged that God "shows lovingkindness to thousands" (32:18). Perhaps he was thinking about those who keep God's commandments (Ex. 20:6). God also expresses His love for those who are ignorant of Him or have rejected Him (Mt. 5:44, 45; Acts 14:16, 17; 17:26–28; 2 Pet. 3:9).

3. *Punitive.* God "repays the iniquity of fathers into the bosom of their children after them" (32:18). He is a just God who punishes evildoers at the proper time. One wicked generation often influences the next, calling down the wrath of God (16:11–13).

4. *Perceptive.* The Lord is "great in counsel," and His "eyes are open to all the ways of the sons of men" (32:19). This language describes God's omniscience. His perfect knowledge ensures His righteous judgments.

5. *Proven.* Jeremiah appealed to God's "signs and wonders" in Egypt (32:20). These great deeds established the Lord's name in Egypt, in Israel, and among the nations. His mighty hand had demonstrated that He is the only true God.

6. *Protective.* God safely brought His people out of Egyptian bondage. He protected them from their enemies by "a strong hand" and "an outstretched arm" (32:21). The psalmist described God as his "rock," "fortress," "deliverer," "shield," "horn of . . . salvation," and "stronghold" (Ps. 18:2).

7. *Philanthropic.* The Lord generously gave Israel the land of Canaan, "a land flowing with milk and honey" (32:22). He provided them with a land where they could plant their crops, sustain their flocks and herds, and raise their families.

These seven attributes are combined to capture the essence of God's identity. He is still the same God—and is worthy of our praise today!

All Things Made New (32:36–44)

God made several promises to His people, describing a new order for them: (1) They would enjoy a new security in the land (32:37, 41–44). (2) God would have a new relationship with His people (32:38). (3) They would have a new commitment to God (32:39). (4) God would make a new covenant with His people

JEREMIAH 32

(32:40). (5) He would express a new joy over them (32:41).[14]

The Goodness and Severity of God in Contrast (32:36–44; see Rom. 11:22; KJV))

The last section of the chapter, 32:36–44, emphasizes the character of God. For example, the repeated use of the first person ("I," "Me, and "My") underscores His power and authority over our lives.

Another attribute that surfaces is God's goodness. We are indeed dependent upon Him for the blessings in our lives. God is great, and we rely on Him for every good thing (Jas. 1:17).

This passage also teaches us that God is just. He punishes the disobedient and richly blesses those who obey Him (1 Pet. 3:10–12). The temporary decisions of this life are linked to everlasting rewards or consequences, which will bring either eternal rejoicing or eternal regret (Mt. 25:31–46; Jn. 5:28, 29; 12:48; 2 Cor. 5:10–15).

The goodness and the severity of God (see Rom. 11:22; KJV) can be seen from the following parallel, which shows both sides of God's nature.

His Goodness	His Severity
"Behold, I will gather them out of all the lands" (32:37).	Judah shall be "given into the hand of the king of Babylon . . ." (32:36).
"I will . . . make them dwell in safety" (32:37).	". . . by sword, by famine and by pestilence" (32:36).
"I will bring them back to this place" (32:37).	"I have driven them . . ." (32:37).
"I will give them one heart and one way . . . for their own good and for the good of their children after them" (32:39).	". . . in My anger, in My wrath and in great indignation" (32:37).

---

[14]Adapted from Smith, 555–57.

"I will make an everlasting covenant with them. . . . I will rejoice over them to do them good" (32:40, 41).	I turned away from them (implied; 32:40).
"I am going to bring on them all the good that I am promising them" (32:42).	"I brought all this great disaster on this people" (32:42).
"I . . . will faithfully plant them in this land. . . . Fields will be bought in this land . . . of Benjamin . . . Jerusalem . . . cities of Judah" (32:41, 43, 44).	"[Their land] is a desolation, without man or beast" (32:43).
"I will restore their fortunes" (32:44).	"[Their land] is given into the hand of the Chaldeans" (32:43).

God's severity should warn us against doing evil, while His goodness should elicit our praise and thanksgiving. Because He is gracious and kind, we can have hope for tomorrow.

Chapter 33
God's Visit of His Prophet In Prison

Chapter 33 concludes what has been called "The Book of Consolation" (chs. 30—33). In this chapter, God once again visited His prophet in prison (33:1). His most positive promises and reinforcement came during Jeremiah's confinement.

God spoke to Jeremiah during a time of great despair. As the Babylonian siege of Jerusalem continued its destruction (33:4, 5), those left in Judah charged God with total rejection (33:24). It may have seemed that all hope had faded, but Jeremiah and the people were not to forget God's plans for them.

This chapter continues with encouragement and an emphasis on the benefits people would receive upon submitting to God's scheme of redemption. The first half of the chapter focuses on God's news of restoration and prosperity (33:1–13). The second half reveals the greater news of a messianic plan assuring a reign of righteousness (33:14–26).

A PREDICTION OF RESTORATION (33:1–13)

The Call of the Creator (33:1–5)

¹Then the word of the Lord came to Jeremiah the second time, while he was still confined in the court of the guard, saying, ²"Thus says the Lord who made the earth, the Lord who formed it to establish it, the Lord is His name, ³'Call to Me and I will answer you, and I will tell you great and mighty things, which you do not know.' ⁴For thus says the Lord God of Israel

concerning the houses of this city, and concerning the houses of the kings of Judah which are broken down to make a defense against the siege ramps and against the sword, ⁵'While they are coming to fight with the Chaldeans and to fill them with the corpses of men whom I have slain in My anger and in My wrath, and I have hidden My face from this city because of all their wickedness.'"

Verse 1. As the chapter begins, **Jeremiah . . . was still confined in the court of the guard.** A similar description is found in the previous chapter, where God spoke to the prophet (see comments on 32:1, 2). Here God revealed His message to Jeremiah for a **second time.**

Verse 2. God prefaced His words by identifying Himself as the Creator: **"Thus says the LORD who made the earth, the LORD who formed it to establish it"** (see 10:12; 31:35; 32:17, 27). "Formed" comes from the term יָצַר (*yatsar*), which means "form" or "fashion." It can be used for "a potter who forms out of clay a vessel."[1] The word first appears in the Old Testament when "the LORD God formed man of dust from the ground" (Gen. 2:7). In verse 2, God described Himself as shaping the whole earth.

God also identified Himself by His personal **name, the LORD.** The Hebrew word for "LORD" is יהוה (*YHWH*), which can be transliterated as "Yahweh." This name, which is similar to "I AM" in Hebrew (Ex. 3:14, 15), may indicate God's eternal nature or His continuous action in human affairs.[2]

Verse 3. God invited Jeremiah to ask Him for answers concerning the future: **"Call to Me and I will answer you, and I will tell you great and mighty things, which you do not know"** (see Is. 48:6). The Scriptures emphasize that God hears and answers the prayers of His faithful servants (Ps. 3:4; 4:3; 18:6; 27:7, 8; 28:1, 2; 30:8; 34:4, 15–18; 55:17; Mt. 7:7; 1 Pet. 3:12). In the case of Jeremiah, the Lord would reveal an inspired message. "Mighty

---

[1]Francis Brown, S. R. Driver, and Charles A. Briggs, *A Hebrew and English Lexicon of the Old Testament* (Oxford: Clarendon Press, 1972), 427–28.

[2]For more information, see Coy D. Roper, *Exodus*, Truth for Today Commentary (Searcy, Ark.: Resource Publications, 2008), 59–60.

things" comes from the word בָּצַר (*batsar*), which means "cut off" or "make inaccessible." The term is sometimes used for a wall or height that is impenetrable or unscalable. Here it is used for knowledge that is unavailable to mankind—that is, "secrets" or "mysteries."[3] These "unsearchable things" (NIV) involved God's restoration of His people.

Verse 4. The desperate conditions in Jerusalem explained God's desire for Jeremiah to call on Him. The general setting of the Babylonian siege is obvious, but the exact meaning of verse 4 is uncertain. Two different interpretations have been adopted, as seen by comparing English versions (which add a phrase to the verse). The first is represented by the TEV: "The houses of Jerusalem and the royal palace of Judah will be torn down *as a result of* the siege and the attack" (emphasis added). Houses would especially be affected if they were built into the city wall.[4] The second possibility is found in the NASB: **The houses of this city, and . . . the houses of the kings of Judah . . . are broken down** *to make a defense against* **the siege ramps and against the sword** (emphasis added). In this case, God's people were tearing down their own homes in Jerusalem in order to have materials to fill the gaps in the walls made by the Babylonian forces (see Is. 22:10). "The houses of the kings of Judah" refers to "the royal palace which was a collection of buildings."[5] (For "siege ramps," see comments on 6:6; 32:24.)

Verse 5. Jerusalem was disintegrating from within and being bombarded from without. While the destruction of buildings tore at the heart, the city was being filled with **the corpses of men** (see 7:33; 9:22; 21:4–7; 31:40; 34:20).

God wanted Jeremiah to recognize two important truths: (1) The destruction was happening because of His **anger**. He had **hidden** [His] **face** from protecting His people. Judah had

---

[3]Brown, Driver, and Briggs, 130–31; Ludwig Koehler and Walter Baumgartner, *The Hebrew and Aramaic Lexicon of the Old Testament*, study ed., trans. and ed. M. E. J. Richardson (Boston: Brill, 2001), 1:148.

[4]Anthony L. Ash, *Jeremiah and Lamentations*, The Living Word Commentary (Abilene, Tex.: ACU Press, 1987), 238.

[5]Douglas Rawlinson Jones, *Jeremiah*, The New Century Bible Commentary (Grand Rapids, Mich.: Wm. B. Eerdmans Publishing Co., 1992), 421.

turned their backs on the Lord, so He had hidden His face from the slaughter (32:28–35). (2) This was happening because of Judah's **wickedness**. For about forty years, God had warned them through Jeremiah, but they would not change (1:16; 2:19; 3:2; 4:14, 18; 6:7; 7:12; 8:6; 12:4; 14:16; 22:22; 23:11, 14). God wanted His people to see that His righteousness and justice demanded the desolation now descending on Jerusalem. Both God's statements and Jeremiah's insight acknowledged that this hour had to come (see Dan. 9:1–19).

God's Clarification of the Purpose For the Conflict (33:6–13)

⁶"'Behold, I will bring to it health and healing, and I will heal them; and I will reveal to them an abundance of peace and truth. ⁷I will restore the fortunes of Judah and the fortunes of Israel and will rebuild them as they were at first. ⁸I will cleanse them from all their iniquity by which they have sinned against Me, and I will pardon all their iniquities by which they have sinned against Me and by which they have transgressed against Me. ⁹It will be to Me a name of joy, praise and glory before all the nations of the earth which will hear of all the good that I do for them, and they will fear and tremble because of all the good and all the peace that I make for it.'

¹⁰"Thus says the LORD, 'Yet again there will be heard in this place, of which you say, "It is a waste, without man and without beast," that is, in the cities of Judah and in the streets of Jerusalem that are desolate, without man and without inhabitant and without beast, ¹¹the voice of joy and the voice of gladness, the voice of the bridegroom and the voice of the bride, the voice of those who say,

"Give thanks to the LORD of hosts,
For the LORD is good,
For His lovingkindness is everlasting";
and of those who bring a thank offering into the house of the LORD. For I will restore the fortunes of the land as they were at first,' says the LORD.

¹²"Thus says the LORD of hosts, 'There will again be in this

place which is waste, without man or beast, and in all its cities, a habitation of shepherds who rest their flocks. ¹³In the cities of the hill country, in the cities of the lowland, in the cities of the Negev, in the land of Benjamin, in the environs of Jerusalem and in the cities of Judah, the flocks will again pass under the hands of the one who numbers them,' says the LORD."

Verse 6. God wanted Jeremiah to understand that this horror was part of a cleansing. It held a golden thread of hope for the future, since God would bring **health and healing** to His people. "Health" is from the Hebrew word אֲרוּכָה (*ᵃrukah*), which indicates "new flesh growing on a healing wound."⁶ The divine doctor knew what was required to correct their evil condition.

The Lord said that He would **reveal to them an abundance of peace and truth**. The Hebrew word translated "abundance," עֲתֶרֶת (*ᵃthereth*), appears only this one time in the Old Testament. The meaning of the word is uncertain,⁷ but many English versions use the term "abundance" or "abundant." Some versions simply do not translate the word at all.

A contrast can be made between God's message and that of the false prophets. They dealt deceitfully with the people, proclaiming peace when there was none to be found. These deceivers treated the wound of the people superficially (6:13, 14). God, however, seriously addressed their wound, performing radical surgery—the destruction of Jerusalem and the Babylonian captivity. As a result, the people would someday enjoy true peace in their land.

Verse 7. Once more, God promised to **restore the fortunes** of His people (29:14; 30:3, 18; 31:23; 32:44; 33:11, 26). He mentioned both **Judah** and **Israel**, that is, all of His chosen people. He would **rebuild them as they were at first**.

Verse 8. As a penitent people, they could receive God's promise: He would **cleanse** and **pardon** them. "Cleanse" is from טָהֵר (*taher*), meaning "be clean, pure." It can relate to physical, cere-

---

⁶Koehler and Baumgartner, 1:85. The word *ᵃrukah* also appears in 8:22 and 30:17.

⁷Ibid., 1:906; Brown, Driver, and Briggs, 801.

monial, or moral purification.[8] The last of these is in view here. "Pardon" is from סָלַח (*salach*), which only appears in the Scriptures concerning God's forgiveness of man. It is never used for people forgiving each other.[9] God would give His people moral purity and forgiveness in place of their sin.

Verse 9. These divine plans would produce much fruit. The surrounding **nations** would learn of the internal and external renovation of God's restored people. The result would be **joy** and **praise** for what God had done for that land and His people, especially in Jerusalem. Those nations would give **glory** to God for the manner in which He blessed His people (see 13:11). His plan for renewal would result in international respect.

The nations would demonstrate a sense of awe and reverence: **They will fear and tremble because of all the good and all the peace that I make for it.** This is the kind of fear mentioned in Ecclesiastes 12:13, 14 that leads to conversion and salvation. Indeed, the nations would witness the Lord's blessings and come to know that the He is God (see Ezek. 28:25, 26; 36:22–38). Some would even seek a relationship with Him (see Zech. 8:18–23).

Verses 10, 11. Rejoicing would return to **the cities of Judah** and to **the streets of Jerusalem**, which the Babylonian forces had left **desolate, without man and without inhabitant and without beast** (32:43). God's curse, which removed the celebration of weddings (7:34; 16:9; 25:10, 11), would be lifted. Due to His blessing, **the voice of joy and the voice of gladness, the voice of the bridegroom and the voice of the bride** would once again be heard in the Promised Land.

The sounds of celebration and worship would reverberate on the temple mount in Jerusalem. God's people would praise Him in song as they brought **a thank offering** (see 30:19; 31:6). In language reminiscent of the Psalms (Ps. 100:5; 106:1; 107:1; 118:1; 136:1), they would sing,

Give thanks to the Lord of hosts,
For the Lord is good,

---

[8]Brown, Driver, and Briggs, 372.
[9]Ibid., 699.

For His lovingkindness is everlasting.

This rejoicing could only take place because of God's promises to **restore the fortunes of the land as they were at first** (see comments on 33:7). These promises appear several times in the book (17:26; 29:14; 30:3, 18–22; 31:4–6, 12–14, 23, 24; 32:44; 33:7, 10–13, 26). Indeed, the Babylonian exiles did rejoice when God brought them back to Jerusalem. After they had laid the foundation for the temple, the people gave thanks to God, saying, "For He is good, for His lovingkindness is upon Israel forever" (Ezra 3:11). Later, they celebrated the Passover and Feast of Unleavened Bread with joy (Ezra 6:19–22). Later still, they participated in the Feast of Tabernacles with "great rejoicing" (Neh. 8:17). After the wall was rebuilt, the people "offered great sacrifices and rejoiced because God had given them great joy, even the women and children rejoiced, so that the joy of Jerusalem was heard from afar" (Neh. 12:43).

Verses 12, 13. Once more, God promised to overrule the curse of desolation. Even though the land had become a **waste, without man or beast** (see 32:43; 33:10), He would restore the flocks and make the **shepherds** prosper. R. K. Harrison wrote, "Once again sheep will pass under the hands of the shepherd, this being the normal way of counting them as they entered the fold for the night."[10] In this way, the shepherd would make sure that none of them were missing. (For the geographical listing, see comments on 32:43, 44.)

A PROMISE OF A REIGN OF RIGHTEOUSNESS (33:14–26)

A Prophetic Preview of the Righteous Branch of David (33:14–18)

¹⁴"'**Behold, days are coming,' declares the LORD, 'when I will fulfill the good word which I have spoken concerning the**

---

[10]R. K. Harrison, *Jeremiah and Lamentations: An Introduction and Commentary*, Tyndale Old Testament Commentaries (Downers Grove, Ill.: Inter-Varsity Press, 1973), 144. (See Lev. 27:32; Ezek. 20:37.)

house of Israel and the house of Judah. ¹⁵In those days and at that time I will cause a righteous Branch of David to spring forth; and He shall execute justice and righteousness on the earth. ¹⁶In those days Judah will be saved and Jerusalem will dwell in safety; and this is the name by which she will be called: the LORD is our righteousness.' ¹⁷For thus says the LORD, 'David shall never lack a man to sit on the throne of the house of Israel; ¹⁸and the Levitical priests shall never lack a man before Me to offer burnt offerings, to burn grain offerings and to prepare sacrifices continually.'"

Verse 14. With the introductory phrase **Behold, days are coming,** God pointed to the future time when His promise of the coming Messiah would be realized. This precious promise is referred to here as **the good word which I have spoken concerning the house of Israel and the house of Judah** under the leadership of God's chosen king.

Verses 15, 16. These verses echo the language of 23:5, 6, a text that also predicts the coming of the Messiah (see comments on 23:5, 6). J. A. Thompson considered it strange that some English versions have verses 15 and 16 printed as prose, whereas 23:5, 6 is arranged as poetry.[11] This inconsistency is evident in the NASB. However, several translations now print both passages as poetry (NIV; NKJV; NJB; CEV; NCV; NLT).

The Messiah, Jesus Christ, is spoken of as the **righteous Branch** coming from **David**. This figure of speech is prominent in God's unfolding plans for His people (23:5, 6; Is. 4:2; 11:1–4; Zech. 3:8–10; 6:12, 13). The Messiah's reign would be characterized by **justice and righteousness** (23:5, 6; Is. 9:6, 7). Jack Cottrell underscored the importance of the terms "justice" (מִשְׁפָּט, *mishpat*) and "righteousness" (צְדָקָה, *tsᵉdaqah*) by showing their use in other prophetic passages:

In Hosea 2:19 God tells his erring people that he will

---

[11]J. A. Thompson, *The Book of Jeremiah*, The New International Commentary on the Old Testament (Grand Rapids, Mich.: Wm. B. Eerdmans Publishing Co., 1980), 601.

receive them back, and "I will betroth you to Me in righteousness and in justice [*tsedeq* and *mishpāt*]." In Hosea 10:12 the people are told "to seek the Lord until He comes to rain righteousness [*tsedeq*] on you." Micah declares, "I will bear the indignation of the Lord because I have sinned against Him, until He pleads my case and executes justice [*mishpāt*] for me. He will bring me out to the light, and I will see His righteousness [*tsedāqāh*]" (Micah 7:9). See Zechariah 8:8; 9:9.[12]

In the time of the Messiah, the people of God, symbolized by **Judah** and **Jerusalem**, would truly be delivered from their oppressors, enjoying peace, security, and **safety**. Literal Israel and Judah never reestablished an independent nation under a Davidic ruler following the return to their homeland.[13] God had something better and greater in mind. "Judah" and "Jerusalem," as God's people then, must be understood as representing the spiritual unfolding Christ made possible through the church (the kingdom of God), which enables souls to be reconciled to God (Acts 2:29–47; 13:32–39; 2 Cor. 5:17–21; Gal. 4:21–31; Col. 1:12–14; 1 Thess. 1:1; 2:12; Rev. 21:1, 2, 10). The name given to the Messiah in 23:6 is here applied to the people of God: **The Lord is our righteousness.**

Verse 17. God's plans for the throne of David had been repeatedly expressed (2 Sam. 7:8, 12–16; 1 Kings 2:1–4; 8:25; 9:5; Ps. 89:20, 21, 26–29, 33–37), but those earlier promises had come when David's rule was strong. The promise to Jeremiah was shocking in the middle of the Babylonian conquest of God's people. The idea that **David** [would] **never lack a man to sit on the throne of the house of Israel** seemed quite unlikely, yet God's promises had never failed. The unbroken succession of

---

[12]Jack Cottrell, *God the Redeemer*, What the Bible Says Series (Joplin, Mo.: College Press Publishing Co., 1987), 229.

[13]During the Intertestamental period, the Hasmoneans (a priestly family) ruled over an independent Israel (142–63 B.C.). They had cast off the oppression of the Seleucids, the Syrian rulers to the north who tried to Hellenize them. However, Israel's independence came to an end due to the conquest of the Roman army led by Pompey (63 B.C.).

David's line was replaced with a higher fulfillment: Christ's continuous sovereignty as the true Son of David (Amos 9:11, 12; Mt. 1:1, 6–18; Mk. 11:9, 10; Lk. 1:30–33; 22:29, 30; Acts 2:22–36; 13:22, 23, 33–39; 15:15–17; Rev. 5:5–10).

Verse 18. In addition to the monarchy, God had made a promise regarding the priesthood: **"The Levitical priests shall never lack a man before Me to offer burnt offerings, to burn grain offerings and to prepare sacrifices continually."** The background of this promise is the time just after Israel's exodus from Egypt, when the Lord appointed Aaron and his sons to serve at the altar of the tabernacle (Ex. 28:1, 41). Aaron and his descendants, who came from the tribe of Levi, were to "have the priesthood by a perpetual statute" (Ex. 29:9; see Num. 3:10; 16:40; 18:1–7; 25:10–13; Neh. 13:29; Mal. 2:4).

The promise of perpetual sacrifices may have also seemed shocking, since burnt offerings and grain offerings would cease to be made when the Babylonians destroyed Jerusalem and the temple. However, after the Jews returned from captivity, they built a new altar and the Levitical priests resumed sacrifices (Ezra 3:2, 3); they also built a new temple (Ezra 6:14, 15). Generally speaking, sacrifices continued to be made until the fall of Jerusalem and the destruction of the temple at the hands of the Romans in A.D. 70.[14]

Like the promise of kingship given to David, the promise concerning perpetual priesthood is also fulfilled in Jesus Christ. He became a high priest after the order of Melchizedek, who was both king and priest, and not of the Levitical lineage (Heb. 7:1–4, 11–17). Jesus Christ, as both high priest and king, forever serves and reigns over God's spiritual kingdom (Jn. 14:6; 18:36, 37; Heb. 1:1–12; 3:1; Rev. 17:14; 19:11–16).

Jesus, the great high priest, offered Himself as a sin offering once for all time and for all people when He died on the cross

---

[14]One exception to this statement is when sacrifices ceased for more than three years during the Intertestamental period (168–165 B.C.). The temple was looted and desecrated by the Seleucid ruler Antiochus IV (Epiphanes). The rededication of the temple by the Jews after that time serves as the background for Hanukkah (1 Maccabees 1:20–62; 4:36–61). In the New Testament, this celebration is called "the Feast of the Dedication" (Jn. 10:22).

(Heb. 7:26, 27; 9:11, 12, 24–28; 10:10; 1 Pet. 3:18; 1 Jn. 2:1, 2). For one to attempt to offer any other sacrifice of *atonement* would be futile. Under the new covenant, those who are baptized into Christ—whether male or female—become a part of His holy priesthood (1 Pet. 2:4–10; Heb. 10:19–23). They are called to offer spiritual sacrifices that show gratitude to God. Such sacrifices include singing songs of praise and showing kindness to others (Heb. 13:15, 16). Christians give themselves as living sacrifices in spiritual service to the Lord (Rom. 12:1, 2).

Therefore, verse 18 presents old covenant symbols to identify an unending spiritual service by God's people, offering spiritual sacrifices through Christ, the "Branch of David" (33:15). Jeremiah had earlier indicated a dramatic change in priestly rituals when he declared that the ark of the covenant would not be a part of the messianic age (3:16). The ark was crucial to the worship patterns under the old covenant (2 Chron. 5:2–10; Heb. 9:3–14). The removal of that ark, therefore, pointed to "a complete change in the nature of the priesthood."[15] What Jeremiah gives in 33:14–18 opens the door of glorious hope with several changes, when "Judah will be saved" (33:16; see Acts 2:14–21).

Assurance That God's Promises Are True (33:19–26)

[19]The word of the LORD came to Jeremiah, saying, [20]"Thus says the LORD, 'If you can break My covenant for the day and My covenant for the night, so that day and night will not be at their appointed time, [21]then My covenant may also be broken with David My servant so that he will not have a son to reign on his throne, and with the Levitical priests, My ministers. [22]As the host of heaven cannot be counted and the sand of the sea cannot be measured, so I will multiply the descendants of David My servant and the Levites who minister to Me.'"

[23]And the word of the LORD came to Jeremiah, saying, [24]"Have you not observed what this people have spoken, saying,

---

[15]James E. Smith, *Jeremiah and Lamentations*, Bible Study Textbook Series (Joplin, Mo.: College Press, 1972), 568.

'The two families which the LORD chose, He has rejected them'? Thus they despise My people, no longer are they as a nation in their sight. ²⁵Thus says the LORD, 'If My covenant for day and night stand not, and the fixed patterns of heaven and earth I have not established, ²⁶then I would reject the descendants of Jacob and David My servant, not taking from his descendants rulers over the descendants of Abraham, Isaac and Jacob. But I will restore their fortunes and will have mercy on them.'"

During these dark days of destruction, God surrounded His confined spokesman with salvation, security, revival, hope, and loyalty. Recognizing that this situation might seem too good to be true, God responded by giving repeated assurance in verses 19 through 26. (The pattern of great promises followed by reassurance appears earlier in 31:31–40.)

Verses 19–21. These verses, which constitute an **if . . . then** statement, form an argument based on the constancy of creation (see 31:35–37). God affirmed that His **covenant** promises to **David** and **the Levitical priests** were as solid as His **covenant for the day** and His **covenant for the night** (Gen. 1:3–5). As long as day and night continued to exist, the people could know that God's promises to David and His priestly plans through the tribe of Levi would prevail.

Verse 22. God would **multiply the descendants of David . . . and the Levites who minister** as **the host of heaven . . . and the sand of the sea**. The stars of heaven and sand of the sea were often used in proverbial expressions to indicate a vast number that could not be counted (Gen. 15:5; 22:17; 26:4; Ex. 32:13; Deut. 1:10; 10:22; 28:62; Josh. 11:4; Judg. 7:12). In this context, God's infinite creation also provided evidence that He could raise up leaders and descendants for the kingly and priestly duties, even in those dark days.

As previously indicated, such promises point to the reign of Christ and His people. Christians have been consecrated as a kingdom of priests who reign with Christ (Rom. 5:17; 8:17; 2 Tim. 2:12; 1 Pet. 2:5, 9; Rev. 1:6; 3:21; 5:10; 20:5, 6; 22:5).

Verses 23, 24. God addressed the negative message that His prophet had been hearing. Some were claiming, **"The two fami-**

lies which the LORD chose, He has rejected them." Two questions arise when interpreting this message. First, who are the **people** who actually said it? They could be either those from foreign nations or "those within Israel who had ceased to believe in Yahweh's election of his people."[16] Second, to whom do "the two families" refer? In the preceding verses, God had been discussing the families of David (kings) and Aaron (Levitical priests). The references to **My people** and **a nation**, however, seem to indicate that "the two families" refer to Judah and Israel. Together, these groups comprised God's chosen people.

Verses 25, 26. These verses comprise another **if . . . then** statement, drawing on the constancy of creation. Once again, God appealed to His **covenant** of **day and night** (see 33:19–21). In addition, He mentioned **the fixed patterns of heaven and earth**. The natural laws established at creation serve as signs of God's faithfulness to His promises.

While the Assyrian and Babylonian captivities gave the appearance that God had abandoned His people, He had not utterly rejected them (6:30; 7:29; 14:19; Lam. 1:15; 2:7; 3:17, 21–26; 5:21, 22). God alluded to His promises and faithfulness to this people, going all the way back to **Abraham, Isaac and Jacob** (Gen. 12:1–3; 15:5, 17–21; 22:17, 18; 26:1–5; 32:12; Ex. 3:14–18; Josh. 21:43–45). His long-term fidelity served as further evidence that He would **have mercy on** His people and **restore their fortunes** (29:14; 30:3; 31:23; 32:44). Because of their great iniquities, they deserved to be cast off forever. Nevertheless, God would offer salvation and hope.

APPLICATION

Understanding and Treasuring God's Promises (Ch. 33)

This positive portion of Jeremiah (chs. 30—33) offers a ray of sunshine in a dark hour, a foundation for hope in the midst of slaughter. In this chaos, remembering the Lord's covenant promises was most reassuring.

---

[16]Thompson, 603.

A great lesson to be gleaned from chapter 33 is that we need to accurately handle God's Word (2 Tim. 2:15). The prophets repeatedly used Mosaic terminology to describe the spiritual realities that would be found in Christ's covenant. In 33:14–18, Jeremiah used the terminology and concepts of his own day so that his message would be meaningful to the people who first received it.

The prophets predicted many things about salvation and the scheme of redemption through Christ that they did not fully understand; even "angels long[ed] to look" into these things (1 Pet. 1:10–12). Since a true prophet's message came from God, he did not have to fully understand it in order to proclaim it to the people.

The prophets' messages were sometimes explained by their fulfillment in the new covenant. We have given repeated references from the New Testament that show the fulfillment of what Jeremiah affirmed would happen in chapter 33. Each Bible student should recognize and accept those fulfillments on the one hand, and avoid a misapplication of any prophetic utterance on the other. For example, Hebrews 7 makes it abundantly clear that Christ's priesthood is after the order of Melchizedek, not after the order of Levi. This is necessary because Jesus descended from the tribe of Judah, not Levi. Hebrews 9 and 10 also teach that Christ's priesthood is far superior to the Levitical priesthood of Aaron. By accepting the interpretation found in Hebrews concerning the priestly promises spoken by Jeremiah, we can avoid some incorrect teachings.

The legitimacy of the Levitical, priestly system ended when Christ became High Priest and King after His resurrection. Therefore, His reign renders false any claims for a continuation of the Levitical system today. Any child of God through Christ, whether male or female, is a part of Christ's priesthood (Gal. 3:26–29; 1 Pet. 1:1, 2; 2:4–10).

We should allow the fulfillment of Jeremiah's prophecies—which took place about six hundred years later through Christ—to strengthen our faith. Jeremiah was indeed God's prophet, and the Bible is truly God's Word. Human resources are inept when it comes to accurately predicting the future (Deut. 18:15–22).

JEREMIAH 33

God's Invitation to Pray (33:3)

God told Jeremiah, "Call to Me and I will answer you, and I will tell you great and mighty things, which you do not know" (33:3). The Lord wanted His prophet to trust in Him and to seek Him for guidance. God also wants us to call on Him in prayer today (Col. 4:2; 1 Thess. 5:17, 18). Peter wrote, "Cast all your anxiety on him because he cares for you" (1 Pet. 5:7; NIV). It should mean so much to us to be able to contact God anytime and anywhere. He can hear us wherever we may be.

CHAPTER 34
DISOBEDIENCE LEADING TO DEFEAT

Chapters 34 through 36 primarily present different stages of disobedience by God's people. They are not in chronological order. Of the events recorded, the ones in chapter 34 occurred in the days of King Zedekiah, those in chapter 35 took place "in the days of Jehoiakim" (35:1), and those in chapter 36 occurred "in the fourth year of Jehoiakim" (36:1). These three chapters identify different ways God's people departed from His directions.

Chapter 34 provides a personality study, sadly demonstrating man's weakness and fickleness. The price of waywardness is portrayed, and Judah's failure to fulfill their covenant responsibilities is illustrated. The overall theme is God's justification for punishing these rebellious people.

Two distinct messages from the Lord were given to Jeremiah in chapter 34. The first related to the downfall of Jerusalem, the defeat and death of Zedekiah (34:1–7). The second, which was for all the people, concerned their disobedience to the covenant rules for releasing servants (34:8–22).

THE DECREE OF DEATH FOR ZEDEKIAH (34:1–7)

¹**The word which came to Jeremiah from the LORD, when Nebuchadnezzar king of Babylon and all his army, with all the kingdoms of the earth that were under his dominion and all the peoples, were fighting against Jerusalem and against all its cities, saying,** ²**"Thus says the LORD God of Israel, 'Go and speak to Zedekiah king of Judah and say to him: "Thus says the LORD,**

'Behold, I am giving this city into the hand of the king of Babylon, and he will burn it with fire. ³You will not escape from his hand, for you will surely be captured and delivered into his hand; and you will see the king of Babylon eye to eye, and he will speak with you face to face, and you will go to Babylon."'
⁴Yet hear the word of the LORD, O Zedekiah king of Judah! Thus says the LORD concerning you, 'You will not die by the sword. ⁵You will die in peace; and as spices were burned for your fathers, the former kings who were before you, so they will burn spices for you; and they will lament for you, "Alas, lord!"' For I have spoken the word," declares the LORD.
⁶Then Jeremiah the prophet spoke all these words to Zedekiah king of Judah in Jerusalem ⁷when the army of the king of Babylon was fighting against Jerusalem and against all the remaining cities of Judah, that is, Lachish and Azekah, for they alone remained as fortified cities among the cities of Judah.

Verse 1. This chapter begins by generally dating the prophecy given to **Jeremiah** to the time **when Nebuchadnezzar king of Babylon and all his army** were attacking **Jerusalem** and the surrounding **cities** of Judah (588–586 B.C.). Nebuchadnezzar's army included soldiers from **all the kingdoms of the earth that were under his dominion**. As he conquered nation after nation, Nebuchadnezzar enlisted men suitable for battle into his army for the next stage of conquest (see 2 Kings 24:1–3). Anthony L. Ash emphasized the exchange that took place between vassal and overlord: "Vassal treaties of the day often agreed that a vassal would provide an overlord with military assistance, in exchange for the overlord's protection of the vassal against enemies."[1] This practice probably serves as the background for Nebuchadnezzar's combined army in verse 1.

---

[1]Anthony L. Ash, *Jeremiah and Lamentations*, The Living Word Commentary (Abilene, Tex.: ACU Press, 1987), 244. For an example of a treaty in which the overlord required military assistance from the vassal, see James B. Pritchard, ed. *Ancient Near Eastern Texts: Relating to the Old Testament*, 3d ed. (Princeton, N.J.: Princeton University Press, 1969), 204; William W. Hallo, ed., *The Context of Scripture* (Boston: Brill, 2003), 2:96–97.

Verse 2. As the Babylonian armies maneuvered outside Jerusalem, **God** sent Jeremiah to **speak to Zedekiah** within the city. This event must have preceded the prophet's confinement (see comments on 32:1, 2; 33:1), taking place in the earlier part of the siege (588 B.C.).

The divine message given to the **king of Judah** foretold the losses he would sustain from Nebuchadnezzar, **the king of Babylon**. God was giving the **city** of Jerusalem over to the Babylonian king, and **he** [would] **burn it with fire**. To see one's city surrendered to an enemy would be awful. Even worse would be to witness the burning of stately buildings full of tradition. The greatest of tragedies for the Jews, no doubt, was to witness the burning of God's holy temple (39:8; 2 Kings 25:8–10; 2 Chron. 36:17–19).

Verse 3. In addition to losing his nation, the king would also lose his own liberty. He would **not escape from** Nebuchadnezzar, but **be captured and delivered into his hand** (32:4, 5; Ezek. 12:12, 13; 17:11–20). The fulfillment of this prediction is detailed in 39:1–7: After attempting to escape and hide, Zedekiah was captured and brought before Nebuchadnezzar. He was able to **see the king of Babylon eye to eye** and **speak with** [him] **face to face** (see comments on 32:4). After being blinded, Zedekiah was taken away **to Babylon**. He is a classic example of a man who would not heed the truth. He lived in constant fear and denial, always looking for an escape or some easy, immediate solution.

Verses 4, 5. God's message also contained details about the death of **Zedekiah**. Unlike many Jews living in Jerusalem, the **king** would **not die by the sword**. He would **die in peace** in Babylon and receive a royal funeral. Zedekiah was told, **"As spices were burned for your fathers, . . . so they will burn spices for you."** This custom was a means of expressing honor (2 Chron. 16:14; 21:19). The people would also **lament** for him, saying, **"Alas, lord!"** While the people would perform these rituals for Zedekiah at his death, we should not conclude that he was blessed with royal pomp and splendor. It was more likely a tribute of pity. At least he would have someone honor him at his passing. His brother, Jehoiakim, received none of these benefits (see comments on 22:18, 19).

Verses 6, 7. Jeremiah obeyed God by speaking **all these words to Zedekiah** (34:2). The prophet continued to display great courage as he confronted the king. His prophecy is more specifically dated to the time the Babylonians were **fighting against Jerusalem** and the **fortified cities** of **Lachish and Azekah**. By this time, all the other **cities of Judah** had been defeated.

Lachish was located nearly thirty miles southwest of Jerusalem, on the way to Gaza, and Azekah was about twelve miles north of Lachish. Azekah was "an isolated fortress city situated in the Shephelah of Judah . . . , controlling the entrance to the valley."[2] Lachish was "one of the principal cities of Judah and a royal fortress protecting the southern Judean hill country from invasion from the southern Philistine plain."[3] Both of these cities are listed in the allotment of land given to the tribe of Judah (Josh. 15:35, 39).

Lachish is well known from the reliefs discovered at the palace of Sennacherib in Nineveh. This Assyrian king overtook Lachish and made it his base of operations in 701 B.C., as he mounted an attack on King Hezekiah and Jerusalem (2 Kings 18:13, 14; Is. 36:1, 2). One scene from the reliefs depicts Lachish under siege, men being impaled, and captives being led away.[4]

Another archaeological discovery is more relevant to the present text. Excavations of Lachish in 1935 revealed a collection of letters on potsherds in a guardroom between the inner and outer city gate. *Letter 4*, written to the rulers of Lachish from another site, suggests that Lachish and Jerusalem may have been the only fortified cities remaining. The author of the letter wrote, "We are watching the (fire)-signals of Lachish according to the code which my lord gave us, for we cannot see Azeqah."[5] If Azekah had already fallen to the Babylonians, *Lachish Letter 4*

---

[2] Frederick E. Young, "Azekah," in *The International Standard Bible Encyclopedia*, rev. ed., ed. Geoffrey W. Bromiley (Grand Rapids, Mich.: Wm. B. Eerdmans Publishing Co., 1979), 1:375.

[3] Victor Roland Gold and Keith N. Schoville, "Lachish," in *The International Standard Bible Encyclopedia*, rev. ed., ed. Geoffrey W. Bromiley (Grand Rapids, Mich.: Wm. B. Eerdmans Publishing Co., 1986), 3:55.

[4] Ibid, 3:56.

[5] Hallo, 3:80; see Pritchard, 322.

was written after Jeremiah's prophecy in 34:1–7. Lachish, too, eventually fell to the determined army of Nebuchadnezzar.

THEIR DISOBEDIENCE TO GOD'S COMMAND TO RELEASE SLAVES (34:8–16)

⁸The word which came to Jeremiah from the LORD after King Zedekiah had made a covenant with all the people who were in Jerusalem to proclaim release to them: ⁹that each man should set free his male servant and each man his female servant, a Hebrew man or a Hebrew woman; so that no one should keep them, a Jew his brother, in bondage. ¹⁰And all the officials and all the people obeyed who had entered into the covenant that each man should set free his male servant and each man his female servant, so that no one should keep them any longer in bondage; they obeyed, and set them free. ¹¹But afterward they turned around and took back the male servants and the female servants whom they had set free, and brought them into subjection for male servants and for female servants.

¹²Then the word of the LORD came to Jeremiah from the LORD, saying, ¹³"Thus says the LORD God of Israel, 'I made a covenant with your forefathers in the day that I brought them out of the land of Egypt, from the house of bondage, saying, ¹⁴"At the end of seven years each of you shall set free his Hebrew brother who has been sold to you and has served you six years, you shall send him out free from you; but your forefathers did not obey Me or incline their ear to Me. ¹⁵Although recently you had turned and done what is right in My sight, each man proclaiming release to his neighbor, and you had made a covenant before Me in the house which is called by My name. ¹⁶Yet you turned and profaned My name, and each man took back his male servant and each man his female servant whom you had set free according to their desire, and you brought them into subjection to be your male servants and female servants."'"

At various times, the Book of Jeremiah gives glimpses of Judah which show that they knew enough of God's will to do better than they did. This section is one such case.

JEREMIAH 34

Verses 8, 9. The Law spoke regarding Israelites who became slaves, offering release from servitude at specific intervals. Exodus 21:1–11 explains the plan for Hebrew slaves to be set free after six years (see Deut. 15:12–18). Difficult economic conditions or bad management might lead an Israelite to succumb to enslavement. Circumstances such as war, natural disasters (like famine; 14:1–9), or poor health might send a man and his family into poverty. The repeated invasions by Babylon could certainly have produced difficult times for many in Judah.

Those in Jerusalem had disregarded God's law concerning the release of the slaves in the seventh year. Responding to this situation, **King Zedekiah had made a covenant with all the people who were in Jerusalem to proclaim release to them**. If a **man** owned a slave who was **a Hebrew**, whether **male** or **female**, he was instructed to **set** that person **free;** a fellow **Jew** was not to be kept **in bondage**.

Verse 10. Those **who had entered into the covenant** with Zedekiah, including **all the officials and all the people**, initially followed through with their commitment, releasing their slaves. What motivated the king and his subjects to comply with God's law at this point in time? Was it a true desire to serve God or something else? The fact that they soon turned back to their old ways seems to indicate that their repentance was less than genuine (34:11). How, then, can the people's ulterior motives be explained? With the Babylonian army pounding on the city gates, some may have attempted to repent just enough to avoid exile. They may have thought that their obedience to this law would lead God to intervene and spare the city. Apparently, it was after their release of the slaves that Egyptian forces did come to the relief of Jerusalem. In 588 B.C., the siege of Jerusalem was temporarily lifted because of Pharaoh's army (37:5–11).

Another motivation for freeing the slaves has also been suggested. Slaves may have been set free because there was little service they could render under the current circumstances. Famine was part of the siege (19:9). Therefore, it was difficult for slave owners to feed their own families, without the added burden of slaves. The care and protection of slaves may have become more of a liability than an asset. In this case, obeying God's law to set slaves free was more a matter of convenience than of conviction or respect for God's commandment.

Verse 11. When the people concluded that the Babylonian threat was gone, the slaves who had been **set free** were enslaved again. Perhaps their services were needed once more as work in the fields and vineyards outside the city resumed.

Different forms of the verb שׁוּב (*shub*) are used here to make a play on words. They are respectively translated **turned around** and **took back**. *Shub*, which means "return," is often used in the Old Testament to signify repentance. However, in this verse, the people's return was to their evil ways.

Verses 12, 13. When the people took their slaves back into subjection, **God** called their attention to the **covenant** He had **made** with their **forefathers** when He **brought them out of the land of Egypt**. God had been faithful to this covenant, but they had been unfaithful to theirs.

Egypt's description as **the house of bondage** reminded the people that God had delivered their ancestors from slavery (11:3, 4; Ex. 13:3, 14; 20:2; Deut. 5:6; 6:12; 7:8; 8:14; 13:5, 10; Josh. 24:17; Judg. 6:8). The fair treatment of slaves in the legislation of Deuteronomy 15:15 is, in fact, grounded upon this history: "You shall remember that you were a slave in the land of Egypt, and the LORD your God redeemed you."

Verse 14. God summarized the laws of Exodus 21:2 and Deuteronomy 15:12 in these words: **"At the end of seven years each of you shall set free his Hebrew brother who has been sold to you and has served you six years, you shall send him out free from you."** The phrase "at the end of seven years" is unusual,[6] since the parallel texts read "in the seventh year" (NIV). "At the end of every seven years" does, however, appear in Deuteronomy 15:1, regarding the canceling of debts. Some suggest that, in verse 14, the phrase was intended to mean "in the seventh year," while others contend that the freeing of slaves actually took place "at the end of seven years."

The release of Hebrew slaves in the seventh year not only

---

[6]Based on the Septuagint, the RSV reads "six" instead of "seven." The CEV and NLT also remove the number "seven" from verse 14.

assured the slave of freedom, but it required that the former owner "furnish him liberally from your flock and from your threshing floor and from your wine vat," making those gifts "as the LORD your God has blessed you" (Deut. 15:14). Such a liberal send off was no doubt difficult during these hard times.

Verses 15, 16. It is tragic when people do what is right—proving that they know God's command—but then turn it into wrong. God was still watching as the people of Jerusalem **took back** the slaves they had released. The Lord rebuked them for not keeping their commitment and subjecting their neighbors to slavery a second time. He said, **"Although recently you had turned and done what is right in My sight, . . . you turned and profaned My name."**

Once more, *shub* is repeated in these verses (see comments on 34:11). The first turning of the people was in repentance to God, whereas the second turning was away from Him. "Profaned" comes from חָלַל (*chalal*), which can mean "pollute, defile," "violate," or "treat as common."[7] They defiled the Lord's name by breaking the **covenant** they had made in His presence at the temple. A. S. Peake said that "the edict of emancipation was not merely a civil proclamation, it was an oath sworn with all the solemnities of religion, and thus placed under the protection of Yahweh."[8] Since the people had made a covenant **before** God, in His **house**, and by His **name**, the reversal of their action had profaned God's name.

THE DESOLATION RESULTING FROM THEIR DEPARTURE (34:17–22)

[17]"Therefore thus says the LORD, 'You have not obeyed Me in proclaiming release each man to his brother and each man to his neighbor. Behold, I am proclaiming a release to you,' declares the LORD, 'to the sword, to the pestilence and to the

---

[7]Francis Brown, S. R. Driver, and Charles A. Briggs, *A Hebrew and English Lexicon of the Old Testament* (Oxford: Clarendon Press, 1972), 320.

[8]A. S. Peake, *Jeremiah and Lamentations*, vol. 2, The Century Bible (Edinburgh: T. C. & E. C. Jack, 1911), 138.

famine; and I will make you a terror to all the kingdoms of the earth. ¹⁸I will give the men who have transgressed My covenant, who have not fulfilled the words of the covenant which they made before Me, when they cut the calf in two and passed between its parts—¹⁹the officials of Judah and the officials of Jerusalem, the court officers and the priests and all the people of the land who passed between the parts of the calf—²⁰I will give them into the hand of their enemies and into the hand of those who seek their life. And their dead bodies will be food for the birds of the sky and the beasts of the earth. ²¹Zedekiah king of Judah and his officials I will give into the hand of their enemies and into the hand of those who seek their life, and into the hand of the army of the king of Babylon which has gone away from you. ²²Behold, I am going to command,' declares the LORD, 'and I will bring them back to this city; and they will fight against it and take it and burn it with fire; and I will make the cities of Judah a desolation without inhabitant.'"

Verse 17. God responded to the people's disobedience with satire. Since they had not provided a **release** for their slaves, God would cause **a release** for them. "Release" is from the Hebrew word דְּרוֹר (d^eror), which means "flowing," "free run," or "liberty."[9] However, their release would be **to the sword, to the pestilence and to the famine**. Timothy M. Willis referred to these three punishments as "the familiar triad of disaster"[10] (see comments on 14:12). Ultimately, God would make the people **a terror to all the kingdoms of the earth**.

Verse 18. The Lord reminded the people of the solemnity of **the covenant which they made before** [Him]. The ceremony at the temple in Jerusalem was charged with meaning to assure their commitment to the promise of releasing their slaves. A **calf** was killed and **cut** down the middle. One half was laid opposite the other with a passageway, and the people **passed between its**

---
[9]Brown, Driver, and Briggs, 204.
[10]Timothy M. Willis, *Jeremiah-Lamentations*, The College Press NIV Commentary (Joplin, Mo.: College Press Publishing Co., 2002), 281.

parts. This custom, which is also illustrated by God's covenant with Abraham in Genesis 15, lies behind the expression "cutting a covenant" (see comments on 31:31). J. A. Thompson defined it: "The meaning of the rite seems to have been that the parties to the covenant thereby called down an imprecation on themselves. The fate of the animal was a picture of the fate that would befall them if they broke the covenant."[11] After such a solemn ceremony, to reverse the pledged release by putting the freed people back into subjection was sheer hypocrisy.

Another play on words appears here. God indicted those who had "passed" between the parts of the calf, saying that they had **transgressed** [His] **covenant**. Both "passed" and "transgressed" are from the same Hebrew root, עָבַר (*'abar*). Among its many definitions, it can mean "pass through" or "pass over" ("transgress").[12] Ironically, those who had passed through the parts of the calf, which signified the covenant, had passed over the boundaries of that covenant.

Verses 19, 20. God affirmed that those who had broken the covenant would be slaughtered (like the calf) and put to shame. No one who transgressed His covenant—**officials, court officers, priests**, or common **people**—would be spared. They would die at **the hand of their enemies** and bear the added shame of **their dead bodies** being left unburied. Their corpses would serve as **food for the birds of the sky and the beasts of the earth** (7:33; 12:9; 14:15, 16; 16:4; 19:7).

Verses 21, 22. The Lord assured **Zedekiah, his officials**, and the people of Jerusalem of their coming defeat. The Babylonians' withdrawal from the siege to deal with the Egyptians would only be temporary (37:5–11). God would return the Babylonians to Jerusalem to **fight against it** and **burn it with fire**. With the destruction of the capital, the **desolation** of **the cities of Judah** would be complete (see 4:27; 6:8; 9:11; 10:22; 12:11; 18:16; 19:8; 22:5; 25:9–11; 32:43).

---

[11] J. A. Thompson, *The Book of Jeremiah*, The New International Commentary on the Old Testament (Grand Rapids, Mich.: Wm. B. Eerdmans Publishing Co., 1980), 613. Thompson cited an example from an ancient treaty (n. 22).

[12] Brown, Driver, and Briggs, 716–18.

The severity of the destruction and desolation of Judah has been explained by W. F. Albright:

> Many towns were destroyed at the beginning of the sixth century B.C. and never again occupied; others were destroyed at that time and partly reoccupied at some later date; still others were destroyed and reoccupied after a long period of abandonment, marked by a sharp change of stratum and by intervening indications of use for non-urban purposes. There is not a single known case where a town of Judah proper was continuously occupied through the exilic period.[13]

This section is another example of how God referred to one incident to demonstrate the complete corruption characterized by Judah. They failed to find one man who would do justice and seek the truth in 5:1–6. We read of their gross idolatry in 10:1–16. We see their failure to keep one command, the Sabbath, in 17:19–27. Here, we see how they refused to grant liberty to their fellow Jews as God had commanded. They rebelled in many ways, bringing judgment on themselves.

APPLICATION

The Path of Partial Obedience (Ch. 34)

Are there some commands that we have refused to obey? How does God view our obedience or our disobedience? From Judah's wavering pattern of obedience and disobedience, we should learn this lesson: The reason we do something is as important as what we do! How many people obey God when it is convenient, rather than devotedly obeying Him because He so commanded? (See Acts 24:24–26.) This chapter reveals the danger of giving God temporary obedience only as it is convenient (see Heb. 5:8, 9).

The Book of James warns us about not respecting persons—

---

[13]W. F. Albright, *The Archaeology of Palestine*, 3d ed. (Baltimore: Penguin Books, 1956), 141–42.

as many failed to do in 34:16—and about keeping part of God's commands but ignoring others (Jas. 2:1–13). It is amazing how subtle Satan has been in propagating partial obedience. One of the battlegrounds among those who claim to follow Christ centers around the command to be baptized. Some correctly emphasize that we need to believe in Jesus, but then ignore or deny the necessity of baptism, even though it was commanded by Jesus Himself (Mt. 28:18, 19; Mk. 16:15, 16; Jn. 3:5).

The purposes of baptism are also frequently overlooked. These include the following: (1) to get into Christ (Rom. 6:3, 4); (2) to get into the one body, the church (1 Cor. 12:13; Eph. 1:22, 23); (3) to receive the forgiveness of sins (Acts 2:38); and (4) to be saved (Mk. 16:16; 1 Pet. 3:21). If baptism is not necessary, then it is not important to get into Christ, be a member of His church, receive forgiveness from God, or be saved.

All Satan needs to do to succeed in this subtle arena of partial obedience is change the coordinating conjunction "and" to "or"! However, we must recognize that under Christ's covenant it is not belief *or* baptism, but belief *and* baptism (plus doing it for the right purpose—Mk. 16:16).

Have we been ensnared to submit to some of Satan's subtle schemes of partial obedience? Jeremiah 34 shows us the danger of such a course before God. We must not surrender to it!

Contrasting Two Kings (34:1–7)

After attempting to escape from the Babylonians, Zedekiah was brought face to face with Nebuchadnezzar (39:4–7). A great contrast is seen as these two kings stood "eye to eye" and "face to face" (34:3). One was a natural leader and conqueror, and—strangely enough—a pagan ruler who paid more tribute to God and His prophet than Jeremiah's own king did (39:11–14; Dan. 3:28–30; 4:34–37). Zedekiah, on the other hand, was weak and vacillating, without conviction. He was unwilling to take a stand for righteousness. Nebuchadnezzar, with power and conviction, killed the sons of Zedekiah before his eyes. He then put out Zedekiah's eyes and led him, blind, into captivity (39:5–7). How long he lived in captivity is unknown, but his weakness and failure must have haunted his memory. Could his blindness have led to faith, allowing him to see the truth? Did he honor God more as a blind captive than as a free king? It may be that his penitence led to the respect given at his funeral, or perhaps the people pitied him for his weaknesses. Regardless, 34:5 indicates that he received some type of tribute that he surely did not deserve, since he had led Judah into its final fall.

CHAPTER 35
THE RECHABITES VERSUS JUDAH

Jeremiah's survey of obedience and disobedience, which began in chapter 34, continues in chapter 35. The geographical setting is the same, but the time reverts to the days of Jehoiakim, who ruled from 609 to 598 B.C.[1]

Jehoiakim began his reign as a vassal of Egypt (2 Kings 23:34–37). After the battle of Carchemish in 605 B.C., he gave allegiance to Nebuchadnezzar until 601 B.C. (2 Kings 24:1). When Egypt rallied against Babylon, Jehoiakim rebelled against Nebuchadnezzar. As a result, Babylonian forces were joined by Arameans, Moabites, and Ammonites to overcome Jehoiakim, leading to his capture and death (2 Kings 24:2–6; 2 Chron. 36:5–8; Jer. 22:18, 19). The incidents in chapter 35 likely occurred toward the end of Jehoiakim's reign.

Chapter 35 contains one of the greatest examples ever recorded of a man's influence upon his posterity. The commands of Jonadab, one of the Rechabites, were being followed by his descendants over two centuries after he had given them (35:1–11). In stark contrast to this unswerving obedience, Judah was unfaithful to God's divine commands, even though He had repeatedly sent prophets to call them to repentance (35:12–16). The chapter concludes by stating the punishment of Judah for disobeying God and the reward of the Rechabites for obeying their ancestor (35:17–19).

---

[1]While the events of chapter 34 are set in the days of Zedekiah (34:1, 2), both chapters 35 and 36 deal with the earlier time of Jehoiakim (35:1; 36:1). Chapter 37 returns to the reign of Zedekiah (37:1).

THE RECHABITES' EXAMPLE OF FAITHFULNESS (35:1–11)

¹The word which came to Jeremiah from the Lord in the days of Jehoiakim the son of Josiah, king of Judah, saying, ²"Go to the house of the Rechabites and speak to them, and bring them into the house of the Lord, into one of the chambers, and give them wine to drink." ³Then I took Jaazaniah the son of Jeremiah, son of Habazziniah, and his brothers and all his sons and the whole house of the Rechabites, ⁴and I brought them into the house of the Lord, into the chamber of the sons of Hanan the son of Igdaliah, the man of God, which was near the chamber of the officials, which was above the chamber of Maaseiah the son of Shallum, the doorkeeper. ⁵Then I set before the men of the house of the Rechabites pitchers full of wine and cups; and I said to them, "Drink wine!" ⁶But they said, "We will not drink wine, for Jonadab the son of Rechab, our father, commanded us, saying, 'You shall not drink wine, you or your sons, forever. ⁷You shall not build a house, and you shall not sow seed and you shall not plant a vineyard or own one; but in tents you shall dwell all your days, that you may live many days in the land where you sojourn.' ⁸We have obeyed the voice of Jonadab the son of Rechab, our father, in all that he commanded us, not to drink wine all our days, we, our wives, our sons or our daughters, ⁹nor to build ourselves houses to dwell in; and we do not have vineyard or field or seed. ¹⁰We have only dwelt in tents, and have obeyed and have done according to all that Jonadab our father commanded us. ¹¹But when Nebuchadnezzar king of Babylon came up against the land, we said, 'Come and let us go to Jerusalem before the army of the Chaldeans and before the army of the Arameans.' So we have dwelt in Jerusalem."

Verses 1, 2. Jeremiah's actions in this section serve as an acted parable. Just as he was instructed to go to the potter in chapter 18, here the prophet was told to go to **the house of the Rechabites**. These people were related to the Kenites (1 Chron. 2:55). The Kenites, who were relatives of Moses, had joined the Israelites at the time of their exodus from Egypt (Num. 10:29–32; Judg. 1:16). Some of the Kenites lived among the northern tribes (Judg. 4:11, 17; 5:24), while others lived among the Amalekites in the south (1 Sam. 15:5, 6).

Due to the term "house" (בַּיִת, *bayith*), some may conclude that the Rechabites—a nomadic people—were living in more permanent dwellings made of wood and stone in Jerusalem. However, the same term appears in verse 5, where it obviously has a different meaning. John Bright contended, "'House' does not here refer to a dwelling, but to the members of a clan or, better, a community."[2]

After finding the Rechabites, Jeremiah was to (1) **speak to them**, (2) **bring them into the house of the LORD**, and (3) **give them wine to drink** (see comments on 35:4, 5).

Verse 3. Jeremiah went and spoke to **the whole house of the the Rechabites**, and they agreed to go with him. One of their leaders is mentioned by name: **Jaazaniah the son of Jeremiah, son of Habazziniah**. Apparently, "Jaazaniah," which means "Yahweh hears," was a common name in that period (40:8; 42:1; 2 Kings 25:23; Ezek. 8:11; 11:1).[3] Archaeologists have found it on a seal at Tell en-Nasbeh (likely ancient Mizpah) from about 600 B.C.[4] The name also appears in *Lachish Letter* 1, written a few years before the destruction of Jerusalem in 586 B.C.[5]

Verse 4. Jeremiah **brought** the Rechabites to the temple, and they entered **the chamber of the sons of Hanan the son of Igdaliah, the man of God**. Charles J. Ellicott wrote,

> The Temple of Solomon appears from 1 Kings 6:5 to have had, like a cathedral, apartments constructed in its precincts which were assigned, by special favour, for the residence of conspicuous priests or prophets.... In this case the chamber was occupied by the sons of Hanan. He, or

---

[2]John Bright, *Jeremiah*, The Anchor Bible (Garden City, N.Y.: Doubleday & Company, 1965), 189.

[3]An alternate spelling is "Jezaniah."

[4]D. Winton Thomas, ed., *Documents from Old Testament Times*, illust. ed. (New York: Harper & Row, Publishers, 1961), 222, plate 13.

[5]Ibid., 213.

Igdaliah (the Hebrew punctuation is decisive in favour of Hanan), is described as "a man of God"—*i.e.*, as a prophet—and therefore sympathising, we may believe, with Jeremiah's work (Deut. 33:1; 1 Sam. 2:27; 1 Kings 13:1; 20:28; 2 Kings 4:7, 9; 1 Chron. 23:14; 2 Chron. 11:2).[6]

The meeting chamber used by Jeremiah is further identified as being **near the chamber of the officials, which was above the chamber of Maaseiah the son of Shallum**. The language indicates an upper room. Apparently, two other men named Maaseiah are mentioned in the Book of Jeremiah: the father of Zedekiah the false prophet (29:21) and the father of Zephaniah the priest (21:1; 29:25; 37:3). It is possible, however, that this Maaseiah was the father of Zephaniah due to his connection with the temple. Some identify him with an "official of the city" commissioned to repair the temple during Josiah's reign, but this is doubtful (2 Chron. 34:8, 9). The man named Maaseiah in verse 4 is referred to as **the doorkeeper** (שֹׁמֵר הַסַּף, *shomer hassap*). This was an important office in Jerusalem, which three men held at the same time (52:24; see 2 Kings 12:9, 10; 22:4; 23:4; 25:18).[7]

Verse 5. After entering the chamber of the sons of Hanan, Jeremiah offered **the Rechabites pitchers full of wine and cups**. The Hebrew term גְּבִיעַ (*gabia'*), which stands behind "pitchers," "is an Egyptian loan-word (*qbḥw*) used of a large container from which the wine was poured into cups or bowls."[8] Timothy M. Willis suggested that the wine used on this occasion had been brought by worshipers to the temple as tithe-offerings, showing gratitude to the Lord for His abundant provision. Such offerings

---

[6]Charles J. Ellicott, *Ellicott's Commentary on the Whole Bible*, vol. 5 (Grand Rapids, Mich.: Zondervan Publishing House, 1959), 121. In addition to living quarters, the side rooms of the temple were also used for storing offerings for the Levites and the priests (1 Chron. 28:12, 13; 2 Chron. 31:11, 12; Neh. 13:4, 5).

[7]See Ludwig Koehler and Walter Baumgartner, *The Hebrew and Aramaic Lexicon of the Old Testament*, study ed., trans. and ed. M. E. J. Richardson (Boston: Brill, 2001), 1:763.

[8]R. K. Harrison, *Jeremiah and Lamentations: An Introduction and Commentary*, Tyndale Old Testament Commentaries (Downers Grove, Ill.: Inter-Varsity Press, 1973), 149; see Koehler and Baumgartner, 1:173.

were typically used by the priests or distributed to those who were less fortunate.⁹

Verse 6. The Rechabites rejected Jeremiah's offer, saying, **"We will not drink wine, for Jonadab the son of Rechab, our father, commanded us, saying, 'You shall not drink wine, you or your sons, forever.'"** This response centered on the command of an ancestor, Jonadab (or Jehonadab[10]), who was a worshiper of God (2 Kings 10:15–31). He had sided with Jehu in the revolution against the evil and idolatry of Ahab and Jezebel about 840 B.C. In this chapter, Jonadab is named seven times (35:6, 8, 10, 14, 16, 18, 19), identified as "father" six times (35:6, 8, 10, 14, 16, 18), and referred to by the pronouns "he" and "his" six times (35:8, 14, 16, 18)—a total of nineteen references in nineteen verses. The number of times he is mentioned reflects the nature and impact of his influence. The power of his influence is also demonstrated by the fact that his commands were still being respected by his descendants over two hundred years later.

Jeremiah's offer to the Rechabites should not be interpreted as placing a stumbling block in front of a weaker brother (see Rom. 14:13, 21). His actions were not intended to entice these men to sin. God, and likely Jeremiah, knew that the Rechabites were committed to rigid rules that included abstaining from wine. This directive was given by God through Jeremiah in order that the loyalty and obedience of the Rechabites might be vividly portrayed for the benefit of "the men of Judah and the inhabitants of Jerusalem" (35:13).[11]

The term "forever" (עוֹלָם, 'olam) indicates that, as long as Rechabites existed, this rule not to drink wine was to be enforced. Surely, some of their lineage must have had a longing for wine, but all had honorably respected the rule and refused to drink. They set a standard in self-control and dedicated obedience.

---

⁹Timothy M. Willis, *Jeremiah-Lamentations*, The College Press NIV Commentary (Joplin, Mo.: College Press Publishing Co., 2002), 287.

[10]The name is spelled two ways in the Hebrew text of this passage. The NASB has consistently used the shorter name, "Jonadab," to avoid confusion. The longer name, "Jehonadab," appears in 2 Kings 10:15–28.

[11]James E. Smith, *Jeremiah and Lamentations*, Bible Study Textbook Series (Joplin, Mo.: College Press, 1972), 590.

Verse 7. In addition to abstinence from wine, Jonadab had forbidden his descendants from participating in other aspects of a sedentary life: **"You shall not build a house, . . . but in tents you shall dwell all your days."** Following these instructions would provide his descendants with a measure of security. As nomads, they would rarely be attacked or robbed because their material wealth would be so meager that the gain would not be worth the effort for marauding bands.

Jonadab also told them, **"You shall not sow seed and you shall not plant a vineyard or own one."** Sowing seed in fields and planting vineyards were typical of the settled way of life. In contrast, nomads were shepherds who moved their flocks from place to place. Of course, the choice not to plant a vineyard and the choice to abstain from wine went hand in hand.

Why had Jonadab given these instructions to his descendants? Some suggest that he had wanted to preserve the customs of the Wilderness Wandering. It is likely that the ancestors of Jonadab, who were related to the Kenites (1 Chron. 2:55), had continued to live in tents until his day (see Judg. 4:11, 17; 5:24; 1 Sam. 15:5, 6). Perhaps he saw the stability of that lifestyle and wanted to pass it down to his offspring.

A deeper explanation may be found when the cultural background of Canaan is considered. Jonadab had been a staunch opponent of Baal (2 Kings 10:15-28), the male fertility god whom the Canaanites worshiped. Those among the Israelites who planted fields and vineyards were often tempted to call on Baal to send rain on their crops. The worship of Baal involved both cult prostitution and excessive drinking; it was an invitation to immorality. The austere pattern given by Jonadab was a rebuke to any Israelite who might yield to the tantalizing temptation to join in these sensual practices. Like Nazarites, the Rechabites set a standard of commitment to God concerning any abuses related to wine or pagan orgies (see Num. 6:1-4, 13-21).[12]

Jonadab's ultimate objective had been that his descendants would **live many days in the land where** [they] **sojourn**[ed]. His regulations had not been intended to remove joy from them, but

---

[12]Ibid., 591.

to provide long-term benefits of living many days in the land. The language here is strikingly similar to the fifth commandment: "Honor your father and your mother, *that your days may be prolonged in the land* which the LORD your God gives you" (Ex. 20:12; emphasis added). Obedience to God and one's parents would bring longevity and blessings in the Promised Land (Deut. 4:40; 5:16, 33; 11:8, 9, 18–21).

Verses 8–10. The Rechabites said they had fully **obeyed the voice** of their ancestor **Jonadab** by abstaining from drinking **wine** and building **houses**. They had not planted a **vineyard** or sown **seed** in a field. They had continued to be nomads, **dwell[ing] in tents. All** of Jonadab's commands had been kept by all the members of every family (**we, our wives, our sons or our daughters**) for their entire lifetimes (**all our days**).

Verse 11. The Rechabites clarified their presence in Jerusalem: "**When Nebuchadnezzar king of Babylon came up against the land, we said, 'Come and let us go to Jerusalem before the army of the Chaldeans and before the army of the Arameans.' So we have dwelt in Jerusalem.**" This nomadic group had recently come into Jerusalem, fleeing for safety from the raiding Babylonians ("Chaldeans") and Syrians ("Arameans") (see 2 Kings 24:1–7). R. K. Harrison wrote, "While the Babylonians were regrouping after the battle with Egypt in 601 BC, they made sporadic raids on selected sites in Judah between 599 and 597 BC, to which verse 11 refers."[13]

The fact that the Rechabites were living in Jerusalem does not necessarily mean they were living in houses. It is possible that they had pitched their tents within the city walls. Nevertheless, living in the city was certainly not their preference.

JUDAH'S REFUSAL TO LISTEN
(35:12–16)

[12]**Then the word of the LORD came to Jeremiah, saying,** [13]**"Thus says the LORD of hosts, the God of Israel, 'Go and say to the men of Judah and the inhabitants of Jerusalem, "Will**

---

[13]Harrison, 147–48.

you not receive instruction by listening to My words?" declares the LORD. ¹⁴"The words of Jonadab the son of Rechab, which he commanded his sons not to drink wine, are observed. So they do not drink wine to this day, for they have obeyed their father's command. But I have spoken to you again and again; yet you have not listened to Me. ¹⁵Also I have sent to you all My servants the prophets, sending them again and again, saying: 'Turn now every man from his evil way and amend your deeds, and do not go after other gods to worship them. Then you will dwell in the land which I have given to you and to your forefathers; but you have not inclined your ear or listened to Me. ¹⁶Indeed, the sons of Jonadab the son of Rechab have observed the command of their father which he commanded them, but this people has not listened to Me.'"'"

Verses 12, 13. With the strange but significant standard of Rechabite obedience standing before them, **Judah** and **Jerusalem** heard God's appeal: **"Will you not receive instruction by listening to My words?"** "Instruction" comes from מוּסָר (*musar*), meaning "discipline," "chastisement," "training," "exhortation," or "warning."¹⁴

Verse 14. God must have hungered for Judah to respond to His commands in obedience as the Rechabites had done to **Jonadab**. The Hebrew word for **obeyed** is שָׁמַע (*shama‘*), which includes hearing, understanding, accepting, and obeying.¹⁵ Surely God desired and demanded obedience (3:13, 25; 7:23, 28; 9:13; 11:3, 4, 7, 8; 12:17; 17:23; 22:21; 26:13; 32:23; 34:10, 11).

This verse also says that they **observed** Jonadab's commands. "Observed" comes from קוּם (*qum*), which can mean "arise," "stand up," "raise up," "establish," or "endure."¹⁶ More than just looking at what Jonadab required, the Rechabites established his rules as a lifestyle.

At this point, a contrast is made between the obedient Recha-

---

¹⁴Koehler and Baumgartner, 1:557.
¹⁵Ibid., 2:1570–72.
¹⁶Ibid., 2:1086–88; Francis Brown, S. R. Driver, and Charles A. Briggs, *A Hebrew and English Lexicon of the Old Testament* (Oxford: Clarendon Press, 1972), 877–79.

bites and disobedient Judah. Concerning Judah, God lamented, **"I have spoken to you again and again; yet you have not listened to Me."** The phrase "again and again" can more literally be translated "rising up early" (see comments on 7:13).

Verse 15. The Lord had frequently sent His **servants the prophets** to urge the people to obey (7:25; 25:4; 26:5; 29:19; 44:4). The sentiments of His message are repeated frequently: (1) **Turn now every man from his evil way** (18:11; 25:5; 26:3; 36:3). (2) **Amend your deeds** (7:3; 18:11; 26:13). (3) **Do not go after other gods to worship them** (7:6, 9; 11:10; 13:10; 16:11; 25:6). (4) **Then you will dwell in the land which I have given to you and to your forefathers** (16:15; 24:10; 25:5). (5) **You have not inclined your ear or listened to Me** (7:24, 26; 11:8; 17:23; 25:4; 34:14).

Verse 16. Ironically, the Rechabites, **the sons of Jonadab the son of Rechab**, showed more respect for the human traditions of **their father** Jonadab than Judah had to the divine commands of Almighty God. The Lord had sent His prophets to generation after generation, but Judah, referred to as **this people**, had continually **not listened** to His warnings.

The people of Judah and Jerusalem had not obeyed their heavenly Father, who had blessed them so richly in the land He had given to them. They were strikingly different from the small clan of the Rechabites, who were so faithful to their forefather. Even though the Rechabites possessed little of this earth's treasure, they had a few binding rules and the basic wisdom to follow them.

THE LORD'S REWARD AND PUNISHMENT (35:17–19)

[17]**"Therefore thus says the LORD, the God of hosts, the God of Israel, 'Behold, I am bringing on Judah and on all the inhabitants of Jerusalem all the disaster that I have pronounced against them; because I spoke to them but they did not listen, and I have called them but they did not answer.'"**

[18]**Then Jeremiah said to the house of the Rechabites, "Thus says the LORD of hosts, the God of Israel, 'Because you have obeyed the command of Jonadab your father, kept all his com-**

mands and done according to all that he commanded you; ¹⁹therefore thus says the LORD of hosts, the God of Israel, "Jonadab the son of Rechab shall not lack a man to stand before Me always."'"

Verse 17. As the prophetic message was given to the people, **God** required a positive response in order for a reward to follow. However, they paid no attention and offered no action (7:25–28). God's covenant with Judah and His special blessings to them should have been a dual cause to respect and obey Him, but they did not. As a result, **Judah** and **Jerusalem** would receive their just punishment. God was **bringing on** them **all the disaster** He had **pronounced against them** (6:19; 11:11–15; 18:11, 17; 19:3–6, 15; 25:29; 26:3; 32:23, 42; 36:31).

Verses 18, 19. God was equally faithful to reward obedience. The submission of **the Rechabites** to their ancestor **Jonadab** had not gone unrecognized. God promised these people, **"Jonadab the son of Rechab shall not lack a man to stand before Me always."** Similar language was used in regard to the kings descending from David and the Levitical priests descending from Aaron (see comments on 33:17, 18). "To stand before" God meant more than the continuity of a name. It involved the sort of faithfulness to convictions and obedience that the descendants of Jonadab had demonstrated (see 1 Kings 17:1; 18:15; 2 Kings 3:14).

The fulfillment of God's promise can be assumed, although little is said about the Rechabites after the destruction of Jerusalem in 586 B.C. One passage from the post-exilic period may mention a Rechabite who dishonored the vow. Nehemiah 3:14 says that "Malchijah the son of Rechab, the official of the district of Beth-haccerem repaired the Refuse Gate" in Jerusalem. This man had authority over a district south of Jerusalem whose name meant "House of the Vineyard." However, it is uncertain if he descended from the same Rechab discussed in Jeremiah 35. According to Jewish tradition, in later times the Rechabites were among select people in Israel who brought wood offerings to the temple.[17]

---

[17]Mishnah *Taanith* 4.5.

APPLICATION

Setting an Example (Ch. 35)

While chapter 35 is heartening proof that God recognizes and rewards genuine obedience, the primary theme of the chapter centers on the example of the Rechabites. An example is a powerful influence. It emanates from every person, as surely as air breathed in must be exhaled. Whatever else we may be, rest assured that we are an example and an influence. Paul gave an inspired truth when he wrote, "We do not live to ourselves, and we do not die to ourselves" (Rom. 14:7; NRSV). Each of us is an example in some way to someone.

The great impact of an example is emphasized in many Scriptures. Let us consider a few passages from the Old Testament:

> "You shall not follow the masses in doing evil, nor shall you testify in a dispute so as to turn aside after a multitude in order to pervert justice" (Ex. 23:2).

> ... they were inclined to follow Abimelech, for they said, "He is our relative" (Judg. 9:3).

> "Behold, everyone who quotes proverbs will quote this proverb concerning you, saying, 'Like mother, like daughter'" (Ezek. 16:44).

It is obvious that everybody follows someone. In the New Testament, Paul wrote the these words:

> [We] offer ourselves as a model for you, so that you would follow our example (2 Thess. 3:9).

> Let no one look down on your youthfulness, but rather in speech, conduct, love, faith and purity, show yourself an example of those who believe (1 Tim. 4:12).

> In all this I have given you an example that by such work we must support the weak, remembering the words of the Lord Jesus (Acts 20:35; NRSV).

Concerning Jesus, Peter wrote,

> ... Christ also suffered for you, leaving you an example for you to follow in His steps, who committed no sin, nor was any deceit found in His mouth (1 Pet. 2:21, 22).

What kind of example are we demonstrating at home, at school, at work, in the community, and in the church? May God's use of the Rechabites in Jeremiah 35 inspire us to be obedient to God and worthy examples to those around us. A religious revival and the restoration of a nation begins by obedience to God, who waits to redeem and reward (1 Cor. 15:58; Eph. 1:3–7; Col. 1:12–14).

Models of Obedience (Ch. 35)
The Rechabites, who serve as an example of obedience, demonstrated a devout and dedicated spirit. Their lifestyle went beyond the legal response of law, for they had a loving and respectful appreciation for the lawgiver. More than duty, their lifestyle was one of gratitude. This spirit corresponds meaningfully to the disposition of our true standard-setter, Jesus Christ. Jesus repeatedly affirmed His fidelity to please the Father, stating, "I always do the things that are pleasing to Him" (Jn. 8:29). Jesus also said, "Whatever the Father does, these things the Son also does in like manner" (Jn. 5:19; see 4:34). As surely as God is the demonstration of perfect fatherhood, so Jesus Christ is the embodiment of perfect sonship. That sonship was tested under the severest of pressure, but Jesus never failed to demonstrate His loyalty to the Father. What a dramatic demonstration of trust and fidelity springs from the cross! Just after Jesus cried out those words in agony, "My God, My God, why have You forsaken Me?" (Mk. 15:34), He added in faith, "Father, into Your hands I commit My spirit" (Lk. 23:46). In Jesus we surely see our model of obedience, and in His exaltation we see God's faithful, rewarding ways (Acts 2:32, 33; Phil. 2:5–11; Heb. 5:7–10).

Receiving Instruction (35:12, 13)
God knows us and instructs us according to our needs. His

instruction may include doctrine for the immature, encouragement for the faint-hearted, admonition to ones going astray, an example to help another, or discipline for the disobedient. His Word fits each person's needs (2 Tim. 3:16, 17), and we should anxiously receive His directions.

Obeying Our Father (35:16)

In 35:16, God made a parallel between His relationship to Judah and Jonadab as a father to the Rechabites. The fact that Almighty God, the Creator of the universe, is also our Father should be viewed with great appreciation. The fatherhood of God, rather than relaxing our obedient response to Him, should deepen our devotion and determination to be obedient to His requests. A king hardly knows his subjects. A government official seldom leaves his administrative surroundings to be with the people. In contrast, a father dwells with, knows, and daily deals with his own. The closeness should be comforting, but it can also be challenging. A father has rights and relationships, plans and purposes geared to growth and guidance more specific than any other tie in a child's life. For years the child is wholly dependent on parents, who sustain, protect, provide, and work endless hours for the welfare of their offspring. The unique characteristics of God toward us mentioned by Paul best fits God's role as Father: "In Him we live and move and exist" (Acts 17:28), and "He is not far from each one of us" (Acts 17:27).

The constancy of His care, the longsuffering nature of His love, and the fidelity of His fatherhood should capture our interest in His every directive (1 Jn. 4:19; see Jn. 14:15). Such parental vigilance (2 Chron. 16:9), love (Rom. 5:6–10), and the supreme sacrifice (Jn. 3:16; 2 Cor. 5:21) should stimulate the deepest gratitude in our souls. Repayment for all His good gifts (Jas. 1:17, 18) would be impossible and is not required, but the least we can do is offer dedicated obedience. As the Ruler of the universe, He could demand it, but as a loving Father "He causes His sun to rise on the evil and the good, and sends rain on the righteous and unrighteous" (Mt. 5:45), longing to hear an obedient response that so seldom has come.

CHAPTER 36
THE POWER AND IMPACT OF GOD'S MESSAGE

"The fourth year of Jehoiakim" (605 B.C.) is frequently mentioned as a prominent year in Judah's history and Jeremiah's ministry (25:1; 36:1; 45:1; 46:1, 2). In that year, the battle of Carchemish determined which power would rule the ancient Near East for the next half-century. The Babylonians defeated the remaining armies of Assyria, who had joined forces with the Egyptians (46:2). This victory solidified Babylonian control over the Fertile Crescent. Later that year, Nebuchadnezzar also conquered Jerusalem for the first time, taking captives to Babylon (2 Kings 24:1; Dan. 1:1, 2).

Chapter 36 recounts God's plan for Jeremiah to record his prophecies from the days of Josiah to this year in the reign of Jehoiakim. The prophet carried out God's will by dictating to Baruch, a scribe (36:1-7). The effect of this well-prepared message is the central theme of the chapter. While some officials reacted to it in humility and fear (36:8-20), Jehoiakim and his servants did not. The king brazenly mutilated and burned God's divine word (36:21-26). As a result, God pronounced judgment on the wicked king and commissioned Jeremiah to make another copy of His message (36:27-32).

THE MESSAGE TRANSCRIBED (36:1-7)

¹**In the fourth year of Jehoiakim the son of Josiah, king of Judah, this word came to Jeremiah from the LORD, saying,** ²**"Take a scroll and write on it all the words which I have spoken to you concerning Israel and concerning Judah, and con-**

cerning all the nations, from the day I first spoke to you, from the days of Josiah, even to this day. ³Perhaps the house of Judah will hear all the calamity which I plan to bring on them, in order that every man will turn from his evil way; then I will forgive their iniquity and their sin."

⁴Then Jeremiah called Baruch the son of Neriah, and Baruch wrote on a scroll at the dictation of Jeremiah all the words of the LORD which He had spoken to him. ⁵Jeremiah commanded Baruch, saying, "I am restricted; I cannot go into the house of the LORD. ⁶So you go and read from the scroll which you have written at my dictation the words of the LORD to the people in the LORD's house on a fast day. And also you shall read them to all the people of Judah who come from their cities. ⁷Perhaps their supplication will come before the LORD, and everyone will turn from his evil way, for great is the anger and the wrath that the LORD has pronounced against this people."

Verse 1. The **word** of God **came to Jeremiah** during **the fourth year of Jehoiakim the son of Josiah, king of Judah**. As previously noted, this was 605 B.C., an important year in the history of the ancient Near East. Not only did Nebuchadnezzar defeat the Assyrians and Egyptians, he also became the king of Babylonia and the ruler over the Babylonian Empire (see comments on 25:1).

Verse 2. The Lord instructed Jeremiah to **take a scroll** and record the prophetic messages He had given to him (see comments on 30:1, 2). The Hebrew phrase translated "scroll," מְגִלַּת־סֵפֶר (*mᵉgillath seper*), is more literally "a scroll of a book" (NKJV). This Hebrew phrase also appears in Psalm 40:7[8] and Ezekiel 2:9. Some think that it is a technical term for an official scroll that was of fine quality. Such a scroll could have been made from either parchment or papyrus (see comments on 36:23).

On the scroll, Jeremiah was instructed to record prophecies **concerning Israel and concerning Judah, and concerning all the nations**. While the bulk of prophecies in the Book of Jeremiah deal with Judah, some may have addressed Israel—even though they were taken into captivity in 722 B.C. Jeremiah also spoke God's word to the nations (see 1:10).

The prophecies that Jeremiah would record dated from the time God **first spoke** to the prophet in **the days of Josiah** until **this day**. Jeremiah's ministry began in "the thirteenth year of Josiah" (627 B.C.), and it was now "the fourth year of Jehoiakim" (605 B.C.)—a period of twenty-three years (25:1-3; see 1:1, 2). This was about half of Jeremiah's ministry.

The actual contents of the scroll after the prophecies were recorded is uncertain. R. K. Harrison believed that it was "fairly short" compared to the Book of Jeremiah, since it was read three times on the same day (36:10, 15, 21).[1] The phrase **all the words**, however, indicates that it was not merely a synopsis. Anthony L. Ash wrote, "It is generally assumed that the contents were part, perhaps most, of the contents of Jeremiah 1—25. Some think, because of the reference to *all the nations*, that chapters 46—51 may also have been included, or at least part of them."[2]

Verse 3. The purpose of recording the prophecies on a scroll was so they could be read to the people, and, as a result, the people would repent. God said, **"Perhaps the house of Judah will hear all the calamity which I plan to bring on them, in order that every man will turn from his evil way."** At this point in time, repentance was still a possibility. God was willing to **forgive their iniquity**.

Verse 4. To help him fulfill God's command, **Jeremiah called Baruch the son of Neriah**. Baruch played a prominent role by recording the message dictated by the prophet and later reading the message to certain groups of people. He was a trusted and helpful coworker (32:12, 13, 16; 43:1-3, 6, 7; 45:1-3). While Jeremiah could do his own writing (32:10; 51:60), Baruch was a professional scribe. According to Josephus, he was "of a very eminent family, and exceeding[ly] skilful in the language of his country."[3] Later in the book, Baruch's brother, Seraiah, was in the royal service with King Zedekiah (51:59).

---

[1] R. K. Harrison, *Jeremiah and Lamentations: An Introduction and Commentary*, Tyndale Old Testament Commentaries (Downers Grove, Ill.: Inter-Varsity Press, 1973), 150.

[2] Anthony L. Ash, *Jeremiah and Lamentations*, The Living Word Commentary (Abilene, Tex.: ACU Press, 1987), 252.

[3] Josephus *Antiquities* 10.9.1.

Interestingly, the name "Baruch son of Neriah" is attested on two bullae (seal impressions) from the seventh century B.C. These are pieces of clay that were used to seal documents, having been stamped by their owner (see 32:10; 1 Kings 21:8; Esther 8:8; Job 38:14; Is. 29:11). The seal impressions both read: "(Belonging) to Berechyahu son of Neriyahu the scribe."[4] Most likely, these belonged to Baruch, the scribe summoned by Jeremiah.

Verse 5. **Jeremiah** was unable to go to the temple, so he chose to send **Baruch** in his place. The prophet stated, **"I am restricted; I cannot go into the house of the LORD."** The Hebrew word for "restricted," עָצַר (*'atsar*), is sometimes used for Jeremiah's confinement (33:1; 39:15). However, it is obvious that he was not under arrest at this time (36:19, 26). Instead, he was prevented from entering the temple courts and speaking to the people. If he attempted to do so, he would be thrown out or arrested.

Verse 6. Jeremiah instructed Baruch to **go and read from the scroll** that he had **written** while receiving the prophet's **dictation**. **The words of the LORD** (the right message) were to be given **to all the people of Judah** (the right audience) at **the LORD's house** (the right place) **on a fast day** (the right time).

The only fast day prescribed in the Law was Yom Kippur, the Day of Atonement (Lev. 16:29–31; 23:27, 29, 32). Verse 9 indicates a different time—a special, proclaimed fast that related to all the people of Jerusalem and Judah. This type of fast would imply a time of national distress (see 1 Kings 21:8–10; 2 Chron. 20:3, 4; Joel 1:14, 15; Zech. 7:5–7). It was a time when the courts of the temple would be thronged with people, who hopefully would be in a frame of mind to listen to warnings and exhortations related to national repentance and reform.[5]

Verse 7. The ultimate goal was that the people would repent, offering to God **their supplication** (the right disposition). By turning away from **evil**, they could escape from God's **anger** and

---

[4]William W. Hallo, ed., *The Context of Scripture* (Boston: Brill, 2003), 2:197. For a photograph of the seal impression, see Philip J. King, *Jeremiah: An Archaeological Companion* (Louisville, Ky.: Westminster/John Knox Press, 1993), 96.

[5]Charles J. Ellicott, *Ellicott's Commentary on the Whole Bible*, vol. 5 (Grand Rapids, Mich.: Zondervan Publishing House, 1959), 124.

wrath. "Anger" comes from the Hebrew word אַף (*'ap*), which can mean "nose," "face," or "anger." The nose is symbolic of anger because "in anger there is heavy breathing through the nose," causing one's nostrils to flare. The statement "his nose became hot" is used many times in the Old Testament for God. It is an anthropomorphism that means "his anger was kindled."[6] The word "wrath" is from חֵמָה (*chemah*), meaning "heat," "poison," "venom," "rage," or "wrath."[7] These two heated terms for God's indignation sharply contrast His loving spirit, which would, upon their repentance, forgive their iniquity (36:3). The difference between these two features of God's disposition made Judah's response a most significant decision.

THE MESSAGE'S IMPACT ON VARIOUS PEOPLE (36:8–20)

The First Presentation By Baruch in the Lord's House (36:8–10)

⁸Baruch the son of Neriah did according to all that Jeremiah the prophet commanded him, reading from the book the words of the Lord in the Lord's house.

⁹Now in the fifth year of Jehoiakim the son of Josiah, king of Judah, in the ninth month, all the people in Jerusalem and all the people who came from the cities of Judah to Jerusalem proclaimed a fast before the Lord. ¹⁰Then Baruch read from the book the words of Jeremiah in the house of the Lord in the chamber of Gemariah the son of Shaphan the scribe, in the upper court, at the entry of the New Gate of the Lord's house, to all the people.

Verse 8. Baruch carried out the commands of **Jeremiah the prophet**. He went to the temple and read from the scroll containing **the words of the Lord**. His faithfulness shows that Jeremiah

---

[6]Ludwig Koehler and Walter Baumgartner, *The Hebrew and Aramaic Lexicon of the Old Testament*, study ed., trans. and ed. M. E. J. Richardson (Boston: Brill, 2001), 1:76.
[7]Ibid., 1:326.

was not the only righteous person in Jerusalem at that time.

Verse 9. Baruch's reading at the temple came at least nine months after the original assignment was made. God's directions given to Jeremiah came "in the fourth year of Jehoiakim" (36:1), whereas Baruch's reading took place **in the fifth year of Jehoiakim . . . , in the ninth month**. Some of the time that elapsed was spent recording the message on the scroll. After it was completed, Baruch had to wait for an opportunity when **the people** were gathered in **Jerusalem** for **a fast before the** LORD (36:6).

"The fifth year . . . the ninth month" was December 604 B.C. The Babylonians had just leveled the city of Ashkelon on the Philistine coast. It may be that the people of Judah feared that they would be next on the list. Perhaps such fear led to this proclaimed fast.[8]

Verse 10. Baruch read the scroll containing **the words of Jeremiah** before **all** Jerusalem and Judah **in the house of the** LORD, speaking from **the chamber of Gemariah**. Apparently, this room overlooked the courtyards, and it was a place where Baruch could easily be seen and heard.

Gemariah was obviously favorable to the prophet Jeremiah; he was a man of good heritage and devout patriotism. His father, **Shaphan the scribe**, was active in repairing the temple during the reign of the good king Josiah. Shaphan was a close coworker to Hilkiah, the high priest, and a key figure in promoting the newly-discovered book of the law (2 Kings 22:3–13). As a scribe, he would have been engaged in study and proclamation of the edicts for the restoration of true worship under Josiah. Gemariah's brother, Ahikam, was instrumental in sparing Jeremiah's life during one of his severe trials (26:24). Another brother, Elasah, delivered Jeremiah's letter to exiles in Babylon (29:3). In this context, both Gemariah and his son Micaiah were key personalities who gave consideration to the special message Jeremiah had dictated to Baruch (36:11, 12). As in the case of Baruch, the name "Gemaryahu son of Shaphan" is preserved on a clay seal impression.[9]

---

[8]Ash, 254.
[9]King, 94.

The Second and Third Presentations
Through Micaiah and Baruch (36:11-15)

> [11]Now when Micaiah the son of Gemariah, the son of Shaphan, had heard all the words of the Lord from the book, [12]he went down to the king's house, into the scribe's chamber. And behold, all the officials were sitting there—Elishama the scribe, and Delaiah the son of Shemaiah, and Elnathan the son of Achbor, and Gemariah the son of Shaphan, and Zedekiah the son of Hananiah, and all the other officials. [13]Micaiah declared to them all the words that he had heard when Baruch read from the book to the people. [14]Then all the officials sent Jehudi the son of Nethaniah, the son of Shelemiah, the son of Cushi, to Baruch, saying, "Take in your hand the scroll from which you have read to the people and come." So Baruch the son of Neriah took the scroll in his hand and went to them. [15]They said to him, "Sit down, please, and read it to us." So Baruch read it to them.

A stirring message occasionally results in a request for it to be presented to another audience. Baruch's message from Jeremiah (and from God) had such an impact on its hearers. Altogether, the message was presented five times: It was read aloud three times and summarized twice.

Verses 11–13. The effect the message had on **Micaiah** is especially noted. After listening to Baruch at the temple, **he went to the king's house, into the scribe's chamber**, and repeated what he **had heard** to **the officials**—including his father **Gemariah**. This was the second presentation of the message.

Not only was **Micaiah** moved to share, but he **declared to them all the words that he had heard when Baruch read from the book to the people**. If the writing on the scroll was extensive (see comments on 36:2), the reference to "all the words" may be hyperbole. The masterful message touched Micaiah's heart and made an indelible impression on his mind. Apparently, he gave an extensive summary of Baruch's reading.

Of the officials mentioned in verse 12, **Elishama the scribe** was likely a member of the royal family and the grandfather of

Ishmael, who later assassinated Gedaliah, the governor (41:1, 2; 2 Kings 25:25). **Elnathan the son of Achbor** was the leader of the group that brought the prophet Uriah back from Egypt to be sentenced to death (26:20–23). It is interesting that he took a stand for the prophet Jeremiah (36:25). Nothing else is known about **Delaiah the son of Shemaiah** and **Zedekiah the son of Hananiah** beyond what is written in chapter 36.

Verses 14, 15. The influence of the message continued as **the officials sent** a representative **to Baruch**, urging that **the scroll** be brought and **read** to them. They trusted Micaiah enough to seek out Baruch, but they wanted to hear the message from its original source. As **Baruch read** the message to them, we are informed of its third presentation.

The representative sent to find Baruch was named **Jehudi**, which means "a Jew." Harrison commented, "His name, along with that of his great-grandfather Cushi (i.e., 'Ethiopian'), is noteworthy, indicating foreign origin of the family and the possible naturalization of Jehudi."[10]

The Third Presentation, Leading to the Fourth by the Officials (36:16–20)

[16]**When they had heard all the words, they turned in fear one to another and said to Baruch, "We will surely report all these words to the king."** [17]**And they asked Baruch, saying, "Tell us, please, how did you write all these words? Was it at his dictation?"** [18]**Then Baruch said to them, "He dictated all these words to me, and I wrote them with ink on the book."** [19]**Then the officials said to Baruch, "Go, hide yourself, you and Jeremiah, and do not let anyone know where you are."**

[20]**So they went to the king in the court, but they had deposited the scroll in the chamber of Elishama the scribe, and they reported all the words to the king.**

---

[10]R. K. Harrison, "Jehudi," in *The International Standard Bible Encyclopedia*, rev. ed., ed. Geoffrey W. Bromiley (Grand Rapids, Mich.: Wm. B. Eerdmans Publishing Co., 1982), 2:983.

Verse 16. After Baruch read the scroll to the officials, **they turned in fear one to another.** "Turned in fear" comes from the Hebrew verb פָּחַד (*pachad*), meaning "be startled," "tremble," "approach in trepidation," or "be in terror."[11] J. A. Thompson noted that "the total impact of these oracles which had been delivered over a number of years was terrifying."[12] The officials' internal reaction resulted in physical action. They asserted, **"We will surely report all these words to the king."**

Verses 17, 18. Before approaching Jehoiakim, the officials wanted to verify the source of the information they had just heard. **They asked Baruch, saying, "Tell us, please, how did you write all these words? Was it at his dictation?"** While not specifically naming Jeremiah, this was certainly who they had in mind. **Baruch** acknowledged that Jeremiah was the one who had **dictated** the **words** to him. The scribe had written these on the scroll **with ink.** This is the only occurrence of the word "ink" (דְּיוֹ, *d*e*yo*) in the Old Testament (see 2 Cor. 3:3; 2 Jn. 12; 3 Jn. 13).

Verse 19. When **the officials** confirmed the details concerning how **Baruch** received this message, they urged him to **hide,** along with **Jeremiah.** (As verse 5 demonstrates, the prophet was restricted from the house of the Lord, but he was not confined at this time.) The officials did not think that Jehoiakim would receive the message well, and they wanted to protect these two righteous men. Their fears were not unfounded. The king had gone to great lengths to find the prophet Uriah in Egypt in order to execute him (26:20–23). Since the king had the power and means of gathering information, they also advised Baruch, **"Do not let anyone know where you are."**

Verse 20. The officials then **deposited the scroll in the chamber of Elishama the scribe** (36:12), probably wanting to keep it out of the king's hands. After the scroll was secure, **they** entered the palace **court** and **reported all the words to the king.** That

---

[11] Koehler and Baumgartner, 2:922.

[12] J. A. Thompson, *The Book of Jeremiah*, The New International Commentary on the Old Testament (Grand Rapids, Mich.: Wm. B. Eerdmans Publishing Co., 1980), 626.

summary was the message's fourth presentation. Once again, the message had made such an impression on the listeners that they were able to recall and repeat it (see comments on 36:11–13).

THE MESSAGE'S IMPACT ON THE KING (36:21–26)

The Fifth Presentation to Jehoiakim And the Burning of the Scroll (36:21–25)

²¹Then the king sent Jehudi to get the scroll, and he took it out of the chamber of Elishama the scribe. And Jehudi read it to the king as well as to all the officials who stood beside the king. ²²Now the king was sitting in the winter house in the ninth month, with a fire burning in the brazier before him. ²³When Jehudi had read three or four columns, the king cut it with a scribe's knife and threw it into the fire that was in the brazier, until all the scroll was consumed in the fire that was in the brazier. ²⁴Yet the king and all his servants who heard all these words were not afraid, nor did they rend their garments. ²⁵Even though Elnathan and Delaiah and Gemariah pleaded with the king not to burn the scroll, he would not listen to them.

Verse 21. Jehoiakim was not a good king, but he was a leader. He wanted to hear Jeremiah's message from the **scroll** itself, so he instructed **Jehudi** (36:14) to retrieve it from **the chamber of Elishama** (36:20). After securing the scroll, **Jehudi read it to the king as well as to all the officials who stood beside the king**. As he read, Jehoiakim realized that the report to him about those words was accurate. Perhaps the personal condemnation of the king found in 22:13–19 incited him to the action that followed. This fifth presentation now excited even more emotion than the previous four had done.

Verse 22. Since it was **the ninth month** (36:9), or December, **the king was sitting in the winter house**. The phrase "winter house" could refer to a separate residence used by the king during the cold season (see Amos 3:15). However, it more likely refers to a lower level of a two-story building that was heated in the winter (see Judg. 3:20). In that place, the king had **a fire burning in the brazier before him**. A "brazier" (אָח, *'ach*) was a pot or pan made of metal or clay that held burning coals.[13] Perhaps the brazier was centrally located in the room to allow for the heat to be more evenly distributed.

Verse 23. When Jehudi had read three or four columns, the king cut it with a scribe's knife and threw it into the fire that was in the brazier. The text of ancient Hebrew scrolls was written in parallel columns, which made it necessary to unroll them as they were read.[14] "Columns" comes from דֶּלֶת (*deleth*), which is literally translated "door." James E. Smith suggested that the uniform width and height of these columns bore a resemblance to doors, which explains the figurative use of the word.[15] A "scribe's knife" was used for cutting papyrus rolls and sharpening reed pens.[16] The fact that the king burned the scroll indoors likely indicates that it was made from papyrus, not parchment (animal skin). William Sanford LaSor pointed out that "burning that much leather in a closed room in winter would have made the place practically uninhabitable for hours or even days."[17]

The king kept cutting and burning sections of **the scroll** until all of it **was consumed in the fire**. He surely did this out of disdain and disrespect for the message. In addition, it is possible that he burned the scroll in an attempt to annul or reverse the power of Jeremiah's message. Thompson thought this might be the case. He wrote,

> It may even be that Jehoiakim believed that he would destroy the power of the prophetic word by destroying the recorded words in a kind of execrating act. He may

---

[13]Koehler and Baumgartner, 1:29.

[14]Harrison, *Jeremiah and Lamentations*, 150.

[15]James E. Smith, *Jeremiah and Lamentations*, Bible Study Textbook Series (Joplin, Mo.: College Press, 1972), 605, n. 1.

[16]Harrison, *Jeremiah and Lamentations*, 152; Ash, 256.

[17]William Sanford LaSor, "Scroll," in *The International Standard Bible Encyclopedia*, rev. ed., ed. Geoffrey W. Bromiley (Grand Rapids, Mich.: Wm. B. Eerdmans Publishing Co., 1988), 4:364.

have entertained some hope that his nominal Egyptian overlord might yet come to the aid of his vassal despite Jeremiah's prophecies about the foe from the north.[18]

Verse 24. Unlike the officials in verse 16, **the king and all his servants who heard all these words were not afraid**. These men did not **rend their garments** in repentance, as the good king Josiah had done after he heard the reading of the lost book of the law (2 Kings 22:11). Instead of tearing his clothes, Jehoiakim cut up the scroll!

Verse 25. Though wiser leaders—**Elnathan**, **Delaiah**, and **Gemariah** (36:12)—respected God's words and **pleaded with the king not to burn the scroll**, this audacious king defied God's warning. He refused to **listen** to their advice.

The Attempt to Arrest Jeremiah (36:26)

[26]And the king commanded Jerahmeel the king's son, Seraiah the son of Azriel, and Shelemiah the son of Abdeel to seize Baruch the scribe and Jeremiah the prophet, but the LORD hid them.

Verse 26. After destroying the message, **the king** went after the messengers, **Jeremiah the prophet** and **Baruch the scribe**. As he had earlier done with the prophet Uriah (26:20–23), the king sent his men **to seize** them so that he could kill them. Timothy M. Willis described the irony of this situation: "Jeremiah is viewed as a threat to the well-being of the city, even though he is the one presenting the only way the city's well-being can actually be preserved."[19] The king's plans to destroy Jeremiah and Baruch were foiled. Through God's providence, His protection was extended to His faithful servants (1:17–19; 45:1–5).

Three men were commissioned to arrest Jeremiah and Baruch. The first is identified as **Jerahmeel the king's son**. Since King

---

[18]Thompson, 627.
[19]Timothy M. Willis, *Jeremiah-Lamentations*, The College Press NIV Commentary (Joplin, Mo.: College Press Publishing Co., 2002), 294.

Jehoiakim was only about thirty years old at this time (36:9; 2 Kings 23:36), it is doubtful that Jerahmeel was his literal son. He may have descended from royal blood and/or been a member of the king's court (see 38:6; 1 Kings 22:26). A seal impression bearing his name has been discovered, which reads, "(Belonging) to Jerahmeel the king's son."[20] Beyond their mission in verse 26, nothing else is known about the other two men, **Seraiah the son of Azriel** and **Shelemiah the son of Abdeel.**

THE MESSAGE REWRITTEN AND PUNISHMENT FOR THE KING (36:27–32)

[27]Then the word of the LORD came to Jeremiah after the king had burned the scroll and the words which Baruch had written at the dictation of Jeremiah, saying, [28]"Take again another scroll and write on it all the former words that were on the first scroll which Jehoiakim the king of Judah burned. [29]And concerning Jehoiakim king of Judah you shall say, 'Thus says the LORD, "You have burned this scroll, saying, 'Why have you written on it that the king of Babylon will certainly come and destroy this land, and will make man and beast to cease from it?'" [30]Therefore thus says the LORD concerning Jehoiakim king of Judah, "He shall have no one to sit on the throne of David, and his dead body shall be cast out to the heat of the day and the frost of the night. [31]I will also punish him and his descendants and his servants for their iniquity, and I will bring on them and the inhabitants of Jerusalem and the men of Judah all the calamity that I have declared to them—but they did not listen."'"

[32]Then Jeremiah took another scroll and gave it to Baruch the son of Neriah, the scribe, and he wrote on it at the dictation of Jeremiah all the words of the book which Jehoiakim king of Judah had burned in the fire; and many similar words were added to them.

Verses 27, 28. Man cannot destroy God's word or diminish

---

[20]Hallo, 2:198; King, 97.

its effect (Is. 55:10, 11; Mt. 24:35). Even though **the king had burned the scroll**, he could not reverse its message; the prophet's words would stand. Therefore, God told Jeremiah to **take again another scroll and write on it all the former words that were on the first scroll** (see 36:32).

Verse 29. Jeremiah recorded the very words that **Jehoiakim** had spoken as he **burned** the original **scroll**. In his winter house, the king had said concerning the prophet, **"Why have you written on it that the king of Babylon will certainly come and destroy this land, and will make man and beast to cease from it?"** These words were revealed by God to Jeremiah, who was in hiding with Baruch (36:19, 26). Since God is everywhere (23:23, 24; Eccles. 12:13, 14; Heb. 4:13), He could supply His prophet with any secret. This insight once again proved Jeremiah to be a true prophet under the care and protection of Almighty God (1:17–19).

It has been suggested that Jehoiakim actually had someone else burn the scroll. However, the repeated references to the king seem to indicate that he personally performed the deed. Moreover, in verse 29, the pronoun **you** in the statement "You have burned this scroll" is emphatic. John Bright offered this translation: "You have dared to burn this scroll."[21]

Verse 30. God stated that **Jehoiakim** would **have no one to sit on the throne of David**. Jehoiachin (Coniah), a son of Jehoiakim, did have a brief three-month reign, but he was taken captive to Babylon in 597 B.C. (2 Kings 24:6–15). He was also rejected by God and told that "no man of his descendants [would] prosper sitting on the throne of David or ruling again in Judah" (see comments on 22:30). Jehoiachin was replaced by his uncle, Zedekiah (37:1; 2 Kings 24:17). The language of verse 30 ("have no one to sit on the throne of David") stands in stark contrast to the ending of the previous chapter, where the faithful Rechabites would "not lack a man to stand before [God] always" (35:19).

In addition, God said that Jehoiakim's **dead body** [would] **be cast out to the heat of the day and the frost of the night** (see

---

[21]John Bright, *Jeremiah*, The Anchor Bible (Garden City, N.Y.: Doubleday & Company, 1965), 178, 181.

comments on 22:18, 19). The Hebrew word translated "cast out" is שָׁלַךְ (*shalak*), the same word used in verse 23 when Jehoiakim "threw" the pieces of paper into the fire. As he had thrown God's word into the brazier to be burned, his corpse would be thrown out in disgrace (see 16:4).

Verse 31. This chapter begins and ends with a reference to **all the calamity** that God had promised to shower on **Judah** and **Jerusalem** because **they did not listen** (36:3, 31). "Listen," from the Hebrew word שָׁמַע (*shama‘*), means so much more than just hearing. It implies the need to understand and obey (see 7:24, 26, 27; 11:11; 16:12; 17:24, 27; 18:19; 23:16; 25:3, 4, 7; 26:3, 4, 5). With leaders like Jehoiakim, Judah had lost interest in what God said. Jehoiakim had surrounded himself with people of similar character, and they would all suffer **for their iniquity** (see 3:13; 5:25; 11:10; 13:22; 14:10, 20; 16:10, 17, 18; 18:23; 22:22).

Verse 32. Jeremiah wasted no time in obeying God's command. He **took another scroll and gave it to Baruch**, who recorded his **dictation**. This new scroll was not simply a copy of the first; it included other oracles the prophet had delivered up until that time. Very likely, this second scroll became the basis for the Book of Jeremiah we have today.

APPLICATION

Responses to God's Word (Ch. 36)

Both the power of God's revealed message and the human response to His message stand out in this chapter. The apostle Peter reminded Christians of the weak and temporary nature of the flesh in contrast to the lasting power of God's eternal Word (1 Pet. 1:23–25). We should be drawn like magnets to His reviving and refreshing message (Mt. 4:4). God's revealed Word has lasting power that must not be ignored, and it has doomed to failure every human effort to destroy it (see Ps. 119:89; Heb. 13:20, 21).

Jehoiakim was neither the first nor the last to seek to destroy God's message. All who have attempted to so do will face the fact that "the grass withers, the flower fades, but the word of our God stands forever" (Is. 40:8). Kings and rulers may burn the

Scriptures, but when judged by those Scriptures they themselves will burn (see Mt. 25:41–46; Rev. 19:20, 21; 20:10; 21:8). People have been killed because of a determination to do God's will, Christ Jesus being the supreme example (Mt. 26:38–45; 2 Cor. 5:21; 1 Pet. 2:24). His Word may be refused or abused, but it will be around when heaven and earth have passed away, serving as the standard for judging one and all (Mt. 24:35; Jn. 12:48; Rev. 20:11–15).

The foregoing facts underscore the importance of our various responses to God's message. As we look at these responses in chapter 36, we should consider our own disposition toward God's Word (2 Cor. 13:5; see Acts 17:11).

First, Jeremiah and Baruch represent those who are teaching God's message to others, seeking to turn them from sin (36:1–10). While the Holy Spirit guided Christ's apostles into all the truth (Jn. 16:13), so that no more revelation from heaven will be given (1 Cor. 13:8–10; Eph. 2:19, 20; 3:3–5; Jude 3), the spreading of His message is an ongoing responsibility of every generation (Mt. 28:18–20; Mk. 16:15, 16; Acts 8:4). Are we, like Jeremiah and Baruch, among those today trying to get His message to others? (See 2 Tim. 2:2, 24; 4:1–5.)

Second, people like Elishama, Delaiah, Elnathan, Gemariah, and Zedekiah gathered with interest to hear the message of God (36:11–15). Do we consistently assemble to hear God's Word, hungering to know His will for our lives? (See Mt. 5:6; Jn. 7:17; Heb. 10:23–25.) More than simply assembling, the attitude we have when we assemble is important (1 Pet. 1:22—2:3).

Third, the officials put forth special effort, vocally calling for the message to be shared with others, even the king (36:16). Are we, by our financial contributions and our words, doing what we can to see that others hear the gospel of Christ? (See 1 Cor. 9:9–16; Gal. 6:6; 3 Jn. 5–8.)

Fourth, some were concerned about the source of those words (36:17–19). Have we diligently searched the Word for the truth that it is from God? (See Mk. 16:15–20; Eph. 3:3–5; Heb. 1:1–4; 2:1–4; 2 Pet. 1:20, 21.) We are certainly warned that many will seek to lead souls astray (Gal. 1:6–12; 1 Tim. 6:3–5; 2 Pet. 2:1–3; 1 Jn. 4:1). Is our faith built on truth or family tradition? (See

Jn. 8:31, 32; Rom. 10:17, 18; 2 Jn. 9, 10.) Truth never fears investigation, and honestly searching the Scriptures is a most noble enterprise (Jn. 7:17; Acts 17:11).

Fifth, some individuals heard God's message, did not fear it, and openly sought to destroy it. King Jehoiakim was the primary one, but others joined in his rebellious spirit (36:20–26). To stand in defiance to God's Word, seeking to abolish any of His teaching, is dangerous. We should remember the end of King Jehoiakim, who did not receive a proper burial and was not mourned by his family and fellow countrymen (22:18, 19).

Several responses to God's Word can be found in this chapter. Which responses do we identify with the most? Are we where God wants us to be in relationship to His Word, being blessed by it? (See Ps. 1:1–3.)

Going to the House of the Lord (36:5)

Jeremiah's restriction from entering the temple courts is sad. One who had been so loyal to God, so dedicated to worship, and so disposed to help in those troubled times was the very one restricted from such outreach to his countrymen. Confinement of one so willing to serve stands in stark contrast to those today who, because of indifference, voluntarily keep themselves from worship assemblies.

Have we allowed distractions to restrict us from assembling? If so, our situation is equally sad. Jeremiah's restriction by others was no more grave or somber than the situation of one who is able to go but excuses himself (see Lk. 14:15–24). If we are able to gather with others for worship, we should do so with joy (see Ps. 122:1; Heb. 10:23–25).

CHAPTER 37
PAYMENT FOR PROPHESYING: IMPRISONMENT

Chapter 37 begins a series of events just before the final fall of Judah and Jerusalem. These incidents are dated to the reign of Zedekiah (37:1), who was king over Judah 597–586 B.C. (2 Kings 24:17–20). More specifically, they belong toward the end of Zedekiah's reign (588–586 B.C.). During this time, the Babylonians were besieging Jerusalem, but they temporarily lifted the siege in order to deal with the Egyptians, who had come to assist Judah (37:5, 7, 11).

Other passages in Jeremiah also relate to this time period. For example, in 21:1–14, Zedekiah sent and asked Jeremiah to inquire of the Lord on their behalf, just as he did in 37:3–10. The prophet's slightly different responses in the two passages indicate that 37:1–10 reports a later inquiry. The likely sequence of events from 588 to 586 B.C. can be found below:

DATE	PASSAGE	EVENT
588 B.C. (early)	34:1–7	Babylon was fighting against Jerusalem, Lachish, and Azekah (34:7).
588 B.C.	21:1–14	Babylon was warring against Jerusalem (21:2).
588–587 B.C.	37:1–10; 34:20–22	The Jews believed the Babylonians would leave. They left temporarily (34:21), lifting the siege to deal with Egypt (37:5, 7, 11).
588–587 B.C.	37:11–21	Jeremiah was placed in the dungeon and then in the court of the guardhouse.
587–586 B.C.	38:1–13, 28	Jeremiah was cast into the cistern and then returned to the court of the guardhouse until the capture of Jerusalem.

GOD'S MESSAGE SOUGHT BUT NOT ACCEPTED (37:1–5)

¹Now Zedekiah the son of Josiah whom Nebuchadnezzar king of Babylon had made king in the land of Judah, reigned as king in place of Coniah the son of Jehoiakim. ²But neither he nor his servants nor the people of the land listened to the words of the Lord which He spoke through Jeremiah the prophet.

³Yet King Zedekiah sent Jehucal the son of Shelemiah, and Zephaniah the son of Maaseiah, the priest, to Jeremiah the prophet, saying, "Please pray to the Lord our God on our behalf." ⁴Now Jeremiah was still coming in and going out among the people, for they had not yet put him in the prison. ⁵Meanwhile, Pharaoh's army had set out from Egypt; and when the Chaldeans who had been besieging Jerusalem heard the report about them, they lifted the siege from Jerusalem.

Verse 1. The events of this chapter are dated to the reign of **Zedekiah** (597–586 B.C.). He was preceded on the throne by his father **Josiah** (640–609 B.C.), his brother Jehoahaz (609 B.C.), his brother **Jehoiakim** (609–598 B.C.), and his nephew **Coniah** (598–597 B.C.). Coniah, also known as Jehoiachin or Jeconiah, only reigned for three months before **Nebuchadnezzar** removed him from the throne and took him as a captive. The **king of Babylon**, and not God, made Zedekiah **king in the land of Judah** (2 Kings 24:17).

Verse 2. Judah had a long-standing problem of not listening to God's commands. Once again, the king, **his servants**, and **the people** ignored the **words of the Lord** spoken **through Jeremiah the prophet**. Second Kings 24:19 characterizes Zedekiah by these words: "He did evil in the sight of the Lord, according to all that Jehoiakim had done."

Verse 3. Ironically, even though **King Zedekiah** did not listen to the divine prophecies, he **sent** some officials to have **Jeremiah the prophet . . . pray to the Lord** for them. Similarly, King Hezekiah had asked the prophet Isaiah to pray for Judah during the Assyrian siege of Jerusalem in 701 B.C. (2 Kings 19:1–7; Is. 37:1–7). The Hebrew word for "pray," פָּלַל (*palal*), can mean

JEREMIAH 37

"act as an advocate" or "make intercession."[1] In verse 7, the term "inquire" (דָּרַשׁ, *darash*) is used as a loose synonym. In this context, it means "seek a word from" the Lord.[2] Zedekiah not only wanted Jeremiah to intercede for Jerusalem, the king also wanted him to ask for an oracle from God concerning the city's future (see comments on 21:1, 2). Timothy M. Willis commented, "This exposes the truly tragic nature of Zedekiah's character. He represents those who yearn to 'hear' the word of the LORD and yet are not willing to 'hear' that word when it comes. He has 'ears to hear,' but he does not 'hear.'"[3]

One of the messengers sent by Zedekiah was **Jehucal the son of Shelemiah.** The shortened form of his name, Jucal, appears in the next chapter (38:1). This man was an opponent of Jeremiah who eventually called for his death (38:4). The other messenger was **Zephaniah the son of Maaseiah**, a high-ranking **priest** (52:24; 2 Kings 25:18). He had accompanied Pashhur on a similar mission (21:1, 2). Zephaniah was more compassionate toward Jeremiah than his associates were (29:24–32).

Verse 4. Jehucal and Zephaniah were sent to find the prophet at a time when he maintained his freedom: **Now Jeremiah was still coming in and going out among the people, for they had not yet put him in the prison** (see 37:15, 16, 21; 38:6, 13, 28). J. A. Thompson identified the phrase "coming in and going out" as a common expression that was typically used in three ways: (1) for military operations (Josh. 14:11; 1 Sam. 29:6); (2) for sacred ceremonies (Ex. 28:35; Ezek. 46:10); and (3) for everyday movements (Deut. 28:6; 2 Kings 19:27).[4] The last of these is in view here, as the prophet moved "among the people."

Verse 5. As the messengers sought out Jeremiah for an oracle

---

[1]Ludwig Koehler and Walter Baumgartner, *The Hebrew and Aramaic Lexicon of the Old Testament*, study ed., trans. and ed. M. E. J. Richardson (Boston: Brill, 2001), 2:933–34.

[2]Ibid., 1:233.

[3]Timothy M. Willis, *Jeremiah-Lamentations*, The College Press NIV Commentary (Joplin, Mo.: College Press Publishing Co., 2002), 299.

[4]J. A. Thompson, *The Book of Jeremiah*, The New International Commentary on the Old Testament (Grand Rapids, Mich.: Wm. B. Eerdmans Publishing Co., 1980), 632, n. 6.

from God, **Pharaoh's army had set out from Egypt**. Apparently, Zedekiah was exploring all of his options; he was seeking help from the Lord as well as the king of Egypt. The pharaoh at that time was Hophra (44:30), also known as Apries, who reigned from 589 to 570 B.C. Ezekiel 17:15 indicates that Zedekiah had sent "envoys to Egypt that they might give him horses and many troops." In addition, *Lachish Letter* 3 mentions a general who had "moved south in order to enter Egypt" and had sent messengers to summon some men.[5] Initially, the Egyptians responded to Zedekiah's plea and came out to fight the Babylonians. Having **heard** that the Egyptians were rallying their troops, the Babylonians temporarily **lifted the siege from Jerusalem**. They redirected their energies toward this more powerful enemy.

GOD'S PROMISE OF PUNISHMENT (37:6–10)

⁶Then the word of the Lord came to Jeremiah the prophet, saying, ⁷"Thus says the Lord God of Israel, 'Thus you are to say to the king of Judah, who sent you to Me to inquire of Me: "Behold, Pharaoh's army which has come out for your assistance is going to return to its own land of Egypt. ⁸The Chaldeans will also return and fight against this city, and they will capture it and burn it with fire."' ⁹Thus says the Lord, 'Do not deceive yourselves, saying, "The Chaldeans will surely go away from us," for they will not go. ¹⁰For even if you had defeated the entire army of Chaldeans who were fighting against you, and there were only wounded men left among them, each man in his tent, they would rise up and burn this city with fire.'"

Verses 6–8. Apparently, **Jeremiah** fulfilled their request, even though he had been commanded not to pray for his people on previous occasions (7:16; 11:14; 14:11). In response, **the prophet** received a **word** from **the Lord**.

Jehucal and Zephaniah were about to get a similar message

---

[5]William W. Hallo, ed., *The Context of Scripture* (Boston: Brill, 2003), 3:79.

to what Pashhur and Zephaniah had heard in 21:1–14. Zephaniah heard a message of doom for Jerusalem on each occasion. One of those destined to perish was his own brother, Zedekiah, who was a false prophet (29:21, 22, 25). Zephaniah himself would also die, being struck down before Nebuchadnezzar at Riblah after Jerusalem's destruction (52:24–27).

Jeremiah instructed these messengers to tell Zedekiah that **Pharaoh's army** would **return to its own land of Egypt**. The Egyptians had rallied their troops to assist Judah, having **come out** to fight the Babylonians. Nevertheless, they would retreat (see Ezek. 17:17; 29:6, 7; 30:20–22), and the Babylonian forces would resume the siege against Jerusalem. Their army would **capture** the city and **burn it with fire** (39:1–10; 52:6–30).

Verses 9, 10. Zedekiah was surely hoping for a message of deliverance from the Lord like King Hezekiah had received through the prophet Isaiah over a century earlier:

> "Therefore, thus says the LORD concerning the king of Assyria, 'He will not come to this city or shoot an arrow there; and he will not come before it with a shield, or throw up a siege ramp against it. By the way that he came, by the same he will return, and he will not come to this city,' declares the LORD. 'For I will defend this city to save it for My own sake and for My servant David's sake'" (Is. 37:33–35; see 2 Kings 19:32–34).

In 701 B.C., the angel of the Lord struck down 185,000 Assyrians who had encircled Jerusalem, causing King Sennacherib to return home to Nineveh (Is. 37:36, 37; see 2 Kings 19:35, 36).

While Zedekiah and Jerusalem hungered for hope, Jeremiah declared only doom. The prophet told them not to **deceive** themselves because of military shifts that might seem favorable to them. Zedekiah repeatedly ignored warnings from God. That rebellion meant doom for him and the nation. In 21:7–9, God offered Zedekiah and Judah life by surrendering to Babylon. They did not listen. Now they were being warned again not to be deceived by an expected deliverance supplied by Egypt. Help from Egypt was a deceptive assumption. They were conjuring up hope without a foundation, ignoring God's repeated warnings.

A bold hyperbole underscored the divine oracle: Even if the **entire army** of Babylon were **defeated**, with **only wounded men left** in their tents, **they would rise up and burn** Jerusalem (21:10). God was blunt when His people chose to not heed His warnings. This message certainly did not increase the popularity of God's prophet.

GOD'S PROPHET INCARCERATED
(37:11–16)

> ¹¹Now it happened when the army of the Chaldeans had lifted the siege from Jerusalem because of Pharaoh's army, ¹²that Jeremiah went out from Jerusalem to go to the land of Benjamin in order to take possession of some property there among the people. ¹³While he was at the Gate of Benjamin, a captain of the guard whose name was Irijah, the son of Shelemiah the son of Hananiah was there; and he arrested Jeremiah the prophet, saying, "You are going over to the Chaldeans!" ¹⁴But Jeremiah said, "A lie! I am not going over to the Chaldeans"; yet he would not listen to him. So Irijah arrested Jeremiah and brought him to the officials. ¹⁵Then the officials were angry at Jeremiah and beat him, and they put him in jail in the house of Jonathan the scribe, which they had made into the prison. ¹⁶For Jeremiah had come into the dungeon, that is, the vaulted cell; and Jeremiah stayed there many days.

Verses 11, 12. While the Babylonians **had lifted the siege from Jerusalem** to deal with the Egyptian threat, **Jeremiah** left **Jerusalem to go to the land of Benjamin**. It is likely that he was on his way to Anathoth, his hometown which was only about three miles northeast of Jerusalem (1:1).

The purpose of Jeremiah's journey was **to take possession of some property there among the people**. The phrase "take possession of some property" translates the word חָלַק (*chalaq*), which can mean "divide," "have one's share," "apportion," or "distribute."⁶ The exact meaning in this context is uncertain. One possibility is that the transaction involved the property of his cousin Hanamel, which he later redeemed while imprisoned (32:1–15). Thompson wrote, "He may, of course, have known of the possibility of inheriting Hanamel's property and been on his way to Anathoth to arrange this when he was arrested."⁷ It could be, however, that the transaction involved a separate matter.

Verse 13. Jeremiah never completed his journey; he did not even get all the way out of Jerusalem. At **the Gate of Benjamin** (see comments on 20:1, 2), the prophet was **arrested** by **Irijah**, a **captain of the guard**. Since he and Jehucal are both identified as **the son of Shelemiah** (37:3), it is possible that the two men were brothers.

Irijah charged **Jeremiah**, saying, **"You are going over to the Chaldeans!"** In the Hebrew text, "you" is emphatic. "Going over" comes from נָפַל (*napal*), which literally means "fall down."⁸ The image here is one of surrender. Other versions use the terms "deserting" (TEV; NIV; NRSV; NJB) and "defecting" (NKJV; NJPSV; NLT). Irijah was charging Jeremiah with treason. While this charge was false, it is understandable in light of Jeremiah's advice to others. In 21:9, the prophet had said, "He who dwells in this city will die by the sword and by famine and by pestilence; but he who goes out and *falls away to the Chaldeans* who are besieging you will live, and he will have his own life as booty" (emphasis added). The same advice is echoed in 38:2. Indeed, some heeded Jeremiah's words, surrendering themselves to the Babylonians and sparing their own lives (38:19; 39:9; 52:15).

Verse 14. Jeremiah answered this charge by claiming that it was **a lie**. Even still, **Irijah** refused to **listen**. Having **arrested** him, the captain of the guard **brought him to the officials**.

Verses 15, 16. The officials were angry at Jeremiah, supposing that he was defecting to the Babylonians. Moreover, they did not appreciate his message of doom (37:6–10). They wanted to silence him, ending his influence. Previously, some had schemed

---

⁶Koehler and Baumgartner, 1:322–33.
⁷Thompson, 633.
⁸Koehler and Baumgartner, 1:709–10.

against Jeremiah, threatening his life (18:18). He had also been beaten and placed in the stocks (20:1, 2). On this occasion, as a result of their anger, they **beat him** and **put him in jail**. This action was taken without any proof of treason and without any legal rules being followed.

The prison was located **in the house of Jonathan the scribe**. The reason for using this particular house as a place of confinement is not stated. Jonathan may have functioned as a minister of police. The fact that a scribe's work was not limited to copying manuscripts is evident from 52:25. On the other hand, this man's house may have been used because Jerusalem was in a state of emergency. Since all the other cities of Judah had been captured by the Babylonians, Jewish survivors had fled to Jerusalem, causing it to be overcrowded.

The place of confinement is further described as a **dungeon, that is, the vaulted cell**. The Hebrew word for "dungeon" is בּוֹר (*bor*), which can also be translated "pit" or "cistern."[9] Subterranean pits or cisterns were commonly used in the ancient Near Eastern as prisons (38:6; Gen. 40:15; Ex. 12:29; Is. 24:22).

While these events occurred on the same day, **Jeremiah** was left in the dungeon for **many days**. No specific statements are given about Jeremiah's treatment at the house of Jonathan, but the fact he made an impassioned entreaty to the king not to be taken back there would indicate it was not a pleasant experience. Indeed, he envisioned he could die there (37:20).

In this dark pit, one might ask himself, "Why am I here? What else will they do to me? Why is my good work repaid by evil treatment? Where is God's promised protection?" (See 1:17–19; 15:19–21.) However, nothing indicates that Jeremiah asked any of those questions at this time. After he faced persecution with great resolve in chapter 20, Jeremiah's treatment only worsened. Nevertheless, he, like Jesus after His Garden of Gethsemane experience, never uttered a doubt or made a complaint to God. This took tremendous trust, courage, and character in the face of unfair conduct.

---

[9]Francis Brown, S. R. Driver, and Charles A. Briggs, *A Hebrew and English Lexicon of the Old Testament* (Oxford: Clarendon Press, 1972), 92.

JEREMIAH 37

GOD'S PROVIDENCE FOR HIS PROPHET (37:17–21)

¹⁷Now King Zedekiah sent and took him out; and in his palace the king secretly asked him and said, "Is there a word from the Lord?" And Jeremiah said, "There is!" Then he said, "You will be given into the hand of the king of Babylon!" ¹⁸Moreover Jeremiah said to King Zedekiah, "In what way have I sinned against you, or against your servants, or against this people, that you have put me in prison? ¹⁹Where then are your prophets who prophesied to you, saying, 'The king of Babylon will not come against you or against this land'? ²⁰But now, please listen, O my lord the king; please let my petition come before you and do not make me return to the house of Jonathan the scribe, that I may not die there." ²¹Then King Zedekiah gave commandment, and they committed Jeremiah to the court of the guardhouse and gave him a loaf of bread daily from the bakers' street, until all the bread in the city was gone. So Jeremiah remained in the court of the guardhouse.

With the return of Babylon's army and the renewed siege, it seems that the king on the throne was more insecure than the prophet in the pit. Faith is stronger than a kingship, and God-given trust is mightier than a throne (see Eccles. 9:17, 18; Heb. 13:5, 6; 1 Jn. 5:4, 5).

Verse 17. Zedekiah sent for Jeremiah, taking **him out** of the dungeon to the confines of the **palace.** There **the king secretly asked** him, **"Is there a word from the Lord?"** This request indicates that Zedekiah knew he was a true prophet. Sadly, the king had wandered so far from God that he no longer revered or feared His spokesman. A drowning man will reach for any reprieve or relief from ruin. The coming days would dramatically prove that calling for Jeremiah was no conversion to the prophet's comments or God's governing principles.

Jeremiah firmly responded to the king, saying, **"There is!" Then he said, "You will be given into the hand of the king of Babylon!"** (see 21:6, 7). He consistently spoke God's divine truth throughout his prophetic ministry, and this response was no exception. His answer proved his trust, integrity, boldness, and determination to declare whatever the Lord gave him to reveal. This prophet was consistent and courageous. He had just been brought from the pit, where he was doomed to stay because of a similar pronouncement (see Acts 5:19, 20; 5:40–42; 2 Tim. 4:16–18).

Verse 18. Jeremiah did not invite his many trials and punishment. The rest of the chapter is a well-structured argument by Jeremiah seeking an end to the injustice against him. He did not want to be a martyr, but he would be one if the Lord's cause demanded it.

In his own defense, Jeremiah challenged the justice of his incarceration. He asked, **"In what way have I sinned against you, or against your servants, or against this people, that you have put me in prison?"** The three categories mentioned here ("you," "your servants," and "this people") mirror those listed in verse 2, where they are indicted for not listening to the Lord and His prophet. "Sinned" is from the Hebrew term חָטָא (*chata'*), which means "go wrong," "miss the mark," "miss the way," or "miss the goal or path of right and duty."[10] Jeremiah was not guilty of any violation. Indeed, he was imprisoned for telling the truth.

Verse 19. Jeremiah also challenged the so-called **prophets** of peace (6:13, 14; 14:13–16), who had declared that **the king of Babylon** would not attack Jerusalem (28:1–4). With Babylon occupying Judah and many from Judah already in captivity, these prophets had been proven to be liars (see Deut. 18:22). Jeremiah's argument was valid and time-tested. Only Judah's injustice could account for the freedom of lying prophets while Jeremiah, the prophet of truth, had been in the pit.

Verse 20. Having established his argument, Jeremiah respectfully entreated **the king** that he would not have to **return to the house of Jonathan the scribe**. The living conditions were certainly dark and miserable in the dungeon. Without proper ventilation, the prophet would have lacked clean air to breathe. Without the light of day, the underground cell would have been cold

---

[10]Ibid., 306–7.

and damp. In addition, verse 21 implies that Jeremiah had not been fed regularly. The prophet believed that if he went back to the dungeon, he would **die there**. The misery of the pit was his motivation for this strong plea against returning.

Verse 21. The prophet's plea and God's providence (1:17–19) resulted in a double blessing. Instead of sending **Jeremiah** back to Jonathan's house, **Zedekiah** allowed him to be held in **the court of the guardhouse** (see comments on 32:2–5). This was a much better environment. Moreover, the king provided him with a ration of food: **a loaf of bread daily from the bakers' street**. R. K. Harrison said, "The *baker's street* was a name typical of the Orient, where each trade or craft was usually restricted to a particular street."[11] Jeremiah received this ration **until all the bread in the city was gone**.

APPLICATION

Weakness and Strength (Ch. 37)

Chapter 37 teaches the nature of a true prophet and the sadness of weak leadership. Jeremiah demonstrated the responses of a faithful spokesman for God. A faithful spokesman asks not what the safe or easy path may be, but "What is God's path?" Hebrews 11:24—12:4 illustrates for us the pain and problems, trials and tests, hurts and horrors endured by a gallery of faith's heroes. This great text is climaxed by Christ and the cross. Paul put great success and great stress together in one setting in 1 Corinthians 16:9: "For a wide door for effective service has opened to me, *and there are many adversaries*" (emphasis added). Zedekiah's secret conversation with Jeremiah was a demonstration of weakness by leadership, whereas Jeremiah's bold announcement of that leader's downfall was a demonstration of strength under stress (37:17).

Speaking truth, upholding eternal realities, facing the challenge of fundamental duties, daring to do what God declares

---

[11]R. K. Harrison, *Jeremiah and Lamentations: An Introduction and Commentary*, Tyndale Old Testament Commentaries (Downers Grove, Ill.: Inter-Varsity Press, 1973), 154.

must be done to maintain faithfulness—these represent the sobering stand that must be taken by any true spokesman for God, or anyone who would follow in the footsteps of Jesus or His faithful apostles and prophets. Has this been the path that we have taken? (See 2 Tim. 4:1–5, 16–18.)

The other side of this story—weakness—is also demonstrated in chapter 37. One weakness was a refusal to listen to the words of the Lord (37:2), while still trying to relate to God's spokesman (37:3). One cannot make progress while torn between truth and tradition (see Mk. 7:9–13), the Lord's law and personal preference (see Lk. 9:23; Acts 4:19, 20; 5:29; 1 Pet. 4:11).

Weakness can be seen when Irijah arrested Jeremiah, and the officials joined in to beat him and confine him (37:13–15). This was a weakness in the failure to apply fairness, facts, and justice. It was the kind of weakness Pilate followed when he had Christ scourged and crucified, surrendering truth and justice to mob action (Mk. 15:12–32; Jn. 19:1–22). It is sad when people in a position of power weakly surrender to evil influences and impose pain on others.

This chapter shows both weakness and strength—and the reality of the devil's efforts to undermine faithfulness in the face of trials. May the faithfulness and strength exhibited by Jeremiah be characteristic of our conduct.

Chapter 38
Zedekiah:
A Weak and Wavering King

A careful reading of 37:11–21 and chapter 38 reveals that they contain a number of similarities. Some believe the two chapters contain alternative accounts of the same events. J. A. Thompson thought this to be the case and listed these similarities between the chapters: (1) Jeremiah was arrested in Jerusalem, turned over to officials, and charged (37:11–14; 38:1–5); (2) he was imprisoned in a "dungeon" or "cistern," the same Hebrew word (בּוֹר, *bor*) being used in 37:15, 16 and 38:6–13; (3) he had a private conversation with King Zedekiah each time (37:17–20; 38:14–27); and (4) afterward, Jeremiah experienced further imprisonment in the court of the guardhouse (37:21; 38:28).[1]

Thompson also noted some dissimilarities. For instance, the dungeon in 37:15, 16 is located in the house of Jonathan the secretary, while in 38:6 the cistern belonged to Malchijah the king's son and was in the court of the guardhouse.[2] James Burton Coffman listed differences involving circumstances (37:11; 38:2), the interviews with the king (37:17–20; 38:14–26), and the duration of the imprisonments (37:16; 38:6, 7), among others. While the events in the two chapters have similarities, the accounts will be treated as separate incidents.[3]

Three key personalties—Zedekiah, Jeremiah, and Ebed-

---

[1] J. A. Thompson, *The Book of Jeremiah*, The New International Commentary on the Old Testament (Grand Rapids, Mich.: Wm. B. Eerdmans Publishing Co., 1980), 636.

[2] Ibid.

[3] James Burton Coffman and Thelma B. Coffman, *Commentary on Jeremiah*, James Burton Coffman Commentaries (Abilene, Tex.: ACU Press, 1990), 417–18.

melech—are featured in chapter 38. The central figure is Zedekiah. This king showed weakness by changing his mind several times. First, he agreed to charges against Jeremiah (38:1–6). Next, he supported an official's suggestion for Jeremiah's release (38:7–13). Then, he sought counsel from Jeremiah (38:14–23). Finally, the king desired Jeremiah's silence, fearing what others would do if they knew he had spoken to the prophet (38:24–28). Regrettably, the king had prominence but lacked the courage to execute his authority.

HIS CONSENT TO CHARGES AGAINST JEREMIAH (38:1–6)

¹Now Shephatiah the son of Mattan, and Gedaliah the son of Pashhur, and Jucal the son of Shelemiah, and Pashhur the son of Malchijah heard the words that Jeremiah was speaking to all the people, saying, ²"Thus says the Lord, 'He who stays in this city will die by the sword and by famine and by pestilence, but he who goes out to the Chaldeans will live and have his own life as booty and stay alive.' ³Thus says the Lord, 'This city will certainly be given into the hand of the army of the king of Babylon and he will capture it.'" ⁴Then the officials said to the king, "Now let this man be put to death, inasmuch as he is discouraging the men of war who are left in this city and all the people, by speaking such words to them; for this man is not seeking the well-being of this people but rather their harm." ⁵So King Zedekiah said, "Behold, he is in your hands; for the king can do nothing against you." ⁶Then they took Jeremiah and cast him into the cistern of Malchijah the king's son, which was in the court of the guardhouse; and they let Jeremiah down with ropes. Now in the cistern there was no water but only mud, and Jeremiah sank into the mud.

Verse 1. The chapter begins by identifying four officials who were hostile to Jeremiah. **Shephatiah the son of Mattan** is mentioned nowhere else in the Scriptures. **Gedaliah the son of Pashhur** may have been from a priestly family. His father could have been the Pashhur who had Jeremiah beaten and placed in the stocks (20:1, 2). **Jucal the son of Shelemiah** was the same one Zedekiah had sent, along with Zephaniah the priest, to ask Jeremiah to inquire of the Lord (37:3). **Pashhur the son of Malchijah** had also been sent on a mission, along with Zephaniah, to speak to the prophet (21:1, 2).

These men **heard the words that Jeremiah was speaking to all the people**. The text does not say where the prophet spoke these words. Jeremiah was free to receive visitors and to speak to people (32:8, 12). It is possible that he was "still coming in and going out among the people" (37:4). The four men mentioned in verse 1 could have been the officials to whom Jeremiah was taken after being arrested by Irijah (37:13, 14). These men were angry with Jeremiah and beat him (37:15).

Verses 2, 3. As he spoke to the people, Jeremiah expressed the lifesaving option of surrendering to the Babylonians. To ignore that option and remain in Jerusalem would result in death by **the sword**, **famine**, and **pestilence** (see comments on 14:12). This was not the only occasion on which the prophet gave this warning (see comments on 21:9; 27:12, 13).

If the people chose not to surrender, God would not relent from bringing calamity on Jerusalem: **This city will certainly be given into the hand of the army of the king of Babylon and he will capture it** (see 21:7; 34:2, 22; 37:8). The key word "hand" (יָד, *yad*), which symbolizes power and authority, appears many times in chapters 37 and 38. Concerning this feature, Timothy M. Willis wrote,

> The LORD declares repeatedly "by the hand of" Jeremiah (37:2) that King Zedekiah and the city will be given "into the hand of" the Babylonian king and his army (37:17; 38:3, 18). Zedekiah places Jeremiah "into the hands of" his officials (38:5 . . .), but then "into the hand of" Ebed-melech (38:10–11). Zedekiah is afraid of falling "into the hand of" his own people more than being captured by the Babylonians (38:19, 23). It is as if everyone's life is "in the hand of" someone else.[4]

---

[4]Timothy M. Willis, *Jeremiah-Lamentations*, The College Press NIV Commentary (Joplin, Mo.: College Press Publishing Co., 2002), 307.

Verse 4. The four **officials** charged Jeremiah with treason before **the king,** and called for his **death**. They claimed that he was **discouraging the men of war** and **all the people** who were left in Jerusalem. This statement reveals that some, perhaps many, had already died or had defected. Jeremiah's message was supposedly "discouraging" the rest. The Hebrew text literally says that he "weakens the hands of" the people (NKJV). This idiom appears in *Lachish Letter* 6, which accuses certain officials of discouraging the men during this same crisis.[5] It is also found in Ezra 4:4 (see KJV), where the mixed people who had been settled in Israel discouraged the Jews who returned to Jerusalem from rebuilding the temple (see Is. 35:3; Heb. 12:12).

Jeremiah was also charged with **not seeking the well-being of this people but rather their harm**. Anthony L. Ash thought that these four officials were pro-Egyptian in their policies.[6] They apparently thought that Jerusalem would be rescued by the Egyptian army. However, this strategy was doomed for failure (see comments on 37:5–8).

The prophet's message may have seemed treasonous, but God was giving Jerusalem over to the Babylonians. Surrender would put an end to the bloodshed. In truth, Jeremiah was offering the only message of hope and peace. The term "well-being" is from שָׁלוֹם (*shalom*), whose definitions include "personal safety, welfare, state of health" and "deliverance, salvation."[7] The four officials, however, branded the prophet's message as "harm." The Hebrew word is רָעָה (*ra'ah*), which means "evil," "wickedness," "misfortune," or "calamity, disaster."[8]

The officials wanted the people to take courage, when their real need was to surrender and correct their ways. God's message was not for their ruin, as idolatry had already brought that

---

[5] William W. Hallo, ed., *The Context of Scripture* (Boston: Brill, 2003), 3:81.

[6] Anthony L. Ash, *Jeremiah and Lamentations*, The Living Word Commentary (Abilene, Tex.: ACU Press, 1987), 263.

[7] Ludwig Koehler and Walter Baumgartner, *The Hebrew and Aramaic Lexicon of the Old Testament*, study ed., trans. and ed. M. E. J. Richardson (Boston: Brill, 2001), 2:1506–10.

[8] Ibid., 2:1262–64.

upon them. Rather, His message was for their repentance. Jeremiah told the truth but was called a traitor!

Verse 5. The wavering ruler submitted to the wickedness of these men. **King Zedekiah said, "Behold, he is in your hands; for the king can do nothing against you."** This weak leader could "do nothing" because he lacked nerve, not because he lacked authority (38:25, 26).

Verse 6. The ultimate aim of these officials was to put the prophet to death (38:4). However, they did not do so immediately, either by stoning him or by cutting him down with the sword. Instead, **they took Jeremiah and cast him into the cistern of Malchijah the king's son, which was in the court of the guardhouse.** Again, Jeremiah was confined, this time in a dark, slimy "cistern" (בּוֹר, bor). Most houses in Jerusalem were equipped with private cisterns (2 Kings 18:31; Prov. 5:15). These were used for storing water from rainfall or springs in order to survive through the dry months (see comments on 14:3). "Malchijah" was likely the father of Pashhur, one of the four officials who was persecuting Jeremiah (see comments on 38:1). "The king's son" is an honorary title and should not be taken literally. This man was probably from royal blood and/or a member of the king's court (see comments on 36:26).

The officials **let Jeremiah down** through the narrow opening **with ropes** (see 38:13). This **cistern** was apparently deep, and it was almost empty: **There was no water but only mud.** This lack of water could reflect the conditions throughout the city during the siege.[9]

What is the mindset of men who would put any human being into such a place? A cistern might be a convenient place to deposit a dead body (41:4–7), but to cast a live person into such a damp, dark, mud pit is piling abuse on top of incarceration. This cistern was partly dried up, but there was a thick deposit of slimy soil sufficiently deep that **Jeremiah sank into the mud.** The misery was intensified by the prevailing perils of no food (38:9). Were these officials too cowardly to carry out a public exe-

---

[9] Ash, 264.

cution? Were they seeking to kill the prophet without shedding his blood? Jeremiah's death by starvation could easily be rationalized as a death by disease.

Jeremiah's source of strength and God's response to this cruel conduct may be seen in Lamentations 3:53–66. As the following verses show, God had not forgotten His prophet.

HIS SUPPORT OF A EUNUCH'S SUGGESTION FOR JEREMIAH (38:7–13)

⁷But Ebed-melech the Ethiopian, a eunuch, while he was in the king's palace, heard that they had put Jeremiah into the cistern. Now the king was sitting in the Gate of Benjamin; ⁸and Ebed-melech went out from the king's palace and spoke to the king, saying, ⁹"My lord the king, these men have acted wickedly in all that they have done to Jeremiah the prophet whom they have cast into the cistern; and he will die right where he is because of the famine, for there is no more bread in the city." ¹⁰Then the king commanded Ebed-melech the Ethiopian, saying, "Take thirty men from here under your authority and bring up Jeremiah the prophet from the cistern before he dies." ¹¹So Ebed-melech took the men under his authority and went into the king's palace to a place beneath the storeroom and took from there worn-out clothes and worn-out rags and let them down by ropes into the cistern to Jeremiah. ¹²Then Ebed-melech the Ethiopian said to Jeremiah, "Now put these worn-out clothes and rags under your armpits under the ropes"; and Jeremiah did so. ¹³So they pulled Jeremiah up with the ropes and lifted him out of the cistern, and Jeremiah stayed in the court of the guardhouse.

This section contrasts courage and cowardice. The king, too weak to do anything for Jeremiah, is set in opposition to Ebed-melech, an Ethiopian servant who would do something.

Verses 7, 8. Although the people of Jerusalem are characterized as being corrupt (5:1–6), a few righteous individuals actually stood up for Jeremiah and his cause, such as Ahikam (26:24) and Baruch (36:4–8). Here we are introduced to another person who showed compassion to the prophet. His compound name, **Ebed-melech**, means "servant of the king." Concerning this name, William Ewing wrote,

> From the early monarchy the description of a court official as "slave" helped to differentiate him from those who were functioning in their capacity of tribal elders. Sometimes it was indicated that the "slave" was a paid official. The practice originated in Babylonia, and among the Assyrians "Ebed-melech" became a proper name.[10]

This official connected with **the king's palace** is further described as **the Ethiopian** (see comments on 13:23) and **a eunuch** (סָרִים, *saris*). This word can refer to a "high official" or a "eunuch,"[11] that is, a castrated man (see comments on 52:25). The practice of making men eunuchs probably goes back to ancient Mesopotamia, where they were in charge of the king's harem. Eunuchs came to serve in many other capacities. Some kings, such as Cyrus the Great, preferred to have eunuchs as their officials because these men were more devoted, not being distracted by family ties.[12]

Because of his palace connections, Ebed-melech **heard that they had put Jeremiah into the cistern**, and he resolved to intervene on behalf of the prophet. When he approached Zedekiah, **the king was sitting in the Gate of Benjamin**. This was the same location where Jeremiah had been arrested (37:13). Zedekiah's "sitting" (יָשַׁב, *yashab*) probably refers to being seated on a throne as king and judge.[13] Apparently, it was customary for kings to sit in the gate complex to hear complaints and judge court cases (see 2 Sam. 15:2–4). This gave Ebed-melech an opportunity to approach the king, something he may not have done in the pal-

---

[10]William Ewing, "Ebed-melech," in *The International Standard Bible Encyclopedia*, rev. ed., ed. Geoffrey W. Bromiley (Grand Rapids, Mich.: Wm. B. Eerdmans Publishing Co., 1982), 2:8.

[11]Koehler and Baumgartner, 1:769–70.

[12]Xenophon *Cyropaedia* 7.5.60–65.

[13]Francis Brown, S. R. Driver, and Charles A. Briggs, *A Hebrew and English Lexicon of the Old Testament* (Oxford: Clarendon Press, 1972), 442.

ace without an invitation.[14] If the king was indeed sitting in judgment at this time, then his hypocrisy is even more extreme. The only step toward justice was taken by an Ethiopian eunuch who dared to approach the king about the cruelty being suffered by Jeremiah. Since Ebed-melech trusted in the Lord, his life would be spared in the downfall of Jerusalem (39:18).

Verse 9. Ebed-melech brought charges against the officials, saying, **"My lord the king, these men have acted wickedly in all that they have done to Jeremiah the prophet whom they have cast into the cistern."** The Hebrew word for "acted wickedly" (רֵעַע, ra'a') is related to the word for "harm" (רָעָה, ra'ah) in verse 4. The four officials had accused Jeremiah of bringing calamity on the people, yet they were the real evildoers.

The Ethiopian eunuch was concerned that Jeremiah would **die** if he remained in the cistern (see 37:20). The eunuch contended that Jerusalem was experiencing **famine, for there** [was] **no more bread in the city.** This statement is difficult to interpret. (1) In light of 37:21 and 52:6, 7, some have understood it as hyperbole. Apparently, the food supply totally ran out later on, just prior to the breaching of the walls. (2) The statement could simply mean that "the public stores of grain were exhausted."[15] What little food there was in the city would not reach him in the cistern. Why bother feeding a condemned prisoner when food supplies are extremely limited? (3) Instead of "for," some versions render the conjunction כִּי (ki) as "when," which is a legitimate translation.[16] The NEB says that "*when* there is no more bread in the city he will die of hunger where he lies" (emphasis added). Trapped in the cistern, he could not escape death.

Verse 10. Surprisingly, **the king commanded Ebed-melech** to **take thirty men** and rescue **Jeremiah**, saving him from death. The eunuch's position as an official is evident here by the **authority** he possessed. Based on a textual variant, some versions read

---

[14]John Bright, *Jeremiah*, The Anchor Bible (Garden City, N.Y.: Doubleday & Company, 1965), 231.

[15]James E. Smith, *Jeremiah and Lamentations*, Bible Study Textbook Series (Joplin, Mo.: College Press, 1972), 628.

[16]See Koehler and Baumgartner, 1:470–71.

"three men" instead of "thirty" (RSV; NRSV; TEV; NEB; REB). "Thirty" and "three" are spelled similarly in Hebrew, which would explain a scribal error. While "three men" probably would have been a sufficient number to pull Jeremiah out of the cistern, "thirty" could have more ably defended the operation against any opposition.

Verse 11. Ebed-melech made some plans by which to lift the prophet from **the cistern**. He stopped by a **storeroom**—perhaps a wardrobe room (see 2 Kings 10:22)—in **the king's palace**, taking from there some **worn-out clothes** and **rags**, plus **ropes** sufficiently long enough to reach down to **Jeremiah**.

Verse 12. The gentleness of **the Ethiopian** in the rescue mission is clearly seen. The **rags** would serve as a softening pad **under** Jeremiah's **armpits**. Therefore, a lift would be formed around Jeremiah's body that would be strong but not abrasive. It was thoughtful and caring for this official to design a method to lessen the tremendous strain that would be on Jeremiah's arms during the lifting process. Rough ropes would have cut and burned the prophet's flesh, with the possible danger of tearing his arms from their sockets.

Verse 13. The thirty men who had joined in this rescue effort (38:10) **pulled Jeremiah up with the ropes and lifted him out of the cistern**. Their sizable number made possible a slow, steady, gentle hoisting of God's prophet to light, fresh air, and a firm foundation under his feet.

After that time, **Jeremiah stayed in the court of the guardhouse** (see 32:2). This was the same place where he was confined after being removed from the dungeon in the previous chapter (37:21).

HIS REQUEST FOR COUNSEL FROM JEREMIAH (38:14–23)

A Plea for Providential Provisions (38:14–20)

¹⁴Then King Zedekiah sent and had Jeremiah the prophet brought to him at the third entrance that is in the house of the

LORD; and the king said to Jeremiah, "I am going to ask you something; do not hide anything from me." ¹⁵Then Jeremiah said to Zedekiah, "If I tell you, will you not certainly put me to death? Besides, if I give you advice, you will not listen to me." ¹⁶But King Zedekiah swore to Jeremiah in secret saying, "As the LORD lives, who made this life for us, surely I will not put you to death nor will I give you over to the hand of these men who are seeking your life."

¹⁷Then Jeremiah said to Zedekiah, "Thus says the LORD God of hosts, the God of Israel, 'If you will indeed go out to the officers of the king of Babylon, then you will live, this city will not be burned with fire, and you and your household will survive. ¹⁸But if you will not go out to the officers of the king of Babylon, then this city will be given over to the hand of the Chaldeans; and they will burn it with fire, and you yourself will not escape from their hand.'" ¹⁹Then King Zedekiah said to Jeremiah, "I dread the Jews who have gone over to the Chaldeans, for they may give me over into their hand and they will abuse me." ²⁰But Jeremiah said, "They will not give you over. Please obey the LORD in what I am saying to you, that it may go well with you and you may live."

Verse 14. With the siege of Jerusalem daily becoming more grave, the weak **King Zedekiah** longed for encouragement and divine help. He **sent** for **Jeremiah**, having him **brought to . . . the third entrance that is in the house of the LORD**. Seeking counsel with **the prophet**, Zedekiah said, **"I am going to ask you something."** The Hebrew term translated "something" is דָּבָר (*dabar*), which also means "word."[17] The NJB has "I want to ask you for a word." The context indicates that **the king** was seeking a divine oracle (38:17, 18). Zedekiah urged **Jeremiah**, saying, **"Do not hide anything from me."** Like many weak leaders, he was desperate yet distrustful.

Verse 15. Having released **Jeremiah** from the cistern, **Zedekiah** surely hoped for better news. Jeremiah made two candid observations. Since his message had not changed, he asked

---

[17]Koehler and Baumgartner, 1:211–12.

Zedekiah, **"If I tell you, will you not certainly put me to death?"** Then, basing his thoughts on past experience, he added, **"Besides, if I give you advice, you will not listen to me."** This was clear-cut and compact.

Verse 16. Concerning the prophet's first concern, **Zedekiah swore to Jeremiah** that he would not be executed or given to others who wanted to kill him. This oath was taken in the name of **the LORD**, recognizing both His existence (He **lives**) and His creative power (He **made this life**[18] **for us**). The conversation took place **in secret**, a detail which becomes more important as the chapter progresses (38:24–27).

Verses 17, 18. The prophet's second concern proved valid; **Zedekiah** would not listen to or heed the message. **Jeremiah** declared God's solution, telling the king that his surrender to **Babylon** would ensure three benefits: (1) **"You will live"**; (2) **"this city will not be burned with fire"**; and (3) **"you and your household will survive."** While these were promising benefits, stubborn refusal would result in suffering for all. Jerusalem would be destroyed **by fire**, and the king would **not escape** from the Babylonians. This divine oracle was consistent with Jeremiah's previous prophecies; the message had not changed (38:2, 3).

Verses 19, 20. The following exchange provides a dramatic example of how weak faith, deaf ears, and shortsightedness lead to disaster. A great difference existed between Zedekiah's fears, which kept him from obeying the Lord, and Jeremiah's faithfulness to the Lord's word. **King Zedekiah said to Jeremiah, "I dread the Jews who have gone over to the Chaldeans, for they may give me over into their hand and they will abuse me."** Zedekiah was afraid that, if he surrendered, the Babylonians would turn him over to the Jews who had already deserted (52:15). **But Jeremiah said, "They will not give you over."** He then urged, **"Please obey the LORD in what I am saying to you, that it may go well with you and you may live."** The language here is similar to Deuteronomy 4:40; 5:16; and 19:13. Willis con-

---

[18]"Life" is from the complex term נֶפֶשׁ (*nepesh*). In this passage, other versions translate the word as "soul" (KJV) or "breath" (NIV). It seems that the life principle is in view here.

cluded that the similarity "implies that the blessings previously promised for those who lived in the Promised Land are being perpetuated in a different land, the land of the Babylonians."[19]

A Price to Be Paid for Procrastination (38:21–23)

²¹"But if you keep refusing to go out, this is the word which the LORD has shown me: ²²'Then behold, all of the women who have been left in the palace of the king of Judah are going to be brought out to the officers of the king of Babylon; and those women will say,
"Your close friends
Have misled and overpowered you;
While your feet were sunk in the mire,
They turned back."
²³'They will also bring out all your wives and your sons to the Chaldeans, and you yourself will not escape from their hand, but will be seized by the hand of the king of Babylon, and this city will be burned with fire.'"

Verse 21. Jeremiah warned that the king's refusal to surrender (**go out**) to the Babylonians would lead to dire consequences. Zedekiah could not afford to procrastinate any longer. If he would not obey God's message, disaster was inevitable. The descriptive images found in verses 22 and 23 were **the word which the LORD [had] shown** the prophet. In other words, Jeremiah had received this divine message in a vision (see 1:11–16; 24:1).

Verse 22. Jeremiah was specific, giving the source of the mockery that would be heaped upon Zedekiah. **The king** would be shamed by **all of the women who [had] been left in the palace**. This number would include his wives, concubines, other female relatives, and servants. Later, when the walls of Jerusalem were breached, Zedekiah abandoned these women and fled for his own life (39:4; 52:7, 8).

The women would **be brought out to the officers of the king of Babylon**, to their camp outside Jerusalem. Some of them may

---

[19]Willis, 311.

have been taken as wives by the Babylonian officers (see Judg. 5:30). As the women went out, they would sing a taunting song which emphasized that Zedekiah's **close friends** [had] **misled and overpowered** him. "Close friends" could literally be rendered "men of your peace" (שָׁלוֹם, *shalom*). Those officials had proclaimed "peace," but it was all a lie (see comments on 38:4). Their influence dictated the king's actions; he listened to them instead of God's prophet.

The women would also sing, **"While your feet were sunk in the mire, they turned back."** This language brings to mind Jeremiah's own recent experience at the bottom of the cistern (38:6). Of course, being "sunk in the mire" is used here as a metaphor for great distress (see Ps. 40:2; 69:2, 14). Having misled Zedekiah, his closest friends would abandon him in a time of crisis. The language may point to the fact that, after fleeing from Jerusalem, the king was overtaken by the Babylonian army near Jericho and "all his army was scattered from him" (52:8).

Verse 23. The Babylonians would capture **all** of Zedekiah's **wives** and his **sons** (or "children"; NIV; NJPSV). His family would not escape their grasp. Further, Zedekiah himself would **not escape from their hand**. Instead, the king of Judah would **be seized by the hand of the king of Babylon** (see 37:17). Indeed, after capturing Zedekiah, the Babylonian army took him to Riblah, where he faced the wrath of Nebuchadnezzar (see comments on 52:9–11). Ultimately, Jerusalem would **be burned with fire** (21:10; 32:29; 34:2, 22; 37:8, 10; 39:8; 52:13).

HIS DEMAND FOR JEREMIAH'S SILENCE (38:24–28)

24Then Zedekiah said to Jeremiah, "Let no man know about these words and you will not die. 25But if the officials hear that I have talked with you and come to you and say to you, 'Tell us now what you said to the king and what the king said to you; do not hide it from us and we will not put you to death,' 26then you are to say to them, 'I was presenting my petition before the king, not to make me return to the house of Jonathan to die there.'" 27Then all the officials came to Jeremiah and

questioned him. So he reported to them in accordance with all these words which the king had commanded; and they ceased speaking with him, since the conversation had not been overheard. [28]So Jeremiah stayed in the court of the guardhouse until the day that Jerusalem was captured.

Verse 24. Zedekiah wanted to keep his conversation with **Jeremiah** a secret. Since the prophet was confined and had to be escorted from place to place, news was likely to spread from his guards that he had met with the king. Zedekiah did not want others to hear the oracle, so he told Jeremiah, **"Let no man know about these words and you will not die."** His promise to protect Jeremiah matches his previous oath (38:16).

Verse 25. The king's mind was so busy imagining what others might say or do that his ears seemed deaf to the facts and promises offered by Jeremiah from God. He anticipated that his **officials** would learn about this meeting with Jeremiah and seek more information about it from the prophet. He was deeply concerned about what Jeremiah might say to the officials when he saw them and how they would react. The officials would not hesitate to use Jeremiah's life as a bargaining chip in their quest for information. They would say, **"Tell us now what you said to the king and what the king said to you; do not hide it from us and we will not put you to death."**

Verses 26, 27. At the meeting in 37:20, Jeremiah had pleaded with Zedekiah, "Do not make me return to the house of Jonathan the scribe, that I may not die there." Possibly recalling this earlier request, Zedekiah instructed Jeremiah to tell his officials, **"I was presenting my petition before the king, not to make me return to the house of Jonathan to die there."**

Jeremiah did not jeopardize his own safety by revealing to **the officials** the divine oracle he had spoken to the king. Instead, **he reported to them in accordance with all these words which the king had commanded.** These words were true, even though they were not the whole truth. There are times when wisdom dictates that not everything needs to be spoken (see Mk. 14:57–61; Jn. 19:8, 9). Jeremiah's response satisfied the officials, since they had no other knowledge of **the conversation.**

Verse 28. Chapter 38 concludes in the same manner as chapter 37: **So Jeremiah stayed in the court of the guardhouse.** This time, the confinement lasted **until the day that Jerusalem was captured.**

APPLICATION

The Ethiopian Eunuch (38:7–13)
The spirit and skills of this Ethiopian eunuch are commendable: (1) He dared to face the king for Jeremiah's welfare (38:7–9). (2) He thought ahead of what equipment and supplies would be needed for this project, knowing where those supplies could be found (38:11). (3) He was able to clearly communicate to Jeremiah how the rescue events would unfold (38:12). (4) He utilized the personnel he was given to accomplish this task in a gentle, caring, carefully executed process (38:10, 13). (5) He knew where to take Jeremiah for safety and security when the rescue was completed (38:13).

Uplifting Others (38:10)
The king's command deserves special attention: "Bring up Jeremiah the prophet from the cistern before he dies" (38:10). A valuable application is seen here. We need to "bring up" men (Rom. 14:19; 1 Thess. 5:11). Many people are depressed and despondent, in all kinds of dungeons. People who caringly lift up burdened brethren, restoring hope and purpose to their lives are precious indeed (Gal. 6:2; Heb. 12:12, 13). We need to take people out of their prisons (Gal. 5:1; Jude 20–23). This vital work must be done before these souls perish (see Heb. 9:27).

Principles for Personal Work (38:20)
Jeremiah's appeal to Zedekiah in 38:20 contains several valuable lessons for sharing the gospel with others.

1. *Helping to calm the prospect*—"You shall not be given to them" (RSV). Removing fear prepares the soil where faith can grow.

2. *Showing concern*—"Please." The Hebrew term, נָא (na'), denotes genuine concern or an urgent appeal (see Acts 20:31).

3. *Teaching commands*—"obey." This term, שָׁמַע (*shama‘*), urges people to listen, give heed to, care for, and understand God's message. It is intended to stimulate both concern and action. A halfhearted presentation or a halfhearted hearing will never satisfy the urgency in this context.

4. *Understanding the Source*—"the voice of the LORD" (KJV). These are not matters of personal preference, but divine directives. God has spoken, and men must hear (Heb. 2:1–3; 12:25; 1 Pet. 4:11).

5. *Communicating clearly*—"in what I am saying to you." We should know well those with whom we are studying and communicate wherever they may be mentally, morally, emotionally, and spiritually. This step does not include tickling their ears or appeasing their weaknesses, but the one sharing God's Word with others does need to be conscious of how people will hear and evaluate the truth presented (see 1 Cor. 3:1–3; Heb. 5:11–14). We should be like Timothy and truly care for their welfare (Phil. 2:20).

6. *Considering the cause for these comments*—"that it may go well with you" (enriching for life) and "that . . . you may live" (extension of time) (Mt 4:4; Jn. 10:10).

As we relate with others, have we taken this type of interest? Have we sought to follow these practical principles for personal work?

A Sad Song (38:22)

True songs not only tell a story, they may also taunt their victims. Four messages spring from the brief lines Jeremiah delivered concerning the king (38:22).

1. The king's "close friends"—his princes and counselors—became the controlling influence in this true life episode.

2. "Your close friends have misled . . . you." What a tragic combination—close friends and misleading friends! The Scriptures warn about bad company that can corrupt even good morals (1 Cor. 15:33). We are repeatedly warned about individuals who produce division, pervert God's principles, and draw others to their deceptive, dangerous ways (Ex. 23:1, 2; Prov. 1:10–19; 6:16–19; Mt. 24:24–26; Acts 20:29, 30; Rom. 16:17, 18; 1 Jn. 4:1).

3. "Your close friends have . . . overpowered you." This is not a tragedy in the making; it is a disaster that had already developed. It would just require a little more time to see Zedekiah fall and fail (39:4–8). God does not allow one to be tempted beyond what that person can bear (1 Cor. 10:13), but neither does He destroy our wills by which our weaknesses may cave in to eternally damaging courses of conduct (1 Cor. 10:12; Tit. 1:10, 11; Heb. 12:14–17).

4. The disastrous consequences are described by a figure of speech in satire: "Your feet were sunk in the mire." The very method which the king allowed Jeremiah to endure would be akin to the curse imposed on Zedekiah. He was not thrown into a slimy cistern, but he would be as totally helpless, facing his fate, as Jeremiah was when officials cast him into the muddy mire. Who would come to Zedekiah's mind when these women shamed him about being stuck in the mud? Jeremiah, of course.

Zedekiah's Failures (38:23)

King Zedekiah failed in many areas of his life. Four of these can be seen from 38:23.

1. *He failed as a husband.* His wives were taken into Babylon as captives. He abandoned them to save his own life, rather than cherishing and protecting them (see Eph. 5:25–33).

2. *He failed as a father.* His children became captives. His sons were killed (39:6; 52:10), and his daughters were taken into Egypt (43:6, 7). It must have hurt Zedekiah deeply to watch his sons be killed and to have those images as his last visual memories.

3. *He failed as a man*—He was "seized by the hand of the king of Babylon," blinded, bound in bronze fetters, and taken into captivity (39:7; 52:11).

4. *He failed as a king*—Jeremiah told him, "This city will be burned with fire," and it did (39:8; 52:13).

In no area of influence did this king succeed. His life was a bundle of mistaken fear. He feared the Jews and the Babylonians more than he feared God. He feared that the Jewish deserters would mock and abuse him (38:19). He wanted to hear everything (38:14), but he would not heed anything he heard from God or His prophet.

CHAPTER 39

JERUSALEM'S FALL TO BABYLON

The wrathful judgment of God and the destructive power of the Babylonian army merge together in this climactic chapter. After many years, the divine oracles spoken against Judah's rebellion were fulfilled as the holy city of Jerusalem was destroyed.

Chapter 39 primarily centers on three personalities. The first is Zedekiah, whose weakness and rebellion were typical of his corrupt kingdom. Jerusalem would now reap what had been sown (39:1–10). The second personality is Jeremiah, whose dedication in the midst of despair over the people's disobedience was providentially rewarded. God's tender care for Jeremiah is nowhere better seen than during this time when his native country was crumbling (39:11–14). The third personality is Ebed-melech, the Ethiopian eunuch, who exemplifies God's interest in anyone who will stand for what is right. A touching gentleness is seen in God's provision for this man of faith (39:15–18).

Although God is not mentioned in the chapter until verse 15, His justice and judgments, as well as His compassion and care, are evident. While the rebellious king and nation were ruined by their unrighteousness, both Jeremiah and Ebed-melech were protected due to their faithfulness.

GOD'S PROPHECY CONCERNING JERUSALEM FULFILLED (39:1–10)

The destruction of Jerusalem in 586 B.C. was a monumental event in Israel's history, and it is recorded in three other passages (52:1–30; 2 Kings 24:18—25:21; 2 Chron. 36:15–21). At times, these other accounts provide additional details that are not found in 39:1–10. A more comprehensive picture of Jerusalem's downfall can be gained by studying this section alongside these parallel passages.

Besieged Jerusalem Finally Falls (39:1–3)

¹**Now when Jerusalem was captured in the ninth year of Zedekiah king of Judah, in the tenth month, Nebuchadnezzar king of Babylon and all his army came to Jerusalem and laid siege to it;** ²**in the eleventh year of Zedekiah, in the fourth month, in the ninth day of the month, the city wall was breached.** ³**Then all the officials of the king of Babylon came in and sat down at the Middle Gate: Nergal-sar-ezer, Samgar-nebu, Sar-sekim the Rab-saris, Nergal-sar-ezer the Rab-mag, and all the rest of the officials of the king of Babylon.**

Year after year, with God patiently waiting, Jeremiah had warned Judah to repent. For some forty years Jeremiah's prophetic pleas for penitence had been spoken, but rejection and continued rebellion had prevailed. God was now acting, and Babylon's forces were ready to enact violence and destruction (52:3; 2 Kings 24:20).

Verse 1. The beginning of the **siege** of **Jerusalem** is dated to **the tenth month** of **the ninth year of Zedekiah king of Judah**. Jeremiah 52:4 adds that it was "the tenth day." This date has been calculated to be January 15, 588 B.C.[1] The text indicates that **Nebuchadnezzar** and **all his army** were initially involved. Later, however, the **king of Babylon** stayed at Riblah, where he oversaw his operations throughout Palestine (39:6).

Verse 2. Jerusalem had undergone an awful attack by Babylon's bombarding forces. The siege had been temporarily lifted as the Babylonians dealt with the army marching from Egypt (37:5). However, the Egyptians eventually turned back, and the

---

[1] William Sanford LaSor, "Jerusalem," in *The International Standard Bible Encyclopedia*, rev. ed., ed. Geoffrey W. Bromiley (Grand Rapids, Mich.: Wm. B. Eerdmans Publishing Co., 1982), 2:1016.

Babylonians encircled Jerusalem once more (37:7, 8). Finally, **in the eleventh year of Zedekiah, in the fourth month, in the ninth day of the month**—July 18, 586[2]—**the city wall was breached.**

Verse 3. After the walls were breached, Babylon's **officials** entered the city and met **at the Middle Gate**. This is the only reference to a gate by this name in the Old Testament. One suggestion is that it was located in the wall separating Mount Zion from the lower city. In this case, it was a strategic meeting place in the central part of Jerusalem—which agrees with the prophecy of 21:4. Another possibility is that it was in the middle of the northern wall of the city, which was most vulnerable to attack.

Some of these **officials** are mentioned by name. **Nergal-sar-ezer** may be the same person as Neriglissar, who later seized the throne from Nebuchadnezzar's son Evil-merodach and reigned over the Babylonian Empire from 560 to 556 B.C. (see comments on 27:7; 52:31).

The next name listed is **Samgar-nebu**. This name has not been discovered in Babylonian documents, yet "Nergal-sar-ezer" does appear as a governor of Sin-magir. For this reason, some versions attach "Samgar" to "Nergal-sar-ezer" above and "nebu" to "Sar-sekim" below.[3] For example, the NCV has "Nergal-Sharezer of the district of Samgar" and "Nebo-Sarsekim" (see NEB; REB; CEV; NLT).

The name **Sar-sekim**, or better "Nebo-Sarsekim" (NCV), has recently been discovered on a Babylonian cuneiform tablet dating to about 595 B.C. It records a man by this name—perhaps the same person—making a payment to the temple of his god at Sippar near Babylon.[4] The title **Rab-saris**, which is a transliteration, has been variously translated as "chief official" (NIV), "chief officer" (NCV), or "chief eunuch" (NEB). This term designates a high-ranking official who was close to the king.

The final name listed here, which also appears in verse 13, is

---

[2]Ibid.

[3]D. J. Wiseman, "Samgar-Nebo," in *The International Standard Bible Encyclopedia*, rev. ed., ed. Geoffrey W. Bromiley (Grand Rapids, Mich.: Wm. B. Eerdmans Publishing Co., 1988), 4:308.

[4]Laura Sexton, "Nebo-Sarsekim Cuneiform Tablet" (http://www.archaeology.org/0801/topten/cuneiform.html; Internet, accessed 16 June 2011).

Nergal-sar-ezer. He is distinguished from the first man in the list by the title **Rab-mag**. Concerning this term, D. J. Wiseman wrote, "While the precise nature of this court office is unknown, it is likely the same as the Assyrian and Bab[ylonian] *rab mu(n)gi*, used of a high military official who occasionally served as a special envoy to foreign rulers."[5]

King Zedekiah's Flight from Jerusalem (39:4–10)

⁴When Zedekiah the king of Judah and all the men of war saw them, they fled and went out of the city at night by way of the king's garden through the gate between the two walls; and he went out toward the Arabah. ⁵But the army of the Chaldeans pursued them and overtook Zedekiah in the plains of Jericho; and they seized him and brought him up to Nebuchadnezzar king of Babylon at Riblah in the land of Hamath, and he passed sentence on him. ⁶Then the king of Babylon slew the sons of Zedekiah before his eyes at Riblah; the king of Babylon also slew all the nobles of Judah. ⁷He then blinded Zedekiah's eyes and bound him in fetters of bronze to bring him to Babylon. ⁸The Chaldeans also burned with fire the king's palace and the houses of the people, and they broke down the walls of Jerusalem. ⁹As for the rest of the people who were left in the city, the deserters who had gone over to him and the rest of the people who remained, Nebuzaradan the captain of the bodyguard carried them into exile in Babylon. ¹⁰But some of the poorest people who had nothing, Nebuzaradan the captain of the bodyguard left behind in the land of Judah, and gave them vineyards and fields at that time.

Verse 4. After the city wall was broken through, **Zedekiah** and **all the men of war** fled from the Babylonians. They did this stealthily **at night**, so as not to get caught. Perhaps they used a secret **gate between the two walls** that was near **the king's garden**. This was on the southeastern side of the city by the Kidron

---

[5]D. J. Wiseman, "Rabmag," in *The International Standard Bible Encyclopedia*, 4:30.

Valley (Neh. 3:15). (For **Arabah**, see comments on 52:7.)

Verse 5. Zedekiah, attempting to escape, found that he could not do so (32:4; 34:3; 38:18). On **the plains of Jericho**, he was overtaken and **seized**. It appears that he was trying to cross over the Jordan River and find refuge in Moab or Ammon.

Zedekiah was then taken to **Nebuchadnezzar**, who was stationed **at Riblah**. This city, located about two hundred miles north of Jerusalem, served as Nebuchadnezzar's headquarters as he oversaw military operations in Palestine and Egypt (see comments on 52:9).

No way of escape was possible for Zedekiah or for his people (16:16–18). The king of Judah was brought face to face with the **king of Babylon**. Then Nebuchadnezzar **passed sentence on him**.

Verse 6. The folly and weakness of the king of Judah caused him to lose his sons (see 38:23), as they were slaughtered **before his eyes**. While the text says that **the king of Babylon slew the sons of Zedekiah**, it is doubtful that Nebuchadnezzar personally carried out the deed. More likely, he ordered the executions, and his men fulfilled his commands. **The nobles of Judah** were also put to death.

Verse 7. Then **Zedekiah's eyes** were put out. His last visual memories of the executions of his sons and noblemen must have haunted him for the rest of his life. Moreover, the words of the prophecies about him coming eye to eye with Nebuchadnezzar must have reverberated in his mind (32:4; 34:3; see 38:23).

After being **blinded**, Zedekiah was **bound . . . in fetters of bronze** and led on the long journey **to Babylon**. As he traveled along, the sobering message that he would not see that land must have tormented his soul (Ezek. 12:12–16). His future promised only a plague of problems. Eventually, Zedekiah died in prison in Babylon (see comments on 52:10, 11).

Verse 8. The scene shifts back to **Jerusalem**, where the city was **burned with fire** (21:10; 34:2; 37:10; 38:18, 23) and **the walls** were torn **down**. Jeremiah 52:12 indicates that Nebuzaradan, the captain of the bodyguard, was sent by Nebuchadnezzar to orchestrate the destruction of the city, which took place about a month after the wall was breached.

According to the NASB, the buildings that were burned with fire included **the king's palace and the houses of the people**. It is surprising that the temple of the Lord is not specifically mentioned here, as it is in 52:13, for it was the most important structure in Jerusalem. Some think that the temple is included under the umbrella of "the king's palace," for the two structures were adjacent to each other and were both heavily fortified. Others point out that the term "houses" is actually singular in the Hebrew text. "House" could be understood collectively (as most versions have), or it may point to a scribal eyeskip. The NEB and REB suggest that the original text read "the royal palace and the house *of the* LORD *and the houses* of the people" (emphasis added). In this case, the italicized portion has dropped out of the Hebrew text.

Verse 9. After carrying out the destruction of Jerusalem, **Nebuzaradan** deported the following groups to **Babylon**: (1) **the people who were left in the city**, (2) **the deserters who had gone over to him**, and (3) **the rest of the people who remained**. Based on the parallel in 52:15, some believe that the last category should read "artisans" instead of "people" (see NEB; REB; NJB).

Verse 10. Not all of the Jews were killed or taken captive. Instead, **some of the poorest people** were **left behind in the land of Judah**. These were given **vineyards and fields** to work, which indicates a redistribution of the land. The fact that these people **had nothing** emphasizes the total devastation and poverty of Judah. The poor were left behind because they lacked skills that would benefit Babylon. Moreover, without wealth or education, they posed little threat to the Babylonians.

GOD'S PROVIDENCE FOR HIS PROPHET (39:11–14)

¹¹Now Nebuchadnezzar king of Babylon gave orders about Jeremiah through Nebuzaradan the captain of the bodyguard, saying, ¹²"Take him and look after him, and do nothing harmful to him, but rather deal with him just as he tells you." ¹³So Nebuzaradan the captain of the bodyguard sent word, along with Nebushazban the Rab-saris, and Nergal-sar-ezer the Rab-

mag, and all the leading officers of the king of Babylon; ¹⁴they even sent and took Jeremiah out of the court of the guardhouse and entrusted him to Gedaliah, the son of Ahikam, the son of Shaphan, to take him home. So he stayed among the people.**

God's care and protection for Jeremiah were promised from the beginning (1:17–19). The promise was reaffirmed in 15:19–21, and Jeremiah finally learned to rely on it in 20:7–13, after twenty years of prophesying. It became a glorious reality another twenty years after that, unfolding as Jerusalem fell to Babylon.

Verse 11. How did **Jeremiah** gain so much respect in the eyes of **Nebuchadnezzar**? This king had slaughtered nations and put out the eyes of Zedekiah. Why did he show so much care and gentleness toward Jeremiah? (1) Perhaps Nebuchadnezzar had heard of Jeremiah's messages for Judah to surrender to Babylon (20:4–6; 21:3, 4; 38:1–3). (2) It may have been because Jeremiah had prophesied that Judah and the surrounding nations would be subject to Babylon (25:15–29; 27:6–11). In either case, this information may have come from Jewish deserters who had surrendered to the Babylonians.[6] (3) Jeremiah had possibly met Nebuchadnezzar when he went to the Euphrates River much earlier (13:4–7). Whatever the reason, the **king of Babylon gave orders** to protect the prophet **through Nebuzaradan the captain of the bodyguard.**

Verse 12. The orders of the king benefited Jeremiah in three ways: (1) *His provisions*— **"Take him and look after him"**; (2) *His protection*—**"Do nothing harmful to him"**; (3) *His position*—**"Deal with him just as he tells you."** The prophet ultimately got to choose between staying in the land or staying with Nebuzaradan (39:14; 40:4, 5).

Verse 13. These instructions were specific and God's providential care was impressive. God can work through the ruler of a great empire, who is truly His servant (27:6), and through mil-

---

[6]In the fourth year of Jehoiakim, Jeremiah had also prophesied that God would punish the king of Babylon and that nation, making it "an everlasting desolation" (25:1, 12–14). Later chapters indicate that he prophesied of the end of Babylon (50:1—51:58) in the fourth year of Zedekiah (51:59–64). None of this would boost Jeremiah's favor before Nebuchadnezzar.

itary men bent on international destruction, enacting a gentle graciousness to an incarcerated prophet.

These directions were distributed to the commanding **officers** and were dutifully carried out. Besides **Nebuzaradan the captain of the bodyguard**, who appears throughout the preceding verses, two other men are mentioned: **Nebushazban the Rab-saris** and **Nergal-sar-ezer the Rab-mag**. The latter individual is mentioned in verse 3. Some think that "Nebushazban" may be an alternate name for "Nebo-Sarsekim" (NCV) in verse 3; both names are modified by the same title, "Rab-saris."

Verse 14. Jeremiah was taken **out of the court of the guardhouse**, where he had been confined (see 32:2; 37:21; 38:28), and placed in the hands of **Gedaliah**. It is ironic that Jeremiah's own people had beaten him and kept him in prison, while the enemy set him free so he could go **home**.

Gedaliah was **the son of Ahikam, the son of Shaphan**. Shaphan, the grandfather of Gedaliah, was a high-ranking scribe during King Josiah's administration (see comments on 36:10). Ahikam, the father of Gedaliah, was the one who had earlier saved Jeremiah's life (see comments on 26:24). Gedaliah himself was later made the governor over those left in the land (40:5). A seal impression has been found at Lachish which bears his name. It says, "(Belonging) to Gedalyahu, over(seer of) the (royal) house."[7]

GOD'S PROVISION FOR A TRUSTING EUNUCH (39:15–18)

15Now the word of the LORD had come to Jeremiah while he was confined in the court of the guardhouse, saying, 16"Go and speak to Ebed-melech the Ethiopian, saying, 'Thus says the LORD of hosts, the God of Israel, "Behold, I am about to bring My words on this city for disaster and not for prosper-

---

[7]William W. Hallo, ed., *The Context of Scripture* (Boston: Brill, 2003), 2:198. For a photograph, see Steven Voth, "Jeremiah," in *Zondervan's Illustrated Bible Backgrounds Commentary*, vol. 4, *Isaiah, Jeremiah, Lamentations, Ezekiel, Daniel*, ed. John H. Walton (Grand Rapids, Mich.: Zondervan, 2009), 325.

ity; and they will take place before you on that day. ¹⁷**But I will deliver you on that day,"** declares the Lord, **"and you will not be given into the hand of the men whom you dread.** ¹⁸**For I will certainly rescue you, and you will not fall by the sword; but you will have your own life as booty, because you have trusted in Me,"** declares the Lord.'"

Verse 15. In the previous section, **Jeremiah** was released into the care of Gedaliah. Now the reader is taken back to a time shortly before the destruction of Jerusalem, when the prophet was still **confined in the court of the guardhouse.** There **the word of the Lord** came to him.

Verse 16. God instructed Jeremiah, saying, **"Go and speak to Ebed-melech the Ethiopian."** Even though he was confined, the prophet was allowed to have visitors and speak to those nearby. Ebed-melech has already been introduced as an important character, having rescued Jeremiah from the muddy cistern (38:7–13).

Jeremiah was to speak God's words to this eunuch regarding the downfall of Jerusalem: **"Behold, I am about to bring My words on this city for disaster and not for prosperity; and they will take place before you on that day."** Indeed, Ebed-melech would witness the breaching of the wall, the infiltration of the enemy, and perhaps even the burning of the city (39:2, 3, 8).

Verse 17. God promised His protection before the Babylonians conquered the city. He would **deliver** Ebed-melech. "Deliver" is from the Hebrew word נָצַל (*natsal*), which can also be translated "snatch away." It suggests the image of a shepherd snatching away his sheep from the mouths of wolves (1 Sam. 17:35; Ezek. 34:10; Amos 3:12).[8] This word implies that Ebed-melech would be in a dangerous situation.

By God's providence, Ebed-melech would **not be given into the hand of the men** that he feared. It has been suggested that he was afraid of the evil officials who were against Jeremiah

---

[8]Ludwig Koehler and Walter Baumgartner, *The Hebrew and Aramaic Lexicon of the Old Testament*, study ed., trans. and ed. M. E. J. Richardson (Boston: Brill, 2001), 1:717.

(38:1–4). After all, he had said that they had "acted wickedly" (38:9), and he had retrieved the prophet from the cistern to which they had consigned him (38:10–13). Nevertheless, the phrase **on that day**, repeated from verse 16, indicates that Ebed-melech was afraid of the Babylonian forces. Since he was an official in the king's palace (see comments on 38:7, 8), he feared being put to death. His fears were not unfounded, since many from the king's court were captured and executed (39:6; 52:10, 24–27).

Verse 18. God's promise of deliverance is further emphasized: **"For I will certainly rescue you."** In Hebrew, two different forms of the root word מָלַט (*malat*) appear together, underscoring the idea by repetition. This term is variously defined as "slip away," "escape," and "deliver."[9] Ironically, King Zedekiah could not escape from the Babylonians (39:4, 5), but God would deliver this official.

God would **not** allow Ebed-melech to **fall by the sword** of the Babylonians. Rather, he would **have** [his] **own life as booty**—that is, he would be preserved alive (21:9; 38:2; 45:5). This man was blessed because he **trusted** in the Lord. His reliance upon God is evident from the actions he took to spare Jeremiah's life in 38:7–13. Such trust builds conviction, which is the very foundation for commitment to the Creator.

APPLICATION

The Justice of God (Ch. 39)

God is not impassive, unfeeling, or unconcerned. He loves us. He cares about us (1 Pet. 5:7; 1 Jn. 4:8). He is a just and righteous God (Is. 45:21; Zeph. 3:5; 2 Tim. 4:8), who loves righteousness and hates iniquity (Ps. 45:6, 7; Prov. 6:16–19). While His patience may seem limitless, His justice demands that He take vengeance on evil deeds and evildoers (Deut. 32:35–39; Rom. 12:19). Too often people today, like Judah, depend on God's patience, developing ears that are deaf to His warnings. That arouses God's anger. God has a large arsenal from which He may

---

[9]Francis Brown, S. R. Driver, and Charles A. Briggs, *A Hebrew and English Lexicon of the Old Testament* (Oxford: Clarendon Press, 1972), 572.

attack to enact His justice. Since Nebuchadnezzar was God's servant (27:6), God had a powerful ally willing and ready to enact a day of justice and judgment on Judah. Blindness to danger and deaf ears to repeated warnings, while continuing with a mind set on idolatry and rebellion (44:14–23), offers no escape from the inevitable justice of the Lord. For any city or nation that persists in unfaithfulness and idolatry, there will always arrive an eleventh year, a fourth month and a ninth day—a day of reckoning with the Ruler of the universe (39:2; Gen. 15:13–16; 18:20–33; 19:24, 25; Ps. 66:5–7; Amos 1:2–10).

God's justice is encouraging and necessary in a world where all have sinned and fall short of the glory of God (Rom. 3:23). Punishment for crime and evil is in the best interest of free men (Eccles. 8:11, 12). Hell is an eternal warning that crime does not pay, and heaven is the harbor of hope for the righteous. If God took no action against evil and wrongdoing, all our tomorrows would be draped with a cloud of depression. One part of the God of love (1 Jn. 4:8) is a hate for folly and forces that hurt and divide (Prov. 6:16–19). If we are denied the inspired truth concerning His justice and judgments toward ungodliness, then we are left with a mantle of insecurity and hopelessness. However, if we are given His revelation of being enthroned over men and nations (Ps. 9:7–10; 103:19–22; Mt. 28:18–20; Rev. 3:21), that He will bring every thought and deed into His just judgment, with every secret thing (17:9, 10; Eccles. 12:13, 14), then confidence is restored that the righteous Judge will not tolerate that which blights and blasts, corrupts and condemns (Mt. 25:41–46; Rom. 14:10–12; 2 Cor. 5:10). Ultimately, all that is high and noble and pure will prevail (2 Cor. 6:14—7:1).

Certainly, we should not view the punishment being enacted on Jerusalem and its king as a vindictive, irresponsible, enjoyable act by God. Both time and revelation repeatedly tell the story of His longsuffering spirit, acting only when rebellious souls refuse to repent (2 Pet. 3:9). This fact was so dramatically demonstrated centuries later when Jesus stood at the edge of Jerusalem and tearfully lamented those words:

> Jerusalem, Jerusalem, who kills the prophets and stones

those who are sent to her! How often I wanted to gather your children together, the way a hen gathers her chicks under her wings, and you were unwilling. Behold, your house is being left to you desolate! (Mt. 23:37, 38; see Lk. 19:41).

Christ's sentence that day was quite similar to God's charge in Jeremiah's day, and the intervening centuries become a sobering echo of His patience and justice.

The Price Zedekiah Paid (39:1–8)
The downfall of this city, which God had set aside as the place to meet His people, had to be a horrifying and heart-rending experience. It had to be difficult for this weak king, who had repeatedly sought the easy way out.

Suddenly responsibilities he had dodged and divine revelations he had refused to face became reality. Consider the burdens he had to bear, gleaning a lesson on the painful price of shirked responsibility: (1) The city was given into the hands of the king of Babylon (39:1–3; see 21:4–14; 32:3). (2) Jerusalem was ultimately burned with fire, and its walls were broken down (39:8; see 34:2; 38:18, 23). (3) Zedekiah, attempting to escape, found that he could not do so (39:4, 5; see 32:4; 34:3; 38:18). (4) He was brought face to face with King Nebuchadnezzar (39:5). (5) Zedekiah's folly and weakness caused him to lose his sons, as they were slaughtered before his eyes (39:6; see 38:23). (6) He surely was taunted and mocked by women—even his wives—in this awful hour of slaughter and defeat (38:22). (7) Zedekiah's eyes were put out (39:7). At that moment, he must have had a haunting memory of those words about coming eye to eye with Nebuchadnezzar (32:4; 34:3). (8) As the blinded king walked in chains to Babylon, the sobering message that he would not see that land must have scorched his soul (Ezek. 12:12–16). His future promised only a plague of problems.

Did Zedekiah remember, with a sense of gratitude for God's mercy and grace, that he would die in peace and be honored in his death? (See 34:4, 5.) Does this mean that the wavering king finally mustered enough courage to repent of his many wrongs?

These questions are not answered by the text. Instead, it impresses upon us the gravity of sin's consequences. What a price Zedekiah paid for his weakness, waywardness, and wickedness!

Jeremiah and Jesus (39:14)

As Jerusalem was being destroyed, God providentially cared for Jeremiah. The Babylonians removed him from imprisonment and entrusted him to Gedaliah's care. A great statement about God's prophet is found in 39:14, which says, "So he stayed among the people." These words give us additional insights into Jeremiah's character.

He gave up a good life to suffer alongside his people. The next chapter says that Jeremiah had the option to go to Babylon under the care of Nebuzaradan, the head of Babylon's military forces (40:4, 5). He would have stayed in the officer's quarters, but he opted to stay in a destroyed region among his rebellious fellow countrymen.

He remained with them, even though they would reject his message. About forty years of ministry had proven that to be their true nature (7:27, 28), and the succeeding months would verify they had not changed (43:1, 2; 44:1–5).

He stayed with them, and they treated him poorly. The people forced Jeremiah to go into Egypt against his own divinely given orders (42:15, 16; 43:1–4). He loved them, even though they did not love him.

Truly, Jeremiah was a man of God. Every influence he had faced and would yet face among these people echoed a message of futility so far as gaining their favor was concerned. The response of those people identified no reason to stay with them. It had to be loyalty to God, not loyalty from those people, that led him to stay and continue to speak God's message to them.

Is there any parallel similar to this? Yes. Jesus labored among a people who would not believe Him (Mt. 13:14, 15; Jn. 5:39, 40), who were referred to repeatedly as "hypocrites" and "blind guides" (Mt. 23:13, 15, 16, 23, 25, 27, 29), and who would by force pressure rulers to crucify Him (Mt. 27:22–26; Jn. 19:4–16).

Why would Jeremiah and Jesus willingly work among such people? Because such a standard in service and sacrifice in time verifies God's love and helps redeem souls (see Dan. 9:1–19; Lk. 23:34; Acts 2:36–41; 6:7; 2 Cor. 5:14–17; 1 Jn. 4:19).

How are we affected by the examples of Jeremiah and Jesus, manifesting a determined devotion to still serve among those people? How does it affect us to know God loves us that much? (See Rom. 5:6–11.)

CHAPTER 40

THE FOLLOW-UP AFTER JERUSALEM'S FALL

Chapter 40 tells about the events that unfolded after Jerusalem fell to the Babylonian forces in 586 B.C. The first section records Jeremiah's movement from Jerusalem to Mizpah and his choice to stay with the remnant there (40:1-5). The second section informs us about the provincial government set up by Babylon, with Gedaliah serving as governor over the people (40:6-12). The final section reveals a potential assassination threat to Gedaliah's life, along with a proposed solution by Johanan (40:13-16).

JEREMIAH SET FREE (40:1-5)

The Military Commander's Grasp Of the Situation (40:1-3)

¹**The word which came to Jeremiah from the L**ORD **after Nebuzaradan captain of the bodyguard had released him from Ramah, when he had taken him bound in chains among all the exiles of Jerusalem and Judah who were being exiled to Babylon.** ²**Now the captain of the bodyguard had taken Jeremiah and said to him, "The L**ORD **your God promised this calamity against this place;** ³**and the L**ORD **has brought it on and done just as He promised. Because you people sinned against the L**ORD **and did not listen to His voice, therefore this thing has happened to you."**

Verse 1. In 39:11-14, **Nebuzaradan captain of the bodyguard**

JEREMIAH 40

had been instructed by Nebuchadnezzar to take care of **Jeremiah**, treating him with kindness. As a result, he released the prophet from the court of the guardhouse and entrusted him to the care of Gedaliah. Therefore, what is the meaning of verse 1, which says that Jeremiah had been transported to **Ramah**, along with **all the exiles of Jerusalem and Judah, bound in chains**? Some think that the prophet was released in Jerusalem, accidentally arrested again, taken to Ramah, and then released again. J. A. Thompson referred to this possible re-arrest as "an embarrassing mistake" made by the Babylonian soldiers.[1] Others, however, believe that 39:14 is a summary recording the beginning and ending of the Babylonian's treatment of Jeremiah. In this reconstruction, which is more likely, he was taken from the court of the guardhouse, transported along with the exiles in fetters to Ramah, and then released into Gedaliah's care.

Ramah was located about five miles north of Jerusalem (see comments on 31:15). R. K. Harrison referred to this place as "a general staging-area from which the deportees would leave for Babylonia."[2]

After Jeremiah had been **released** at Ramah, he was given a message **from the LORD**. However, the only message in this context is found on the lips of Nebuzaradan, the captain of the body guard (40:2–5). It is possible that God communicated His word to Jeremiah through this pagan commander.

Verses 2, 3. Nebuzaradan showed detailed insight concerning *what* was happening to Judah and *why* it was happening. Was this pagan military leader so well informed because **Jeremiah** had been commissioned by God as "a prophet to the nations" (1:5)? We should not be surprised concerning Nebuzaradan's grasp of this situation. Numerous biblical examples show how foreign rulers and dignitaries were acquainted with divine inten-

---

[1] J. A. Thompson, *The Book of Jeremiah*, The New International Commentary on the Old Testament (Grand Rapids, Mich.: Wm. B. Eerdmans Publishing Co., 1980), 651.

[2] R. K. Harrison, *Jeremiah and Lamentations: An Introduction and Commentary*, Tyndale Old Testament Commentaries (Downers Grove, Ill.: Inter-Varsity Press, 1973), 159.

tions.³ It may even be that God spoke directly to Nebuzaradan. Regardless of how the information came, he knew that **the Lord** had **promised this calamity against** Judah and Jerusalem (19:15; 23:12; 32:23). He also knew why it was being done: Because the **people** had **sinned against the Lord** and refused to **listen to His voice** (37:2). They had no respect for God and made no response to God. Sometimes the people of the world have a better grasp of God's will than His own people do (see Mt. 23:23, 24; Lk. 16:8).

The Military Commander's Care for Jeremiah (40:4, 5)

⁴"But now, behold, I am freeing you today from the chains which are on your hands. If you would prefer to come with me to Babylon, come along, and I will look after you; but if you would prefer not to come with me to Babylon, never mind. Look, the whole land is before you; go wherever it seems good and right for you to go." ⁵As Jeremiah was still not going back, he said, "Go on back then to Gedaliah the son of Ahikam, the son of Shaphan, whom the king of Babylon has appointed over the cities of Judah, and stay with him among the people; or else go anywhere it seems right for you to go." So the captain of the bodyguard gave him a ration and a gift and let him go.

Verse 4. Jeremiah had been threatened, mocked, beaten, imprisoned, and placed in chains (11:18–20; 18:18–23; 20:2, 7, 8; 32:2; 37:13–16, 21; 38:6, 13, 28; 40:1). These ordeals must have made him especially grateful when Nebuzaradan offered him kindness and a choice. Nebuzaradan said, **"I am freeing you today from the chains which are on your hands."** Most people live and die without ever being placed in chains. Those who have been bound know what a special moment it is when one is set free. Jeremiah surely knew many who would not be set free that day, but were just beginning a long, trying journey to Babylon.

One option granted to Jeremiah was this: **"If you would pre-**

---

³These rulers include: Cyrus (Ezra 1:1–4; Is. 44:26–28); Darius the Mede (Ezra 6:1–14); Huram, king of Tyre (2 Chron. 2:11–16); and Pharaoh Neco (2 Chron. 35:20, 21).

fer to come with me to Babylon, come along, and I will look after you." The phrase "look after you" echoes the instructions given by Nebuchadnezzar ("look after him") in 39:12. Nebuzaradan was saying that he would extend compassion, pay attention to, and take care of the prophet.[4] This offer was inviting, considering the environment and the circumstances in which Jeremiah had been living. He was being offered the luxuries Babylon could supply, much as Moses was offered the pleasures of Egypt (Heb. 11:24–27). He had the opportunity to live at the same level of the leader of Babylon's mighty armed forces. The fact that Jeremiah refused the offer proves forcefully that he was not "going over to the Chaldeans" (37:13). He was God's man all the way.

Another option was presented to Jeremiah: **"If you would prefer not to come with me to Babylon, never mind. Look, the whole land is before you; go wherever it seems good and right for you to go."** This language is reminiscent of Abraham's conversation with Lot when the two men parted ways. Giving his nephew the first choice, he asked, "Is not the whole land before you?" (Gen. 13:9). The choice given to Jeremiah by Nebuzaradan reflects Nebuchadnezzar's instructions to "deal with him just as he tells you" (39:12). The terms "good" and "right" may also reveal the high level of respect Nebuzaradan had for Jeremiah. Knowing he was a man of convictions, this military commander knew that the prophet's life could not be tranquil until he was in the right place.

Verse 5. As Jeremiah was still not going back is one rendering of a difficult Hebrew phrase, whose meaning is uncertain. The NCV has "Before Jeremiah turned to leave," whereas the AB has "While [Jeremiah] was hesitating." Apparently, the prophet did not make an immediate decision.

Nebuzaradan gave a third option which was more specific: **"Go on back then to Gedaliah the son of Ahikam, the son of Shaphan, whom the king of Babylon has appointed over the cities of Judah, and stay with him among the people."** Nebuchadnezzar had appointed Gedaliah as governor over the poor

---

[4]Since Jeremiah was a genuine prophet, being his benefactor may have added to Nebuzaradan's status in Babylonia. (Harrison, 159–60.)

people left in the land (2 Kings 25:22). This appeared to be a wise selection, since for three generations his family members had been influential and had conducted themselves in a commendable way. They had also been loyal friends to Jeremiah (see comments on 26:24; 29:3; 36:10, 25; 39:14).

Jeremiah decided to live among his people, under the rule of Gedaliah. It seems that he wanted to stay and be a part of Judah's future in the land. Nebuzaradan **gave him a ration** of food (see 52:33, 34) as well as **a gift** (see Esther 2:18), and then he **let him go.** Jeremiah had boldly and clearly prophesied of the end of Babylon (25:12–16; 50:1—51:58). Nevertheless, by the providence of God, he was shown special favor from the leader of the enemy forces (see Ps. 23:5). Indeed, he was even rewarded by the military power that had crushed his homeland. God truly provided for and protected His prophet.

JUDAH'S PROVINCIAL GOVERNMENT SET UP BY BABYLON (40:6–12)

⁶Then Jeremiah went to Mizpah to Gedaliah the son of Ahikam and stayed with him among the people who were left in the land.

⁷Now all the commanders of the forces that were in the field, they and their men, heard that the king of Babylon had appointed Gedaliah the son of Ahikam over the land and that he had put him in charge of the men, women and children, those of the poorest of the land who had not been exiled to Babylon. ⁸So they came to Gedaliah at Mizpah, along with Ishmael the son of Nethaniah, and Johanan and Jonathan the sons of Kareah, and Seraiah the son of Tanhumeth, and the sons of Ephai the Netophathite, and Jezaniah the son of the Maacathite, both they and their men. ⁹Then Gedaliah the son of Ahikam, the son of Shaphan, swore to them and to their men, saying, "Do not be afraid of serving the Chaldeans; stay in the land and serve the king of Babylon, that it may go well with you. ¹⁰Now as for me, behold, I am going to stay at Mizpah to stand for you before the Chaldeans who come to us; but as for you, gather in wine and summer fruit and oil and put them in your

storage vessels, and live in your cities that you have taken over." ¹¹Likewise, also all the Jews who were in Moab and among the sons of Ammon and in Edom and who were in all the other countries, heard that the king of Babylon had left a remnant for Judah, and that he had appointed over them Gedaliah the son of Ahikam, the son of Shaphan. ¹²Then all the Jews returned from all the places to which they had been driven away and came to the land of Judah, to Gedaliah at Mizpah, and gathered in wine and summer fruit in great abundance.

Verse 6. Jeremiah left Ramah, where the Jewish exiles had been taken in preparation for their journey to Babylonia (40:1). He **went to Mizpah**, which is usually identified with Tell en-Nasbeh. It was located a few miles north of Ramah, that is, seven or eight miles north of Jerusalem. This fortified site was situated in the northern territory of Benjamin (Josh. 18:21, 26). Mizpah had been an important place for Israel's sacred assemblies prior to the establishment of the monarchy (Judg. 20:1; 21:1; 1 Sam. 7:5–12). In fact, Saul had been anointed there as Israel's first king by the prophet Samuel (1 Sam. 10:17–25). Now, with Jerusalem in ruins, Mizpah regained importance, serving as the location for Judah's government. Jeremiah went there to stay with **Gedaliah**, who had been appointed governor over what was left of the cities of Judah (40:5).

Verse 7. After **Gedaliah** took office, news of his appointment over **the poorest of the land** (39:10) reached **all the commanders of the forces that were in the field, they and their men**. Who were these soldiers? John Bright described them as "the wreckage of Judah's army, isolated detachments of which had escaped the Babylonian 'mop-up' and still maintained themselves in out-of-the-way places."[5] Apparently, the Babylonians did not view these isolated units as a serious threat.

Verse 8. The commanders and their troops **came to Gedaliah at Mizpah**, appearing to place themselves under his authority. However, as the narrative proceeds, it becomes evident that

---

[5]John Bright, *Jeremiah*, The Anchor Bible (Garden City, N.Y.: Doubleday & Company, 1965), 253.

not everyone was on his side. Time would prove that he was too trusting to serve well as the leader of this rebel remnant.

The first man on the list of commanders, **Ishmael the son of Nethaniah,** would eventually assassinate Gedaliah (40:14; 41:1, 2). He is described as belonging to "the royal family" and being "one of the chief officers of the king" (41:1). A clay seal impression (bulla) has been discovered from the end of the seventh or early sixth century B.C. which says, "Belonging to Ishmael, the king's son."[6] It likely refers to the man in this verse. In this case, "the king's son" is probably used figuratively (see comments on 36:26; 38:6).

Next on the list are two brothers, **Johanan and Jonathan the sons of Kareah.** Johanan was the one who tried to warn Gedaliah of the plot against his life. He even volunteered to intervene by killing Ishmael, but Gedaliah would not believe his message (40:13–16). After Gedaliah's demise, Johanan chased after Ishmael and recovered the Jewish people who had been taken captive (41:11–16). This commander was instrumental in leading the remnant into Egypt (41:17—43:7).

Others mentioned include **Seraiah the son of Tanhumeth** and **the sons of Ephai the Netophathite.** The words "the sons of Ephai" are missing from 2 Kings 25:23, which simply has "Seraiah the son of Tanhumeth the Netophathite." Netophah was a village about three miles southeast of Bethlehem, on the way to Tekoa (see Ezra 2:21, 22; Neh. 7:26). The people who lived there had descended from Caleb (1 Chron. 2:50, 54), who had faithfully served God during the periods of Wilderness Wandering and Conquest.

The last name on the list is **Jezaniah the son of the Maacathite.** Archaeologists have discovered an ancient seal at Tell en-Nasbeh (Mizpah) bearing the name "Jezaniah," along with the title "servant of the king." It may have belonged to this man (see comments on 35:3).

Verse 9. Gedaliah made an oath to these men, promising that if they would **stay in the land and serve the king of Baby-**

---

[6]Gabriel Barkay, "A Bulla of Ishmael, the King's Son," *Bulletin of the American Schools of Oriental Research*, no. 290, 291 (May–August 1993): 109.

lon, things would **go well** for them (see comments on 38:19, 20). Gedaliah was discouraging these men from planning any counter-attacks against the Babylonian army or making alliances with other nations to fight against them. Gedaliah's charge stands parallel to the preaching of Jeremiah, who urged the people to surrender to the yoke of Nebuchadnezzar and live (27:11, 12; 29:5–7). God planned for Judah to serve Babylon as part of the reformation process to ultimately redeem His people. Respect for God and respect for their captors were two reasons to pursue that course.

Verse 10. Gedaliah promised to fulfill his intercessory role, remaining **at Mizpah to stand for** the people of Judah **before the Chaldeans who** came to monitor the region's activities.[7] He would faithfully carry out his responsibilities as their governor, living and working at that location.

For this arrangement to be successful, the commanders and their men would have to settle into a normal way of life. Gedaliah gave them this counsel: **"Gather in wine and summer fruit and oil and put them in your storage vessels, and live in your cities that you have taken over."** Jerusalem fell in the summer of 586 B.C., just before the harvest of grapes, figs, and pomegranates. The Gezer Calendar indicates that the summer fruit was harvested from the middle of August to the middle of September, whereas the olive crop was brought in from the middle of September to the middle of November.[8]

Verse 11. In addition to the commanders and their troops, other **Jews** learned that Nebuchadnezzar **had left a remnant for Judah** in the land and that **he had appointed over them Gedaliah**. These people had escaped from Judah and Jerusalem and had taken refuge **in Moab**, in **Ammon**, and **in Edom**—the bordering countries to the east and the south. Zedekiah himself had been fleeing to Ammon or Moab when he was caught near Jericho (39:4, 5).

Verse 12. These **Jews** left the countries where they found ref-

---

[7]In 15:1, Moses and Samuel are hypothetically portrayed as "stand[ing] before" God in an intercessory role.

[8]For a translation, interpretation, and photographs of the Gezer Calendar, see G. Ernest Wright, *Biblical Archaeology*, rev. and exp. ed. (Philadelphia: The Westminster Press, 1962), 183–87.

uge and went back to **Judah**. They gave their allegiance **to Gedaliah at Mizpah**, and peace prevailed in the land. They settled in various towns and worked vigorously. God blessed their harvest, as they **gathered in wine and summer fruit in great abundance**. Part of this harvest would have been given to the king of Babylon as tribute.[9]

All of this sounds good and encouraging. God's mercy was granting these surviving souls another chance. Sadly, the evil influences that had doomed the nation would surface to breed disaster among those remaining in the land.

JOHANAN'S ATTEMPT TO PROTECT GEDALIAH (40:13–16)

¹³Now Johanan the son of Kareah and all the commanders of the forces that were in the field came to Gedaliah at Mizpah ¹⁴and said to him, "Are you well aware that Baalis the king of the sons of Ammon has sent Ishmael the son of Nethaniah to take your life?" But Gedaliah the son of Ahikam did not believe them. ¹⁵Then Johanan the son of Kareah spoke secretly to Gedaliah in Mizpah, saying, "Let me go and kill Ishmael the son of Nethaniah, and not a man will know! Why should he take your life, so that all the Jews who are gathered to you would be scattered and the remnant of Judah would perish?" ¹⁶But Gedaliah the son of Ahikam said to Johanan the son of Kareah, "Do not do this thing, for you are telling a lie about Ishmael."

Verses 13, 14. Johanan and the other **commanders** (40:8) went **to Gedaliah at Mizpah** with a report about **Baalis**, who was **the king of the sons of Ammon**. While little is known about this Ammonite king, his name has been discovered on two archaeological finds. The first is a small clay cone that may have been used as a stopper for a small jug. An impression on the end of the cone says, "Belonging to Milqom, servant of Ba'alis." Milqom was presumably a high official in King Baalis' administration. The

---

[9]Josephus *Antiquities* 10.9.3.

second find is a royal seal bearing the image of a winged sphinx. Although the script is damaged, scholars are confident that it once read, "Belonging to Ba'alis, King of the Sons of Ammon."[10]

The report of the commanders was that Baalis had **sent Ishmael** (40:8) to kill **Gedaliah**. Although that report proved to be true (41:1, 2), Gedaliah **did not believe them**. Concerning this conspiracy, Philip J. King contended that Baalis was trying to gain more power and influence over the land of Judah, taking advantage of its weakened condition.[11] The plot could also be viewed as a strike against the Babylonians, who had put Gedaliah in power. Baalis was certainly unhappy with Gedaliah's policy of yielding to Nebuchadnezzar (40:9). A few years earlier, the Ammonites had been a part of an anti-Babylonian coalition. They had joined forces with King Zedekiah of Judah and the kings of other neighboring peoples, including Edom, Moab, Tyre, and Sidon (27:3).[12]

Verse 15. After the commanders warned **Gedaliah** of the conspiracy, **Johanan** talked with him **secretly**. He volunteered for a covert operation: **"Let me go and kill Ishmael . . . , and not a man will know!"** Johanan's conduct in this matter is worthy of consideration. He knew the facts about Ishmael's intent and had good reason for removing him from the scene: (1) to save Gedaliah's **life**; (2) to prevent **the Jews** who had returned to Gedaliah from being **scattered**; and (3) to keep **the remnant of Judah** from being destroyed.

Verse 16. Gedaliah answered **Johanan**, saying, **"Do not do this thing, for you are telling a lie about Ishmael."** The response by the governor demonstrates that he was naive about the situation. This kind of disposition can be dangerous when good men get involved in government leadership. One may want to assume the best in others and build confidences among fellow leaders. However, he must deal with all citizens, including both the good

---

[10]Robert Deutsch, "Seal of Ba'alis Surfaces: Ammonite King Plotted Murder of Judahite Governor," *Biblical Archaeology Review*, 25, no. 2 (March–April 1999): 46–49, 66.

[11]Philip J. King, *Jeremiah: An Archaeological Companion* (Louisville, Ky.: Westminster/John Knox Press, 1993), 98.

[12]Ibid.

and the bad. Due to the many corrupt influences in Judah, Jeremiah had warned, "Let everyone be on guard against his neighbor, and do not trust any brother" (9:4). Nevertheless, no record indicates that Gedaliah investigated this matter. In this case, Jeremiah's words went unheeded.

Gedaliah forbade Johanan to pursue the matter; the commander's request to kill Ishmael, ending his plot of treason, was denied. Johanan adhered to Gedaliah's decision, even though it was against his better judgment and even though he had been called a liar. Later, Johanan assumed leadership of those remaining in Judah and refused to listen to the truth himself (43:1–7). Man is indeed frail and fallible!

APPLICATION

Making Godly Decisions (Ch. 40)

In the midst of dark clouds and destruction in the land, in spite of continued waywardness and weakness among those remaining there, we see a ray of devotion to God. Jeremiah's situation here is reminiscent of that significant moment when all the apostles forsook Jesus and fled (Mt. 26:56), yet Christ steadfastly marched forward to the cross (see Lk. 9:51).

Jeremiah 40:1–6 contains a vital message for those who seek to serve the Lord. Jeremiah's choice of where to serve obviously was not a matter of convenience or money. The better possibilities in both areas would have been Nebuzaradan's extended honorable position in the land of exile. However, Jeremiah had a work to do for God among his people, and he stayed to accomplish it. Just as Ezekiel served among God's people in Babylon, so Jeremiah would serve among this remnant that eventually went to Egypt. In both areas, God's mission would be fulfilled—"They will know that a prophet has been among them" (Ezek. 2:5).

In modern times, preachers of the gospel often face the dilemma of where to live and serve. Heads of families in our mobile age often face a similar challenge as they deal with travel away from home, job relocation, and promotions in the cooperate chain. How will a move or time away from home affect family members? Jeremiah's example will not supply all the answers to making these difficult decisions, but it demonstrates that consecration before God must take priority over personal preference, prosperity, or position (see Mt. 26:36–46; Acts 18:9–11; 1 Cor. 16:8, 9).

As the Lord's servants, we will wrestle with the decisions of where to go and what service to render. May we always be like Christ and Jeremiah—determined that God's will be done. Providence can then be a divine course-setter.

CHAPTER 41
THE ASSASSINATION OF GEDALIAH

From 605 to 586 B.C., Judah and Jerusalem had been a virtual battleground. Ruination from fighting and fire had left beautiful buildings, including God's temple, a scene of rubble and debris. Most of the inhabitants of Judah and Jerusalem had been taken as captives to wherever Nebuchadnezzar, king of Babylon, had chosen to scatter them throughout his empire. The city had been vacated, with only a few Jews remaining in the city or near the city.

It would be expected that those remaining in Judah would huddle together, pray, and keep every covenant principle God had given them to stabilize their bewildered spirits. If there ever was a time that a calling upon God should be a natural response, this time following the destruction of Jerusalem was that time. Unfortunately, this chapter has a different story to tell. It is a clear warning to those who are living in disobedience. It illustrates that a return to God through penitence and forsaking sin may not always be the chief longing of the those who are suffering (see Heb. 6:1–6).

The narrative of those who remained in Judah bears witness to several atrocities. Ironically, it begins with a fellowship meal which became the setting for an assassination (41:1–3). The killing, however, did not end with the murder of Judah's governor, Gedaliah. His close associates were also viciously killed (41:4–10), as the murder developed into a massacre. Then, the chapter climaxes with the taking of hostages, a brief civil war, and a regrouping for a trip to Egypt (41:11–18). Even though this chapter is short in length, it involves much bloodshed and rebellion.

JEREMIAH 41

THE MURDER AT MEALTIME (41:1–3)

¹**In the seventh month Ishmael the son of Nethaniah, the son of Elishama, of the royal family and one of the chief officers of the king, along with ten men, came to Mizpah to Gedaliah the son of Ahikam. While they were eating bread together there in Mizpah,** ²**Ishmael the son of Nethaniah and the ten men who were with him arose and struck down Gedaliah the son of Ahikam, the son of Shaphan, with the sword and put to death the one whom the king of Babylon had appointed over the land.** ³**Ishmael also struck down all the Jews who were with him, that is with Gedaliah at Mizpah, and the Chaldeans who were found there, the men of war.**

Earlier, Johanan had warned Gedaliah that some officers around him might seek to kill him. Johanan was especially concerned about the sinister designs of Ishmael, a fellow commander, who, with Johanan, had joined Gedaliah at Mizpah (40:13, 14). Because of the threats Ishmael had made, Johanan had even offered to kill him and get him out of the way (40:15). Gedaliah had refused to believe that a trusted soldier like Ishmael had made such threats. He, therefore, would not allow Johanan to lay a hand on Ishmael (40:16). However, all that Johanan had predicted about Ishmael's intent unfolded in this awful scene at Mizpah.

Verse 1. The time reference given for this event is simply **In the seventh month**—that is, it occurred in the month of Tishri (September–October). From Jeremiah's account in 39:1, 2, it is clear that Jerusalem fell in Zedekiah's eleventh year, the fourth month, the ninth day (July 18, 586 B.C.). It is possible that only some three months later, in the seventh month, the events of this verse began to take place. It is also possible that a few years passed before these events took place. After all, the last Jewish exile by the Babylonians in 582 B.C. could have been a response to the atrocities in this chapter (see comments on 52:28–30).

Ishmael was **one of the chief officers**, and he belonged to **the royal family**. He had blue blood in his veins and should have possessed sterling character. However, he is seen here to be an ambitious, ruthless, violent character. Ishmael is also described as the grandson of **Elishama**, a scribe who had heard the scroll read by Baruch (36:12–26).

Ishmael and **ten men** came to **Gedaliah** at **Mizpah**. As a governor whose heart went out to all who had been left behind when Jerusalem fell, Gedaliah invited Ishmael and his men to sit down with him for a fellowship meal. **While they were eating,** a murderous intent was carried out. All the togetherness, stability, and prosperity that Gedaliah had fostered among the remnant living in the land began to unravel (see 40:12). One evil deed followed another.

Verse 2. Ishmael . . . and the ten men who were with him perpetrated the crime. At an opportune moment, they **struck down Gedaliah the son of Ahikam, the son of Shaphan, with the sword** [putting] **to death the one whom the king of Babylon had appointed over the land**. This murder of Gedaliah—Babylon's appointee, the man in charge of bringing peace, order, and leadership to this devastated region—was catastrophic. Gedaliah had made some inroads toward rebuilding what remained; but, with his death, all seemed to be lost.

Ishmael's actions bordered on insanity. It could well be that he believed that he had been slighted when Nebuchadnezzar appointed a governor outside the royal seed. Driven by blinding hatred and jealousy, he yielded to the evil that sought to control him. How insidious jealousy is!

Verse 3. The victims of this assassination plot fell in three stages of destruction. The first to fall was Gedaliah (41:2). Next came **all the Jews . . . with Gedaliah**. Perhaps these were just the ones who were sharing in the festivities at that banquet. Apparently, Ishmael had resolved that no witnesses would remain alive. Third, the Babylonian soldiers or bodyguards, **the men of war**, were killed. These men may have represented the armed forces who were active in that area. Ishmael did not want any interference from them, so he removed them with his sword. Because of the nature of the occasion, armaments (except those involved in the plot) would have been laid aside. Gedaliah, in sacred hospitality, welcomed Ishmael and his men to his table. Killing him was a cunning and devilish, ruthless, and senseless deed. It also violated one of the most hallowed characteristics of that time—the shelter of hospitality extended by one man to another. However, Ishmael's killings had just begun.

THE MURDERS THAT FOLLOWED (41:4–10)

⁴Now it happened on the next day after the killing of Gedaliah, when no one knew about it, ⁵that eighty men came from Shechem, from Shiloh, and from Samaria with their beards shaved off and their clothes torn and their bodies gashed, having grain offerings and incense in their hands to bring to the house of the LORD. ⁶Then Ishmael the son of Nethaniah went out from Mizpah to meet them, weeping as he went; and as he met them, he said to them, "Come to Gedaliah the son of Ahikam!" ⁷Yet it turned out that as soon as they came inside the city, Ishmael the son of Nethaniah and the men that were with him slaughtered them and cast them into the cistern. ⁸But ten men who were found among them said to Ishmael, "Do not put us to death; for we have stores of wheat, barley, oil and honey hidden in the field." So he refrained and did not put them to death along with their companions.

⁹Now as for the cistern where Ishmael had cast all the corpses of the men whom he had struck down because of Gedaliah, it was the one that King Asa had made on account of Baasha, king of Israel; Ishmael the son of Nethaniah filled it with the slain. ¹⁰Then Ishmael took captive all the remnant of the people who were in Mizpah, the king's daughters and all the people who were left in Mizpah, whom Nebuzaradan the captain of the bodyguard had put under the charge of Gedaliah the son of Ahikam; thus Ishmael the son of Nethaniah took them captive and proceeded to cross over to the sons of Ammon.

Verse 4. Somehow, the foregoing deeds were kept secret a little while, for **the next day after the killing of Gedaliah, . . . no one knew about it**. Ishmael was managing to keep his murderous escapades quiet until he had received an opportunity to move on to his next conquests. His ultimate goals are uncertain, but it must be that he was seeking to take control of the whole area.

Verse 5. Eighty men, obviously in mourning, arrived from **Shechem, Shiloh,** and **Samaria.** They came **with their beards shaved off and their clothes torn and their bodies gashed**, indicating that they were in great grief. Their bodies had been "gashed," an action they had taken even though such conduct as this was condemned in God's Old Testament laws (Lev. 19:27, 28; Deut. 14:1; see 1 Kings 18:28; Is. 15:2). They had come expressing the greatest of sorrow over the destruction of the temple and Jerusalem. They were on their way to "the house of the LORD," which at that time lay in rubble, to make some **grain offerings and incense**, which would express their broken spirits over Jerusalem. It is possible that some types of offerings were still being made at the location of the temple—maybe not blood sacrifices, but cereal and incense offerings. Since it was the seventh month, these offerings could have been related to the Feast of Tabernacles (Lev. 23:34; see Zech. 7:5).

Verse 6. Word about these mourners reached Ishmael. He went out to meet them, **weeping as he went**, feigning deep grief at what had happened, and welcomed them to come and express their condolences to Gedaliah. **He said to them, "Come to Gedaliah the son of Ahikam!"** Ishmael, deceptive in each move, decided that he could not allow these eighty men to live. Their presence confused his plans and called for the use of his sword.

Verse 7. What a dramatic, conniving character Ishmael was! He used a good name for a bad cause, urging these men to come and meet with Gedaliah. **As soon as they came inside the city, Ishmael** seduced them into his trap and killed seventy of them, disposing of the bodies of these slain men by casting them **into the cistern**. Immediately hiding the bodies was Ishmael's method of concealing his dastardly deed. Through death, these men went to meet Gedaliah! They must have been innocent men who had come to pay their respects concerning the great destruction, but they had shown up at the wrong time.

Verse 8. It is clear that the massacre was systematically carried out, with even some time being allowed for discussion and dialogue. **Ten men . . . found among them** cried out. Seeing they were next in line for slaughter, these men pleaded for a hearing.

They offered their possessions for their lives. They urged, **"Do not put us to death; for we have stores of wheat, barley, oil and honey hidden in the field."** They would gladly give up the produce they had in storage to avoid the merciless end met by those whose bodies were in the nearby cistern. Perhaps Ishmael needed supplies to carry out the next phase of his plan. Agreeing to such a exchange, **he refrained and did not put them to death along with their companions**. Their produce might even be a bargaining point that Ishmael could use when he made his way "over to the sons of Ammon" and sought to link up with them (41:10; see 40:14).

Verse 9. The **cistern** became a significant landmark in this chain of notorious events. It was **where Ishmael had cast all the corpses of the men whom he had struck down because of Gedaliah**. The phrase "because of Gedaliah" is somewhat obscure to us. The Hebrew has "by the hand [יָד, *yad*] of Gedaliah." The NASB begins the phrase with "because," but the writer may have intended a figurative use of the phrase which would mean "alongside of." The ASV has "by the side of." It appears that the seventy bodies were thrown into the cistern where the body of Gedaliah had already been cast.

In a historical aside, Jeremiah said that the "cistern" **was the one that King Asa had made on account of Baasha, king of Israel**. This "cistern" had been built some three hundred years earlier by King Asa, apparently when he was fortifying or renovating Geba and Mizpah. Baasha had made Ramah into a blockade to prevent his citizens from migrating to southern Israel. After Baasha had been driven from Ramah by Asa and Ben-hadad, Asa took the materials that Baasha had used at Ramah and used them to refurbish these two cities (1 Kings 15:17–22; 2 Chron. 16:1–6). In the process of completing these building projects, he must have dug this cistern.

Verse 10. Ishmael took captive all the remnant of the people who were in Mizpah, the king's daughters and all the people who were left in Mizpah. These were people who were staying around Gedaliah because of the hope his governorship had brought them. The captives Ishmael took included "the king's daughters." The Hebrew word for "daughter," בַּת (*bath*), can have a wide range of meanings. It can refer to a daughter, maiden, princess, half-sister, or granddaughter. Any female offspring of the wives, servants, or concubines of King Zedekiah could have been included in the word.[1] Zedekiah's sons were all killed (39:5, 6), and his "daughters," whoever they were, remained in the land (see 38:22).

Those left in and around Jerusalem had been placed under the care of **Nebuzaradan the captain of the bodyguard**, the chief officer of Nebuchadnezzar, who oversaw the final details of the capture and destruction of Jerusalem (39:9–14; 40:1–5; 52:12–30). He had chosen to put them **under the charge of Gedaliah the son of Ahikam**. These men, women, and children had no local, civic leadership other than Gedaliah. In light of who they were and what he could do with them, **Ishmael . . . took them captive**. He then **proceeded to cross over to the sons of Ammon**. Herding his captives like chattel, Ishmael was headed to Baalis, the Ammonite king, for further negotiations.

THE MULTIPLIED TRAGEDY (41:11–18)

Ishmael's Escape (41:11–15)

[11]But Johanan the son of Kareah and all the commanders of the forces that were with him heard of all the evil that Ishmael the son of Nethaniah had done. [12]So they took all the men and went to fight with Ishmael the son of Nethaniah and they found him by the great pool that is in Gibeon. [13]Now as soon as all the people who were with Ishmael saw Johanan the son of Kareah and the commanders of the forces that were with him, they were glad. [14]So all the people whom Ishmael had taken captive from Mizpah turned around and came back, and went to Johanan the son of Kareah. [15]But Ishmael the son of

---

[1]Francis Brown, S. R. Driver, and Charles A. Briggs, *A Hebrew and English Lexicon of the Old Testament* (Oxford: Clarendon Press, 1972), 123.

Nethaniah escaped from Johanan with eight men and went to the sons of Ammon.

Verse 11. Ishmael was bold as he attacked defenseless people, but there is no indication that he was ready for a face-to-face confrontation with **Johanan . . . and all the commanders of the forces that were with him**. Johanan, in contrast, was ready to take action when he found out what had happened. Having **heard of all the evil that Ishmael . . . had done**, Johanan was obviously ready to attack whenever he confronted him. His confident air was indicated by his earlier recommendation that Gedaliah allow him to kill Ishmael (40:15).

Verse 12. Johanan and his forces traveled hurriedly to Gibeon, a city of the tribe of Benjamin (Josh. 18:21–25). They arrived, ready **to fight with Ishmael**. Johanan **found him by the great pool that is in Gibeon**. The captives were no doubt distraught as they made their way along, not knowing what they were going to face next. The "great pool" could well be the rock-hewn pool that has been found at el-Jib, thought to be ancient Gibeon (see 2 Sam. 2:13).[2]

Verse 13. As soon as all the people who were with Ishmael saw Johanan . . . they were glad. Their glimpse of Johanan brought them hope, life, and possibilities that they thought had been lost at Mizpah.

Verse 14. At the sight of their possible deliverers, they broke from those who controlled them, leaving Ishmael behind them, and ran toward Johanan. **So all the people . . . turned around and came back, and went to Johanan.** In a rush of confidence, they seized the opportunity, fled, and left Ishmael to face his pursuers.

Verse 15. Ishmael . . . escaped from Johanan with eight men. Ishmael had ten men at first (41:1), but apparently two were killed before they could join the others and head toward Ammon. Ishmael was running for cover to "escape" (מָלַט, *malat*) the fierce army of Johanan. (For *malat*, see comments on 39:18.)

And [he] **went to the sons of Ammon.** That Ishmael had

---

[2]James B. Pritchard, "The Water System at Gibeon," *Biblical Archaeologist* 19 (1956): 66.

catered to the Ammonites was a sure sign that he had little care or concern for his own people. The Ammonites had originated through the offspring of Lot by his daughter (Gen. 19:38). Tracing their history in the biblical record, it is seen that there was constant conflict between God's people and the Ammonites.[3] Ishmael was not only a mass murderer, but he was also a traitor. In keeping with his selfish nature, Ishmael slipped speedily away, and he is not heard from again in the Book of Jeremiah.

The Remnant's Move Toward Egypt (41:16–18)

[16]**Then Johanan the son of Kareah and all the commanders of the forces that were with him took from Mizpah all the remnant of the people whom he had recovered from Ishmael the son of Nethaniah, after he had struck down Gedaliah the son of Ahikam, that is, the men who were soldiers, the women, the children, and the eunuchs, whom he had brought back from Gibeon.** [17]**And they went and stayed in Geruth Chimham, which is beside Bethlehem, in order to proceed into Egypt** [18]**because of the Chaldeans; for they were afraid of them, since Ishmael the son of Nethaniah had struck down Gedaliah the son of Ahikam, whom the king of Babylon had appointed over the land.**

Verse 16. After the rescue at Gibeon, Johanan gathered up **all the remnant**, that is, **the men who were soldiers, the women, the children, and the eunuchs,** and organized them for travel to Egypt. In their minds, **Gibeon**, some five miles northwest of Jerusalem, was no place to stay.

Verse 17. This small contingent of people left Gibeon and made their way to **Geruth Chimham, which is beside Bethlehem.** Here they sought to make the necessary arrangements so that they could **proceed into Egypt.** "Geruth" (גֵּרוּת) could refer to a temporary "lodging place" or a "fief" (land given in trust).[4]

---

[3]See Deut. 23:3–5; Judg. 10:11; 11:4–15, 32, 33; 1 Sam. 11:1–11; 2 Sam. 10:1–14; 12:26–31; 1 Kings 11:7, 31–33; 2 Kings 23:13; Neh. 2:10, 19; 4:7, 8; 13:1, 2.

[4]Ludwig Koehler and Walter Baumgartner, *The Hebrew and Aramaic Lexicon of the Old Testament,* study ed., trans. and ed. M. E. J. Richardson (Boston: Brill, 2001), 1:202.

JEREMIAH 41

It may have been some kind of convenient place for travelers to stay or a field where they could camp. "Chimham" is a name that is connected to the son of Barzillai, an attendant of David's, who brought great encouragement to David in the aftermath of his battle against his son, Absalom (2 Sam. 19:40). The designation does not appear to have anymore significance in this text than to identify the camping place for the group as they made future plans.

This small group that is now left in the land is a sad sight! Their situation was like moving from a tragedy to an even greater tragedy. They are a people who are lingering in rebellion against God. Their lives can only get worse as they figuratively bite, devour, and consume one another (see Gal. 5:13–15). The fact that Ishmael and his henchmen were gone does not mean that the rest were pure-hearted people. The next three chapters expose them as being carnal-minded, idol-driven, and unwilling to heed God's messages to them.

Verse 18. However, we are not to assume that all the Jews who were rescued from Ishmael were in favor of going to Egypt. Some of them went because of fear. **The Chaldeans** were naturally on the minds of Johanan and the people with him. **They were afraid of them, since Ishmael . . . had struck down Gedaliah . . . , whom the king of Babylon had appointed over the land.** They knew that Gedaliah had been appointed by Nebuzaradan and they might be unjustly blamed for his murder.

For obvious reasons, freedom now gave way to fear: (1) Babylon and Nebuchadnezzar had set up a government under Gedaliah at Mizpah, not Gibeon (40:1–6); (2) Gedaliah, the governor of Babylon's appointment, had been killed without justification or approval (41:1–3); (3) Chaldean officials had been killed by Ishmael (41:3); and (4) Ishmael, the cowardly murderer, had fled the scene. This left the small remnant at Gibeon unable to try that traitor, punish him, or prove to any incoming forces from Babylon that Ishmael was the culprit.

Somewhere not far from all this killing, chaos, and murky planning was Jeremiah, the great prophet who is not even named in this chapter. He appears again in later scenes, giving divine directions but still being rejected. Evil escalated as this rebellious remnant set its sights toward Egypt.

APPLICATION

Making the Right Move (Ch. 41)

The move at the end of chapter 41 was a move in the wrong direction, as the people turned toward Geruth Chimham, beside Bethlehem. That was just a step on their way to Egypt (41:17, 18). Their reasoning was that they must escape from the anticipated wrath of Babylon's forces, who would eventually learn what had happened. Even if the remnant was not guilty, they had neither proof nor an answer that they believed would be acceptable to Babylon. They were victims of guilt by association (see 1 Cor. 15:33). How often has that curse led people deeper into dangers? Are we now trying to cling to friends who will only lead us into wrongdoing and damage our souls before God? We must turn from them and turn to God (see Ex. 23:2; Heb. 13:5, 6).

Actually, three groups are seen in chapter 41. The first group could be classified as *destructive*. Ishmael plus the ten henchmen with him represent this group. They slaughtered Gedaliah, a number of Jews, and the mourners from Shechem, Shiloh, and Samaria (41:1–7). Every major community has a criminal element in it, those who seek gain by violence. Proverbs 1:8–19 contains a sobering message from a father to his son, instructing him concerning the dangerous disposition of these sinners: "Keep your feet from their path" (Prov. 1:15).

The second group could be defined as *defenders*. Johanan and the men with him dared to confront Ishmael and his henchmen (41:11–16). These acts by Johanan and his men not only stopped the killing but saved many who were in danger while with Ishmael. God ordained that there be governing authorities for the very purpose of showing strength sufficient to put fear in the wicked and to bring wrath on evildoers. The Christian should honor and respect those governing authorities who serve well because they are ordained of God (Rom. 13:1–7; 1 Pet. 2:13–17). One word of caution is in order: Not all governments and ruling authorities do as God directs, nor were they ordained of God. Government officials should remember that God truly is sovereign. They are obligated to honor Him and to surrender to His principles (Mt. 28:18–20; Eph. 1:20–23; 1 Tim. 1:17; 6:17–19).

The third group could be recognized as the *defenseless*. They are identified in 41:16 as the remnant of the women, the children, and the eunuchs. These had been held by Ishmael, and they rushed over to the side of Johanan and his forces. They had no personal strength or defense in either camp. In most communities, congregations, and social settings, certain individuals lack leadership and have limited moral or spiritual strength.

The whole goal of the Christian system is to enable formerly defenseless souls and sinners (Rom. 3:23) to become stable and strong against all elements of evil, through righteous living and God's grace and care (Eph. 6:10–18; 2 Tim. 1:7–9; 1 Pet. 3:8–16). Having the divine promises and challenges in His Word, we no longer are to be as children tossed here and there, but speak the truth in love (Eph. 4:14, 15). We are to set the standard for good and against evil. Matthew 5:13–16 says,

> "You are the salt of the earth; but if the salt has become tasteless, how can it be made salty again? It is no longer good for anything, except to be thrown out and trampled under foot by men.
>
> "You are the light of the world. A city set on a hill cannot be hidden; nor does anyone light a lamp and put it under a basket, but on the lampstand, and it gives light to all who are in the house. Let your light shine before men in such a way that they may see your good works, and glorify your Father who is in heaven."

Let us make the right move. God has promised, "I will never desert you, nor will I ever forsake you" (Heb. 13:5).

CHAPTER 42
THE REMNANT'S COURSE

Jeremiah and Baruch were among the people camped at Geruth Chimham, near Bethlehem (41:17). Probably, they had also been with them at Mizpah; they must have been somewhere on the outskirts of everything that had happened there. Perhaps they had followed behind the group and joined them at Geruth Chimham.

In Jeremiah's relationship with these people, he at times could see a glimmer of a submissive spirit in them (3:22–25; 14:19–22; 37:3; 38:14; 2 Kings 23:2, 3). However, beneath their words of commitment, a spirit of rebellion clamored for dominance. God had repeatedly urged them to repent and obey Him in a genuine way. Through famine, Israel's fall and captivity, and the warning that they could be treated like those at Shiloh (26:6, 9), God had called them to repentance; but they had continued in disobedience.

In this chapter, Jeremiah again heard what he wanted to hear from the people, only to see these rebels do the opposite of what God was directing them to do. For this reason, the chapter at first tells of a hearing that encouraged Jeremiah, but later the chapter describes a meeting that broke his heart because of the people's response of rejection.

The remnant left in Geruth Chimham presented a united front as Johanan and all the people, small and great, came to Jeremiah (42:1). Their coming indicated a general respect for Jeremiah as a true prophet of God, which should have been uplifting to him. Since Jeremiah had been beaten, thrown into a cistern, and left in the guardhouse until Jerusalem fell, this united, favorable approach must have impressed him with beautiful possibilities. Still, the events in this chapter eventually fall into Judah's oft-repeated pattern.

Jeremiah was urged to pray for the people, and the people promised to obey what God would tell them. Their seemingly submissive spirit constrained them to appeal to God through Jeremiah to answer their question, "What should we do?" (42:1–6). After ten days, God's answer was a pointed command: "Stay in this land, and then I will build you up." This direction would offer them peace for obedience or punishment for disobedience (42:7–18). The chapter closes with Jeremiah's rebuke of a people who had chosen to be disobedient (42:19–22).

THE PEOPLE'S QUESTION: "WHAT SHOULD WE DO?" (42:1–6)

¹Then all the commanders of the forces, Johanan the son of Kareah, Jezaniah the son of Hoshaiah, and all the people both small and great approached ²and said to Jeremiah the prophet, "Please let our petition come before you, and pray for us to the LORD your God, that is for all this remnant; because we are left but a few out of many, as your own eyes now see us, ³that the LORD your God may tell us the way in which we should walk and the thing that we should do." ⁴Then Jeremiah the prophet said to them, "I have heard you. Behold, I am going to pray to the LORD your God in accordance with your words; and I will tell you the whole message which the LORD will answer you. I will not keep back a word from you." ⁵Then they said to Jeremiah, "May the LORD be a true and faithful witness against us if we do not act in accordance with the whole message with which the LORD your God will send you to us. ⁶Whether it is pleasant or unpleasant, we will listen to the voice of the LORD our God to whom we are sending you, so that it may go well with us when we listen to the voice of the LORD our God."

Verse 1. A bewildered group of people came to Jeremiah. **All the people both small and great approached** the prophet. Leaders as well followers, women as well men, were involved in making a request. **Jezaniah the son of Hoshaiah** must be a different man from the one mentioned in 40:8, who was the son of the Maacathite. This Jezaniah is frequently identified with Azariah in 43:2, under the assumption that he is called by two names.

Verse 2. Realizing they were few in number and confused on what to do next, all the people asked Jeremiah to pray for them. Their words appear to be sincere: **"Please let our petition come before you, and pray for us to the LORD your God, that is for all this remnant; because we are left but a few out of many, as your own eyes now see us."** Driven by desperation, they turned to the prayers of God's true prophet. They came with a "petition." This is the Hebrew word for "supplication" (תְּחִנָּה, *th͗echinnah*), which involves a strong appeal for a favor (see 36:7; 37:20; 38:26; 42:9). They were urging the prophet to "pray" (פָּלַל, *palal*), to make a request for them to the Lord God (see comments on 37:3). The very terms they used indicated that they were hungry for guidance.

Verse 3. They pleaded for God to tell them **the way in which [they] should walk and the thing that [they] should do**. Apparently, they were making the right request. So far they were walking in the way of penitence. Their approach to Jeremiah suggested that they knew how to obey God; and at that point in time, they were willing to bring their wills into submission to Him. They were asking God to give them the type of direction for which they asked on more than one occasion (7:3, 5; 18:11; 26:13).

Verse 4. Jeremiah told them that he would pray, and when God answered him, he would come back to them and reveal to them whatever message God had given him (see Acts 20:20). He said that they would get his prayers and God's answer. His promise was that his conduct toward them would be unimpeachable: **"I will tell you the whole message which the LORD will answer you. I will not keep back a word from you."** His response to them was going to be the response of a true prophet. Micaiah, a prophet of a similar attitude, told the man who urged him to be one of the crowd of the false prophets and agree with them, "As the LORD lives, what the LORD says to me, that I shall speak" (1 Kings 22:14).

Verse 5. The people affirmed that they would listen to what God would tell them. If they were not obedient, they said, **"May the Lord be a true and faithful witness against us."** Thinking of God as a potential "witness" against them, the people assured Jeremiah that they would **act in accordance with the whole message** that the Lord God would send to them.

Three elements to their response stand out. One is their evident sincerity: They agreed that the Lord would "be a true and faithful witness," either for or against them.

Verse 6. Another element is their commitment: **"Whether it is pleasant or unpleasant, we will listen to the voice of the Lord our God."** The Hebrew word for "listen" is שָׁמַע (*shama‘*). The KJV and ASV have "obey" instead of "listen," which may be a more appropriate translation in this context. A third element is their realization of prosperity: **"That it may go well with us when we listen to the voice of the Lord our God."** The word "well" (יָטַב, *yatab*) also appears in 7:23; 38:20; and 40:9. It includes the idea of what is good, the action of doing the right thing, and being joyful as a result of what has been done.[1] It covers both the act and the attitude. They were confessing that they knew that obedience brought God's approval and disobedience brought His rejection.

In view of their own words, can anyone doubt that these people were aware of how they should relate to God? They knew their basic responsibilities. Thus far they appear to be well on the road to a genuine return to God.

GOD'S ANSWER: "STAY IN THIS LAND!" (42:7–18)

God's Positive Plan and Promise (42:7–12)

⁷**Now at the end of ten days the word of the Lord came to Jeremiah.** ⁸**Then he called for Johanan the son of Kareah and**

---

[1] See Ludwig Koehler and Walter Baumgartner, *The Hebrew and Aramaic Lexicon of the Old Testament*, study ed., trans. and ed. M. E. J. Richardson (Boston: Brill, 2001), 1:408–9.

all the commanders of the forces that were with him, and for all the people both small and great, ⁹and said to them, "Thus says the LORD the God of Israel, to whom you sent me to present your petition before Him: ¹⁰'If you will indeed stay in this land, then I will build you up and not tear you down, and I will plant you and not uproot you; for I will relent concerning the calamity that I have inflicted on you. ¹¹Do not be afraid of the king of Babylon, whom you are now fearing; do not be afraid of him,' declares the LORD, 'for I am with you to save you and deliver you from his hand. ¹²I will also show you compassion, so that he will have compassion on you and restore you to your own soil.'"**

Verse 7. Perhaps for the purpose of testing, God allowed some time to go by before He answered them. **Now at the end of ten days the word of the LORD came to Jeremiah.** God, in grace, gave them a clear reply to their entreaty.

Verse 8. After receiving the answer, Jeremiah gathered the group and prepared them for the answer that would be given. He called for **Johanan, all the commanders of the forces,** and **all the people both small and great.** It was now time to see whether or not there was real sincerity behind their request for guidance. Just as the request was made by all, Jeremiah's answer would be given to all. A vital lesson is seen in what was done. Everyone should be informed because God carries out His plan through the entire congregation (27:5–7; 1 Sam. 17:42, 28, 33–36, 46; Is. 11:6; Mt. 18:2). Also, without communication, real togetherness cannot exist (see 1 Cor. 1:10). Only truth can enable a community to dwell together in unity (2 Tim. 2:2; 1 Pet. 2:2).

Verse 9. Jeremiah began with a dynamic exclamation: **"Thus says the LORD the God of Israel."** They were seeking God's answer, and it is His answer that they would receive.

Verse 10. While so much tragedy had already come to this remnant, God's patience was manifested once again as He assured them that peace and prosperity were still possible. They were told, **"If you will indeed stay in this land, then I will build you up and not tear you down, and I will plant you and not uproot you."**

JEREMIAH 42

They received an answer and a promise. What they needed to do and what would be done for them were clearly delineated. Several expressions identify the gracious, goodness of God that would follow their obedience. The benevolent spirit of God emanated from the two promises "I will" and "I am." It is easy to see why this section of the chapter can be entitled "God's Offer." He was the preeminent supplier of these benefits that they would receive (see Jas. 1:17).

If they obeyed, contentment would be theirs. Should they "stay in this land," He would give them growth. God promised, "I will build you up" and "I will plant you."

God was willing to **relent concerning the calamity** that He had threatened if they would do as He directed. The word "relent" (נָחַם, *nacham*), translated "repent" in the KJV and ASV, relates more to God's nature than to faulty conduct that must be rectified. In 18:8 and 26:3, God manifested a similar willingness to alter His avowed intent, providing the people would adhere to His principles and commandments. Jeremiah's counsel from God was, as it had been all along, that these people should accept the punishment God had inflicted on them, staying in the land even though it lay in devastation. A response such as this called for trust in God's care. Suspicion were doubt were out of place.

Verse 11. However, there is more. He would also give them peace. He urged them, **"Do not be afraid of the king of Babylon, whom you are now fearing."** When God surrounds His people, even the great Nebuchadnezzar cannot not get to them. His great promise to be their Savior and Redeemer, **"I am with you to save you and deliver you,"** should remove all their fears. His words could be rephrased to say, "I will snatch you out of all danger."

Verse 12. God would manifest **compassion** in another way. He promised that the king himself, Nebuchadnezzar, would **have compassion** on them. With both God and the king of Babylon showing "compassion" on the remnant, they would be standing both in earthly and heavenly grace. They would be **restore**[d] to their **own soil**, the soil of Judah and Jerusalem.

This dual blessing not only included safety from Babylon and compassion from that foreign emperor, but the people would be made happy by the King of kings, as He built and planted them. The divinely stated mission of Jeremiah (1:10) indicated that God's people would be constructed like a beautiful, firmly founded building. Here again is seen the great work of God by which He raises up beauty from ashes by the restoration and reestablishment of His people. For His great work, He should be glorified (see Is. 61:2, 3; KJV). If God's people would have but realized the fulfillment of such promises, they would have seen that His demands and their duty were indeed privileges that were filled with precious promises.

**God's Punishment Promised
For Rejecting the Plan (42:13–18)**

¹³"'But if you are going to say, "We will not stay in this land," so as not to listen to the voice of the LORD your God, ¹⁴saying, "No, but we will go to the land of Egypt, where we will not see war or hear the sound of a trumpet or hunger for bread, and we will stay there"; ¹⁵then in that case listen to the word of the LORD, O remnant of Judah. Thus says the LORD of hosts, the God of Israel, "If you really set your mind to enter Egypt and go in to reside there, ¹⁶then the sword, which you are afraid of, will overtake you there in the land of Egypt; and the famine, about which you are anxious, will follow closely after you there in Egypt, and you will die there. ¹⁷So all the men who set their mind to go to Egypt to reside there will die by the sword, by famine and by pestilence; and they will have no survivors or refugees from the calamity that I am going to bring on them."'"

¹⁸For thus says the LORD of hosts, the God of Israel, "As My anger and wrath have been poured out on the inhabitants of Jerusalem, so My wrath will be poured out on you when you enter Egypt. And you will become a curse, an object of horror, an imprecation and a reproach; and you will see this place no more."

Verse 13. God warned against disobedience. He always does, for He expects His servants to follow His guidance. Punishment was promised to those who rejected His gracious benefits. God was specific with them, using the very words He knew they would use in their rejection: **"But if you are going to say, 'We will not stay in this land,'"** then "the sword . . . will overtake you" (42:16). If they refused to **listen to the voice of the LORD**, then God would be constrained to pour out His wrath on them, as it had been poured out on Jerusalem.

Verse 14. If they persisted in saying, **"We will go to the land of Egypt,"** then God would have no choice but to fulfill His threat to make them "a curse" (42:18).

What the remnant thought and what God had planned for them were two different things. These people surmised that they would not **see war or hear the sound of a trumpet** in Egypt. They further believed, **"We will not . . . hunger for bread, and we will stay there."**

Verses 15–17. The people thought that, in their fleeing to Egypt, they were entering safety. The reality was that they were rushing into the very calamities they feared the most. The Lord warned, **"The sword, which you are afraid of, will overtake you . . . the famine, about which you are anxious, will follow closely after you . . . and you will die there."** Their disobedient descent into Egypt, would so decimate them that they would **have no survivors or refugees**.

The tone in this chapter has changed from compassion (42:10–12) to **calamity** (42:16, 17), from salvation to starvation! God's warning of what He would **bring on them** should have been enough motivation for these people to rectify any wrongs they were committing, turn to the right decisions, and resolve to stay in the land.

Verse 18. However, in truth, God's description foretold an even greater tragedy. If they were determined to go to Egypt in disobedience to what they had been commanded, they would experience far-reaching manifestations of His fury.

The prophet must have cringed with pain and withdrew in fear as he related what was coming to them. They would become detested; they would suffer **a curse** (אָלָה, *'alah*). (See Num. 5:21; Is. 24:6.) His passionate fury would result in their becoming despicable, **an object of horror** (שַׁמָּה, *shammah*). They would be viewed as repugnant and disgusting, even as **an imprecation** (קְלָלָה, *qᵉlalah*), an accursed thing. The nations would make verbal aspersions against them. They would be tauntingly denounced and regarded as **a reproach** (חֶרְפָּה, *cherpah*) among people.

What was left of Judah would stand socially and publicly rejected by men, and they would be forced to live in total isolation from their homeland. They could never again enter the Promised Land. God's words restricted them to foreign lands: **"You will see this place no more."** For the rebels who came under this curse, any hope to return to Jerusalem or participate in rebuilding the temple would be out of the question. The place where they had annually gone for worship and atonement would be forbidden to them.

Only a devout Jew could realize the sorrow related to this loss. It would be difficult to level a heavier penalty on a Jew than what God had given in these warnings. Daily life under that imposed punishment would induce consistent shame and suffering, perpetual hurt and degradation. Every day that dawned would be a day of disappointment and depression. As the story is followed through chapter 44, it becomes obvious that God meant what He said. By continued rebellion, the people would sink lower and lower into dark despair and shame.

JEREMIAH'S WORD TO THE DISOBEDIENT: "YOU WILL DIE!" (42:19–22)

¹⁹**The LORD has spoken to you, O remnant of Judah, "Do not go into Egypt!" You should clearly understand that today I have testified against you. ²⁰For you have only deceived yourselves; for it is you who sent me to the LORD your God, saying, "Pray for us to the LORD our God; and whatever the LORD our God says, tell us so, and we will do it." ²¹So I have told you today, but you have not obeyed the LORD your God, even in whatever He has sent me to tell you. ²²Therefore you should now clearly understand that you will die by the sword, by famine and by pestilence, in the place where you wish to go to reside.**

Verse 19. Jeremiah concluded his prophetic judgment with a reminder of its source: **The Lord has spoken to you, O remnant of Judah.** God's promises of peace and prosperity (on the basis of obedience) or punishment (on the basis of disobedience) had been clearly given through the mouth of Jeremiah. The "remnant" in Judah had stood in the valley of decision. Because the decision was so vast in its implications, Jeremiah made a plaintive plea: **You should clearly understand that today I have testified against you.** The Hebrew word for "testified," עוּד (*'ud*), has repetition embedded within it.[2] Jeremiah had reiterated God's warnings so that they could not be misunderstood.

Verse 20. As evidence of finality, Jeremiah reviewed with the people what they had requested of him and what he had done for them. **It is you**, he said, **who sent me to the Lord your God, saying, "Pray for us to the Lord our God; and whatever the Lord our God says, tell us so, and we will do it."** With a broken spirit he had to say to them, **You have only deceived yourselves**. Truly, they were wandering, erring, and in the process of making a disastrous journey. These people lied in their hearts by pretending with their tongues that they would obey God.

Verse 21. God had faithfully told them what to do. Jeremiah had candidly reported to them God's revelation. They had been privileged to come face to face with the truth. Now, God had become their witness that they were not going to obey Him (see 42:5, 6). The verdict of their decision became plain to Jeremiah: **You have not obeyed the Lord your God, even in whatever He has sent me to tell you.**

Verse 22. The judgment of God that they would face was horrible to think about. They would **die by the sword, by famine and by pestilence** (see comments on 14:12). All this sorrow and suffering would come on them because they had not lived up to the pledge, "we will listen to the voice of the Lord our God," that they had made.

These tragedies that were to prevail upon them would come to them **in the place where** [they wished] **to go to reside**. In other words, these calamities would befall them in Egypt. They chose

---

[2]See Francis Brown, S. R. Driver, and Charles A. Briggs, *A Hebrew and English Lexicon of the Old Testament* (Oxford: Clarendon Press, 1972), 728–29.

to follow their human judgment and the advice of the false prophets. In the place that they had chosen they would eat the fruits of their disobedience (42:15-17; see Mt. 7:15-20).

Considering God's promises of compassion if they stayed where they were, as opposed to the catastrophes that awaited them in Egypt, why did these survivors have any desire to journey into Egypt? The answer is unmistakable. They had chosen to walk by sight, not by faith (see 2 Cor. 5:7; Heb. 11:17-19). God's promises were ignored because, in their own vain imagination, they concluded that Babylonian officials would return to punish them mercilessly for the atrocities at Mizpah (which had been none of their doing). The promises of God's and Nebuchadnezzar's compassion (42:11, 12) were not heard (or not believed) because the people had stopped listening to God. They were living by the code of their own thinking (7:24, 26, 27; 25:3, 4; 26:5; 44:16-18). When people reach this state, they truly have eyes but do not see and ears but do not hear (Is. 6:9, 10; Mt. 13:14, 15).

APPLICATION

Walking in His Promises (Ch. 42)

Do we walk by faith in God's promises? Do we distrust God, making decisions by assumption and sight? How often do we approach God or His Word seeking only what we want to hear? Metaphorically speaking, have we ever headed for Egypt when God wanted us to stay where He directed through His principles and promises?

This chapter challenges us to grow in faith to the level of obeying God's law, even when it is counter to our culture or convenience. God's ways are not our ways, and His thoughts are not our thoughts (Is. 55:6-9). We may easily understand His moral law as sane and sensible (see Rom. 13:8-10), but His divine law may not be so easily grasped. For example, the directions to offer Isaac as a sacrifice went beyond all logic, but Abraham trusted God and obediently acted by faith (Heb. 11:17-19). To us, baptism of a believer for the forgiveness of sins may not seem logical. However, Christ said to do it, attaching precious promises to such obedience (Mk. 16:15, 16; Acts 2:38; Rom. 6:3,

4; Gal. 3:26, 27; 1 Cor. 12:13). The Lord's Supper on the first day of the week is insufficient as a meal. In men's eyes, it may not even seem to be a fitting memorial. Nevertheless, Christ said to do it and told us why we are to do it (Lk. 22:17–20; 1 Cor. 11:23–26). He also warned us that we can eat and drink condemnation to ourselves if we "discern not the body" (1 Cor. 11:29; ASV).

Do we walk by faith or by sight, by human reasoning or by divine principles (Is. 1:18)? In 42:4, we find basic guidelines for teachers. Let us take these guidelines to heart.

Seek information. Jeremiah told the people, "I have heard you." We should listen carefully and digest a person's comments and question's before dispensing information or giving an answer.

Make intercession. Jeremiah said, "I am going to pray to the Lord . . . in accordance with your words." It is appropriate to talk with God about the needs of others. Not only should we solicit His help, but talking to Him may also help us better understand and comprehend their words. Paul highly commended Timothy when he wrote to the Christians in Philippi, "I have no one else of kindred spirit who will genuinely be concerned for your welfare" (Phil. 2:20). It is easy to respond to others on the basis of our thinking rather than understanding what they were thinking. Even more sobering is the task of properly blending their thinking with God's principles.

Give an exact declaration. Jeremiah said, "I will tell you the whole message which the Lord will answer you." While we may need wisdom to know what others can handle (see 1 Cor. 3:2, 3), we are not really free from the blood of all men unless we declare unto them the whole counsel of God (see Acts 20:26, 27). There are various levels of response: We may talk to others about what the Lord said concerning them; we may tell them what we think the Lord wants them to do; we may tell them part of the Lord's message; or we may, like Jeremiah and Paul, give them the whole message of the Lord.

Attempt a complete proclamation. Jeremiah told them, "I will not keep back a word from you." God trained Jeremiah that way (1:7, 17; 26:1, 2). Repeatedly, the prophet declared what the people needed to do, plus the blessings they would receive if they did it. He foresaw how people might rebel, and he indicated the punishment God would impose if they responded in a disobedient manner.

Know that God's message confidently affirms that it is God's message (42:7). The inspired record informs us that ten days passed before Jeremiah got an answer from God for those people. While prophecy as given to Jeremiah is not God's method of revelation today, we do need to study God's Word and handle it accurately (2 Tim. 2:15), or "rightly divide it" (KJV), being sure that what we are sharing with others is God's message for them. Paul severely rebuked some would-be teachers for the Lord who confidently affirmed the message when they did not understand what they were saying (Rom. 10:1–3; 1 Tim. 1:6, 7). Surely, Jeremiah must have done some inquiring about God's message before those ten days passed, but it is obvious that he did not speak God's word until he knew it was God's word. Any teacher for God should go forth and do likewise.

How have we served in this area of sharing God's whole counsel with those around us? As Jesus sent out the Twelve, He urged that they be "shrewd as serpents and innocent as doves" (Mt. 10:16), knowing when to strike and how to do so with gentleness. (See the description of Jesus as a teacher in Mt. 12:18–21.)

CHAPTER 43
MIGRATING TO EGYPT

The remnant's pattern of disobedience continued to prevail. In Geruth Chimham (41:17), two basic needs should have surfaced. In the first place they should have realize the importance of their destiny. When one runs from God, he runs toward ruin. In Egypt the remnant found this out, as Jonah learned it at sea (Jon. 1:4). In addition, it was paramount for them to identify their underlying problem—rebellion against God. They were running from Him, not from any physical, material, or international power.

Babylon's forces would come to Egypt to inflict the very destruction that God's people had hoped to escape. One does not escape danger by merely departing from God. In fact, how can one run away from God, when God is everywhere? (See 23:23, 24; Ps. 139:1–16.) As with Jonah, everyone who flees from God must eventually face a storm.

Chapter 43 naturally separates into three parts: the rejection of Jeremiah's message (43:1–4), the remnant's entering into Egypt (43:5–7), and the prophecy of Babylon's coming to Egypt (43:8–13).

REJECTING THE PROPHET'S MESSAGE (43:1–4)

¹**But as soon as Jeremiah, whom the LORD their God had sent, had finished telling all the people all the words of the LORD their God—that is, all these words—**²**Azariah the son of Hoshaiah, and Johanan the son of Kareah, and all the arrogant men**

said to Jeremiah, "You are telling a lie! The LORD our God has not sent you to say, 'You are not to enter Egypt to reside there'; ³but Baruch the son of Neriah is inciting you against us to give us over into the hand of the Chaldeans, so they will put us to death or exile us to Babylon." ⁴So Johanan the son of Kareah and all the commanders of the forces, and all the people, did not obey the voice of the LORD to stay in the land of Judah.

Verse 1. Jeremiah faithfully accomplished the mission upon which **God had sent** him. He **finished telling** the inspired message to **all the people**, both men and women (42:1). "Finished" is from כָּלָה (*kalah*), which gives the sense of "complete," "accomplished," or "fulfilled."[1] The text emphasizes that he did not hold anything back (42:4); he spoke **all the words of the LORD their God** to them. However, **as soon as** he finished speaking, the prophet and his message were met with rejection. The superficiality of their earlier question surfaced. Their request and response show that degenerate roots may reside beneath noble words and appropriate questions (7:3, 5; 18:11; 26:13).

Verse 2. The remnant reached the wrong conclusion, and they were going to stay with that conclusion at all costs. They accused Jeremiah of **telling a lie**. Who would draw such a conclusion concerning God's truth? The message did not fulfill their desires or alleviate their fears, so they looked for some disparaging way to discard it. **Azariah, Johanan,** and **all the arrogant men** spoke up. The group of resisters seems to have been led by Azariah. The phrase "arrogant men" is a designation for the leaders who had risen to rebuke Jeremiah. The Hebrew word for "arrogant" is זֵד (*zed*), meaning "insolent" or "presumptuous."[2] This adjective is often used by itself (without a noun) as a technical term for "godless, rebellious men."[3] Of the several words for "pride" or "arrogance," this is one of the worst. With their

---

[1]Francis Brown, S. R. Driver, and Charles A. Briggs, *A Hebrew and English Lexicon of the Old Testament* (Oxford: Clarendon Press, 1972), 477–78.

[2]Ludwig Koehler and Walter Baumgartner, *The Hebrew and Aramaic Lexicon of the Old Testament*, study ed., trans. and ed. M. E. J. Richardson (Boston: Brill, 2001), 1:263.

[3]Brown, Driver, and Briggs, 267.

"arrogant" attitude, it is not surprising that these men charged Jeremiah with falsehood a short time after pleading with him to approach God for them (42:1–3, 6). It is sad when leaders are so fickle and confused in their thinking that they refer to good as evil and label truth a lie (see Is. 5:20; 1 Tim. 1:5–7).

They argued that Jeremiah had told them the opposite of what God wanted him to say: **"The Lord our God has not sent you to say, 'You are not to enter Egypt to reside there.'"** It is always the highest type of evil to deny what the Lord has said. When people have no counter arguments, they often attack the credibility of the speaker. The disobedient do not have a reason for opposing God's direction, so they made one up.

Verse 3. These men not only asserted that Jeremiah had lied (when he had not), but they also claimed that the underlying cause came from Baruch (when it did not). They said, **"Baruch the son of Neriah is inciting you against us to give us over into the hand of the Chaldeans, so they will put us to death or exile us to Babylon."** These men were rabidly grabbing at any suspicion or imagined rationale for rejecting Jeremiah's message (see Mk. 14:55–59, 63, 64). Their rebellious minds conjured up the fear that Jeremiah was somehow courting the favor of the Babylonians. They assumed that he intended to deliver the remnant into enemy hands so they could put them to death or send them into exile in Babylon.

Verse 4. Obviously, the remnant had made their decision. Consequently, it was necessary for Jeremiah to state tersely and historically what they had done: **So Johanan the son of Kareah and all the commanders of the forces, and all the people, did not obey the voice of the Lord to stay in the land of Judah.** God had given them His commandment on what to do, but they had answered, "We will not do it." We see here a clear case of disobedience in the divine record.

ENTERING EGYPT (43:5–7)

⁵But Johanan the son of Kareah and all the commanders of the forces took the entire remnant of Judah who had returned from all the nations to which they had been driven away, in order

to reside in the land of Judah—⁶the men, the women, the children, the king's daughters and every person that Nebuzaradan the captain of the bodyguard had left with Gedaliah the son of Ahikam and grandson of Shaphan, together with Jeremiah the prophet and Baruch the son of Neriah—⁷and they entered the land of Egypt (for they did not obey the voice of the LORD) and went in as far as Tahpanhes.

Verse 5. Johanan, the very man who had courageously sought to save the remnant shortly before (40:13–16), became one of the men who led the people on their rebellious course. The exact number of people who had decided to go to Egypt is uncertain. During the ten days of waiting (42:7), word had spread and all the remnant in and around Jerusalem had come together. An all-inclusive phrase is used in connection with the number taken. Johanan and the military forces **took the entire remnant of Judah**. This comprehensive word, "entire" (כֹּל, *kol*) or "whole" must be understood literally. Among its many definitions, the word "took" (לָקַח, *laqach*) can mean "capture," "seize," or "carry off."[4] For some people, the journey to Egypt was one of coercion.

These people included those who had been left when the deportation took place at the fall of Jerusalem as well as those **who had returned from all the nations to which they had been driven away**. This latter group included people who had left Jerusalem sometime before its fall, spent time in neighboring countries, and returned after the destruction of the city. They had come back to Judah, pledged their allegiance to Gedaliah, and joined in the harvest of the summer fruit (see comments on 40:12). These people were brought together and made a part of the company that was going to Egypt.

No one was left out. Had they stayed, perhaps God would have used these people to begin the process of rebuilding Jerusalem. Now, the city was going to be left more desolate than ever. It would lie in ruins until the remnant came from Babylon with Sheshbazzer and Zerubbabel (Ezra 1:1—2:2).

Verse 6. A repetition of the group's diversity is given to stress

---

[4] Ibid., 542–44.

the brutal reality of what had happened. Jeremiah related that **the men, the women, the children, the king's daughters and every person that Nebuzaradan the captain of the bodyguard had left with Gedaliah ... together with Jeremiah the prophet and Baruch** were taken. In this encompassing picture stood faithful people who did not want to go. These had resolved to do what God had commanded but were being compelled to go. They were constrained against their will to fall in line and do what the others had decided to do. Jeremiah and Baruch were two of the dissenters. This forced journey against what he knew to be the will of God became a climactic conclusion to the abuse he had suffered at the hands of His people.

Nowhere do we find that Jeremiah approved of this journey to Egypt. He did not preach one way and then live another. It must be true that these two men have been sent with the band of travelers by God Himself so that they would continue to know that a prophet was among them.

As the group departed for Egypt, a message given by Moses should have been ringing in their ears. The warning was given at the time when the people sought to set up a king over the nation. The king was not to get horses from Egypt, as Solomon had done (1 Kings 10:26–29). Moses conveyed to them God's solemn charge: "You shall never again return that way" (Deut. 17:16). Nearly nine hundred years later, these descendants of Abraham were, as a rebellious remnant, headed back to suffer and die in that place where their forefathers had suffered in slavery (44:26, 27). God had been faithful and patient. Years before, the lineage of Abraham had witnessed God's divine power to overcome Egypt through plagues and pestilences, granting liberty to the enslaved. Nevertheless, God's people in the environs of Jerusalem were returning to Egypt.

Verse 7. Now comes one of the Old Testament's saddest lines: **And they entered the land of Egypt (for they did not obey the voice of the Lord).** Their rejection of the Lord's plan is a repeat of Jonah's refusal to fulfill the commission he had been given (Jon. 1:2, 3). While one Jonah is sad picture, a whole caravan of Jonahs is one of the most tragic portrayals of apostasy in the Bible.

They **went in as far as Tahpanhes**. God could have kept Jeremiah and Baruch from going on this journey had He so desired, as surely as He had cared for them when Babylon conquered Judah. However, the rest of this chapter and chapter 44 show that God still had prophetic work for Jeremiah to do. Some prophets, including Daniel and Ezekiel, were among the captives taken to Babylon. Jeremiah's task, by providential plan, was to be with the remnant that continued their rebellious move into Egypt. Through Jeremiah, God repeatedly declared to them what they would face and why they would face it. His word was true, even though his words meant their utter judgment.

PROPHECY UTTERED IN EGYPT
(43:8–13)

The exact time the remnant immigrated to Egypt cannot be determined. It has already been seen (ch. 41) that the armies of Nebuchadnezzar returned to the land of Judah in 582 or 581 B.C., around five years after the fall, to enact judgments on the remnant for events surrounding Gedaliah's death. The date of 583 or 582 B.C. would be fairly accurate. The end of chapter 43 contains the last recorded oracle of Jeremiah, which he gave before the death of Pharaoh Hophra in 569 B.C. The material in 43:8–44:30, therefore, relates to a maximum period of thirteen years (583–570 B.C.). The middle of those years, likely, closes the last inspired account we have of Jeremiah's prophetic life.

The Prophetic Plan Presented for Egypt's Fall
(43:8–11)

⁸Then the word of the LORD came to Jeremiah in Tahpanhes, saying, ⁹"Take some large stones in your hands and hide them in the mortar in the brick terrace which is at the entrance of Pharaoh's palace in Tahpanhes, in the sight of some of the Jews; ¹⁰and say to them, 'Thus says the LORD of hosts, the God of Israel, "Behold, I am going to send and get Nebuchadnezzar the king of Babylon, My servant, and I am going to set his throne right over these stones that I have hidden; and he will

spread his canopy over them. ¹¹He will also come and strike the land of Egypt; those who are meant for death will be given over to death, and those for captivity to captivity, and those for the sword to the sword."'"

Verse 8. God, therefore, sent His **word** with the remnant in the person of **Jeremiah**. In this great prophet resided further evidence of God's persistence and compassion. Even in the face of complete rebellion, He made sure that His prophet would be among these who had cast aside His directions.

Tahpanhes, the city where Jeremiah resumed his prophetic work, was at the edge of the Egyptian delta, some seven miles west of what is now the Suez Canal. James E. Smith described the excavation of it:

> This site was excavated by Sir Flinders Petrie, the famous British archaeologist, in 1886. He found the native name of the place to be Qsar Bent el Yehudi, "palace of the Jew's daughter." This name had for centuries preserved the memory of the visit of Zedekiah's daughters following the collapse of the kingdom of Judah.[5]

Verse 9. God had given Jeremiah specific instructions regarding taking **large stones** in his **hands** and placing them **in the mortar** at an exact spot **in the brick terrace which is at the entrance of Pharaoh's palace**. Evidence is lacking on exactly what he did. It is only known that Jeremiah put "large stones" near a "palace" often used by Pharaoh. The Hebrew word for "mortar" (מֶלֶט, *melet*) is used only this one time in the Old Testament. Its rarity has made it elusive of translation. While the NASB has "mortar,"[6] other versions have "clay" (KJV; NIV; NRSV).[7]

While excavating the fortress of **Tahpanhes**, Petrie found a large brick platform at the main entrance. It is thought by some

---

[5]James E. Smith, *Jeremiah and Lamentations*, Bible Study Textbook Series (Joplin, Mo.: College Press, 1972), 673.

[6]See Brown, Driver, and Briggs, 572.

[7]See Koehler and Baumgartner, 1:590.

that the platform may have been the very place where God instructed Jeremiah to bury the stones.[8]

Through the bricks, Jeremiah was to give another dramatic demonstration to God's people (see 13:1–11; 19:1–13; 25:15–31; 27:1—28:17; 32:6–15; 35:1–19; 51:59–64). The instructions required him to do this act **in the sight of some of the Jews**. God never tires of putting before people the evidence of His name.

Verse 10. Jeremiah was even given guidance on what to say as he hid the bricks. This declaration constitutes his first recorded message in Egypt. He was to announce that **the Lord of hosts, the God of Israel**, said, **"I am going to send and get Nebuchadnezzar the king of Babylon, My servant, and I am going to set his throne right over these stones that I have hidden; and he will spread his canopy over them."** The prophecy testified to the truth that Nebuchadnezzar was God's "servant" (27:6). God would take this great king and "send" him to Egypt, and He would "set his throne" on the specific spot where Jeremiah had implanted the stones. That emperor would "spread his canopy" over the stones Jeremiah had placed in that entrance to the palace. The word for "canopy" (שַׁפְרוּר, *shaprur*) is also used only once in the Old Testament. The KJV and ASV have "pavilion"; the NASB and NIV have "canopy." The message for the Jews who stood watching was that Egypt was not going to be the place to seek safety from Nebuchadnezzar.

Just as Johanan and his followers had forced Jeremiah to go into Egypt, God would bring Nebuchadnezzar into Egypt. The word translated "get" (לָקַח, *laqach*) is the same Hebrew word rendered "took" in 43:5.

Verse 11. Jeremiah was to further reveal that the great king would **also come and strike the land of Egypt**. God would use Nebuchadnezzar to do His will more easily than Johanan had taken Jeremiah into Egypt.

While God is all powerful, He permits man's free will. This implies that Nebuchadnezzar would choose to "strike the land of Egypt" (see Dan. 2:20, 21; Hos. 8:2–4). Nebuchadnezzar would choose to act; God would use the act. He did not use Nebuchad-

---

[8]Smith, 673.

nezzar as a willing agent, but as an unaware instrument.

The doom pronounced on Egypt is similar to that pronounced on Judah. **Those who are meant for death will be given over to death, and those for captivity to captivity, and those for the sword to the sword** (see comments on 15:2). Some of the Jews would be killed by "the sword"; some would be taken to other places for "captivity." Tragedy wears many faces. The situation would be fraught with danger—swords would be in use, soldiers would be coming through the city, and death would be on the prowl. Certain destruction and death lay ahead.

Judgment Would Come to Egypt's Idols (43:12, 13)

¹²"'"And I shall set fire to the temples of the gods of Egypt, and he will burn them and take them captive. So he will wrap himself with the land of Egypt as a shepherd wraps himself with his garment, and he will depart from there safely. ¹³He will also shatter the obelisks of Heliopolis, which is in the land of Egypt; and the temples of the gods of Egypt he will burn with fire."'"

Verse 12. God said, **"And I shall set fire to the temples of the gods of Egypt, and he** [Nebuchadnezzar] **will burn them and take them captive."** With Nebuchadnezzar as His servant and hand of judgment, God was about to take action again against all the idolatry of Egypt. In God's plan, this was just another move against widespread falsehood (see Ezek. 30:1–26). From Nebuchadnezzar's viewpoint, the removal of Egypt's idols resulted in promoting his own domination and power.

How would this great warrior do his work? God said, **"He will wrap himself with the land of Egypt as a shepherd wraps himself with his garment, and he will depart from there safely."** Nebuchadnezzar would come with ease, do his will as easily as a shepherd dons his outer mantel, and then move on to another place without suffering the slightest interference and inconvenience. He would come in with a swinging of his power and might and would leave the same way.

Verse 13. Egypt's cities and gods would melt before Nebuchadnezzar. The centers of idolatry would be powerless before him. **He will also shatter the obelisks of Heliopolis, which is in the land of Egypt; and the temples of the gods of Egypt he will burn with fire.** All the gods of Egypt put together could not stop this army.

The phrase "the obelisks of Heliopolis" is unique and revealing. "Obelisks" is from the Hebrew word מַצֵּבָה (*matstsebah*), which refers to a "memorial stone" that was set upright.[9] In an Egyptian context, it denotes an "obelisk"—a towering stone monument that was tapered at the top. Edwin M. Yamauchi said that "the obelisk symbolized the primeval hill at the beginning of creation. It became the symbol of the sun-god, guaranteeing life and prosperity to the pharaohs."[10] A red granite obelisk from the reign of Senusret I (1971–1926 B.C.) can be seen at Heliopolis today.[11]

"Heliopolis" is a translation of two Hebrew words, בֵּית שֶׁמֶשׁ (*Beyth Shemesh*), which literally mean "House of [the] Sun."[12] The NASB uses the Greek rendering taken from the Septuagint (LXX). "Heliopolis" (Ἡλιούπολις) is a compound name: The Greek word for "sun" is ἥλιος (*hēlios*), and the word for "city" is πόλις (*polis*). This city, also known as On, was located near Memphis on the Nile River; the site is presently in a suburb of Cairo. It was the epitome of idolatrous worship, being "the center for the worship of the sun god Atum-Re."[13]

In spite of any warnings from Jeremiah, the remnant did not turn from their rebellious and idolatrous ways. The prophet continued to point out their sin and speak against their shameful actions. They were surrounded by the gods of Egypt. For God's people, their journey into Egypt was just another of the several roads to ruin.

---

[9]Koehler and Baumgartner, 1:620–21.

[10]Edwin M. Yamauchi, "Obelisk," in *The International Standard Bible Encyclopedia*, rev. ed., ed. Geoffrey W. Bromiley (Grand Rapids, Mich.: Wm. B. Eerdmans Publishing Co., 1986), 3:577–78.

[11]Jimmy Dunn, "The Area of Ancient Heliopolis Today" (http://www.touregypt.net/featurestories/on.htm; Internet, accessed 29 June 2011).

[12]Other cities located in Palestine were also known as "Beth-shemesh" (Josh. 15:10; 19:22, 38).

[13]Steven Voth, "Jeremiah," in *Zondervan's Illustrated Bible Backgrounds Commentary*, vol. 4, *Isaiah, Jeremiah, Lamentations, Ezekiel, Daniel*, ed. John H. Walton (Grand Rapids, Mich.: Zondervan, 2009), 332.

JEREMIAH 43

APPLICATION

Continuing in Sin (Ch. 43)

The tracing of Judah's prolonged rebellion warns us about the dangers of continuing in sin. Sinful habits are like threads, winding together daily until a strong cord is formed and cannot be broken (see Eccl. 4:12; Heb. 6:6; 1 Jn. 5:16, 17). That is the situation Judah had created, and they continued in it. Instead of following their destructive pattern, we must flee immediately to the grace of God for cleansing (Ps. 119:59, 60; see Acts 22:16; Rom. 5:6–11; 6:1–7, 16–18; 1 Cor. 15:55–58; 1 Jn 1:6–10).

To develop courage and strength to overcome our temptations, let us consider this summary of the deepening degrees of the trial Jeremiah endured to be faithful to God.

They laughed at his messages (17:15). To have others laugh at our efforts to speak truth is difficult. Nevertheless, Jeremiah did what God wanted him to do. His message said what God wanted him to say.

They redefined his messages, striking at him with their tongues, determining not to heed what he said (18:18). Other people, by twisting our words and refusing to listen us, can be intimidating. Jeremiah endured such words and continued to respond faithfully with his "Thus says the LORD."

They laid plots to ensnare him in his words (20:10). It can break our spirits to know that people are zealously watching for us to make mistakes. Jeremiah rose above that pattern and was faithful to God (Heb. 13:5, 6).

The king took his written work and burned the message he had given (36:22, 23). If people destroyed some precious, personal possession of ours, we might become depressed. However, when this happened to Jeremiah, he resumed his responsibilities before God (28:10–17; 36:27–32).

They labeled him a liar and his words a lie (43:2). For one to continue to serve God among those who call him a liar would be a sobering challenge. Nevertheless, Jeremiah remained faithful to God, and centuries later we still salute him for his steadfast, serving spirit.

The prophet's steadfast faithfulness should encourage us to

overcome, by God's grace, every weakness that would harm us (see 2 Cor. 12:7–10).

Going Back to Egypt (Ch. 43)

Thomas Moore gave a unique treatment to the triumphant song of deliverance that was sung after Israel had crossed the Red Sea:

> Sound the loud timbrel o'er Egypt's dark sea!
> Jehovah has triumph'd—His people are free!
> Sing—for the pride of the tyrant is broken,
> His chariots, his horsemen, all splendid and brave.
> How vain was their boasting—the Lord hath but spoken,
> And chariots and horsemen are sunk in the wave.
> Sound the loud timbrel o'er Egypt's dark sea!
> Jehovah has triumph'd—His people are free![14]

It is sad that after nine hundred years, an arrogant remnant of exiles, fleeing in fear and rebellion, disobediently returned to that forbidden land, rejecting the message of God from His faithful prophet. How awful arrogance can be! It led Pharaoh and his army to drown in the Red Sea, and that same insidious attitude now compelled the remnant to return to Egypt as exiles of evil (43:2, 3).

Jeremiah, A Model Preacher (43:1)

The message that Jeremiah delivered in 42:8–22 was not given to gain popularity. However, the brief summation in 43:1 of what he had done and said is an evangelistic model for making the message known. Each expression contains a rich homiletical nugget.

How he preached: "as soon as Jeremiah . . . had finished telling." Jeremiah told the people *everything* that God instructed him to say. While too many sermons are half-delivered and halfheartedly presented, Jeremiah's message was a thorough, finished product.

---

[14]http://www.litscape.com/author/Thomas_Moore/Sound_The_Loud_Timbrel.html; Internet, accessed 11 July 2011.

To whom he preached: "all the people." Jeremiah spoke to all who had gathered. Messages from God are not to be spoken into the empty air. They are to be spoken to an individual or a group. Good gospel preaching reveals God's message to a gathering of people.

What he preached: "all the words of the Lord their God." That was also Paul's approach (Acts 20:26, 27). Partial preaching and partial obedience are unacceptable to the Lord. Peter may not have fully grasped all that he said on the day of Pentecost in Acts 2 (compare Acts 2:39 with Acts 10:1–5, 9–16, 28–35), but he still said what God wanted him to say. That enabled the inspired word to do its work, even though Peter did not grasp that the promise he was making "for all who are far off" included the Gentiles. We need more ministers who saturate their sermons with appropriately arranged Scriptures, as they declare the whole counsel of God. When we release God's Word to do its work, we have met our responsibility as God's representatives.

Why he preached: "the Lord their God had sent [him]." Jeremiah was doing much more than just mouthing words. He was an ambassador for God. He was saying what needed to be said for the reason that God wanted it said. His was a God-sent message. God's goals for the gospel—including the place and purpose of His Son—must be kept in view if we are to proclaim His precepts acceptably.

The Suffering of Jeremiah (43:5–7)

Jeremiah was forced to go to Egypt, along with the remnant. This was one of many ways that he suffered for the truth. God provided him with strength to endure great suffering during his lifelong ministry: (1) Jeremiah was rejected by his family (12:6); (2) he was rebuked for being a discourager (38:4); (3) he was considered a traitor (37:11–15); (4) he was punished as a false prophet (20:1–5); (5) he was called a "madman" (29:26); (6) he was left alone and depressed, being mocked daily (15:10; 20:7); (7) he was beaten and put in stocks (20:2); (8) he was beaten and put in the dungeon (37:15, 16); (9) he was cast into a muddy cistern (38:6); and (10) he was threatened with death (26:8, 11).

Chapter 44
A Final Glimpse of Jeremiah

Between chapters 43 and 44, enough time had passed for the remnant to scatter out in Egypt. These rebellious souls had not escaped God by going to Egypt, for He rules in every place wherever one might try to hide.

Strategically located, the clause "thus says the Lord of hosts" is included four times in the context of this chapter. In each case, God is further identified as "the God of Israel" (44:2, 7, 11, 25). The word "Lord" in Hebrew is יהוה (*YHWH*), or "Yahweh." This is "the proper name of the God of Israel," the "giver of existence" and "the absolute and unchangeable one."[1] He is truly the Lord of "hosts." The Hebrew word for "hosts" is צָבָא (*tsaba'*), meaning "army," "host (organized body) of angels," or "the host of heaven."[2] He was the "God" (אֱלֹהִים, *'Elohim*) of Israel.[3] This remnant should have worshiped the Lord. He was their God; and He was Yahweh, the Lord of hosts, which means that He was the Lord over all the earth, even Egypt.

The prophet Jeremiah is uniquely coupled with God in this chapter. Though several chapters remain in the book, chapters that contain messages spoken to the nations, Jeremiah here deliv-

---

[1] Francis Brown, S. R. Driver, and Charles A. Briggs, *A Hebrew and English Lexicon of the Old Testament* (Oxford: Clarendon Press, 1972), 217–18.

[2] Ibid., 838–39.

[3] "Yahweh is God in truth" (Jer. 10:10); "righteous God" (Ps. 7:11); "living God" (Jer. 23:36); "Israel's God" (Jer. 35:17); "God of the Hebrews" (Ex. 3:18); "everlasting God" (Is. 40:28); "true God" (2 Chron. 15:3); "God of all flesh" (Jer. 32:27); "God of heaven" (Gen. 24:7); "God of my salvation" (Ps. 18:46); and "God who is my praise" (Ps. 109:1). (Ibid., 44.)

ered his last prophetic words to this small group of his people. The remnant continued in total rebellion to the final hour. One glimmer of hope appears in 44:28, but Jeremiah's message was like a fading beacon in the darkness.

Chapter 44, then, gives us our last glimpse of Jeremiah. As a loyal and courageous soldier, he fought for God's will to be heard and heeded, appealing as long as he was able to a disobedient people. He was faithful to the end, even to this unfaithful band of Jews. In judgment they will surely know that a true prophet of God had stood among them (see Ezek. 2:5; 33:33).

As we come to this climactic moment in the book, it is appropriate to retrace the unparalleled work of this mighty man of God. The tenderhearted, timid youth had become for Yahweh a fortified city, like a pillar of iron and walls of bronze to the whole nation. Many had died, others had been exiled to whatever places Babylon dictated, and the small remnant had further rebelled in making its journey into Egypt. As a fanatical rabble led by treacherous men, their wayward attitude was matched by one stalwart servant of God who boldly and bluntly declared their doom through another "thus says the LORD" (44:20–30). Loyally, manfully, with unflinching prophecies from God, Jeremiah faced that assembly with a graphic description of their destiny. He showed faith, courage, love, and loyalty down to his final prophecy.

The chapter can be divided according to the use of the words "therefore," as it presents God's warnings to these people (44:6, 11, 23); and "then," as it introduces the reasoning of God, the remnant, and Jeremiah (44:7, 15, 20, 24). These key words mark the dividing points, but they do not convey the content. The following divisions give a basic grasp of the chapter: their past punishment (44:1–6); their current condition (44:7–14); their persistent rebellion (44:15–19); the divine perception (44:20–27); and the promise of God's power (44:28–30).

THEIR PAST PUNISHMENT (44:1–6)

¹**The word that came to Jeremiah for all the Jews living in the land of Egypt, those who were living in Migdol, Tahpanhes, Memphis, and the land of Pathros, saying,** ²**"Thus says**

the LORD of hosts, the God of Israel, 'You yourselves have seen all the calamity that I have brought on Jerusalem and all the cities of Judah; and behold, this day they are in ruins and no one lives in them, ³because of their wickedness which they committed so as to provoke Me to anger by continuing to burn sacrifices and to serve other gods whom they had not known, neither they, you, nor your fathers. ⁴Yet I sent you all My servants the prophets, again and again, saying, "Oh, do not do this abominable thing which I hate." ⁵But they did not listen or incline their ears to turn from their wickedness, so as not to burn sacrifices to other gods. ⁶Therefore My wrath and My anger were poured out and burned in the cities of Judah and in the streets of Jerusalem, so they have become a ruin and a desolation as it is this day.'"

Verse 1. In **Egypt**, Jeremiah received a special message to give to the Jews **who were living in Migdol, Tahpanhes, Memphis, and the land of Pathros**. These landmarks indicate that Jews had spread out in the land. "Migdol" was near "Tahpanhes," the city mentioned in 43:8, 9. From these places in the northeastern delta, some had traveled to "Memphis" ("Noph"). This city was located on the west side of the Nile River about 125 miles south of the Mediterranean Sea. Others had migrated much farther south to "the land of Pathros." This place was known as the "land of the South" and also called "Upper Egypt."

Verse 2. God's promised calamity on Jerusalem and all the cities of Judah had become a reality (44:23; see 19:15; 25:29; 36:3; 40:1–3). Since these people had personally experienced the destruction, God could say to them, **"You yourselves have seen all the calamity that I have brought on Jerusalem and all the cities of Judah."** As a consequence, the land was ruined, and the place was uninhabited.

Verse 3. Not only had this remnant seen it, but God's prophet had informed them numerous times of why this horrifying event had come to pass. They had suffered this judgment **because of their wickedness** of **continuing to burn sacrifices and to serve other gods whom they had not known**. They had "not known" any of these gods. These were non-entities who had not spo-

JEREMIAH 44

ken to them, guided them, or delivered them. In their yielding to sin, they had been led into this evil of idolatry by the nations around them.

Verse 4. God clearly identified this terrible practice as a despicable activity. He related how He had sought to lead them out of such wickedness: **"Yet I sent you all My servants the prophets, again and again, saying, 'Oh, do not do this abominable thing which I hate'"** (see comments on 7:25; 26:4–6). The Hebrew word for "abominable," תּוֹעֵבָה (*thoʻebah*), refers to that which is "corrupted" or "polluted." Acts described as detestable to God in the Old Testament include idolatry, child sacrifices, and sexual perversion.[4]

The different stages of this abomination are indicated. To begin with, they had permitted themselves to be taught to serve the gods "they had not known" (44:3). Serving humanly devised idols was not a practice that came from God (see 2:8; 32:33, 34; Deut. 29:10–29). Even further, the people had pursued this course of continuing "to burn sacrifices and to serve other gods" (44:3; Ex. 20:3–5).

Verse 5. Underlying their sin, was their disobedience to the prophetic message. When Jeremiah and others were preaching, **they did not listen or incline their ears to turn from their wickedness, so as not to burn sacrifices to other gods**. God's prophets from Moses to Jeremiah had been rebuffed, rejected, and even persecuted (see 1:16; 2:19; 3:2; 4:14, 18; 8:6; 14:6; 22:22; 23:11, 14; 33:5).

No words can describe what these violations had meant to God. However, He did sum up His feelings in one candid expression concerning His outlook on their idolatry: "which I hate" (44:4). The love of holiness demands hatred of all that is contrary to it or all that destroys it. Bowing before and serving other gods in the presence of God was disloyalty, hypocrisy, and mockery. It reflected abused relationships, a broken covenant, a lost love for God, and shattered promises, all rolled into one shameful violation. Both sides of God's principles and pain are summarized by Jack Cottrell:

---

[4]Ludwig Koehler and Walter Baumgartner, *The Hebrew and Aramaic Lexicon of the Old Testament*, study ed., trans. and ed. M. E. J. Richardson (Boston: Brill, 2001), 2:1702–4.

"Thou hast loved righteousness, and hated wickedness," says the Psalmist to the divine Messiah (Ps. 45:7; cf. Heb. 1:9). The Canaanites were destroyed because "every abominable act which the Lord hates they have done for their gods" (Deut. 12:31). Specific sins hated and detested by God are idolatry (Deut. 7:25; 16:22; Jer. 44:4); occultism (Deut. 18:9–14); haughty eyes, a lying tongue, hands that shed innocent blood, hearts that devise wicked plans, feet that run to do evil (Prov. 6: 16–18; cf. Prov. 12:22; 15:26); false weights (Prov. 11:1); hypocritical ceremonialism in worship (Amos 5:21; Isa. 1:14); arrogance and false trust (Amos 6:8); lying and injustice (Zech. 8:17); divorce (Mal. 2:16); and "the deeds of the Nicolaitans" (Rev. 2:6).[5]

Verse 6. The wickedness of God's people brought the **therefore** of judgment. Distraught with His people, God **poured out** His **wrath** and **anger** upon them (see 7:20; 21:5; 23:19, 20; 30:23; 33:5; 36:7; 42:18). He left Judah and Jerusalem in a state of unbelievable **ruin** and **desolation**. The land that had flowed with milk and honey was already—**as it is this day**, said Jeremiah—a scene of misery, murder, and horror (see 7:33, 34; 14:16; 18:16; 19:8). The response God made should engender in us a deep respect for His wrath.

THEIR CURRENT CONDITION (44:7–14)

Self-imposed Pain (44:7–9)

[7]"'Now then thus says the LORD God of hosts, the God of Israel, "Why are you doing great harm to yourselves, so as to cut off from you man and woman, child and infant, from among Judah, leaving yourselves without remnant, [8]provoking Me to anger with the works of your hands, burning sacrifices to other gods in the land of Egypt, where you are entering to reside, so that

---

[5]Jack Cottrell, *God the Redeemer* (Joplin, Mo.: College Press Publishing Co., 1991), 253.

JEREMIAH 44

you might be cut off and become a curse and a reproach among all the nations of the earth? ⁹Have you forgotten the wickedness of your fathers, the wickedness of the kings of Judah, and the wickedness of their wives, your own wickedness, and the wickedness of your wives, which they committed in the land of Judah and in the streets of Jerusalem?'"'"

Verse 7. God had continually sought to reason with His people (see Is. 1:18). His great patience with this small remnant is evident, as He asked, **"Why are you doing great harm to yourselves . . . ?"** "Doing" comes from עָשָׂה (*'asah*), which can also be translated "make," "work," "perform," or "act."⁶ The KJV uses the word "commit." The Hebrew term for "harm," רָעָה (*ra'ah*), can also be translated "evil" (see comments on 18:8). If there is such a thing as malignant evil or harm, this was it. As they engaged in the enterprise of destroying themselves,⁷ the evil spread to every area of their lives.

"Great harm" comes to one's life when evil influences are present. Such influences cause one's mind to become warped, deceived, and confused, rendering it irrational and unable to make right decisions in the future (see Prov. 14:12; 20:24; Rom. 1:18–23; 2 Tim. 3:13). What happened to Judah and Jerusalem echoes the danger to anyone who opens the door to evil.

In this case, harm would come to all the people—**man and woman, child and infant**. Unfortunately, the decisions of parents would negatively impact their children. Because they had left **Judah** and fled to Egypt, these people would cease to be a **remnant** of God's people (44:14, 27).

Verse 8. Their actions had not only severed their relations with God, but they had also broken His heart, **provoking** [Him] **to anger**. The people continued to incur God's wrath by making **sacrifices to other gods in the land of Egypt**. They would neither listen to the prophet nor learn from him; they refused to respect God and would not return to Him.

---

⁶Koehler and Baumgartner, 1:889–92.
⁷"Yourselves" comes from the word נֶפֶשׁ (*nepesh*), which can mean "breath," "living being," "person," or "soul." (Ibid., 1:711–13.)

Through their disobedience to God, their reputations as righteous people had been destroyed. Instead of light, they had **become a curse and a reproach among all the nations of the earth** (42:18; 44:12). Wherever these people looked—within themselves, up to God, or out to those around them—only a hiss and byword could be heard.

Verse 9. Jeremiah asked the people if they had **forgotten the wickedness** committed by their **fathers, the kings of Judah** and **their wives**, and themselves and their own **wives ... in the land of Judah and in the streets of Jerusalem**. In a few words Judah's history of disobedience is summarized. God pointed to the wicked parents, wicked leaders, and wicked wives. They were unashamed, committing their evil for all to see. Their condition provided no place for hope or happiness.

The Causes for This Shame (44:10)

¹⁰"'"But they have not become contrite even to this day, nor have they feared nor walked in My law or My statutes, which I have set before you and before your fathers."'"

Verse 10. How had such evil conduct developed? Three shortcomings of character and life are named. First, no "contrition" is mentioned: **But they have not become contrite even to this day**. The Hebrew word for "contrite" is דָּכָא (*daka'*), meaning "crushed," "broken in pieces," or "shattered." Here it is used figuratively for being "contrite" or "humble."[8] The people lacked the sense of regret or remorse that might lead to reform. They were committed to the corrupt and had no pangs of conscience that would lead to another path.

Second, they had no "fear": **Nor have they feared**. "Feared" is from יָרֵא (*yare'*), which means "be afraid," "stand in awe of," or "reverence."[9] Having no reverence for the godly, they would neither flee from evil nor proceed toward righteousness. The bold and shameful acts and the attitude of King Jehoiakim viv-

---

[8]Brown, Driver, and Briggs, 193–94.
[9]Ibid., 431.

idly illustrated this trait among these people (36:22–26).

Third, He accused them of being disobedient: They did not walk in His **law** or **statutes** which He had **set before** them and their **fathers**. They remained rebels without any remorse as a nation and as a remnant.

The Promised Punishment (44:11–14)

¹¹"Therefore thus says the LORD of hosts, the God of Israel, 'Behold, I am going to set My face against you for woe, even to cut off all Judah. ¹²And I will take away the remnant of Judah who have set their mind on entering the land of Egypt to reside there, and they will all meet their end in the land of Egypt; they will fall by the sword and meet their end by famine. Both small and great will die by the sword and famine; and they will become a curse, an object of horror, an imprecation and a reproach. ¹³And I will punish those who live in the land of Egypt, as I have punished Jerusalem, with the sword, with famine and with pestilence. ¹⁴So there will be no refugees or survivors for the remnant of Judah who have entered the land of Egypt to reside there and then to return to the land of Judah, to which they are longing to return and live; for none will return except a few refugees.'"

Verse 11. Therefore affirms a conclusion God had reached because of Judah's corruption. Verses 11 through 14 suggest that the remnant had been left to anticipate God's punishment. Their steps had led them to the promised condemnation.

The verdict of God would soon arrive. The Lord said, **"Behold, I am going to set My face against you for woe, even to cut off all Judah"** (see 21:10). Any separation or withdrawal from human beings has overtones of pain; but separation from God—the source of life and love, hope and happiness, salvation and success—is heart-rending! The greatest possible loss has come to those who have lost the Lord.

Verse 12. With their separation from God came suffering: **They will all meet their end in the land of Egypt; they will fall by the sword and meet their end by famine.** Sword or famine would affect all who had **set their mind on entering the land of Egypt to reside there**. Not all wanted to go to Egypt (42:7–12), but the ones determined to do so would "meet their end" or "be consumed" (KJV) in that place. The Hebrew word used here, as well as in 44:18, 27, is תָּמַם (*thamam*), which means "be (become) completed," "come to an end," "be consumed," or "perish."[10] The language identifies a form of destruction that always goes to its intended fulfillment. Everything God had promised in regard to punishment would come to pass.

Along with suffering came a shame of the worst sort: **And they will become a curse, an object of horror, an imprecation and a reproach**. This predicted humiliation (42:17, 18) would become a reality. The degeneration was to deepen as the situation went from becoming "a curse" to "an object of horror" and then to "an imprecation," culminating in being "a reproach" (see comments on 42:18).

Verse 13. At the end of this decline, no survivors would be found. Those who chose to go to Egypt would find no escape there: **And I will punish those who live in the land of Egypt**. Before they left Judah, these misguided people had been warned by Jeremiah that tragedy would befall them in Egypt (42:13–22). Their trials would be similar to those experienced by **Jerusalem** in the time of its siege.

Verse 14. Not only would there be **no refugees or survivors for the remnant of Judah**, but any **longing to return** would be fruitless. The Hebrew word for "longing," נָשָׂא (*nasa'*), has a variety of meanings, including "carry," "lift up," "lift up the head," and "raise his face."[11] For the Jews in Egypt to raise their faces and fix their eyes on Judah in eager expectation would be futile. As life in Egypt continue, they would regret, remember, and long to go back, but their wishes would be in vain. Only a foolish person would bid farewell to what would one day be his foremost "longing." Disobedience brings regret. These people would be without any ability or hope of returning to what they had rejected (see Heb. 12:14–17).

---

[10] Koehler and Baumgartner, 2:1752–54.
[11] Ibid., 1:724–27.

For none will return except a few refugees. These "few" people, the ones who would later be allowed to return, were the ones who had been forced to go to Egypt (see comments on 43:5). No definite proof is available concerning who did return, but God's promise given here was surely fulfilled.

THEIR PERSISTENT REBELLION (44:15–19)

¹⁵Then all the men who were aware that their wives were burning sacrifices to other gods, along with all the women who were standing by, as a large assembly, including all the people who were living in Pathros in the land of Egypt, responded to Jeremiah, saying, ¹⁶"As for the message that you have spoken to us in the name of the LORD, we are not going to listen to you! ¹⁷But rather we will certainly carry out every word that has proceeded from our mouths, by burning sacrifices to the queen of heaven and pouring out drink offerings to her, just as we ourselves, our forefathers, our kings and our princes did in the cities of Judah and in the streets of Jerusalem; for then we had plenty of food and were well off and saw no misfortune. ¹⁸But since we stopped burning sacrifices to the queen of heaven and pouring out drink offerings to her, we have lacked everything and have met our end by the sword and by famine. ¹⁹And," said the women, "when we were burning sacrifices to the queen of heaven and were pouring out drink offerings to her, was it without our husbands that we made for her sacrificial cakes in her image and poured out drink offerings to her?"

Verse 15. A large assembly of Jews, including both **men** and **women**, had been listening to Jeremiah's bold preaching. The exact location of this gathering is not stated, but the text does indicate that the crowd included **all the people who were living in Pathros** (see comments on 44:1). These hearers should have been brought to repentance. They should have been able to easily see their wickedness. After all, some of the men had **wives** who **were burning sacrifices to other gods**.

Verse 16. The people resisted the **message that** [had been] **spoken to** them by this prophet **in the name of the** LORD. Jeremiah simply did not get the response he desired from the people. With an equally bold bluntness, this assembly responded, **"We are not going to listen to you!"**

Apparently, Jeremiah's warnings were not even considered by the remnant. By not listening, they were rejecting God as well as Jeremiah (see 6:16, 17; 1 Sam. 8:6, 7; Lk. 10:16; Jn. 13:20). The tragedies these people had undergone had brought no penitence or pain to their hearts. Both Babylon and sinful behavior had beaten the people down, but neither of these beatings had brought submission. Jeremiah's prophecies surfaced the true hardness of their hearts. With a stiff, stubborn, bragging spirit, they continued to rebel.

Verse 17. With total disregard for what God had said through Jeremiah, they had chosen their course. They responded with these words: **"We will certainly carry out every word that has proceeded from our mouths."** Their decision revealed that the remnant was completely self-centered. They had forgotten the covenant of their Creator. Paganism and humanism had become their guides (see Lev. 11:44, 45; 19:2; 20:7).

The rationalizing people seen here were like those described in Romans 1:21, who "became futile in their speculations, and their foolish heart was darkened" (see Rom. 1:18–25). Multitudes of people have ignored God, but it takes a deeper degree of rebellion to gloat openly over one's own greatness as these people did (see 2:11; 10:23; Prov. 14:12, 14, 16; Rom. 3:4; 10:3; 2 Cor. 10:12, 13).

The text identifies the rationalizations. They reasoned that their long-standing and widespread practices must be right. They chose to follow in the footsteps of their **forefathers, kings,** and **princes,** who practiced idolatry **in the cities of Judah and in the streets of Jerusalem.** Their response defiantly echoes the warning given by Jeremiah in verse 9.

On the basis of tradition, they decided that the **sacrifices to the queen of heaven** were justifiable. They were worshiping this deity in Egypt, just as they had done in Judah and Jerusalem. At the time Jeremiah spoke to them, the "large assembly" (44:15) may have been having a religious festival in her honor. "The queen of heaven" could be identified with the Canaanite goddess Astarte or the Babylonian goddess Ishtar (see comments on 7:17, 18).

JEREMIAH 44

Verse 18. In addition, the people had misplaced the Source of their blessings. They said, **"But since we stopped burning sacrifices to the queen of heaven and pouring out drink offerings to her, we have lacked everything and have met our end by the sword and by famine."** They argued that sacrifices to "the queen of heaven" had been the real source of their prosperity and success in the past. How mistaken they were! Israel had not bowed to "the queen of heaven" as they left Egyptian bondage, nor had they been doing so when they entered the Promised Land. Rather, as they journeyed out of Egypt, the true God had blessed them (Ex. 19:1–9; Ps. 78; see Jas. 1:17). "The queen of heaven" was not the God of their fathers. Abraham, Isaac, and Jacob worshiped the Lord. How could this remnant ignore that God and that heritage and bow down to "the queen of heaven" as the source of success and prosperity?

While God may grant material prosperity, physical health, and national peace, those factors are no divine measuring rod to prove righteousness in people. More than once, when God's people were "fat" that they abandoned their faith in God, bringing on tragic failure (see Deut. 31:19–21; 32:15; Ps. 78:27–37). Material prosperity can never stand as righteousness or give us assurance before God (see Ps. 62:10, 11; 52:7). This remnant had become so deluded that they called truth a lie, good evil, and evil good (see 4:22; 5:21, 30, 31; 10:8–11; 16:10–12; Is. 5:20).

These people were looking for prosperity when penitence was needed. They rationalized that God's punishment (by famine and sword; 44:11–13) was a lack of power on His part to provide for them. Blaming God for their problems, they issued a bold statement of intent to follow the words of their own mouths. After worshiping man-made gods for so long, they now sought to treat the Lord Almighty in the same way. They reasoned that it would be wrong to stop burning sacrifices to "the queen of heaven" (see 44:8).

Verse 19. The wives in the assembly asked, **"Was it without our husbands that we made for her sacrificial cakes in her image and poured out drink offerings to her?"** Women took the leading role in the worship of "the queen of heaven," just as they did in weeping for Tammuz (Ezek. 8:14, 15). These wives argued that their actions were right because their husbands had given them their approval (7:17-19). They emphasized that it was in cooperation with their husbands that they had burned sacrifices, poured out drink offerings, and made sacrificial cakes to the image of "the queen of heaven."[12] However, such actions resulted from turning to corruption rather than living in harmony with God's covenant (Ex. 20:1-5; see Acts 5:1-11).

The boldness of these women, the error of the remnant's reasoning, and their unity in idolatrous acts are all part of the sad scene of a disintegrating nation. Thinking themselves to be wise, they became fools (see Rom. 1:21-23; 1 Cor. 1:26-29).

THE DIVINE PERCEPTION (44:20-27)

God's Explanation (44:20-23)

[20]**Then Jeremiah said to all the people, to the men and women—even to all the people who were giving him such an answer—saying,** [21]**"As for the smoking sacrifices that you burned in the cities of Judah and in the streets of Jerusalem, you and your forefathers, your kings and your princes, and the people of the land, did not the** LORD **remember them and did not all this come into His mind?** [22]**So the** LORD **was no longer able to endure it, because of the evil of your deeds, because of the abominations which you have committed; thus your land has become a ruin, an object of horror and a curse, without an inhabitant, as it is this day.** [23]**Because you have burned sacrifices and have sinned against the** LORD **and not obeyed the voice of the** LORD **or walked in His law, His statutes or His testimonies, therefore this calamity has befallen you, as it has this day."**

Verse 20. Jeremiah countered the rejection of **the people**. He told them that they had received a just judgment from God.

Verse 21. God had remembered their **smoking sacrifices**. He

---

[12]A cake mold representing a goddess (perhaps Ishtar) has been found at Mari in the Middle Euphrates region. For a photograph, see Philip J. King, *Jeremiah: An Archaeological Companion* (Louisville, Ky.: Westminster/John Knox Press, 1993), 105.

JEREMIAH 44

saw everything that they, their **forefathers**, their **kings** and **princes**, and **the people of the land** had done. He called these things to **mind** and announced God's judgment upon them.

Verse 22. When He saw the **evil of** [their] **deeds**, the **abominations which** [they had] **committed**, He **was no longer able to endure it**. He could no longer tolerate their sin or withhold His judgment from it. "Endure" is from נָשָׂא (*naśa'*), the same Hebrew word translated "longing" in verse 14. In this context, the term means "lift up" or "bear" (KJV; NRSV). The definition of this term tells the story. It was no longer possible for Him to "lift up" these people. He had no confidence in them. Even God's great patience has a limit (see Prov. 1:24–33; Amos 1:3, 6, 9, 11, 13). He could not pardon their sin because there had been no repentance (see Heb. 6:1–6). How could He relate to them when they had committed such an "abomination" against Him through spiritual adultery with "the queen of heaven" and other gods? (See 3:1–5.)

They had not only polluted themselves, but they had also defiled their **land**. God's justice brought to them stages of deteriorating conditions. They would be without prosperity because the land was in a state of **ruin**. They would have no pleasure, for the land was **an object of horror**, wasting away. It was desolate and provoked astonishment in the viewer (see 25:11, 18; 29:18). The land was already—**this day**—a barren place and was to be left **without an inhabitant**.

Verse 23. The word **because** introduces the reasons those terrible conditions had occurred. Their mistakes had branched out into three areas. First, they were failures with regard to their focus on the material things. The people had **burned sacrifices** to other gods because they said that they lacked food (44:8, 17–19). This criticism indicates how much their minds were occupied with material benefits. They had a greater need for faith than for food (Heb. 11:6).

Second, they had failed in walking with God. They had **sinned against the** Lord (see 1 Sam. 8:6, 7; 1 Chron. 5:25; Dan. 11:32–36; Hos. 13:16; Mt. 12:30). On several occasions, Jeremiah reminded these people that they had provoked God to anger by their idolatrous conduct (7:18, 19; 8:19; 25:6, 7; 32:30; 44:3).

Third, they had forsaken His message. The verdict concerning them was a tragic indictment: They had not **obeyed the voice of the LORD** (see Deut. 28:14–45; Judg. 2:20–23; Ps. 81:10–13). They had listened to His law but had not obeyed it: They had not **walked in His law, His statutes or His testimonies** (see comments on 11:3). Obedience requires deeds to be done and steps to be taken. Both our beliefs and our daily behavior are important to Him (Ps. 1; Mt. 12:36, 37; 1 Pet. 3:10–12).

The Remnant's Response (44:24, 25)

²⁴**Then Jeremiah said to all the people, including all the women, "Hear the word of the LORD, all Judah who are in the land of Egypt, ²⁵thus says the LORD of hosts, the God of Israel, as follows: 'As for you and your wives, you have spoken with your mouths and fulfilled it with your hands, saying, "We will certainly perform our vows that we have vowed, to burn sacrifices to the queen of heaven and pour out drink offerings to her." Go ahead and confirm your vows, and certainly perform your vows!'"**

Verse 24. Jeremiah continued to speak **to all the people, including all the women**. In this large assembly, the prophet not only declared the evil these people had practiced (44:20–23), but he also reflected on their resolve to continue in idolatry (44:24, 25). His comments were prefaced by an authoritative admonition: **"Hear the word of the LORD, a ll Judah who are in the land of Egypt."**

Verse 25. Both by the vows **spoken with** [their] **mouths** and the acts **fulfilled ... with** [their] **hands**, they had made it clear that their devotion would continue to be to **the queen of heaven**. The Jews in Egypt served idols with greater loyalty than they had ever shown for the one true God when the nation of Judah was still standing (44:17–19; see 8:1, 2). They had said, **"We will certainly perform our vows that we have vowed."** They had made a commitment, and they were determined to keep it. They had resolved to **burn sacrifices** to "the queen of heaven" and **pour out drink offerings**.

With a touch of satire and sarcasm, Jeremiah urged these idolaters to keep these vows they had made to "the queen of heaven." God told them, **"Go ahead and confirm your vows, and certainly perform your vows!"** The time comes when a determined course is all too evident. The cliché "dyed-in-the-wool" has come to identify one whose mind seems to be unchangeable regarding a course he has decided to pursue. Such were these people. Jeremiah implied, "Enough is enough! Go on with what you are doing. Yes, go on into your ruin!" In Revelation 22:10–12, John closed out Christ's covenant with a similar scene of insistence on continuing in sin (see Heb. 6:4–6).

God's Promise (44:26, 27)

²⁶**"Nevertheless hear the word of the LORD, all Judah who are living in the land of Egypt, 'Behold, I have sworn by My great name,' says the LORD, 'never shall My name be invoked again by the mouth of any man of Judah in all the land of Egypt, saying, "As the Lord GOD lives." ²⁷Behold, I am watching over them for harm and not for good, and all the men of Judah who are in the land of Egypt will meet their end by the sword and by famine until they are completely gone.'"**

Verse 26. God's punishment of these people was to be twofold. First, God would remove His name from their lips: **"Behold, I have sworn by My great name," says the LORD, "never shall My name be invoked again by the mouth of any man of Judah in all the land of Egypt."** God punished them by removing one of their highest privileges. Three possible views have been suggested for the meaning of God's statement. (1) His people would not be able to mention God's name because no Jews would be left alive in Egypt. (2) By rejecting God and His covenant, they had lost the right to call upon His name. (3) God punished their apostasy by allowing them to sink so deeply into a state of secularism that they no longer even thought of God.

Verse 27. Second, God told this rebellious remnant that He would oversee their destruction: **"Behold, I am watching over them for harm and not for good, and all the men of Judah who**

are in the land of Egypt will meet their end by the sword and by famine until they are completely gone." He would punish them by releasing upon them the evils He had been withholding from them. When God—the giver of every good and perfect gift (Jas. 1:17)—withdraws all good from us, we are left to the subtle, inadequate supply Satan offers (Jn. 8:44; Rom. 7:18–25; 1 Pet. 5:8). Hopeless tomorrows were projected for these Jews.

Truly, the death knell had been sounded. All the Jews who had sought security in Egypt would suffer and die there by famine and the sword. God's words always stand, while the words from the mouths of these disobedient people were sure to fail.

THE PROMISE OF GOD'S POWER (44:28–30)

[28]"'Those who escape the sword will return out of the land of Egypt to the land of Judah few in number. Then all the remnant of Judah who have gone to the land of Egypt to reside there will know whose word will stand, Mine or theirs. [29]This will be the sign to you,' declares the Lord, 'that I am going to punish you in this place, so that you may know that My words will surely stand against you for harm.' [30]Thus says the Lord, 'Behold, I am going to give over Pharaoh Hophra king of Egypt to the hand of his enemies, to the hand of those who seek his life, just as I gave over Zedekiah king of Judah to the hand of Nebuchadnezzar king of Babylon, who was his enemy and was seeking his life.'"

Verse 28. Jeremiah reminded them of what God had said about coming back: **"Then all the remnant of Judah who have gone to the land of Egypt to reside there will know whose word will stand, Mine or theirs."** They had been told that only a **few**, perhaps those who did not want to go to Egypt in the first place, would be returning. "When it is time for the few to come back," Jeremiah was saying, "then you will know who has told you the truth." From a human standpoint, an onlooker in Jeremiah's time might have found it difficult to know if the words of God and Jeremiah would stand. Would God's word be true, or would the

JEREMIAH 44

equally bold declarations of the remnant be true? Time would tell. Without trust in God's revelation, many situations become merely one person's word against another's.

Verse 29. "This will be the sign to you," declares the LORD. The timeless God, in His own time, would remove any doubt. God promised to give the remnant a "sign" (אוֹת, *'oth*), which would confirm the truth of His earlier prediction.

Verse 30. In this case, God named particular people and specific events. **Pharaoh Hophra king of Egypt** would be given into **the hand[s] of his enemies**, just as **Zedekiah** had been given into **the hand of Nebuchadnezzar**.

Pharaoh Hophra, also known as Apries, was the Egyptian king whose army caused the Babylonians to temporarily lift the siege of Jerusalem in 588 B.C. (37:5). Hophra reigned over Egypt from 589 to 570 B.C. According to the Greek historian Herodotus, the Egyptian army rebelled against Hophra (Apries) and appointed Amasis to be the next Pharaoh. They captured Hophra and imprisoned him. After a while, the Egyptians insisted that he be put to death. As a result, Amasis gave him over to them, and they strangled him.[13]

God's judgment against the Jews in Egypt was at least partially carried out by Nebuchadnezzar, who invaded Egypt twice during this period. According to Josephus' report, the first time was around 582 B.C.[14] Fragments of a Babylonian record indicate that the second invasion of Egypt came in about 568 B.C.,[15] nearly twenty years after the fall of Judah. Even though the details of these invasions are lacking, it is clear that they took place.

---

[13]Herodotus *Histories* 2.161–163, 169–170; see Diodorus *Library of History* 1.68.

[14]Josephus, a Jewish historian of the first century A.D., stated that God signified to Jeremiah about this invasion by Nebuchadnezzar and "commanded him to foretell to the people that Egypt should be taken, and the king of Babylon should slay some of them, and should take others captive, and bring them to Babylon; which things came to pass accordingly; for on the fifth year after the destruction of Jerusalem, which was the twenty-third of the reign of Nebuchadnezzar . . . he took those Jews that were there captives, and led them away to Babylon" (*Antiquities* 10.9.7).

[15]James B. Pritchard, ed., *Ancient Near Eastern Texts: Relating to the Old Testament*, 3d ed. (Princeton, N.J.: Princeton University Press, 1969), 308.

The imprisonment of Hophra in 570 B.C. occurred prior to Nebuchadnezzar's second invasion in 568 B.C., serving as God's "sign" for the remnant. When the Jews witnessed Hophra's downfall, just as God had promised, they then would know that His words would stand against them for harm. However, when they finally faced reality (see 43:10–13), it would be too late to escape the consequences.

Where was Jeremiah the day they faced this reality? We do not know. Surely, when that day came, they realized that a prophet of God had been among them. He had neither faltered nor failed them. God had faithfully communicated to them through a persevering prophet.

APPLICATION

Rejection or Repentance? (Ch. 44)

Chapter 44 shouts the warning that humans may wander so far in sin that their minds are no longer rational or reliable. These souls will face doom and destruction, perilous surroundings, and eternal separation from God. What causes these tragedies? From where do they come? Three sources may instigate this sad situation. It behoves God-fearing people to look carefully at these origins so that they can avoid them at all costs.

The devil may do it. Referring to Satan as "the god of this world," Paul wrote,

> And even if our gospel is veiled, it is veiled to those who are perishing, in whose case the god of this world has blinded the minds of the unbelieving so that they might not see the light of the gospel of the glory of Christ, who is the image of God (2 Cor. 4:3, 4).

Without that gospel, mankind has no hope for salvation or redemption (Rom. 1:16–18). Deceived minds through the devil's influence may pursue a course that seems right, but it is a way that leads to death (Prov. 14:12; Rom. 6:23; Rev. 21:8).

God may do it. When people will not receive, or have a love for, the truth, Paul plainly stated that "God will send upon them a deluding influence so that they will believe what is false" (2 Thess. 2:8–11). While God does not want anyone to perish (see Ezek. 18:30–32; 2 Pet. 3:9), neither does He force His will on those whose sin causes them to favor lies over the law of the Lord.

People may do it. In 2 Timothy 3:8, Paul wrote of Jannes and Jambres, who opposed Moses and the truth. These "men of depraved minds" rejected the faith. Stephen referred to some as "stiff-necked and uncircumcised in heart and ears" because they "resist[ed] the Holy Spirit" (Acts 7:51). Jesus identified certain individuals as being children of the devil, saying, "You are of your father the devil, and you want to do the desires of your father" (Jn. 8:44). People can reject God's Word and His scheme of redemption through many channels—whether it be by human selfishness (Rom. 10:1–3), indifference (Is. 32:9–14; Amos 6:1–7; Zech. 1:15; Mt. 13:22), fear of responsibility (Mt. 25:24, 25), or just seeking human approval (Jn. 12:42, 43). Some actually believe they can outwit God (Ps. 50:16–23; 94:7–11).

Whether deluding influences come from God, the devil, or the mixed-up minds of men, destruction awaits anyone who surrenders to them. How can humanity retain hope in view of these ensnaring influences? God would have all people to be saved (1 Tim. 2:4). He sent Christ to be the Savior of the world (Jn. 3:16; 1 Jn. 4:14); and He is the author of eternal salvation to all who would obey Him (2 Cor. 5:20, 21; Heb. 5:8, 9; 1 Pet. 2:24). Christ's covenant contains the good news that is God's power unto salvation to every one who will believe and obey (Rom. 1:16; Heb. 13:20, 21). That covenant is to be preached to all creation under heaven (Mt. 28:18–20; Acts 1:8; Col. 1:23) and is so designed that we can understand it, even as Paul did (Eph. 3:3–5; 2 Tim. 2:4).

Just as God warned the rebellious Jews in Egypt, so He has warned us:

> The Lord Jesus will be revealed from heaven with His mighty angels in flaming fire, dealing out retribution to those who do not obey the gospel of our Lord Jesus; these will pay the penalty of eternal destruction away from the presence of the Lord and from the glory of His power (2 Thess. 1:7–9).

God has always wanted those who are sick in sin to turn penitently to His will and words, so that they do not perish.

If there ever were souls more steeped in sin than this remnant of God's people who persecuted Jeremiah, it surely must have been the Jews to whom Peter preached on the day of Pentecost in Acts 2. Peter addressed some of the very men who had helped to crucify God's sinless Son (Acts 2:22–24, 36). When those shameful sinners recognized their pitiful plight and cried out for a solution, Peter answered, "Repent and each of you be baptized in the name of Jesus Christ for the forgiveness of your sins; and you will receive the gift of the Holy Spirit" (Acts 2:37, 38). Some three thousand that day gladly received Christ's saving solution: They turned from sin and were baptized, being added by the Lord to the church (Acts 2:41–47; NKJV).

Is there any way our sins could be greater or graver than those of the people who crucified God's Son? Peter's comments prove that anyone can be saved and added to the church—the body of people Christ promises to save and one day present to Himself as a glorious church (Acts 20:28; Eph. 5:25–27). With Christ's eternal covenant before us in this day, let us reach out to receive these promises (Mk. 16:15, 16; 1 Pet. 1:18–25). In contrast to the rebellious Jews in Jeremiah 44, we should avoid God's punishments, which will come through His Son (Jn. 5:28, 29; 12:46–48; Rev. 20:11–15). We should be like the Jews in Acts 2, whose lives were changed by the message they heard.

Chapter 45
God's Message to Baruch

In chapter 45, we are again confronted with the realization that Jeremiah's book does not unfold in a chronological sequence. Even though it does not naturally follow after chapter 44, it is not necessarily out of place. A few observations on the author's purpose may clear away some confusion regarding the discontinuity between this chapter and the flow of the narrative preceding it.

The context makes it fairly clear that chapter 45 is not intended to be a continuation of chapters 43 and 44. These two chapters place the aged Jeremiah with a small Jewish remnant in Egypt. The journey into Egypt occurred some time after the fall of Jerusalem in 586 B.C. In contrast, the events in this chapter transpired during "the fourth year" of Jehoiakim's reign (45:1), that is, 605 B.C., almost twenty years before Jerusalem's fall.

Rather than proceeding with the story of chapters 43 and 44, the chapter serves as an introduction to a new section, namely, Jeremiah's prophecies to the nations which involve the next six chapters (chs. 46—51). As an introduction to God's pronouncements "on all flesh" (45:5), chapter 45 is strategically located.

The events of chapter 45 occurred during the same period as those in chapter 36. At that time, Jeremiah was restricted from the temple, being unable to go before the people (36:1, 5). Nevertheless, he dictated to Baruch a stirring message. Chapter 45 indicates that the message which Baruch had written down as Jeremiah's scribe had powerfully influenced him. The scroll caused tremors of concern among the officials, and King Jehoiakim himself threw it into a fire and burned it (36:16, 20–23).

No one can fully imagine Baruch's feelings. He had a deep concern about the prophetic tragedies he had recorded at Jeremiah's dictation, and he experienced emotional trauma when the hot-tempered king burned that scroll. The king was so upset with Jeremiah and Baruch that these two were forced to go into hiding (36:19, 26). After that experience, Jeremiah dared, under God's directions, to have Baruch rewrite those moving messages, along with some additional ones (36:32). In the destroyed text, God had forecast disaster for the nation; and the updated copy contained a clear statement of the tragic death that would be suffered by King Jehoiakim (36:29–32). Such bold messages of doom for the nation and the king could not be ignored by the people in authority.

The unreceptive king identified this compilation of messages of coming destruction as a most ominous document. Baruch, the bewildered writer of those messages, was unable to remain calm in these unsettling hours. When death stalks and forces one into hiding, it is no small matter! Baruch's reaction becomes the subject of revelation, not speculation. His anxiety clearly comes to light and is dealt with in this brief chapter.

During Baruch's time of need, God gave him the encouragement his battered spirit required so that he could grow and mature as His servant. God did this for Baruch, even as He had done it for Jeremiah in chapters 11 through 20. This portion of the Book of Jeremiah is a personality profile, in which one finds God expressing His concern and mercy for Baruch.

HIS INTEREST IN BARUCH
(45:1, 2)

¹**This is the message which Jeremiah the prophet spoke to Baruch the son of Neriah, when he had written down these words in a book at Jeremiah's dictation, in the fourth year of Jehoiakim the son of Josiah, king of Judah, saying:** ²**"Thus says the LORD the God of Israel to you, O Baruch."**

Verse 1. With its opening words, the content of this chapter is identified as being a **message which Jeremiah the prophet**

spoke to Baruch the son of Neriah. With this beginning, the question of inspiration is eliminated, and the destiny of the revelation is clarified. Also, this opening of the chapter not only dates the writing to **the fourth year of Jehoiakim** (see 25:1; 36:1; 46:2), but it also adds an important setting or context: **when [Baruch] had written down these words in a book at Jeremiah's dictation**. This notation provides the chronological setting as well as an introduction to Jeremiah's prophecy to the nations (chs. 46—51). In those chapters, God presented His judgment upon the Gentile nations.

"Jeremiah the prophet" and "Baruch the son of Neriah" shared some extremely trying times in their service to the Lord. The early stages of their labor together included the trials faced when Baruch wrote the scroll and delivered it to the officials and the king. The first part of this chapter probably relates to the time when the writing of the scroll was completed (ch. 36). Later in time, although earlier in the book, Baruch assisted the imprisoned Jeremiah as he purchased property at Anathoth (ch. 32). Then, when Johanan forced the people to go into Egypt, Baruch and Jeremiah were together for that unfortunate journey (43:1–7). They shared many struggles, and these stories are supplied for us throughout the Book of Jeremiah.

Verse 2. Seemingly, it was while Jeremiah and Baruch were hiding from King Jehoiakim that these words came to the prophet and were dictated to his scribe. No doubt is left about the subject of this personal correspondence: **"Thus says the Lord the God of Israel to you, O Baruch."** God was directing these words squarely at Baruch. The thoughts were from God, not Jeremiah, and they had Baruch's name on them. The message was divine and specific. Few men on earth have received a special communication from God, but Baruch did.

HIS INSIGHT INTO BARUCH'S MOOD
(45:3)

³"'You said, "Ah, woe is me! For the Lord has added sorrow to my pain; I am weary with my groaning and have found no rest."'"

Verse 3. Not only can God give us a message, but He also can see through us and know our states, both mental and physical (Ps. 139:1–12). He knows our thoughts and our words (17:10; Mt. 12:35–37). As is seen here, God can be stunningly personal. His intimate perception was evident in the way He identified all the "I," "me," and "my" words that Baruch used in one sentence. Looking into his heart, God detected an attitude bordering on self-pity. Baruch needed to change his outlook before he would be ready for the more trying days that lay ahead (see 12:5, 6).

Baruch showed four signs of depression in this verse. First, he was troubled. He said, **"Ah, woe is me!"** The Hebrew word translated "woe" is אוֹי (*'oy*). Here is a lamentation that has with it a cry of despair. Jeremiah had been in that same situation (4:31; 10:19; 15:10). Such inner concerns and cries can be uttered on behalf of others, but Baruch's trouble concerned how he saw his own circumstances.

Furthermore, he said, **"For the LORD has added sorrow to my pain."** "Pain" (מַכְאוֹב, *mak'ob*) can refer to a wide variety of physical or mental distresses.[1] This was not just pain on top of pain, or grief added to suffering. Baruch was in a mood to blame God. Several prominent biblical figures exhibited this disposition. Elijah expressed similar sentiments as he sat under his juniper tree (1 Kings 19:4). Jonah had a despondent moment because of the loss of a shade-giving plant (Jon. 4:5–11). Some of the psalms fit this frame of mind (see Ps. 73:2–24). Most developed and striking is the response of Job to his suffering (Job 7:3–20; 10:1–8; 16:6–17; 23:1–17).

Jeremiah had been depressed at one stage of his life (15:17, 18; 18:19–23; 20:7–9). He had reacted to God with doubt and disappointment when struggling with trials in earlier years. He had been in the condition Baruch was now experiencing. God was seeking to help Baruch move toward the same degree of maturity that Jeremiah had developed. We must depend on God's patience, mercy, and grace as we seek to take on His divine nature (see Heb. 5:11–14; 2 Pet. 1:2–4).

---

[1] Francis Brown, S. R. Driver, and Charles A. Briggs, *A Hebrew and English Lexicon of the Old Testament* (Oxford: Clarendon Press, 1972), 456.

Still further, Baruch was tired. He complained, **"I am weary with my groaning."** The Hebrew word for "weary" (יָגַע, *yaga'*) means to be tired or exhausted. The KJV says, "I fainted in my sighing." Baruch had experienced all the ordeals and traumas associated with writing Jeremiah's message and delivering it to different groups. He had also just heard that the king had burned it. Had this affected Baruch? Who would not have been exhausted physically and emotionally after all that he had been through? His good intentions had made him a fugitive. He was having to run into hiding to save his life.

Last, but not least, he was burdened with tension. He had **found no rest**. His mind was too unsettled for sleep to come. Whether this was caused by fear, doubt, confusion, anger, exhaustion, or out-of-control imagination, Baruch wanted relief. He could not "rest; his burdened soul would not relax. It was at this time that the God of all comfort came to his rescue.

HIS MESSAGE FOR BARUCH
(45:4)

⁴**"Thus you are to say to him, 'Thus says the Lord, "Behold, what I have built I am about to tear down, and what I have planted I am about to uproot, that is, the whole land."'"**

Verse 4. God wanted Baruch to view the situation as He saw it. The scribe was asked to see some important truths relative to coming events.

To begin with, God would **tear down** what He had **built**. What He had **planted**, He was **about to uproot**.[2] For two reasons, Baruch needed to meditate on this. Any stress, hurt, or depression that Baruch was feeling about the tragedies prophesied against his homeland, God was experiencing with a deeper love and broader insight that included **the whole land**. God had

---

[2]The Book of Jeremiah began with these words for Jeremiah from the Lord: "See, I have appointed you this day over the nations and over the kingdoms, to pluck up and to break down, to destroy and to overthrow, to build and to plant" (1:10; see 18:7–10; 31:27, 28, 40).

stated this same fact earlier to help Jeremiah (12:7–11). Further, if Baruch thought these tragedies could be averted or would not come to pass (especially, if he had any idea that he might change God's mind), God was assuring him that the tearing down and uprooting were part of His plan and were sure to occur.

HIS MERCY TO BARUCH (45:5)

⁵"'But you, are you seeking great things for yourself? Do not seek them; for behold, I am going to bring disaster on all flesh,' declares the LORD, 'but I will give your life to you as booty in all the places where you may go.'"

Verse 5. With divine insight, God recognized a pride problem that called for correction. He approached the problem with this question: **"But you, are you seeking great things for yourself?"** We are not given a complete picture of the great things Baruch had in mind for himself. However, God's question implies that Baruch had a selfish spirit. Ambitions of the human heart often run counter to the plans and purposes of God.

Had Baruch, as Jeremiah's scribe, been affected by his writing down this tremendous book of prophecies? Had it built in him lofty ambitions regarding his writing skills? Did he long to come out of hiding so he could once again prove his power with the pen? We do not know, but God saw something that required adjustment.

Baruch needed to understand that he must not aspire to do great things for himself because God intended **to bring disaster on all flesh**. The calamity that God was bringing had kept Jeremiah from taking a wife or entering certain houses (16:1–8). Would Baruch not have to also make sacrifices in this situation?

What was Baruch to avoid? We are not told, but surely he knew what God was requiring of him. His personal, selfish, ambitious plans did not fit into God's designs. By not being specific, God provided wise counsel for all of us to avoid selfishness in whatever direction we may be tempted to go. W. H. Bennett surmised that Baruch would have to curb his aspirations to excel in popularity and sophistication:

JEREMIAH 45

We gather from the tone of the chapter that Baruch's aspirations were unduly tinged with personal ambition. While kings, priests, and prophets were sinking into a common ruin from which even the most devoted servants of Jehovah would not escape, Baruch was indulging himself in visions of the honor to be obtained from a glorious mission, successfully accomplished. Jeremiah reminds him that he will have to take his share in the common misery. Instead of setting his heart upon "great things," which are not according to the Divine purpose, he must be prepared to endure with resignation the evil which Jehovah "is bringing upon all flesh."[3]

Though God had been straightforward in His perceptive comments concerning Baruch's problems, He was also gracious and merciful in His projection for Baruch's future. These words were given almost twenty years before Judah fell and the people went into Egypt. Numerous trials occurred within that time frame. Baruch was, through God's guidance, able to triumph over despondency and curtail his ambitious intents, so that he might conform to God's will. No reference to Baruch's complaining is found hereafter. We see him standing faithfully beside Jeremiah through each abusive or disappointing incident. What God said to Baruch in the fourth year of Jehoiakim's reign must have remained with him through all the tragedies that were connected to Judah's fall and to the subsequent journey into Egypt.

What God promised Baruch, as he viewed the slaughter and strife around him, was a precious expression of concern: "I will give your life to you as booty in all the places where you may go" (see 21:9; 38:2; 39:18). Following this special revelation, we know Baruch went to several places, and God's promise went with him every step of that troublesome way. This assurance to Baruch that he would continue to live under and for God had to be a great blessing. He made a heavy sacrifice when he became Jeremiah's scribe, but God gave him the promise that his life

---

[3]W. H. Bennett, *The Book of Jeremiah: Chapters 21—52*, The Expositor's Bible, ed. W. Robertson Nicoll (New York: A. C. Armstrong and Son, 1902), 60–61.

would be preserved. At that time, with all the surrounding devastation and death, this promise was one of the highest order.

What happened to Baruch? We do not know beyond his stay in Egypt with Jeremiah (43:1–7). One tradition, preserved by Jerome, is that Baruch died in Egypt.[4] Another tradition, found in Jewish writings, is that he was taken to Babylon and died there.[5] Bennett referred to these as "mere attempts of wistful imagination to supply unwelcome blanks in history."[6]

APPLICATION

Man's Moods and God's Mercy (Ch. 45)

This brief chapter has a great lesson that incorporates man's moods and weaknesses with God's mercy and sufficiency (see 2 Cor. 3:4–6; 12:7–10). Perry Tanksley captured the message succinctly in the lines of his poem "Standing Up to Life":

> Don't run away and hide
> From troubles that you see;
> You'll multiply the woes
> From which you try to flee.
> We ought to meet our troubles
> Head-on and unafraid;
> It makes our courage grow,
> And helps our fears to fade.
> And if we dauntless face
> The frightful, dreaded foe,
> We'll find by being brave
> Our courage starts to grow;
> And soon discover, too,
> By standing up to life
> That every trouble conquered
> Equips for future strife.

---

[4]Jerome *On Isaiah* 30.6–7. Some believe that Jeremiah died in Egypt as well. One tradition in the Pseudepigrapha says that he was stoned in Tahpanhes by the Jewish people (*The Lives of the Prophets* 2.1).

[5]See Talmud *Megillah* 16b; *Song of Songs Rabbah* 5.5.

[6]Bennett, 57.

> Yet if you should forget
> And fearful run away,
> You'll find, unsolved, each woe
> Will seek you out one day.[7]

Jeremiah and Baruch, discovering that truly God is our helper (Heb. 13:5, 6), stood with courage and set a standard. Surely, with Christ as our helper, we can faithfully march forward, doing the same (Phil. 4:10–13).

The Big Word "Seeking" (45:5)

It is appropriate for us to raise three pertinent questions about what God said to Baruch regarding "seeking."

The first question is "Are we seeking?" Some people just do not seek, and this failure can be a major problem.

The second question is "Are we seeking great things for God?" Let us consider the following passages that deal with seeking great things for Him: Matthew 6:33; 28:5; Mark 16:16; 2 Corinthians 12:14, 15.

The third question is "Are we seeking great things for ourselves?" Selfish seeking can never truly satisfy (see Mt. 20:20–28; Jn. 5:30, 44; 8:50; Phil. 2:21).

---

[7]Perry Tanksley, *Love Gift* (Old Tappan, N.J.: Fleming H. Revell Company, 1971), 67.

Chapter 46
The Judgment of Egypt

By God's plan, Jeremiah was a prophet to all the world. While he was in the womb of his mother, God appointed him to be "a prophet to the nations" (1:5, 10; 46:1). Every prophetic book of the Old Testament (except Hosea) contains some revelations concerning one or more of the nations neighboring Israel. Judgments against the nations can be found in Jeremiah 46—51; Isaiah 13—23; 34; Ezekiel 25—32; 38; 39; Amos 1; 2; and Jonah 1—4.

God has always been interested in the nations, even though He made His special covenant with Abraham and Israel. He watched over a chosen nation so that, through its lineage, the Messiah would come into the world to save us. Beyond this, He is the God of all people (Gen. 12:1–3; 17:4–9; 22:17, 18; 26:1–4; 28:13, 14; Ex. 19:1–8; Deut. 18:15–19; Mt. 1:1–17; Acts 3:18–26; Gal. 3:6–9). God's great love radiated out to the Gentile nations through His chosen people, and He and they were greatly involved in the rise and fall of those nations. As the prophets emphasized God's universal sovereignty—His rule over all the earth—they made known His plans for the future involving those nations.

The prophecies concerning the nations did not present a specific law or code for their behavior, but they did set forth principles from "the Lord of hosts" (see Dan. 4:24–37; 5:18–31; Jon. 1:1, 2; 3:1–10; 4:1, 2, 11; Rom. 1:16—2:16). This guidance is evident in the oracles of judgment that Jeremiah gave concerning the nations in chapters 46 through 51.

Jeremiah 46:2 chronologically sets the stage for the beginning of these prophetic utterances with a judgment against Egypt. It was the fourth year of the reign of Jehoiakim, king of Judah (46:2). Hostile feelings between Egypt and Babylon had existed for some time. Each had ambitions of conquest and supreme power. Judah was geographically located between them and had recently become involved in their battles (2 Chron. 35:20–27). Jehoiakim was appointed to rule over Judah by Pharaoh Neco, the Egyptian ruler (2 Chron. 36:1–4). Therefore, Jeremiah's announcements in the fourth year of Jehoiakim related to the current conflicts, which were matters of grave concern to Judah. He wanted both Judah and Egypt to realize that all of this was part of God's judgment against them (46:10).

In earlier messages, God had promised the remnant in Egypt that Pharaoh Hophra would be overcome by Nebuchadnezzar. Chapter 46 falls into two parts, covering two time periods. The earlier conquest of Egypt by Babylon at Carchemish in 605 B.C. (46:2) was prophetically covered by Jeremiah in the fourth year of Jehoiakim in 46:1–12. The latter part of the prophecy, in 46:13–26, relates to the final conquest by Nebuchadnezzar in 568 B.C. and is more parallel with the prophetic material found in 43:7–13 and 44:29, 30. This second stage of the conquest was pertinent to Judah because the small remnant had fled to Egypt after Judah's fall (43:1–7). These prophecies should have convinced the people that Jeremiah was a true prophet of God and that God would use Nebuchadnezzar to complete His vengeance on Egypt. (See the prophecy against the nations in 27:1–11.)

This great oracle of judgment served as a warning both to Egypt and to the remnant of Judah who were in Egypt. The prophecy has three parts: (1) Egypt's fall to Nebuchadnezzar at Carchemish in 605 B.C. (46:1–12); (2) Egypt's ultimate fall when Nebuchadnezzar invaded Egypt in 568 B.C. (46:13–26); and (3) the encouragement from God for His scattered people (46:27, 28).

THE FALL AT CARCHEMISH (46:1–12)

Preparation of the Egyptian Forces (46:1–4)

¹That which came as the word of the Lord to Jeremiah the prophet concerning the nations.

²To Egypt, concerning the army of Pharaoh Neco king of Egypt, which was by the Euphrates River at Carchemish, which Nebuchadnezzar king of Babylon defeated in the fourth year of Jehoiakim the son of Josiah, king of Judah:
³"Line up the shield and buckler,
And draw near for the battle!
⁴Harness the horses,
And mount the steeds,
And take your stand with helmets on!
Polish the spears,
Put on the scale-armor!"

Verse 1. **Jeremiah**, under God's direction, as **the prophet concerning the nations**, was to give an oracle of judgment to Egypt. He began this unpleasant task by confirming the authenticity of what he was saying. This prophecy, he said, was **that which came as the word of the LORD** to him (see comments on 46:1 and 49:34). As a kind of preface to these six chapters, he referred to himself as a prophet to the Gentile "nations."

Verse 2. His list began with the great nation of **Egypt**. Psammetichus I, Neco II, Psammetichus II, and Hophra of the Twenty-Sixth Dynasty were Egypt's kings who were contemporaneous with Jeremiah. Toward the end of the Assyrian Empire, when growing difficulties at home compelled Assyria to relax her hold on distant territories, Egypt renewed something of her former quest for power and control. Rebounding from the heavy oppression of Sennacherib, the nation resumed its ancient forms of life and government. Unity and independence were restored, and Egypt was again a rival power to Babylon for the domination of Western Asia.[1]

At its beginning, the oracle discussed specifically **the army of Pharaoh Neco king of Egypt** at **the Euphrates River at Carchemish**. It was here that **Nebuchadnezzar king of Babylon defeated** [Egypt] **in the fourth year of Jehoiakim the son of Josiah, king of Judah.**

---

[1]W. H. Bennett, *The Book of Jeremiah: Chapters 21—52*, The Expositor's Bible, ed. W. Robertson Nicoll (New York: A. C. Armstrong and Son, 1902), 220.

JEREMIAH 46

The year was 605 B.C. A battle with unbelievable dimensions was developing. Carchemish, the last Assyrian capital, was the site of the conflict as Assyria tried to retard Babylon's rise to world dominance. With a confident air, the forces of Neco made their preparation to join Assyria in this decisive battle against Babylon.

Jeremiah may have been writing this oracle near the time of the battle. If he wrote shortly before it, he was writing prophecy; if he was writing shortly after it, he was giving a divine interpretation of what had happened.

Verse 3. In prophetic form, Jeremiah wrote from the battlefield itself. A charge was given to the armies to muster their forces: **"Line up the shield and buckler, and draw near for the battle!"** The "buckler" (מָגֵן, *magen*) must have been the small, circular shield, while the "shield" (צִנָּה, *tsinnah*) provided almost full body-length protection.[2] The NIV says, "Prepare your shields, both large and small." Jeremiah, with a tinge of satire, described their enthusiastic binding on of the battle equipment. Egypt was poised and ready for the conflict.

Verse 4. Next, the cavalry was commanded to take their places: **"Harness the horses, and mount the steeds."** Then the call came: **"Take your stand with helmets on!"** The soldiers' helmets, probably made of metal or leather, were fastened into place.[3] Wearing their protective gear, the men awaited the signal to march. Another charge was also issued: **"Polish the spears, put on the scale-armor!"** Spears had to be polished or sharpened beforehand, even as the scale-armor had to be donned before the troops stepped into battle alignment. Prophetic images were sometimes oblivious to time. In the flow of the descriptions, past, present, and future tenses merged in the liveliness of the picture (see Nahum 3:1–10).

---

[2]Ludwig Koehler and Walter Baumgartner, *The Hebrew and Aramaic Lexicon of the Old Testament*, study ed., trans. and ed. M. E. J. Richardson (Boston: Brill, 2001), 2:1037. For more information about shields, see Steven Voth, "Jeremiah," in *Zondervan's Illustrated Bible Backgrounds Commentary*, vol. 4, *Isaiah, Jeremiah, Lamentations, Ezekiel, Daniel*, ed. John H. Walton (Grand Rapids, Mich.: Zondervan, 2009), 336.

[3]Voth, 337.

Neco was defeated and forced to retreat from Nebuchadnezzar (2 Kings 24:7). This battle had major implications for Neco. He did not try to confront Nebuchadnezzar again.

A Sudden Turn of Events (46:5, 6)

> ⁵"Why have I seen it?
> They are terrified,
> They are drawing back,
> And their mighty men are defeated
> And have taken refuge in flight,
> Without facing back;
> Terror is on every side!"
> Declares the LORD.
> ⁶Let not the swift man flee,
> Nor the mighty man escape;
> In the north beside the river Euphrates
> They have stumbled and fallen.

Verse 5. The scene suddenly changed in verses 5 and 6. The previous imagery was the preparation for battle, while this picture is the turn of the tide on the field of battle. Apparently, these were the words of Neco: **"Why have I seen it?"** He was amazed that the advantage in battle was so decisively in Babylon's favor. It is as if he were asking, "How can this be?"

Taking a look at his army, he said, **"They are terrified, they are drawing back."** He saw that his **mighty men** [were] **defeated** and** [had] **taken refuge in flight, without facing back**. The prophet's words suggest astonishment that such a well-trained, well-equipped, and well-disciplined army could be defeated. In this prophecy Jeremiah included a frequently used figure of speech: **"Terror is on every side!"** (see 6:25; 20:4, 10; 49:29).

Verse 6. The battle turned into a lopsided victory for Babylon. Even the best warriors could not escape: **Let not the swift man flee, nor the mighty man escape**. The bravest and strongest of the soldiers had met their match.

In the north beside the river Euphrates, where the battle was being fought, they had **stumbled and fallen**. The great event occurred at one significant place, and the outcome was decided by the end of that battle.

We must not doubt this unexpected scene because the source is reliable. The One describing these events to us is the Lord. Egypt was going down in defeat, falling and stumbling beside the Euphrates River in Babylon.

The Opposition Displayed (46:7-9)

> ⁷Who is this that rises like the Nile,
> Like the rivers whose waters surge about?
> ⁸Egypt rises like the Nile,
> Even like the rivers whose waters surge about;
> And He has said, "I will rise and cover that land;
> I will surely destroy the city and its inhabitants."
> ⁹Go up, you horses, and drive madly, you chariots,
> That the mighty men may march forward:
> Ethiopia and Put, that handle the shield,
> And the Lydians, that handle and bend the bow.

Verse 7. The text reverts in verses 7 through 9 to describing Egypt's strength and readiness for this battle. This was a formidable nation, possessing raging power, like the mighty Nile. The prophet asked, **Who is this that rises like the Nile, like the rivers whose waters surge about?** The Nile at flood stage cannot be hedged in. It overruns its banks and covers the land. This is an apt metaphor for an invincible army.

Verse 8. How mighty was this army? Who could stand in its way? With this flashing imagery, it would be difficult not to hear Pharaoh Neco saying, **"I will rise and cover that land; I will surely destroy the city and its inhabitants."** Many versions generally attribute this statement to Egypt (NIV; NRSV; TEV; NCV; CEV; REB; NJPSV). The NASB, however, capitalizes the pronoun **He,** apparently crediting God with this statement. In this case, the Lord would overthrow mighty Egypt.

Verse 9. As the horses and chariots madly moved to conquer, the people echoed Neco's ambitious, proud spirit: **Go up, you horses, and drive madly, you chariots, that the mighty men may**

march forward. This is a classic example of man's mistaken calculations (see Lk. 14:31–33).

The oracle refers next to **Ethiopia and Put, that handle the shield, and the Lydians, that handle and bend the bow.** The places mentioned here had supplied Pharaoh's mercenary troops. From the days of Pharaoh Psammetichus I (664–610 B.C.), these mercenaries had been a formidable force that made up the major part of the Egyptian army. "Ethiopia" or "Cush" refers to the area just south of Egypt, that is, modern-day Sudan (see comments on 13:23). "Put" is likely the equivalent of Libya, located west of Egypt. Soldiers from these areas were apparently adept at handling the sword and the shield. "Lydians" could refer to men who also came from Libya,[4] or perhaps they were from the kingdom of Lydia in Asia Minor.[5] These soldiers were famous for their archery skills (Is. 66:19; KJV; NIV; NRSV).

Who could withstand such a huge, heavily armed host? Pharaoh was making his boast, but could he deliver the results he anticipated? He should have remembered that these mercenaries, who made up a large part of his army, had no national loyalty to Egypt. If the battle became too fierce, they might flee to the hills for safety.

The Lord's Victory Guaranteed (46:10–12)

> [10]For that day belongs to the Lord GOD of hosts,
> A day of vengeance, so as to avenge Himself on His foes;
> And the sword will devour and be satiated
> And drink its fill of their blood;
> For there will be a slaughter for the Lord GOD of hosts,
> In the land of the north by the river Euphrates.
> [11]Go up to Gilead and obtain balm,
> O virgin daughter of Egypt!
> In vain have you multiplied remedies;
> There is no healing for you.

---

[4]R. K. Harrison, *Jeremiah and Lamentations: An Introduction and Commentary*, Tyndale Old Testament Commentaries (Downers Grove, Ill.: Inter-Varsity Press, 1973), 171.

[5]Voth, 338.

¹²The nations have heard of your shame,
And the earth is full of your cry of distress;
For one warrior has stumbled over another,
And both of them have fallen down together.

Verse 10. Beginning with this verse, we see another marked contrast. In spite of their pomp and power, Egypt's forces suddenly turned into a defeated army and became **slaughter for the Lord GOD of hosts, in the land of the north by the river Euphrates**. Why was this the case? **For that day belong[ed] to the Lord GOD of hosts, a day of vengeance, so as to avenge Himself on His foes.** God, not Egypt or Babylon, rules the world (Is. 24:21; 54:5; Zech. 14:16–18). God's own **sword** was attacking Egypt, and that sword would **devour and be satiated and drink its fill of [the] blood** of Egypt.

Egypt is referred to here as God's "foes," but not because they had held God's people captive in the days of Moses. God had settled that issue with ten disastrous plagues and a mighty deliverance at the Red Sea (Ex. 7—12; 14).

In more recent years, Egypt had been a constant source of irritation to God and His people. For instance, Pharaoh had shown favor to Hadad the Edomite, an enemy to King Solomon (1 Kings 11:14–22). Shishak, the king of Egypt, had warred against God's people (1 Kings 14:25–27); and Egyptian rulers had tried to usurp God's place as Judah's protector (2 Kings 18:19–24). Pharaoh Neco had killed good King Josiah and banished Josiah's son, Jehoahaz, to Egypt (2 Kings 23:29–34). He had even extended a gesture of hope to Zedekiah and the few remaining in Judah—all in defiance of Jeremiah's prophecies concerning the conquest by Nebuchadnezzar (27:1–11; 37:3–11; 43:1–7). Egypt, a constant source of conflict between God and His people, was viewed as God's foe.

Verse 11. Because of the severity of the conflict, there was no cure for Egypt. The people could not **go up to Gilead**, a place known for its healing **balm** (see comments on 8:22). The balm of Gilead would not solve Judah's sins, and it certainly would offer no healing for Egypt. She had even been known as being a land of healing **remedies** of all sorts; but in this battle, there was **no**

healing for her. No cures were available; only agonizing cries of distress awaited them.

Verse 12. The nations have heard of your shame. Egypt's disgrace and stumbling had spread to all the nations. Her cry of agony and defeat had become the subject of conversation in the neighboring nations. Word had spread, and **the earth** [was] **full of** [her] **cry of distress.**

Egypt's infantrymen, skilled with the latest techniques of warfare, **stumbled over** [one] **another.** Instead of marching like seasoned soldiers, they wobbled like blind beggars.

This message, given in the fourth year of Jehoiakim, would certainly have warned those remaining in Judah (after its fall) that Egypt was no place to seek security. Here is another dramatic proof that either Judah was not listening to Jeremiah, or else those few refugees who later forced him to go to Egypt did not remember the prophecy about the Egypt's plight.

EGYPT'S ULTIMATE FALL (46:13–26)

Egypt's Mighty Ones Humbled (46:13–17)

¹³This is the message which the LORD spoke to Jeremiah the prophet about the coming of Nebuchadnezzar king of Babylon to smite the land of Egypt:
¹⁴"Declare in Egypt and proclaim in Migdol,
Proclaim also in Memphis and Tahpanhes;
Say, 'Take your stand and get yourself ready,
For the sword has devoured those around you.'
¹⁵Why have your mighty ones become prostrate?
They do not stand because the LORD has thrust them down.
¹⁶They have repeatedly stumbled;
Indeed, they have fallen one against another.
Then they said, 'Get up! And let us go back
To our own people and our native land
Away from the sword of the oppressor.'
¹⁷They cried there, 'Pharaoh king of Egypt is but a big noise;
He has let the appointed time pass by!'"

Verse 13. This verse introduces a different phase of the oracle, as its preface indicates: **This is the message which the LORD spoke to Jeremiah the prophet about the coming of Nebuchadnezzar king of Babylon.** The Babylonian forces were no longer near the Euphrates River at Carchemish. By this time, Nebuchadnezzar was coming **to smite the land of Egypt.**

Nebuchadnezzar's "coming" has been given three different dates: One is 605 B.C., when he pursued Neco for a short time after the battle of Carchemish.[6] The second is 601 B.C., when Nebuchadnezzar and Neco fought again on the border of Egypt.[7] That battle was indecisive. The third is 568 B.C., when Nebuchadnezzar invaded Egypt and achieved a complete victory.[8] That battle seems to be the burden of this oracle.

If the date for the battle was 568 B.C., it occurred some thirty-seven years after the battle at Carchemish. Not long after the destruction of Jerusalem (586 B.C.), the remnant of Judah had gone down into Egypt, seeking security from Babylon (43:1–7). If the remnant believed that they would have security while living in Egypt, then they had ignored Jeremiah's plain prophecies to the contrary (43:8–13; 44:26, 27, 30).

Verse 14. The oracle warned the cities to which the remnant had gone to prepare for Nebuchadnezzar's coming. The proclamation of the ensuing campaign was to be **declare**[d] in the cities of **Migdol, Memphis,** and **Tahpanhes.** These same cities were named in 44:1 as the locations in Egypt where the remnant went. "The land of Pathros," although included in the list in 44:1, does not appear here. The message for the cities was **"the sword has devoured those around you."** The time had come; the warning Jeremiah had given the remnant before they left Jerusalem was soon to be fulfilled.

Verse 15. Jeremiah's prophecy announced—as if it were

---

[6]See William W. Hallo, ed., *The Context of Scripture* (Boston: Brill, 2003), 1:467–68.

[7]See Kenneth A. Kitchen, "Neco," in *The International Standard Bible Encyclopedia*, rev. ed., ed. Geoffrey W. Bromiley (Grand Rapids, Mich.: Wm. B. Eerdmans Publishing Co., 1986), 3:510.

[8]See James B. Pritchard, ed., *Ancient Near Eastern Texts: Relating to the Old Testament,* 3d ed. (Princeton, N.J.: Princeton University Press, 1969), 308.

already happening—a major defeat that Egypt would experience. When the battered and beleaguered forces of Egypt returned from the battlefield, their cry went up: **"Why have your mighty ones become prostrate?"** The LXX has "Why has Apis fled?" This translation has been utilized by several English versions (RSV; NRSV; NEB; REB; TEV; NJB; CEV). To arrive at this phrasing, the translators arbitrarily divided the Hebrew verb into a verb and a noun. The verb in the Masoretic Text (MT) is נִסְחַף (*nis-chap*), which means "become prostrate." In dividing the verb, the LXX came out with נָס (*nas*), a verb meaning "fled,"[9] and חַף (*chap*), which is the noun for "Apis," the sacred bull of Egypt. If the LXX is correct, this rendering involves victory over an Egyptian deity. As R. K. Harrison pointed out, "In ancient Near Eastern thought the conquest of a nation entailed the defeat of its gods."[10] However, if one holds to the MT, the line is a characterization of Pharaoh or his soldiers falling as the battle goes to the Babylonians.

The answer that fills the air is the name of the Lord of hosts: The Egyptian soldiers and gods could **not stand because the LORD** [had] **thrust them down.** "Thrust" is from the Hebrew word הָדַף (*hadap*), which means "thrust away," "drive out," and "depose."[11] Truly, the weak things of God cast down the strong forces of men, and those who deem themselves wise before God's judgments prove to be foolish (see Lev. 26:7, 8; Deut. 32:28–31; 1 Sam. 17:26–52; 1 Cor. 1:26–29).

Verse 16. The idea of stumbling stands for inability, confusion, and disorganization. In the throes of the battle, **they** [had] **repeatedly stumbled; indeed,** [many of them had] **fallen one against another.** In the mire of defeat, they urged one another to retreat to safety. To those who had fallen, **they said, "Get up! And let us go back to our own people and our native land away from the sword of the oppressor."** The reference here must be to the mercenary soldiers who fought for Egypt (46:9). These

---

[9]The lexical form is נוּס (*nus*).
[10]Harrison, 172.
[11]Francis Brown, S. R. Driver, and Charles A. Briggs, *A Hebrew and English Lexicon of the Old Testament* (Oxford: Clarendon Press, 1972), 213.

paid warriors had experienced enough; they were going home. The battle was too much for them.

Verse 17. When Egypt's forces returned in defeat, they cried, **"Pharaoh king of Egypt is but a big noise"** (see Is. 30:7). The word for "noise" (שָׁאוֹן, *sha'on*) indicates a loud sound, like the roar of rushing waters (Is. 17:12). The pharaoh had bragged about the size and strength of his army, but now the braggart was having to admit defeat. The mockery is a parallel to the cliché "Big cloud! Loud Thunder! No Rain!" When a nation loses trust in its leaders, the core of that nation's strength has crumbled. The expression **he has let the appointed time pass by** reflects a conviction that Pharaoh had not taken advantage of his earlier opportunities with Babylon. With shattered morale and wearied bodies, Egypt's forces declared that Pharaoh should give up the battle.

Egypt's Final Fall Before the Lord and Babylon (46:18–24)

> ¹⁸"As I live," declares the King
> Whose name is the LORD of hosts,
> "Surely one shall come who looms up like Tabor among the mountains,
> Or like Carmel by the sea.
> ¹⁹Make your baggage ready for exile,
> O daughter dwelling in Egypt,
> For Memphis will become a desolation;
> It will even be burned down and bereft of inhabitants.
> ²⁰Egypt is a pretty heifer,
> But a horsefly is coming from the north—it is coming!
> ²¹Also her mercenaries in her midst
> Are like fattened calves,
> For even they too have turned back and have fled away together;
> They did not stand their ground.
> For the day of their calamity has come upon them,
> The time of their punishment.
> ²²Its sound moves along like a serpent;
> For they move on like an army
> And come to her as woodcutters with axes.

> ²³"They have cut down her forest," declares the LORD;
> "Surely it will no more be found,
> Even though they are now more numerous than locusts
> And are without number.
> ²⁴The daughter of Egypt has been put to shame,
> Given over to the power of the people of the north."

Verse 18. This part of the oracle presents God as speaking. During the time of the battle, **the King whose name is the LORD of hosts** declared that He was the real warrior that Egypt was fighting. **"As I live,"** He said, **"one shall come who looms up like Tabor among the mountains, or like Carmel by the sea."** These two mountains in northern Israel are conspicuous on the landscape. They tower upward, with nothing around equal to them. Similarly, Nebuchadnezzar's great power and might would be unexcelled; the Babylonians would bring about exile on one hand and destruction on the other.

Verse 19. Those dwelling in Egypt were headed for exile. With these words, the fulfillment of the prophecy to the exiles was given: **"Make your baggage ready for exile, O daughter dwelling in Egypt."** They would see that the Lord's word was good; the claims of the false prophets could not compare with the divine message.

Memphis ("Noph"; KJV) would be burned and left uninhabited. It would **become a desolation,** being **burned down and bereft of inhabitants.**

Verse 20. Another metaphor is introduced here, depicting **Egypt** as **a pretty heifer.** This nation was beautiful, sleek, and well-fed, having wealth and luxury. However, **a horsefly** [was] **coming from the north**—the Babylonian army—and it would attack her. This "horsefly" was known for biting cattle, causing wounds and festering irritations. The Hebrew word is קֶרֶץ (*qerets*), meaning "a nipping or stinging insect."[12] The root term carries the idea of gnawing, biting, or tearing away. The figure suggests that Egypt was about to be stung all over.

Verse 21. Egypt's **mercenaries** were **like fattened calves**—

---

[12]Ibid., 903.

JEREMIAH 46

well-fed but being led to slaughter, not to victory. The figure may also include their turning on the nation and fattening themselves on anything that could be taken.[13] Warfare was their business, but these men had **turned back** and had **fled away together**. These battle-wise soldiers could **not stand their ground** before the superior warriors of Babylon. **The day of their calamity** [had] **come**, and **the time of their punishment** had arrived.

Verse 22. Egypt had no defense left. **Its sound move**[d] **along like a serpent**. The defeated armies slipped away in a line, making only a hissing sound like a slithering snake. As their king had done earlier, they made a humming sound of retreat rather than the tumultuous noise of an attack. They hissed, but they could no longer bite. This was true of Egypt, but not of Babylon. Nebuchadnezzar's force **move**[d] **on like an army and** [came] **to her as woodcutters with axes**. The Babylonians, like "woodcutters," cleared the land of people, property, and precious things (see comments on 5:17; 6:6).

Verse 23. Like innumerable locusts, they gleaned everything good and left the rest in ruins. **"They have cut down her forest," declares the** Lord; **"surely it will no more be found, even though they are now more numerous than locusts and are without number."** Every figure here used by God describes devastation and destruction. Egypt was left helpless, poor, and hurting.

Verse 24. The completeness of the victory is given in a summary statement: **The daughter of Egypt has been put to shame, given over to the power of the people of the north**. Egypt had finally succumbed to the power of Babylon.

Egypt's Punishment and Promise (46:25, 26)

²⁵**The** Lord **of hosts, the God of Israel, says, "Behold, I am going to punish Amon of Thebes, and Pharaoh, and Egypt along with her gods and her kings, even Pharaoh and those who trust in him.** ²⁶**I shall give them over to the power of those who are seeking their lives, even into the hand of Nebuchad-**

---

[13]Theo. Laetsch, *Jeremiah*, Bible Commentary (St. Louis: Concordia Publishing House, 1965), 329.

nezzar king of Babylon and into the hand of his officers. Afterwards, however, it will be inhabited as in the days of old," declares the LORD.

Verse 25. If there was anything more horrifying than the cruel force from "the north," it was the message that Egypt's fall was because **the LORD of hosts, the God of Israel** had willed their destruction.

The hearers of the prophecy were taken behind the scene of battle alignments and military strength to see the real power that had defeated Egypt. God said that He had a score to settle with these people: **"Behold, I am going to punish Amon of Thebes, and Pharaoh, and Egypt along with her gods and her kings, even Pharaoh and those who trust in him."**

Concerning Thebes, Steven Voth wrote of its location and prestige:

> It was the most important city in Egypt after Memphis and was located on the Nile River 438 miles south of the Mediterranean.... It served as the capital city of Egypt from the Middle Kingdom (ca. 2100 B.C.) up until the Assyrian invasion led by Ashurbanipal (ca. 663/661 B.C.). In Egyptian texts Thebes is referred to as "the city of Amon."[14]

Ezekiel had prophesied, "Thebes will be breached" (Ezek. 30:16); history affirms that his words were literally fulfilled. In this way, God attacked and destroyed "Amon of Thebes"—the sun god that for centuries was "the chief god of the Egyptian pantheon."[15]

From Jeremiah's time up to the third century of the Christian Era, Thebes faced a succession of attacks by foreigners and insurrections from local sources. Nebuchadnezzar (568–567 B.C.) was an early force that attacked. Next came Cambyses II in 525 B.C., who plundered Thebes, burned its temples, and ravaged the city. Her former prominence was never regained. An

---

[14]Voth, 339.
[15]Laetsch, 329.

insurrection at Thebes was mercilessly quelled by the Persians in 335 B.C. The next conquest was brought by Alexander the Great, when he conquered Egypt in 332 B.C. Ptolemy IX, in the first pre-Christian century, seeking to stop an uprising, completely destroyed Thebes. No city walls can be seen amidst the ancient ruins now. Some gateways and pylons mark the places where walls once stood when the famous city flourished. Jeremiah and Ezekiel once again stand as true prophets of God's judgments on that city.

Verse 26. God was the divine source of power, and Nebuchadnezzar was the instrument. He said, **"I shall give them over to the power of those who are seeking their lives, even into the hand of Nebuchadnezzar king of Babylon and into the hand of his officers."** This was a promise, and the promise was kept by the Most High.

God also said, **"Afterwards, however, it will be inhabited as in the days of old."** The "afterwards" may parallel phrases like "the latter days" (see 48:47; 49:6, 39), when God would bring out of captivity many of these peoples. "The latter days" could be symbolizing the Messianic Age, for similar phrases are so used in the New Testament (Acts 2:17; Heb. 1:1, 2; 1 Pet. 1:18–20; 1 Jn. 2:18). Regardless of the exact age meant in this verse, it is a matter of history that Egypt did submit to Nebuchadnezzar and a biblical fact that God was the one who gave Egypt into Babylon's hands.

GOD'S ENCOURAGEMENT FOR HIS SCATTERED PEOPLE (46:27, 28)

[27]"But as for you, O Jacob My servant, do not fear,
Nor be dismayed, O Israel!
For, see, I am going to save you from afar,
And your descendants from the land of their captivity;
And Jacob will return and be undisturbed
And secure, with no one making him tremble.
[28]O Jacob My servant, do not fear," declares the LORD,
"For I am with you.
For I will make a full end of all the nations

> Where I have driven you,
> Yet I will not make a full end of you;
> But I will correct you properly
> And by no means leave you unpunished."

Verse 27. Comments concerning God's judgment against Egypt were of more than just national interest. The remnant of Judah (including Jeremiah) had come to reside there, and God (along with Jeremiah) was still greatly concerned about these people. Therefore, at the close of this oracle, God included a **but**, as the NASB puts it. Egypt was to become a desolation, making it foolish for the remnant to hope or trust in that land and its rulers for their security. Still, God's people, wherever they had been scattered, were **not** to **fear** or **be dismayed**. They are referred to here as **Israel** and **Jacob** (see comments on 30:10, 11; 31:7–9).

After spending years in captivity because of their rebellion, God's people were nearing the time when they would finally listen to God so He could **save** them. Wherever the **captivity** had taken them, His people would **return and be undisturbed and secure**. They would have no need to **tremble** again.

Verse 28. This great Egyptian oracle ends with the promise that God would abide among His faithful servants. He is ever seeking to give eternal hope to those who trust in Him. The Lord spoke in tones of forgiveness and restoration, **"O Jacob My servant, do not fear, . . . for I am with you."**

It is true that God brought His people out of captivity, but He continued to use the rod of discipline when it was needed. God judged the **nations** who had taken His people captive, bringing those nations to **a full end**. However, this was not to be so for His people; He would **not make a full end** of them. His promise to His followers was certain and abiding, corrective and redemptive: **"I will correct you properly and by no means leave you unpunished."** The Hebrew word for "correct" (יָסַר, *yasar*) means "discipline," "chasten," or "admonish."[16]

When Jeremiah's words were first written, how grateful those people should have been! God's promise did not waver for over

---

[16]Brown, Driver, and Briggs, 415–16.

a half-century, even though they continued in their impenitence. God was able and ready to bless them, whenever they were ready to obey. It is sad that they took so long to search for Him wholeheartedly (see 29:10–14).

APPLICATION

God's Promise of Renewal (46:28)

In 46:28, God made a touching promise to His people in Egypt. This is a promise that we also need to consider.

The Promise of Comfort—"For I am with you." Among the many things God is to man, He is the God of comfort (2 Cor. 1:3–7; see Mt. 28:20; Rom. 8:31–39; Heb. 13:5, 6). Anyone who has wandered from God's principles and has delayed repentance should drink deeply of the statement God made to these people, even as they maintained their sinful ways. While He chastened them and pursued a course to break their stubborn will, He was still beside them with positive goals. God wanted them back.

The Promise of Continuation—"For . . . I will not make a full end of you." God's promises do not fail. His plans will be completed. God has often salvaged and saved penitent people who wandered afar from His will and ways. He ever longs to lift up, redeem, and restore the fallen (see Num. 6:26, 27; Ps. 10:12; Is. 1:26; 49:22; Jer. 30:17; Jas. 4:10).

The Promise of Correction—"I will correct you properly and by no means leave you unpunished." God can do this in many different ways. Whatever procedure He uses, we need to recognize that His intents and purposes are pure and proper. Various Scriptures emphasize the disciplinary relationship God has always maintained with His people. In both the old and the new covenants, this principle is clearly stated: "My son, do not reject the discipline of the Lord or loathe His reproof, for whom the Lord loves He reproves, even as a father corrects the son in whom he delights" (Prov. 3:11, 12; see Heb. 12:5, 6). Peter said that, if it is necessary, God will distress us with various trials to prove and build our faith (1 Pet. 1:6, 7). God so disciplines His people for their good (Heb. 12:9–11). He knows us better than we know ourselves, enabling Him to apply proper corrective measures at the right time and place. He stated, "When it is My desire, I will chastise them; and the peoples will be gathered against them when they are bound for their double guilt" (Hos. 10:10). While the devil tempts us to break us, God disciplines us to make us (Jas. 1:12–15). Because of His chastening and corrective acts, we are able to endure (Heb. 12:7). The psalmist recognized this and said, "Before I was afflicted, I went astray, but now I keep Your word. . . . It is good for me that I was afflicted that I might learn Your statutes" (Ps. 119:67, 71).

The insertion of this special promise for God's people (46:28) in the midst of Jeremiah's prophecies to the nations teaches us that God has always had an interest in all nations and all peoples. His core concern is for His principles to prevail in human hearts. He has consistently worked (and continues to work) for the redemption of wayward souls. Each of these inspired statements to the nations is proof of God's moral and spiritual interest in every heart. While God worked in a special way with the seed of Abraham to bring the Redeemer to men through that lineage (Mt. 1:1–17; Gal. 3:8–29; 4:1–6), that Redeemer died for all (2 Cor. 5:14–21; 1 Pet. 2:21–25). Therefore, these prophecies to the nations are just one of the living monuments of God's interest and concern for great empires or small sovereign states.

God is over all as the Lord of hosts. Ultimately, every knee will bow before Him, and every tongue will confess that Christ is Lord, with the whole transaction being to the glory of God (Rom. 14:10–12; Phil. 2:5–11). Seated at God's right hand, Christ is now King of kings and Lord of lords (Rev. 19:11–16). In the midst of earthly kingdoms and governments, He is now King over His kingdom and head over His body, the church (Mk. 9:1; Lk. 24:44–49; Acts 1:1–8; 2:22–47; 1 Cor. 15:20–28; Eph. 1:18–23; 5:23–27; Col. 1:12–20).

The call is to be sounded to people of all nations, exhorting them to enter His eternal kingdom or church (Mt. 28:18–20; Jn. 3:3–5; 1 Thess. 1:1; 2:12; Heb. 12:22–29). Christ has the right to make such a call, having died for all, and He builds a glorious and righteous relationship with all who submissively obey Him.

CHAPTER 47
THE JUDGMENT OF PHILISTIA

The Philistines were descendants of Ham (Gen. 10:6, 13, 14), who, it seems, came from the country of "Caphtor" (כַּפְתּוֹר, *Kaphtor*; see 47:4; Amos 9:7). This is generally believed to be the isle of Crete and related islands.[1] These people moved into the coastal region of Palestine and gave their name to the entire land.

That God would make an announcement of judgment like the one announced for the Philistines in chapter 47 comes as no surprise. As early as the days of Abraham, these people had been in conflict with God's chosen people (Gen. 21:32–34; 26:1–18). They were a constant military menace to Israel.

Ezekiel, a prophet contemporaneous with Jeremiah, gave two reasons that Philistia was deserving of judgment (Ezek. 25:15–17). First, he said they were due judgment because of the evil spirit of revenge they had continually demonstrated (see Deut. 32:35; Rom. 12:17–19). In addition, Ezekiel said that God would judge them for a teaching purpose. He wanted to show them the power and identity of the true God: "They will know that I am the LORD when I lay My vengeance on them" (Ezek. 25:17). Other prophecies against Philistia were made in Isaiah 14:28–31; Amos 1:6–8; and Zephaniah 2:5–7.

---

[1] Merrill C. Tenney saw evidence in the Scriptures for an ancient connection between Crete and Philistia. (See Ezek. 25:16 and Zeph. 2:5, where the LXX renders Cherethites as "Cretans.") The Philistines were called "Cherethites." "It is possible," Tenney said, "that Caphtor includes with Crete also the other islands in the vicinity, including Caria and Lycia" (Merrill C. Tenney, *Zondervan Pictorial Dictionary of the Bible* [Grand Rapids, Mich.: Zondervan Publishing House, 1967], 147).

AUTHORITY AND DESTINATION (47:1)

¹That which came as the word of the LORD to Jeremiah the prophet concerning the Philistines, before Pharaoh conquered Gaza.

Verse 1. In this second judgment oracle that **came as the word of the LORD to Jeremiah the prophet**, a vivid warning was delivered **concerning the Philistines**. The introductory formula here is parallel to the formulas in 46:1 and 49:34.

The time element is supplied in the words **before Pharaoh conquered Gaza**. The significance of this note was likely clear to those who lived in his era, but its meaning remains obscure to us. The LXX has omitted the phrase entirely. Some help on this question may be found in Jeremiah's reference to the force "from the north" in the next verse. That expression was Jeremiah's way of identifying Babylon and Nebuchadnezzar in the fourth year of Jehoiakim, before the battle of Carchemish in 605 B.C. (1:13, 14; 4:6; 6:22; 46:1, 2). After that battle, Jeremiah freely and specifically named Babylon and Nebuchadnezzar (20:4; 21:9; 25:11–13; 27:8, 13; 28:4, 11; 29:10, 15). Based on that understanding, it is a reasonable conclusion that the message in 47:1–7 was one of Jeremiah's earlier prophecies.

The pharaoh who reigned during this period was Neco II (610–595 B.C.). It is possible that Neco attacked Gaza on his way to fight the Babylonians, prior to 605 B.C. However, C. F. Keil concluded that Neco left Egypt, went beyond Gaza on his way to invade the Babylonian forces, and then returned from the north to Gaza, conquering it in order to keep that area open as "the high road to Egypt," the route of his return.[2] This would place the attack on Gaza a little after 605 B.C. It is possible also that the reference to Pharaoh's conquering of Gaza may point to some other occasion.

---

[2]C. F. Keil and F. Delitzsch, *Commentary on the Old Testament*, vol. 8, *Jeremiah, Lamentations* (Grand Rapids, Mich.: Wm. B. Eerdmans Publishing Co., n.d.), 199.

JEREMIAH 47

THE POWER COMING "FROM THE NORTH"
(47:2, 3)

²Thus says the LORD:
"Behold, waters are going to rise from the north
And become an overflowing torrent,
And overflow the land and all its fullness,
The city and those who live in it;
And the men will cry out,
And every inhabitant of the land will wail.
³Because of the noise of the galloping hoofs of his stallions,
The tumult of his chariots, and the rumbling of his wheels,
The fathers have not turned back for their children,
Because of the limpness of their hands."

Verse 2. What did **the** LORD say about the Philistines? He said, in effect, "I am sending a force **from the north** upon you." This enemy "from the north" undoubtably refers to Babylon and its leader Nebuchadnezzar (20:4–6; 25:1–9; 27:1–8). The powerful nature of this army is vividly described in verses 2 and 3. All that Egypt had pretended and claimed to be, Babylon actually was—and that power would be brought upon Philistia.

The invasion by Babylon is pictured as a raging torrent of destructive, overpowering **waters**. The metaphor of surging waters, one of the greatest powers known to man, is used for the mighty invasion of Babylon in 46:8. This metaphor is used of Assyria in Isaiah 8:7, 8, and of the disasters of life in Psalm 93:3, 4. The water figure emphasizes swiftness, engulfing strength, and expansive coverage. These waters would **become an overflowing torrent, and overflow the land and all its fullness**.

Grown **men** [would] **cry out** in the face of the Babylonian assault, and **every inhabitant of the land** [would] **wail**. In this parallelism, the words "cry out" (זָעַק, za'aq) and "wail" (יָלַל, yalal) are used synonymously to describe their deep affliction. The word *za'aq* refers to a "call for help."³ The word *yalal* means

---

³Ludwig Koehler and Walter Baumgartner, *The Hebrew and Aramaic Lexicon of the Old Testament*, study ed., trans. and ed. M. E. J. Richardson (Boston: Brill, 2001), 1:277.

"howl" or "lament."[4] It is an onomatopoetic term,[5] that is, a word imitating the sound of what it denotes. Such weeping was associated with the deepest forms of crying, causing a sufferer to shout out his strongest feelings of pain and distress. This type of anguish was not only characteristic of mourning for the dead, but it was also used of a man who pled for someone to help him bear his personal pain. Whether this pain was caused by danger, shame, sickness, or stress, it was a most intense suffering.

Using the figure of swelling waters that would **rise** in the north, Jeremiah envisioned "an overflowing torrent" as it swept southward. Like a widespread flood, it would leave ruin and destruction in its path across the outlying land and **the city** itself. Every section of soil and every soul would be affected.

Verse 3. As Jeremiah continued his description of the **tumult**, he spoke of **the noise of the galloping hoofs of** [the] **stallions** and **the rumbling of** [the] **wheels** of approaching **chariots**. Each citizen would shout and shriek as charging horsemen brought bloodshed and captivity, death and destruction. Truly, the Babylonian army was formidable and impossible to resist.

Graphic descriptions of the destroyer's invasion are given. Defeat and humiliation would fall upon the Philistines. These images accent the most intense stage of chaos, disarray, and devastation. Men blinded by horror would abandon their wives and neglect their **children**. The impulse of natural affection that drives a father to seek above all else to save his children was abandoned in the frantic effort to avoid death. Even the strongest **hands** suffered **limpness**, according to an Hebrew idiom (see 6:24; 50:43; Ezek. 7:17; Zeph. 3:16), as people fled hopelessly from the destruction.

THE COMPLETE FALL (47:4, 5)

4"**On account of the day that is coming
To destroy all the Philistines,**

---

[4]Ibid., 1:413.
[5]Francis Brown, S. R. Driver, and Charles A. Briggs, *A Hebrew and English Lexicon of the Old Testament* (Oxford: Clarendon Press, 1972), 410.

To cut off from Tyre and Sidon
Every ally that is left;
For the LORD is going to destroy the Philistines,
The remnant of the coastland of Caphtor.
⁵Baldness has come upon Gaza;
Ashkelon has been ruined.
O remnant of their valley,
How long will you gash yourself?"

Verse 4. Such a scene reinforced Jeremiah's prediction that this conquest was coming **to destroy all the Philistines**. Conditions would be the worst imaginable. The proud, rich commercial cities of **Tyre and Sidon** would offer no aid or comfort. These were not Philistine cities, but they must have been allies who had at times assisted them. **Every** remaining **ally** was **cut off** (כָּרַת, *karath*)—quickly, decisively, and completely. This term has no other message to give us than the highest tragedy.[6] The loss was so extensive that those named became powerless and could render absolutely no aid to their neighbors. The slaughter would leave few inhabitants among the **Philistines**, just a small **remnant of the coastland of Caphtor**, where the Philistines had their beginning.

Verse 5. The **baldness** that would **come upon Gaza** most likely refers to the ritual of shaving one's head due to sorrow and humiliation (7:29; 16:6; 48:37; Mic. 1:16). It could also be a figurative way of referring to the city becoming barren. **Ashkelon**, another key Philistine city, was to be **ruined** or "destroyed" (NJPSV). The Hebrew word דָּמָה (*damah*) also means "be silenced" (NIV).[7] It was common for mourners to sit in silence (Job 2:13).

The phrase **remnant of their valley** is a good translation of the Hebrew text, being found in several other versions (KJV; NKJV; ASV; NJPSV; see NJB; NCV). "Their valley" refers to "the plain" (NIV) of "the Mediterranean coast" (NLT) where the Philistines lived. The translators of the RSV and the CEV have followed the LXX, which has "Anakim" instead of "their valley." This read-

---

[6]Koehler and Baumgartner, 1:500–1; Brown, Driver, and Briggs, 503–4.
[7]Koehler and Baumgartner, 1:225; Brown, Driver, and Briggs, 198.

ing is based on a slight alteration of the Hebrew text: "Anakim" (עֲנָקִים) resembles "their valley" (עִמְקָם, *'imqam*). The Anakim were a formidable people who inhabited southern Palestine, including Philistia (Deut. 2:10, 21; Josh. 11:21, 22). One other translation of the Hebrew text has been advocated: Some versions have "their strength" (NEB) or "power" (NRSV; REB).[8]

Those remaining would express the intensity of their pain as they **gash**[ed] themselves in mourning (see 16:6; 41:5). God's people were forbidden to cut themselves in keeping with the pagan tradition of lancing oneself during times of deep anguish and mourning (Lev. 19:28; Deut. 14:1, 2; 1 Kings 18:27, 28).

THE CRY OF "ENOUGH!" (47:6, 7)

⁶"Ah, sword of the LORD,
How long will you not be quiet?
Withdraw into your sheath;
Be at rest and stay still.
⁷How can it be quiet,
When the LORD has given it an order?
Against Ashkelon and against the seacoast—
There He has assigned it."

Verse 6. The Philistines knew the reason for their punishment. These people for generations had been told that their problems were related to their abuse of the principles of the God of Israel (see 1 Sam. 5:1–12; 6:1–21). In the days of both Samuel and Jeremiah, the Philistines were ready to acknowledge God as being supreme over their tribal and national gods. In the throes of judgment, their cry would be a plea for cessation: **"Ah, sword of the LORD, how long will you not be quiet? Withdraw into your sheath; be at rest and stay still."** They had experienced enough conflict and were begging for relief.

Could verse 6 actually be Jeremiah's cry for God to cease the slaughter? The evidence is against this view. The next verse is a

---

[8]See Koehler and Baumgartner, 1:847.

clear reminder that Jeremiah knew God's judgment must run its course. Therefore, it seems more likely that he had heard the Philistines' cry for God's sword of justice to be put into its sheath and was responding with a certain announcement that the disaster must be completed.

Verse 7. The force from the north would not be turning back. It could not **be quiet**; it would march because **the LORD** [had] **given it an order**. The devastation had to be fulfilled from **Ashkelon** to **the seacoast**—that is, throughout Philistia. This was the divine command to Babylon, who functioned as a sword in God's hand. God had **assigned** (יָעַד, *ya'ad*) it, or "appointed it,"[9] to do this work. He had decreed the degree to which the Philistines would suffer, knowing that His planned vengeance would parallel the work of Nebuchadnezzar and his army.[10]

Other prophets spoke of the downfall and ruin of Philistia (Is. 14:29–31; Ezek. 25:15–17; Amos 1:6–8; Zeph. 2:4–7). Their words, along with those in this chapter, echoed the darkness of doom for these enemies of God's people.

APPLICATION

Hope for the Hopeless (Ch. 47)
Was there any hope for Philistia?

The promise. Though no gesture of hope is recorded in this chapter, Zechariah pointed to a day beyond the destruction when that region would be populated by a people who would "be a remnant for our God" (Zech. 9:5–7). Even in Philistia, God's mercy would be found. The promised Messiah died for all people (2 Cor. 5:14, 15). Surely, Zechariah's prophecy was fulfilled when Philistia heard the gospel message and many in that region believed in Christ, were baptized, and became citizens of the kingdom of God (see Acts 8:40; 9:32–43). At that time, they would have reason to be grateful to God for His goodness. When Peter

---

[9]See Brown, Driver, and Briggs, 416–17.

[10]This plan does not rule out free will among people. God knows human nature. Babylon's going against Philistia was most satisfactory to Nebuchadnezzar, for world conquest was his goal.

brought the gospel message to that area, it was surely a case of light shining in a dark place (see 2 Pet. 1:17–21).

The demonstration. The Philistines became one of the dramatic demonstrations of God's patience and grace. From the first book of the Bible and the days of Abraham, it is evident through his association with Abimelech (Gen. 21:32, 33) that these people had an opportunity to be acquainted with God. In that early period, Abraham had been concerned among them, having observed, ". . . there is no fear of God in this place, and they will kill me because of my wife" (Gen. 20:11). While that did not happen, these statements indicate an acquaintance with God but a lack of respect for Him.

The Philistines had been in conflict with God's people from the time of Abraham until the days of Jeremiah—a period of some fifteen hundred years. The Philistines had many opportunities to consider God during those years. The tragedy is that they continued to reject God and react against His people. The fact that God still would extend to them a ray of hope and redemptive benefits (Ezek. 25:17; Zech. 9:5–7) is an amazing tribute to His patience, mercy, and grace.

The invitation. Anyone who has a heritage of rebellion should take note, gain courage, and rest assured that God will receive anyone who penitently turns to Him and obeys His will (Acts 10:34, 35; 2 Cor. 5:4–21). God, through Christ, even embraced Paul, who labeled himself as the chief of sinners (1 Tim. 1:12–16; NKJV), appointing him as an apostle to the Gentiles and guiding him through the Spirit to write almost half of the books in the New Testament. What a loving, merciful, forgiving God! His longsuffering spirit benefits us as it did the Philistines.

Each of us should appropriate God's goodness through Christ. To all who obey Him, He is "the source of eternal salvation" (Heb. 5:8, 9; see Acts 2:36–47).

CHAPTER 48
THE JUDGMENT OF MOAB

The small nation of Moab can be traced to the son produced by the incestuous union of Lot and his older daughter (Gen. 19:29–38). The Moabites lived just east of the Dead Sea. The exact borders to the north, south, and east varied according to their power and prosperity over the years of their history. Jeremiah listed at least twenty-four Moabite cities in this oracle of judgment. Eight of them are also mentioned in the Book of Joshua, as part of the inheritances of Reuben and Gad (Josh. 13:15–28).

Strife and enmity were common patterns of conduct between Israel and Moab. As Moses led Israel toward the land that God had promised them, their first encounter with the Moabites occurred. After the conquest of the Amorites, great fear came upon King Balak of Moab, prompting him to ask the prophet Balaam to place a curse on Israel as they came near Moab (Num. 21:24—24:25). Instead of a curse, Balaam pronounced a blessing on God's people, prophesying that one from Israel would "crush through the forehead of Moab" (Num. 24:17). Then God's people "began to play the harlot with the daughters of Moab," joining themselves "to Baal of Peor" (Num. 25:1, 3). Twenty-four thousand Israelites died from the plague God imposed on His people because of this wicked fellowship (Num. 25:9).

Through the years, chaos and conflict were the general conditions between Israel and Moab. The only interruption of the repeated hostilities between these two groups of people were the two occasions when Elimelech (Ruth 1:1, 2) and David took refuge in Moab (1 Sam. 22:3, 4).

Before Jeremiah, several prophets had uttered messages

against Moab. Balaam was directed by the Spirit of God to prophesy against Moab (Num. 22). Amos, Isaiah, and Zephaniah also prophesied against this nation (Amos 2:1-3; Is. 15:1-7; 16:6-12; 25:10-12; Zeph. 2:8-11). Jeremiah obviously used some phrasing from these earlier prophets, but no other prophet gave as much information or named as many specific cities as did Jeremiah.

The geographic location of Moab separated it from the frequently traveled path to the powerful lands of the ancient Near East—Aram, Assyria, and Babylon—that waged repeated battles with each other and with Egypt. Moab was too insignificant to attract their special attention. As a result, during certain periods when Judah was burdened by these forces, Moab enlarged her borders, expanding in wealth and power. This success, in turn, led to pride. Throughout Jeremiah's prophecy, we see a clear condemnation of their arrogance.

Their great success was challenged as Jeremiah opened with a message from "the LORD of hosts," beginning with the foreboding word "Woe." Then he spoke of Moab's self-sufficient spirit (48:1-6), their inability to escape (48:7-10), their being disturbed (48:11-25), their shame and reproach (48:26-29), God's lament over them (48:30-39), the coming of the conqueror (48:40-46), and their hope of restoration (48:47).

SELF-SUFFICIENCY (48:1-6)

¹**Concerning Moab.**
Thus says the LORD of hosts, the God of Israel,
"Woe to Nebo, for it has been destroyed;
Kiriathaim has been put to shame, it has been captured;
The lofty stronghold has been put to shame and shattered.
²**There is praise for Moab no longer;**
In Heshbon they have devised calamity against her:
'Come and let us cut her off from being a nation!'
You too, Madmen, will be silenced;
The sword will follow after you.
³**The sound of an outcry from Horonaim,**
'Devastation and great destruction!'
⁴**Moab is broken,**

JEREMIAH 48

Her little ones have sounded out a cry of distress.
⁵For by the ascent of Luhith
They will ascend with continual weeping;
For at the descent of Horonaim
They have heard the anguished cry of destruction.
⁶Flee, save your lives,
That you may be like a juniper in the wilderness."

Verse 1. This judgment oracle **concerning Moab** was the message of **the Lord of hosts, the God of Israel** and the judge of all the earth. Depending on how the Hebrew text is translated, God pronounced judgment on either two or three locations in this verse. **Nebo** was not the mountain where Moses had stood (Deut. 32:49), but a town in that region. The Moabite Stone (c. 830 B.C.) reports that King Mesha had taken this city from the Israelites.[1] The site of **Kiriathaim**, meaning "double city," is uncertain. However, many identify it with modern el-Qereiyat, about five miles northwest of Dibon.[2] Kiriathaim is also mentioned on the Moabite Stone; it was under construction during Mesha's reign.[3] **The lofty stronghold** (מִשְׂגָּב, *miśgab*) may refer to a heavily fortified area within Kiriathaim. In this case, it is used as a parallel term for that city. However, the KJV takes the word as a proper name, "Misgab." Merrill C. Tenney believed this to be another name for Moab's capital, Kir-Moab.[4]

The beginning word **woe** indicates that shocking doom was coming. The land would be **destroyed** (שָׁדַד, *shadad*), that is, "devastated" or "utterly ruined."[5] The people would be **put to shame** (בּוֹשׁ, *bosh*), completely humiliated. The KJV has "confounded." The cities would be **shattered** (חָתַת, *chathath*). This

---

[1] William W. Hallo, ed., *The Context of Scripture* (Boston: Brill, 2003), 2:138.
[2] William Sanford LaSor, "Kiriathaim," in *The International Standard Bible Encyclopedia*, rev. ed., ed. Geoffrey W. Bromiley (Grand Rapids, Mich.: Wm. B. Eerdmans Publishing Co., 1986), 3:42.
[3] Hallo, 2:137.
[4] Merrill C. Tenney, *Zondervan Pictorial Dictionary of the Bible* (Grand Rapids, Mich.: Zondervan Publishing House, 1967), 547.
[5] Francis Brown, S. R. Driver, and Charles A. Briggs, *A Hebrew and English Lexicon of the Old Testament* (Oxford: Clarendon Press, 1972), 994.

term can also mean "be dismayed" or "filled with terror."⁶ The Moabite people would be **captured** (לָכַד, *lakad*). Combined, these terms specify total desolation and describe the terrifying hostility of the invading forces. This disaster would be staggering to this small nation.

Verse 2. The people in cities on the borders of **Moab**, like **Heshbon**, located six miles northeast of Mount Nebo, would be devising or plotting **calamity** to take place in her. Perhaps there is a wordplay using the Hebrew terms for "Heshbon" (חֶשְׁבּוֹן, *Cheshbon*) and **devised** (חָשַׁב, *chashab*). Instead of having **praise** for her, the nations were planning a disaster for her. This city may have been where Nebuchadnezzar planned his attack upon parts of Moab. The attacking army would seek to **cut her off from being a nation**. The **sword** that the Moabites had used on others would come back to attack them.

Madmen (מַדְמֵן, *Madmen*), a word meaning "dung hill," stands for an unknown city of Moab. This city would **be silenced** (דָּמַם, *damam*). These Hebrew terms may also form a wordplay.

Verses 3, 4. The cry going up in cities like **Horonaim**—a city mentioned on the Moabite Stone⁷—was a shout of **devastation and great destruction**. Even the **little ones** would cry out because of the severity of the **distress**. "Little ones" may not be a reference to the children as much as to the distressed villages that had been reduced to nothing. Instead of "little ones," the LXX has "as far as Zoar" (see Is. 15:5).⁸ This rendering is followed by the RSV, NEB, and REB.

Verse 5. People would travel up **the ascent of Luhith,** weeping as they went, and then go down **the descent of Horonaim**, uttering **the anguished cry of destruction** (see Is. 15:5). These places were apparently located near the southern end of the Dead Sea.

---

⁶Ludwig Koehler and Walter Baumgartner, *The Hebrew and Aramaic Lexicon of the Old Testament*, study ed., trans. and ed. M. E. J. Richardson (Boston: Brill, 2001), 1:365.

⁷Hallo, 2:138.

⁸See R. K. Harrison, *Jeremiah and Lamentations: An Introduction and Commentary*, Tyndale Old Testament Commentaries (Downers Grove, Ill.: InterVarsity Press, 1973), 174.

Verse 6. The people would be advised, **"Flee, save your lives that you may be like a juniper in the wilderness."** The admonition for the people to preserve their lives is clear (see 39:18; 45:5). However, the precise translation and interpretation of the comparison that follows it is more difficult. The Hebrew term rendered "juniper," עֲרוֹעֵר (*ᵃroʿer*), may refer to some type of tree (KJV) or "bush" (NIV). However, this word also identifies a particular Moabite city, "Aroer" (NJPSV; see 48:19). Some versions follow the LXX, which slightly alters the Hebrew text; they have "wild ass" (NRSV) or "wild donkey" (NJB).[9] Of these three options, the word probably refers here to a tree or bush that exists "in the wilderness" (see comments on 17:6). R. K. Harrison wrote, "The point appears to be that safety lies only in isolation."[10]

NO ESCAPE (48:7–10)

[7]"For because of your trust in your own achievements and treasures,
Even you yourself will be captured;
And Chemosh will go off into exile
Together with his priests and his princes.
[8]A destroyer will come to every city,
So that no city will escape;
The valley also will be ruined
And the plateau will be destroyed,
As the LORD has said.
[9]Give wings to Moab,
For she will flee away;
And her cities will become a desolation,
Without inhabitants in them.
[10]Cursed be the one who does the LORD's work negligently,
And cursed be the one who restrains his sword from blood."

Verse 7. Moab is an example of man's inability to direct his own steps. What seems right and safe to human understanding

---
[9]See Koehler and Baumgartner, 1:883.
[10]Harrison, 175.

leads to death (Prov. 14:12). Moab was told that they were in trouble **because of** [their] **trust in** [their] **own achievements and treasures**. While arrogantly assuming they were secure, the people of Moab were mentally and spiritually taking all the wrong steps to attain security. They put their faith in their own performance.

Chemosh, their national deity, could not protect the people of Moab from going into exile. This god they worshiped is mentioned several times on the Moabite Stone, where he is given credit for King Mesha's victories.[11] The people, **priests**, and **princes**, along with the idols of their god, would be taken into exile (see 48:13, 46; Num. 21:29, 30; 1 Kings 11:7, 33; 2 Kings 23:13). Removing a nation's idols symbolized the defeat of their gods (see comments on 43:12).

Verse 8. No city [would] **escape**, for **a destroyer** would be sent **to every city**. Even the choice regions of their land would be destroyed. **The** [Jordan] **valley**, on Moab's west, would **be ruined**; and **the plateau**, where nearly all of Moab's cities were located, would **be destroyed**. The Lord had spoken, and His word cannot fail.

Verse 9. It would be as if **Moab** had been given **wings** so that she could fly away as a bird to the hills, never to be heard from again. Instead of giving "wings," other versions have "give a warning signal to" (REB), "set up a tombstone for" (TEV), and "put salt on" (NIV).[12] This last suggestion points to the ancient custom of sowing salt on conquered cities (Judg. 9:45). The Hebrew text has wings (ציץ, *tsiyts*). With her cities **a desolation**, her existence would be only a memory.

Verse 10. A curse was uttered upon those who delayed in implementing the destruction God had decreed. His sentence of judgment would not be carried out **negligently**. The people of Moab had a calling to do the will of the Creator, like all other nations; but they had rejected their mission. Judgment had to

---

[11]Hallo, 2:137–38.

[12]For more information, see Harrison, 175; Douglas Rawlinson Jones, *Jeremiah*, The New Century Bible Commentary (Grand Rapids, Mich.: Wm. B. Eerdmans Publishing Co., 1992), 502.

JEREMIAH 48

come, and **cursed** [was] **the one who restrain**[ed] **his sword from blood** as he carried out God's mission. God's instruments of judgment could not refrain from bringing the full measure of retribution to Moab. Obedience would have brought security to them.

DISTURBED (48:11–25)

Moab was due the pain and punishment that God had planned for them. Their carnality and corruption had brought judgment upon them. These steps to ruin have been repeated by other nations, with the same consequences.

Deception and Assumption (48:11, 12)

¹¹"Moab has been at ease since his youth;
He has also been undisturbed, like wine on its dregs,
And he has not been emptied from vessel to vessel,
Nor has he gone into exile.
Therefore he retains his flavor,
And his aroma has not changed.
¹²Therefore behold, the days are coming," declares the LORD, "when I will send to him those who tip vessels, and they will tip him over, and they will empty his vessels and shatter his jars."

Verse 11. Moab was satisfied and self-sufficient. From its **youth**, this nation had been **at ease** and **undisturbed, like wine on its dregs**. The people were compared to grape juice that had rested unmoved on its "dregs" or "lees," maturing into strong wine. Moab had **retain**[ed] **his flavor, and his aroma** [had] **not changed**. Located a safe distance from the route generally traveled by conquering nations, Moab had not suffered any kind of captivity. The nation had experienced peace, but instead of using the opportunity for good, the people had used it for the development of evil. Oblivious to the warnings that had come, Moab became ripe for judgment.

Verse 12. Further extending the wine figure, the prophet said that Moab would be disturbed. Upheaval would come. He had long remained in the same place, prospering, developing confidence, and mellowing like wine—but that was soon to change. God said, **"I will send to him those who tip vessels, and they will tip him over."** Life, for the Moabites, had a good flavor that had led them to a false sense of security.

Nevertheless, that security was in the past; a new day was approaching: **"Therefore behold, the days are coming,"** declares the Lord. Prosperity is no proof of character, and mansions do not guarantee righteousness. Moab, the proud and undisturbed nation, was assured by God that it was about to be shattered. He was sending to Moab those who would **empty his vessels and shatter his jars** (see 19:10–12).

Tragedy and Terror (48:13)

¹³**"And Moab will be ashamed of Chemosh, as the house of Israel was ashamed of Bethel, their confidence."**

Verse 13. Chemosh, Moab's national god, would leave the people **ashamed**. Triumph and power would be replaced with terror and tragedy. The nation of **Israel** had become similarly **ashamed** of the calf idol at **Bethel** and the false religion established by Jeroboam I (1 Kings 12:28–30; Amos 3:14; 4:4; 5:5). When the time of testing came, their false worship did not protect them from deportation by the Assyrians (722 B.C.). "Chemosh," being unable to walk or talk, to see or save (Ps. 115:3–8), was a great delusion; yet this idol had been the source of **their confidence.** Religion that is wrong leads to ruin.

Slaughter and Assumed Splendor (48:14–25)

¹⁴**"How can you say, 'We are mighty warriors,
And men valiant for battle'?
¹⁵Moab has been destroyed and men have gone up to his cities;
His choicest young men have also gone down to the slaughter,"
Declares the King, whose name is the Lord of hosts.**

¹⁶"The disaster of Moab will soon come,
And his calamity has swiftly hastened.
¹⁷Mourn for him, all you who live around him,
Even all of you who know his name;
Say, 'How has the mighty scepter been broken,
A staff of splendor!'
¹⁸Come down from your glory
And sit on the parched ground,
O daughter dwelling in Dibon,
For the destroyer of Moab has come up against you,
He has ruined your strongholds.
¹⁹Stand by the road and keep watch,
O inhabitant of Aroer;
Ask him who flees and her who escapes
And say, 'What has happened?'
²⁰Moab has been put to shame, for it has been shattered.
Wail and cry out;
Declare by the Arnon
That Moab has been destroyed.
²¹"Judgment has also come upon the plain, upon Holon, Jahzah and against Mephaath, ²²against Dibon, Nebo and Beth-diblathaim, ²³against Kiriathaim, Beth-gamul and Beth-meon, ²⁴against Kerioth, Bozrah and all the cities of the land of Moab, far and near. ²⁵The horn of Moab has been cut off and his arm broken," declares the LORD.

Verse 14. Moab, in one sense, had no **mighty warriors**, no **men valiant for battle**. They thought they did, but the day of battle would show them to be woefully inadequate. Confidence in military might, without a right relationship with God, leads to disaster. As surely as they had misplaced their trust in their god Chemosh, they also had miscalculated what their military might could do for them. In comparison to the invading force from the north, they had no "mighty warriors."

Verse 15. Moab has been destroyed and men have gone up to his cities. The LORD **of hosts** was in charge of battle. At the time of His choosing, Moab's **choicest young men** would go **down to the slaughter**.

Verse 16. Instead of Moab's having a firm defense and plenty of time to assess his strength and readjust, **his calamity** was **swiftly** coming (see Deut. 32:35). Instead of being safe and secure, Moab was headed for defeat.

Verse 17. Moab's dilemma would evoke mourning from **all who live around him** and **who know his name**, from remote and nearby peoples. They had placed their confidence in their power and numbers; but they would see the **mighty scepter**, the **staff of splendor**, the glory of their nation, **broken**. Truly, "pride goes before destruction, and a haughty spirit before a fall" (Prov. 16:18; NIV).

Verse 18. A listing of thirteen specific cities now begins. Almost all of these also appear in the Pentateuch and in Joshua. Each one suffered the impact of the predicted devastation.

The first is **Dibon**, a city on two hills. It was located thirteen miles east of the Dead Sea near the Arnon River. This place served as the capital during the reign of Mesha (ninth century B.C.) and is where the Moabite Stone was found in 1868.[13] When disaster came, Jeremiah warned, the dwellers of this city would **come down from** their high places and **sit** in mourning on **parched ground**. The Hebrew word used here, צָמָא (*tsama'*), actually means "thirst" (KJV; NJPSV). The NASB, along with several other versions, gives an interpretative rendering of the word.[14] Instead of "parched ground," some translations have "dust" (TEV; NLT). This understanding of the text is supported by a similar statement in Isaiah 47:1. **The destroyer of Moab** would drive the people from their places of safety and their routines of life.

Verse 19. Next is **Aroer**, which was located on the north side of the Arnon River near Dibon. It was the southernmost city of Reuben (Josh. 13:15, 16). The Moabite Stone records that it was later controlled by the Moabites.[15]

As the battle raged, those fleeing from the enemy would be

---

[13]Hallo, 2:137.

[14]The image of a "thirsty" or "parched" land is found several times in the Old Testament (Deut. 8:15; Ps. 143:6; Is. 32:2; 35:7; 44:3; Ezek. 19:13; Hos. 2:3; Joel 2:20).

[15]Hallo, 2:138.

asked, **"What has happened?"** The questioner would be an **inhabitant** of the city who was stationed as a watchman **by the road**. This likely refers to the King's Highway, which flanked the west side of the city (see Num. 20:17; 21:22).

Verse 20. The truth was to be heralded abroad that **Moab** had been **shattered**. By the **Arnon** River the story was to be told. The fall predicted in this context is more than a fall from a high plane to a lower level. These people would see real power, and it would ruin their strongholds. God was not doing this just to cause their fall; this was His means of bringing them into proper focus with Him.

Verse 21. To show the completeness of the overthrow, other cities are identified. Many of these were allocated to Reuben during the days of Joshua (Josh. 13:15–23). **Judgment** came **upon the plain** (מִישׁוֹר, *mishor*), that is, "the tableland" (NRSV) or "the plateau" (NIV) where the majority of these towns were located.

Holon, meaning "sandy," was a town whose location is unknown. **Jahzah** (Jahaz), meaning "trodden under foot," is the Amorite city which the invading Israelites took in Numbers 21:23–25. The Moabite Stone says that, during the ninth century B.C., Israel's king rebuilt the city and stayed there while fighting the Moabites, but King Mesha took it from him.[16] The exact location of Jahzah is uncertain, although passages associating it with other cities may suggest an area in the southeast of the Amorite territory (Josh. 13:17, 18; 21:36, 37). **Mephaath**, meaning "splendor," was a Reubenite town that had been assigned along with Jahaz to the Levites (Josh. 21:36, 37).

Verse 22. Beth-diblathaim, meaning "house of the fig cakes," is probably the same site as Almon-diblathaim, which is mentioned as a resting place for Israel on their way to Canaan (Num. 33:46, 47). In this case, it was located between Dibon and Nebo. According to the Moabite Stone, Beth-diblathaim was under construction during the reign of Mesha.[17] The other cities listed in this verse are **Dibon** (see comments on 48:18) and **Nebo** (see comments on 48:1).

---

[16]Ibid.
[17]Ibid.

Verse 23. Kiriathaim is mentioned once again (see comments on 48:1). **Beth-gamul**, meaning "house of recompense," was probably located about six miles east of Dibon. **Beth-meon**, meaning "house of habitation," is the same place as Baal-meon or Beth-baal-meon (Josh. 13:17). It was an Amorite city that the Reubenites had taken and rebuilt (Num. 32:37, 38). The Moabite Stone says that it was later occupied by the Moabites; Mesha rebuilt the city (adding a water reservoir) and brought flocks there.[18] Beth-meon, often identified with the later Roman ruins of Ma'in, was probably located about seven miles south of Mount Nebo.

Verse 24. Kerioth is a word meaning "cities." Apparently, it was an important place where the Moabites worshiped Chemosh. The Moabite Stone reports that, after conquering the Israelites in Ataroth, Mesha hauled an altar hearth back to Kerioth. It was brought "before the face of" Chemosh, which suggests that a sanctuary was built there in honor of Moab's national god.[19]

The **Bozrah** listed here was not the city that belonged to Edom (Gen. 36:33). It may, however, be identical to Bezer, a city in Reuben's territory set apart for the Levites and as a place of refuge (Josh. 20:8; 21:36).[20] If this association is correct, then it may have been located at Umm el-'Amad, about eight miles east of Medeba. The name Bozrah means "fortified place" or "sheepfold."

This catalog of cities was not intended to be all-inclusive. Instead, these places were representative of **all the cities of the land of Moab, far and near**.

Verse 25. The series ends with a sweeping affirmation: **The horn of Moab has been cut off**. The metaphor of a "horn" is often used in Old Testament literature to indicate strength or power. Moab, personified as a soldier who had come from battle, is pictured as having had **his arm broken**. The nation had been rendered incapable of further warfare. This decree of prophetic judgment was declared by **the LORD**; therefore, it stood secure and certain.

---

[18]Ibid., 2:137–38.
[19]Ibid.
[20]Bezer is also referred to on the Moabite Stone. Mesha had rebuilt it because it had laid in ruins. (Ibid., 2:138.)

SHAME AND REPROACH (48:26–29)

²⁶"Make him drunk, for he has become arrogant toward the LORD; so Moab will wallow in his vomit, and he also will become a laughingstock. ²⁷Now was not Israel a laughingstock to you? Or was he caught among thieves? For each time you speak about him you shake your head in scorn.
²⁸Leave the cities and dwell among the crags,
O inhabitants of Moab,
And be like a dove that nests
Beyond the mouth of the chasm.
²⁹We have heard of the pride of Moab—he is very proud—
Of his haughtiness, his pride, his arrogance and his self-exaltation."

Verse 26. Shame, degradation, and reproach would overwhelm **Moab**. God's directive was clearly given: **"Make him drunk, for he has become arrogant toward the LORD."** The rejection and debasing would drive them to the depths of humiliation. The Moabites would stumble and wobble under the blows of the enemy. They would become senseless, like a drunken man. Their humiliation would be so horrible that their state could be compared to one **wallow**[ing] **in his vomit**. It is indeed humbling for a proud person to be seen wallowing in vomit (see 2 Pet. 2:20–22). Their demise would bring with it extreme reproach; they would be **a laughingstock** to other nations.

Verse 27. Moab had mocked **Israel** in the past. He would look at Israel and **shake** [his] **head in scorn**, treating God's people as if they had been found **among thieves** and had been arrested. The tables would be turned. Moab was to become the object of scorn. Cries of contempt fill this scene of humiliation.

Verse 28. So serious would be the desolation that it would be good for its inhabitants to **leave the cities** and make their homes in the mountains. Having left a luxurious life in a prosperous city, these denigrated souls would seek to take refuge or **dwell among the crags** ("rocks"; NIV).

Pushed from their houses and cities, they would desire to **be like a dove**, able to fly away to another place of habitation that would be hard to reach and would provide safety. They needed to get as far away from the disaster as possible. Their new abode might well be a forsaken place, like a cleft or cave in the mountain. Residing on the edge of a precipice, at **the mouth of the chasm** (or "in the sides of the cave's mouth"; NKJV), would provide the necessary shelter.

Verse 29. Moab had all the sordid characteristics of **pride—haughtiness, arrogance,** and **self-exaltation**. Their attitude was one that Jesus taught against: He told of a person who chose a chief seat at a marriage feast and the shame that followed when he was asked to move to a lower place. The lesson was "Everyone who exalts himself will be humbled" (Lk. 14:11). The proud Moabites saw that type of shame as they heard the cry, "Come down from your glory and sit on the parched ground" (48:18). They left their abundance, their splendor, and came down to starvation.

THE LAMENT OF GOD (48:30–39)

Futile Fury (48:30–34)

> ³⁰"I know his fury," declares the LORD,
> "But it is futile;
> His idle boasts have accomplished nothing.
> ³¹Therefore I will wail for Moab,
> Even for all Moab will I cry out;
> I will moan for the men of Kir-heres.
> ³²More than the weeping for Jazer
> I will weep for you, O vine of Sibmah!
> Your tendrils stretched across the sea,
> They reached to the sea of Jazer;
> Upon your summer fruits and your grape harvest
> The destroyer has fallen.
> ³³So gladness and joy are taken away
> From the fruitful field, even from the land of Moab.
> And I have made the wine to cease from the wine presses;
> No one will tread them with shouting,
> The shouting will not be shouts of joy.

³⁴**From the outcry at Heshbon even to Elealeh, even to Jahaz they have raised their voice, from Zoar even to Horonaim and to Eglath-shelishiyah; for even the waters of Nimrim will become desolate."**

Verse 30. The major theme in this divine judgment on Moab is the charge of national arrogance. **"I know his fury," declares the Lord.** God recognized that Moab was filled with "fury," but **his idle boasts** were **futile;** they **accomplished nothing.** Arrogance is both damaging and deceitful. It seems to build up, while in actuality it tears down.

Verse 31. What did it all mean? How bad was it? The destruction was so total and so deep that God Himself would **wail for Moab** (see 4:8; 25:34; 47:2), crying out **for all Moab**.[21] The crying would be directed toward the desperate needs of the people. God said He would mourn **for the men of Kir-heres.** The name of this place, also spelled Kir-hareseth (2 Kings 3:25), meant "city of earthenware." It is best identified with the chief fortification of southern Moab, located some eleven miles east of the Dead Sea. This place was also called Kir of Moab (Is. 15:1).

Verse 32. Weeping follows in this verse. God would weep over **Jazer** because of its ruined vineyards. Jazer, whose name means "fortified," was one of the Amorite cities that had been conquered by Israel (Num. 21:32). Located about ten miles north of Heshbon, it had been included in Gad's allotment (Josh. 13:24, 25) and set apart for the Levites (Josh. 21:39). At some point, Jazer had come under Moabite control.

God would **weep** even more for **Sibmah.** Also known as Sebam (Num. 32:3), this place was located only a few miles from Heshbon. It had been one of the richest and most productive farm areas for vineyards. Figuratively speaking, its tender vines **stretched across the sea,** that is, the Dead Sea. The expression **the sea of Jazer** is considered by some to be a scribal error, since

---

[21]In the parallel passage, Isaiah 16:6, 7, it is Moab who wails. See a comparison of the passages in Timothy M. Willis, *Jeremiah-Lamentations*, The College Press NIV Commentary (Joplin, Mo.: College Press Publishing Co., 2002), 359–60.

no significant body of water is found in the vicinity. In that case, the word "sea" (יָם, *yam*) was accidentally repeated from the previous clause. It is omitted in the LXX and in the parallel in Isaiah 16:8; the latter simply has "as far as Jazer." Several versions omit "sea" from the phrase here, also reading "as far as Jazer" (RSV; NRSV; NEB; REB; TEV; see NJB; NJPSV). Others think that a small lake was located near Jazer in ancient times, but no longer exists today. Sibmah was situated between the Dead Sea, which was about ten miles to the west, and Jazer, which was about ten miles to the north (see CEV).

God's heart was broken because the **summer fruits** and the **grape harvest** (see comments on 40:10) had been trampled down by **the destroyer**. The expressions in verses 31 and 32—"wail" "cry out," "moan," and "weep"—convey intense agony.

Verse 33. The emphasis is how favored cities and fertile fields had been torn and terrorized, falling before the advancing foe. Production had been replaced with pain, and **shouts of joy** were being replaced with cries of suffering. Good times had been turned into bad times of gruesome destruction.

The aftermath of war would include a time of drought, with **gladness and joy . . . taken away from the fruitful field**. The **wine presses** would be empty, and the harvest song would no longer be heard in the land. This verse begins with **so** or "therefore," implying a summation. The review consists of a trail of tears.

Verse 34. According to this depiction, the voices of seven cities were raised in an **outcry**. In the north, the sound went out from **Heshbon . . . to Elealeh**, a short distance away, **even to Jahaz**, which was much farther away, southeast of Heshbon.

The wailing went out **from Zoar . . . to Horonaim**, two cities in the southern part of Moab, and on **to Eglath-shelishiyah**, which means "the third Eglath" or "Eglath in three places." This compound word may indicate that there were three different places by the same name.

Even the waters of Nimrim will become desolate. These waters were to be "desolate" (מְשַׁמָּה, *mᵉshammah*), either because they had become corrupted so that no one could drink them, or maybe they were resort pools and lakes that had been abandoned. Former places of pleasure had lost their appeal because they had become ravaged ruins.

A Divine Lamentation (48:35–39)

³⁵"I will make an end of Moab," declares the LORD, "the one who offers sacrifice on the high place and the one who burns incense to his gods. ³⁶"Therefore My heart wails for Moab like flutes; My heart also wails like flutes for the men of Kir-heres. Therefore they have lost the abundance it produced. ³⁷For every head is bald and every beard cut short; there are gashes on all the hands and sackcloth on the loins. ³⁸On all the housetops of Moab and in its streets there is lamentation everywhere; for I have broken Moab like an undesirable vessel," declares the LORD. ³⁹"How shattered it is! How they have wailed! How Moab has turned his back—he is ashamed! So Moab will become a laughingstock and an object of terror to all around him."

Verses 35, 36. Those who worshiped the idols, who were said to **sacrifice on the high place** and burn **incense**, recognized that God was bringing in the **end**. Both of these verses reveal that God, too, gave an outcry, as His **heart wail**[ed] **for Moab like** [the] **flutes**, or reed pipes, of funeral mourning (see Mt. 9:23, 24). He wailed **for the men of Kir-heres**.

Isaiah 15 and 16 present a parallel to Jeremiah 48, as it pertains to Moab's punishment, not in time but in fact. The "three years" of Isaiah 16:14 likely refers to the time when Sennacherib and the Assyrian forces came to Jerusalem in the days of King Hezekiah (Is. 10:24, 28–32). While Moab suffered in that siege, a remnant was left (Is. 16:14); but when Nebuchadnezzar came in the days of Jeremiah, as reflected in this chapter, no remnant would be left.

Here we find proof of God's deep concern for nations other than His covenant people. If God brings an end or pain to any people, He does so with wailing and weeping that grows out of their failure to repent (see Ezek. 18:30–32; 2 Pet. 3:9).

Verse 37. Images of mournful music, wailing cries, **bald**

heads, cut **beard[s]**, **gashes** on bodies, and **sackcloth** identify miserable, pagan mourners and a distressed prophet who shared in this sorrow (see 4:8; 6:26; 7:29; 16:6; 41:5; 47:5).

Verse 38. There is lamentation everywhere. Mournful sounds of lamentation could be heard from the **streets** and the **housetops**. In addition, Isaiah 16:9, 11, like a musical intonation of mourning, presents God's sorrow over the devastation of Moab. God said **Moab** had been broken **like an undesirable vessel** (see 22:28). The figure is the potter who takes a misshapen piece of pottery and breaks it because it is of no value.

Verse 39. In a moment of prophetic review, the oracle looks back and surveys the rubbish of Moab and its people: **How shattered it is! How they have wailed! How Moab has turned his back—he is ashamed!** "Shattered" souls wailed in shame, having **become a laughingstock and an object of terror to all around** them.

THE CONQUEROR'S ARRIVAL (48:40–46)

Moab's Warning (48:40–42)

⁴⁰For thus says the LORD:
"Behold, one will fly swiftly like an eagle
And spread out his wings against Moab.
⁴¹Kerioth has been captured
And the strongholds have been seized,
So the hearts of the mighty men of Moab in that day
Will be like the heart of a woman in labor.
⁴²Moab will be destroyed from being a people
Because he has become arrogant toward the LORD."

Verse 40. God's warning was this: The conquest was coming **swiftly like an eagle** (or vulture). Nebuchadnezzar would come through Moab, Ammon, and the land of the neighboring peoples in 582 or 581 B.C.

Verse 41. Kerioth (see 48:24) was **captured and the strongholds** were **seized**. Nebuchadnezzar's mighty army would strike in Moab's **mighty men** fear and terror similar to **the heart of a**

woman in labor. Instead of new life, this meant the end of life for Moab as a nation.

Verse 42. The cause is clear. This happened to **Moab** because "he . . . magnified himself against the LORD" (KJV). The word for **become arrogant** is גָּדַל (*gadal*), which is a general term with multiple meanings. Here it means to make oneself "big," that is, to brag. This same phrasing in verse 26 may be partially explained by Zephaniah 2:8: "I have heard the taunting of Moab and the revilings of the sons of Ammon, with which they have taunted My people and become arrogant against their territory." This magnifying of themselves or becoming arrogant against **the LORD** may imply an attempt to dominate Israel, to seek to regain possession of the land God had given to His people (Judg. 3:28–30; 11:32, 33). By harassing Israel, they were reacting against and challenging God Himself.

Moab's Fall (48:43–46)

> ⁴³"Terror, pit and snare are coming upon you,
> O inhabitant of Moab," declares the LORD.
> ⁴⁴"The one who flees from the terror
> Will fall into the pit,
> And the one who climbs up out of the pit
> Will be caught in the snare;
> For I shall bring upon her, even upon Moab,
> The year of their punishment," declares the LORD.
> ⁴⁵"In the shadow of Heshbon
> The fugitives stand without strength;
> For a fire has gone forth from Heshbon
> And a flame from the midst of Sihon,
> And it has devoured the forehead of Moab
> And the scalps of the riotous revelers.
> ⁴⁶Woe to you, Moab!
> The people of Chemosh have perished;
> For your sons have been taken away captive
> And your daughters into captivity."

Verse 43. The following verses give a unique description of the certain annihilation that these people were to suffer. God began by saying, **"Terror, pit and snare are coming upon you."**

Verse 44. The impossibility of escape is graphically given. God warned, **"The one who flees from the terror will fall into the pit."** Moreover, anyone fortunate enough to rise from the pit, He said, would **be caught in the snare**. Punishment had been divinely decreed and would be poured forth on all (see 21:3–7; 37:6–10).

Verse 45. The **fugitives** would flee into **fire** that would devour **the forehead of Moab and the scalps of the riotous revelers**. "The forehead of Moab" is a difficult figure of speech, but in this context it seems to point to the unprotected part, where no armament was to save those fleeing fugitives (see 1 Sam. 17:49, 50). Their loud, boastful talk would not lead to triumph, but to tragedy (see 46:17; 48:14). These individuals are described as "riotous revelers" or "sons of destruction," people who were not devoted to duty (see 1 Pet. 4:3, 4). Moab's military might, likely centered at **Heshbon** and **Sihon**, had faltered and failed.

Verse 46. The oracle ends as it began, by pronouncing a **woe** upon **Moab** (see 48:1). The false spiritual security, placed in **Chemosh**, resulted in **sons** and **daughters** going **into captivity** as the nation perished.

Moab had lost her national identity. When Israel returned from Babylonian captivity, only two brief references were made concerning these people. These were in Ezra 9:1 and Nehemiah 13:1, 23, where God's people were charged with having Moabite wives. After this point, no Old Testament reference ever again gave them the status of a nation.

THE HOPE OF RESTORATION (48:47)

47"**Yet I will restore the fortunes of Moab
In the latter days," declares the** Lord.
Thus far the judgment on Moab.

Verse 47. What Chemosh, the god of the proud Moabites, could not do, the Creator of heaven and earth would do: **"Yet I will restore the fortunes of Moab in the latter days," declares the** Lord.

God's promise did not relate to a restoration of Moab as a nation. A greater fortune for these people was the plan of redemption that would come, presenting the Christ as the Savior of the world (1 Jn. 2:1, 2; 4:14). Through the gospel preached to all creation under heaven (Col. 1:23), descendants of Moab would have an opportunity to enter God's eternal kingdom (2 Pet. 1:1–4, 10, 11). Similar predictions of God's intent are made concerning Ammon (49:6), Elam (49:39), and the nations that harassed the people of God (12:14–17). That the people of Moab would have such an opportunity is another tribute to the grace and mercy of God.

Thus far the judgment on Moab is Jeremiah's final literary notation. It announces the end of the judgment by means of a backward look.

APPLICATION

Our Sufficiency and God's Sufficiency (Ch. 48)

Pride or arrogance is a fundamental error which produces multiple tragic consequences.

With pride or arrogance, a person assumes a security or sufficiency that does not exist. Verses 29 and 30 mention Moab's self-exaltation and her fury, but verse 45 warns that they were without strength. In this manner, "pride goes before destruction and a haughty spirit before stumbling" (Prov. 16:18). God warned, "Let not a wise man boast of his wisdom, and let not the mighty man boast of his might, let not a rich man boast of his riches" (9:23). Many ensnared by this sin have faltered and failed. Paul's warning is pertinent: "Therefore let him who thinks he stands take heed that he does not fall" (1 Cor. 10:12).

Because of pride or arrogance, one is inclined to be lazy, turning deaf ears to facts that he later must face and ignoring needs that should be supplied. This led the Moabites to be "at ease" and make "idle boasts" (48:11, 30), resulting in their becoming drunk, wallowing in their vomit, and being a laughingstock (48:26). Solomon presented a graphic lesson about the slothful, who lacked sense, resulting in negligence and needs that were never met (Prov. 6:6–11; see 13:4; 20:4; 26:16). Through pride come negligence and unpreparedness. How many have been entrapped here, so that real needs were never met and assumptions led to sorrow (Lk. 12:16–21)?

With pride or arrogance, a person invariably assumes a self-sufficiency that pits him against God. It is a basic truth that God resists the proud (48:42; 1 Pet. 5:5–7). Surely, the greatest demonstrations of the sin of pride are the first three kings of Israel. Each of these men possessed humility at the first, but each drifted into sin and shame when pride entered his life. Saul became proud, and God rejected his kingship (1 Sam. 9:21; 10:17–24; 15:17–23). David was so humble at the beginning (1 Sam. 16:1–13), but, as a powerful king, he pridefully wanted to display the number of his forces (2 Sam. 24:1–15). This resulted in the death of seventy thousand of God's people scattered from Dan to Beersheba. Solomon pursued this same path, beginning with a humble prayer for God's wisdom to be given to him so that he might properly govern God's people (1 Kings 3:5–15); but later he rebelled and broke every rule God had called for His appointed king to follow (Deut. 17:14–20; 1 Kings 4:26–28; 10:26–29; 11:1–6).

If these kings fell victim to pride so that they disobeyed God's principles and sinned, how can any of us dare to take this temptation lightly? The plight of King Herod, who pridefully failed to give God the glory, should serve as a sobering lesson for us (Acts 12:20–24).

In spite of the deceit and dangers inherent in a mindset of pride or arrogance, *God's compassion and mercy are still extended to any pride-filled person who will repent and humbly seek God as his sufficiency.* Moab would be given another opportunity to gain God's fortunes (48:47; see Acts 2:36–47; 2 Pet. 3:9). God is gracious to extend hope to those who are hurting (Mt. 11:28–30; Rev. 22:17).

The Downfall of Moab (48:7–10)

A parallel which pinpoints the foolishness of these people can be seen. We can observe the course taken by Moab and the consequences that were suffered (48:7–10).

The wrong response—"trust in your own achievements" (48:7). All their works ("cities") were destroyed (48:8, 9), and they themselves were captured (48:7).

The wrong remedy—"trust in your own . . . treasures" (48:7). All their land was left desolate (48:9; see Eccles. 10:19).

The wrong religion—in Chemosh (48:7). All were cursed because of negligence (48:10).

Pride (48:30)

As soon as arrogance settles in the heart, the trap is set for the fall. Being "puffed up" (1 Cor. 13:4; KJV) is like a disease that makes everybody else as sick as the one who has it. Some people grow under responsibility, but not the proud—they swell. The fruit of subtle influence was well expressed by Alexander Pope:

> Of all the causes which conspire to blind
> Man's erring judgment, and misguide the mind,
> What the weak head with strongest bias rules,
> Is Pride, the never-failing vice of fools![22]

---

[22]Quoted in Albert M. Wells, Jr., ed., *Inspiring Quotations* (Nashville: Thomas Nelson Publishers, 1988), 165–66.

CHAPTER 49

THE JUDGMENT OF OTHER NATIONS

In the oracle concerning the "other" nations in chapter 49, the phrase "the LORD" is dominant. "The LORD" appears 19 times in the phrases "declares the LORD," "says the LORD," "declares the LORD [God] of hosts," and "says the LORD of hosts." These phrases appear 5 times regarding Ammon, 5 times with Edom, once with Damascus, 4 times relative to Kedar and Hazor, and 4 times concerning Elam. Beyond these phrases, "the LORD" occurs 3 additional times in the chapter. References to God are also seen in the pronouns "I" (24 times), "Me" (4 times), "My" (3 times), "Myself" (once), "He" (4 times), and "His" (2 times). That makes a total of sixty references to God in these thirty-nine verses. God was the One in charge of these judgments, regardless of whom He would be using to enact the punishment.

A pattern of announcement is repeated for each geographic region. The literary order first includes God's calling for each nation to consider its circumstances. Second, a curse from God is pronounced upon them. Third, a specific cause for the curse is given. The final part of each is the promised punishment. In some cases, comfort for the future is given (see 49:6, 39).

One after the other, God reviewed the sins that had been committed and then pronounced divine sentences upon Ammon (49:1–6), Edom (49:7–22), Damascus (49:23–27), Kedar and Hazor (49:28–33), and Elam (49:34–39).

AMMON TO THE EAST (49:1–6)

The Ammonites lived just north of Moab and east of the

Jordan River. Their capital, Rabbah, was near the Jabbok River. When God granted that territory to Israel, it was allocated to the tribe of Gad (Num. 21:21–31; 32:1–39).

Ammon had engaged in conflicts with Israel as early as the days of Jephthah (Judg. 11:12–28). Problems continued in the days of King David (2 Sam. 8:9–15; 10:1–19) and King Solomon (1 Kings 11:1–7, 29–33). After the kingdom had divided and Israel had gone into Assyrian captivity, the Ammonites took control. Even following Judah's fall, they were still a source of trouble (40:1, 2, 11–14; 41:1–15). In this oracle, God brought these disturbing people to account.

The Conditions Briefly Stated (49:1)

> [1] **Concerning the sons of Ammon.**
> **Thus says the Lord:**
> **"Does Israel have no sons?**
> **Or has he no heirs?**
> **Why then has Malcam taken possession of Gad**
> **And his people settled in its cities?"**

Verse 1. Each judgment oracle except one is introduced with the word **concerning**, indicating new subject matter. Of the "other" nations, **Ammon** is mentioned first.

It is as if God debated with Ammon, saying, "Come . . . let us reason together," as in Isaiah 1:18. He asked, **"Does Israel have no sons? Or has he no heirs?"** The Lord had given the territory to Gad, so why should there be a change in His rule or the heirship of His people over that territory? He further asked, **"Why then has Malcam taken possession of Gad?"** The Hebrew word for "take possession," יָרַשׁ (*yarash*), is translated "inherit" in the KJV. While the word can have either meaning,[1] the context implies a forceful takeover. "Malcam" is an allusion to their false god that had to be removed so that God might rule (1 Kings

---

[1] Ludwig Koehler and Walter Baumgartner, *The Hebrew and Aramaic Lexicon of the Old Testament*, study ed., trans. and ed. M. E. J. Richardson (Boston: Brill, 2001), 1:441.

11:5, 7, 33; see Ex. 20:3, 5). This god was also known as "Molech," "Moloch," "Muluk," and "Malik."

God's Curse Stated (49:2, 3)

> ²"Therefore behold, the days are coming," declares the LORD,
> "That I will cause a trumpet blast of war to be heard
> Against Rabbah of the sons of Ammon;
> And it will become a desolate heap,
> And her towns will be set on fire.
> Then Israel will take possession of his possessors,"
> Says the LORD.
> ³"Wail, O Heshbon, for Ai has been destroyed!
> Cry out, O daughters of Rabbah,
> Gird yourselves with sackcloth and lament,
> And rush back and forth inside the walls;
> For Malcam will go into exile
> Together with his priests and his princes."

Verse 2. In coming **days**, the prophecy said, **a trumpet blast of war** would **be heard** in **Rabbah**. God's curse would result in **a desolate heap** (שְׁמָמָה, sh^emamah). Ammon was sinking into a deserted, appalling ruination. God said that **her towns** [would] **be set on fire** and laid waste. In Hebrew, the villages next to Rabbah are designated as her "daughters" (see KJV). The term for "daughter" is בַּת (bath) (see comments on 41:10). It is used because these towns or villages were viewed as "belonging to"[2] Rabbah, just as a daughter belongs to her father. All of these surrounding places would be burned.

Then, when this tragedy took place, **Israel** [would] **take possession of his possessors** by recovering some of the territory that had been lost to the Ammonites.

Verse 3. The judgment was so certain to come that the cities might as well begin their mourning. They could see the destruction that had occurred at **Ai** as well as other places. This was not the Ai near Jericho, but rather an unknown site. **Wail**[ing] and

---

[2]Ibid., 1:166.

donning **sackcloth** was in order, for what had happened to others was soon to happen to **Heshbon** and **Rabbah**. Heshbon was so close to the borders of two territories that its ownership fluctuated with the land conquests of those two territories. In 48:2, it is referred to as a Moabite city.

Rush back and forth inside the walls, a phrase that depicts panic during the attack, has been variously translated. "Walls" is from גְּדֵרָה (*gᵉderah*), a non-specific word that can be understood as a "border," "enclosure," or "hedge." While the NASB has "walls," the ASV has "fences," and the KJV has "hedges." The NLT portrays the people "hiding in the hedges," while the NJB has them "run[ning] to and fro among the sheep-pens." Some slightly alter the Hebrew text to read "with gashes" (NEB; REB), similar to 48:37, but this is unneccessary. Their leaders, **priests**, and **princes**, as well as **Malcam**, their god, would **go into exile together**.

The Cause for the Curse (49:4)

> ⁴"How boastful you are about the valleys!
> Your valley is flowing away,
> O backsliding daughter
> Who trusts in her treasures, saying,
> 'Who will come against me?'"

Verse 4. The cause of the judgment is here highlighted. **How boastful you are about the valleys!** To begin with, the Ammonites were "boastful," glorying in their fertile valleys. "Boastful" is translated from הָלַל (*halal*), which is the Hebrew word often translated "praise." In this verse, it refers to an infatuation with one's personal worth or possessions.[3] They, like the Moabites, had fallen victim to pride and would be cursed because of it (48:7, 14, 16, 29, 30).

Further, they had misplaced their trust: **who trusts in her treasures** (see Ps. 52:7; 62:10; Mt. 6:19–21). They had made the mistake of putting their faith in material things.

---

[3]Ibid., 1:249.

Still further, a problem with morality is named: They were saying, **"Who will come against me?"** Amos 1:13–15 notes Ammon's inhumanity toward others as they went out to "enlarge their borders." By this sort of abuse, they demonstrated not only the lowest moral conduct, but also the cheap value they had placed on human life. Divine principles were sacrificed to acquire more land.

The Conclusion: "Terror Is Coming" (49:5)

> **⁵"Behold, I am going to bring terror upon you,"**
> **Declares the Lord GOD of hosts,**
> **"From all directions around you;**
> **And each of you will be driven out headlong,**
> **With no one to gather the fugitives together."**

Verse 5. Terror would come upon them **from all directions**. This punishment fit the crime (see Gal. 6:7, 8). Whereas they had boastfully sought prosperity and security, they now would face "terror" and insecurity. They had gloried in their beautiful land, but now they would **be driven out headlong** into captivity. Although they had possessed and controlled others, their god and leaders would be taken away, leaving them as **fugitives**, with no protecting hand to **gather** them.

A Word of Comfort (49:6)

> **⁶"But afterward I will restore**
> **The fortunes of the sons of Ammon,"**
> **Declares the LORD.**

Verse 6. Despite their departure from the one true God, they would be extended an opportunity of grace at some point in the future. It would come **afterward** (see 48:47).

Because **the LORD** uttered the promise of restoration, we must accept it as being true. When and how this was done is not expressed in either biblical or secular history. After the exile, when God's people were rebuilding the walls of Jerusalem, an

Ammonite mocked their efforts (Neh. 4:1–3). Perhaps many of the Ammonites had already received **the fortunes**, and some of them had already gone astray.

EDOM IN THE HEIGHTS (49:7–22)[4]

The Edomites were descendants of Esau (Gen. 25:30; 36). Esau's jealousy and hatred of his brother Jacob (Gen. 27) later led to conflicts between the Edomites and Jacob's descendants, the Israelites (Num. 20:14–21; 1 Kings 11:14–25; 2 Kings 8:20–22; 14:7). While Jacob and Esau were reconciled (Gen. 33), the Israelites and the Edomites never found that reconciliation, for seldom did they experience peace with one another.

The Zered River served as a boundary between Moab and Edom. Edom's northern border was at the southern tip of the Dead Sea. The Arabian desert was its eastern border, and the Arabah served as the general border on the west. Their land, the mountain country of Edom, was rich in iron and copper.

Human Wisdom (49:7–15)

> [7]**Concerning Edom.**
> **Thus says the Lord of hosts,**
> **"Is there no longer any wisdom in Teman?**
> **Has good counsel been lost to the prudent?**
> **Has their wisdom decayed?**
> [8]**Flee away, turn back, dwell in the depths,**
> **O inhabitants of Dedan,**
> **For I will bring the disaster of Esau upon him**
> **At the time I punish him.**
> [9]**If grape gatherers came to you,**
> **Would they not leave gleanings?**
> **If thieves came by night,**
> **They would destroy only until they had enough.**

---

[4]The Book of Obadiah focuses on another prophecy of judgment for Edom.

¹⁰"But I have stripped Esau bare,
I have uncovered his hiding places
So that he will not be able to conceal himself;
His offspring has been destroyed along with his relatives
And his neighbors, and he is no more.
¹¹Leave your orphans behind, I will keep them alive;
And let your widows trust in Me."
¹²For thus says the LORD, "Behold, those who were not sentenced to drink the cup will certainly drink it, and are you the one who will be completely acquitted? You will not be acquitted, but you will certainly drink it. ¹³For I have sworn by Myself," declares the LORD, "that Bozrah will become an object of horror, a reproach, a ruin and a curse; and all its cities will become perpetual ruins."
¹⁴I have heard a message from the LORD,
And an envoy is sent among the nations, saying,
"Gather yourselves together and come against her,
And rise up for battle!"
¹⁵"For behold, I have made you small among the nations,
Despised among men."

Verse 7. This oracle **concerning Edom** is much longer than the previous judgment against Ammon. The prophet began by using three rhetorical questions to show that Edom's counsel and **wisdom** had **decayed**. "Decayed" is from סָרַח (*sarach*), a word which means "be stinking, rotting."[5] Had they dismissed their wisdom, or did they no longer use it? Jeremiah insisted that **there [was] no longer any wisdom in Teman**. The city or region of "Teman"—a name given to Esau's grandson (Gen. 36:8–11)—had become known as a place where many wise people lived (Ezek. 25:13; Obad. 6–9). It was located in northern Edom and was the home of Eliphaz (Job 2:11). Jeremiah said that **good counsel [had] been lost to the prudent**. The people of Edom had acted lightheartedly on matters that called for discretion. A darkness had come over them because Edom had no wise ones to lead them.

---

[5]Koehler and Baumgartner, 1:769.

Verse 8. God intended to **bring** disaster upon them, as He would upon Egypt (46:20, 21) and Moab (48:16). The Hebrew word translated "bring," בּוֹא (*boʾ*), is repeatedly seen in Jeremiah in the sense of bringing in judgment (4:6; 5:15; 6:19; 11:8, 11; 17:18; 19:3; 23:12). God's people heard this word so often that they mockingly urged Jeremiah to "bring it on" or "let it come now" (17:15).

Dedan was an Arabian city or region just outside Edom's border. The people living there were urged to withdraw from their relationships with Edom and run to safety. Their only hope was to **flee away, turn back, dwell in the depths**, or hidden places of safety. The Hebrew word for "depths," עָמֹק (*ʿamoq*), suggests "land in a valley," such as "a plain between two mountain ridges, or between a mountain and the water."[6] This may have been a call to move deeper into the desert, south and east. By distancing themselves, the people could hope to escape the overwhelming flood of destruction that would pour over Edom.[7] God in His grace was giving them fair warning. The invasion would be no light attack. If Dedan did not flee, **the disaster of Esau** would also fall upon them.

Verse 9. Using the figure of gleaning grapes and the coming of thieves (see Obad. 5, 6), Jeremiah assured Edom that this destruction would be complete. **Grape gatherers** and **thieves** do not take everything available to them; they seize only what they desire. In the sweep of God's judgment upon Edom, however, nothing would be left behind.

Verse 10. The people would be **stripped . . . bare**. Even their **hiding places** would be **uncovered**. One's immediate family, **his offspring, his relatives**, and **his neighbors** would all be victims of what was coming.

Verse 11. Widows and **orphans** alone were offered hope of survival. They would be left in the land and would have to depend upon God to protect them. Such **trust** had been missing in this nation (see 5:17; 7:4, 8; 9:4; 13:25; 46:25; 48:7; 49:4). The

---

[6]Ibid., 1:847.

[7]A few versions, however, suggest that the reference is to hiding in "deep caves" (NIV; NCV).

defenseless, "widows" and "orphans," were offered security; whereas the wise, pompous, and seemingly strong would fall and be left bare or ruined.

Verse 12. Jeremiah reused the figure of **drink[ing] the cup** of wrath which was used in 13:12; 25:15, 21, 28. He was assuring Edom that they would indeed "drink" of God's wrath. If He did not spare His own people from drinking such a cup of wrath during the fall of Jerusalem, would He spare Edom? They would **not be acquitted, but** [would] **certainly drink it.**

Verse 13. The punishment of **Bozrah** was also certain to come. God had **sworn** this to be the case. The well-known capital of Edom (Gen. 36:33) would **become an object of horror, a reproach, a ruin and a curse.** Likewise, **its cities** [would] **become perpetual ruins.**

Verse 14. Jeremiah incorporated the more vivid words of the prophecy of Obadiah into this part of the oracle (see Obad. 1–3). A prophetic **message** (שְׁמוּעָה, *sh^emu'ah*) had gone out **from the Lord.** Obadiah said that the prophets had heard this message, but Jeremiah only noted he had heard it. The message indicated that **an envoy,** an ambassador for God, had called upon **the nations** to rise up against Edom. They were told to **gather** [themselves] **together** and **rise up for battle.** He had stirred the nations to turn against Edom and become His instrument of judgment.

Verse 15. Living in the hills, the Edomites had come to think of themselves as invincible. Nevertheless, the prophecy predicts humiliation for them. Using a perfect verb, the Lord is pictured as saying, **"I have made you small among the nations, despised among men."** The prophecy was so certain to occur that it was spoken of as having already been completed.

Arrogance and Pride (49:16)

> [16]"As for the terror of you,
> The arrogance of your heart has deceived you,
> O you who live in the clefts of the rock,
> Who occupy the height of the hill.
> Though you make your nest as high as an eagle's,
> I will bring you down from there," declares the Lord.

Verse 16. The cause for Edom's punishment is identified. Much like Moab (48:14, 15), Edom had viewed themselves as a **terror** to others; but they were **deceived**. They believed no one could reach them to overcome them. Their cities were located **in the clefts** of mountainous **rock**, or, to say it another way, upon **the height of the hill**. They had been built in such places so that the ravines, canyon walls, and precipices around it would make them unapproachable by an enemy. They would hide in their rocky fortresses and pick off anyone trying to attack them. The people believed their security was unequaled. That deception had led to an **arrogance** that not only left them vulnerable as human beings, but it also required God's plans and power to be set against them (see 1 Pet. 5:5–7). In time, their high and lofty defenses would fall to God's judgment. He promised them that He would **bring** [them] **down from** their high perch of confidence. Indeed, they would be defeated.

God's Curse (49:17, 18)

¹⁷"**Edom will become an object of horror; everyone who passes by it will be horrified and will hiss at all its wounds. ¹⁸Like the overthrow of Sodom and Gomorrah with its neighbors,**" says the LORD, "**no one will live there, nor will a son of man reside in it.**"

Verse 17. Specific factors and forces would be involved in Edom's downfall. For example, they would suffer **wounds**. The word מַכָּה (*makkah*) can mean "blow," "wound," "slaughter," or "defeat." It sometimes denotes a "beating" or a "scourging."[8] The term emphasizes that the people would experience great physical suffering. They would also be despised. All who saw them would be **horrified** and would **hiss** at them. This phrasing is similar to the description of Judah's fall in 19:8.

Verse 18. Edom would become desolate like the overthrown cities of **Sodom** and **Gomorrah** (Gen. 13:13; 18:20; 19:1–28) and

---

[8]Francis Brown, S. R. Driver, and Charles A. Briggs, *A Hebrew and English Lexicon of the Old Testament* (Oxford: Clarendon Press, 1972), 646–47.

their **neighbors**, Admah and Zeboiim (Gen. 10:19; Deut. 29:23–25; Hos. 11:8). No person would **live** or **reside** there. No statement of future hope is offered in Edom's case (see 48:47; 49:6).

Certain Punishment to Follow (49:19–22)

¹⁹"Behold, one will come up like a lion from the thickets of the Jordan against a perennially watered pasture; for in an instant I will make him run away from it, and whoever is chosen I shall appoint over it. For who is like Me, and who will summon Me into court? And who then is the shepherd who can stand against Me?"
²⁰Therefore hear the plan of the LORD which He has planned against Edom, and His purposes which He has purposed against the inhabitants of Teman: surely they will drag them off, even the little ones of the flock; surely He will make their pasture desolate because of them. ²¹The earth has quaked at the noise of their downfall. There is an outcry! The noise of it has been heard at the Red Sea. ²²Behold, He will mount up and swoop like an eagle and spread out His wings against Bozrah; and the hearts of the mighty men of Edom in that day will be like the heart of a woman in labor.

Verse 19. With the figure of **a lion** coming up **from the thickets of the Jordan** (see 2:15; 4:7; 5:6; 12:5, 8; 25:38), the prophecy indicates that the hunt to death was ready to begin. The phrase **perennially watered pasture** pictured prosperity and an ideal setting. Because of grave danger, people would flee, and no one would be able to alter that flight, for God was to be the One making them flee. This would happen even if God chose someone to be His servant in this process. He could even **appoint** another nation to be in charge of removing them.

Deep irony is seen in God's question **"Who will summon Me into court?"** Until this moment, no one had ever taken God to court for His actions; and, of course, no one would be able to do it in this situation either. God punctuated His meaning by asking one more question: **"Who then is the shepherd who can stand against Me?"**

Verse 20. All of these actions were part of God's purposes. This movement was no accident; it was a matter of divine intent. God had **planned** and **purposed** all these tragedies **against** them. The security of **Edom** and the wisdom of **Teman** would not protect them. He would **drag . . . off** their sheep, both large and small, significant leaders as well as the insignificant ones. The pasture land inhabited by this **flock** would become **desolate**.

While the phrase **their pasture** differs in various translations, three facts are certain: (1) An outside force was to invade Edom; (2) "their pasture" is a satirical allusion to Edom's assumed strength; and (3) no one could stop this action, for it was the fulfillment of God's purpose. The Edomites would run, but they would be dragged off like helpless sheep.

Verse 21. The cries coming from the conquest would be a thundering **noise** (קוֹל, *qol*). At the fall of Edom, **the earth** would quake. The price the Edomites paid would be acoustical, making its sound to be heard all the way to **the Red Sea**. Cities such as Elath (2 Kings 14:21, 22) and Ezion-geber (1 Kings 9:26) would hear the sound, since they were located at the head of the Gulf of Aqabah. The crushing fall of Edom was a newsworthy moment, and faraway places would hear of it.

Verse 22. The Edomites had nested as an eagle does (49:16), and God would invade **like an eagle**. He would **mount up and swoop** down **and spread out His wings against Bozrah. The mighty men of Edom** would become as fainthearted as women in childbirth (see comments on 13:21).

DAMASCUS TO THE NORTH (49:23–27)

²³Concerning Damascus.
"Hamath and Arpad are put to shame,
For they have heard bad news;
They are disheartened.
There is anxiety by the sea,
It cannot be calmed.
²⁴Damascus has become helpless;
She has turned away to flee,
And panic has gripped her;

> Distress and pangs have taken hold of her
> Like a woman in childbirth.
> ²⁵How the city of praise has not been deserted,
> The town of My joy!
> ²⁶Therefore, her young men will fall in her streets,
> And all the men of war will be silenced in that day," declares the Lord of hosts.
> ²⁷"I will set fire to the wall of Damascus,
> And it will devour the fortified towers of Ben-hadad."

Judgment was next announced for three cities of Syria (Aram). Damascus was the capital of Syria; Hamath and Arpad were major sister cities (Is. 36:19; 37:13). The relationship of Damascus to Israel is mentioned often in the Old Testament (Gen. 10:18; Num. 34:8; Josh. 13:5; 1 Kings 4:21–24; 2 Kings 14:28; 18:34; 19:13; 2 Chron. 8:4; Is. 10:9; Amos 6:2). No reason for this judgment oracle is given in the text.

Verse 23. The prophet began this first part of his announcement with **Hamath**, which was about a hundred miles north of the city of **Damascus**, and **Arpad**, which was about one hundred miles north of Hamath. The description of these places emphasizes the depressing conditions that would arise because of the judgment sentence. They are pictured as experiencing an embarrassing **shame** (בּוֹשׁ, *bosh*). Because of the **bad news** they had received, they were left lifeless, unable to fight or to take a stand. The terrifying sights they had seen caused their hearts to faint. They are described as **disheartened** (מוּג, *mug*), as if their spirits had melted.[9] For them, at this point, the fight was over. They no longer had a will for the war that they faced. They were filled with **anxiety** (דְּאָגָה, *deʿagah*)—that is, "worry" and "concern"[10]— and their dread could not **be calmed**.

Verse 24. **Damascus** is portrayed as **helpless**. The Hebrew word is רָפָה (*rapah*), which means "grow slack," "wither," or "collapse." It sometimes appears in the idiom "the hands grow slack,"

---

[9]Ibid., 556.
[10]Koehler and Baumgartner, 1:207.

which means that a person's "courage fails."[11] **She . . . turned away** from the approaching attackers **to flee, and panic . . . gripped her**. According to this description, she became filled with **distress**, and **pangs** of fear took **hold of her like a woman in childbirth** (see comments on 13:21). From the very beginning of humanity, fear has led to fleeing and hiding (Gen. 3:6–10; Mt. 26:56; Lk. 22:54–62).

Verse 25. The translation and interpretation of this verse are difficult. According to the NASB, which follows the MT, God said, **"How the city of praise has not been deserted, the town of My joy!"** The presence of the word "not" (לֹא, *lo'*) seems out of place in this context. For this reason, a few versions drop it from the text (RSV; NRSV; NJB). John Bright suggested that *lo'* is a scribal error for the emphatic lamed (לְ, *lᵉ*), meaning "utterly."[12] In this case, the text would say, "How the city of praise has been *utterly* deserted." Another option is to accept the text as it stands and attempt to make sense of it. Perhaps the thought is one of amazement that the people had not yet fled from the city in order to save their lives (see NIV; NCV).

Verse 26. The city of Damascus had once enjoyed beauty, promise, and appeal. Nevertheless, the people, even the **young men**, would **fall in her streets**, and the **men of war** would be put to silence. When the military men fall, there remains no defense for a city.

Verse 27. The promise of this prophecy was that God would **set fire to the wall**[s] and that fire would **devour the fortified towers** that had been built by or in honor of **Ben-hadad**. This was possibly a dynastic name or title for the kings of Syria (1 Kings 15:18; 20:1; 2 Kings 6:24; 8:7; 13:3). It is difficult to know who was intended here, other than a Syrian king. Regarding both men and material fortifications, no defense would be left.

Prevailing power had been in the clutches of Damascus. This city's potential had been a marvel. However, because of sin, judgment was coming. Its fortified places would be set on fire, its mil-

---

[11]Ibid., 2:1277.
[12]John Bright, *Jeremiah*, The Anchor Bible (Garden City, N.Y.: Doubleday & Company, 1965), 333, n.

itary forces would fall in the streets, and the fear-stricken people would flee, leaving the city forsaken. The conquest would be complete. God's wrath is a terrible thing.

KEDAR AND HAZOR (49:28–33)

Kedar, a descendant of Ishmael (Gen. 25:13–16), was of the Arabian tribes. His tribe was located north and east of the Ammonites. These people are also mentioned in several other passages (2:10–13; Ps. 120:5; Is. 21:16, 17; 42:11; 60:7; Ezek. 27:21). Exact details concerning those from Hazor (a Hazor that is unidentified) are unknown. We know that they were "men of the east" (49:28), and the name appears several times as a location in Palestine (Josh. 11:1; 15:23; 19:36); but their being related to Kedar fits with none of those passages.

Conditions Surveyed (49:28–30)

²⁸**Concerning Kedar and the kingdoms of Hazor, which Nebuchadnezzar king of Babylon defeated. Thus says the** L<small>ORD</small>**,**
"Arise, go up to Kedar
And devastate the men of the east.
²⁹**They will take away their tents and their flocks;**
They will carry off for themselves
Their tent curtains, all their goods and their camels,
And they will call out to one another, 'Terror on every side!'
³⁰**Run away, flee! Dwell in the depths,**
O inhabitants of Hazor," declares the L<small>ORD</small>;
"For Nebuchadnezzar king of Babylon has formed a plan
  against you
And devised a scheme against you."

Verse 28. The perfect verb translated **defeated** in this introductory verse probably indicates that, when Jeremiah's oral prophecy was finally recorded, the actual conquest of these people by **Nebuchadnezzar** had already occurred. What follows in verses 29 through 33 describes conditions and circumstances that

JEREMIAH 49

came to pass under Babylon's rule.

The command **"Arise, go up to Kedar"** was given to Nebuchadnezzar. He was given the charge to **devastate the men of the east**. These people inhabited **Kedar and the kingdoms of Hazor**. That same destruction also affected the Philistines (47:4) and the Moabites (48:8, 18, 32).

Verse 29. These nomadic people owned little more than their **tents, flocks,** and **camels**. All their possessions were to be carried away. The cruel, merciless manner in which it was done called forth that common cry from Jeremiah: **"Terror on every side!"** (6:25; 20:3, 10; 46:5).

Verse 30. That God exhorted them to **flee** and **dwell in the depths** (see comments on 49:8) is another proof that the central goal of the judgment was removal, not death. The people could slip away for survival and avoid execution. **Nebuchadnezzar king of Babylon** was too powerful. He had devised **a plan**, and his **scheme** was too strong to overcome.

The Cause of Their Fall (49:31–33)

> ³¹"Arise, go up against a nation which is at ease,
> Which lives securely," declares the LORD.
> "It has no gates or bars;
> They dwell alone.
> ³²Their camels will become plunder,
> And their many cattle for booty,
> And I will scatter to all the winds those who cut the corners of their hair;
> And I will bring their disaster from every side," declares the LORD.
> ³³"Hazor will become a haunt of jackals,
> A desolation forever;
> No one will live there,
> Nor will a son of man reside in it."

Verse 31. Why had such a curse been placed on these people? The cause identified in verses 31 through 33 is the same basic

375

problem that had plagued each group mentioned in this oracle: They were **at ease** (שָׁלֵו, *shalew*), enjoying tranquility and rest.[13] Others who were carefree, prosperous, and at ease are mentioned in the Scriptures (Job 16:12; 21:23; Ps. 73:12; Ezek. 23:42; Zech. 7:7). The satire is obvious in the Lord's declaration that this **nation** lived **securely** (בֶּטַח, *betach*). They were living a "carefree" life, being "undisturbed" in their safe environment.[14] They were indifferent to dangers—whether physical, moral, or spiritual.

Verse 32. In reality, they had no gates, so **their camels [would] become plunder.** They had no bars, so the multitude of their **cattle [would become] booty.** The people would face **disaster from every side.** The slaughter would be severe, the land would become a desolation with no one residing there any more—at least not **those who cut the corners of their hair** in worship of a pagan god (see comments on 9:25, 26; 25:23).

Verse 33. The city of **Hazor** was to become **a desolation forever.** The Hebrew term translated "forever" is עוֹלָם (*'olam*), which means "age-lasting." A "long time" is implied. The duration of *'olam* is "usually eternal, . . . but not in a philosophical sense."[15] The term was used in relation to the Sabbath in 17:19–22. Whatever age God had in mind here was obviously long enough to be a sobering sentence for these people. The land would become a barren place where only wild animals lived and roamed. It would lose its human population. Not even **a son of man** would **reside in it.**

ELAM, FAR TO THE EAST (49:34–39)

Elam was related to Noah's son Shem (Gen. 10:22; 14:1–11). His posterity emerged as a strong nation north and east of the Persian Gulf, west of Persia, south of Media, and east of Babylon. The capital, Sushan or Susa (Neh. 1:1; Esther 1:2, 5; Dan. 8:2), was about 250 miles east of Babylon.

Prior to the prophecy of chapter 49, the Elamites joined forces

---

[13]Koehler and Baumgartner, 2:1505.
[14]Ibid., 1:120–21.
[15]Ibid., 1:798.

with Assyria against Israel (Is. 22:6–10). Years later, the Lord used Elam and Media to overthrow Babylon (Is. 21:1–10). Theo. Laetsch observed that, "after the fall of Nineveh (612 B.C.), the Medes subjugated Elam, and Cyrus embodied it in his vast empire."[16] Adam Clarke thought that "the Elamites and Persians were two distinct people, and continued so till blended under Cyrus."[17]

Since Elam was a nation so distant from Judah, why did Jeremiah include a prophecy concerning these people? Obviously, one answer is that the prophet's message was "the word of the LORD" to the nations (see 49:38, 39). God put His words in Jeremiah's mouth, and that determined his message (1:7–10). This prophecy may have related to the days of Zedekiah. A recent deportation of many Jews to Babylon in 597 B.C. (22:24–30; 2 Kings 24:10–18) was referred to in the false prophets' claims of an imminent return of the Jews to Palestine (27:9–20; 28:1–4; 29:1–23). Maybe Jeremiah was countering a false hope that was being generated among those in exile.

Some records indicate that Elam was reacting against Nebuchadnezzar at this time. With false prophets speaking to God's people left in Judah and in exile about a speedy return, Elam could have offered prospects for the false predictions to come true. Therefore, God directed Jeremiah to give this brief oracle against Elam to set the record straight, removing any illusions or delusions about Elam's influence at that time relative to Babylon's conquests.

The Reason for Judgment (49:34, 35)

³⁴That which came as the word of the LORD to Jeremiah the prophet concerning Elam, at the beginning of the reign of Zedekiah king of Judah, saying:
³⁵"Thus says the LORD of hosts,
'Behold, I am going to break the bow of Elam,
The finest of their might.'"

---

[16]Theo. Laetsch, *Jeremiah*, Bible Commentary (St. Louis: Concordia Publishing House, 1965), 351.

[17]Adam Clarke, *The Holy Bible With a Commentary and Critical Notes*, vol. 4, *Isaiah to Malachi* (New York: Abingdon-Cokesbury Press, n.d.), 381.

Verse 34. That which came as the word of the Lord to Jeremiah the prophet once again serves as the introductory formula (see 46:1; 47:1). Babylonian operations against **Elam** seem to have been conducted in 596 B.C., which would have been in **the beginning of the reign of Zedekiah.**

Verse 35. Both the conditions and the cause of this judgment may be covered in this sweeping promise. God's plan to **break the bow** of the Elamites would be a devastating blow to the heart of their military power. Elam was widely known for its skilled archers. Herodotus said that three skills were taught to the youth of Persia: (1) to ride, (2) to draw the bow, (3) and to speak the truth.[18] This weapon, the deadly bow **of Elam**, was regarded as **the finest of their might**. While archery was the finest strength of their arsenal, breaking it was no strong challenge to the Lord of lords and King of kings (see 1 Tim. 6:15, 16).

The Curse of the Judgment (49:36–38)

> 36"'I will bring upon Elam the four winds
> From the four ends of heaven,
> And will scatter them to all these winds;
> And there will be no nation
> To which the outcasts of Elam will not go.
> 37So I will shatter Elam before their enemies
> And before those who seek their lives;
> And I will bring calamity upon them,
> Even My fierce anger,' declares the LORD,
> 'And I will send out the sword after them
> Until I have consumed them.
> 38Then I will set My throne in Elam
> And destroy out of it king and princes,'
> Declares the LORD."

Verse 36. The **scatter**[ing] of the Elamites by **the four winds** would be so extensive that it would take them to all nations; **no nation** would be left out. That scattering could have been

---

[18]Herodotus *Histories* 1.136.

throughout the 127 provinces that were organized after the Babylonian Empire (Esther 1:1, 2; Dan. 6:1). The prophecy may also have been a hyperbolic prediction for a major scattering.

"The four winds" and **the four ends of heaven** are figures of speech that are frequently used in the Bible (Ezek. 37:9; Dan. 7:2; 8:8; Zech. 2:6; Mt. 24:31; Rev. 7:1). They imply forces of heaven and earth, coming from all directions, being powerful enough to disperse the Elamites to all parts of the earth. It is no wonder that the Elamites would undergo trembling and terror as they experienced this trauma.

Verse 37. The scared souls would be dismayed **before their enemies** as the **calamity** came upon them. God's pronouncement is in the first person, for He was the One who would **shatter** (חָתַת, *chathath*) Elam (see comments on 48:1). The Lord vowed to release His **fierce anger** and **send out the sword after them** (15:2; 44:13). When wickedness is widespread, God's sentence of judgment rises to the highest level of fright (Gen. 6:5, 17, 18; 9:6).

Verse 38. They were subjected not just to men but also to God Himself, for He would **set [His] throne in Elam**. The enactment of the judgment would be according to His dominion and sovereignty. God would **destroy** its **king and princes** because evil must be removed before righteousness can take root.

How would God set His throne in Elam? Charles J. Ellicott paralleled this setting of His throne to 25:13–25 and 43:10, attributing the fulfillment of the prophecy to Nebuchadnezzar, as God's servant.[19] Clarke looked at it from a different slant, as he wrote, "This is spoken either of Nebuchadnezzar or Cyrus. It is certain that Cyrus did render himself master of Elymais and Media, which are in the land of Elam."[20] James E. Smith thought that it might have been a territorial fulfillment: "When Cyrus, the anointed of the Lord (Isaiah 44:28; 45:1), incorporated Elam as a province in his vast empire, the present prophecy was fulfilled."[21] Another possibility is that God's use of the phrase

---

[19]Charles J. Ellicott, *Ellicott's Commentary on the Whole Bible*, vol. 5 (Grand Rapids, Mich.: Zondervan Publishing House, 1959), 161.
[20]Clarke, 381.
[21]James E. Smith, *Jeremiah and Lamentations*, Bible Study Textbook Series (Joplin, Mo.: College Press, 1972), 750.

"My throne in Elam" could allude to His plan that His principles would prevail in that place (see 27:6–11). Certainly, that was God's ultimate intent.

A Ray of Hope (49:39)

> [39]"'But it will come about in the last days
> That I will restore the fortunes of Elam,'"
> Declares the LORD.

Verse 39. In spite of the curse God placed on Elam, a ray of hope and comfort was extended in this prophecy. **In the last days**, the days of the Messiah (Acts 2:14–21; Joel 2:28–32), God promised to **restore the fortunes of Elam**. This far-reaching promise emphasized that the all-powerful God is not just in the desolation and destruction business. It further proves that God is always working with a plan and a purpose. When we work with God, His plan always works for good, seeking to restore welfare and happiness to people (48:47; Rom. 8:28–39; Jas. 1:17).

APPLICATION

A Hope for the Future (Ch. 49)
How often, just in the Book of Jeremiah, God patiently offered a way for people to avoid His punishment, while offering them His precious promises! (See 4:1–4; 6:16–19; 9:7–9; 29:10–14; 30:18–22; 31:17–34.) It is important to go beyond the promise and realize that people from Elam were present on the Day of Pentecost when Peter preached the gospel (Acts 2:9). On that day, salvation was offered to those gathered through the Savior, who left heaven to live, love, die, and give His blood to redeem Elamites—along with all men—who would penitently be baptized in His name for the removal of sins (Acts 2:23–39; 22:16).

As Elamites heard the gospel message, God's divine and prophetic plans were unfolding. Paul gave emphasis to that fact as he wrote, "I will call those who were not My people, 'My people,' and her who was not beloved, 'Beloved.' And it shall be that in the place where it was said to them, 'You are not My people,' there they shall be called sons of the living God" (Rom. 9:25, 26; see Hos. 2:23; 1:10).

The call comes to each of us. We should ask, "Have I honored and obeyed that mighty, loving, caring God?" May all the earth hear and heed His call! (See Mt. 11:28–30; Mk. 16:15, 16; Rev. 22:17.)

The Responsibility of Using Money (Ch. 49)

Helmut Thielicke boldly said, "Our pocketbooks have more to do with heaven and also with hell than our hymnbooks."[22] Did he mean that money is more powerful than worship? No, he meant that the emphasis people often give to each shows an improper balance. Too many have fallen victim to the words the writer of Ecclesiastes wrote in satire: "Money is the answer to everything!" (Eccles. 10:19). We must not believe it! Money brings food but not appetite, medicine but not health, acquaintances but not friends, days of laughter but not peace.

Leaders That Lead (49:26)

Great damage is done when leaders are either deceitful or irresponsible (see 1 Tim. 1:3–7). A leader who fails to act wisely will be responsible for the followers whom he has led astray. How often those who thought they were wise have proven to be operating with decayed wisdom! (See Is. 3:1–8; 19:11–14; 29:13–16; Rom. 1:18–25; 1 Cor. 1:26–29.) While no one of us lives to himself or dies to himself (Rom. 14:7), a leader has an extended circle of influence for which he holds a special responsibility. A leader is one who "knows the way, goes the way, and shows the way."[23] This is especially true in matters of morality and spirituality. Jesus Christ qualified perfectly in that regard (Jn. 10:9, 10; 14:1–6; 1 Pet. 2:21–25).

---

[22]Quoted in Albert M. Wells, Jr., ed., *Inspiring Quotations* (Nashville: Thomas Nelson Publishers, 1988), 135.

[23]Lloyd Cory, *Quotable Quotations* (Wheaton, Ill.: Victor Books, 1994), 210.

CHAPTER 50
THE JUDGMENT OF BABYLON, 1

Chapters 50 and 51, when counted together, contain 110 verses. These two chapters stand as a unit. They foretell the judgment of the nation and city of Babylon, which is one of the main topics throughout Jeremiah's prophetic work (1:14–16; 20:4; 21:2; 24:1; 25:1). He has pursued this theme no doubt because of Babylon's relation to Israel. In light of this fact, it is only fitting that his prophecy conclude with a detailed depiction of the retribution of Babylon, the great destroyer of Israel.

The words of this prophecy were written and read aloud in the fourth year of Zedekiah, the year when this king was taken to Babylon (51:59). Judah had already fallen to Nebuchadnezzar, who was at the height of his empire-building career. Other nations were yet to be conquered by Nebuchadnezzar, but his power and prominence were already established. Even God was using him as His instrument in the conquests that he was decreeing (27:1–8).

In these two chapters, Jeremiah, in a land which had already fallen victim to the emperor, was openly declaring the downfall of the greatest ruler and army of that day. The prophet was proclaiming the coming conquest of the conqueror. He had selected as his spokesman Seraiah, who is referred to as a "quartermaster" (51:59). He transported this scroll of Babylon's prophecy, and, on occasions, read it aloud (51:61). He was surely delivering an explosive message. As is often the case, God's power was being manifested through the weakness of man (see 1 Cor. 1:26–29).

Jeremiah's unusual book showed that he was working for God rather than Babylon (see 37:6–21). If he had not been speaking for God, his words would have been foolish. He was striking out against his own people (who wanted to kill him) and against the victorious invading army of Babylon. Neither his message nor the current situation was likely to bring him friendship from either side. His trust had to be in God! The courageous prophet had to look to heaven for his encouragement (25:29–33).

What punishment was proclaimed for Babylon? Just as severe treatment came from Babylon, severe punishment would come to Babylon (see *Appendix: Parallels in the Book of Jeremiah Between Severe Treatment by Babylon & the Punishment of Babylon*, page 576). Her destruction provides thought-provoking testimony of the divine principle of sowing and reaping (Gal. 6:7, 8).

Why was this punishment prescribed for Babylon? Specific sins and violations of Babylon can be gleaned from Jeremiah's coverage in these two chapters. God was indeed justified in responding to Babylon as He did. Though Babylon and Nebuchadnezzar may have acted as God's servants (25:9; 27:6–8; 43:10–13; Is. 13:1–6; 44:26–28) to punish other nations, the Babylonians became embedded in evil which demanded that they face divine judgment. Jeremiah proved that this was the case with the thundering indictment, "For she has sinned against the LORD" (50:14). In this affirmation, he showed that God holds nations accountable to Him in ways other than the covenant He made with Israel (18:5–10).

Jeremiah also preached, "You have engaged in conflict with the LORD" (50:24). Babylon's disobedient spirit is identified as a "conflict" (גָּרָה, *garah*), as "strife,"[1] with the Creator (see Deut. 2:5, 19; Prov. 28:4; Dan. 11:10, 25). He said, "She has become arrogant against the LORD" (50:29; see 50:31, 32; 13:15). When the creature so responds to the Creator, a disastrous brand of humanism is manifested.

Jeremiah then said of Babylon, "It is a land of idols, and they are mad over fearsome idols" (50:38; see 51:17, 18, 44, 47, 52). "Mad" is from הָלַל (*halal*), which can mean "praise," "boast,"

---

[1] Ludwig Koehler and Walter Baumgartner, *The Hebrew and Aramaic Lexicon of the Old Testament*, study ed., trans. and ed. M. E. J. Richardson (Boston: Brill, 2001), 1:202.

"make [one] look foolish," or "act like a madman."[2] Babylon, with pomp and splendor, attributed great honor and glory to false gods. Two passages, 50:38 and 51:17–52, contain a sobering condemnation of idols and all who bow before them. The Hebrew term, translated by the NASB as "fearsome" in 50:38, is אֵימָה (*'eymah*), which embodies the ideas of "fright," "horror," "dread," and "terror."[3] Cruelty and immorality usually accompanied idolatrous worship.

Highly cultured and sophisticated Babylon had insanely embraced these pagan lifestyles. They could have received the wisdom and knowledge that would bring them to God, but they chose idols instead. Spurning the truth, they went into error. Even Nebuchadnezzar himself had been given opportunities to learn the truth (see Dan. 2:46–49; 3:28–30; 4:27–37). Paul's words aptly describe Babylon: "Professing to be wise, they became fools, and exchanged the glory of the incorruptible God for an image in the form of corruptible man and of birds and four-footed animals and crawling creatures" (Rom. 1:22, 23). In truth, the prophets "applied healing to Babylon, but she was not healed" (51:9; see 50:34). The Babylonian people resisted God as their Redeemer.[4]

It was necessary, then, for Jeremiah to say, "O you who dwell by many waters, abundant in treasures, your end has come" (51:13a). Babylon's greed and selfishness had turned her conquests into opportunities to indulge her "covetousness" (51:13b; KJV). While those conquered by Babylon no doubt deserved punishment for their sinful ways, their guilt did not justify Babylon's

---

[2]Ibid., 1:248–49.

[3]Ibid., 41; Francis Brown, S. R. Driver, and Charles A. Briggs, *A Hebrew and English Lexicon of the Old Testament* (Oxford: Clarendon Press, 1972), 33–34.

[4]"'I will help you,' declares the Lord, 'and your Redeemer is the Holy One of Israel'" (Isa. 41:14). In similar contexts where he promises redemption, God names himself as the *Gō'ēl*. He is 'the Lord your Redeemer, the Holy One of Israel' (Isa. 43:14; 48:17). . . . Twice this designation is accompanied by the reference to God as a rock: 'And they remembered that God was their rock, and the Most High God their Redeemer' (Ps. 78:35); he is 'my rock and my Redeemer' (Ps. 19:14)" (Jack Cottrell, *God the Redeemer* [Joplin, Mo.: College Press Publishing Co., 1991], 17–18).

sinful plundering of their conquered peoples. God said of Babylon, "I will repay Babylon ... for all their evil that they have done in Zion" (51:24; see 51:34, 35; 25:12–14). To be sure, Babylon fell "for the slain of Israel" (51:49).

In these two chapters, Jeremiah repeatedly moved between Babylon's vicious conquests and a ray of hope for God's people. Babylon's evil deeds against Judah had to be done to bring His people to repentance. However, the cruel treatment from Babylon was not approved by God, even though He used it to produce good in His people. Jeremiah announced that the judgment on Babylon was justified.

When did the punishment of Babylon take place? In 539 B.C., Babylon fell to the armies of Cyrus, king of the new Medo-Persian Empire, without a battle. However, the complete destruction of the city came in several parts after numerous sieges (see Dan. 5:18–31).

AUTHORSHIP QUESTIONS

That chapters 50 and 51 were actually written by Jeremiah has been doubted by some. This has been the case even though the book contains the clear statement that God spoke this message "through Jeremiah the prophet" (50:1; 51:59–61, 64). Questions have been raised and speculations offered, but no authentic proof has actually been discovered. Diligent students of God's Word should not dwell on this skepticism or give credence to it. Sufficient evidence exists to support the biblical claim that Jeremiah was the writer.

It has also been argued that the events in these chapters did not occur in the fourth year of Zedekiah, as the oracle claims. After all, the prophecy pictures God's people as already being in exile (50:4, 5). It implies that the temple had already been destroyed (50:23; 51:11), and it says that the current disasters were the embodiment of God's vengeance (51:11). The noise of Babylon's fall had been already sounded (50:8–10; 51:24). Do these contentions comprise a valid argument? Let us not forget that this is a prophetic book, given by the God who knows the future. He knew how to describe these events with precision and exactness long before they happened (25:1, 12–14; see 43:8–13).

Another argument is that Jeremiah's attitude about Babylon was different in 50:8, 9 and 51:9, 10 than in 29:4–10. What can be said about this view? This claim may be true; but in 25:12–14, Jeremiah spoke differently about Babylon than he did to the captives in 29:4–10. He was describing current conditions in 29:4–10, but chapters 50 and 51 reveal the future judgment and the fall of Babylon. Jeremiah had urged the captives to yield to Babylon (29:5–7), and later he had instructed them to return from Babylon (29:12–14). In a prophetic book, the past, present, and future events may be blended together into one presentation. Prophecy sometimes amalgamates the times and tenses as the eternal God sees events in relation to Himself, not years.

It is further suggested that too much repetition occurs in chapters 50 and 51. The attack and approaching desolations of Babylon are mentioned 11 times, the conquest and destruction of Babylon are brought up 9 times, Israel's or Judah's return to Jerusalem is mentioned 7 times, and the approach of the enemy from the north is addressed 4 times (50:3, 9, 41; 51:48). Does this argument have any validity? Repetition does not destroy authenticity or authorship. From chapters 1 to 50, Jeremiah used repetition about Judah's sins, God's plans, idolatry, and Babylon as the force to punish God's people. Chapters 50 and 51 fit Jeremiah's literary pattern more than they support the idea that Jeremiah was not the writer. Where are all of Jeremiah's words that he "pronounced against" Babylon and "prophesied against all the nations" (25:13), if they are not in chapters 50 and 51?

God's servant must study these two chapters as a divine message of judgment for Babylon, given through Jeremiah, and try to glean what God prepared for our instruction and learning.

BABYLON'S FALL (50:1, 2)

¹**The word which the LORD spoke concerning Babylon, the land of the Chaldeans, through Jeremiah the prophet:**
²**"Declare and proclaim among the nations.
Proclaim it and lift up a standard.
Do not conceal it but say,**

'Babylon has been captured,
Bel has been put to shame, Marduk has been shattered;
Her images have been put to shame, her idols have been shattered.'"

Verse 1. At the beginning of this last oracle, a superscription is given for the whole prophecy (chs. 50; 51). It clarifies that what Jeremiah had written was God's oracle, not his own. The judgment, as to origin, was **the word which the L**ORD **spoke concerning Babylon**. As with the other oracles, God spoke **through** [literally, "by the hand of"] **Jeremiah the prophet**. For some reason, the LXX omits this authorship designation.

"Babylon" is a place name that refers to the chief city of the great empire of that time, while **Chaldeans** refers more to the race of people who had come to live in the lower region of the land between the Euphrates and the Tigris Rivers, commonly called "Mesopotamia." J. A. Thompson noted,

> The father of Nebuchadrezzar, Nabopolassar, was a native Chaldean who took the throne of Babylon in 626 B.C. and gave rise to the neo-Babylonian period which lasted till 539 B.C. Nebuchadrezzar was the most illustrious and longest reigning of these kings.[5]

Because of Babylon's prominence in the fourth year of Zedekiah, this announcement that the mighty nation would fall was the biggest secular news that appeared in Jeremiah's writings.

Verse 2. God decreed that this oracle be given worldwide publicity, that it be **declare**[d] **and proclaim**[ed] **among the nations**. The breaking news was to be written on **a standard** (נֵס, *nes*), that is, a "flag" or "ensign,"[6] for the world to see (51:12, 27). Its message was short, but it was earthshaking news: **Babylon has been captured**. This was to be a revelation, not a conceal-

---

[5]J. A. Thompson, *The Book of Jeremiah*, The New International Commentary on the Old Testament (Grand Rapids, Mich.: Wm. B. Eerdmans Publishing Co., 1980), 732.
[6]Koehler and Baumgartner, 1:701.

ment. Babylon, having captured so many nations, would now itself be captured.

Bel was the Baal of the Babylonians. The name means "Lord." The Babylonian "Hymn to Bel," translated from cuneiform script, reveals that he was recognized as the supreme ruler. He was viewed as the life-giver, the god of justice, the one who held society together by controlling the elements, particularly fire (51:44; Is. 46:1).[7]

Ancient inscriptions provide proof that the two names "Bel" and **Marduk** came to represent the same deity:

> Bel appears in the names of the two great walls of Babylon, Imgur-Bel and Nimetti-Bel, the latter name, in the form of Marduk, appears as lord of heaven and earth, and Nebo is subordinate to him. Nebuchadnezzar's devotion to him is indicated by the name he gave his son, Evil-merodach (chap. 52:31). He further exalts him by describing himself as "worshipper of Marduk."[8]

The disease of idolatry (50:2, 38; 51:17, 18, 44, 47, 52) was the cause of Babylon's fall. Bel would be **put to shame**, and Marduk was going to be **shattered**. A lengthy description of the futility of idols is given later, in contrast to the power and might of the true God (51:14–23).

THE OPEN DOOR (50:3–10)

³"For a nation has come up against her out of the north; it will make her land an object of horror, and there will be no inhabitant in it. Both man and beast have wandered off, they have gone away!

⁴"In those days and at that time," declares the LORD, "the sons of Israel will come, both they and the sons of Judah as

---

[7]Merrill C. Tenney, *Zondervan Pictorial Dictionary of the Bible* (Grand Rapids, Mich.: Zondervan, 1967), 103.

[8]Charles J. Ellicott, *Ellicott's Commentary on the Whole Bible*, vol. 5 (Grand Rapids, Mich.: Zondervan Publishing House, 1959), 162.

well; they will go along weeping as they go, and it will be the Lord their God they will seek. ⁵They will ask for the way to Zion, turning their faces in its direction; they will come that they may join themselves to the Lord in an everlasting covenant that will not be forgotten.

⁶"My people have become lost sheep;
Their shepherds have led them astray.
They have made them turn aside on the mountains;
They have gone along from mountain to hill
And have forgotten their resting place.
⁷All who came upon them have devoured them;
And their adversaries have said, 'We are not guilty,
Inasmuch as they have sinned against the Lord who is the habitation of righteousness,
Even the Lord, the hope of their fathers.'
⁸"Wander away from the midst of Babylon
And go forth from the land of the Chaldeans;
Be also like male goats at the head of the flock.
⁹For behold, I am going to arouse and bring up against Babylon
A horde of great nations from the land of the north,
And they will draw up their battle lines against her;
From there she will be taken captive.
Their arrows will be like an expert warrior
Who does not return empty-handed.
¹⁰Chaldea will become plunder;
All who plunder her will have enough," declares the Lord.

Verse 3. The conquering force in this case is described as **a nation . . . out of the north** (see 50:9, 41). It is identified further as "the Medes" in 51:11, 28. Daniel also prophetically foretold of the Medes' and the Persians' conquest of Babylon (Dan. 5:28, 31; 8:20). The desolation would be so complete that neither **man** nor **beast** would remain in the place. After its destruction, even the wild animals that roamed the forests and fields would **have gone away**.

Verse 4. The favor to be shown to **the sons of Israel** and **Judah** in **those days** and at **that time** is the focal point of this part of the prophecy. That Jeremiah emphasized this truth early in his account was no accident. Psalm 137 is a verbal cry expressing the captives' inner longing for Zion: "How can we sing the LORD's song in a foreign land?" (Ps. 137:4). The desire to get back to Jerusalem placed a heavy emotional burden on their hearts. If permitted, they would **go** back, **weeping** as they went, to **seek their God.**

Verse 5. The fall of Babylon and the redemption and restoration of God's people to their homeland are significant events in the account of the fall of Babylon. Though Jews might be weeping as they went to Jerusalem, they would make the trip in order to seek **the LORD** their God (29:11–14). He had been waiting to see and hear this heart-hunger on the part of His people.

Zion was the place on their minds. They were asking **the way to Zion, turning their faces in its direction** (see Neh. 1:1—2:20). The grammatical construction **they will come** indicates that the writer was in Zion. This is another characteristic of the book that favors Jeremiah as the writer.

This restoration was more than a return to the land. It was a return to "the LORD" and to **an everlasting covenant that will not be forgotten** (32:40; 2 Sam. 7:12–16; Is. 55:3; Heb. 13:20, 21).

Verse 6. The metaphor of **lost sheep** is the prophet's description of God's people and how He would make their return possible. One of their difficulties had been **shepherds** who had **led them astray** by teaching them the wicked practices of idolatry. They had been led **from mountain to hill** in their worship of Baal. These idolatrous pursuits had caused them to forget **their resting place** (see 31:10–14; 33:12; 50:19; Is. 65:8–10), their peaceful dwelling in the true God. Without an anchor to hold them in place, these people had become easy prey for the evil influences surrounding them in the land (see Ezek. 34:1–10).

Verse 7. The **adversaries** of Judah justified their crushing actions against God's people by saying, **"We are not guilty, inasmuch as they have sinned against the LORD who is the habitation of righteousness"** (see 40:1–3). They used the unfaithfulness of Judah to justify their mistreatment of Judah. They would argue, "Those who claim fellowship with the LORD of righteousness but worship idols should not expect righteous treatment."

Even though **the LORD** was their hope and **the hope of their fathers**, they had forsaken Him and had been a reproach to the nations.

Verse 8. With the fall of Babylon, freedom would come for the exiles to return to Judea. They would return with confidence. The instructions God had given to guide them through seventy years of captivity (29:4–14) would be replaced by a command to **wander away from the midst of Babylon. Like male goats** leading **the flock**, God's people were to lead others to Jerusalem, setting the standard for other nations returning to their homelands (50:16; Ezra 1:1–11).

Verse 9. The possibilities of the future included Babylon's fall before **a horde of great nations from the land of the north** (Is. 13:17–22). God would be the One bringing about the whole event. He would stir up the "nations," who would come against her as one force. They would **draw up their battle lines against her**, overpower her, and take her **captive**. Their effectiveness at war was compared to **arrows** in the hands of **an expert warrior who does not return empty-handed**.

Verse 10. Chaldea, who had in the past mastered the art of plundering others, would now be thoroughly plundered. The nations who would **plunder her** would recover ample booty to make the effort worth their time. These victories would provide an opening for God's plan for His people in captivity to be enacted.

A HERITAGE OF SHAME (50:11–13)

¹¹"Because you are glad, because you are jubilant,
O you who pillage My heritage,
Because you skip about like a threshing heifer
And neigh like stallions,
¹²Your mother will be greatly ashamed,
She who gave you birth will be humiliated.
Behold, she will be the least of the nations,
A wilderness, a parched land and a desert.
¹³Because of the indignation of the LORD she will not be inhabited,

> But she will be completely desolate;
> Everyone who passes by Babylon will be horrified
> And will hiss because of all her wounds."

Verse 11. In the workings of God, Babylon's haughtiness would be turned into humiliation and shame. The Babylonians were the ones who had pillaged God's people with jubilance. They had jumped about in the process **like a threshing heifer**, and their rejoicing tones had sounded like the **neigh**[s] of strong **stallions**.

Verse 12. The fall of Babylon would bring the greatest degradation and desolation. Figuratively speaking, Babylon's **mother**, perhaps the city of Babylon, would become **greatly ashamed**. The great Babylon, when it was all over, would be **the least of the nations, a wilderness, a parched land and a desert**.

Verse 13. Because of the Lord's **indignation** (קֶצֶף, *qetsep*), that is, His "anger" and "wrath,"[9] the world-renowned nation would become **completely desolate**. Everyone who passed by would **hiss** and **be horrified** because of Babylon's **wounds**. A world empire that had plunged into nothingness struck all who looked at her with shock and surprise.

THE VENGEANCE OF THE LORD (50:14–16)

> [14]"Draw up your battle lines against Babylon on every side,
> All you who bend the bow;
> Shoot at her, do not be sparing with your arrows,
> For she has sinned against the LORD.
> [15]Raise your battle cry against her on every side!
> She has given herself up, her pillars have fallen,
> Her walls have been torn down.
> For this is the vengeance of the LORD:
> Take vengeance on her;
> As she has done to others, so do to her.
> [16]Cut off the sower from Babylon

---

[9]Koehler and Baumgartner, 2:1124–25; Brown, Driver, and Briggs, 893.

> And the one who wields the sickle at the time of harvest;
> From before the sword of the oppressor
> They will each turn back to his own people
> And they will each flee to his own land."

Verse 14. God called upon others to be His instruments of vengeance. The bowmen were given freedom to attack. All who **bend the bow** were to **shoot at her**. The warriors made their attack from every side. **Babylon** had **sinned against the Lord** and must receive her judgment.

Verse 15. The Lord of **vengeance** had given a command: "Take vengeance on her; as she has done to others, so do to her." The vengeance-seekers could openly satisfy their desires. Even Babylon's **pillars** and **walls** would be torn down.

Verse 16. **The sower** and **the one who wields the sickle at the time of harvest** would be free to go home. Slaves of the soil would stop their plowing and planting, as **the sword of the oppressor** gave them release from their servitude in the fields. All the commanding and demanding days of **Babylon** would be over. The invading force did to the Babylonians what they had been doing to others (50:29).

The destruction of Babylon described in these verses should not be seen as a single act. These are prophetic allusions to several different sieges on Babylon. These verses obviously were not all fulfilled with the fall of Babylon in 539 B.C. Cyrus did not raze the walls of the city. He was careful to spare the rural regions of Babylonia. These elements of the prophecy must point to subsequent attacks on the city.

What was the cause of this unexpected turn of events? A mighty God had watched the jubilant abuse and pillage of His people. His "indignation," His "wrath," had been stirred until His vengeance was finally satisfied.

Both the old and the new covenants teach that vengeance belongs to God (Deut. 32:35; Rom. 12:19). No stronger expression of God's sovereignty is given than His confident ability and intent to enact vengeance on any nation or adversary. God, as the Mighty One, affirms, "I will be relieved of My adversaries and avenge Myself on My foes" (Is. 1:24). His justice is summarized in Isaiah 59:18: "According to their deeds, so He will repay, wrath to His adversaries, recompense to His enemies."

His vengeance will be expressed against nations whether they are small or great: It came against Midian (Num. 31:3); Ammon (Judg. 11:36); the Philistines (Ezek. 25:15–17); Edom (Ezek. 25:14); Egypt (46:2, 10); Nineveh (Nahum); and it came against even mighty Babylon (50:15, 28; 51:6, 11, 36; Is. 47:1–3). Nahum 1:1–3 says that it must be understood that "a jealous and avenging God is the LORD; the LORD is avenging and wrathful. The LORD takes vengeance on His adversaries, and He reserves wrath for His enemies. . . . the LORD will by no means leave the guilty unpunished." Paul reminded us that a even greater judgment will take place when Jesus comes again: "Rendering vengeance to them that know not God, and to them that obey not the gospel of our Lord Jesus; who shall suffer punishment, even eternal destruction from the face of the Lord and from the glory of his might" (2 Thess. 1:8, 9; ASV).

A SCATTERED FLOCK (50:17–19)

17"Israel is a scattered flock, the lions have driven them away. The first one who devoured him was the king of Assyria, and this last one who has broken his bones is Nebuchadnezzar king of Babylon. 18Therefore thus says the LORD of hosts, the God of Israel: 'Behold, I am going to punish the king of Babylon and his land, just as I punished the king of Assyria. 19And I will bring Israel back to his pasture and he will graze on Carmel and Bashan, and his desire will be satisfied in the hill country of Ephraim and Gilead.'"

Verse 17. All of God's aggressive acts are overlaid with a sweeping concern for the condition of His people. His all-seeing eye could with only a glance look from 722 to 540 B.C. Obviously, this is possible only for the timeless Creator of heaven and earth (see 2 Pet. 3:8). God's nation had become **a scattered flock**. Oppressive nations, figuratively spoken of as vicious **lions**, had **driven them away**. From Israel's fall to **the king of Assyria** in 722 B.C. to Judah's seventy-year captivity, from 605 B.C. to 536

B.C., under **Nebuchadnezzar king of Babylon** (referred to as **this last one**), His flock had been **broken** and beaten, scattered and made to suffer the pain of two different captivities.

Verse 18. Punishment for the punishers was now in order. **Therefore** (כֵּן, *ken*), or "accordingly," Babylon would receive back the same treatment she had given others. Nebuchadnezzar, **the king of Babylon**, and Shalmaneser, a past **king of Assyria**, had been used as God's instruments; but now they would become the objects of God's wrath. The carnage and conquest of verses 11 through 18 were part of God's overarching plan to return His people to their pasture.

Verse 19. The remnant's return would be pleasant and satisfying. It is characterized as sheep being brought **back** to their special **pasture**. They would return to the land they had previously occupied. This "pasture" is symbolized with **Carmel** and **the hill country of Ephraim**, which were on the west side of the Jordan River, plus **Bashan** and **Gilead**, which were on the east side. These places were well known for their rich pastures (22:6; Song 4:1; Is. 33:9; Ezek. 34:14; Mic. 7:14).

THE DAY HAS COME (50:20–32)

[20]"'In those days and at that time,' declares the Lord, 'search will be made for the iniquity of Israel, but there will be none; and for the sins of Judah, but they will not be found; for I will pardon those whom I leave as a remnant.'
[21]"Against the land of Merathaim, go up against it,
And against the inhabitants of Pekod.
Slay and utterly destroy them," declares the Lord,
"And do according to all that I have commanded you.
[22]The noise of battle is in the land,
And great destruction.
[23]How the hammer of the whole earth
Has been cut off and broken!
How Babylon has become
An object of horror among the nations!
[24]I set a snare for you and you were also caught, O Babylon,
While you yourself were not aware;

You have been found and also seized
Because you have engaged in conflict with the Lord."
²⁵The Lord has opened His armory
And has brought forth the weapons of His indignation,
For it is a work of the Lord God of hosts
In the land of the Chaldeans.
²⁶Come to her from the farthest border;
Open up her barns,
Pile her up like heaps
And utterly destroy her,
Let nothing be left to her.
²⁷Put all her young bulls to the sword;
Let them go down to the slaughter!
Woe be upon them, for their day has come,
The time of their punishment.
²⁸There is a sound of fugitives and refugees from the land of Babylon,
To declare in Zion the vengeance of the Lord our God,
Vengeance for His temple.
²⁹"Summon many against Babylon,
All those who bend the bow:
Encamp against her on every side,
Let there be no escape.
Repay her according to her work;
According to all that she has done, so do to her;
For she has become arrogant against the Lord,
Against the Holy One of Israel.
³⁰Therefore her young men will fall in her streets,
And all her men of war will be silenced in that day," declares the Lord.
³¹"Behold, I am against you, O arrogant one,"
Declares the Lord God of hosts,
"For your day has come,
The time when I will punish you.
³²The arrogant one will stumble and fall
With no one to raise him up;
And I will set fire to his cities
And it will devour all his environs."

JEREMIAH 50

This entire text (50:20–32) is given as a unit. Sprinkled through it are the answers to three significant questions: "Who did this to Babylon?"; "Why was it done to Babylon?"; and "What was done to this city?"

Verse 20. The time that God would bring His people back is clearly stated: **In those days and at that time.** Then one could check **for the iniquity of Israel** or **the sins of Judah**, but he would find **none**. Why would no sins be found? Israel and Judah were the blessed benefactors of God's grace and goodness. They had been the recipients of God's promised **pardon** (see 29:10–14). The term "pardon" (סָלַח, *salach*) has bound up in it the ideas of forgiveness, mercy, gentleness, and restoration. It underscores the caring and compassionate nature of our Creator. The glorious promises of 31:28–34 are incorporated here. This picture of God's restored people and the blessed fruits they would enjoy bring into focus the purpose He had for the captivity.

Verse 21. As the judgment scene unfolds, which places are listed as targets? **Merathaim** is the first to be mentioned. The Hebrew designation, מְרָתַיִם (*Merathayim*), is apparently an epithet that stresses Babylonia's spirit of rebellion. "Double rebellion" is actually implied in the word.[10] "Merathaim" represented "the region of *Mat Marratim* at the head of the Persian Gulf where the Tigris and Euphrates rivers meet."[11] **Pekod**, a place in southeast Babylonia (see Ezek. 23:22–27), would be attacked as well.

The force that would be going against Merathaim and Pekod is not mentioned here, nor is the reason for their judgment. Against this land of these two peoples would come God's instrument of retribution to **slay and utterly destroy them**, . . . **according to all that** [the Lord had] **commanded**.

Verse 22. Babylon's time had come. Her army had brought destruction to other cities, and now similar destruction would devastate her. Her people would hear that **the noise of battle** [was] **in the land** and understand that **great destruction** had come upon them.

Verse 23. This force, this great city, had been **the hammer of**

---

[10] Brown, Driver, and Briggs, 601.
[11] Thompson, 741.

the whole earth; but "the hammer" was to be **cut off and broken**. Babylon, because of the judgment being brought down on her, would **become an object of horror among the nations**. In line with the cyclic nature of moral law, Babylon would suffer what she had meted out to other nations.

Verse 24. As **Babylon** climbed the hill of conquest, snaring other nations became its modus operandi in its rise to domination of the ancient Near East. However, by a divinely planned **snare** (יָקֹשׁ, *yaqosh*), Babylon would be **caught** (תָּפַשׂ, *thapaś*), captured like an animal or bird (see 48:41; 51:41). In the turn of events, Babylon found herself fighting against God. No one—not even Babylon—can be strong enough to carry on such a battle with God (see Acts 5:38, 39).

Verse 25. Who did this **in the land of the Chaldeans**? Jeremiah was careful to make sure that the source of this carnage and suffering was understood: **The LORD has opened His armory**, he said, and **brought forth [His] weapons**. He "set a snare" for Babylon (50:21, 24). **His indignation** was behind it all. It was the **work of the Lord GOD of hosts**.

Verse 26. As the Lord's instrument, the enemy would come **from the farthest border** and devastate Babylon's holdings. These storehouses of supplies, **her barns**, would be opened and looted. The Hebrew term מַאֲבוּס (*ma'abus*) refers to a "granary" or similar storage place.[12] Babylon had been prosperous and had prepared well for the future; but of her vast resources, nothing was to be left. Babylon, as a reservoir of produce and goods, would be taken apart, dismantled, and piled up **like heaps**.

Verse 27. The **young bulls**, perhaps a reference to youthful soldiers (see Ps. 22:12; Is. 34:7; Jer. 48:15), would be put **to the sword**. The army would be taken **down to the slaughter**. This **woe . . . upon them** had come because it was **the time of their punishment**.

Verse 28. The aftermath of the conflict would be the **sound of fugitives and refugees** fleeing **from the land of Babylon**. In the symbolism of Hebrew poetry, they would make their way to Zion **to declare** in it that great Babylon had received **the ven-**

---

[12]Koehler and Baumgartner, 1:538.

geance of the LORD our God, vengeance for His temple. God judges sin wherever it is found, whether in His people or in His instruments of judgment.

Verse 29. The reason given for Babylon's judgment is that she was **arrogant against the** LORD, **against the Holy One of Israel**. Military forces would be encamped **on every side**, allowing no opportunity for escape. She was to be repaid **according to her work; according to all that she** [had] **done**.

Verse 30. **Young,** energetic **men** would **fall in** [the] **streets**, and war-hardened soldiers were to be **silenced in that day**. To be "silenced" means that their military power would have been soundly defeated.

Verse 31. God had announced His opposition to this nation: "**Behold, I am against you, O arrogant one.**" Pride cannot stand before God. This time of judgment is called Babylon's **day**, the time that had been decreed in the divine counsels for her punishment. When God comes against a city, no defense can deter the attack.

Verse 32. Babylon, like all **arrogant one**[s], would **stumble and fall**. No one would be able to **raise him up**. The **fire** of the Lord would go out to the nearby **cities**, consuming **all** [its] **environs**. They would be **devour**[ed] (אָכַל, 'akal), a term depicting the consuming violence of a fire that races out in all directions, bringing total devastation (21:14).[13]

A SONG OF REDEMPTION (50:33, 34)

[33]Thus says the LORD of hosts,
"The sons of Israel are oppressed,
And the sons of Judah as well;
And all who took them captive have held them fast,
They have refused to let them go.
[34]Their Redeemer is strong, the LORD of hosts is His name;
He will vigorously plead their case
So that He may bring rest to the earth,
But turmoil to the inhabitants of Babylon."

---

[13]Ibid., 1:46–47.

Verse 33. Those who had brought God's people into captivity had **held them fast** and **refused to let them go**. However, Babylon's grip was now loosed, and Judah's captives were freed. Without God's intervention, there would have been no release or return.

Verse 34. God acted as a **strong** attorney for His people, and He **vigorously plead**[ed] **their case** (see comments on 12:1). In this exodus, God once again served in the vital role of **their Redeemer**. Without His intervening grace and mercy, Judah would not have been the avenue of the Messiah's coming into the world. God's people had been redeemed from the enemy, captivity, perils, and sin. Through the judgment of Babylon, God had redeemed His people from captivity and oppression, as well as from sin.

THE MIGHTY SWORD (50:35–37)

> [35]"A sword against the Chaldeans," declares the LORD,
> "And against the inhabitants of Babylon
> And against her officials and her wise men!
> [36]A sword against the oracle priests, and they will become fools!
> A sword against her mighty men, and they will be shattered!
> [37]A sword against their horses and against their chariots
> And against all the foreigners who are in the midst of her,
> And they will become women!
> A sword against her treasures, and they will be plundered!"

Verses 35–37. God would call forth **a sword against the Chaldeans** to strike all the people making up their communities—the **inhabitants, officials, wise men, oracle priests, mighty men, horses,** and **foreigners**. A network of people such as this contributed stability to a nation or an empire. With the calling forth of "the sword," God would be giving assurance that all stabilizing forces in Babylon would be repulsed and destroyed.

A sword would bring down their intellectual leadership. While a true wise man might save a city (see Eccles. 9:15), one who is wise only in his own eyes can only bring in evil that destroys. False, fleshly wisdom ultimately brings destruction.

A sword would bring down their mystics and "mighty men." Their "oracle priests" would **become fools** and their mighty men would **be shattered** (see 8:9). "Oracle priests" comes from the Hebrew term בַּד (*bad*), which has a negative connotation to it. It can refer to "empty, idle talk," "imaginary pretensions or claims," "boastings," or "false prophets."[14] "Become fools" is from the verb יָאַל (*ya'al*). In this context, it likely means that these wicked men would be shown to be fools.[15] Such men should have offered insight for survival, but they were neither reliable nor ready to fulfill a leadership role.

A sword would bring down their military arsenal and weaken the forces taken from other nations. When Babylon conquered a nation, all able men of that nation were assigned to Babylon's growing military force (see 2 Kings 24:1–3), but these would melt before the army, becoming as **women**—an implication of their weakness and inability to engage in combat. Their lack of readiness for combat is described in 50:43 and 51:30 (see 48:41).

A sword brought **against** their material **treasures** would allow them to be **plundered** and scattered. All stages of normal defense would be cut away by this most active sword of the Lord.

THE IDOL (50:38–40)

> [38]"A drought on her waters, and they will be dried up!
> For it is a land of idols,
> And they are mad over fearsome idols.
> [39]"Therefore the desert creatures will live there along with
>   the jackals;
> The ostriches also will live in it,
> And it will never again be inhabited
> Or dwelt in from generation to generation.
> [40]As when God overthrew Sodom
> And Gomorrah with its neighbors," declares the Lord,

---

[14]Brown, Driver, and Briggs, 95.
[15]Ibid., 383.

"No man will live there,
Nor will any son of man reside in it."

Verse 38. Their **mad**[ness] **over . . . idols** was also a major factor in Babylon's defenseless condition. Those who made, and submitted to, idols became like them—powerless (51:17, 18; Ps. 115:4–8). Idols cannot move, speak, or act for good or evil (10:3–5). They illustrate futility. Because of the people's idolatry, **a drought** would come upon the **waters**, and they would **be dried up**. The impact of such conditions are far-reaching (see 14:1–7).

Verse 39. When Babylon's demise occurred, nothing would be left. Her inhabitants would be replaced by **the desert creatures, the jackals**, and **the ostriches**. The great city would **never again be inhabited or dwelt in from generation to generation**. The thriving population would deteriorate into bleakness and barrenness.

Verse 40. Babylon's overthrow would be much like the destruction of **Sodom and Gomorrah** [and] **its neighbors**. In summary, God said, **"No man will live there, nor will any son of man reside in it"** (see 49:18; Gen. 19:24–28).

FORCES AND SOURCES (50:41–46)

⁴¹"Behold, a people is coming from the north,
And a great nation and many kings
Will be aroused from the remote parts of the earth.
⁴²They seize their bow and javelin;
They are cruel and have no mercy.
Their voice roars like the sea;
And they ride on horses,
Marshalled like a man for the battle
Against you, O daughter of Babylon.
⁴³The king of Babylon has heard the report about them,
And his hands hang limp;
Distress has gripped him,
Agony like a woman in childbirth.
⁴⁴"Behold, one will come up like a lion from the thicket of the Jordan to a perennially watered pasture; for in an instant

I will make them run away from it, and whoever is chosen I will appoint over it. For who is like Me, and who will summon Me into court? And who then is the shepherd who can stand before Me?" ⁴⁵Therefore hear the plan of the LORD which He has planned against Babylon, and His purposes which He has purposed against the land of the Chaldeans: surely they will drag them off, even the little ones of the flock; surely He will make their pasture desolate because of them. ⁴⁶At the shout, "Babylon has been seized!" the earth is shaken, and an outcry is heard among the nations.

Verse 41. How was Babylon to be destroyed? The description given reveals **a people . . . coming from the north**. The Medes and the Persians did come "from the north" as the city itself was taken. However, **many kings** came from other directions. The mention of the "north" may involve some poetic liberty, illustrating that as Babylon had come from the north to Jerusalem, so—figuratively speaking—would disaster come from the north to Babylon. Over time "many kings" would **be aroused from the remote parts of the earth** and become a part of the dismantling of Babylon.

Verse 42. The attacking armies would be well equipped; they would be **cruel** and act without **mercy**. They would be as loud as the roar of **the sea** with their soldiers riding **on horses**. The "many kings" would approach the battle as if they were one army under one commander. The expression **O daughter of Babylon** is an exact parallel to Judah, when Babylon came so forcefully upon their unprepared people (see 6:2, 23). The very disposition and destructive trends that Babylon had imposed on other nations would now be visited on them.

Verse 43. **The king of Babylon . . . heard the report about** the approaching kings. Terror would paralyze him, making **his hands hang limp. Distress** would grip him, and **agony** would quickly seize him **like a woman in childbirth**. In the midst of the conflict, Babylon was going to have forces working against her from without and from within. The external forces would be the fierce armies; internally, the people would suffer the debilitation of fear, shock, and shame.

Verse 44. The words of the next part of the judgment repeat, almost verbatim, the judgment of Edom (49:19–21). Having been applied to Edom, these same words are now used to refer to Babylon; for the principles of God's judgment remain constant. God will judge every nation by the standard of righteousness.

The gravest force Babylon ever faced came from above, from God's throne. After all, He, the Judge of all the earth, was the One Master mind behind it all (see 5:21–29).

The imagery used here portrays the disaster that would come upon Babylon as **a lion** springs up from a **thicket** near **the Jordan** (see comments on 49:19). Cyrus is symbolized by the "lion," leaping among the sheep as they graze unawares in a **pasture** that is **perennially watered** and contains the choicest grass. God could strike all the sheep **in an instant** of time; His forces are invincible. He also chooses whomever He wishes to do His work. He appoints whomever He needs, for He is the supreme commander. No one is like Him. Who can stand against Him? Who can add to His plans or improve His thoughts? No **shepherd** will ever **stand** over Him or counsel Him.

Verse 45. In this prophecy, **the Lord** announced His **plan . . . which He has planned against Babylon**. The next line, in an occurrence of synonymous parallelism, adds, **His purposes which He has purposed against the land of the Chaldeans**. These plans would not fail. The army God sent would **drag** away the inhabitants of Babylon, **even the little ones of the flock**. This phrase is perhaps figurative for villages, hamlets, or insignificant civilians. The fulfillment of His designs would **make their pasture** [or living places] **desolate because of them**.

Whatever was happening outside or inside Babylon was being carefully observed from above. Indeed, the unfolding of events related to a master "plan," and the master "purposes" were drawn up by the Lord of hosts. Jeremiah had used similar language before. (Compare 50:41–43 with 6:22–24, and compare 50:44–46 with Edom's plight in 49:19–21.) Babylon might try to run from this mighty force out of the north, but she would not escape. As Babylon had treated King Zedekiah of Judah, so Babylon would be treated (39:1–7; 50:15, 29).

Verse 46. The prophet said that, after the defeat was accomplished and the report of it had gone out to the nations, the populated earth would tremble at what had happened. At the announcement **"Babylon has been seized!" the earth** [would be] **shaken, and an outcry** would rise up from **the nations**. Babylon, an example of limitless might, would become an example of the matchless power of God. The Lord sustains a relationship with every existing nation as Creator, King, and Judge. Each person and each nation should be absolutely clear regarding the answer to the final question of eternal judgment: "Who can stand before Him?" (see 49:19; 50:44).

APPLICATION

Sowing and Reaping (Ch. 50)

A feature of God's judgment on Babylon is the sobering way they reaped as they had sown. Every method of conquest they had used for others would be visited upon them.

One of God's rules of judgment is that He searches our hearts and rewards us according to our deeds (17:10; see Eccl. 12:13, 14; 2 Cor. 5:10). This rule will be applied to all people, both great and small.

Let us consider the dimensions of the moral law of sowing. (1) We will definitely reap (Gal. 6:7, 8). (2) We will reap what we have sown. (3) We will reap more than we have sown. (4) We will reap longer than we have sown. (5) Not only will we reap what we have sown, but also others around us will be affected by what we have sown.

CHAPTER 51
THE JUDGMENT OF BABYLON, 2

Although chapters 50 and 51 may appear to be repetitious, they do not contain meaningless repetition. Some ideas must be repeated so that they can be more effectively comprehended.

In the fourth year of Zedekiah (51:59), when these words were being delivered, Babylon was at the height of its power and still in pursuit of other national conquests. To suggest that this powerful nation would fall—not to mention predicting that the fabled palaces and luscious gardens would become desolate (51:2, 29, 43)—seemed tremendously farfetched. To declare that the mighty military force (51:3, 4, 14, 30, 53, 56) would become exhausted, be captured, and be left defenseless must have seemed absurd.

God, knowing the response that His people would give, provided duplicated proof in chapter 51 that the destruction of Babylon was His own plan. In reading this chapter, one needs to note the emphasis on God. His name is given as "the LORD" 23 times, "the LORD of hosts" 5 times, "God" 4 times, "King" once, and "the Holy One of Israel" once. Altogether, God is specifically named 34 times. Including the pronouns referring to God ("I," "Me," "He," "His," "My," and "Himself"), He is mentioned 87 times in these sixty-four verses. These facts indicate that the repetition of the prophecy is a divine affirmation that what happened to Babylon was God's planned action. Both God's people and the nations of the earth would recognize that God was the real administrator when Babylon fell. A similar emphasis on God's desire that people know Him and what He is doing can be traced through this expression in Ezekiel: "Then they will know that I am the Lord."[1] God wants to be known and recognized. This is not a selfish whim on His part, but His hunger to help us learn what is true and best for us (see Jn. 17:3).

"THE SPIRIT OF A DESTROYER" (51:1-14)

[1] Thus says the Lord:
"Behold, I am going to arouse against Babylon
And against the inhabitants of Leb-kamai
The spirit of a destroyer.
[2] I will dispatch foreigners to Babylon that they may winnow her
And may devastate her land;
For on every side they will be opposed to her
In the day of her calamity.
[3] Let not him who bends his bow bend it,
Nor let him rise up in his scale-armor;
So do not spare her young men;
Devote all her army to destruction.
[4] They will fall down slain in the land of the Chaldeans,
And pierced through in their streets."
[5] For neither Israel nor Judah has been forsaken
By his God, the Lord of hosts,
Although their land is full of guilt
Before the Holy One of Israel.
[6] Flee from the midst of Babylon,
And each of you save his life!
Do not be destroyed in her punishment,
For this is the Lord's time of vengeance;
He is going to render recompense to her.
[7] Babylon has been a golden cup in the hand of the Lord,
Intoxicating all the earth.
The nations have drunk of her wine;
Therefore the nations are going mad.
[8] Suddenly Babylon has fallen and been broken;

---

[1] For example, see Ezek. 6:7, 10, 13, 14; 7:4, 9, 27; 11:10; 12:15, 16, 20; 13:9, 14, 21, 23; 14:8; 15:7; 16:62; 17:21, 24; 20:12, 20, 26, 38, 42, 44.

> Wail over her!
> Bring balm for her pain;
> Perhaps she may be healed.
> ⁹We applied healing to Babylon, but she was not healed;
> Forsake her and let us each go to his own country,
> For her judgment has reached to heaven
> And towers up to the very skies.
> ¹⁰The LORD has brought about our vindication;
> Come and let us recount in Zion
> The work of the LORD our God!
> ¹¹Sharpen the arrows, fill the quivers!
> The LORD has aroused the spirit of the kings of the Medes,
> Because His purpose is against Babylon to destroy it;
> For it is the vengeance of the LORD, vengeance for His temple.
> ¹²Lift up a signal against the walls of Babylon;
> Post a strong guard,
> Station sentries,
> Place men in ambush!
> For the LORD has both purposed and performed
> What He spoke concerning the inhabitants of Babylon.
> ¹³O you who dwell by many waters,
> Abundant in treasures,
> Your end has come,
> The measure of your end.
> ¹⁴The LORD of hosts has sworn by Himself:
> "Surely I will fill you with a population like locusts,
> And they will cry out with shouts of victory over you."

In this section, the totality of what was going to happen to Babylon is reviewed from five viewpoints. Mention is made of who would be executing the destruction (51:1–4), why the judgment was being given (51:5, 6), what part God Himself would take in the action (51:7–9), how God's people would respond to the destruction (51:10), and how Babylon was to fall (51:11–14). God is always the central figure through these different viewpoints.

Verse 1. The oracle against Babylon continues. The first line of this second part also names **the LORD** as its author. The point

JEREMIAH 51

is that God uttered this prophecy, and He would see that it is fulfilled. The Lord was specific about what He was going to do. He intended to **arouse . . . the spirit of a destroyer** in foreign forces or nations **against Babylon**. They were to be the instruments of God's judgment.

Verse 1 also indicates that the invading armies were coming against the people of **Leb-kamai**. This name, לֵב קָמָי (*leb qamay*), has a dual meaning. First, it is another athbash cipher, functioning in the sentence as a cryptic way of referring to the Chaldeans (see comments on 25:26). The consonants of "Leb-kamai" (לבקמי, *lbqmy*) have been substituted for the consonants of "Chaldeans" (כשׂדים, *kśdym*). The name, then, parallels "Babylon" in the previous line. Second, "Leb-kamai" means "the heart of those who rise up against Me." In His search of Babylon's heart (17:10), God had seen that she had turned away from Him. She had risen up against Him.

Verse 2. Foreigners (see 51:11, 28) would arrive at God's bidding to **winnow** Babylon (see 4:11–13; 15:7–9). They would use a process similar to sifting chaff from grain, as they eliminated vain people and valueless practices from the social and civic scene. From every side, forces would come and **devastate her land**. "Devastate" (בָּקַק, *baqaq*), carries within it the meaning of emptying the land by laying waste to it and by scattering the people of its cities.[2] This term includes the destruction of people, places, and defenses. **The day** of Babylon's **calamity** had come.

Verses 3, 4. The expressions about not arising in his **scale-armor** ("coat of mail"; NRSV) and not bending the **bow** imply a sudden attack on the one hand and an inept opponent (Babylon) on the other. **Young men** would not be **spare**[d] because of their youth. Soldiers would die in the **streets** before they could put on their layers of equipment or find a protective wall for their defense. Military might would be destroyed, and the slaying of soldiers and the dispersing of her armaments would leave the cities defenseless.

---

[2]Francis Brown, S. R. Driver, and Charles A. Briggs, *A Hebrew and English Lexicon of the Old Testament* (Oxford: Clarendon Press, 1972), 132.

Verse 5. God had not forgotten or **forsaken** His people. As **the Holy One of Israel**, He knew about their **guilt**; but His grace and their repentance had brought regeneration and restoration (see 51:19, 20).

Verse 6. God called for His people to **flee from the midst of Babylon**, so that they might escape the difficult conditions that were arising. Timely flight would save their lives. God did not want His people to **be destroyed in her punishment**. It was **the LORD's time of vengeance** upon Babylon. His people had already been punished; this coming destruction was **recompense** for Babylon. He had used her lust for conquest as His instrument of discipline, but now she must give an accounting for her sins. He had both used and refused Babylon.

Verse 7. Babylon had been God's **golden cup**. She was comparable to an expensive goblet in the sense of extravagance and luxury. She is spoken of as God's "cup" because He had used her as His instrument of disciplinary judgment upon His people. In spite of her wickedness, some **nations** had followed Babylon; they had **drunk . . . her wine** and had become intoxicated with it. They had gone **mad** with lust and greed. In the wake of such a response to Babylon, God would pour out His blazing wrath on these wicked nations as well (25:15–28; 27:1–11).

Verses 8, 9. Babylon was doomed to fall because of her arrogance and sin (50:9–14, 29–32). The benevolence and mercy of God were **applied** to her as healing **balm for her pain**[s], but Babylon would not be **healed** (see 3:22; 17:14; 33:6). Therefore, God's judgment and punishment of Babylon had **reached to heaven** and **tower**[ed] **up to the very skies**. The judgment would be colossal in its consequences.

Verse 10. As God's people began to **recount** or "declare" (NRSV) their place in His plans, we see the word **vindication** coming into use. **God** was restoring His **work** with them. He had made them righteous again. They knew that God was working wonders in their behalf even in the midst of this tragedy. As a result of His blessings and His concern for them, they offered Him praise.

Verse 11. God's purpose was to be fulfilled by the Medes (51:28; see 50:41). He would achieve this by blending His **ven-**

geance with **the spirit of the kings of the Medes**. Daniel pictured in another prophecy the coming of the Medes and the Persians against Babylon and the capturing of the city in 539 B.C.

This is a clear case of God's view of a national force that would be ideal for doing what He wanted done. Again, He utilized the devices of temporal powers as an effective means of executing His judgment. God's justice was upheld, and man's free will was maintained. A dual purpose is further seen in that **Babylon** would be punished for her iniquity (50:14, 18) and God's **vengeance** for what Babylon had done to **His temple** would be satisfied (see 2 Kings 24:11–13; 25:8–10; 2 Chron. 36:16–19).

Verse 12. These forces were to be as thick as locusts. Babylon's strong **walls** would be attacked and taken. The enemy would use **a strong guard** and **station sentries** to do their work. The abundance of Babylon's treasures could not halt or hinder the shouts of victory over her defeat. God had **both purposed** (זָמַם, *zamam*) and **performed** (עָשָׂה, *'asah*) what He had spoken. These two terms reemphasize God's nature and offer assurance that God's action is never an accident, but is always a well-planned intent (see 50:15, 29; 51:24, 47, 49).

Verse 13. Babylon, who dwelt **by many waters** (the waters of the Tigris and Euphrates Rivers) and had accumulated an abundance **in treasures**, was told that her **end** [had] **come**. God, the absolutely reliable One, had not only stated it, but had also measured it out according to His wisdom.

Verse 14. The Lord **of hosts** [had] **sworn by** the only one by whom He can swear: **Himself** (see Heb. 6:13). God's unfailing promise on this occasion was that the enemy would **cry out with shouts of victory over** Babylon. Nothing could prevent this outcome. The greatest army of the earth trembles before the mighty judgment of God. His word is true, and His oath cannot be broken.

GOD, THE GREAT JUDGE (51:15–26)

15 It is He who made the earth by His power,
Who established the world by His wisdom,
And by His understanding He stretched out the heavens.

> ¹⁶When He utters His voice, there is a tumult of waters in the heavens,
> And He causes the clouds to ascend from the end of the earth;
> He makes lightning for the rain
> And brings forth the wind from His storehouses.
> ¹⁷All mankind is stupid, devoid of knowledge;
> Every goldsmith is put to shame by his idols,
> For his molten images are deceitful,
> And there is no breath in them.
> ¹⁸They are worthless, a work of mockery;
> In the time of their punishment they will perish.
> ¹⁹The portion of Jacob is not like these;
> For the Maker of all is He,
> And of the tribe of His inheritance;
> The LORD of hosts is His name.
> ²⁰He says, "You are My war-club, My weapon of war;
> And with you I shatter nations,
> And with you I destroy kingdoms.
> ²¹With you I shatter the horse and his rider,
> And with you I shatter the chariot and its rider,
> ²²And with you I shatter man and woman,
> And with you I shatter old man and youth,
> And with you I shatter young man and virgin,
> ²³And with you I shatter the shepherd and his flock,
> And with you I shatter the farmer and his team,
> And with you I shatter governors and prefects.
> ²⁴"But I will repay Babylon and all the inhabitants of Chaldea for all their evil that they have done in Zion before your eyes," declares the LORD.
> ²⁵"Behold, I am against you, O destroying mountain,
> Who destroys the whole earth," declares the LORD,
> "And I will stretch out My hand against you,
> And roll you down from the crags,
> And I will make you a burnt out mountain.
> ²⁶They will not take from you even a stone for a corner
> Nor a stone for foundations,
> But you will be desolate forever," declares the LORD.

JEREMIAH 51

Like a golden thread woven throughout, an extended description of God and His ways characterizes 51:15–26. The verses do not veer far from the topic of the nature of God: They stress who He is, what He had done, what He would do, and how He would do it.

In connection with the powerlessness of idols (51:15–19), Jeremiah put God's greatness into sharp contrast with man's limitations and futility. God, being almighty, was certainly able to bring judgment to Babylon and her gods. To make this point, the prophet used basically the same words he had said in 10:12–16. The only deviation is in the omission of "Israel" from the phrase "the tribe of His inheritance" in 51:19. The differences between God and man show God to be the authentic Judge of all the earth. Empty things like idols would be recognized as worthless when God released His wrath upon the Babylonians.

Verse 15. God **made the earth by His power**. He **established** [כּוּן, *kun*] **the world**, that is, He "arranged" and "ordered" it.[3] He "established" it **by His wisdom**; and **by His understanding He stretched out the heavens**. This poetic repetition stresses God's creative power and design.

Verse 16. He commands and controls **the clouds**, **lightning**, and **the wind**. He **utters His voice**, and a mass of waters appears **in the heavens**. Man has very little control over the natural world of the weather and the heavens above us.

Verse 17. On the highest level, **all mankind is stupid** (בָּעַר, *ba'ar*) or "senseless" (NIV), **devoid of knowledge**. This truth is illustrated with the picture of **every goldsmith** [being] **put to shame by his idols**. "Put to shame" is from בּוֹשׁ (*bosh*), a word that suggests disgrace, confusion, disillusionment, and humiliation (see comments on 12:13). In this context, it underscores the sad futility of man's best effort when compared to God's great universe. Such a craftsman puts his ability, precious metals, and art into the creation of an idol that is **deceitful** to him and has **no breath** in it. He is humiliated by the work of his hands, for his effort is a worthless waste of his time and talent.

Verse 18. His idols are nothing. What can be said? They are

---

[3]Ibid., 465–66.

deceitful, **worthless, a work of mockery**. When God's judgment came upon Babylon, the idols would **perish** like everything else there.

Verse 19. Israel's God, **the portion of Jacob**, is **not like** idols. God is **the Maker of all** people and things. Who made **the tribe of His inheritance? The L**ORD **of hosts is His name.** Idols cannot even say their own names! How could they serve as lords over the people who made them?

Verses 20–23. What God had accomplished through Babylon is incorporated in this part of the oracle. Babylon had been an instrument in God's hands. He had made Nebuchadnezzar His **war-club** (מַפֵּץ, *mappets*), His **weapon of war** to destroy nations and kingdoms (see 1:13–15; 25:8–29; 27:1–11). These conquests had an impact on every segment of the population: **man** and **woman**, **old man** and **youth, shepherd**[s] and **flock**[s], **farmer**[s] and their **team**[s], and **governors** and **prefects**. He had **shatter**[ed] or destroyed, the military power, including **horse, rider,** and **chariot.** The Hebrew word for "shatter" is נָפַץ (*napats*), which means "smash to pieces" or "destroy."[4] In this context, the term stands for slaughter, scattering, and captivity.

The message is that the international spread of Babylon's great empire was in reality God's action among men. Because God was sovereign in these massive ventures, Nebuchadnezzar is repeatedly referred to by the Lord of hosts as "My servant" (25:9; 27:6; 43:10).

Verse 24. Even though God had used **Babylon** to accomplish His purposes, she would receive God's judgment **for all** the **evil** that she had done.

Verse 25. In this sense, God was **against** her and would **roll** [her] **down** from her place of preeminence. He would make her **a burnt out mountain**. Though Babylon had carried out God's judgments on Judah, the way in which this had been done led God to take action against Babylon (50:14, 24, 29). Babylon is depicted here as a mighty mountain that destroys the whole

---

[4]Ludwig Koehler and Walter Baumgartner, *The Hebrew and Aramaic Lexicon of the Old Testament*, study ed., trans. and ed. M. E. J. Richardson (Boston: Brill, 2001), 1:711.

earth; but then God's outstretched hand pulls it down and pulverizes it into dust, powder, and ashes. God's punishment would be decisive and devastating.

Verse 26. She would be completely destroyed. Not even debris from her would be gathered up and used for building projects in other cities. Not a single **stone** could be found that would serve as a foundation or cornerstone. Never again would Babylon rise; her years as an empire were over. God's decree was that she would **be desolate forever**.

The description of what God had done through Babylon is enlarged in these verses to include what God would do to Babylon. God's action against Babylon was taken especially because of the evil she had done in Zion (Jerusalem and Judah) before Jeremiah's eyes (51:24). An extended view of what Jeremiah had seen Babylon do to Judah and Jerusalem is given in Lamentations, where God's Spirit tells what happened and why it happened.

THE CONSECRATION OF NATIONS (51:27–33)

²⁷Lift up a signal in the land,
Blow a trumpet among the nations!
Consecrate the nations against her,
Summon against her the kingdoms of Ararat, Minni and Ashkenaz;
Appoint a marshal against her,
Bring up the horses like bristly locusts.
²⁸Consecrate the nations against her,
The kings of the Medes,
Their governors and all their prefects,
And every land of their dominion.
²⁹So the land quakes and writhes,
For the purposes of the LORD against Babylon stand,
To make the land of Babylon
A desolation without inhabitants.
³⁰The mighty men of Babylon have ceased fighting,
They stay in the strongholds;

> Their strength is exhausted,
> They are becoming like women;
> Their dwelling places are set on fire,
> The bars of her gates are broken.
> ³¹One courier runs to meet another,
> And one messenger to meet another,
> To tell the king of Babylon
> That his city has been captured from end to end;
> ³²The fords also have been seized,
> And they have burned the marshes with fire,
> And the men of war are terrified.
> ³³For thus says the Lord of hosts, the God of Israel:
> "The daughter of Babylon is like a threshing floor
> At the time it is stamped firm;
> Yet in a little while the time of harvest will come for her."

Verses 27, 28. How God planned to destroy Babylon and who would be affected by the destruction are covered in detail in verses 27 through 58, with a kind of summary being given in the beginning, in verses 27 and 28.

A mustering of the nations against Babylon was to take place. Twice in these verses, God ordered, **Consecrate the nations against her.** "Consecrate" is from קָדַשׁ (*qadash*), meaning "set apart," "treat as holy," or "subject to special treatment."[5] While we generally think of the term "consecrate" in a spiritual sense of dedication to Deity, here it obviously has more than direct spiritual connotations. Still, it is related to God's purpose.

In a dedicated, consecrated way, the Medes would **marshal** forces together to enact God's judgments on Babylon. "The nations" gathered against Babylon were to include **the kings of the Medes, their governors and all their prefects, and every land of their dominion.** Other regions such as **Ararat, Minni and Ashkenaz**, located in present-day Armenia, became the northern allies of the Medes. The cavalry which would play such an important role in the conquest of Babylon is compared to a plague of **locusts.**

---

[5]Ibid., 2:1072–73.

Verse 29. God's view of things is evident in 51:29–33. His purpose would be achieved because He knew how Babylon would react. As **the purposes of the Lord against Babylon** were fulfilled, the nation **quake[d] and writhe[d]** in pain. The blows of war would not stop until **Babylon** became **a desolation without inhabitants**.

Verse 30. The once-dominant military power had been forced to submit and cease **fighting**. The soldiers had slipped away from the field of battle to **stay in the strongholds** or hiding places. **Their strength** [was] **exhausted** (נָשְׁתָה, *nashath*), or "dried up."[6] They were more **like women** than soldiers (see 50:37). These men were no longer ready to mount any defense, much less launch an offensive attack. Their **dwelling places** [were] **set on fire**. The **bars** to the **gates** of their cities were **broken**, leaving them defenseless and exposed to looters.

Verse 31. In this scenario, **one courier** [ran] **to meet another** (in a relay) in order to report to **the king** the latest defeat. This occurred time after time; the streets were thick with **messenger[s]** scurrying with the most recent news. The **city** of **Babylon** was being **captured from end to end**.

Verse 32. The fords (מַעְבָּרָה, *ma'barah*) had been **seized**. Most likely, the Euphrates River did not have any "fords" per se (see comments on 51:36, 37). It was too deep for that, and vessels like ferries would have been required. Instead of "fords," the CEV has "river crossings," and the NLT has "escape routes." These places—bridges, ferries, and other ways of passage—were captured. Since Babylon was surrounded by a moat that was fed by the Euphrates,[7] the people were trapped inside the city.

Anyone seeking refuge in **marshes** or reedy swamps would face **fire** which would eliminate their places of hiding. **The men of war** [were] **terrified** because they knew the death sentence awaited them.

Verse 33. The daughter of Babylon [was] **like a threshing**

---

[6]Ibid., 1:732.
[7]Herodotus *Histories* 1.178. See the city map in D. J. Wiseman, "Babylon," in *The International Standard Bible Encyclopedia*, rev. ed., ed. Geoffrey W. Bromiley (Grand Rapids, Mich.: Wm. B. Eerdmans Publishing Co., 1979), 1:386.

floor ready to be firmly trampled to remove the chaff from the grain. **In a little while**, Babylon would be harvested. The symbols of harvesting and threshing are both used in the Scriptures to describe God's judgments upon nations and men (Is. 41:15, 16; Joel 3:13–17; Mic. 4:12, 13; Rev. 14:14–20).

THE CAUSE FOR CONQUEST (51:34-44)

³⁴"Nebuchadnezzar king of Babylon has devoured me and crushed me,
He has set me down like an empty vessel;
He has swallowed me like a monster,
He has filled his stomach with my delicacies;
He has washed me away.
³⁵May the violence done to me and to my flesh be upon Babylon,"
The inhabitant of Zion will say;
And, "May my blood be upon the inhabitants of Chaldea,"
Jerusalem will say.
³⁶Therefore thus says the LORD,
"Behold, I am going to plead your case
And exact full vengeance for you;
And I will dry up her sea
And make her fountain dry.
³⁷Babylon will become a heap of ruins, a haunt of jackals,
An object of horror and hissing, without inhabitants.
³⁸They will roar together like young lions,
They will growl like lions' cubs.
³⁹When they become heated up, I will serve them their banquet
And make them drunk, that they may become jubilant
And may sleep a perpetual sleep
And not wake up," declares the LORD.
⁴⁰"I will bring them down like lambs to the slaughter,
Like rams together with male goats.
⁴¹How Sheshak has been captured,
And the praise of the whole earth been seized!

How Babylon has become an object of horror among the
    nations!
⁴²The sea has come up over Babylon;
She has been engulfed with its tumultuous waves.
⁴³Her cities have become an object of horror,
A parched land and a desert,
A land in which no man lives
And through which no son of man passes.
⁴⁴I will punish Bel in Babylon,
And I will make what he has swallowed come out of his
    mouth;
And the nations will no longer stream to him.
Even the wall of Babylon has fallen down!"

Verse 34. God knew His people would have something to say during these developments (51:34–36). For seventy years (25:12), they had been plagued by the power of **Babylon**. They had been **crushed** and **devoured** by Nebuchadnezzar. Like a canned product, they had been emptied; like a drink, they had been **swallowed**; like a delicacy, they had been eaten. This formidable enemy had swallowed them up as a sea-**monster** would. They had been used and abused. Each figure of speech in this verse shows that they had been treated like objects, not people. In whatever way they could benefit Nebuchadnezzar or Babylon, they had been so used. Their land and their lives had been selfishly sacrificed to enrich Babylon.

The expression **he has washed me away** suggests the cruel, heartless attitude Babylon had toward God's people. The Hebrew word for "wash away," דּוּחַ (*duach*), means "rinse" or "cleanse away by washing."[8] This, no doubt, was the general treatment of the captives—at least at first (see comments on 29:4–7). However, Daniel and others like him held special posts of duty and were honored (Dan. 1:3–7, 17–21; 2:47–49; 3:28–30; 6:1–3).

Verse 35. The captives called for **Babylon** to face the same **violence** they had imposed on Judah. They asked that Judah's **blood be upon the inhabitants of Chaldea** (see Gen. 9:4).

---

[8]Koehler and Baumgartner, 1:216; Brown, Driver, and Briggs, 188.

Verses 36, 37. God's promise of what He would do to Babylon is reasserted (51:36–44). Beginning in verse 36, God used the first person pronoun **I** five times (51:36, 39, 40, 44), along with seven verbs to specify what He would do to Babylon.

God assured His people that He would **plead** [their] **case. Full vengeance** would be executed. **Babylon** would pay a price for their abuses (50:14, 29–32). God would **dry up her sea** and **make her fountain dry**. This figure may refer to the luxurious way the Babylonians had lived and the elaborate water system that had granted their land fertility and prosperity. Babylon had developed an elaborate irrigation and water control system, but it was to be destroyed. With this abundant water supply gone, Babylon would quickly become an uninhabited desert. Remaining ones would see a ghastly **heap of ruins, a haunt of jackals** (see 9:11; 10:22; 49:33), causing a **horror and hissing** by any who remembered the once proud metropolis (see 18:16; 19:8; 25:9, 18; 29:18).

"Dry up her sea" could more specifically refer to Cyrus' attack on Babylon. Herodotus reported that he and his army diverted water from the Euphrates River into a marshy lake. This strategic move lowered the water level in the moat surrounding Babylon and allowed the army to gain entrance into the city. It took the Babylonians by surprise and led to their demise.[9]

Verse 38. Another figure, **young lions,** is used in this forecast of Babylon's fall. The city is symbolized as "young lions" that **roar** and **growl** over their prowess and prey, gloating over their victory.

Verse 39. The figure of lions is joined with a demonstration and celebration comparable to a victory feast (see 51:57). The Lord said, **"When they become heated up, I will serve them their banquet and make them drunk."** Special irony is seen in this inspired pronouncement. As they reveled in assumed prosperity, "heated up" with wine and lust (see Hos. 7:4–7), God would direct their attention to a banquet of another kind. The wine cup that would "make them drunk" would contain His wrath (25:16, 17), and their riotous celebration would turn into

---

[9]Herodotus *Histories* 1.191.

a perpetual sleep from which they would never awaken. Herodotus wrote that Cyrus took the city while the inhabitants were sharing a feast with revelry (see Dan. 5:1–31).[10]

Verse 40. Babylon's fall is further described as being brought down like lambs to the slaughter. This characterization emphasizes how sudden and unexpected the destruction would be (50:24; 51:8).

Verse 41. The nations' reaction to the fall of Babylon is covered in 51:41–44. Babylon is referred to under the cryptic name Sheshak (see comments on 25:26; 51:1). The changes that were to come upon this place that had been the praise of the whole earth would horrify the nations. Looking on, they would be confounded that disaster could come to such a nation as Babylon.

Verse 42. It would be as if the sea [had] come up over Babylon and completely engulfed her. This language calls up the image of a whole sea of nations overwhelming this mighty empire (46:6–10; 51:2; Is. 8:7, 8; 17:12–14).

Verses 43, 44. Her cities have become an object of horror, a parched land and a desert, a land in which no man lives. This change from Babylon's prosperity to being a parched land would be sobering to anyone who saw it. The formerly beautiful land would be barren; the delightful city would become a desolate desert where no one would pass.

In the preview given here, even the massive wall of Babylon [had] fallen down (see 50:15). Two great walls encircled the city. One bore the name of Imgur-Bel (meaning "Bel protects"), and the other was Nimetti-Bel (meaning "the dwelling of Bel"). As the names indicate, these walls were specifically consecrated to Bel (or Marduk), the national deity.

"I will punish Bel in Babylon, . . . and the nations will no longer stream to him," God said. His defiance of idolatry comes to the center stage in this scene of slaughter and desolation (see 50:1–10). A core cause of Babylon's corruption and cockiness was their worship of false gods, with their foremost god in Babylon being "Bel." Among the plunder that had been confiscated for

---

[10]Ibid.

this god during Babylon's conquests were the vessels from the temple of God in Jerusalem. These vessels had been figuratively **swallowed** when they were placed in Bel's temple. God reasserted His place and power by declaring that what Bel had taken into his greedy jaws would **come out of his mouth**. We have an account of how that was fulfilled in Ezra 1:7–11, as those vessels were returned in total to Jerusalem.

FINAL INSTRUCTIONS (51:45–51)

⁴⁵"Come forth from her midst, My people,
And each of you save yourselves
From the fierce anger of the Lord.
⁴⁶Now so that your heart does not grow faint,
And you are not afraid at the report that will be heard in the land—
For the report will come one year,
And after that another report in another year,
And violence will be in the land
With ruler against ruler—
⁴⁷Therefore behold, days are coming
When I will punish the idols of Babylon;
And her whole land will be put to shame
And all her slain will fall in her midst.
⁴⁸Then heaven and earth and all that is in them
Will shout for joy over Babylon,
For the destroyers will come to her from the north,"
Declares the Lord.
⁴⁹Indeed Babylon is to fall for the slain of Israel,
As also for Babylon the slain of all the earth have fallen.
⁵⁰You who have escaped the sword,
Depart! Do not stay!
Remember the Lord from afar,
And let Jerusalem come to your mind.
⁵¹We are ashamed because we have heard reproach;
Disgrace has covered our faces,
For aliens have entered
The holy places of the Lord's house.

Verse 45. God had prepared His **people** for the gradual fall of Babylon by giving two directives: **"Come forth from** [the] **midst** [of Babylon]" (see 50:8; 51:6, 9; Rev. 18:2–21), and **"Save yourselves from the fierce anger of the Lord."**

Verse 46. It is evident that the news of Babylon's fall and the **violence** accompanying that fall (God's fierce anger) might create such fear that some people would not leave captivity. These events covered an extended period of time. Several upheavals and changes in the throne affected Babylon after the death of Nebuchadnezzar in 562 B.C. Jeremiah warned his people so that those agitations would not create premature hopes of release. Centuries later, Christ gave a similar admonition to His followers about wars and rumors of wars that would occur before the coming of the day of the Lord (Mt. 24:4–14; Mk. 13:5–8). Violence **with ruler against ruler** would come to pass. God's plea was for His people to avoid **grow**[ing] **faint** in **heart** and be prepared to return to their homeland when the door finally opened.

Verse 47. God prepared His people by putting penitence in their hearts. This was God's second concern as He poured forth His fierce anger on **Babylon**. Four factors are given in verses 47 through 51 that could lead God's people to a penitent frame of mind.

First, God would **punish** Babylon for their rank idolatry until they were ashamed of their **idols**. Idols held in the human heart do not leave automatically. The **shame** mentioned would include being silenced, astonished, confounded, disturbed, troubled, and disgraced, with the added elements of paleness and terror. All hope—especially that related to their gods—would be snatched away (see 9:19; 49:23). Watching this happen to Babylon should have rekindled a desire in the captives' hearts to cling again to the true God (51:15–19).

Verses 48, 49. Second, **heaven and earth** would unite to **shout for joy** over Babylon's destruction. Judgment was to fall as retribution for **the slain** of Judah. God's people had lost many loved ones at the hands of Babylon. The fulfillment of God's plan was reassuring within itself, but a sense of justice added to its meaning.

Verse 50. Third, God's people were exhorted to **remember** Him (see Deut. 8:18; 2 Sam. 14:11; Neh. 4:14; Is. 64:5) and **let Jerusalem come to . . . mind**. Those who had **escaped** the disaster were to **depart** for Jerusalem and **not stay** in Babylon (see 24:7; 29:10–14; 50:18–20).

Those in captivity needed to recall God's power and provisions, His greatness and glory, His leadership, loyalty, and love. Recognizing His faithfulness and His judgments—especially in view of the nothingness of Babylon's gods—should have restored their hearts and brought about their return to both God and Jerusalem.

Verse 51. Fourth, the disposition of God's people would be crucial for the preparation needed for their return. Godly sorrow is required for genuine repentance to arise (2 Cor. 7:10; see Ps. 38:17, 18). The iniquity of Babylon had led God's people to be in captivity and had **covered** [their] **faces** with **disgrace**, for the temple was destroyed and the people were defeated. Many had died. The awareness of their guilt should have led them to be **ashamed**. These ingredients—shame, reproach, and disgrace—deep within their souls would stimulate genuine repentance and develop their determination to "save themselves" (51:45).

The importance of this needed change must not be overlooked. The Jews were captives, and **aliens** [had] **entered the holy places of the Lord's house**—which was still standing in the fourth year of Zedekiah (51:59). That put the Jews in a difficult and confusing position. First, it appeared that Babylon's god, Bel, had prevailed over God. Second, insightful Jews knew it was their own sin that had caused these developments. If the facts all snapped into focus, repentance and a return to God—the Lord of hosts—would be natural.

In Nehemiah 1:1—2:18, Nehemiah beautifully displayed the concern and characteristics called for in verse 51. Not only was there a splendid spirit of confessing national wrongs and a glorious tribute to God, but the people had a determination to return to Jerusalem and restore it as a place where God would joyously meet with His people. Nehemiah was one who dutifully did what God directed to be done.

GOD'S SUMMARY (51:52–58)

⁵²"Therefore behold, the days are coming," declares the Lord,
"When I will punish her idols,
And the mortally wounded will groan throughout her land.
⁵³Though Babylon should ascend to the heavens,
And though she should fortify her lofty stronghold,
From Me destroyers will come to her," declares the Lord.
⁵⁴The sound of an outcry from Babylon,
And of great destruction from the land of the Chaldeans!
⁵⁵For the Lord is going to destroy Babylon,
And He will make her loud noise vanish from her.
And their waves will roar like many waters;
The tumult of their voices sounds forth.
⁵⁶For the destroyer is coming against her, against Babylon,
And her mighty men will be captured,
Their bows are shattered;
For the Lord is a God of recompense,
He will fully repay.
⁵⁷"I will make her princes and her wise men drunk,
Her governors, her prefects and her mighty men,
That they may sleep a perpetual sleep and not wake up,"
Declares the King, whose name is the Lord of hosts.
⁵⁸Thus says the Lord of hosts,
"The broad wall of Babylon will be completely razed
And her high gates will be set on fire;
So the peoples will toil for nothing,
And the nations become exhausted only for fire."

Verses 52, 53. The true God prevailed over Babylon's false gods. He said, **"The mortally wounded will groan throughout her land."** For the fourth time in chapter 51, God's words strike at the idolatry in Babylon (51:17, 18, 44, 47, 52). The judgment of Babylon was a classic case of the one true God's taking action against false gods.

Verse 54. The true God prevailed over bragging Babylon. With his keen prophetic ear, Jeremiah heard **the sound of an outcry from Babylon** as **great destruction** came upon the **Chaldeans.**

Verses 55, 56. All the bravado of **Babylon** vanished, and the roaring tumult (see Ps. 124:2-5) of the invading masses moved in to destroy Babylon.

The concept of God's balanced justice has been repeatedly expressed (11:20; 17:10; 20:12; 50:15, 29). Here Jeremiah held up **the LORD** as **a God of recompense** (see Ps. 28:4; 94:2; 137:8; Is. 3:11; 66:6). God would **fully repay** as Babylon's **mighty men** fell.

Verses 57, 58. The true God is, indeed, **the LORD of hosts**. The leading men of Babylon would **sleep a perpetual sleep and not wake up**. The supremacy and significance of God stand out as He is twice in succession referred to as **the LORD of hosts**. His sovereignty echoes in the further affirmation that He is **King**.

God declared that Babylon's defenses would **be completely razed** and that the **gates** would be **set on fire** (Hab. 2:13). The walls and gate complexes of Babylon were impressive structures, offering the city great protection from her enemies. The Greek historian Herodotus reported that one of the walls was 200 royal cubits (350 feet) high and 50 royal cubits (87 feet) wide.[11] However, no excavations have unearthed walls of this magnitude, and many believe that this figure is greatly exaggerated.[12] The historian further mentioned a hundred gates of bronze,[13] whereas Babylonian inscriptions state that access to the inner city was gained by only eight or nine gates.[14] Jean-Claude Margueron wrote,

> Nothing is known about the gates of the outer city wall; there were 9 huge gates in the inner city and the right bank called Ishtar, Sin, Marduk, Zabada, Enlil, Urash, Shamash, Adad, and Lugalgirra. The Ishtar gate, the only

---

[11]Ibid., 1.178.
[12]Wiseman, 1:386.
[13]Herodotus *Histories* 1.179.
[14]"Eight" is the figure given in Wiseman, 1:386.

one that has been excavated, is justly famous for the quality of reliefs in baked, glazed bricks, displaying lions and dragons in interminable lines continuing along the walls of the processional way. This gate has been moved and reconstructed in the Berlin Museum.[15]

When "the Lord of hosts" poured out His wrath, Babylon's gates were attacked, destroyed, and melted by fire.[16] When God's judgment comes, all human efforts and the toil of peoples become as nothing. God's prominent position in the judgments declared against Babylon reached its peak in these closing comments, explaining why we have seen Him identified eighty-seven times in this chapter.

A UNIQUE METHOD (51:59–64)

⁵⁹The message which Jeremiah the prophet commanded Seraiah the son of Neriah, the grandson of Mahseiah, when he went with Zedekiah the king of Judah to Babylon in the fourth year of his reign. (Now Seraiah was quartermaster.) ⁶⁰So Jeremiah wrote in a single scroll all the calamity which would come upon Babylon, that is, all these words which have been written concerning Babylon. ⁶¹Then Jeremiah said to Seraiah, "As soon as you come to Babylon, then see that you read all these words aloud, ⁶²and say, 'You, O Lord, have promised concerning this place to cut it off, so that there will be nothing dwelling in it, whether man or beast, but it will be a perpetual desolation.' ⁶³And as soon as you finish reading this scroll, you will tie a stone to it and throw it into the middle of the Euphrates, ⁶⁴and say, 'Just so shall Babylon sink down and not rise again because of the calamity that I am going to bring upon

---

[15]Jean-Claude Margueron, "Babylon," in *The Anchor Bible Dictionary*, ed. David Noel Freedman (New York: Doubleday, 1992), 1:564. See the photograph of an Ishtar Gate model in Steven Voth, "Jeremiah," in *Zondervan's Illustrated Bible Backgrounds Commentary*, vol. 4, *Isaiah, Jeremiah, Lamentations, Ezekiel, Daniel*, ed. John H. Walton (Grand Rapids, Mich.: Zondervan, 2009), 352.

[16]Perhaps a distinction should be made here between the actual gates (doors) and the gate complexes where they were hung.

her; and they will become exhausted.'" Thus far are the words of Jeremiah.**

God gave a climactic conclusion with a dramatic demonstration. While Zedekiah journeyed to Babylon on some official business, Jeremiah seized the opportunity to unfold another unique prophecy for the nations (see 1:5–10). With Babylon at the zenith of its power in Zedekiah's fourth year, declaring Babylon's doom was no small matter. A seemingly insignificant prophet, opposed by his own people in a country conquered by Babylon, was declaring the doom of the mighty empire. Jeremiah needed great courage to speak his message, even greater courage to write it, and great faith in God to believe it. What a man this prophet was!

Verse 59. The deliverer and the directions for delivering the message were clearly chosen. **Seraiah the son of Neriah, the grandson of Mahseiah,** was Baruch's brother (32:12), and he was selected to transport this unique document and was given specific instructions on what to do with it.

Verses 60, 61. All the calamity [that] **would come upon Babylon** had been written on **a single scroll.** With that document in hand, standing beside the Euphrates River in Babylon, Seraiah was to **read all** of it **aloud.** Not a word was to be omitted (see comments on 26:2; 36:2).

Verse 62. Seraiah assured all who had gathered for the reading that God, not man, had originated these words. The source of the prophecy was neither Zedekiah nor Jeremiah. That assurance was given by these prayerful words: **"You, O Lord, have promised concerning this place to cut it off."** "Cutting off," in this case, meant that neither **man** nor **beast** would thereafter dwell in Babylon. It would be **a perpetual desolation** (see Ps. 137:8, 9).

Verse 63. When Seraiah completed his **reading** of the **scroll,** he was to **tie a stone to it and throw it into the . . . Euphrates** River. The implication by some that this action was to hide the pronounced doom is not credible. Seraiah had just read it aloud for everyone to hear. The real reason for its being cast into the river is given in the next verse.

Verse 64. With the sinking document, those watching saw a shocking summation: the sinking of a great empire! God added a final line of divine judgment: **"Just so shall Babylon sink down and not rise again because of the calamity that I am going to bring upon her."** Babylon would go down in judgment and not rise again because of "the calamity" God was about to bring upon her. That document, as it sank into the river, was a symbol of how Babylon would sink as a nation. From beginning to end, the emphasis was that God's judgment was what would bring Babylon down. Under no other condition would it have made sense to think that this superpower would fall.

Seraiah's closing phrase seems to underscore the tone of the prophecy: **"And they will become exhausted."** The words are almost identical to those closing the great prophecy in 51:58. As Seraiah repeated this last statement of the prophecy—as that declaration of doom passed through his lips—in a dramatic move he was to fling the scroll into the Euphrates. That submersion was the destiny of all the futile labors of men to defend Babylon.

Thus far are the words of Jeremiah (see 48:47). These words may well be the final ones of Jeremiah's messages. The following chapter is perhaps a historical appendix that was added by Jeremiah or an assistant to show the fulfillment of the prophecies that had been uttered. Perhaps it was drawn from 2 Kings 24:18—25:30, which is a depiction of the fall that is almost parallel to chapter 52. It does seem appropriate that Jeremiah, under the leadership of God's Spirit, would have made such a closing comment before adding the narrative of the fall.

APPLICATION

The Message of the Stone (51:59–64)

The stone and its attached message concerning "all the calamity which could come upon Babylon" (51:60) also presents a message for mankind.

The certainty of God's judgments. It is significant that Babylon is still "a wilderness, a parched land and a desert" (50:12). When God chooses to make special marks of His wrath relative to the unrighteousness of men, as with Sodom and Gomorrah (50:40), there remains a blight that no human effort can overcome.

God's clear call to repentance. The central theme of Jeremiah is God's effort through multiple trials to bring repentance among His people, so they would seek Him (29:11-14). Such events surface whenever God wills to preserve and redeem His people (Acts 5:38, 39). However, when God intends to enact a final end, how dark all the tomorrows for that designated region will be! (See 50:39; 51:26, 31; Dan. 7:23-27; Nahum 1:8, 9.) Babylon's barrenness until this day shouts the dreadful possibility of final ruin. All who confidently and selfishly exercise their own will against God's will should shudder at the futility that faces them.

Do God's judgments sober us, scare us, or save us? (See Eccles. 12:13, 14; Acts 2:36-47; 4:12; Heb. 5:8, 9; Rev. 2:10.) God's judgment has a redemptive side that opens the door to wiser ways and better days.

God's open door. Just as God tempts no man (Jas. 1:13-15), neither does He enact judgments or trials on any nation just to manifest His superior power. He is truly Almighty God (Joel 1:15; 2:1-3); but His cry has ever been "Return to Me with all your heart" (Joel 2:12-14; see Jer. 29:10-14), for He is gracious and compassionate. Any divine discipline or destruction is in some way a process of salvation (see Heb. 12:5-11). Even if nations are scattered, human institutions are overthrown, or the temporal lives of some individuals are ended, those who abide faithfully in God—as did Joshua and Caleb (Num. 14:6-9, 26-35; Deut. 1:35-38)—can still be redeemed.

This principle must be considered relative to the message that Seraiah received from God, read to the people, attached to a stone, and threw into the Euphrates River. While this action represented the sinking of a nation, it also presented a divine principle of God's preservation that teaches a lesson even for us today. It is somewhat like Abel in Hebrews 11:4: "Though he is dead, he still speaks." That stone still speaks to all those souls who are self-righteous, self-sufficient, and misguided by idols. It warns those who ignore or rebel against the living God and His principles (see Mt. 7:21; Rom. 1:16-19; 3:4; Heb. 4:12, 13; 13:20, 21).

CHAPTER 52
A REVIEW OF JUDAH'S RUIN

The final chapter of the Book of Jeremiah retells Judah's fall to Babylon as a result of their sin (52:1–11). It recounts the destruction of Jerusalem, along with the temple (52:12–23). In addition, it reminds us that a significant number of prominent people were killed by the Babylonians, while others were taken into exile (52:24–30). The chapter ends with a ray of hope: Jehoiachin was released from prison and enthroned above other subjugated kings in Babylon (52:31–34). This treatment of Jehoiachin gave the exiles hope for a future return to Jerusalem.

This postscript-type chapter to the Book of Jeremiah contains several difficulties that must be carefully examined by the reader. As these problems are considered, it is important not to miss the message of the chapter. While plausible answers can be given to such questions, enough information is not always available to answer them definitively.

One question that arises concerns authorship: Who wrote chapter 52? The Jeremianic authorship of it has been opposed for a combination of reasons. First, the preceding chapter ends with the statement "Thus far are the words of Jeremiah" (51:64), indicating that his writing ended there. This suggests that chapter 52 is a historical appendix added by a later hand. Second, the prophet Jeremiah is neither mentioned by name nor identified by use of the first person ("I," "me," or "my") in chapter 52. Third, the events narrated at the end of the chapter date to at least 560 B.C. (52:31–34). For Jeremiah to have written this section would require that he lived into his eighties or nineties. Fourth, the language of chapter 52 is similar to 2 Kings 24:18—

25:30, which may indicate that these accounts were borrowed from a common source that is no longer available to us (see Josh. 10:13; 1 Kings 11:41). It has been suggested that Jeremiah's scribe, Baruch, inserted the chapter, but we do not know this for certain. Whoever wrote it down was guided by divine inspiration, which means that God was the ultimate author. (See *Appendix: Corresponding Events in Jeremiah 52 (along with 39—41) & 2 Kings 24; 25*, page 579.)

THE LAST KING'S EVIL REIGN
(52:1, 2)

¹**Zedekiah was twenty-one years old when he became king, and he reigned eleven years in Jerusalem; and his mother's name was Hamutal the daughter of Jeremiah of Libnah.** ²**He did evil in the sight of the** L<small>ORD</small> **like all that Jehoiakim had done.**

Verse 1. Zedekiah had been appointed **king** by Nebuchadnezzar, who had removed Jehoiachin (Coniah) from the throne after his brief reign of three months (37:1; 2 Kings 24:8, 17). Zedekiah was **twenty-one years old** at the time of his accession, and **he reigned eleven years in Jerusalem** (597–586 B.C.). His reign is repeatedly discussed in the Book of Jeremiah (chs. 21; 22; 24; 27—29; 32—34; 37—39; 51).

It was a common practice to identify the queen mother alongside the king (see comments on 22:26). In the case of Zedekiah, **his mother's name was Hamutal**. She was one of the wives of Josiah and the mother of both Jehoahaz and Zedekiah (2 Kings 23:31; 24:18). She is further identified as **the daughter of Jeremiah of Libnah**. Libnah was a town located about twenty-five miles southwest of Jerusalem. This man is distinguished from the prophet Jeremiah, who came from Anathoth (1:1).

Verse 2. Zedekiah's reign is characterized as a poor one: **He did evil in the sight of the** L<small>ORD</small>. Frequent references in the Book of Jeremiah provide abundant evidence of his wicked ways (21:1-7; 22:1-9; 27:12-17; 37:1, 2; 38:1-5, 20-23). This last king of Judah was a repulsive combination of weakness and wickedness. His evil ways are compared to the deeds committed by his brother **Jehoiakim**, the king who had cut up Jeremiah's prophecies with a scribe's knife and burned them in the fire (36:20–26). The reigns of these evil men explain why Jerusalem and the temple were ultimately destroyed.

THE LONG SIEGE OF THE CITY (52:3–6)

³For through the anger of the LORD this came about in Jerusalem and Judah until He cast them out from His presence. And Zedekiah rebelled against the king of Babylon. ⁴Now it came about in the ninth year of his reign, on the tenth day of the tenth month, that Nebuchadnezzar king of Babylon came, he and all his army, against Jerusalem, camped against it and built a siege wall all around it. ⁵So the city was under siege until the eleventh year of King Zedekiah. ⁶On the ninth day of the fourth month the famine was so severe in the city that there was no food for the people of the land.

Verse 3. The siege and destruction of **Jerusalem** is attributed to **the anger of the LORD**. God is righteous and cannot tolerate evil, so **He cast them out from His presence**. He had chosen Jerusalem as the place for His divine name to dwell (1 Kings 11:36; 14:21; 2 Kings 21:4, 7), but His people had brought to the city only disgrace and shame (32:31–36). At this point, God finally turned His back on His rebellious people (18:15–17).

The destruction of the holy city is also attributed to the fact that **Zedekiah rebelled against the king of Babylon**. As Jehoiakim had done before him (2 Kings 24:1), Zedekiah also revolted against Nebuchadnezzar. He broke his treaty with Babylon and sent envoys to Egypt to gain horses and troops for defense (Ezek. 17:13–21). The king's rebellion was contrary to the word of the Lord spoken through Jeremiah (27:1–15; 2 Chron. 36:12, 13).

Verse 4. God's warnings about the downfall of Jerusalem had sounded forth through Jeremiah as early as 627 B.C., when the prophet began his ministry (1:1, 2; 6:1–30; 25:3). Almost forty years later, **in the ninth year of** [Zedekiah's] **reign, on the tenth**

day of the tenth month (January 15, 588 B.C.[1]), the Babylonian army came from the north and surrounded Jerusalem. They camped against the holy city, and they built a siege wall all around it (see comments on 6:6; 10:17; 32:24; 33:4).

Verse 4 is one example within the book where another spelling is given for the name **Nebuchadnezzar**. The Hebrew word here is more accurately transliterated "Nebuchadrezzar" (see KJV; RSV). An "r" (ר, *resh*) replaces the "n" (נ, *nun*). To eliminate confusion, the NASB has translated these alternate Hebrew names uniformly as "Nebuchadnezzar." While several theories for the alternate spellings have been advanced, no consensus of opinion exists.

Verses 5, 6. The Babylonian **siege** of Jerusalem lasted **until the eleventh year of King Zedekiah** (586 B.C.). Near the end of the siege, **on the ninth day of the fourth month** (July 18[2]), the situation came to a breaking point. As the Babylonian army pressed forward from the outside, **the people** faced **famine** on the inside. It was **so severe** that **no food** was left (38:9; Lam. 1:19; 2:11, 12, 19; 4:9). The people became so desperate for survival that they ate their own offspring (19:9; Lam. 2:20; 4:10).

THE KING AND HIS SONS SENTENCED (52:7–11)

⁷Then the city was broken into, and all the men of war fled and went forth from the city at night by way of the gate between the two walls which was by the king's garden, though the Chaldeans were all around the city. And they went by way of the Arabah. ⁸But the army of the Chaldeans pursued the king and overtook Zedekiah in the plains of Jericho, and all his army was scattered from him. ⁹Then they captured the king and brought him up to the king of Babylon at Riblah in the land of Hamath, and he passed sentence on him. ¹⁰The king of Babylon slaughtered the sons of Zedekiah before his eyes, and he

---

[1]This is the date provided by William Sanford LaSor, "Jerusalem," in *The International Standard Bible Encyclopedia*, rev. ed., ed. Geoffrey W. Bromiley (Grand Rapids, Mich.: Wm. B. Eerdmans Publishing Co., 1982), 2:1016.
[2]Ibid.

also slaughtered all the princes of Judah in Riblah. ¹¹Then he blinded the eyes of Zedekiah; and the king of Babylon bound him with bronze fetters and brought him to Babylon and put him in prison until the day of his death.

Verse 7. The Babylonian army made a significant breach in the wall (39:2), which would allow their troops to invade Jerusalem. In fear, Judah's **men of war fled . . . from the city**, attempting to escape with their lives. They ran away **at night** in order to go undetected, exiting through **the gate between the two walls which was by the king's garden**. This gate, which may have been a secret passageway, was likely located near the southern corner of the eastern wall, leading out to the Kidron Valley (Neh. 3:15).[3] The term **Arabah** can refer to any part of the Jordan Valley, which extends from Mount Hermon in the north to the Gulf of Aqabah in the south. Since verse 8 mentions "the plains of Jericho," it can be assumed that at least some headed northeast.

Verse 8. At this point, the text informs us that the king had escaped with his men. However, Zedekiah could not run fast enough or far enough to escape God's anger; the Babylonian soldiers fulfilled that certainty (see Lam. 4:19, 20). **The army of the Chaldeans pursued the king and overtook Zedekiah in the plains of Jericho, and all his army was scattered from him.** Zedekiah's men would rather have saved their own lives than be captured with their ruler.

Verse 9. The Babylonian army **captured** Zedekiah, and they **brought him up to the king of Babylon at Riblah in the land of Hamath.** "Riblah" was an ancient Syrian city on the banks of the Orontes River, about two hundred miles north of Jerusalem. It was strategically located at the crossroads of important highways coming from Mesopotamia and Egypt. In 609 B.C., Pharaoh Neco had used the city for his military headquarters (2 Kings 23:29–34). At this time, Nebuchadnezzar occupied Riblah as his base of operations, fighting against Egypt and the countries along the Syrian coast. There **he passed sentence on** Zedekiah.

Verse 10. In the presence of the Babylonian king several exe-

---

[3]Ibid., 2:1011.

cutions took place. The officials (**princes of Judah**) who had been a thorn to Jeremiah (37:11–15; 38:4–6) were killed. Then, a tragedy of tragedies occurred, Zedekiah's **sons** were **slaughtered ... before his eyes**. Who can imagine this scene? For them to brought before their father's view and executed is without doubt the worst moment to which Zedekiah's wicked life led.

Verse 11. Following these horrid events, **Zedekiah** himself was mercilessly **blinded**. This weak king took with him a memory of abused opportunities and neglected responsibility as he stepped into darkness. With an ebony background, his blindness must have blazed and burned with an internal, shame-ridden display of the slaying of his sons and his officials. In this manner, they all met judgment day at Riblah.

After being blinded, Zedekiah was **bound ... with bronze fetters** (נְחֻשְׁתַּיִם, n^e*chosheth*) and **brought ... to Babylon**, where he was thrown **in prison**. Others among God's people had been treated in a similar fashion. Samson had been blinded, bound in bronze fetters, and imprisoned by the Philistines (Judg. 16:21). Another king of Judah, Manasseh, had been bound in bronze fetters by the Assyrian army and taken to Babylon for a time (2 Chron. 33:11). Such fetters are portrayed in Assyrian reliefs.[4] A pair of fetters used to bind a prisoner's wrists were discovered by archaeologists at Nineveh. They weigh eight pounds eleven ounces and are sixteen and a half inches long. The tongs on either end would have been placed around the wrists and then hammered closed.[5]

After making the long, dreadful trek to Babylon, Zedekiah remained in prison **until the day of his death.** His treatment at the hands of Nebuchadnezzar can be contrasted to the treatment given to Jehoiachin (52:31–34). Jehoiachin had surrendered to the Babylonian forces (2 Kings 24:8–12), whereas Zedekiah rebelled, refusing to obey the word of the Lord spoken by His prophet (27:1–11; 38:14–23).

---

[4]See James B. Pritchard, *The Ancient Near East in Pictures: Relating to the Old Testament*, 2d ed. (Princeton, N.J.: Princeton University Press, 1969), 154 (no. 447).

[5]http://www.bible-history.com/past/assyrian_fetters.html; Internet; accessed 3 June 2011.

JERUSALEM AND THE TEMPLE DESTROYED (52:12–23)

The City Burned (52:12–14)

¹²Now on the tenth day of the fifth month, which was the nineteenth year of King Nebuchadnezzar, king of Babylon, Nebuzaradan the captain of the bodyguard, who was in the service of the king of Babylon, came to Jerusalem. ¹³He burned the house of the LORD, the king's house and all the houses of Jerusalem; even every large house he burned with fire. ¹⁴So all the army of the Chaldeans who were with the captain of the guard broke down all the walls around Jerusalem.

Verse 12. Since the walls of Jerusalem had been breached, **Nebuzaradan** was sent by **Nebuchadnezzar** to **Jerusalem** to oversee the demolition of the city (52:13, 14) and the exile of the Jews (52:15, 16). This high-ranking officer is identified as **the captain of the bodyguard, who was in the service of the king of Babylon.** About four years later (582 B.C.), following the assassination of Gedaliah (40:1—41:18), Nebuzaradan returned to Jerusalem for a final deportation (52:30).

Another problem in this chapter involves the date of Nebuzaradan's coming to Jerusalem: **the tenth day of the fifth month, which was the nineteenth year** of King Nebuchadnezzar. The parallel account in 2 Kings 25:8 has "the seventh day" (August 12, 586 B.C.), instead of "the tenth day" (August 15).[6] The simplest solution to this problem seems to involve a closer look at the Hebrew text. No preposition appears before "Jerusalem" in 2 Kings 25:8, whereas the preposition בְּ (b^e) does appear before "Jerusalem" in this verse. The NASB translates this preposition as **to**, whereas the KJV and the ASV have "into"; the latter seems preferable in this context. Apparently, Nebuzaradan came *to* Jerusalem on "the seventh day," where he joined the Babylonians encamped outside the city. Three days later, "on the tenth day,"

---

[6]These dates are provided by LaSor, 2:1016.

he entered *into* the city to destroy it.[7] Perhaps he used the intervening time to organize his men and form a strategy. The demolition of the city began almost a month after the walls were breached on July 18 (52:5–7). This time lapse allows for the capture of Zedekiah and his officials, as well as for travel to and from Nebuchadnezzar's headquarters at Riblah, about two hundred miles north of Jerusalem (52:9).

Verse 13. The major buildings in the city were all destroyed by Nebuzaradan, being **burned with fire**. The most important of these structures was **the house of the L**ORD (Ps. 74:3–10; Lam. 2:6–9), which was the focal point of Judah's religion. So much of their concept of worship to God at that time related to that special meeting place, where God dwelled and would meet with them (1 Kings 8:22–30; 9:1–3; 2 Chron. 6:1–6). The Babylonians showed no fear in destroying the temple of the Lord, since they believed that their own gods were superior to the gods of their enemies.

Although the temple was important, it was not intended to be the focal point of Judah's religion. The center of their faith was to be the Lord. Their hearts had lost touch with the truth of God, putting too much emphasis on the place rather than the the divine Person (7:1–7). Otherwise, this destruction would not have happened.

Next in importance was **the king's house** or "the royal palace" (NIV). The downfall of Judah's government has already been narrated with the sentencing of Zedekiah and the slaughtering of his sons and officials (52:9–11). The burning of the palace completed God's judgment on them. Both government personnel and property were gone.

In addition to religion and government, social life was also affected by the destruction. **All the houses of Jerusalem** were burned, **even every large house**. "Every large house" could also be translated "the houses of the great men" (KJV).[8] The difference in meaning is slight, since wealthy and influential people tend to live in more luxurious homes.

---

[7]The NRSV says that Nebuzaradan "came to Jerusalem" in 2 Kings 25:8 and that he "entered Jerusalem" in Jeremiah 52:12.

[8]The NEB has "the mansion of Gedaliah," which is unwarranted.

JEREMIAH 52

Verse 14. After the buildings were burned, the Babylonian army . . . **broke down all the walls.** They carried out this mission under the direction of Nebuzaradan, **the captain of the guard.** This act left the settlement without any security. In the post-exilic period, Jerusalem lacked protection until the walls were repaired. Therefore, a great emphasis was placed on this undertaking in the days of Nehemiah (Neh. 1:3; 2:17, 18).[9]

Those Exiled and Those Left Behind (52:15, 16)

¹⁵Then Nebuzaradan the captain of the guard carried away into exile some of the poorest of the people, the rest of the people who were left in the city, the deserters who had deserted to the king of Babylon and the rest of the artisans. ¹⁶But Nebuzaradan the captain of the guard left some of the poorest of the land to be vinedressers and plowmen.

Verse 15. Nebuzaradan not only organized the burning of Jerusalem's buildings and the breaking down of the walls, he also was in charge of deporting Jews to Babylonia. These are listed in four separate categories: (1) **Some of the poorest of the people**; (2) **the rest of the people who were left in the city;** (3) **the deserters who had deserted to the king of Babylon** (see 38:2); (4) **the rest of the artisans.**[10] Others who were exiled are mentioned in 52:24–27.

Verse 16. Some of the poorest of the land, however, were **left** in Judah **to be vinedressers and plowmen.** Jeremiah 39:10 says that "some of the poorest people who had nothing" were given "vineyards and fields at that time." These would have possessed little education or skill—as opposed to the nobility and the artisans.

---

[9]Douglas Rawlinson Jones, *Jeremiah*, The New Century Bible Commentary (Grand Rapids, Mich.: Wm. B. Eerdmans Publishing Co., 1992), 550.

[10]The word "artisans" (אָמוֹן, *'amon*) poses some difficulty. Second Kings 25:11 has "people" (הָמוֹן, *hamon*) instead of "artisans." It may be that a scribe copying 2 Kings confused the similar words, since "people" seems redundant and the parallel texts are different. Nevertheless, another parallel in Jeremiah 39:9 has "people" (עַם, *'am*). Craftsmen had previously been deported to Babylon in 597 B.C. (2 Kings 24:14, 16).

Temple Treasures Taken to Babylon (52:17–23)

¹⁷Now the bronze pillars which belonged to the house of the Lord and the stands and the bronze sea, which were in the house of the Lord, the Chaldeans broke in pieces and carried all their bronze to Babylon. ¹⁸They also took away the pots, the shovels, the snuffers, the basins, the pans and all the bronze vessels which were used in temple service. ¹⁹The captain of the guard also took away the bowls, the firepans, the basins, the pots, the lampstands, the pans and the drink offering bowls, what was fine gold and what was fine silver. ²⁰The two pillars, the one sea, and the twelve bronze bulls that were under the sea, and the stands, which King Solomon had made for the house of the Lord—the bronze of all these vessels was beyond weight. ²¹As for the pillars, the height of each pillar was eighteen cubits, and it was twelve cubits in circumference and four fingers in thickness, and hollow. ²²Now a capital of bronze was on it; and the height of each capital was five cubits, with network and pomegranates upon the capital all around, all of bronze. And the second pillar was like these, including pomegranates. ²³There were ninety-six exposed pomegranates; all the pomegranates numbered a hundred on the network all around.

The temple had previously been looted in 597 B.C., when Jehoiachin went into exile (27:16; 2 Kings 24:12, 13; 2 Chron. 36:9, 10), and Jeremiah prophesied that the remaining items would be taken away too (27:19–22). Details are given to emphasize the tragedy involved in the destruction and looting (see 2 Kings 25:13–17; 2 Chron. 36:18). God's people gave up so much because of their disobedience. Their selfish rebellion had hurt them instead of helping them. In addition to that, all quality of life was taken from them.

Verse 17. First on the list of looted items are **the bronze pillars which belonged to the house of the Lord** (1 Kings 7:13–22). The two huge pillars in front of the temple were given names by Solomon (1 Kings 7:21). The right pillar was called Jachin, meaning "He shall establish," and the left was called Boaz, meaning "In it is strength."

Next were **the stands**. These also were made of bronze. These ten stands were intricately designed with images of lions, oxen, and cherubim. They also had two axles and four wheels (1 Kings 7:27–37). The movable stands held basins (1 Kings 7:38, 39) used for washing instruments involved in the sacrifices; five were stationed on the north side of the temple and five on the south (2 Chron. 4:6). Similar, though not identical, stands have been found in Syro-Palestine at Ras Shamra and Megiddo.[11]

The bronze sea was also intricately designed and large in size (1 Kings 7:23–26). It was ten cubits (fifteen feet) in diameter, holding two thousand baths (perhaps eleven thousand gallons) of water. This huge basin was used by the priests for their ceremonial washings (2 Chron. 4:6).

Due to the size and weight of these objects, the Babylonians **broke** [them] **in pieces** in order to transport the **bronze to Babylon**. They were more interested in retaining the precious metal than the design of the object.

Verse 18. The Babylonians also confiscated **all the bronze vessels which were used in temple service**. These were smaller items that were easier to carry. **Pots** and **shovels** had been used to remove ashes from the altar of burnt offering (Ex. 27:3; 38:3; 1 Kings 7:40, 45). **Snuffers** comes from the Hebrew word מְזַמֶּרֶת (*mᵉzammereth*), which refers to "shears used to trim a wick."[12] The priests had utilized these to keep the lamps of the temple burning brightly (1 Kings 7:49, 50). **Basins** were bowls used in the dashing of the blood of sacrifices against the altar (Ex. 27:3; 38:3; 1 Kings 7:40, 45; Zech. 9:15). **Pans** is from כַּף (*kap*), which, in this context, probably refers to a bowl shaped like the palm of a hand.[13] The NASB translates the same word as "spoons" in 1 Kings 7:50. They may have been used for burning incense.[14]

---

[11]For photographs of these stands, see Pritchard, 195 (nos. 587, 588).

[12]Ludwig Koehler and Walter Baumgartner, *The Hebrew and Aramaic Lexicon of the Old Testament*, study ed., trans. and ed. M. E. J. Richardson (Boston: Brill, 2001), 1:566.

[13]Ibid., 1:492.

[14]J. A. Thompson, *The Book of Jeremiah*, The New International Commentary on the Old Testament (Grand Rapids, Mich.: Wm. B. Eerdmans Publishing Co., 1980), 779.

Verse 19. Besides these items, Nebuzaradan, **the captain of the guard**, carried away others made of **fine gold** and **fine silver**. They included small **bowls, firepans** "for carrying burning coals or ashes"[15] (1 Kings 7:50), **basins**, and **pots**. In addition, ten **lampstands** were taken that had been used to illuminate the holy place of the temple—five on the north side and five on the south (1 Kings 7:49). The list ends with **pans** and **drink offering bowls**; the latter were used for pouring out libations (Ex. 25:29; 37:16).

Verse 20. The description of the spoils taken by the Babylonians returns full circle to **the two pillars, the one sea, . . . and the stands, which King Solomon had made for the house of the LORD** (see 52:17). Great emphasis is placed on these **bronze** pieces which were extremely heavy. **The twelve bronze bulls that were under the sea** served as its base, three bulls facing each of the four directions of the compass (1 Kings 7:25). These had been removed by King Ahaz about one hundred and fifty years earlier (2 Kings 16:17). By this time, however, they had been restored to their original position or else new ones had been constructed to replace the originals.[16]

Verses 21–23. The two bronze **pillars** are described here in detail (see 1 Kings 7:15–22). **Each pillar** stood at a **height** of **eighteen cubits** (twenty-seven feet)[17] and had a **circumference** of **twelve cubits** (eighteen feet). Moreover, the pillars were **four fingers in thickness** (three inches) and **hollow**. On top of each one was **a capital of bronze** that was **five cubits** (seven and a half feet). The capitals were both adorned with **pomegranates**, a common decoration in the ancient Near East. The laver stand found at Ras Shamra also has representations of this kind of fruit.[18]

J. A. Thompson pointed out that the goal of this section was

---

[15]Koehler and Baumgartner, 1:572.

[16]Some suggest that Ahaz had given the bronze bulls to Tiglath-pileser III, the king of Assyria, as tribute (see 2 Kings 16:8).

[17]Second Chronicles 3:15 says that the pillars were "thirty-five cubits high." Either this number reflects the combined height of both pillars (see NIV), or it is a scribal error.

[18]See Pritchard, 195 (no. 588).

not to produce an identical list of the items found in 1 Kings 7, when Solomon's temple was constructed. Rather, the author was pointing out the considerable amount of precious metal (especially bronze) and the immense beauty that was lost. The loss of this value and beauty made the destruction of the temple "all the more tragic."[19]

JUDGMENT PASSED (52:24–30)

Prominent People Killed (52:24–27)

[24]Then the captain of the guard took Seraiah the chief priest and Zephaniah the second priest, with the three officers of the temple. [25]He also took from the city one official who was overseer of the men of war, and seven of the king's advisers who were found in the city, and the scribe of the commander of the army who mustered the people of the land, and sixty men of the people of the land who were found in the midst of the city. [26]Nebuzaradan the captain of the guard took them and brought them to the king of Babylon at Riblah. [27]Then the king of Babylon struck them down and put them to death at Riblah in the land of Hamath. So Judah was led away into exile from its land.

Verse 24. Nebuzaradan, **the captain of the guard**, captured the officials who had not fled from Jerusalem with the others (see 52:7–11).

Seraiah the chief priest was related to a noble line of priests. He was the grandson of Hilkiah, the high priest who was involved in King Josiah's massive reforms and the restored worship of the Lord (2 Kings 22, 23). Seraiah's son, Jehozadak, became an exile in Babylon under Nebuchadnezzar (1 Chron. 6:13–15). Loyalty to God must have been continued, because Seraiah's grandson, Joshua, was high priest when the exiles returned to Jerusalem (Hag. 1:1). The great scribe, Ezra, was also a descendant of Seraiah (Ezra 7:1).

---

[19]Thompson, 781.

Zephaniah the second priest was likely the one associated with Jeremiah in several incidents earlier in the book (21:1; 29:25–32; 37:1–3). Apparently, he was not the only person who held the title of "second priest." A group known as "the priests of the second order" are mentioned in 2 Kings 23:4.

The three officers of the temple were literally "doorkeepers" or "keepers of the threshold" (see comments on 35:4). Men who held this office were responsible for funds donated to renovate the temple (2 Kings 12:9, 10; 22:4–7). Perhaps they also were responsible for supervising the four thousand Levites appointed to be gatekeepers (1 Chron. 23:5).[20] In 2 Kings 23:4, the "doorkeepers" are mentioned along with "the high priest" and "the priests of the second order," as they are in verse 24. The "doorkeepers" no doubt held an influential position.

Verse 25. Beyond the priests, Nebuzaradan also captured key leaders from Zedekiah's administration. Those mentioned apparently served in high-level military capacities. **One official ... was overseer of the men of war.** The Hebrew word for "official," סָרִיס (*saris*), can be translated "eunuch" (KJV), which refers to a castrated man (see comments on 38:7, 8). However, the term seems to be used in the more general sense of "official" in this passage.[21] It is noteworthy that the Law excluded eunuchs from "the assembly of the LORD" (Deut. 23:1).

Other administrators included **seven of the king's advisers**. Instead of "advisers," the Hebrew text more literally says "men who appear before the king's face." These were men who had access to the king and offered him counsel (see Esther 1:13, 14). The parallel text in 2 Kings 25:19 has "five" advisers instead of "seven." The reason for this difference is uncertain, although several explanations have been set forth: (1) The number "seven" includes the "overseer" and the "scribe"; (2) "five" of the men were more influential than the other two; (3) "five" were found first, while the other two were discovered later; or (4) one of the numbers is a scribal error.

---

[20]James E. Smith, *Jeremiah and Lamentations*, Bible Study Textbook Series (Joplin, Mo.: College Press, 1972), 828.
[21]See Koehler and Baumgartner, 1:769–70.

The scribe of the commander of the army was the one **who mustered the people of the land**. Obviously, this man's responsibilities far exceeded the copying of legal documents. Scribes were sometimes responsible for numbering and organizing troops for battle (2 Chron. 26:11–13). The meaning of the phrase "the people of the land" is debatable. Some think that it refers to commoners, while others believe that it denotes a wealthier class. **Sixty men** from this group were also captured.

Verse 26. Nebuzaradan took all of these men to Nebuchadnezzar, who was still stationed **at Riblah** (see comments on 52:9). Riblah was on the way to Babylonia, where he was taking the other captives (52:15).

Verse 27. These officials were slaughtered in the cruel fashion characteristic of conquering forces in that day: **The king of Babylon struck them down and put them to death.** The language could be a synonymous parallelism, "struck them down" being equal to "put them to death." Another possibility is that it refers to scourging along with the execution (see NEB).

In the end, **Judah was led away into exile from its land**. This is what had been predicted in the Law (Deut. 28:63) and what had previously happened to Israel at the hands of the Assyrians (2 Kings 17:23). When Judah was exiled, another portion of God's plan and Jeremiah's prophecy was fulfilled (see 15:1–6).

A Declaration of Deportation (52:28–30)

²⁸**These are the people whom Nebuchadnezzar carried away into exile: in the seventh year 3,023 Jews; ²⁹in the eighteenth year of Nebuchadnezzar 832 persons from Jerusalem; ³⁰in the twenty-third year of Nebuchadnezzar, Nebuzaradan the captain of the guard carried into exile 745 Jewish people; there were 4,600 persons in all.**

This section presents a summary of deportations that further fulfilled the prophetic plan. At least four deportations of the Jews took place, yet only three are listed here.

Verses 28–30. The first deportation was in 605 B.C., when Nebuchadnezzar rose to power as the king of Babylon. Daniel

1:1–7 records that Jerusalem was besieged and some of the royal family and the nobles were taken to Babylon. Daniel and his three friends were among this number. This deportation is not recorded in 52:28–30.

The second deportation took place in 597 B.C., when Jehoiachin surrendered to **Nebuchadnezzar**, and his uncle Zedekiah was made king in his place (24:1; 29:2; 2 Kings 24:10–17).[22] This happened **in the seventh year** of Nebuchadnezzar's reign. In 2 Kings 24:12, the event is dated to "the eighth year." This slight variation reflects two different ways of calculating a king's reign. Thompson argued that "the seventh year" "was according to the Babylonian system of reckoning, which omitted the first partial year and began counting the regnal years from the New Year of 604 B.C."[23] This is confirmed by the *Babylonian Chronicle*, which says,

> Year 7: in Kislev the king of Babylonia called out his army and marched to Hattu [the west]. He set his camp against the city of Judah . . . and on 2nd Adar he took the city and captured the king. He appointed a king of his choosing there, took heavy tribute and returned to Babylon.[24]

At that time, Nebuchadnezzar took **3,023 Jews** into Babylonian **exile**. This figure is much lower than the numbers given in 2 Kings 24:14, 16—a total of at least ten thousand captives (and perhaps even eighteen thousand). Suggestions have been made for reconciling the numbers in Jeremiah and 2 Kings, including: (1) The lower number counts the males only; (2) the lower number counts only a segment of the exiles (perhaps Judeans versus citizens of Jerusalem) and is supplemental to the higher number; (3) the higher numbers reflect those taken, whereas the lower numbers represent those who actually made it to Babylonia alive; or (4) some errors have been made in copying the Hebrew text

---

[22]The prophet Ezekiel was also taken captive at this time (Ezek. 1:1–3).
[23]Thompson, 782; see comments on 25:1 (n. 1).
[24]William W. Hallo, ed., *The Context of Scripture* (Boston: Brill, 2003): 1:468.

or another (otherwise unknown) captivity is in view.

The third deportation was in 586 B.C., **the eighteenth year of Nebuchadnezzar**. Again, this reflects the Babylonian way of dating. In 52:12 and in 2 Kings 25:8, the Judean method is used: The destruction of Jerusalem and the Jewish exile are dated to "the nineteenth year." At that time, **832 persons** were taken **from Jerusalem** (see 52:15; 2 Kings 25:11).

The final deportation took place in 582 or 581 B.C., which was **the twenty-third year of Nebuchadnezzar**. This probably happened in response to the murder of Gedaliah, who had been appointed as governor over those left in the land (40:7—41:18; 2 Kings 25:22–26). **Nebuzaradan the captain of the guard**, who had overseen the exile of 586 B.C. (52:12–27), returned to Judah and took an additional **745 Jewish people** captive.

Altogether, **there were 4,600 persons** taken to Babylon. Thompson thought that this number seems small, even if it only included the males or those who survived the journey. He wrote, "Perhaps [these numbers were intended] to make the point that Yahweh could build a new future out of a mere handful of people. The exactness of the figures 3,023, 832, and 745 suggests an authentic recording of the numbers of some kind."[25] It should be pointed out that, when a portion of the Jews returned to Jerusalem about fifty years later, they numbered nearly fifty thousand people (Ezra 2:64, 65).

JEHOIACHIN ENTHRONED IN BABYLON, OFFERING A RAY OF HOPE (52:31–34)

[31]Now it came about in the thirty-seventh year of the exile of Jehoiachin king of Judah, in the twelfth month, on the twenty-fifth of the month, that Evil-merodach king of Babylon, in the first year of his reign, showed favor to Jehoiachin king of Judah and brought him out of prison. [32]Then he spoke kindly to him and set his throne above the thrones of the kings who were with him in Babylon. [33]So Jehoiachin changed his

---

[25]Ibid., 783.

prison clothes, and had his meals in the king's presence regularly all the days of his life. ³⁴For his allowance, a regular allowance was given him by the king of Babylon, a daily portion all the days of his life until the day of his death.

The Book of Jeremiah ends on the positive note that Jehoiachin was released from prison in Babylon. His freedom served as a harbinger of hope for the rest of the Jews, signaling brighter days ahead. God would fulfill the promises He had made through Jeremiah concerning the return and restoration of His people after seventy years of captivity (25:11, 12; 29:10; Dan. 9:2).

Verse 31. Jehoiachin king of Judah is introduced here, where he is portrayed as a prisoner. The mention of his exile to Babylon appears earlier in the book (24:1; 27:20; 29:2; 37:1; see 2 Kings 24:10–17), as he was taken in the second deportation of 597 B.C. Counting from that date, **the thirty-seventh year of the exile** would have been 561 or 560 B.C. An even more specific date is provided: **the twelfth month, on the twenty-fifth of the month**. The parallel in 2 Kings 25:27 has "the twenty-seventh" instead. James E. Smith offered the following explanation:

> Not being in possession of all the details concerning the matter it is most difficult to reconcile these two statements. Perhaps the one account speaks of the day when the official decree was issued which laid the legal foundation for the release; the other account would then refer to the actual day that king Jehoiachin left the prison.[26]

Jehoiachin was shown **favor**, being released from **prison** by **Evil-merodach king of Babylon, in the first year of his reign**. King Nebuchadnezzar had a long reign, lasting forty-four years (605–562 B.C.). After his death, the king was replaced by his son, Evil-merodach, who reigned for only two years before being assassinated (561–560 B.C.) (see comments on 27:7). The fact that this new king released Jehoiachin seems to reflect a difference in policy from the previous administration.

---

[26]Smith, 835–36.

JEREMIAH 52

The name of Nebuchadnezzar's son was actually "Amel-Marduk," which means "man of Marduk." Marduk, also known as "Bel" (50:2), was chief among the Babylonian gods. "Evil-merodach" may simply be a transliteration of the Babylonian name into Hebrew, but some believe it is an intentional corruption of the name used as mockery by the Jews. The Hebrew word for "Evil," אֱוִיל (*ᵉwil*), can mean "fool" or "idiot."[27] "Evil-merodach" may have been intended to mean "the fool who worships Marduk."[28] (For a possible parallel, see comments on 3:24.)

Verse 32. Evil-merodach **spoke kindly to** Jehoiachin, placing **his throne above the thrones of the kings who were with him in Babylon**. The language underscores the fact that the people of Judah were not the only ones who had been uprooted from their land.

Verse 33. At his release, **Jehoiachin changed his prison clothes** (see Gen. 41:14). He had probably been given royal robes to wear that were suitable for a king. Few have likely gone from royal robes to prison clothes, and then back to royal robes. What a contrast and what a unique life! It should be observed that thirty-seven years passed from royal robes to royal robes. He sat in prison longer than he set on thrones.

Jehoiachin ate **his meals in the king's presence regularly all the days of his life**. The text does not indicate that he restricted himself to a kosher diet, as the prophet Daniel had done (Dan. 1:8–16). Since Evil-merodach reigned only a short time, it is reasonable to assume that the Babylonian kings after him continued to have Jehoiachin as a dinner companion.

Verse 34. Jehoiachin also received **a regular allowance** from **the king of Babylon, a daily portion all the days of his life until the day of his death**. Even while he was a prisoner, the king of Judah had been supported by Nebuchadnezzar. It is interesting that documents discovered in the king's palace contain lists of the daily rations of food given to the royal prisoners and hostages from various lands. Jehoiachin and five of his sons are men-

---

[27]Koehler and Baumgartner, 1:21.
[28]Anthony L. Ash, *Jeremiah and Lamentations*, The Living Word Commentary (Abilene, Tex.: ACU Press, 1987), 329.

tioned.[29] From those texts it would seem that Jehoiachin and his sons fared very well under the care of Nebuchadnezzar.

APPLICATION

The Result of Sin and a Ray of Hope (Ch. 52)

The final chapter of the Book of Jeremiah seems to have been written for a twofold purpose. First, it stresses the downfall of Judah and Jerusalem due to their sin. Calamity came upon the people, just as God had spoken through Jeremiah the prophet. Today, we must never underestimate the warnings regarding sin and its consequences (Rom. 6:23; 1 Cor. 10:1–13; Heb. 10:26–31). It has been widely said, "Sin will take you farther than you want to go, keep you longer than you want to stay, and cost you more than you want to pay."

Second, the chapter ends in a positive way with the release and elevation of Jehoiachin. It demonstrated the trend among foreign kings that would someday fulfill the prophecies of a return of God's captive people to their homeland. God's people would rise up, repent, and return (29:10–14). Like ancient Judah, we too "have sinned and fall short of the glory of God" (Rom. 3:23). Nevertheless, He has provided the means for our return to Him through Jesus Christ (Rom. 3:24; 6:3, 4). He has given us a living hope of an eternal inheritance in heaven (1 Pet. 1:3, 4).

While we may have to suffer in this life—just as Judah did in captivity—we must remember that our struggles are only temporary. Paul said that our "momentary, light affliction is producing for us an eternal weight of glory far beyond all comparison" (2 Cor. 4:17). God truly does cause "all things to work together for good to those who love [Him], to those who are called according to His purpose" (Rom. 8:28). We should thank God and be encouraged because of His constant care (Acts 28:15). We should also share the hope we have with a lost and dying world (Mk. 16:15, 16; Eph. 2:12).

---

[29]James B. Pritchard, ed., *Ancient Near Eastern Texts: Relating to the Old Testament*, 3d ed. (Princeton, N.J.: Princeton University Press, 1969), 308.

LAMENTATIONS

INTRODUCTION

The writer of Ecclesiastes wrote, "It is better to go to a house of mourning than to go to a house of feasting, because that is the end of every man, and the living takes it to heart" (Eccles. 7:2). He also wrote, "The mind of the wise is in the house of mourning, while the mind of fools is in the house of pleasure" (Eccles. 7:4). In view of these inspired words, the five-chapter dirge of Lamentations, an extended poem of mourning, surely qualifies as a literary masterpiece on that which is "better."

Lamentations might be called a flowing river of tears, but the images there cannot fully express the Jews' intense sorrow. This small book wears the shroud of grief, echoing a message of the cost of sin. From the very beginning, the lonely city of Jerusalem is portrayed as a woman who weeps bitterly, who sits as a grief-stricken widow under harsh servitude, distress, and mourning (1:1–3). Every sentiment is the cry of a broken heart. The book "may rightly be called the masterpiece of anguish of all the literature of the world."[1]

Jerusalem was destroyed in the eleventh year, fourth month, and ninth day of the reign of King Zedekiah (Jer. 39:1–9). That surely was the most significant tragedy to transpire in the political and religious history of God's people from the exodus out of Egypt until 586 B.C. That event, with its aftermath, precipitated the writing of the Book of Lamentations. Jerusalem, the place where God longed to meet with His faithful people (2 Chron.

---

[1] L. L. Gieger, "Lamentations," *2nd Annual Fort Worth Christian College Lectures* (1961), 324.

7:12–16), was demolished by the orders of Nebuchadnezzar, the Babylonian king. For the people of Judah to see their sacred city go up in flames was a haunting and humiliating experience. Despite repeated prophetic warnings that such a moment was coming (see Jer. 1:15, 16; 7:1–15; 38:17–23), they were totally unprepared for this disaster (Jer. 5:11–13; 16:10; 37:9, 10). Since their deliverance in the days of King Hezekiah, the people had believed that Jerusalem was secure and would never fall (see 2 Kings 19:14–37). Therefore, it was a staggering blow when the walls were breached and the temple was burned. Lamentations is a poetic attempt to portray the devastation and anguish of these conquered people.

THE PROFIT OF THIS STUDY

Before we study specific Scriptures, it may be helpful to notice the following types of people who will be blessed by a study of Lamentations: (1) those who are today bearing heavy burdens, (2) those who have suffered unfair treatment but must keep on doing that which is right, (3) those who are concerned about their relationship with God, (4) those who are not concerned about their relationship with God, (5) those who are deep in sin and need encouragement to restore their hope, (6) those who have relied more on others than on God, (7) those who have suffered tragic loss and need strength to rise above their grief, (8) those who will be able to build faith from a setting of destruction, (9) those who need a warning about how deceived people may become, and (10) those who want to dwell on God's compassionate heart that will never fail us if we trust in Him.

This poem presents the catastrophe that awaits people who forget the imperative of righteousness in the land (see Mt. 6:33; Rom. 6:12, 13, 16–18; 1 Pet. 3:12–22). Let us study it and take to heart its message.

ITS AUTHOR

The writer was prepared for the task not only by God's inspiration, but also by witnessing these crushing events himself.

INTRODUCTION

Lamentations was written shortly after the fall of Jerusalem, so the terrible scenes were fresh in his mind; the horror still flashed before his eyes. As he viewed the city lying in smoldering ruins, he penned this book as if it were a funeral oration, in a manner that supplies us with many lessons.

Internal Evidence

The text does not give the author's name. However, it does give specifics as to his nature, situation, character, and concerns. We are able to deduce who the writer must have been.

1. The writer knew many details about Jerusalem. The city's past standing as "a princess among the provinces" (1:1) had deteriorated until the author said, "She weeps bitterly in the night," (1:2) and perceived that there was no one to comfort her (1:16). He knew current trends in Judah, where, he said, "the roads of Zion are in mourning" (1:4). He gave details about her gates, priests (1:4, 19), virgins, enemies, and disposition. He knew about "the multitude of her transgressions" (1:5; see 1:8, 18, 20, 22). The record of specific action by the elders (2:10) shows that the writer was a man who was present as Jerusalem fell to Babylon.

2. The writer's tears, emotional stress, and personal pain at what he saw and heard from children and mothers (2:11–13) affirmed his love for God's people and His holy city. He was acquainted with the "false and foolish visions" from the past that were the cause of all the sadness (2:14). He surveyed the present perils of "all who pass along the way," clapping their hands "in derision" of Jerusalem (2:15). Not only was the writer enduring the tragic earthly scene, but his pain was intensified by the knowledge that God "in the indignation of His anger" (2:6) had done this. (God's role is stressed by repeated references to "the LORD" and the pronouns "He" and His" in 2:1–9, 17.) Only a man inspired of God could have known these details.

3. In chapter 3, the writer traced his own journey through a personal view of what God had caused him to endure (3:8–18), but then reflected with hope (3:21, 24, 29) on what God was really doing (3:19–38). He then retraced the national and personal period of rebellion and doubt relative to God, concluding that God "drew near when I called on" Him (3:57). The chapter ends

with trust in God (3:64–66). When so viewed, the chapter offers great insight as to the writer of Lamentations. Did any known prophet in that day move through those thought patterns of doubt as he developed a deep trust in God? (See *The Man and His Message: His Trials, 1* in the introduction to Jeremiah.)

4. The writer gave a sweeping survey of the high price to be paid for sin (4:1–10), identifying the reasons for God's wrath and the nation's fall (4:11–22). He understood why God's people would "live among the nations" (4:20); he knew that the captivity was necessary and justified. He knew that God had brought the judgment that He promised to bring if they did not repent.

5. The writer closed with a plea for God to remember the sickening scene that lay before him (5:1–18). He knew that extended sin was the cause of Jerusalem's destruction (5:7, 16). He also recognized God's sovereign position, closing with a plea: "Restore us to You, O LORD" and "renew our days as of old" (5:21). As a loyal patriot, he longed for his people to return to God. Who on the scene would have fit that description?

Even though the book does not name the author, a careful look at the internal evidence, including the nature and character of the writer, leaves little doubt concerning the one inspired man whose character matched these facts. The only true prophet known to have been living in Jerusalem when the nation fell to Babylon was Jeremiah.[2]

When we compare Jeremiah and Lamentations, parallels between them lead us to think that the person who wrote one also wrote the other (see *Appendix: Parallel Phrases in Jeremiah & Lamentations Indicating the Same Author*, page 580). The tone and truths in both books are the same. Both emphasize that punishment came on Judah because of her sins and because of God's judgments against her. The wickedness of prophets and priests is emphasized in both. Consistent phraseology lends itself to one writer as the composer of both.

---

[2]Some who do not accept that Jeremiah wrote Lamentations still date it soon after 586 B.C. and see it as the work of only one author. See F. W. Dobbs-Allsopp, *Lamentations*, Interpretation (Louisville, Ky.: John Knox Press, 2002), 4–5.

INTRODUCTION

External Evidence

The earliest written source to ascribe the book to Jeremiah is the Greek version of Lamentations in the Septuagint (LXX). This translation of Lamentations, probably completed around 200 B.C., contains an introductory note which reads: "And it came to pass, after Israel was taken captive, and Jerusalem was made desolate, that Jeremias sat weeping, and lamented with this lamentation over Jerusalem . . ." (1:1).

The Talmud asserts that "Jeremiah wrote his book, Kings and Lamentations."[3] Early church fathers such as Jerome and Eusebius regarded Jeremiah as the author of Lamentations.[4]

Combining the internal evidence, the parallel tone and thoughts within the Books of Jeremiah and Lamentations, plus the historical evidence, we conclude that Jeremiah was the writer. Modern Old Testament scholars have questioned that Jeremiah wrote it. A review of their arguments can be found in James E. Smith's commentary on Jeremiah and Lamentations.[5] To date, no other name has been supplied as a possible author.

ITS TITLE AND LOCATION

Following the pattern of Old Testament books, Lamentations originally gained its title from the first Hebrew word of the book, the interrogative or exclamatory אֵיכָה (*'eykah*), meaning "Alas! How?" These words of desperation were commonly used as the opening words in the lament.[6] "How" is more than an introductory word of exclamation. It affirms a stunned amazement at the destruction which the writer was called upon to describe. In 1:1, 2:1, and 4:1, that word is used to exclaim how horrifying, how

---

[3]Talmud *Baba Bathra* 14b–15a.
[4]Jerome *Preface to Samuel and Kings*; Eusebius *Ecclesiastical History* 4.25.
[5]James E. Smith, *Jeremiah and Lamentations*, Bible Study Textbook Series (Joplin, Mo.: College Press, 1972), 852.
[6]Ludwig Koehler and Walter Baumgartner, *The Hebrew and Aramaic Lexicon of the Old Testament*, study ed., trans. and ed. M. E. J. Richardson (Boston: Brill, 2001), 1:40. (Biblical references used by Koehler and Baumgartner are based on the Hebrew text. Verse divisions in Lamentations are sometimes different in Hebrew and English.)

catastrophic, and how complete was the ruination of beauty and the lost estate of the elite city of Zion.

Then Jewish rabbis gave the title as קִינוֹת (*Qinoth*), that is, "laments." This rendering may have influenced scholars who later translated the Old Testament into Greek. In the LXX it is named after its contents, Θρῆνοι (*Thrēnoi*), the Greek word meaning "lamentations" or "tears," whereas in the Latin Vulgate it is entitled "The Lamentations of Jeremiah."

Lamentations seems originally to have been located as an appendix to Jeremiah. Josephus wrote that the Hebrews had twenty-two books "considered to be divine."[7] There were five books of Law (Genesis through Deuteronomy), thirteen books of Prophets, and four books containing songs and hymns (Psalms, Proverbs, Ecclesiastes, and Song of Solomon). At that time, 1 and 2 Samuel were one book, as were 1 and 2 Kings, 1 and 2 Chronicles, the twelve minor prophets, and Ezra and Nehemiah. Adding on the four major prophets (Isaiah, Jeremiah, Ezekiel, Daniel), plus Joshua, Judges, Ruth, Job, Esther, and Lamentations, we have fifteen books of prophecy. However, if we consider Judges and Ruth one book and put Lamentations with Jeremiah as one book, we then have thirteen prophetic books, four books of songs and hymns, and the five books of Law (13 + 4 + 5 = 22). In this manner, we arrive at the twenty-two books the Hebrews "considered divine." Also, this shows their conviction that Lamentations is to be associated with Jeremiah. A number of early writers alluded to the twenty-two books of the Hebrew Bible. Among these were Melito of Sardis (A.D. 180), Origen (A.D. 250), Jerome (A.D. 405), and Augustine (A.D. 420).[8] Jerome said that Jeremiah and Lamentations were counted as one book, which suggests that they were written on the same scroll.[9]

Later, Lamentations became a part of the books of *Megilloth*, "the five rolls," which also included Ruth, Esther, Ecclesiastes, and the Song of Solomon. As such, it was prized and frequently read by the Hebrews because it strikingly told of Judah's devas-

---

[7]Josephus *Against Apion* 1.8.
[8]Smith, 847.
[9]Jerome *Preface to Samuel and Kings*.

INTRODUCTION

tation, while containing promises of restoration. It represented the Hebrews' worst horror blended with hope.

This placement of Lamentations among the *Megilloth* emphasized its role in the commemoration of the destruction of the temple in A.D. 70. Jack P. Lewis pictured its use in synagogue:

> In the synagogue, it is traditional [for the Jews] to read Lamentations on the ninth of the month of Ab (July-August), which is the day that commemorates the destruction of the temple both by Nebuchadnezzar (586 B.C.) and by Rome [Titus] (A.D. 70).... In liturgical reading, it is customary to repeat Lam. 5:21 after 5:22 to avoid ending on a despondent note. Liturgical Christian churches use the book in the service preceding Easter to lament the sufferings of Jesus.[10]

ITS FORM AND LITERARY STYLE

Its Poetry

Lamentations is a classic example of Hebrew poetry—a poetry of thought rather than of rhyme. In the English Bible, twenty-two verses are found in chapters 1, 2, 4, and 5, with sixty-six verses in chapter 3. These are translations of a pattern of intent rather than a coincidence. Knowing this can help us grasp the message being given. The second and third lines of each verse in Hebrew relate to, or repeat, the thought of the first line, in different words. This pattern is referred to as synonymous parallelism[11] or, if contrasting the thought of the first line, as antithetic parallelism.

---

[10]Jack P. Lewis, *The Major Prophets* (Henderson, Tenn: Hester Publications, 1999), 90.

[11]The following scholars give good discussions of "parallelism": J. M. LeMon and B. A. Strawn, "Parallelism," in *Dictionary of the Old Testament: Wisdom, Poetry & Writings*, ed. Tremper Longman III and Peter Enns (Downers Grove, Ill.: IVP Academic, 2008), 502–15; Robert Lowth, *Lectures on the Sacred Poetry of the Hebrews* (Oxford: University Press, 1753); and C. Hassell Bullock, *An Introduction to the Poetic Books of the Old Testament* (Chicago: Moody Press, 1979), 43–46, 168–69.

Lamentations in Hebrew has what is called lament rhythm, *Qinah*, which is lost in the English translation. *Qinah* is the basic term for the biblical funeral dirge or eulogy.[12] Generally speaking, the meter in the *Qinah* rhythm finds the second line of each verse one stress shorter than the first line, with the third line like the first. Walter L. McConnell attributed the discovery of this type of Hebrew meter to Jens Budde and said, "It is clear that this pattern is reproduced in many lines in biblical lament. Even so, it would be incorrect to conclude that biblical poets uniformly made use of the 3:2 form in their composition of dirges."[13]

Another unique characteristic of the literary style is that chapters 1 through 4 are in the form of alphabetic acrostics, each section beginning with successive letters of the Hebrew alphabet (twenty-two letters). Norman K. Gottwald has provided a thought-provoking study of the acrostics in Lamentations. He concluded, "Those who entertain this idea of completeness . . . instinctively feel that in naming the whole alphabet one comes as close as man may to a total development of any theme or the complete expression of any emotion or belief."[14] Adele Berlin added, "Those who have studied them have seen them as mnemonic devices, aesthetic devices, or a way to express completeness (everything from A to Z)."[15] Other examples of this form of Hebrew poetry can be found in Psalms 9; 10; 25; 34; 35; 37; 111; 112; 119; 145 and Proverbs 31:10–31. In Psalm 119, the most elaborate example of the acrostic pattern, each letter of the Hebrew alphabet relates to eight lines. Each line of the section in verses 1 through 8 starts with א (*aleph*); the next eight with ב (*beth*), and so on.

Chapters 1 and 2 are identical in form, each consisting of sixty-six lines, organized in groups of three lines in each verse. Each grouping is called a "tricolon." The first line of the first tri-

---

[12]Adele Berlin, *Lamentations*, Old Testament Library (Louisville, Ky.: Westminster John Knox Press, 2004), 2.

[13]Walter L. McConnell III, "Meter," in *Dictionary of the Old Testament: Wisdom, Poetry & Writings*, 476.

[14]Norman K. Gottwald, *Studies in the Book of Lamentations*, Studies in Biblical Theology No. 14, rev. ed. (London: SCM Press, 1962), 29.

[15]Berlin, 4.

INTRODUCTION

colon begins with the Hebrew letter א (*aleph*), while the first line of the second tricolon, verse 2, begins with the second Hebrew letter ב (*beth*), continuing through that pattern until the end of the chapter and the end of the Hebrew alphabet.

Chapter 3, containing sixty-six verses, triples this pattern with a slight variation. Again, there are sixty-six lines—but each of the first three lines begins with א (*aleph*); each of the next three lines begins with ב (*beth*), and so on. In other words, each verse in 3:1–3 begins with א (*aleph*) in Hebrew, while each verse in 3:4–6 begins with ב (*beth*), and the pattern continues so that the Hebrew alphabet is covered in the sixty-six verses.

Chapter 4 is slightly modified. Each verse in the chapter still begins with a different letter of the Hebrew alphabet, but a verse this time consists of only two lines, called a "bicolon."

Chapter 5 is not an acrostic, with each verse beginning with the next consecutive letter. However, it does also have twenty-two verses, the number of characters in the Hebrew alphabet.

Keeping these literary patterns in mind can help the reader to follow the writer's message and emphasis,[16] even when reading from an English translation. The demands and details of this pattern indicate that the composition required deliberation and careful reflection. The form may have been developed for memory purposes, to help the Hebrews in reciting the material. In addition, keeping in mind that the text was inspired by the Holy Spirit (see 2 Pet. 1:20, 21), the reader can rest assured that the form and the content of this lament are worthy of meditation.

Its Pronouns

Another guide for understanding the book's significance is to trace a pattern of collected thoughts centering on an individual or individuals. The emphasis can be detected through the repetition of pronouns, as in the following passages:

---

[16]For further discussion of this Hebrew poetry, see Timothy M. Willis, *Jeremiah-Lamentations*, The College Press NIV Commentary (Joplin, Mo.: College Press Publishing Co., 2002), 393–97, and various articles on Lamentations and Hebrew Poetry in *Dictionary of the Old Testament: Wisdom, Poetry & Writings*.

1:12–15. The emphasis here is on God and His fierce anger as the source of the severe pain inflicted. He is identified by the repeated use of "His" and "He."

2:1–9. God's anger is again emphasized, and it was manifested against "the daughter of Zion." "His" and "He" in reference to the Lord are used 37 times.

2:10–16. The plight of the elders is noted by a repeated use of "they" and "their" in 2:10, 12. The perplexity of the prophet is seen by the use of "my" in 2:11 and "I" in 2:13, while the sad state of the "virgin daughter of Zion" unfolds around "your" and "you" in 2:13–16.

2:17. God and His action are emphasized by the use of "He" and "His" 7 times.

3:1–18. God's action against the prophet is given in swift, repeated statements entwined around the use of "His" and "He" 24 times. In the same verses, the writer decried the affliction imposed on him by using in rapid succession "I," "me," "my," and "who" a total of 34 times.

3:19–24. A switch occurs with the prophet's plea and tribute to God. "My," "me," and "I" are used 10 times. God is named 2 times and is identified by pronouns 3 times.

3:25–38. The tribute to the Lord continues, identifying Him as "Lord," "the Most High," and by pronouns 15 times. Also, there is a switch from the first person in 3:1–24 to "others" (third person) in 3:25–38. The expressions "those who," "person who," "he," "man," "his," "him," "sons of men," "all," and "who" are found 20 times.

3:48–66. In this section the prophet reverted to the trials that were confronting him personally. "My," "me," and "I" are used 27 times. A plea is entwined with expressions of confidence in the Lord. Fifteen times, "You" or "Your" is repeated.

4:1–22. "They," "them," and "their" are often used, generally in reference to God's people as victims of His fierce anger. Beginning in verse 17, the writer injected himself into the scene, identifying personal involvement by "our," "we," and "us."

5:1–22. In this national prayer and appeal to the Lord, the writer asked that God remember and recognize the Jews' sad state. He confessed their sins and acknowledged God as their

INTRODUCTION

hope to be restored to "days as of old" (5:21). The pronoun pattern links the chapter together with "us" (11 times), "we" (8 times), and "our" (18 times).

Pronouns are obviously a key in grasping the emphasis, the core message, the individuals involved, and the details in Lamentations.

Its Near-Eastern Antecedents

Communal lament is not unique to the people of Israel. It was common in the literature of the ancient Near East. Some of the earliest examples are Sumerian poems preserved from the Old Babylonian period (2000–1600 B.C.). Six distinctive Sumerian city laments have been discovered in excavations and published: Ur Lament, Sumer and Ur Lament, Nippur Lament, Uruk Lament, Ekimar Lament and Eridu Lament.[17] Paul W. Ferris, Jr., developed a table of the structure of these laments.[18] Although stylistic structure is similar in these laments and in the Book of Lamentations, no borrowing is evident. We must recognize the fact that Lamentations is an inspired writing, whereas the laments of other people were merely the outpouring of grief because of the destruction of their beloved cities.

ITS PURPOSE AND CONTENT

Any biblical book may serve several purposes, but a dominant theme is usually seen. It may spring from one passage (see Rom. 1:16–18; 1 Tim. 3:14, 15), or it may unfold through accumulated emphasis scattered through the sections or chapters of a book. Lamentations seems to fit the latter pattern. The book moves from one sobering scene to another, climaxing in chapter 5 with the imagery of heaven and earth united in the goal of

---

[17]See the translation of "Lamentation over the Destruction of Ur." Ur fell to the Elamites and Subarians about 2006 B.C. (James B. Pritchard, ed., *Ancient Near Eastern Texts: Relating to the Old Testament*, 3d ed. [Princeton, N.J.: Princeton University Press, 1969], 455–63; William W. Hallo, ed., *The Context of Scripture* [Leiden: Brill, 2003], 1:535–39.)

[18]Paul W. Ferris, Jr., "Lamentations 2: Ancient Near Eastern Background," *Dictionary of the Old Testament: Wisdom, Poetry & Writings*, 412.

grief, a kindred desire in Deity and humanity. As a series of lamentations, it echoes cries of concern from both the Creator and His creatures.

A Chapter-by-Chapter Summary

Each chapter has its own emphasis so that the same scene is viewed from different vantage points, all moving toward meeting God's divine goal.

Chapter 1: *The City, a Scenario of Suffering from Sin*. A person may suffer over sin before he is sorry for sin. The painful price paid because of sin usually precedes penitence for sin. The cost of sin is surveyed using contrasts and comparisons, by stages of suffering.

Chapter 2: *The Creator, the One Who Caused the Destruction and Desolation*. Prominence to God's part in the destruction is given. "The LORD" is named in 2:1, 2, 5–8, 17, and 20.

Chapter 3: *The Cry, as the Distressed Prophet Gained Understanding*. While God is central in the first of these sixty-six verses, the core message is about a prophet whose pain led him to praise God and have confidence in His justice. A striking parallel to Jeremiah's struggle is seen in Jeremiah 11—20.

Chapter 4: *The Cost of Sin, Presented by Internal Decay and Ruin*. Contrasts illustrate how far the nation had fallen. The chapter depicts life in its most horrifying circumstances (4:1–12). Causes for the corruption are identified (4:13–16). The people's dire situation resulted in the prophet's being drawn into their wretchedness (4:17–22).

Chapter 5: *The Cause, Leading to Penitence, and a Plea*. The text provides a survey of where sin had taken God's people. The prophet wanted God to remember Judah's suffering (5:1–10). We see that the price paid by varied groups (5:11–18) had brought God's people to their knees; they were ready to submit to God's reign, seeking His restoration and renewal (5:19–22).

These five chapters show the devastating fruits of sin and enable us to see people in various stages of suffering. The prophet was grieving but growing; the nation was knocked to its knees in stupefying pain. God is both identified as the cause and justified as sin-confessing souls woke up to the truth that the Lord was their portion and their hope (3:24). That is the positive mes-

INTRODUCTION

sage in these scenes of pain and horror. L. L. Gieger summarized the negative aspect of Lamentations:

> Unhappy Judah was in anguish; the fragments of her national glory littered the ground; honor had been dragged in the dirt to Babylon; unbelievers in God were having a field day of mockery; and, each thought in Jeremiah's mind caused a new outburst of tears.[19]

Key Verses

Key verses highlight messages that are contained in the book.

1:8: "Jerusalem sinned greatly, therefore she has become an unclean thing." (See Prov. 6:27; 14:34; Is. 30:1; Jer. 17:1.) We dare not ignore the corrupting nature of sin! Have we decided to be pure in our walk and talk before God and man? (See Tit. 2:7, 8.)

2:5: "The Lord has become like an enemy. He has swallowed up Israel." (See Num. 32:23; Prov. 1:24–32; Is. 59:1, 2; Amos 1:3, 6, 9, 11.) God's mercy only lingers so long; payday will come someday! Have we obtained His grace or mercy for that great day? (See Heb. 4:14–16.)

3:40: "Let us examine and probe our ways, and let us return to the Lord." (See Ps. 119:59, 60; Is. 55:6–9.) To bring His people back to Him has ever been God's good and worthy goal. We must test ourselves to see if we are in the faith. (See 2 Cor. 13:5; Gal. 3:26, 27.)

4:11: "The Lord has accomplished His wrath, He has poured out His fierce anger; and He has kindled a fire in Zion which has consumed its foundation." (See Ex. 34:7; Num. 14:18; Rom. 2:4–9.) Their refusal to repent led to their destruction (see Lk. 13:3, 5). How sad that God had to go that far before righteousness could be restored in the land! (See Gen. 6:5–7; Ps. 14:2, 3; 53:2, 3; Rom. 3:9–11.) Does God need to exercise His wrath toward us, or do we stand in righteousness before Him? (See Eph. 4:22–24; Col. 3:5, 6.)

5:21: "Restore us to You, O Lord, that we may be restored;

---

[19]Gieger, 330.

renew our days as of old." (See Ps. 51:7–13; Is. 58:5–12; Joel 2:12–14.) God's righteous (though destructive) acts are justified by this response of a sinful people, who, like the prodigal (who came to himself), longed for restoration and renewal (see Ezra 1:7, 8; 5:13, 14; 7:9, 19; Is. 1:24–26; Jer. 27:19–22; Lk. 15:11–17). Are we living as Christians (see Rom. 6:3–11; 2 Cor. 5:17), or do we need to come to our senses, to be restored and renewed?

These key verses cover the scope of human relationships before a good, just, and righteous God. From a richly endowed nation that had attained a special place before God and man ("a princess among the provinces"; 1:1), Judah fell to a degenerate and despised people (1:3, 6). This nation represents the separate poles of righteousness and rebellion. The people's iniquity was greater than the sin of Sodom (4:6). With only a memory of her "precious things" (1:7), Judah groveled in confusion and suffered to the point that desperate hunger led women who had once been compassionate to boil and eat their own children (2:20; 4:10).

SUMMARY

All who have been honored (1:8; 2:15) but have fallen shamefully (1:12; 4:3–5); all who have wandered (4:14, 15) and worried (1:20; 2:11); all who have dared to question God (2:20, 21), only to find Him righteous (3:21–25, 55–58); all who would seek restoration to God (5:19–22)—let these come to a study of this book. It presents in a most practical setting the summary of these emotions, these frustrations and fears, these troubles and tears, while holding up a confident trust that God is equal to those occasions. He can lift us up from the greatest tests and trials that we may find in the flesh. Within this book is a broad range of wisdom awaiting the careful student.

THE EXPANDED OUTLINE
LAMENTATIONS

I. **THE CITY, A SCENARIO OF SUFFERING FROM SIN (1)**
   A. The City Seen in Contrasts (1:1)
   B. Conditions of Misery (1:2–5a)
   C. The Cause and Cost of the Conditions (1:5b–9b)
      1. The cause (1:5b)
      2. The cost (1:5c–9b)
   D. The Concern for the Collapse (1:9c–17)
      1. The disaster viewed (1:9c–11)
      2. The afflictions rehearsed (1:12, 13)
      3. The situation assessed (1:14–17)
   E. God's Integrity and Judah's Sin (1:18–22)

II. **THE CREATOR, THE ONE WHO CAUSED THE DESTRUCTION AND DESOLATION (2)**
   A. Scenes of National Disaster (2:1–10)
      1. The scene of the nation (2:1–3)
      2. The scene of the city (2:4, 5)
      3. The scene of the sanctuary (2:6, 7)
      4. The scene of the wall (2:8, 9a)
      5. The scene of the punished leaders (2:9b, 10)
   B. The Prophet's View and the People's Plight (2:11–13)
   C. The Prophets as the Cause (2:14)
   D. The Celebration of the Enemy (2:15, 16)
   E. The Purpose of the Lord (2:17)
   F. The Solemn Need Stated (2:18, 19)
   G. The Prophet's Cry for Relief (2:20–22)

III. THE CRY, AS THE DISTRESSED PROPHET GAINED UNDERSTANDING (3)
A. Cries of Concern—His Pain (3:1–18)
1. The condition of the prophet (3:1a)
2. The cause (in the prophet's eyes) of his pain (3:1b–13)
3. The cost of his relationship with the Creator (3:14–18)
B. Cries of Concern—His Insight (3:19–38)
1. The remembering (3:19–26)
2. The response to the recall (3:27–30)
3. The relationship of God to man now in focus (3:31–38)
C. Cries of Concern—His Confession (3:39–47)
D. Cries of Concern—His Growth (3:48–58)
1. The condition of his incessant weeping (3:48, 49)
2. The cause for the weeping (3:50–54)
3. The call that comforted him (3:55–58)
E. Cries of Concern—His Conviction (3:59–66)

IV. THE COST OF SIN, PRESENTED BY INTERNAL DECAY AND RUIN (4)
A. Pillage and Pain (4:1–10)
1. The temple's destruction (4:1)
2. The people's rejection (4:2)
3. The people's starvation (4:3, 4)
4. The people's degradation (4:5–8)
5. The people's ultimate corruption (4:9, 10)
B. Their Punishment and the Power of God (4:11–16)
1. God's anger (4:11, 12)
2. The leaders' sins (4:13–15)
3. God's scattering (4:16)
C. A Deceived Nation (4:17–20)
D. Hope in the Midst of Punishment (4:21, 22)

V. THE CAUSE, LEADING TO PENITENCE, AND A PLEA (5)
A. "See Our Reproach" (5:1)
B. "We Have Lost 'Our Inheritance'" (5:2–10)

THE EXPANDED OUTLINE

      1. Perils with their property (5:2)
      2. Perils of the people (5:3)
      3. Perils as to supplies (5:4)
      4. Perils from pursuers (5:5)
      5. Perils of starving (5:6)
      6. Perils as to their heritage of iniquity (5:7)
      7. Perils as to social standing (5:8)
      8. Perils of moving about (5:9)
      9. Perils of trying to survive (5:10)
C. "The Crown Has Fallen from Our Head" (5:11–16a)
D. "Woe to Us, for We Have Sinned" (5:16b–18)
E. "You, O Lord, Rule Forever" (5:19–22)

Chapter 1
A City Suffering from Sin

Lamentations portrays pain and destruction. "The first chapter of Lamentations creates a topography of pain. With two voices it maps the heights and depths, the contours and colors of Daughter Zion's suffering."[1] The disaster and desolation that lay before the prophet were viewed from different vantage points and by different personalities within the book, with flickers of hope that a better day would dawn (3:21, 24). These harbingers of hope were largely muffled by cries of concern as the prophet lamented the remains of Judah's golden past. Jeremiah specifically recorded the plights of royalty, priests, mothers, and daughters following the destruction of Jerusalem.

Jerusalem was the focal point for all the sorrow. This is evident by the phrasing in this chapter. "Jerusalem" is named 3 times (1:7, 8, 17), "Zion" 3 times (1:4, 6, 17), and "the city" 2 times (1:1, 19); and pronouns referring to the city ("she," "her," "me," "my," "I," "herself") occur more than 80 times in twenty-two verses.

The personification of a city as a woman is a common metaphor in prophetic literature, but "nowhere is it developed more effectively than in the personification of Jerusalem in this chapter."[2] In verses 1 through 11, the third-person feminine pronominal forms ("she" and "her") dominate.[3]

---

[1] Kathleen M. O'Connor, *Lamentations and the Tears of the World* (Maryknoll, N.Y.: Orbis Books, 2002), 28.

[2] Adele Berlin, *Lamentations*, Old Testament Library (Louisville, Ky.: Westminster John Knox Press, 2004), 47.

[3] F. W. Dobbs-Allsopp, *Lamentations*, Interpretation (Louisville, Ky.: John Knox Press, 2002), 49.

THE CITY SEEN IN CONTRASTS (1:1)

¹How lonely sits the city
That was full of people!
She has become like a widow
Who was once great among the nations!
She who was a princess among the provinces
Has become a forced laborer!

Verse 1. This book opens with a distressing description of Jerusalem. Kathleen M. O'Connor phrased it this way: "Lamentations opens upon a universe of sorrow."[4] The opening word in the Hebrew text, **how** (אֵיכָה, *'eykah*), is exclamatory, not necessarily an interrogative, and frequently introduces distressful or painful circumstances. The prophet Isaiah also used the word in describing Jerusalem's unfaithfulness: "How the faithful city has become a harlot, she who was full of justice! Righteousness once lodged in her, but now murderers" (Is. 1:21; see Jer. 48:17; Eccles. 2:1; 4:1, 2). F. W. Dobbs-Allsopp has said that the figure of the personified **city** is "the most compellingly drawn figure in the whole of Lamentations."[5]

Images of Jerusalem before and after the destruction are contrasted in this verse: before, **full of people** (populated)—after, **lonely** (desolate); before, **great among the nations** (acclaimed, well known)—after, **a widow** (alone, forsaken); before, **a princess among the provinces**[6] (renown)—after, **a forced laborer**[7] (a slave).

---

[4]O'Connor, 17.
[5]Dobbs-Allsopp, 50.
[6]"The opening verse of the book introduces us abruptly to the tragic reversal of Zion. Formerly she was a populous and honoured city, comparable to a princess. Now she is depopulated, humiliated and subject to vassalage, to be likened to a lonely widow" (Norman K. Gottwald, *Studies in the Book of Lamentations*, Studies in Biblical Theology No. 14, rev. ed. [London: SCM Press, 1962], 56).
[7]The Hebrew word מַס (*mas*) is rendered "forced labourer," in reference to "corvée, conscription" (Ludwig Koehler and Walter Baumgartner, *The Hebrew and Aramaic Lexicon of the Old Testament*, study ed., trans and ed. M. E. J. Richardson [Boston: Brill, 2001], 1:603). The NRSV translates the word as "vassal," but Iain Provan said this is a weak translation. (Iain Provan, *Lamentations*, The New Century Bible Commentary [Grand Rapids, Mich.: Wm. B. Eerdmans Publishing Co., 1991], 36.)

The loneliness here is more than being solitary or forsaken. The very word used for "lonely" (בָּדָד, *badad*)[8] implies a cutting or tearing apart from a former situation in which Zion had been filled with prominent, honored people. She now sat in a ghostly solitude of wretchedness, helpless and hopeless, in a monotony of despair. The people had been taken into exile, where they could contemplate what had been lost and painfully measure their failure and faithlessness. They had been battered from significance into slavery. The elite had become the enslaved. What costly contrasts were presented to God's prophet!

CONDITIONS OF MISERY (1:2–5a)

²She weeps bitterly in the night
And her tears are on her cheeks;
She has none to comfort her
Among all her lovers.
All her friends have dealt treacherously with her;
They have become her enemies.
³Judah has gone into exile under affliction
And under harsh servitude;
She dwells among the nations,
But she has found no rest;
All her pursuers have overtaken her
In the midst of distress.
⁴The roads of Zion are in mourning
Because no one comes to the appointed feasts.
All her gates are desolate;
Her priests are groaning,
Her virgins are afflicted,
And she herself is bitter.
⁵ᵃHer adversaries have become her masters,
Her enemies prosper.

---

[8]The basic idea of the Hebrew word is "solitariness," or isolation. (Ernst Jenni and Claus Westermann, "בָּדָד," in *Theological Lexicon of the Old Testament*, trans. Mark E. Biddle [Peabody, Mass.: Hendriksen, 1997], 1:300.)

As a weeping widow, the city was statuesque in sorrow, petrified by fear, remaining terribly awake. "The image gains particular force when we remember the poverty and social stigma of widowhood in the ancient Near East (Isa. 1:23; 10:2; Ezek. 22:7; Lev. 21:14; 1 Kings 17:10–12; Job 24:3, 21)."[9]

Verse 2. In the night she was like one who **weeps bitterly** (בָּכוֹ תִבְכֶּה, *bako thibkeh*; literally, "weeping she weeps"). Such weeping expresses grief, humiliation, and mourning.[10] She had **none to comfort her**. The tragedy of Jerusalem was intensified by reason of its contrast with the previous splendor during the glory days of the shepherd king, David, and the spreading reputation gained through the wisdom, power, and prosperity Solomon had brought to the holy city.

Other rulers loved to draw from her strengths and standards, whereas now **her lovers** and **friends . . . dealt treacherously with her**. The Hebrew word for "treacherously" comes from בָּגַד (*bagad*). Behavior of this type might include dealing "faithlessly, deceitfully in covenants, in word and in general conduct."[11]

This weeping widow imagery served as a backdrop for a coin minted hundreds of years later to commemorate Jerusalem's destruction in A.D. 70, when the Roman emperor Vespasian and his son Titus conquered and razed the city and destroyed the temple. Emperor Vespasian's likeness was on the front of the coin, and the reverse depicted a mourning Jewess and a Roman soldier beside a palm tree (the symbol for Judea).[12]

The husband whom the weeping widow had lost was the Lord Himself, the generous provider, the gentle protector, the God of love. That love, she had refused to respect and return (see Jer. 2:20–22; 3:1–5; Ezek. 16:23–32).[13]

---

[9]Gottwald, 56.

[10]Francis Brown, S. R. Driver, and Charles A. Briggs, *A Hebrew and English Lexicon of the Old Testament* (Oxford: Clarendon Press, 1972), 113.

[11]Ibid., 93.

[12]Several *Judaea Capta* coins were minted by Vespasian in commemoration of the conquest of Judea. His image was on the front of each; the back of one of these coins depicted the soldier, the palm tree, and the mourning Jewess.

[13]John Guest, *Jeremiah, Lamentations*, Communicator's Commentary (Waco, Tex.: Word Books, 1988), 357.

Verse 3. As to her helpers, there were "none to comfort her" (1:2). As to her citizens, they had **gone into exile**. Pain is tripled when one grieves deeply, no one shares in his sorrow, and his calamity finds him on foreign soil. Iain Provan saw the reference to **Judah** as "hyperbolic," indicating that many Judeans went into exile.[14] Jeremiah had seen enough to know that, as to her life, it would be one of **harsh servitude**. This would be slave labor, coupled with the harshness of excessive demands enforced by many blows. As to location, the people had been scattered among Babylon and other **nations**. Keeping the family together was no promised option. In their fear and flight, they were **overtaken** by their **pursuers** ("persecutors"; KJV). "Pursuers" is from רָדַף (*radap*), which means an attempt to "overtake with hostile purpose"; it suggests the idea of chasing a defeated foe (see Deut. 30:7; Jer. 20:11).[15] In taking them captive and relocating them, the conquerors gave no consideration to the preference or convenience of the conquered people.

She has found no rest echoes Deuteronomy 28:64, 65 which is also a description of exile. However we might view these conquered creatures, they were **in the midst of distress**. The word translated "distress," מֵצַר (*metsar*), springs from the Hebrew root idea of binding or tying; it implies being restricted, shut up, cramped, impeded, in straits, or pressed hard.[16] These ideas summarize the combined crunch that the people of Judah felt as they were conquered by Babylon.

Verse 4. No wonder all **the roads of Zion** [were] **in mourning** because of such treatment and **all her gates** were left **desolate**. The Hebrew word for "desolate" is שָׁמֵם (*shamem*), which means to be uninhabited or deserted to the extent of causing onlookers to be appalled or confused.[17] This term pictures both the shameful landscape of nothingness and the jarring impact such a scene makes on anyone who views it. As to the personnel who watched and endured the devastation of Judah, **priests**

---

[14] Provan, 38.
[15] Brown, Driver, and Briggs, 922–23.
[16] Ibid., 865.
[17] Koehler and Baumgartner, 2:1563–66.

[were] **groaning** and **virgins** [were] **afflicted** with grief (1:5, 12), building a disposition that was **bitter** (מָרַר, *marar*). This last term involves becoming distressed, having bitter hostility, or being enraged.[18]

For false prophets and priests to have suffered (see 4:13) seems justified, but how sad it is that virgins were afflicted so! For eighteen to nineteen years Judah and Jerusalem had been under Babylon's domination. Many pure, young women who could have grown gracefully into womanhood were robbed of social favors. Such perils may even have discouraged marriage and motherhood (see Jer. 16:1–9). The final fall of Judah had ushered in complete enslavement and captivity, circumstances in which young women would likely be sexually abused. Therefore, it is not surprising that the prophet would make a special note of virgins being afflicted and grieving.

Verse 5a. Her adversaries (צָר, *tsar*) had become **her masters**. It must have been painful for Judah to see her wicked **enemies prosper**. The word "prosper" (שָׁלָה, *shalah*) is defined as being "quiet," "at ease," "tranquil," "content," or "free."[19] The disposition that is unveiled here begets two-pronged pain. Not only were God's people in deep distress, but to see their adversaries free, at ease, and prospering—with Judah's own treasures and "precious things" (1:7)—doubled the pain.

These conditions made the general populace seethe with hostility. The situation seemed even graver when the prophet viewed the real cause and cost, as covered in the next verses.

THE CAUSE AND COST OF THE CONDITIONS (1:5b–9b)

The Cause (1:5b)

> [5b]**For the LORD has caused her grief**
> **Because of the multitude of her transgressions.**

---

[18]Ibid., 1:638–39.
[19]Brown, Driver, and Briggs, 1017.

Verse 5b. The cause was twofold: **The Lord [had] caused her grief.** The Bible states that God will judge His own people (Deut. 32:35; Heb. 10:30) and scourge every child He receives (Prov. 3:11, 12; Heb. 12:5, 6). In one brief reflection, the prophet looked beyond the visible force of Nebuchadnezzar and his hosts to the truth of God's justice at work in Judah's suffering. This thought would be developed in later descriptions (1:12; 2:1, 3, 22; 4:11, 16); but in this context it left with the suddenness with which it had appeared, permitting the current conditions to be given due emphasis. The prophet repeatedly returned to God's justice as being at work because that fact was the real key to unlocking the mystery of this whole tragedy (see 4:12; Ezek. 33:23–29). God never enacts such scourging without reason.

God had so acted **because of the multitude of her transgressions** (פֶּשַׁע, *pesha'*). Jerusalem had rebelled[20] and sinned greatly (1:8). The term translated "transgressions" is a strong word in Hebrew. It implies much more than erring or crossing over some line. It involves a knowledge of law and willfully rebelling against it. This word "signifies a rebellion against an overlord, in a political sense (2 Kgs 1:1; 3:5), and also, in a religious sense, a rebellion against God."[21] Here Judah's rebellion was being reviewed; the people were now reaping what they had sown (Gal. 6:7, 8). God's anger over Judah's transgressions and sin resulted in a unthinkable cost. Sin is referred to six times in chapter 1, far more frequently than in subsequent chapters. The author was "interested in acknowledging the reality of communal sin and guilt."[22]

The Cost (1:5c–9b)

> [5c]**Her little ones have gone away
> As captives before the adversary.
> [6]All her majesty
> Has departed from the daughter of Zion;**

---

[20]Koehler and Baumgartner, 2:981.
[21]Berlin, 53.
[22]Dobbs-Allsopp, 61.

Her princes have become like deer
That have found no pasture;
And they have fled without strength
Before the pursuer.
⁷In the days of her affliction and homelessness
Jerusalem remembers all her precious things
That were from the days of old,
When her people fell into the hand of the adversary
And no one helped her.
The adversaries saw her,
They mocked at her ruin.
⁸Jerusalem sinned greatly,
Therefore she has become an unclean thing.
All who honored her despise her
Because they have seen her nakedness;
Even she herself groans and turns away.
⁹ᵃ, ᵇHer uncleanness was in her skirts;
She did not consider her future.
Therefore she has fallen astonishingly;
She has no comforter.

Verses 5c, 6. Their **little ones** had gone into captivity **before the adversary**. The little ones were victims of the adults' transgressions, suffering as slaves, not for their own wrongdoing, but because they were the children of rebellious parents. For little ones to be suffering in a strange land under the control of adversaries caused the greatest of sadness. Forms of the word for "adversary" occur at the beginning and at the end of verse 5, surrounding the thoughts of captives just as the enemies had surrounded the city.

All of Judah's grandeur and glory, might and **majesty**, had **departed**. The Hebrew word translated "departed," יָצָא (*yatsa'*), has the connotation of going out "as a criminal" or being "condemned."[23] Her "beauty" (KJV) had been lost. **Her princes**, the natural source for national strength, were seen falling from starvation. Provan says that "princes" in today's usage means

---

[23]Brown, Driver, and Briggs, 422–25.

"sons of kings," which is not true of the Hebrew word here; a better translation would be "leaders."[24]

Verse 7. Homeless and afflicted, her people had only the memory of **her precious things** and the mockery by her **adversaries**—the **mock**[ing] **at her ruin.** The KJV has "sabbaths" in place of "ruin." The word is מִשְׁבַּת (*mishbath*), which means "cessation." The Hebrew term most likely refers to the cessation of their religious rituals. Many of these rituals revolved around the sabbath observances. C. F. Keil and F. Delitzsch seem to have captured the idea better than anyone else:

> The mockery of enemies does not apply to the Jewish celebration of the Sabbath . . . , but to the cessation of the public worship of the Lord, inasmuch as the heathen, by destroying Jerusalem and the temple, fancied they had not only put an end to the worship of the God of the Jews, but also conquered the God of Israel as a helpless national deity, and made a [mockery] of Israel's faith in . . . the only true God.[25]

Verses 8–9b. The sad fact was that Judah had **sinned greatly**, becoming **an unclean thing** in three areas: *She had lost her purity* (1:8). **Her nakedness** was exposed by both physical and spiritual immorality. "Nakedness" is from עֶרְוָה (*'erwah*), implying "shameful exposure," "indecency," or "improper behaviour."[26] She had gone after many gods (Jer. 2:28; 11:13), and adultery had become a common lifestyle, so that **uncleanness was in her skirts** (Jer. 5:6–8; 9:2).

She had lost her vision (1:9a). **She did not consider her future** (see Jer. 5:31). A hunger for the pleasures of the present can crucify any convictions for the future (Mt. 26:24, 25; 27:3–5; Heb. 11:24–26).

She had lost her power (1:9b). From their status as an honor-

---

[24]Provan, 41.
[25]C. F. Keil and F. Delitzsch, *Commentary on the Old Testament*, vol. 8, *Jeremiah, Lamentations* (Grand Rapids, Mich.: Wm. B. Eerdmans Publishing Co., n.d.), 364–65.
[26]Brown, Driver, and Briggs, 788–89.

able and strong nation, they had **fallen astonishingly** (see Deut. 32:23–30). Instead of seeing victory, they had become distressed victims. Sin has ever become the undoing of those who could have had salvation!

THE CONCERN FOR THE COLLAPSE (1:9c–17)

These verses unveil the painful perception of divine retribution upon a sinful city. The people wanted the Lord to see what had happened to them (1:9, 11, 12). They declared that He had brought this tragedy upon them in His fierce anger (1:12), giving His people into the hands of enemies against whom the daughter of Judah could not stand (1:14). Eight times in verses 12 through 17, the pronouns "He" and "His" point to God as the ultimate cause of this disaster. Twenty times, the pronouns "I," "me," and "my" declare that it was Jacob, or the virgin daughter of Judah—metaphors for God's people—to whom these things were done.

The Disaster Viewed (1:9c–11)

⁹ᶜ"See, O Lᴏʀᴅ, my affliction,
For the enemy has magnified himself!"
¹⁰The adversary has stretched out his hand
Over all her precious things,
For she has seen the nations enter her sanctuary,
The ones whom You commanded
That they should not enter into Your congregation.
¹¹All her people groan seeking bread;
They have given their precious things for food
To restore their lives themselves.
"See, O Lᴏʀᴅ, and look,
For I am despised."

Verses 9c–11. The description of this disaster is approached from four viewpoints: The first is *defeat* (1:9c). **The enemy** [had] **magnified himself.** "Magnified" is from גָּדַל (*gadal*), which implies growing up to become great or to do great things.[27] Here we find images of power, pressure, and punishment. The enemy's hands had grabbed Judah's precious possessions.

The second is *desecration* (1:10). The enemy had **enter[ed] into her sanctuary**, the place where only the priests were to go (Num. 18:1–7; Ps. 74:4–8; Is. 64:11; Jer. 51:51). **Precious things** from even the temple were gathered and transported to Babylon for foolish purposes (2 Kings 24:12, 13; 25:8–17; Dan. 5:1–4).

The third is *diet* (1:11). The **people groan[ed], seeking bread**. Various passages identify the severity of starvation: When all bread was gone (Jer. 37:21), hunger pains led women to eat their own children (Jer. 19:9; Lam. 2:20; 4:10). Fellow Jews ate one another! This horror was avoidable, for God had warned the people against these tragic events in the days of Moses (Deut. 28:53–55).

The fourth is *despised* (1:11). They were **despised**. The Hebrew word for "despise," זָלַל (*zalal*), means "be in ruins," "be worthless, in-significant."[28] This term can also be defined, to "cause to shake" or to "be of low value," to "be contemptible" or "vile."[29] As expressed by this term, the people were left trembling and measured as worthless and vile. A careful reading of 1:11–17 shows that the prophet's use of "I," "me," and "my" refers to God's people in the first person. This entire section is an outcry of the woes of "the virgin daughter of Judah" (1:15). It shows what the Lord had commanded concerned Jacob and Jerusalem (1:17). The strong men and young men in verse 15 belonged to Judah, not to Jeremiah. Becoming unclean, God's people had sunk into great shame!

The Afflictions Rehearsed (1:12, 13)

> [12]"Is it nothing to all you who pass this way?
> Look and see if there is any pain like my pain
> Which was severely dealt out to me,

---

[27]Koehler and Baumgartner, 1:179.
[28]Brown, Driver, and Briggs, 272–73.
[29]Koehler and Baumgartner, 1:272.

> Which the L ORD inflicted on the day of His fierce anger.
> ¹³From on high He sent fire into my bones,
> And it prevailed over them.
> He has spread a net for my feet;
> He has turned me back;
> He has made me desolate,
> Faint all day long."

Verse 12. The people longed for their suffering to be seen. From verse 12 to the end of the chapter, Jerusalem is depicted as the speaker. The people were crying for understanding and sympathy. O'Connor argued that the word "passerby" is used frequently in Hebrew poetry "for witnesses of suffering and devastation."[30] The context does not imply injustice, but these hurting souls who longed for some help were met only by taunts. Those who desired for someone to share in their grief heard only roadside gloating (see 2:15; Jer. 18:16; 19:8; Ezek. 33:28, 29). We can almost hear in this verse an agonizing cry like that of Job: "Pity me, pity me, O you my friends, for the hand of God has struck me. Why do you persecute me as God does, and are not satisfied with my flesh?" (Job 19:21, 22).

The source of their suffering is clearly expressed as the Lord's **fierce anger** (2:1, 3, 21, 22; 3:1). Though righteous Job was confused in charging God as the source of his suffering (the devil was the real cause; Job 2:3, 7), Judah's sins had caused His anger to move against them. This was a necessary step to cleanse them from their uncleanness (see Ezek. 23:25–49). When God's anger reaches this level, there can be no arguments—only acceptance. Norman K. Gottwald well said, "Central to the whole matter of the inter-relation of suffering, sin, and wrath is the direct activity of Yahweh in the city's destruction. Sin against God has aroused the divine wrath and that wrath has inflicted punishment without measure or mercy."[31]

Verse 13. The types of suffering are here presented: *It was an internal burning*—**He sent fire into my bones.** This type of wound

---

[30] O'Connor, 25.
[31] Gottwald, 73.

is no superficial or skin-deep suffering. It penetrates to the very marrow, where the pain cannot be quenched. This metaphor is a description of deep misery.

There were external snares—**He has spread a net for my feet.** No feet could be fast enough to escape from His net. This metaphor is of a hunter spreading his net to capture prey.

They faced inescapable justice—**He has turned me back.** The Hebrew word translated "turned back" (שׁוּב, *shub*) can mean to "be repulsed, defeated" or to "turn back to God" in penitence (see 1:8; 3:3; Jer. 3:7).[32] Gottwald insisted that "turn back" and repentance are the same: "It may be assumed that the frequent confession of sin in Lamentations presupposes repentance . . . a turning back to Yahweh."[33] This is a broad term, but in all its usages the implied demands are reassuring that someone—God, in this case—is in control. It is always in His power to repel. Judah hurt because they had refused to obey Him.

Isolated conditions had become a reality—**He has made me desolate.** "Desolate" involves more than being deserted. The deeper meaning is of one devastated, appalled, and awestruck (see comments on 1:2–4). Though Jeremiah and other prophets had warned of this disaster for more than twenty years, Judah and Jerusalem were shockingly unprepared for the crushing blow.

Constant surges of sickness and sadness had come—The people had been made **faint all day long**. The term "faint" (דָּוָה, *daweh*)[34] is, by usage, a blend of sickness, impurity, and uncleanness (see 5:17). It is the weak feeling that especially comes from sickness in the soul and spirit as well as in the body.

The Situation Assessed (1:14–17)

¹⁴"The yoke of my transgressions is bound;
By His hand they are knit together.
They have come upon my neck;
He has made my strength fail.

---

[32]Brown, Driver, and Briggs, 996–1000.
[33]Gottwald, 103.
[34]Brown, Driver, and Briggs, 188.

> The Lord has given me into the hands
> Of those against whom I am not able to stand.
> ¹⁵The Lord has rejected all my strong men
> In my midst;
> He has called an appointed time against me
> To crush my young men;
> The Lord has trodden as in a wine press
> The virgin daughter of Judah.
> ¹⁶For these things I weep;
> My eyes run down with water;
> Because far from me is a comforter,
> One who restores my soul.
> My children are desolate
> Because the enemy has prevailed."
> ¹⁷Zion stretches out her hands;
> There is no one to comfort her;
> The LORD has commanded concerning Jacob
> That the ones round about him should be his adversaries;
> Jerusalem has become an unclean thing among them.

Verse 14. The divine determination was painfully accepted. Judah had absolutely no defense. The people's helplessness is vividly described.

They had been guilty of sin. Like a massive burden bound upon their necks, their **transgressions** ("rebellions") had sapped their **strength**, giving them into the hands of Babylon's forces. Like Samson, when his folly caused God's strength to be taken from him (Judg. 16:5–21), Judah's sins had left them unable **to stand**. R. K. Harrison saw the heaviness of this burden:

> The passage implies that the iniquities of Jerusalem have been compounded, and are weighing her down like a heavy yoke on the neck of an animal. Such a crushing burden effectively prevents the city from eluding the punishment which she so richly deserves.³⁵

---

³⁵R. K. Harrison, *Jeremiah and Lamentations: An Introduction and Commentary*, Tyndale Old Testament Commentaries (Downers Grove, Ill.: Inter-Varsity Press, 1973), 211.

LAMENTATIONS 1

Verse 15. No man or group of men were willing to defend them. Judah's **strong men** and **young men** had all been **rejected** (סָלָה, *salah*). The extent of this rejection is seen in the definition "make light of, toss aside"[36] (see Jer. 5:1–6). There were no redemptive skills or strengths in these souls; they were strapped to the consequences of their own sins. A terrible price was being paid by these polluted people, burdened by sins and crushed by their corruption. The graphic figure of speech portrays **the Lord** as the One who had **trodden as in a wine press the virgin daughter of Judah**. The word "virgin" is likely used in satire to refer to these guilty people (see Jer. 2:35; 8:5, 6; 44:16–19). We see here the scene of a dainty maiden being trampled to death by God as grapes are trampled to squeeze out the juice. Nevertheless, there is no intimation of barbarity, for transgressions hung heavily around their necks. They knew that the judgment of God was justified. Man's guilt is heavier than the Lord's graphic judgment.

Verse 16. The enemy had prevailed. Incessant weeping made tears fall like **water**. The melancholy was profound, being intensified because the **comforter** was far removed from their folly. It is tragic when sin separates souls from God (Is. 59:1, 2). A person's sin can form a mountain barrier between him and his Maker, even though our God is not far from each of us (Acts 17:27, 28).

Verse 17. Their alliances would not speak up for them. Though **Zion stretch[ed] out her hands** in a well-known expression of prayer and an appeal for comfort, both God and man had abandoned this defeated, despondent city and nation. The sad spectacle of surrender had **become an unclean thing**[37] **among them**. Even the pagan military commander who breached their walls and burned their city knew that they were sinners, reaping as they had sown (Jer. 40:1–3). They had manifested an air of holy superiority, holding a unique position with the God of heaven and earth (Ps. 115:1–15). However, they had allowed Satan to make them foul and despicable—in their own eyes (1:4,

---

[36]Brown, Driver, and Briggs, 699.
[37]This image is equivalent to "a menstrual rag" (O'Connor, 27).

8), in the eyes of neighboring nations, and in the eyes of God (Jer. 25:1–9; see Rom. 1:21–25).

GOD'S INTEGRITY AND JUDAH'S SIN (1:18–22)

> ¹⁸"The Lord is righteous;
> For I have rebelled against His command;
> Hear now, all peoples,
> And behold my pain;
> My virgins and my young men
> Have gone into captivity.
> ¹⁹I called to my lovers, but they deceived me;
> My priests and my elders perished in the city
> While they sought food to restore their strength themselves.
> ²⁰See, O Lord, for I am in distress;
> My spirit is greatly troubled;
> My heart is overturned within me,
> For I have been very rebellious.
> In the street the sword slays;
> In the house it is like death.
> ²¹They have heard that I groan;
> There is no one to comfort me;
> All my enemies have heard of my calamity;
> They are glad that You have done it.
> Oh, that You would bring the day which You have proclaimed,
> That they may become like me.
> ²²Let all their wickedness come before You;
> And deal with them as You have dealt with me
> For all my transgressions;
> For my groans are many and my heart is faint."

Beneath the burdens and shame of Judah's trauma, we find quietly woven through this section some fundamental principles. God was building a foundation that, in time, would produce penitence in His people. God's integrity was reaching out to redeem Judah from her iniquity.

Verse 18. A confession of contrast is given: God is **righteous**, but His people (**I**) had **rebelled against His command**. Their confession, seen in the first person singular as offered by Jerusalem, gives no proof that these people were ready to repent or reform. The Book of Jeremiah presents more than one lighthearted confession where no reformation was evident (see Jer. 14:1–10; 42:1–19; 43:1–7). However, confession is the first step that had to be taken in order for wayward children to return to God and His redeeming benefits (Jer. 29:10–14).

The great cost for their rebellion calls upon us to take to heart these events. This tragedy was huge enough, bearing such grave messages, that it ought to be noticed and considered by the nations, or **all peoples**. Uncircumcised heathens should be affected, and aliens were to take note of the crushing of this nation. They were to consider the reason why it had happened. How could God's chosen nation fall into pain and pillage? Shockingly, **young men** and **virgins** paid part of the price, wearing chains into captivity. God cared for these innocent souls, but they bore heavy burdens because of the nation's sin. Dramatic portrayals of God's care for the young captives are given in the Book of Daniel (see, for example, Dan. 1:1–21; 3:1–28).

Verse 19. Confusion came upon the scene because the people had depended on the creature more than the righteous Creator. They had called upon deceptive alliances rather than on Deity (Jer. 3:1, 2; 4:30; 37:6–10). Further, they had depended on degenerate leaders who hastened the nation's fall (Jer. 5:31; 6:13–15; 23:28–34). The fact that **priests** and **elders** had **perished** proved that they were no guarantee of national stability. Their conduct led to national starvation, illustrating the danger of placing undue trust in men (Rom. 3:4; 1 Jn. 4:1).

Verse 20. The people's cry to the Creator identifies their tragic conditions. In the heart of this unit we find the confession of sin and the cause of Judah's suffering: **For I have been very rebellious.** "Rebellious" is from מָרָה (*marah*), which means "contentious" and "disobedient."[38] All the infractions indicated by this broad term of wrongdoing, Judah had done—and even more (see Jer. 7:9, 10; 9:2–6). They wanted the Lord to see their

---

[38]Brown, Driver, and Briggs, 598.

distress, but nowhere do we see evidence that they cried for God to see their evil deeds and debauchery. It is a human characteristic to cry to God when we hurt, but we seek to hide from Him our sinful deeds.

This verse records Zion's appeal for God to observe their "distress": (1) **My spirit is greatly troubled.** Mixed-up and confused, she tried to sort out all the misery. (2) **My heart is overturned within me.** A "heart . . . overturned" within is like a face turning deathly pale (Jer. 30:6), a dance turning into mourning (Lam. 5:15), and comeliness being turned into corruption (Dan. 10:8; KJV). (3) **In the street the sword slays.** Public killings demonstrated the power and control of these pursuers. (4) **In the house it is like death.** In the presence of such violence, the people cowered in fear.

Verse 21. Within and without, the wickedness of war had left misery in its wake. This chapter is unified by an elongated **groan** (see 1:4, 8, 11, 21, 22). There was **no one to comfort** (see Ps. 142:1–4), even though God's wayward people said, **"All my enemies have heard of my calamity."** We might visualize a beaten man lying by the roadside as all those who see the battered, broken body just pass by with victorious disregard (see Lk. 10:30–32).

Indeed, the other nations' awareness of Judah's "calamity" resulted in more than disregard. As they saw this suffering, **they [were] glad.** The term used here expresses exulting and great joy as related to moments of celebration (see Ps. 35:9; Is. 61:10; 65:18; Zeph. 3:17). Judah's adversaries viewed the pillage and pain as marks of achievement, bringing gladness to their hearts. Such a setting lends deeper meaning to the expression that humanity can become so warped in their thinking that they "call evil good" (Is. 5:20).

Verse 22. While no charge is expressed relative to God's part in punishing Judah and Jerusalem for their rebellion and sin (1:5, 14, 18), this chapter unveils a cry for vengeance to be poured forth in equal measure upon their conquerors: **"Let all their wickedness come before You; and deal with them as You have dealt with me."** Any pain Judah had felt, Babylon should feel. Any misery man had imposed on them should be felt by the human agents pouring out God's wrath. Although this may not express the spirit and sentiments of Jesus in the Sermon on the Mount (see Mt. 5:38–42; Rom. 12:20, 21), it is fully within the expressed purpose that God had proclaimed through His prophet (see Jer. 25:9–11, 12–14; 51:24–37).

Overall, this chapter offers no solution for sin and its bitter fruits. Rather, it presents a city suffering, humbled before God. It portrays the pain and punishment imposed on those who had "sinned greatly" (1:8) and had been "very rebellious" (1:20).

APPLICATION

The Cost of Corruption (Ch. 1)

This is a chapter of grief and suffering, a distressed city, and a picture of the pouring out of God's fierce anger. God's sovereignty is introduced in chapter 1 and is more fully developed in chapter 2. Chapter 1 centers primarily on national or city-wide suffering for sin, the people's cries, and the cost of corruption. Here are sobering lessons to be learned.

The strength of sin brings destruction even to powerful and prominent people. In any society, those with such status as a princess (1:1), a prince (1:6), religious leaders (1:4), the honored (1:8), or strong young men (1:15) may—through sin—be brought low. Such people in Judah were left groaning, despised, rejected, subject to forced labor, crushed, starved, and slaughtered. When the clean becomes unclean, he soon falls astonishingly (1:8, 9; 2 Tim. 3:6–9). Sin is like a yoke around one's neck, a burden that saps one's strength, leaving him to weep in shame, unable to stand (1:14, 16). May our leaders, our gifted and blessed people, carefully look at sin's strength and flee from it (see Ps. 11:1–3; Prov. 28:17, 18; Jer. 48:6, 7; Jn. 10:4, 5; 1 Cor. 6:18; 10:14; 1 Tim. 6:10–12).

Sin causes innocent people to suffer. What sin does to the sinner is horrifying enough, but the pain a person's sin can impose on others brings deeper shame on those who practice it. Virgins were afflicted (1:4); and they, along with the young men, were forced to go into captivity (1:5, 18). Later, the text shows how little ones and infants fainted, pleading for food and drink (2:11, 12). They were even eaten by adults (4:10; Jer. 19:8, 9). Such are the fruits of sin. How hollow and unfounded is the sinner's claim that his vile deeds are not hurting anyone! (See Mt. 18:1–7.)

Answering to God is part of the sobering price to be paid for sin. The chapter repeatedly touches on this divine truth (1:5, 12–17, 21, 22). Like a golden thread, this warning is interwoven throughout God's Word (Num. 32:23; Eccles. 12:13, 14; Rom. 14:10–12; 2 Cor. 5:10; Heb. 9:27; Rev. 20:11–15). Each of us will give an answer to God (see Mt. 28:18–20; Acts 4:12; Col. 3:17; Heb. 5:8, 9).

When we are caught in a web of wickedness, God is the only source of comfort. That the fruits of sin cause sinners to cry for comfort is evident. The absence of a comforter is frequently shouted (1:2, 9, 16, 17, 21). The writer had one particular Comforter in mind—the "one who restores my soul" (1:16). However, at this point, He was far away.

Paul affirmed that the Lord is the "God of all comfort" (2 Cor. 1:3–7). Jesus referred to the Holy Spirit as a "Comforter" (ASV) or "Helper" (NASB) in John 14:16, 26; 15:26; 16:7. This source of comfort should be a supreme incentive to obey the Lord so that the Spirit might dwell within us (see Acts 2:38; 5:32; Rom. 5:1–5; 8:26–28; Gal. 5:22; 2 Tim. 1:14). Only then we can have peace instead of pain, and comfort instead of condemnation.

Chapter 2
The City and Its Creator

The second chapter, like the first, starts with the exclamatory "How . . . !" and flows through multiple scenes of misery. In 2:1–10, this consuming fire and crushing defeat are attributed to the Almighty. He is often referred to as "Lord" or "Lord" (8 times), along with the pronouns "He" (23 times) and "His" (14 times). In rapid-fire succession, references associate God with the suffering and slaughter. God is repeatedly identified as the source of the hardships that had come upon this city and its people. In these verses, the victims of this violence (2:6) are identified as "the daughter of Zion" (4 times), "Zion" (once), "daughter of Judah" (2 times), "Judah" (once), "Jacob" (2 times), "Israel" (3 times), or by the pronoun forms "its" (3 times) and "her" (6 times). The motivation for God's march against His people is clearly expressed as His anger, or wrath (2:1 [2 times], 2, 3, 4, 6). John Guest highlighted God as a warrior against His people in 2:1–10:

> God is the dread warrior, not fighting for Jerusalem this time, but against her. The air is filled with smoke because He has blazed against the city wall. It is no longer a great rampart. It burns; houses burn, palaces burn, even the sanctuary burns. Starving infants choke in the street. A mighty arm has swept across Jerusalem, tumbling her walls like a house of cards. The poetry rises to a peak of literary excellence.[1]

---

[1] John Guest, *Jeremiah, Lamentations*, Communicator's Commentary (Waco, Tex.: Word Books, 1988), 351.

Following his graphic portrayal of the scene (2:1–10),[2] the sorrow-stricken prophet expressed his feelings concerning the people's dilemma (2:11–13). The sobering cause of their suffering is given in verse 14, followed by a scene of celebration by the enemy (2:15, 16). The suffering is then summarized as the Lord's purpose (2:17). As horrifying as the hurt had been to Judah, their solemn need was to turn to God, as stated in verses 18 and 19. The closing scene in this lament unfolds as the prophet cried to God for relief (2:20–22).

SCENES OF NATIONAL DISASTER
(2:1–10)

The Scene of the Nation (2:1–3)

> [1]**How the Lord has covered the daughter of Zion**
> **With a cloud in His anger!**
> **He has cast from heaven to earth**
> **The glory of Israel,**
> **And has not remembered His footstool**
> **In the day of His anger.**
> [2]**The Lord has swallowed up; He has not spared**
> **All the habitations of Jacob.**
> **In His wrath He has thrown down**
> **The strongholds of the daughter of Judah;**
> **He has brought them down to the ground;**
> **He has profaned the kingdom and its princes.**
> [3]**In fierce anger He has cut off**
> **All the strength of Israel;**
> **He has drawn back His right hand**
> **From before the enemy.**
> **And He has burned in Jacob like a flaming fire**
> **Consuming round about.**

---

[2]Adele Berlin said of verses 1 through 10, "We are, as it were, witnessing in slow motion the physical demolition of the city" (Adele Berlin, *Lamentations*, Old Testament Library [Louisville, Ky.: Westminster John Knox Press, 2004], 67).

Verse 1. The scenes of this national disaster are **covered ... with a cloud ... from heaven**. The Hebrew word for "covered" is עוּב (*'ub*), meaning "to make dark, to cover with cloud, to scorn."[3] This term suggests undesirable gloom, morbid distress, and excessive melancholy. Disgrace and indignity were being poured out with an intensity that would darken any day and dampen all spirits. It issued from God's anger and robbed Israel of her glory.

Verse 2. The expression that God **has not remembered His footstool** likely points to the mercy seat over the ark of the covenant, which in former days had been His meeting place with His people (Ex. 25:17–22; 29:42–45). The ghastly scene of burning embers was silent testimony that God's meeting place was gone and that the benefits at His mercy seat were forgotten (2 Kings 25:9).

The first scene is of the nation, where **all the habitations of Jacob** had been **swallowed up**. "Swallowed up," from בָּלַע (*bala'*), carries the idea of quickness or suddenness and is used figuratively of greed (Job 20:15) and being overwhelmed by calamity (Ps. 69:16).[4] It is a key term in chapter 2, as is seen in its use in verses 5 and 8. The **strongholds ... of Judah**—the walls as physical protection and the temple as spiritual security (see Jer. 7:4, 12–14)—had been thrown **down**. The **kingdom**, as a scene of shame, was **profaned** (חָלַל, *chalal*), which literally means "desecrate" or "be polluted" in the sense of holy places being defiled (Ezek. 7:24; 25:3). God "defiles or profanes his inheritance by giving it over to Babylon" (Is. 47:6).[5]

Verse 3. Everything that was **round about** had been **consum[ed]** (אָכַל, *'akal*),[6] as by fierce enemies who thirsted after one's blood. Anything or anyone of value (**princes**, the ones who were **the strength of Israel**) had been **cut off**, or consumed.

---

[3]Ludwig Koehler and Walter Baumgartner, *The Hebrew and Aramaic Lexicon of the Old Testament*, study ed., trans. and ed. M. E. J. Richardson (Boston: Brill, 2001), 1:794.

[4]Francis Brown, S. R. Driver, and Charles A. Briggs, *A Hebrew and English Lexicon of the Old Testament* (Oxford: Clarendon Press, 1972), 118.

[5]Ibid., 320.

[6]Ibid., 37–38.

The Scene of the City (2:4, 5)

⁴He has bent His bow like an enemy;
He has set His right hand like an adversary
And slain all that were pleasant to the eye;
In the tent of the daughter of Zion
He has poured out His wrath like fire.
⁵The Lord has become like an enemy.
He has swallowed up Israel;
He has swallowed up all its palaces,
He has destroyed its strongholds
And multiplied in the daughter of Judah
Mourning and moaning.

Verse 4. The next scene is one of sad souls and prominent places in the city. The **pleasant** people, **palaces**, and **strongholds** refer to Judean soldiers and known spots in Jerusalem. God's **right hand** is evident in Exodus as supporting and defending Israel, but here it was set against them. The figure of the **bent... bow** pictures the **enemy** in attack mode, with all before this **adversary** being **slain**.

Verse 5. Those who survived, seeing the slaughter and demolished dwellings, were left in **mourning and moaning**. These two terms are related to each other, springing from the same root in Hebrew. They combine to emphasize weeping and moaning on top of weeping and moaning. The fact that God was Judah's **enemy** and "adversary" intensified the sobering implications of this tragedy.

The Scene of the Sanctuary (2:6, 7)

⁶And He has violently treated His tabernacle like a garden booth;
He has destroyed His appointed meeting place.
The Lord has caused to be forgotten
The appointed feast and sabbath in Zion,
And He has despised king and priest
In the indignation of His anger.

> ⁷The Lord has rejected His altar,
> He has abandoned His sanctuary;
> He has delivered into the hand of the enemy
> The walls of her palaces.
> They have made a noise in the house of the LORD
> As in the day of an appointed feast.

Verse 6. Then the prophet focused on the demolition of the **tabernacle** (temple). This scene of the sanctuary depicts the temple as **a garden booth**.⁷ The attack was like harvest time: Rich produce had been stripped away, leaving behind empty vines (see Jer. 24:1, 2, 8–10). This place where one was to look for forgiveness and security (1 Kings 8:33, 34, 44, 45) had now mercilessly become the point of attack by the Almighty. He had **destroyed** His **meeting place**, **rejected His altar**, and **abandoned His sanctuary**. God would allow His people to follow their false prophets no longer (see Jer. 9:6–9; 14:14–16).

Verse 7. The **sanctuary** and **altar** were treated **violently** (חָמַס, *chamas*). This Hebrew word means "be hard, strict, rigorous" (see Jer. 22:3), "fail to nourish, kill," and can have either a physical or an ethical connotation (see Prov. 8:36).⁸ Both **king and priest** were **delivered into the hand[s] of the enemy** because of their transgressions against God's covenant (Jer. 34:17–22). Where sacred, solemn worship should have been, there would only be heard a **noise** (קוֹל, *qol*).⁹

The Scene of the Wall (2:8, 9a)

> ⁸The LORD determined to destroy
> The wall of the daughter of Zion.
> He has stretched out a line,
> He has not restrained His hand from destroying,

---

⁷"A *sukkâ* is a frail temporary hut in a garden or field used for shelter (Cf. Isa 1:8; Jonah 4:5; Job 27:8); as a metaphor for protection, it is an appellation for the temple" (Berlin, 69).

⁸Brown, Driver, and Briggs, 329.

⁹This sound is a "din," a "noise made by animals [or a] human voice" (Koehler and Baumgartner, 2:1084).

And He has caused rampart and wall to lament;
They have languished together
⁹ᵃHer gates have sunk into the ground,
He has destroyed and broken her bars.

Verse 8. The recognition of complete conquest is evident in the latter part of this verse, where the **wall** is said **to lament**. The **rampart**, erected as a special defensive structure, and the wall, used as a defense, **have languished together**. It was as if these demolished materials had bowed their once fortified heads in humiliated defeat.

Verse 9a. The scene is that of **the wall** suffering destruction, with the **gates . . . sunk into the ground**. The **bars** that should have held this massive fortification together were **broken**.

The Scene of the Punished Leaders (2:9b, 10)

⁹ᵇHer king and her princes are among the nations;
The law is no more.
Also, her prophets find
No vision from the Lord.
¹⁰The elders of the daughter of Zion
Sit on the ground, they are silent.
They have thrown dust on their heads;
They have girded themselves with sackcloth.
The virgins of Jerusalem
Have bowed their heads to the ground.

Verse 9b. Here is the scene is of the punished leaders. The **king[s]** and **princes**, who should have protected God's people from other nations, had been scattered **among the nations**. The **prophets** had received **no vision[s]**, and **the law** [was] **no more**. "The law" (תּוֹרָה, *torah*) was God's instruction through Moses to Israel to govern them with principles of justice and to direct their worship to God. It sealed their covenant with Him.[10] Iain Provan suggested that, without the authorities who mediated the Law,

---

[10]Kathleen M. O'Connor, *Lamentations and the Tears of the World* (Maryknoll, N.Y.: Orbis Books, 2002), 35.

its effect was no longer present.¹¹ The people had neither heard nor obeyed God's Word, so He removed it from them (Jer. 7:23–28; 44:15–22, 26, 27).

Verse 10. The elders, who should have established a testimony in Jacob (Ps. 78:2–8), sat in silence. Jeremiah's prophecy before elders such as these had become a reality (Jer. 19:1–8). They threw **dust on their heads** as an outward act of despondent agony within (Job 2:12; Ezek. 27:30). Such an act might have been an expression of repentance (Job 42:6), but there is no indication that these men had moved in a penitent direction, toward their Maker. They had a sorrow like that of Judas—sorrow which shows regret but does not follow through with reformation of life (see Mt. 27:3–5). In the story of Judas, the Holy Spirit appropriately used the Greek word μεταμέλομαι (*metamelomai*), which relates to regret, instead of μετανοέω (*metanoeō*, "repentance"), which calls for regret plus reformation of life.¹²

The virgins of Jerusalem (see 1:18) had also **bowed their heads to the ground**. This was another expression of the lowest submission, deep depression, or extreme stress (see Is. 60:14; Mt. 26:38, 39; Lk. 24:5).

These five scenes offer a composite of carnage that staggered all who surveyed the city. It is no wonder that the writer injected the impact personally felt as he took another look.

THE PROPHET'S VIEW AND THE PEOPLE'S PLIGHT (2:11–13)

> ¹¹**My eyes fail because of tears,**
> **My spirit is greatly troubled;**
> **My heart is poured out on the earth**
> **Because of the destruction of the daughter of my people,**

---

¹¹Iain Provan, *Lamentations*, The New Century Bible Commentary (Grand Rapids, Mich.: Wm. B. Eerdmans Publishing Co., 1991), 69.

¹²C. G. Wilke and Wilibald Grimm, *A Greek-English Lexicon of the New Testament*, trans. and rev. Joseph H. Thayer (Edinburgh, Scotland: T. & T. Clark, 1901; reprint, Grand Rapids, Mich.: Baker Book House, 1977), 405.

> When little ones and infants faint
> In the streets of the city.
> ¹²They say to their mothers,
> "Where is grain and wine?"
> As they faint like a wounded man
> In the streets of the city,
> As their life is poured out
> On their mothers' bosom.
> ¹³How shall I admonish you?
> To what shall I compare you,
> O daughter of Jerusalem?
> To what shall I liken you as I comfort you,
> O virgin daughter of Zion?
> For your ruin is as vast as the sea;
> Who can heal you?

Verse 11. The prophet's own pain surfaces in this section, which uses the personal pronoun **my** four times in this verse. His **eyes fail**[ed] (כָּלָה, *kalah*). That is, they were "at an end, finished, spent."[13] The word-picture presented here is of a people whose eyes were exhausted from weeping and who had wasted away, unable to find relief or refreshment (see 4:17). The writer's **spirit** [was] **greatly troubled** (חָמַר, *chamar*), a term that basically means to "scorch" or "burn."[14] He identified here an agitated spirit, a disturbed, bewildered mind, flashing with multiple emotions and degrees of misery. He **poured out** his **heart**. He was overflowing with hurt, but he was helpless; there was no solace for his suffering. A tremendous burden was bearing down on him **because of the destruction** of his **people**, depicted as **the daughter** of Jerusalem or Zion.

Verse 12. The people's plight fully justified his tears and trauma. He was looking upon a mountain of misery, highlighted by the sight of the **little ones and infants**. Some were old enough to speak, but all were **faint** (עָטַף, *'atap*) or "swooned" (KJV). This term is found in verses 11, 12, and 19, showing that they were

---

[13]Brown, Driver, and Briggs, 477–78.
[14]Koehler and Baumgartner, 1:330.

feeble and perishing from hunger. Whether it be wreckage from a storm, lives abandoned at sea, or starvation from famine, our piercing pain goes even deeper when little ones are suffering. The pain is yet more severe when a mother must hear the cries of her own child during his dying moments, as she is pressing him against her **bosom**.

Verse 13. The picture is beyond comprehension. These little ones shared the terrifying fate of the famine. The hardship pressed on all, but the children were not the cause for this carnage.

The prophet asked, **How shall I admonish you?** The Hebrew word translated "admonish" is עוּד (*'ud*). This word means "bear witness" in order to warn, exhort, or solemnly charge.[15] The text is uncertain, but the idea is "to produce ... as witness, i.e. in evidence, as an example."[16] It can also be translated, "How can I bear witness for you?"[17] This expression does not properly convey the original language. "Exhort solemnly" might be closer to the idea. The NJPSV reads, "What can I take as a witness to you or liken to you, O Fair Jerusalem?" The writer was overwhelmed with the sad scene and voiced his inability to convey the depth of the suffering. The **ruin** (שֶׁבֶר, *sheber*; the same word translated "destruction" in 2:11) was as unlimited and as unfathomable as the ocean itself. Who can see the extended edge of the ocean, or who can discern its dimensions? This is the image used to describe the suffering of the prophet.

THE PROPHETS AS THE CAUSE
(2:14)

> [14]Your prophets have seen for you
> False and foolish visions;
> And they have not exposed your iniquity
> So as to restore you from captivity,
> But they have seen for you false and misleading oracles.

---

[15]Brown, Driver, and Briggs, 730.
[16]Koehler and Baumgartner, 1:795.
[17]O'Connor, 39.

Verse 14. Three charges were brought against the **prophets** of Judah: First, they had shared **false and foolish visions**. While the Hebrew word for "false," שָׁוְא (*shaw^e*'), emphasizes that their message was evil, empty, and meaningless,[18] the word "foolish" (תָּפֵל, *thapel*) adds the idea that it was tasteless and unsatisfying, offering nothing more than "whitewash."[19] Literally, the latter word means "unsalted," giving here the sense of insipid and dull.[20] Many people pursue paths that are empty, evil, and unsatisfying. God, through His truth, offers us far more in life. Satan is subtle, with His meaningless and miserable messages. He has been effective for a long time.

Second, the prophets had **not exposed** [the people's] **iniquity** (see Jer. 6:13–15; 23:30–32). In God's eyes, there is a time to speak blunt truths and to do something about a problem. God has always given directions coupled with warnings for cases when people did not obey (Gen. 2:15–17; Lev. 26:1–6, 14–18; Deut. 27; 28). Prophets were set aside to teach and follow God's divine principles (2 Chron. 20:20; Neh. 9:30; Amos 1—3). The prophets in this time had sadly failed to teach truth and to warn the nation.

Third, a restoration **from captivity** could never be achieved by false prophets or by people who listened to false prophets. From the fourth year of King Jehoiakim until Jerusalem was destroyed some eighteen years later, Jeremiah had struggled in the face of these false, lying prophets (Jer. 27:14–22; 28:1–17). Babylon's forces had repeatedly carried people from Judah into captivity (see *Appendix: The Deportations from Judah to Exile in Babylon*, page 578), while lying prophets proclaimed hope for a quick return. God's faithful prophet looked over the shattered city and knew that the masses had been deceived by false prophets into further rebellion against God. Jeremiah had given himself completely to the work of prophecy on behalf of God's people. He had lived alone, had wept, had suffered greatly, but had been overruled by false prophets. What haunting and hurting memories he must have had!

---

[18]Brown, Driver, and Briggs, 996.
[19]Provan, 73.
[20]Koehler and Baumgartner, 2:1775–76.

LAMENTATIONS 2

THE CELEBRATION OF THE ENEMY (2:15, 16)

¹⁵All who pass along the way
Clap their hands in derision at you;
They hiss and shake their heads
At the daughter of Jerusalem,
"Is this the city of which they said,
'The perfection of beauty,
A joy to all the earth'?"
¹⁶All your enemies
Have opened their mouths wide against you;
They hiss and gnash their teeth.
They say, "We have swallowed her up!
Surely this is the day for which we waited;
We have reached it, we have seen it."

Verses 15, 16. The conduct of two groups is covered: One was unconcerned foreigners who, as they chanced to **pass** by, would **hiss and shake their heads**. The other was the enemy, who would **hiss and gnash their teeth**. Hissing or "whistling" signifies astonishment and sometimes derision.[21] **Jerusalem** became an object of analysis. Critics gloated over the city's agony. The body language of the former group depicted astonishment, while the latter group displayed anger and conquest. Both groups intermingled mockery in their assessments of Judah's fate.

The enemy's first group spoke in contrasting satire. **The perfection of beauty** likely is from Psalm 50:2, which was written to honor God and glorify Jerusalem. The sordid scene of devastation given in 2:1–13 is a sharp contrast to the psalmist's claim.

The comment by the enemy, **"We have swallowed her up!"** is a bold affirmation of Judah's lost independence and total defeat. God had intended to bless all the people of the earth through this race (Gen. 12:3; Jer. 2:11–13), but at this point the desolate landscape presented them as the surrendered scum of the earth. Nations had **waited** for this scene (see 2 Kings 24:1–3), and now they saw it and relished it.

---

[21]Berlin, 74.

THE PURPOSE OF THE LORD (2:17)

¹⁷The LORD has done what He purposed;
He has accomplished His word
Which He commanded from days of old.
He has thrown down without sparing,
And He has caused the enemy to rejoice over you;
He has exalted the might of your adversaries.

Verse 17. None of those observing this tragic scene—those who passed by, the enemy, and especially God's people—were to be mistaken regarding the real power behind this conquest. On the surface, it looked as if Babylon and the neighboring nations had accomplished the conquest. However, Lamentations clearly affirms, "The Lord has swallowed up" (2:2) and says that He had done so **without sparing**. This verse further emphasizes, **The LORD has done what He purposed** (זָמַם, *zamam*); that is, He had planned this scene.[22] The Hebrew word shows determined intent, fixing one's thought on something devised (Jer. 4:28; 51:12).[23] The multiple use of the pronoun **He** in the verse affirms and reaffirms that God had done this according to **His word**. Truly, a timeless God had **commanded** this **from days of old**, even before His people had entered the land to possess it.[24] The exactness with which this prediction was made, more than eight hundred years before the sad scene unfolded, is a bold testimony to the fact that our timeless God is the true Author of the Bible. He sees the end from the beginning. He moves even history toward the fulfillment of all His plans. Men have no such prophetic powers.

THE SOLEMN NEED STATED (2:18, 19)

¹⁸Their heart cried out to the Lord,
"O wall of the daughter of Zion,

---

[22]Koehler and Baumgartner, 1:273.
[23]Brown, Driver, and Briggs, 273.
[24]See Deut. 28:15–22, 32–37, 45–48, 52–68.

Let your tears run down like a river day and night;
Give yourself no relief,
Let your eyes have no rest.
¹⁹Arise, cry aloud in the night
At the beginning of the night watches;
Pour out your heart like water
Before the presence of the Lord;
Lift up your hands to Him
For the life of your little ones
Who are faint because of hunger
At the head of every street."

Verse 18. The depth of devotion required to reach out to Deity is indicated in the phrasing of verses 18 and 19. Their **tears** were to **run down . . . day and night**, and their **eyes** were to **have no rest**. The mood is reminiscent of that night when Christ's soul was sorrowful, even unto death, and He prayed with such stress and emotion that sweat was heavy on His brow, like drops of blood (Lk. 22:44; see Mt. 26:36–46). The weeping was to be done by **the daughter of Zion**, an identifying term that has already been used, with variations, twelve times in these lamentations (1:6, 15; 2:1, 2, 4, 5, 8, 10, 11, 13 [twice], 15).

The prophet's personification here of the **wall** as crying out rivets the mind of the reader to a strong, secure structure. Some who first read this inspired book surely had refreshed themselves in the shade of that wall. This location had offered protection and pleasantries. The fact that the wall was now shattered caused wailing among all who viewed this war-torn area.

Verse 19. There was a great need for the people of Judah to **pour out** [their] **heart**[s] **like water**, as the prophet had already done (2:11). God had poured out His wrath like fire (2:4), and they were to pour out their souls in repentance. The weeping was to be done **at the beginning of the night watches**. The thought is likely "at the beginning" of each of the three night watches.[25] God's people were hurting, and they needed to seek help **before the presence of the Lord** (see Ps. 27:9; 40:17; 46:1; 71:12, 13).

---

[25]Provan, 76.

As if the prophet could not erase a certain scene from his eyes, he justified his heavy-laden appeal because of the haunting scene of starvation faced by the **little ones**. He saw this heart-rending **hunger at the head of every street**.

THE PROPHET'S CRY FOR RELIEF (2:20–22)

²⁰See, O Lord, and look!
With whom have You dealt thus?
Should women eat their offspring,
The little ones who were born healthy?
Should priest and prophet be slain
In the sanctuary of the Lord?
²¹On the ground in the streets
Lie young and old;
My virgins and my young men
Have fallen by the sword.
You have slain them in the day of Your anger,
You have slaughtered, not sparing.
²²You called as in the day of an appointed feast
My terrors on every side;
And there was no one who escaped or survived
In the day of the Lord's anger.
Those whom I bore and reared,
My enemy annihilated them.

Verse 20. After the stirring plea for the people to pour out their hearts before the presence of the Lord (2:19) comes the burdened cry to the Creator. Carnage bursts forth in this appeal to God: **See, O Lord, and look!** That is the fourth time such a cry has sounded in these laments (see 1:9, 11, 20). As four areas were considered, the bewildered cry came, **With whom have You dealt thus?** Had any other people ever faced all of these calamities?

He asked the Lord to see the sickening, unparalleled sadness of **eat**[ing] **their offspring** (see 4:10; Lev. 26:27–32; Deut. 28:52–57; Is. 9:20; Jer. 19:8, 9; Ezek. 5:10). Surely, this act has seldom, if ever, been repeated in history.

He called upon God to see the shaming of the **sanctuary**, as

LAMENTATIONS 2

priest[s] and prophet[s] [were] slain therein. (See Lev. 21:10–12; Num. 3:38; 2 Chron. 26:16–21; 23:12–15; 36:17 for laws against defiling the temple.) When anything or any place set aside to be holy is desecrated, it is a dark, shameful day for the people or the nation. There is no deeper level of meanness and misery than when blood falls in a place that was supposed to have been sacred.

Verse 21. Next Jeremiah prayed that God might see **the streets** being strewn with those of all ages—**young and old**—who had been **slain** (see Jer. 6:11–13, 21; 7:16–29, 32–34; 9:19–22). Many people are blessed to live their lifetimes without ever seeing a dead body lying in the street. It would be difficult for us to imagine the impact that seeing numerous dead bodies in street after street would have on Jeremiah.

Verse 22. He said that there were **terrors on every side** (see Jer. 6:25; 20:10; 46:5; 49:29). Anywhere the prophet looked, **there was no one who escaped or survived** (see Jer. 15:1–4; 39:1–9). All were either hunted down and slain or placed in chains to be carried to Babylon. Technically, no one escaped. Total collapse and conquest were seen in every direction.

Those whom I bore and reared, my enemy annihilated them. Through his teachings and prophesying, Jeremiah "bore and reared" these people (see Jer. 2:1–7; 33:1–11). God's **anger** and severe discipline are always geared toward redeeming the penitent in a day yet to come (Jer. 29:10–14).

The true message in this hour of lament for God's people was that the enemy had "annihilated" them (כָּלָה, *kalah*; see comments on 2:11) because of their sinfulness. These lamentations are not a collection of thoughts to comfort and console, but a jarring reminder of a just God and the sobering cost of sin against Him.

The day of the Lord had traditionally been understood by the Jews to refer to their triumph over enemies. However, here it had become a day of disaster for them. The prophets also sought to convey to the people the idea that "the day of the Lord" would not always be against their enemies (see Is. 2:12; 13:9; Jer. 4:9; Amos 5:18–20). God's people could suffer a "day of the Lord" just as their enemies would.

APPLICATION

God's Punishment (Ch. 2)

Has the severity of God ever been more forcefully demonstrated than in the scenes in Lamentations 2? From the cloud that covered Zion in His anger (2:1) to the plea in verse 20, this chapter attributes deep agony and horror to the punishment imposed by God on His people. He poured forth His wrath like fire (2:4). His anger is also mentioned in verses 1, 2, 3, 6, 21, and 22. It is no surprise, then, that His action is declared to be like that of "an enemy" (2:4, 5).

Still, we somehow recoil at the thought of God as man's enemy—especially an enemy to His own covenant people. Sobering lessons must be learned in this atmosphere of the smoldering city of Zion, where starvation was so severe that mealtime found maternal figures feasting on their own children. The wrath of the Lord is a terrible thing (see Ps. 88:14–16; Is. 2:19, 21; Zeph. 2:11; Rev. 6:12–17; 14:9, 10). Several truths from this chapter may be applied to our lives.

Lesson one: *As terrible as the scenes of Zion's fall are, nowhere is it implied that the punishment imposed should be labeled an act of injustice.* Instead of allowing this pain to turn them away from God, the people were exhorted to pour out their tears and heart "before the presence of the Lord" (2:19). As repulsive as this pain must have been, it was to be viewed as a steppingstone back to God (see Ps. 119:67, 71; 1 Pet. 1:6–9).

Lesson two: *The reason God poured out His anger, bending His bow as an enemy and allowing His sanctuary to be desecrated, was that His commands, statutes, and judgments must be honored above all else.* These scenes of suffering—with places shattered and God's people starving, dead, or sent into captivity—are a warning that disrespect for His decrees is a sure course for disaster. What God said from the very beginning of His covenant relationship with these people should have been believed and obeyed (see Ex. 19:1–8; Deut. 28:1–65; Jer. 7:16–34). The scene in chapter 2 is proof that God meant what He had said in Jeremiah 7.

Since the Lord is the same yesterday, today, and forever (Heb. 13:8), we surely need today to surrender to His authority and commands for His people in this age (see Mt. 28:18–20; Jn. 12:48; Acts 2:36–47; 4:12; Rom. 1:16–32; 6:1–17; Heb. 5:8, 9; 2 Jn. 9). Christ has all authority in heaven and on earth: "All rule and authority and power and dominion, and every name that is named, not only in this age but also in the one to come" are to be subject to Him, keeping His commandments for them (Eph. 1:18–23; Col. 1:13–20).

Lesson three: *A severe and sobering price must be paid for sin.* Isaiah 59:1–18, viewed alongside Lamentations 2, gives a solid warning that rebellion against God is not the course to take. Is there any part of the pain covered in this chapter that we would invite to be a part of our lives?

Lesson four: *The elders and the leaders in the church should expose sin and carry out biblical discipline* (see 2:14). God knew that, in every age, the unruly would have to be admonished, the fainthearted would require encouragement, and the weak would need help and support (see 1 Thess. 5:12–18). Some, we must keep away from, or withdraw from (2 Thess. 3:6, 7, 10–15; KJV); and we have to reject others (Tit. 3:9–11), even handing some over to Satan (1 Tim. 1:18–20). Jesus initially taught such discipline when sin seeks to raise its ugly head among God's people (Mt. 18:15–17).

The scenes of misery in the chapter voice several lessons of the necessity of reverence for God and obedience of His commands.

Chapter 3
The Cry of the Distressed Prophet

Of the five chapters in Lamentations, chapter 3 is the most detailed in composition, and its spiritual tone is the most elevated. Most of it is in the first person. The writer's thoughts dramatically unfold as the prophet grows in confidence in the Creator. The chapter depicts his coming out of chaos and conflict.

An elaborate acrostic, the chapter contains sixty-six verses which are written in triplets in Hebrew. The three lines of each triplet begin with a letter of the Hebrew alphabet (twenty-two triplets, three lines each, that total sixty-six lines). This unique pattern, read either in Hebrew or in English, is secondary to the significant messages. The poem presents thoughts concerning the Lord, the writer, and the writer's outlook on life because of his relationship with God.

The exegetical problem in chapter 3 revolves around the question of whether this is an individual lament or whether the individual is a personification of the nation. The fact that the writer emphasized "I am the man who . . ." in 3:1 lends evidence to the idea that this was a depiction of the suffering of a particular person.[1] ("Man" is used in 3:1, 27, 35, 39.) Other expressions seem to relate to an individual and his experiences: "I have become a laughingstock" (3:14); "I recall to my mind" (3:21); "O Lord, You have pleaded my soul's cause" (3:58). This conclusion seems

---

[1] "One almost forgets, under the intolerable weight of the misfortunes proclaimed, that this man is not a professional sufferer. He is no ascetic revelling in his self-inflicted deprivations nor a hypochondriac exaggerating his troubles" (Norman K. Gottwald, *Studies in the Book of Lamentations*, Studies in Biblical Theology No. 14, rev. ed. [London: SCM Press, 1962], 59).

even more plausible in light of the use of "we" and "us" in 3:40–47. In that passage the individual drew the nation into his plea for collective action.

Assuming that Jeremiah was the writer of Lamentations, we see some striking parallels between his struggles in chapter 3 and those described in Jeremiah 1—20 (see *Appendix: Similar Struggles Described in Lamentations 3 & Jeremiah 1—20*, page 581). Therefore, we find interwoven in Lamentations 3, as in the early chapters of Jeremiah, a growing awareness that God is just, compassionate, and sufficient. The maturing process of the writer is made evident as the chapter progresses.

Concerning structure, there first came his cries of pain and his view of what God had done (3:1–18). Then his hope of relief in God's mercy became evident. His doubt gave way to more understanding (3:19–38). Next he looked at himself and the nation as sinners before God (3:39–47). Following this, he summarized his past and current condition (3:48–58) and stated his confidence in God and his devotion to Him (3:59–66).

CRIES OF CONCERN—HIS PAIN (3:1–18)

The suffering and despair of the prophet led to a type of indictment against God in 3:1–18. He discussed his condition, the cause of the pain, and the cost of his relationship with God.

The Condition of the Prophet (3:1a)

^{1a}**I am the man who has seen affliction.**

Verse 1a. The man (גֶּבֶר, *geber*)—a young, strong man[2]—is the speaker in verses 1 through 18. He is briefly identified as one who had **seen affliction** (עֳנִי, *ʿoni*) consisting of poverty, oppression, and frustration.[3] This term points to a person in misery, suf-

---

[2] Ludwig Koehler and Walter Baumgartner, *The Hebrew and Aramaic Lexicon of the Old Testament*, study ed., trans. and ed. M. E. J. Richardson (Boston: Brill, 2001), 1:175.

[3] Francis Brown, S. R. Driver, and Charles A. Briggs, *A Hebrew and English Lexicon of the Old Testament* (Oxford: Clarendon Press, 1972), 777; Koehler and Baumgartner, 1:857.

fering in wretchedness. The prophet's struggles and the Lord's involvement in imposing them unfold in a series of pronouns. The prophet is referenced in the words "I" (6 times), "my" (7 times), and "me" (13 times). The Lord is mentioned in the words "He" (20 times) and "His" (4 times) in 3:1–18.

One who gets caught up in what the Lord is said to have done to the prophet may miss a vital key to understanding the overall message in this chapter. While some charges are leveled by the prophet, rephrasing those charges (without changing their meanings) will identify a concerned, chastening God. The Lord knew what discipline the prophet needed for his development (see Heb. 12:9–13; Jas. 1:2–4; 1 Pet. 1:6–9).

The Cause (in the Prophet's Eyes) of His Pain (3:1b–13)

¹ᵇBecause of the rod of His wrath.
²He has driven me and made me walk
In darkness and not in light.
³Surely against me He has turned His hand
Repeatedly all the day.
⁴He has caused my flesh and my skin to waste away,
He has broken my bones.
⁵He has besieged and encompassed me with bitterness and hardship.
⁶In dark places He has made me dwell,
Like those who have long been dead.
⁷He has walled me in so that I cannot go out;
He has made my chain heavy.
⁸Even when I cry out and call for help,
He shuts out my prayer.
⁹He has blocked my ways with hewn stone;
He has made my paths crooked.
¹⁰He is to me like a bear lying in wait,
Like a lion in secret places.
¹¹He has turned aside my ways and torn me to pieces;
He has made me desolate.
¹²He bent His bow
And set me as a target for the arrow.

**¹³He made the arrows of His quiver
To enter into my inward parts.**

As the prophet saw the circumstances confronting him, he realized the type of God he served.

Verse 1b. *An angry God.* Affliction had come **because of the rod of His wrath** (עֶבְרָה, *'ebrah*), His "overflowing rage, fury."[4] The writer indicated that he had seen God's wrath. Statements such as those recorded in Jeremiah 15:14; 17:4; 21:5; 25:7; and 32:37 made it clear to the prophet that God was angry with Judah. That explains why Jeremiah was seeing these afflictions. While it must have been terrible to behold such disaster unfolding all around, we must remember that one—especially God—can be angry and yet not sin (see Mk. 3:5; Eph. 4:26). As Norman K. Gottwald has indicated, God's wrath must be seen as a focal point in Lamentations:

> The Book of Lamentations is distinguished by the repeated emphasis upon the wrath of Yahweh which acts directly in dealing out retribution. Commensurable with the suffering and sin is the anger of Yahweh. . . .
>
> The real dynamic of the motif of Yahweh's wrath, however, is lost unless one studies it in close connection with the contexts where it occurs. Only by detailed analysis of the text of Lamentations can the interpreter grasp the fierceness and violence of the divine punishment. Central to the whole matter of the inter-relation of suffering, sin, and wrath is the direct activity of Yahweh in the city's destruction. Sin against God has aroused the divine wrath and that wrath has inflicted punishment without measure or mercy.[5]

Verse 2. *A demanding God.* The prophet said, **He has driven me and made me walk in darkness** (חֹשֶׁךְ, *choshek*). The reference to "darkness," implying extraordinary darkness and distress

---

[4] Brown, Driver, and Briggs, 720.
[5] Gottwald, 72–73. Gottwald reviewed all of the words related to "anger" and "wrath" in his book.

symbolic of judgment,[6] tells the story of the inner anxiety that was part of Jeremiah's life day after day. He delivered a message of terror and dread, a judgment of Yahweh upon Judah. He did not clearly understand, but God would send him—in fact, drive him out—to deliver another message of doom, which would not be respected (Jer. 7:27, 28; 17:15–18; 18:18–23). It is a perplexing moment when a preacher presents truth but the hearers react with vengeance instead of respect (see Acts 2:39, 40; 10:34–48; 11:1–17; Gal. 2:11–18).

Verse 3. *A directing God.* **Against me He has turned His hand repeatedly all the day.** Like a loving Father, God watched over Jeremiah, hearing his complaints and making demands as needed for his development (see Jer. 15:15–21; 20:7–13; 1 Pet. 1:6–9).

Verse 4. *A physically taxing God.* God had allowed Jeremiah to **waste away** (בָּלָה, *balah*), to be afflicted as if he had "become old."[7] Not only was he worn out and used up, but this word alludes to emaciation caused by famine and hunger.[8] God never said that Jeremiah's assignment would be easy, but He did promise to deliver the prophet and make him equal to his task (Jer. 1:7–10, 17–19). Consider the rigors of forty-plus years of prophetic pressure in a sinful nation, with daily rejections of his message by the leaders and the people. To say that Jeremiah "wasted away," or was "used to the fullest extent," is a mild description of the trying times he endured.

Verse 5. *A stress-assigning God.* **He has besieged and encompassed me with bitterness and hardship** (תְּלָאָה, *tᵉla'ah*).[9] The definition of the term for "hardship" surveys the grueling services Jeremiah rendered. His prayers seemed hopeless (Jer. 11:11, 14; 14:11); he was weary in vain endeavors (Jer. 18:19–23). Though exhausted, he patiently worked among the faithless people of Judah (Jer. 25:2–4; 38:14, 15; 40:1–6). Ironically, if he stopped speaking for God, he grew weary of holding the message within him (Jer. 20:9). Little relief could be found for this dedicated pro-

---

[6]Brown, Driver, and Briggs, 365.

[7]Ibid., 115.

[8]Iain Provan, *Lamentations*, The New Century Bible Commentary (Grand Rapids, Mich.: Wm. B. Eerdmans Publishing Co., 1991), 85.

[9]Brown, Driver, and Briggs, 521.

claimer of God's message.

Verse 6. *An isolating God.* **In dark places He has made me dwell.** This figure identifies a situation in which counsel or encouragement had been withdrawn. The cry of Jeremiah, "I sat alone" (15:17), conveys the loneliness and pain of rejection. At this time, he was blaming God.

Verse 7. *A burden-requiring God.* Being **walled . . . in**, the prophet could see no outlet. As one chained in a cell, he found his **chain heavy**. The word used here refers to that which is burdensome, distressing, difficult, and grievous (כָּבֵד, *kabed*).[10] It suggests the idea of wearing a yoke, which Jeremiah had literally done under the Lord's directions (Jer. 27:2–8; 28:2–17).

Verse 8. *A prayer-training God.* The prophet's claim was that God **shuts out my prayer**. It is evident that Jeremiah's love for the people was often declared to God (see 7:16; 11:14; 14:11; 18:20). Having such emotional ties to them, he was in danger of following their patterns of thought and conduct (see Jer. 15:19). God knew that must not happen. Weaknesses and inclinations subject people to unwise temptations. This explains why, centuries later, the apostles pleaded, "Lord, teach us to pray" (Lk. 11:1–13). He knows how we should pray (see Lk. 18:1–14; Phil. 4:6, 7; 1 Thess. 5:17, 18; Jas. 4:1–3).

Verse 9. *A challenging God.* **He has blocked my ways . . . He has made my paths crooked.** What a lesson for Jeremiah and for us! God "blocked" (גָּדַר, *gadar*) the prophet from marriage, social gatherings, and even mourning (Jer. 16:1–9; see Mt. 8:21, 22), as if he were walled off from society.[11] Marriage, death, and social gatherings have led some to wander from God rather than walking toward Him or with Him. Although marriage is from God and can be a great blessing (Prov. 19:14; Eph. 5:22–33), some have rushed into unwise marriages only to lose their souls. Going to the house of mourning may in some cases be the better course (Eccles. 7:2–4). What may seem like a contradiction in these passages emphasizes that people too often pursue the wrong path. At times God should block some of our paths and overturn some

---

[10] Ibid., 457–58.
[11] Ibid., 154.

of our decisions. When He does so, we may think that He is perverting, or making crooked, our paths (see Ps. 119:9–11, 105; Prov. 14:12; Jer. 10:23; 1 Cor. 10:13; 1 Pet. 5:5–7).

Verses 10, 11. *A powerful, adjusting God.* **He has turned aside my ways . . . He has made me desolate** (שָׁמֵם, *shamem*), presents a sad image of a "deserted"[12] land or person (see comments on 1:2–4). The idea of power is depicted in the hiding **bear** and secluded **lion**, figures indicating unexpected intrusions into one's life that cannot be ignored. The work assignment God had given Jeremiah left him deserted and appalled, with torn emotions (Jer. 9:1, 2; 15:10; 18:19–22; 20:7–9).

Verses 12, 13. *An inner-working God.* The prophet had, figuratively speaking, seen God's **arrows** enter into his **inward parts** (כִּלְיָה, *kilyah*), or "kidneys, . . . the most sensitive and vital part" of man.[13] This phrasing pinpoints God's deep interest in our souls and our spirits (see 1 Thess. 5:23). He is the Father of our spirits (see Eccles. 12:7; Heb. 12:9). However, just as a child may react against a parent who seeks to mold his or her character, so Jeremiah resisted in some ways God's prodding him. Jeremiah ultimately commended God, as a child might a parent, for helping him to grow toward Him with greater insight (see 3:19–24).

The Cost of His Relationship with the Creator (3:14–18)

> [14]**I have become a laughingstock to all my people,**
> **Their mocking song all the day.**
> [15]**He has filled me with bitterness,**
> **He has made me drunk with wormwood.**
> [16]**He has broken my teeth with gravel;**
> **He has made me cower in the dust.**
> [17]**My soul has been rejected from peace;**
> **I have forgotten happiness.**
> [18]**So I say, "My strength has perished,**
> **And so has my hope from the LORD."**

---

[12]Ibid., 1030–31.
[13]Ibid., 480.

Verse 14. To the **people**, the prophet had **become a laughingstock** (שְׂחוֹק, *śᵉchoq*); they subjected him to mockery and derision.[14] This term denotes more than one person, or group, laughing at another person and openly making sport of him. Laughter was intermingled with contempt for who the prophet was and what he said. Jeremiah kept speaking for the Lord, enduring such mockery day after day (Jer. 20:7, 8). The people's derision of his inspired warnings was coupled with a desire to blot out the man—and even a memory of the man (Jer. 11:19; 26:8, 11). Let those who speak for the Lord pause to contemplate how discouraging it would have been to continue to face them day after day. How did the prophet handle it?

Verse 15. As to his inner self, he became **filled . . . with bitterness** (מְרֹד, *maror*). This term springs from the word for a bitter plant; figuratively, it relates to endured experiences and inflicted distress.[15] Jeremiah's bitter times included the incidents when Pashhur had him beaten and put in stocks (Jer. 20:1, 2), when Hananiah broke the yoke around Jeremiah's neck (Jer. 28:10, 11), and when the officials threw him into the cistern (Jer. 38:6). Other heart-wrenching experiences could be added to this list; together, they filled the prophet with bitterness and disgust.

Verse 16. The message coming from the prophet's mouth was like **gravel** grinding on one's **teeth**. Jeremiah 15:16 refers to the word being received with joy because those words proved Jeremiah to be God's spokesman (see Jer. 1:8–10), called by God's name. His service was worthy of honor and glory. However, after facing daily rejection by a rebellious audience that cried out for violence and destruction (Jer. 20:8, 9), his words began to have the effect of gravel against the teeth. He was filled with indignation (Jer. 15:17). His experiences left him **cower**[ing] **in the dust**, or rolling in the ashes—a figure of disgrace and humiliation. He descended into the depths of sorrow and internal pain (see Ps. 102:9; Jer. 6:26; Ezek. 27:30).

Verse 17. The prophet's **soul** had been denied **peace** (שָׁלוֹם, *shalom*), with its accompanying feeling of being intact or com-

---

[14]Koehler and Baumgartner, 2:1315.
[15]Brown, Driver, and Briggs, 601.

plete.¹⁶ He had **forgotten happiness**. In this frame of mind, he thought that everything good, refreshing, or prospering had been denied him. The fact that his welfare seemed forgotten shows his resignation to being in a valley of depression.

Verse 18. The writer's external **strength** had **perished** (אָבַד, *'abad*) and so had his **hope**; His physical strength was depleted; it had vanished.¹⁷ How close this prophet had come to giving up, even on God!

CRIES OF CONCERN—HIS INSIGHT
(3:19–38)

Like his fellow Jews, the prophet struggled to understand why God would bring calamity upon His chosen people. As he cried for God to remember his situation, he himself came to a point of remembering.

The Remembering (3:19–26)

> ¹⁹Remember my affliction and my wandering, the wormwood and bitterness.
> ²⁰Surely my soul remembers
> And is bowed down within me.
> ²¹This I recall to my mind,
> Therefore I have hope.
> ²²The LORD's lovingkindnesses indeed never cease,
> For His compassions never fail.
> ²³They are new every morning;
> Great is Your faithfulness.
> ²⁴"The LORD is my portion," says my soul,
> "Therefore I have hope in Him."
> ²⁵The LORD is good to those who wait for Him,
> To the person who seeks Him.
> ²⁶It is good that he waits silently
> For the salvation of the LORD.

---

¹⁶Koehler and Baumgartner, 2:1506–7.
¹⁷Brown, Driver, and Briggs, 1–2.

LAMENTATIONS 3

Verse 19. The prophet said, **This I recall.** These verses offer a review of what had almost happened. His past **affliction** had led to a **wandering** lifestyle of **bitterness** and **wormwood**.

Verse 20. Circumstances had almost made his soul **bow** (שׁוּחַ, *shuach*) and buckle. The Hebrew term used here points to a soul that would sink down and melt away in a state of depression (see Ps. 42; 43; 49:15).[18]

Verse 21. While the afflictions lingered in the quiet chamber of his memory, the prophet had acquired a depth of soul that removed him far from the raw, superficial character he once had been. How thrilling is the moment when one turns from hopelessness to **hope**! Jeremiah went from depression to devotion, from caving in to having courage. His change is reminiscent of Job's rise from ruin to rejoicing. In deep affliction, he learned of God's grace, goodness, wisdom, and power (Job 19:6–12; 42:1–6, 10–17). Even Jesus learned obedience by the things which He suffered (Heb. 5:5–9). That glorious transition in Jeremiah is evident in the verses that follow.

Verse 22. Beginning with this verse, the thought goes from the accusing agony of 3:1–18 to praise of the Lord's compassion and goodness. The sudden change should not surprise us. Jeremiah 20:1–13 contains an exact parallel—a mood swing from deep depression to praise for God's loving care. Perhaps we should understand this to have been part of the prophet's growing to mature faith in the goodness of God. This seems to be taking place from chapters 12 to 20. However, the new realization was abruptly stated in both cases. Just as Jeremiah was, in a moment, extracted from the cistern (Jer. 38:11–13), so he seems to have leaped in a moment from the pit of accusations into the confidence of God's care.

It is interesting that one of the most meaningful expressions of assurance in God's care appears in the middle of Lamentations.[19] The prophet acknowledged three divine characteristics in a beautiful tribute to God in verses 22 through 24:

---

[18]Ibid., 1001.

[19]F. W. Dobbs-Allsopp saw 3:19–24 as having "pivotal theological significance" (F. W. Dobbs-Allsopp, *Lamentations*, Interpretation [Louisville, Ky.: John Knox Press, 2002], 116).

He recognized that the attitude of God toward His people was—and always would be—one of **lovingkindness** (חֶסֶד, *chesed*).[20] Norman Snaith gave one of the best descriptions of this beautiful word. It is covenant-love and covenant-loyalty. Its basic meaning is steadfastness and constancy of love.[21] Gottwald added, "He [God] brings his anger to an end, but his covenant loyalties are never consumed and his mercies are never exhausted."[22] Love is the very nature of God (see 1 Jn. 4:8).

He spoke of God's **compassions**. The psalmist wrote, "Just as a father has compassion on his children, so the Lord has compassion on those who fear Him" (Ps. 103:13).

Verse 23. This unfailing compassion is expressed in action: He nurtures His children, providing for their needs daily. His acts of mercy **are new every morning**. W. F. Adeney reminds us of the greatness of God's mercies:

> There is something cheering in the poet's idea of the morning as the time when these mercies of God are renewed. God's mercies do not fail, are not interrupted. The emphasis is on the thought that no day is without God's new mercies, not even the day of darkest trouble; and further, there is the suggestion that God is never dilatory in coming to our aid. He does not keep us waiting and wearying while He tarries. He is prompt and early with His grace. The idea may be compared with that of the promise to those who seek God "early," literally, "in the morning" (Prov. 8:17).[23]

The prophet rejoiced in the Lord's **faithfulness**. He is always available when His obedient children call upon Him. He has

---

[20]Gottwald's comment on this verse is important: "We are left confronting the unfathomable divine love and mercy which can never be calculated but comes only as a gift" (Gottwald, 100).

[21]Norman Snaith, *The Distinctive Ideas of the Old Testament* (London: Epworth Press, 1945), 102.

[22]Gottwald, 99.

[23]W. F. Adeney, "The Lamentations of Jeremiah," in *The Biblical Illustrator*, comp. and ed. Joseph S. Exell (Grand Rapids, Mich.: Baker Book House, 1973), 44.

promised never to desert us (Heb. 13:5, 6). What hope is instilled by the prophet's tribute to the Creator's goodness!

Verse 24. There follows one of the most amazing figures in the Scriptures: **"The LORD is my portion," says my soul.** Just as priests had been granted certain portions from the sacrifices when the Promised Land was inherited (see Lev. 7:8, 9; 5:12, 13), so the prophet's soul-strengthening confidence bursts forth in his message: "The LORD is my portion!" He remains a sufficient and satisfying spiritual portion for us today (2 Cor. 3:4–6; Heb. 6:18, 19; see Ps. 145:14–16). No wonder this thought gave the prophet hope (3:21). Our **hope** is **in Him** (see Col. 1:27; Heb. 11:1; 1 Jn. 3:1–3). This is a glorious, faith-building confidence: The Lord can be ours, and we can be His (see Mt. 28:18–20; Gal. 2:20; Jn. 15:4, 5). F. W. Dobbs-Allsopp noted that this "hope" has two outstanding features: It is clearly rooted in God; and it is a statement of faith.[24]

Verses 25, 26. In the Hebrew, verses 25 through 27 all begin with the word טוֹב (*tob*, **good**).[25] The prophet's view of how man should respond to God is seen in this verse.

The Lord's goodness is said to be available **to those who wait for Him** and **to the person who seeks** [דָּרַשׁ, *darash*][26] **Him**, that is, who truly studies and discusses to search out the meaning of his message, a well as spending time with God in prayer and worship. These two phrases remove any idea of waiting in the sense of doing nothing. God's ways are not our ways (Is. 55:7–9), so we may twist and squirm as we seek to discern His thoughts.

Nevertheless, these words drive home the truth that we must dig diligently as we wait, so that we may know His will. How grand it is that our limitations, which require us to wait, can be alleviated by His sufficient provision (see Acts 17:27, 28; 2 Cor. 3:4–6)! The prophet's suggestion here is almost parallel to Jeremiah 6:16, where we see: "stand," "see and ask," walk in [the

---

[24]Dobbs-Allsopp, 118.

[25]Kathleen M. O'Connor suggested that "the three repetitions of the word 'good' create the impression that goodness requires repetition to become convincing" (Kathleen M. O'Connor, *Lamentations and the Tears of the World* [Maryknoll, N.Y.: Orbis Books, 2002], 51).

[26]Brown, Driver, and Briggs, 205.

good way]," and "rest for your souls." Verses 25 and 26 have almost the same wording: "wait," "seeks Him," **waits silently,** and **the salvation of the LORD.**

The Response to the Recall (3:27–30)

> ²⁷**It is good for a man that he should bear**
> **The yoke in his youth.**
> ²⁸**Let him sit alone and be silent**
> **Since He has laid it on him.**
> ²⁹**Let him put his mouth in the dust,**
> **Perhaps there is hope.**
> ³⁰**Let him give his cheek to the smiter,**
> **Let him be filled with reproach.**

The response of the prophet to his recollection is expressed in the form of instructions.

Verse 27. It is good for **man** to receive the Lord's assignment at an early age. The verse affirms that "it is good" for one to **bear the yoke in his youth.** This conviction sprang from a voice of experience. The prophet was reflecting on an earlier day, when he had not understood the wisdom of placing such a heavy burden on a young man (see Jer. 1:6–10). It is good to bear the yoke while young because it is reasonable in God's divine plan (see Ps. 78:1–8; Prov. 22:6); it is honorable (Prov. 10:1–5); it is rewarding (1 Tim. 4:8–16; 2 Tim. 3:14–17); it is the easiest and best way to live (Mt. 11:28–30; Jn. 10:10; 1 Pet. 5:5–7).

Verse 28. He said that one should remain silent until the plan can be seen more clearly. God has **laid** our burden upon us.

Verse 29. A man must trust in Him and accept His tasks for him without arguing against Him. He must **put his mouth in the dust.** An expression of this kind symbolizes being silent before the Lord. It is an expression of extreme reverential humility. **Hope** is seen in this context (3:24; Jer. 12:1–6).

Verse 30. He charged that one should remain faithful, even when smitten on the **cheek** (see Jer. 20:1–13; Mt. 5:38–42; 26:63–68). Turning the other cheek is not a sign of weakness or cowardice. Rather, it is the perfection of true courage and moral strength that will not surrender to carnal conduct. Here, apparent humiliation rises to become mature glorification. It was in this type of behavior that Jesus won a victory through submission (Mt. 20:26–28; Phil. 2:5–11; 1 Pet. 2:21–24).

The Relationship of God to Man Now in Focus (3:31–38)

> ³¹For the Lord will not reject forever,
> ³²For if He causes grief,
> Then He will have compassion
> According to His abundant lovingkindness.
> ³³For He does not afflict willingly
> Or grieve the sons of men.
> ³⁴To crush under His feet
> All the prisoners of the land,
> ³⁵To deprive a man of justice
> In the presence of the Most High,
> ³⁶To defraud a man in his lawsuit—
> Of these things the Lord does not approve.
> ³⁷Who is there who speaks and it comes to pass,
> Unless the Lord has commanded it?
> ³⁸Is it not from the mouth of the Most High
> That both good and ill go forth?

God's relationship to man is in focus in this section. Three reasons are given for waiting on the Lord and submitting to suffering before Him.

Verse 31. First, the prophet said that the suffering is temporary. Although it seemed to him that God had withdrawn from His afflicted servant, it was but for a season (see Jer. 15:15, 18, 19–21; 17:14–18; 18:19–23; 20:7–13). The temporary nature of God's **reject**[ion] or anger was a common concept in Hebrew thinking. In some cases, the idea was stated in God's Word (see Ps. 44:23; 77:7–9; 79:5; 85:5, 6; 103:9; Is. 64:9; Jer. 3:5, 12; Mic. 7:18).

Verse 32. God's **compassion** will soon follow behind one's **grief**. When His compassion comes, it will be **abundant lovingkindness**.

Verse 33. God does not **afflict willingly or grieve the sons of men**. If He grieves, chastens, or scourges an individual, it is to help make that person into what he can and should be. It is by such chastening that one learns endurance (see Heb. 12:5–7; 1 Pet. 1:6–9).

Verse 34. God does not **crush under His feet all the prisoners of the land**. He does not allow any soul to be tested beyond what that soul, through His grace, can endure. God's providential care is evident in 1 Corinthians 10:13: "God is faithful, who will not allow you to be tempted beyond what you are able [preventive providence], but with the temptation will provide the way of escape also [protecting providence], so that you will be able to endure it [perfecting providence]."

Verses 35, 36. The Lord does not approve of injustice, nor will He **deprive a man of justice**. Abraham raised the question "Shall not the Judge of all the earth deal justly?" (Gen. 18:25). The prophet here answered that anyone "in the presence of the Most High" can rest assured that He will neither approve what is evil nor **defraud** one where justice is to be executed. In addition, God will have compassion according to His abundant lovingkindness (3:22, 32).

Verse 37. This verse expresses the prophet's concept of God in relationship to **good and ill**. Man is not in control; God is. What God says **comes to pass**. Not only did that concept serve as the test of a true prophet (Deut. 18:15–22), but the statement is also a tribute to the sovereignty of God. He is over, and in, the affairs of men.

Verse 38. Every good gift is from God (Jas. 1:17, 18), and any **ill** is either His allowance or His assignment. God has allowed sin; He even extends blessings to the good and the evil, the just and the unjust (Mt. 5:44, 45). However, He will search every heart and see that each person is judged according to his works (Jer. 17:9, 10; Rom. 14:10–12; 2 Cor. 5:10). If ill will is assigned by God to some, it is to repay their disobedience. He will bring destruction upon those who have no love for truth and refuse to respond to God's commands (see Deut. 13:1–9; 2 Thess.1:6–10; 2:8–12). Yahweh is a just God, and men reap as they have sown (Gal. 6:7–9).

LAMENTATIONS 3

CRIES OF CONCERN—HIS CONFESSION
(3:39–47)

Having vindicated God and given tribute for His lovingkindness, compassion, and justice (3:21–38), the prophet next turned to look at himself and his people as sinners before the just God. Plural pronouns are used in 3:40–47, further indicating that these thoughts were national, not just personal.

> ³⁹Why should any living mortal, or any man,
> Offer complaint in view of his sins?
> ⁴⁰Let us examine and probe our ways,
> And let us return to the LORD.
> ⁴¹We lift up our heart and hands
> Toward God in heaven.
> ⁴²We have transgressed and rebelled,
> You have not pardoned.
> ⁴³You have covered Yourself with anger
> And pursued us;
> You have slain and have not spared.
> ⁴⁴You have covered Yourself with a cloud
> So that no prayer can pass through.
> ⁴⁵You have made us mere offscouring and refuse
> In the midst of the peoples.
> ⁴⁶All our enemies have opened their mouths against us.
> ⁴⁷Panic and pitfall have befallen us,
> Devastation and destruction.

Verse 39. A conclusion was drawn that mortal man, in his sins, is in no position to **offer complaint** (אָנַן, 'anan), to mourn or groan impiously.[27] A common—and often misapplied—question is "Why did God do this?" First, God may not be the source of the struggle in question. That was the basic mistake Job made: accusing God, when Satan was the real source of his trials (Job 2:1–10; 16:7–17; 19:6–12). Second, man, with his limited facts, has no right to judge God. Third, when a sinner reaps as he has sown,

---
[27]Ibid., 59.

it is no time to mourn impiously and complain to a just God (see Gal. 6:7, 8; 2 Tim. 4:8).

Verse 40. The proper course for sinners to take is threefold: (1) **Let us examine** (חָפַשׂ, *chapaś*) or search, or test,[28] our ways. (2) Let us **probe** (חָקַר, *chaqar*)[29] **our ways**. This is obviously a case of double emphasis: This verse suggests that we need to search and then search again in thorough self-examination. When one is seeking to get right with God, it is no time for lighthearted investigation, partial facts, or half-truths. (3) When one has honestly examined himself, discovering any waywardness or weakness, then it is time to **return to the LORD**. In this verse, which is specifically related to sin and God, the word "return" (שׁוּב, *shub*) means to "turn back to God" or "seek penitently" (see comments on 1:13).

Verse 41. Lifting up **our heart** (internal devotion) and **hands** (external desire and service) demonstrates a sincere longing to get back with God (see 1 Tim. 2:8).

Verse 42. A confession was made that the people of Judah had **transgressed and rebelled** (1:18, 20). Both words, "transgressed" (פָּשַׁע, *pasha'*)[30] and "rebelled," carry the idea of knowing God's will and openly revolting against it. Again, here is a double emphasis on stubborn, disobedient, and offensive conduct. Truly, people with this character and conduct have no right to complain before God or man if punishment comes their way (Lk. 23:39–41).

Verse 43. Jeremiah assessed Judah's condition, in various expressions of tragedy: How God reacted to Judah's sin was part of the sobering scene. Since the people had not repented, God had not "pardoned" them (3:42; see Jer. 29:12–14). God's **anger** (see 1:12; 2:1, 3, 21, 22; 3:1) and His pursuit of justice had caused many to be **slain** and **not spared** (see 2:2, 4, 6).

Verse 44. A **cloud** has often been used as a figure of darkness, gloom, and depression; here it is coupled with God's anger (2:1). This cloud represented a barrier which prayer could not

---

[28]Ibid., 344.
[29]Ibid., 350.
[30]Ibid., 833.

penetrate (see Prov. 1:24–33; Is. 59:1–8; Jer. 7:16; 11:14; 14:11).

God had warned the people that their evil ways would cause Him to turn His back to them (Jer. 15:6; 18:15–17). The prophet now sadly admitted that the moment had come.

Verse 45. How Judah's enemies responded is also stated. To be measured as the **offscouring** [סְחִי, *s^echi*] **and refuse** of human beings is as low as mankind can be, valued no more than filth scraped from the body.[31] In the use of this word, which appears only here in the Old Testament, the people were being equated with "scum," "bodily waste," or "rubbish."[32] It is similar to a dog returning to its vomit (Prov. 26:11; 2 Pet. 2:22).

Verse 46. Added to this estimation of the people's worthlessness was the prophet's statement that enemies had **opened their mouths against us**. The defamation of God's people was complete. In the midst of swords and slaughter, the captors hurled insults and slanderous cursing at captives in chains. What horrifying sights and sounds staggered these defenseless souls!

Verse 47. How Judah responded to this smoldering scene of **devastation and destruction** is summarized as **panic** (פַּחַד, *pachad*). This indicated their dread and terror. Terrors were on every side (2:22). The people were aghast, stupefied, and completely bewildered by what has happened. This sudden fright and agony were fruits borne of their sin.

CRIES OF CONCERN—HIS GROWTH
(3:48–58)

Verses 48 through 58 revert to the first person, which continues until the end of the chapter, with the use of "my" (16 times), "me" (6 times), and "I" (5 times). Two other parties are dominant in the prophet's personal observations. The Lord is named 7 times, and the pronouns "You" (12 times) and "Your" (3 times) are used repeatedly in addressing God, commending Him or calling on Him for help. The reason for these cries to the Lord is

---

[31]Ibid., 695.
[32]Provan, 101.

that the prophet was facing enemies (3:52) and assailants (3:62), who are repeatedly identified by the pronouns "their" (9 times), "them" (5 times), and "they" (once).

The Condition of His Incessant Weeping (3:48, 49)

> ⁴⁸My eyes run down with streams of water
> Because of the destruction of the daughter of my people.
> ⁴⁹My eyes pour down unceasingly,
> Without stopping.

Verses 48, 49. The condition of the writer was one of incessant weeping. With tears running down like **streams of water**, and **pour**[ing] **down unceasingly, without stopping**, could his pain have been any more persistent? Could his agony have been much deeper? If words can lead us to weep with one who weeps (Rom. 12:15), then any reader who ponders this scene should feel sorrow for that suffering soul. What a price this prophet of God had to pay!

Does **the daughter of my people** refer to adjoining cities that had been destroyed? The phrase probably does not mean that here. Like verse 51, it should be interpreted literally. Verse 51 refers to the "daughters of my city," indicating a burdened heart for the defenseless women and the indescribable cruelty they had endured as the city fell before famine and foe (see 2:11–13, 18–20). Those around her had come under the suffering that Jerusalem received.

The Cause for the Weeping (3:50–54)

> ⁵⁰Until the LORD looks down
> And sees from heaven.
> ⁵¹My eyes bring pain to my soul
> Because of all the daughters of my city.
> ⁵²My enemies without cause
> Hunted me down like a bird;
> ⁵³They have silenced me in the pit
> And have placed a stone on me.

⁵⁴Waters flowed over my head;
I said, "I am cut off!"

Verse 50. The prophet would weep **until the Lord looks down and sees from heaven**. This is a key statement.

Verse 51. The reasons for the prophet's weeping relate to more than **the daughters of** [his] **city**. Now knowing that these events were God's judgments, the prophet acknowledged that the only help in this day of devastation would be the Lord God. Judah's rejected Redeemer, their just God, had to be appeased before He would restore them (see Jer. 29:10–14).

Verse 52. The prophet's own helplessness is identified. He recalled how his **enemies** had **hunted** [him] **down like a bird** (see Jer. 37:12–16).

Verses 53, 54. They had **silenced** him by putting him **in the pit** (בּוֹר, *bor*).³³ Not only was Jeremiah in the depths of the cistern, but a lid or **stone** was also over his head in that dark, isolated pit. When anyone mistreats us, we are hurt. It is especially perplexing and heartbreaking when the enemies are our own people (see Ps. 55:4–15; 69:1–12).

No wonder he felt silenced and **cut off**. When help was so much needed and he so much wanted to help his people, being in that pit was painful. He was unable to speak for God or to help those who were hurting up above. His only hope for better days was to look to God.

The Call That Comforted Him (3:55–58)

⁵⁵I called on Your name, O Lord,
Out of the lowest pit.
⁵⁶You have heard my voice,
"Do not hide Your ear from my prayer for relief,
From my cry for help."
⁵⁷You drew near when I called on You;

---

³³This is the word for "cistern" (Koehler and Baumgartner, 1:116). This calls to mind Joseph's being thrown into a pit by his brothers (Gen. 37:24) and Jeremiah's being imprisoned in a dungeon (Jer. 37) and in a muddy cistern (Jer. 38).

You said, "Do not fear!"
⁵⁸O Lord, You have pleaded my soul's cause;
You have redeemed my life.

Verse 55. This verse includes the call (on the **name** of the LORD) that comforted. If this petition came from the **pit** or cistern, it truly echoes the ability of the Almighty to hear us no matter where we are.

Verse 56. His **cry** was for divine **relief** and **help**. One who is stuck in a muddy cistern, with a stone closing off the entrance above, is in no position to say, "I can take care of myself!"

God responded to Jeremiah's cry in five significant ways. First, God heard his voice; He did not **hide** [His] **ear** from the prophet's **prayer** (see Jn. 9:31). Often, there is a big difference between fears and facts. Earlier, when the prophet had cried out for help, he had said of God, "He shuts out my prayer" (3:8). He further charged that God covered Himself as a cloud so that no prayer could pass through (3:44). A difference is noticed in the confidence of the prophet in 3:55–57. Who had changed: God or the prophet?

Verse 57. Second, when the prophet **called**, God **drew near** (see Acts 17:25–28). It has been said that we are near to God at this moment and would be equally near on the other side of the earth, for He is everywhere (Ps. 139:1–18; Jer. 23:23, 24). Nevertheless, the Scriptures identify a moment when God pours out a blessing as a time when He draws near.

Third, God said to Jeremiah, **"Do not fear!"** He is the Almighty God (see Gen. 17:1; 28:3; Ex. 6:3; Ps. 9:1, 3; Rev. 4:8; 19:6). God is love, and perfect love casts out fear (1 Jn. 4:8, 18; see 2 Tim. 1:7; Heb. 13:5, 6). When God says there is no reason to be afraid, His words are backed by unlimited resources and strength to make them meaningful.

Verse 58. Fourth, according to Jeremiah, God had **pleaded** (רִיב, *rib*) his **soul's cause**. The word used here can have legal connotations associated with an appeal in court, but here it likely means merely to cry out or plead one's cause.[34] Whatever the

---

[34]Brown, Driver, and Briggs, 936.

prophet's cause might have been, who is able to argue with Almighty God? (See Job 42:1–6; Ps. 8:1–4.)

Fifth, the prophet gratefully prayed to God, **You have redeemed** [גָּאַל, *ga'al*] **my life.** We can only imagine what it meant to Jeremiah, after being in that pit, to have his life redeemed as Ebed-melech came with thirty men and lifted the prophet out of the cistern (Jer. 38:8–13). The sense here is that of being reclaimed. The word is used extensively in Isaiah, Jeremiah, and Psalms to speak of God's activity in behalf of Israel.[35]

CRIES OF CONCERN—HIS CONVICTION (3:59–66)

⁵⁹O Lord, You have seen my oppression;
Judge my case.
⁶⁰You have seen all their vengeance,
All their schemes against me.
⁶¹You have heard their reproach, O Lord,
All their schemes against me.
⁶²The lips of my assailants and their whispering
Are against me all day long.
⁶³Look on their sitting and their rising;
I am their mocking song.
⁶⁴You will recompense them, O Lord,
According to the work of their hands.
⁶⁵You will give them hardness of heart,
Your curse will be on them.
⁶⁶You will pursue them in anger and destroy them
From under the heavens of the Lord!

Verse 59. The prophet's problems were placed in the Lord's hands. At this point, the phrasing is no longer a plea, but a reality. The Lord was alert; He saw the prophet's **oppression**.

Verses 60–63. The writer now recognized that the Lord had seen his enemies' **vengeance, schemes, reproach**[es], deceptive **lips,** and **whispering**[s]. He had become the object of their mock-

---

[35]Koehler and Baumgartner, 1:169.

ing **all day long**. A striking parallel exists between the charges in 3:59–63 and those in Jeremiah 20:7–13. In the similar phrasing of these passages, the jubilant prophet was expressing confidence in a God-given victory over his assailants. He saw himself as being on the winning side.

Verse 64. The prophet saw God's plan to **recompense** Judah's enemies **according to the work of their hands**. That is God's way in judgment, His way to punish (Jer. 17:9, 10; Ezek. 18:30–32; Gal. 6:7, 8).

Verses 65, 66. The price they would pay is described in 3:66. God would **pursue them in** [His] **anger** (אף, *'ap*) and **destroy them** (see Jer. 18:20–23). This fire-charged term has been repeatedly used in this book (1:12; 2:1, 3, 6, 21, 22; 3:43). God's action would **give them hardness of heart**, and His **curse** [would] **be on them**. This is no Calvinistic doctrine that God foreordains so many to be lost and so many to be saved, denying man of his own free will. God does not desire that any be lost, but He does command people to repent of their rebellious ways (Ezek. 18:30–32; Acts 17:30, 31; 2 Pet. 3:9). If a person resists God's longsuffering spirit and mercy, being unwilling to develop a love for the truth, he will face the consequences of rebellion (see Prov. 1:23–33; 2 Thess. 2:9–12).

In this manner God hardened Pharaoh's heart (Ex. 7:3; 9:12; 10:1), but it is clearly stated that stubborn Pharaoh hardened his own heart (Ex. 7:13, 14; 8:15, 32; 9:34). When the sun shines on wax and concrete, one is softened and the other is hardened. In the same way, God's truth may soften one to grateful obedience, while another receiving the same truth becomes hardened and rebels.

The writer was no longer making a plea for God to act, but was making a confident statement to God. **You will** is used three times in quick succession in 3:64–66. He was resting his heart upon God's faithfulness.

This chapter shows the transition from an agonizing and afflicted prophet (3:1) to a prophet confident in God's care. It is appropriate that the lament ends with a phrase affirming the prophet's growing faith, acknowledging that this was **of the LORD**.

APPLICATION

Growth in Insight (3:1–18, 55–66)

A message in chapter 3 that must not be overlooked is the prophet's presentation of *what God had done to him* (3:1–18), which ends with gratitude because of *what God had done for him* (3:55–66). The altered view came not so much from a change in God's pattern, but from a deeper insight gained by the prophet. The change was not in God's care or concern, but in the prophet's grasp of the circumstances. God promised Jeremiah His care and deliverance in Jeremiah 1:17–19, but Jeremiah did not recognize the fulfillment of the promise for some twenty years (see Jer. 20:7–13). Likewise, in chapter 3 the prophet moved from complaining and doubt to confidence in God and devotion to Him.

How do we think of God and His response to our circumstances? Would we rather be like the prophet at the beginning of chapter 3 or at the end?

Another great example of this same principle is Psalm 73. Verses 1 through 16 express the psalmist's complaints. He was envious of the wicked, who seemed to be prospering and trouble-free until the writer "came into the sanctuary of God" (73:17a). There he was able to put things in the proper focus and perceive the end of the wicked. He closed the psalm with a confession of his own senseless shortsightedness, along with a glowing tribute to God, who provided his strength (73:17b–28).

In the valley of affliction, we can gain the perception of God's promises and provisions. This is not a claim that facing hardship is the only way one can focus on God's favor and care, but numerous passages and incidents prove our need to recognize that growth may come from grief and affliction. Deeper perception may come from pain. Jesus learned obedience from suffering (Heb. 5:7–9), and it was through his thorn in the flesh that Paul grasped God's grace, recognizing that weakness leads us to lay hold on God's strength (2 Cor. 12:7–10). Likewise, it was out of affliction that the psalmist came to learn and live according to God's Word (Ps. 119:67, 71). We should not be surprised if God allows us to face grief through trials for the strengthening and proving of our faith (Gen. 22:1–14; Heb. 11:17–19; 1 Pet. 1:6–9).

"The Steadfast Love of the Lord" (3:22–24)

A wonderful song is based on this passage of Scripture:

> The steadfast love of the Lord never ceases,
> His mercies never come to an end;
> They are new ev'ry morning;
> Great is Thy faithfulness.
> "The Lord is my portion," says my soul,
> "Therefore I will hope in Him."[36]

Don Shackelford taught for many years at a Christian university. He recalls that the students loved to sing this song in expressing their faith, but when asked over the years where this thought was expressed in the Bible, they did not know.

How wonderful it is that, in the very midst of anguished cries of a funeral dirge, Jeremiah could express this profound faith in the Lord! With his world crumbling around him, Jeremiah did not lose hope, and neither should we. The Lord's steadfast love, mercies, and faithfulness never cease.

"Do Not Fear!" (3:57)

The power of God's Word can be observed in the richness of a brief promise that can alter our entire outlook on life. Three key words are "Do not fear!" in 3:57. Let us not forget the setting: The prophet was in "the lowest pit" (3:55); yet, knowing that God would draw near to him, he moved to a confident trust in God's redeeming benefits (3:58). God makes a big difference through just a few words.

This principle has prevailed to work wonders for people. God comforted Abraham in Genesis 15:1: "Do not fear, Abram." He did the same for Isaac: "Do not fear, for I am with you" (Gen. 26:24). God gave the same instruction to Moses before the conquest of a king: "Do not fear him" (Num. 21:34). When Joshua faced all the kings of the Amorites, God calmly said, "Do not fear them" (Josh. 10:8). While Judah and Jerusalem were facing a

---

[36]"The Steadfast Love of the Lord," *Songs of Faith and Praise*, comp. and ed. Alton H. Howard (West Monroe, La.: Howard Publishing Co., 1994).

great multitude, God said, "Do not fear . . . because of this great multitude, for the battle is not yours but God's" (2 Chron. 20:15). Through Isaiah, God spoke to Israel in a time of trouble, saying, "Do not fear, for I am with you" (Is. 41:10). An angel was sent to Daniel in captivity to say, "Do not be afraid, Daniel" (Dan. 10:12). When God's people came out of their captivity, God said, "Do not fear!" (Hag. 2:5; Zech. 8:13). When it was time for Jesus to be born, God said through an angel, "Do not be afraid, Mary" (Lk. 1:30). As Jesus selected Peter and others to go out for Him, He said, "Do not fear" (Lk. 5:10). When Paul faced a shipwreck, God sent the message "Do not be afraid, Paul" (Acts 27:24). Appearing before John as the amazing, glorified, resurrected Son of God, the Lord in splendor said, "Do not be afraid" (Rev. 1:17).

From the beginning to the end of God's message to men, the cry and call to creatures of earth has been "Do not fear!" These words repel fear and strengthen the faith within us (see Mt. 28:20; Jn. 14:1–3, 6; 1 Cor. 15:50–58; Heb. 5:8, 9).

"The Lord Is My Portion"

In *The Biblical Illustrator*, D. Wilcox gave ten significant benefits for the one who is truly converted to the idea that "the Lord is my portion": (1) When he grasps God's worth and the need for Him, it leads that person to be "incapable of being satisfied without Him, or taking up with anything else." (2) He "has entered into covenant with Him." (3) He "loves Him, above all, or with a superlative affection." (4) He "values communion with Him more than any sensible enjoyment." (5) He "is greatly thankful for the direction and grace that inclined and enabled him to make the happy choice which he would not now exchange for all the world." (6) One who recognizes the significance of Him as his portion "feels the greatest grief for the apprehended loss of Him, or when in the dark as to an interest in Him." (7) He "will, by prayer and supplication, frequently go to Him, and be more earnest for His favour and grace than for any lower good." (8) He "will make Him the ground of his trust and triumph, when outward comforts may be withdrawn or denied (Hab. 3:17, 18)." (9) He will take "care to please and serve Him with the inward man," and be careful to maintain a fear of offending Him, "even in the thoughts, or things that do not come under the eye of the world." (10) He will be "breathing after that world and state where it shall have the full enjoyment of Him; and frequently, with pleasure, taken up in the believing thoughts and hopes of it . . . when this world is to be for ever left, and all lower sensual delights at an end."[37]

---

[37]D. Wilcox, "The Lamentations of Jeremiah," in *The Biblical Illustrator*, comp. and ed. Joseph S. Exell (Grand Rapids, Mich.: Baker Book House, 1973), 52.

CHAPTER 4
THE COST OF SIN

Chapter 4 contains a series of scenes showing the calamity that had come upon Judah (4:1–10). The cause for the calamity (4:11–16) and a summary of the complete destruction is given (4:17–20). At the end, a ray of hope appears (4:21, 22). This nation was mourned by the prophet (4:1–10), mocked by other nations (4:12, 21, 22), and rejected by God (4:11, 16). The initial scene is one of cruel contrasts between what His people once had been and what they had become (see *Appendix: The "Before" & "After" Pictures of God's People [Lam. 4:1–8]*, page 582). While chapter 3 portrayed the exile from the perspective of the individual, chapter 4 focuses on the community during the siege. This chapter is the most graphic in depicting the physical suffering of the people.[1]

In the Hebrew, verses 1 through 6 form a unit that presents certain contrasts, plus the cause of Judah's destruction. Verses 7 through 10 present more contrasts, and a reminder of the cause is given in verse 11. The prepositions "for" at the beginning of verse 6 and "because" in verse 10 introduce the causal statements.

Scholars have noticed that chapters 4 and 5 are shortened in form from earlier chapters. This could well be true because Jeremiah was winding down in cries of concern to God. His pain and lament before God had ascended to its apex and now was diminishing to a calmer state.[2]

---

[1] Adele Berlin, *Lamentations*, Old Testament Library (Louisville, Ky.: Westminster John Knox Press, 2004), 102–3.
[2] Kathleen M. O'Connor, *Lamentations and the Tears of the World* (Maryknoll, N.Y.: Orbis Books, 2002), 58.

PILLAGE AND PAIN (4:1–10)

Once a beautiful and prosperous land, Judah now lay in ruin. The contrasts drawn between the former prosperity of the land and its current state seem to double the tragedy. The pillage appears amplified as the people are pictured in their agony: "the precious sons of Zion" (4:2), "the daughter of my people" (4:3, 6), infants (4:4), and mothers who went from compassion to cannibalism (4:10). These images climax the scene of starvation and slaughter of the besieged city in 4:1–10. Norman K. Gottwald emphasized this contrast: "As with the earlier poems, so with the fourth, we meet the dramatic contrast between past and present. One by one the various groups pass in review."[3]

The Temple's Destruction (4:1)

> [1]**How dark the gold has become,**
> **How the pure gold has changed!**
> **The sacred stones are poured out**
> **At the corner of every street.**

Verse 1. The temple had been ripped apart and left in shambles. Conquest had changed Jerusalem's former glory into the gory scene of a decimated city. John Guest described how he thought Jeremiah may have observed this setting:

> He looks at each stone, having been so carefully hewn, so brilliantly fitted together, now wrenched from its position and tumbled carelessly into the streets of Jerusalem as though they were random chunks of nothing. He was pained to see them out of place, no longer joined together for the glory of God.[4]

---

[3]Norman K. Gottwald, *Studies in the Book of Lamentations*, Studies in Biblical Theology No. 14, rev. ed. (London: SCM Press, 1962), 59.

[4]John Guest, *Jeremiah, Lamentations*, Communicator's Commentary (Waco, Tex.: Word Books, 1988), 381.

The **sacred stones** and the structure of the temple are depicted as **poured out** (שָׁפַךְ, *shapak*). This phrasing in Hebrew offers a word-picture of stones lying around as if they had been spilled.[5] The term is freely used in Lamentations and is always expressive of grave, eye-catching stages of tragedy. The "sacred stones" were from structures that had been precious to the Jews—structures that had been reduced to rubble, with scattered pieces disrespectfully thrown into the **street**[s]. Are the "sacred stones" a metaphor for the "precious sons" mentioned in verse 2? Probably not, for other biblical records give us ample reason to see in these words the scattered remains of the temple structure (1 Kings 7:49–51; 2 Kings 24:12, 13; 25:9, 13–17; 2 Chron. 36:6, 7, 10, 17–19; Jer. 27:21, 22; 52:13–23).

Three Hebrew terms are used in 4:1, 2 to identify the gold that had been plundered: (1) זָהָב (*zahab*), for the general term **gold**, (2) כֶּתֶם (*kethem*), translated **pure gold**, and (3) פַּז (*paz*), for "fine gold." All are used to identify specific parts of the former beauty that the prophet now viewed as stained, **dark**, and **changed**. Something so precious losing its value and being scattered on street corners shows the degree to which the social and spiritual landscape of Judah had exploded. Once again, Guest described how the tarnished scene must have looked:

> The temple no longer glistens in the sunlight. Her golden age has passed into blackened streets where temple stones have been tumbled and all the brilliant things of God have become cheap and common. The sons of Zion are no longer precious, no longer mortised together as living stones of the spiritual house. The daughters too have lost their glory, have become less than human. They eat their dying infants in order to survive.[6]

---

[5]Ludwig Koehler and Walter Baumgartner, *The Hebrew and Aramaic Lexicon of the Old Testament*, study ed., trans. and ed. M. E. J. Richardson (Boston: Brill, 2001), 2:1629.

[6]Guest, 351.

The People's Rejection (4:2)

> ²The precious sons of Zion,
> Weighed against fine gold,
> How they are regarded as earthen jars,
> The work of a potter's hands!

Verse 2. The precious sons of Zion, set apart to be a kingdom of priests and a holy nation, were now rejected and ignored. The ones who had been compared to **fine gold** had become like cheap **earthen jars**. Valuable objects of gold were now counted as having no more worth than broken pieces of pottery, "by all odds the commonest and cheapest refuse of ancient city life."[7] Individuals who had been majestic and splendid went unnoticed and unwanted. The bloodline that was supposed to have been a noble blessing to all nations had been reduced to nothing and had become no nation (see Gen. 26:1–4; Jer. 13:9–11).

The People's Starvation (4:3, 4)

> ³Even jackals offer the breast,
> They nurse their young;
> But the daughter of my people has become cruel
> Like ostriches in the wilderness.
> ⁴The tongue of the infant cleaves
> To the roof of its mouth because of thirst;
> The little ones ask for bread,
> But no one breaks it for them.

Verse 3. The domestic scene was one of hunger and thirst. The people cried for sustenance that could not and would not be supplied. **Even jackals**, the wild, roving beasts of prey, were said to give food to their **young**; but the prophet said that **the daughter of my people**—the mothers in Judah—had **become cruel**. The Hebrew word for "cruel," אַכְזָר (*'akzar*), is associated with fierce, harsh, even savage treatment (see Job 30:21; Prov. 5:9; 17:11; Is.

---

[7]Gottwald, 59.

13:9; Jer. 30:14).⁸ The conduct suggested by this term is blended with the charge that they were **like ostriches in the wilderness**. Theo. Laetsch observed, "While the stork is called *avis pia*, 'the pious bird,' the ostrich was regarded as a symbol of maternal neglect and cruelty (cp. Job 39:13b–16)."⁹

Verse 4. Even greater vividness is used: **The tongue of the infant cleaves to the roof of its mouth because of thirst.** The water is gone and people are dying of thirst. **The little ones ask for bread, but no one breaks it for them.** Judah's agony reached such a wretched level that mothers became stoic and insensitive to the suffering of their own children.

The People's Degradation (4:5–8)

> ⁵Those who ate delicacies
> Are desolate in the streets;
> Those reared in purple
> Embrace ash pits.
> ⁶For the iniquity of the daughter of my people
> Is greater than the sin of Sodom,
> Which was overthrown as in a moment,
> And no hands were turned toward her.
> ⁷Her consecrated ones were purer than snow,
> They were whiter than milk;
> They were more ruddy in body than corals,
> Their polishing was like lapis lazuli.
> ⁸Their appearance is blacker than soot,
> They are not recognized in the streets;
> Their skin is shriveled on their bones,
> It is withered, it has become like wood.

Verse 5. The social scene added to the sadness. Members of the aristocracy, who had been accustomed to living luxuriously, were seen wandering about debris-strewn **streets**, seeking some-

---

⁸Francis Brown, S. R. Driver, and Charles A. Briggs, *A Hebrew and English Lexicon of the Old Testament* (Oxford: Clarendon Press, 1972), 470.

⁹Theo. Laetsch, *Jeremiah*, Bible Commentary (St. Louis: Concordia Publishing House, 1965), 397.

thing to sustain their starving bodies. Their **desolate** state is mentioned repeatedly (1:4, 13, 16; 3:11). In luxury, they had reclined on scarlet couches; they now **embrace**[d] **ash pits** (אַשְׁפֹּת, *'ashpoth*), or "dunghills" (KJV), places normally used for cooking pots,[10] for their beds. In some countries, women still pick up dung and pat it into cakes to be used as fuel for cooking.

Verse 6. The prophet explained what had led to this conduct and lifestyle: **the iniquity** (עָוֹן, *'awon*) **of my people**. Their sin was **greater than the sin of Sodom**. The people of Sodom were guilty of vile sins (see Gen. 19:1–29; Jer. 23:1–15; 16:9–13), but the shame of Sodom had been eclipsed by the rebellion of the city once most favored by heaven.

Verse 7. Further contrasts follow, showing what the people had been and what they had become. The **consecrated ones**, rulers and princes dedicated to God, had been **purer than snow**. Their former state is described as **more ruddy in body than corals** ("rubies"; KJV) and polished **like lapis lazuli**. The term for "corals" (פְּנִינִים, *peninim*)[11] has been related to coral (Job 28:18) or pearls or jewels (Prov. 3:15; 8:11; 31:10).[12] While the translation may vary, the message in this context is clear: Young leaders who were polished and pure had once guided Judah. The Lord had led them to great victories and brought them into a productive land (see Lev. 26:6–13; Deut. 32:7–14; Is. 63:11–14).

Verse 8. How shocking it must have been to see the plight of the people reversed! **Their appearance** [was] **blacker than soot**. Starvation had turned handsome human beings into people whose **skin** [was] **shriveled on their bones**. Their **withered**, wrinkled flesh was hard and warped **like wood**. No one seemed to care about them. They went staggering about, **not recognized** (נָכַר, *nakar*) **in the streets**. They had gone from being nobility to becoming someone who was "not recognized" at all. A graphic picture of burned-out, worn-out, thrown-away people is seen here.

---

[10]Koehler and Baumgartner, 1:96.
[11]These have been defined as "pearls of coral" (Ibid., 2:946).
[12]Brown, Driver, and Briggs, 819.

LAMENTATIONS 4

The People's Ultimate Corruption (4:9, 10)

⁹Better are those slain with the sword
Than those slain with hunger;
For they pine away, being stricken
For lack of the fruits of the field.
¹⁰The hands of compassionate women
Boiled their own children;
They became food for them
Because of the destruction of the daughter of my people.

Verse 9. The time came when slaughter was preferable to starvation. Being attacked with a **sword** is a terrifying thought (1 Sam. 31:3–6); but the slow process of starvation is prolonged, with no prospects of recovery. The thought of **being stricken** is from a Hebrew term, דָּקַר (*daqar*), that means "to pierce through."[13] One "stricken" with starvation faces ongoing, piercing **hunger** pangs.

Verse 10. The section 4:1–10 closes with a climax of corruption. A pathetic case of satire is penned in this scene of Judah's mothers **boil**[ing] and eating **their own children** (see 2:20; Deut. 28:47–57; 2 Kings 6:24–30; Jer. 19:8, 9). This desperate act came at the hands of those who were labeled as **compassionate women**. Here is a Hebrew term for "compassionate," רַחֲמָנִי (*rachᵃmani*),[14] found only in Lamentations 4:10; but it springs from a basic root, רָחַם (*racham*), that is repeatedly translated as "mercy," "compassion," "pity," and "love" (Ps. 18:2; 103:13; Jer. 12:15; 31:20; 33:26). The ironic description is an echoing shout to warn us how far humanity can descend. People lost in sin can sink so low that their compassion gives way to cannibalism. The unbelievable must be believed. The price that must be paid for promiscuous, rebellious, stubborn conduct should steer rational souls away from sin. Truly, those who sow to the flesh shall reap corrup-

---

[13]Ibid., 201.
[14]Ibid., 933. Kathleen M. O'Connor said, "The merciful nature of the mothers turned to cannibalism of their own children adds one more detail of communal abasement in the destroyed society" (O'Connor, 62).

tion, just as Judah met **destruction** (Gal. 6:7, 8; see Is. 13:16–22; Jer. 4:30, 31; 9:17–22).

THEIR PUNISHMENT AND THE POWER OF GOD (4:11–16)

The painful scene described in 4:1–10 was no accident. Rather, it was God's intent. Verses 11 and 16 emphasize that these punishments were part of a divine plan.

While it is an undesirable thought for God's people to entertain, both the Old and the New Testaments speak of God's wrath. Verse 11 says that the Lord "kindled a fire in Zion." Hebrews 12:29 reads, "Our God is a consuming fire." He judges His people, according to Deuteronomy 32:36 and Hebrews 10:30; and His punishment is neither feeble nor ineffectual (see Ezek. 23:35–49).

God's Anger (4:11, 12)

> ¹¹**The LORD has accomplished His wrath,**
> **He has poured out His fierce anger;**
> **And He has kindled a fire in Zion**
> **Which has consumed its foundations.**
> ¹²**The kings of the earth did not believe,**
> **Nor did any of the inhabitants of the world,**
> **That the adversary and the enemy**
> **Could enter the gates of Jerusalem.**

Verse 11. What God's seething **anger** had purposed, He had now **accomplished** (see 2:11–13). Ezekiel 5:13–16 provided a graphic rationale for what God was doing. He said that God did what He did for this reason: ". . . they will know that I, the LORD, have spoken in My zeal when I have spent My wrath upon them" (Ezek. 5:13).

It is sad that God had to go so far before these people would honor Him as Lord and turn from their wicked ways. The degree of the destruction is seen in the statement that the **fire in Zion . . . has consumed** [אָכַל, *'akal*] **its foundations** (see comments on 2:1–3).

LAMENTATIONS 4

Verse 12. Other nations were surprised that **the enemy could enter the gates of Jerusalem**. This mountain city dedicated to Yahweh had gained a reputation as an impregnable fortress. Not only had Zion's citizens forgotten God, but surrounding nations had failed to consider what can happen when God sets His face against a city (see Jer. 21:1–14).

The fact that God could protect His city from powerful forces had been dramatically demonstrated. The emperor Sennacherib and his massive forces from Assyria had crumbled before a single angel of the Almighty. In one night, 185,000 Assyrian soldiers had died (Is. 37:6–38). The seemingly impossible became a reality when God's anger turned against Jerusalem and Judah.

The Leaders' Sins (4:13–15)

> ¹³**Because of the sins of her prophets
> And the iniquities of her priests,
> Who have shed in her midst
> The blood of the righteous;
> ¹⁴They wandered, blind, in the streets;
> They were defiled with blood
> So that no one could touch their garments.
> ¹⁵"Depart! Unclean!" they cried of themselves.
> "Depart, depart, do not touch!"
> So they fled and wandered;
> Men among the nations said,
> "They shall not continue to dwell with us."**

Verse 13. A primary interpretative point of the Book of Lamentations is that the **sins** of Jerusalem's leaders were the cause of this calamity. **Prophets**, **priests**, and kings had **shed . . . the blood of the righteous** and the innocent (see 2 Kings 21:1–6; 24:3, 4; Jer. 2:26–30, 34, 35; 19:1–4). They were guilty of lying and gross immorality (Jer. 6:13–15; 27:14–22; 29:21–23).

Verse 14. These shamed, stunned souls had become untouchables; they were **defiled** (גֹּאֲלוּ, *ga'al*)—stained and polluted[15]—

---

[15]Brown, Driver, and Briggs, 146.

with blood. When Jerusalem fell, these false, crying prophets and priests were unmasked so that their countrymen treated them as they would treat unclean lepers (Lev. 13:45).

Verse 15. How sad and ironic that the very people who should have helped Judah to be pure and clean were forced to move about in shame, crying of themselves, **"Depart! Unclean!"** The ones who should have offered strength and stability to the people became shaking and scared, running about aimlessly. They are described as straying souls who, incapable of doing anything else, **wandered** [נוּעַ, *nua'*][16] **blind, in the streets.** These helpless, blind wanderers became tottering vagabonds. Adele Berlin said, "There is a certain irony in prophets—visionaries—being blind."[17] From their positions of leadership, they had gone to wandering and being unwanted. Once the favored people of God, they had become filthy, defiled, and defenseless.

God's Scattering (4:16)

> [16]**The presence of the LORD has scattered them,**
> **He will not continue to regard them;**
> **They did not honor the priests,**
> **They did not favor the elders.**

Verse 16. It is here stated that God **scattered them**. The action of Judah's enemies came from **the presence of the LORD**. The term translated "scattered" (חָלַק, *chalaq*) primarily carries the force of "being divided." Jeremiah 27—29 makes evident that God, by scattering His people in the exile, was also dividing those who had joined in deceit. False prophets were being identified and given the death sentence. God would no longer **regard** or respect them. The process of separation was already underway; the people at that time **did not honor the priests** and **did not favor the elders.** The Hebrew term for "favor" (חָנַן, *chanan*), when joined with "not," shows no yearning for, no mercy, no

---

[16]Ibid., 631.
[17]Berlin, 111.

compassion, no pity.¹⁸ No longer would the people look favorably upon those deceivers.

A DECEIVED NATION (4:17–20)

¹⁷Yet our eyes failed,
Looking for help was useless;
In our watching we have watched
For a nation that could not save.
¹⁸They hunted our steps
So that we could not walk in our streets;
Our end drew near,
Our days were finished
For our end had come.
¹⁹Our pursuers were swifter
Than the eagles of the sky;
They chased us on the mountains,
They waited in ambush for us in the wilderness.
²⁰The breath of our nostrils, the LORD's anointed,
Was captured in their pits,
Of whom we had said, "Under his shadow
We shall live among the nations."

Verse 17. The prophet himself was active in the narrative of this section (4:17–20). It shifts from third person ("they" and "them") to first person plural ("our," "us," and "we").

The summation of a deceived nation is presented next in four scenes.

Scene 1: "We sought foreign alliances to save us—but it did not work!" (See 1:7; Jer. 2:16–19, 25; 42:9–19.) The tendency of these people to seek help from other nations rather than from God had been a mistaken pattern for a long time. An Assyrian commander had expected them to do so in the days of Hezekiah (see Is. 36:1–9). In Jeremiah's day, it was still part of the nation's folly (Jer. 37:6–8). They needed **help**, but they sought it from a **useless** source.

---

¹⁸Brown, Driver, and Briggs, 335–36.

Verse 18. *Scene 2:* "The strength of our adversaries overwhelmed us—and we were destroyed!" Suddenly, the people were faced with a nightmare of unexpected destruction (Jer. 39:1–3; 52:12–27). Actually, obstinacy made the Jews hold out for so long against Babylon. Jeremiah had described their downfall for more than twenty years, but the people had not listened (Jer. 25:1–11). For about fifteen more years, the prophetic message called for them to turn to God and not seek help from other nations (Jer. 37:1–10). Even the final thrust by Babylon's forces lasted eighteen months, and the beleaguered forces of Judah still refused to repent or apply reason to their sad state (Jer. 39:1–9). They seemed stunned. They continued in their stubbornness until the temple itself was torn down and burned. The prophet, speaking for these deceived souls, said, **our days were finished for our end had come**.

Verse 19. *Scene 3:* "Swift pursuers ensnared us—and we were devoured!" (See Is. 5:26–30; 30:15–17.) The enemy came like hunters; the people and their property were devoured (Jer. 5:15–17; 16:16–18). Jeremiah had long before prophetically described how they would respond, as a ruined people, when the speedy forces came upon them (Jer. 4:11–13). Like **eagles** swooping in for the kill, so the forces of Babylon descended upon Judah.

Verse 20. *Scene 4:* "Shallow leadership left us defenseless—and we were defeated!" **The Lord's anointed** surely is a reference to King Zedekiah, the last king of Judah to occupy the throne. God was supposed to appoint the kings of His people (see Deut. 17:14, 15; 1 Sam. 9: 15–17; 16:1, 11–13); but, technically, God did not select Zedekiah. That act was carried out by the conquering king, Nebuchadnezzar (2 Kings 24:17–20). However, the people of Judah considered Zedekiah their king (Jer. 37:1–3). Even though he failed as a king, a husband, a father, and a man (Jer. 38:17–23; 39:1–8), the position he occupied led the people of Judah to view him as **the breath of our nostrils**. He was their lifeline. Zedekiah was to them the current representative of the house of David, and many were deluded into believing that God would never allow the house of David to be overthrown (see 2 Sam. 7:5, 12–16; Acts 2:22–32).

God's intent to provide spiritual salvation through Jesus, the

Messiah, was far from the expectations of these material-minded and sin-driven people. A temporal kingdom dominated their thinking. In their shortsighted stubbornness, they insisted on viewing Zedekiah as "the breath of our nostrils," their link to survival. He was their **shadow** of salvation to care for them as a nation **among nations**. Their grave mistake was that they had placed their trust in man, not in their Maker, and in a place, not in the Person who gave significance to that place (see Jer. 7:1–11). The figure of speech depicting refuge as a shadow was common to the Hebrews (see Ps. 17:8; 36:7; 57:1; 63:7, 8; 91:1–4; Is. 49:1–4; 51:15, 16). God had warned His people about choosing the wrong refuge (Is. 30:1–3; Hos. 14:1–7).

HOPE IN THE MIDST OF PUNISHMENT (4:21, 22)

> ²¹Rejoice and be glad, O daughter of Edom,
> Who dwells in the land of Uz;
> But the cup will come around to you as well,
> You will become drunk and make yourself naked.
> ²²The punishment of your iniquity has been completed, O daughter of Zion;
> He will exile you no longer.
> But He will punish your iniquity, O daughter of Edom;
> He will expose your sins!

Verse 21. One might wonder if, while the prophet was viewing the scenes of degradation and degeneration about him, a foreigner came along. Perhaps someone from **Edom** walked by, uttering a joyous word of satisfaction because Judah had gotten what she deserved (see 2:15, 16).

Judah's downfall brought **rejoic**[ing] and **glad**[ness] to the neighboring nation of Edom. Edom had not yet fallen to Babylon's conquests, but the prophet gave assurance that they would. He knew that those who enjoyed their drunken, immoral lifestyle would surely be visited by God's wrath (see Jer. 25:21, 27–29; 49:7–22).

Verse 22. God would **expose** and reveal Edom's **sins**. The amazing note of hope in this scene must not be overlooked. God's cycle of punishment and purpose are briefly, but significantly, stated in this context. The **punishment** of Judah's **iniquity** had been prophetically **completed** (תָּמַם, *thamam*), implying a strong sense of closure[19] (see 3:48; 4:3, 6, 10). The plan for captivity, with the relocating of God's fallen people, was now complete as well. No more movements were necessary to achieve God's goal of bringing on repentance and cleansing for His people (see Jer. 27:21, 22; 29:10–14; 31:16–21; 50:17–20; 52:15–30). Certainly, they would be punished for their sin (Jer. 30:10, 11), but a beautiful ray of hope is seen in this promise: **He will exile you no longer.** Though Edom's overthrow would be like that of Sodom and Gomorrah—so that no man would reside therein (Jer. 49:17, 18)—Judah's exile would end after seventy years. Then some would joyfully return to their homeland. That was more than a promise: It became a reality (Ezra 1:1–11).

APPLICATION

"Take Heed" (Ch. 4)

This chapter is proof that sin is no respecter of persons. We find here a glaring demonstration of the principle in 1 Corinthians 10:12: "Therefore let him who thinks he stands take heed that he does not fall."

Various expressions identify a special people who had possessed commendable qualities but had changed, becoming degenerate creatures whom God had to reject. Every human or divine measurement of success was attributed to them. They were "precious sons of Zion" (4:2); "those who ate delicacies . . . those reared in purple" (4:5); "consecrated ones . . . purer than snow" (4:7); "compassionate women" (4:10); and "the LORD's anointed" (4:20). On the surface, such splendid souls seemed unlikely to falter. Ignorance of the true knowledge of God fostered a quick and dangerous journey into all kinds of sin (see Hos. 4:6). Their iniquity was "greater than the sin of Sodom" (4:6). (See the phrases

---

[19]F. W. Dobbs-Allsopp, *Lamentations*, Interpretation (Louisville, Ky.: John Knox Press, 2002), 138.

describing the divine sentence against them in 4:10, 14, 15.) God completed the punishment of their iniquity (4:22).

Listening to false prophets and priests was a major factor in their fall (4:13). Whom do we accept as our religious instructors? (See Acts 17:10, 11; 2 Pet. 2:1–9; 1 Jn. 4:1.) We must measure any teaching we receive by our Master's message (Jn. 8:31, 32; Rom. 3:4; 2 Jn. 9).

Self-Examination, not Rejoicing (4:21, 22)

A significant principle is presented by Edom's attitude at the end of chapter 4. Rejoicing over vengeance enacted on another is no proof of personal purity or security. Edom's response to Judah's fall reflects a dangerous disposition. Edom was gloating over Judah's fall, completely ignoring the danger of God's wrath to be poured out upon them when God exposed their sins (4:21, 22).

How prone people have been to see the sins of others, and even rejoice "when they got what was coming to them," while ignoring their own waywardness. Paul warned, "You, therefore, who teach another, do you not teach yourself? You who preach that one shall not steal, do you steal?" (Rom. 2:21–23). Jesus stated, "For in the way you judge, you will be judged; and by your standard of measure, it will be measured to you. . . . Or how can you say to your brother, 'Let me take the speck out of your eye,' and behold, the log is in your own eye?" (Mt. 7:2–5). In Christ's great lesson about the two sons in Luke 15:11–32, the younger sinned greatly but recognized his sin and penitently sought forgiveness. The older brother judgmentally refused to forgive and blindly became guilty himself (see Mt. 6:14, 15). Are we ever inclined to act as Edom did? Do we help to redeem others, or do we stand aside and self-righteously rejoice when they fall? (See Lk. 18:9–14.)

CHAPTER 5
A PENITENT PLEA

The punishment had been completed (4:22); the nation of Judah had been brought to its knees and was getting ready for restoration. The delay before the restoration would find the prophet and the nation depressed and desolate. While chapter 5 has the overtones of a lament, it is a pleading prayer of penitence. The people longed for God to see their suffering so that He, in His mercy, might restore the "good old days" (see 5:21; Jer. 6:16). This final poem in Lamentations is a petition for the compassion of God, a request for His help. From the beginning to the end, its contents are addressed to God in the first-person voice of the people. They were calling for God to join in the prophet's meditation of misery, seeking His action as the only power, the only Person, who could give relief and restoration. The chapter is laced together with three cries of "O LORD" (5:1, 19, 21).

"SEE OUR REPROACH" (5:1)

¹**Remember, O LORD, what has befallen us;
Look, and see our reproach!**

Verse 1. The plea presented here called on the Lord to **remember** (זְכֹר, *zakar*). The Hebrew word covers more than a recollection; it includes the ideas of observing, caring, being concerned, protecting, and delivering. A concern for God's remembering was already expressed in 2:1 and 3:19. Asking God to remember, or stating that He remembered, was common in the Old Testament eras (see Gen. 9:15, 16; Lev. 26:40–42; 1 Sam. 1:11–20; 2 Kings

20:1–3; Ps. 98:1–3; 105:8–10; 106:44–46; 111:4–6; 136:23–26; Jer. 14:19–21; 18:19–23; Hab. 3:2).[1] At this time, the prophet especially appealed for God to **see** their **reproach** (חֶרְפָּה, *cherpah*) caused by taunting, disgrace, and shame.[2] This is a broad term of sad circumstances of taunting, as itemized in the verses that follow. Three Hebrew imperatives are used: "Remember," "Look," and "See."

"WE HAVE LOST 'OUR INHERITANCE'" (5:2–10)

Nine different kinds of imminent danger are presented in this section, relating to varied stages of Judah's circumstances.

Perils with Their Property (5:2)

²**Our inheritance has been turned over to strangers,
Our houses to aliens.**

Verse 2. The people had been **turned over to strangers** and **aliens**. These two terms relate to both foreigners and to people who are unknown. Their **inheritance**, both tribal property and personal possessions, was in the hands of one stranger after another.[3] This situation alone must have been overwhelming and depressing. To relate to the emotional impact this tragedy had on God's people, we would have to lose our most prized possessions. They had watch what they held most dear go up in smoke before their eyes.

---

[1]Francis Brown, S. R. Driver, and Charles A. Briggs, *A Hebrew and English Lexicon of the Old Testament* (Oxford: Clarendon Press, 1972), 269–71.

[2]Ludwig Koehler and Walter Baumgartner, *The Hebrew and Aramaic Lexicon of the Old Testament*, study ed., trans. and ed. M. E. J. Richardson (Boston: Brill, 2001), 1:356.

[3]The property that God promised to Israel as they prepared to enter the Promised Land (Num. 26:53; Deut. 4:38) had now been given to those who had no claim to it. (Iain Provan, *Lamentations*, The New Century Bible Commentary [Grand Rapids, Mich.: Wm. B. Eerdmans Publishing Co., 1991], 125.)

Perils of the People (5:3)

> ³**We have become orphans without a father,**
> **Our mothers are like widows.**

Verse 3. The people were like **orphans**, having no **father** (see Jer. 15:8; 18:21), and their **mothers** were **like widows**. Fathers and husbands were either dead or, as captives, totally helpless to render assistance to those nearest and dearest to them (see 2:11, 12; 4:3–5, 9, 10). This verse focuses on the "disintegration of the basic family unit."[4]

Perils as to Supplies (5:4)

> ⁴**We have to pay for our drinking water,**
> **Our wood comes to us at a price.**

Verse 4. Items like **water** and **wood** were essential—one to sustain the body when it began to thirst, and the other for preparing food to avoid starvation. All of the ponds, wells, fruit trees, and forests were currently possessed by the enemy. The writer emphasized that it was the water and wood that belonged to them with the word **our**. The blessings of the Promised Land had been freely given to God's people; but now these precious commodities for survival had to be purchased. The reality of facing slow death by starvation (4:9, 10) drives home the painful struggles that these people had undergone.

Perils from Pursuers (5:5)

> ⁵**Our pursuers are at our necks;**
> **We are worn out, there is no rest for us.**

Verse 5. The expression **at our necks** ("hotly pursued"; NJPSV; "under persecution"; KJV) fits the idea of being yoked

---

[4]F. W. Dobbs-Allsopp, *Lamentations*, Interpretation (Louisville, Ky.: John Knox Press, 2002), 145.

or enslaved and that they were totally at the mercy of their adversaries. God's people were fleeing from these adversaries; they were **worn out**, yet they dared not pause in their flight. In the tragic scene in Jeremiah 39:4–8, even the king tried to flee.

Perils of Starving (5:6)

> ⁶**We have submitted to Egypt and Assyria to get enough bread.**

Verse 6. Starvation pressured the people to turn to evil alliances to sustain them. They had **submitted** [נָתַנּוּ יָד, *nathannu yad*] **to Egypt and Assyria**; that is, they had handed themselves over to these foreign forces, seeking **bread**. Literally, this phrase means that they had "given the hand" to these enemies. The idea of submitting also implies humiliation (3:30), but who would not have submitted in this way to keep from starving? Neither the Egyptians nor the Assyrians were friendly to these Jews; but when a person is hungry, he gets bread anywhere he can beg or buy it. This is just another dismal proof that these souls were subjected to the complete control of others. Basically, they had nothing.

Perils as to Their Heritage of Iniquity (5:7)

> ⁷**Our fathers sinned, and are no more;**
> **It is we who have borne their iniquities.**

Verse 7. The captives' pain was intensified because of the power of influence. The prophet reviewed the extended impact of sin on the current generation. While each sinner is to be punished before God for his own sin (see Jer. 31:30; Ezek. 18:19–24), terrible circumstances imposed by men cannot always be avoided but must sometimes be endured by others. If a drunken driver survives a car wreck that kills a small child, that innocent child has suffered pain and death because of the driver's sin of drunkenness. Also, because of the power of influence, children may follow in the paths of wicked fathers, and daughters may repeat the sins of their mothers (see Ezek. 16:44–47). The prophet took a historical look at the sinning **fathers** and affirmed, **it is we who have borne their iniquities**.

Penalties may come from neglecting opportunities, setting aside covenant commandments, or ignoring warnings. We may suffer for our own sins (Mt. 23:14; Mk. 12:38–40; Lk. 20:46, 47; Jas. 3:1). However, even the Son of God demonstrated how the innocent may suffer with and for the guilty, as He bore our sins in His body on the cross (Rom. 5:6–10; 1 Pet. 2:24). That was part of God's great scheme of redemption (Is. 53:4–6; 2 Cor. 5:14–18).

Perils as to Social Standing (5:8)

> **⁸Slaves rule over us;**
> **There is no one to deliver us from their hand.**

Verse 8. Even **slaves** could **rule over**[5] the captives: How low they had descended on the social ladder of life! This pitiful plight was intensified by the fact that there was **no one to deliver** (פָּרַק, *paraq*) them. This Hebrew word involves "tearing away," "breaking off," or "liberating."[6] It implies a strong binding, such as being in chains (see Jer. 40:4; Lam. 3:7; Ezek. 7:23–26). These captives were the recipients of God's wrath (1:5, 12; 2:1, 3, 21, 22), and no man or nation was able to save them (4:16, 17). Of course, it was horrible to suffer and starve, but their agony must have been magnified by their subjected state in the hands of slaves. The truth of Psalm 121 showed that they needed the Lord to be the source of their help.

Perils of Moving About (5:9)

> **⁹We get our bread at the risk of our lives**
> **Because of the sword in the wilderness.**

Verse 9. While some were subjected to slaves, others cow-

---

[5]Proverbs 30:21–23 lists this as one of the four worst things that could happen to a people: to be "under a slave when he becomes king."
[6]Koehler and Baumgartner, 2:973.

ered in caves and hiding places, knowing that to emerge to find **bread** would likely mean facing a **sword**. Even **in the wilderness**, these fugitives were on the "wanted" list. If found, their fate would be settled with a sword (4:19; see Jer. 40:9—41:8). God had intended for His people to pay for their iniquity for a long time (Jer. 14:1–12).

Perils of Trying to Survive (5:10)

> ¹⁰Our skin has become as hot as an oven,
> Because of the burning heat of famine.

Verse 10. Survival efforts were complicated by the devastation of **famine**. The terror of hunger has been repeatedly mentioned (5:4, 6, 9; see 1:11, 19; 2:11, 12, 19, 20; 4:4, 5, 9, 10). The human body cannot build immunity without proper food. Famine breeds illness and produces pestilence (see Jer. 14:2–4, 12; 21:5–7; 24:10; 27:12, 13). The people's blackened **skin**, withered like wood (4:8), is described with the figure of the glowing, burning **heat** of an **oven**. Anyone near these feverish victims could feel the **burning** of their bodies. The prophet pleaded for God to look mercifully upon these loathsome souls.

"THE CROWN HAS FALLEN FROM OUR HEAD" (5:11–16a)

> ¹¹They ravished the women in Zion,
> The virgins in the cities of Judah.
> ¹²Princes were hung by their hands;
> Elders were not respected.
> ¹³Young men worked at the grinding mill,
> And youths stumbled under loads of wood.
> ¹⁴Elders are gone from the gate,
> Young men from their music.
> ¹⁵The joy of our hearts has ceased;
> Our dancing has been turned into mourning.
> ¹⁶ᵃThe crown has fallen from our head.

Several descriptions of punishment are presented in 5:11–16a. As horrendous as these wretched acts would have been, no cry against the perpetrators was voiced. No question was raised as to why God, in His anger, would allow this to be done. Earlier, the prophet had expressed a desire that the enemies pay the price God had promised (1:21, 22). The absence of such a plea in this lament could well be like the comments of the thief on the cross when Christ died. Internal honesty led that thief to say to his fellow-thief regarding their condition, "We . . . are receiving what we deserve for our deeds" (Lk. 23:41). The conclusion of this section is not a cry of injustice or even for vengeance, but a confession of woe for the sin and shame of these rebellious souls.

Verse 11. The punishment fell upon women, whether young or old. **They ravished the women in Zion, the virgins in the cities of Judah.** The story pains good hearts; for, both in Zion (Jerusalem) and in the cities of Judah, these women were "ravished" (עָנָה, *'anah*). This broad term not only includes rape and sexual shame, but numerous other abusive and humiliating ways that men might torment female captives.[7] The fact that the prophet specifically mentioned "virgins" assures us that some innocent souls were devastated in the affliction imposed on Judah by Babylon. This again reminds us of how the innocent suffer with the guilty (see Jer. 51:19–23).

Verse 12. The punishment came upon **princes**, as they **were hung by their hands**. High poles or stakes were dressed with prominent human bodies. The victims' hands were usually tied to these poles to ensure slow, agonizing death (see Deut. 21:22, 23; Jn. 19:31–37). The usual **respect** that would be extended to princes and **elders** was denied (see 4:16; Jer. 52:24–27). Neither handsome nor old and tired bodies were extended any mercy (4:7, 8; Is. 47:6).

Verse 13. Punishment fell on **young men** who **worked at the grinding mill, and youths** [who] **stumbled under loads of wood.** The hardship on young men was so heavy that they "stumbled." This was no accidental stumping of the toe; heavy burdens were

---

[7]Koehler and Baumgartner, 1:852–53.

imposed until the flesh was feeble, tottering, injured, or ruined![8] Even on young bodies, such stresses and strains would impose pain and humiliation (see Judg. 16:21–30).

Verse 14. Punishment extended so far that there was no place to relax or be refreshed. **Elders are gone from the gate, young men from their music.**[9] The practice of having elders at the gate, having a gathering place to be refreshed and to enjoy social interchange, was gone (see Josh. 20:4; Ruth 4:1, 2; Prov. 31:23). Elders were the very bedrock of Israelite society. They met for discussion and deliberation at the gates of the cities. These opportunities were no longer available to them, and no time for merrymaking was left (see Is. 24:6–12; Jer. 7:34; 16:8–12; 25:10, 11). As the prophet had asked God to remember (5:1), he himself recalled Judah's past. Evidently, the writer was reminiscing about times past, when normal functions and activities were associated with certain places. Surely, his memories broke his heart; every recollection of good moments with varied groups in these locations had become heart-rending misery.

Verse 15. Punishment could be summarized in three poignant expressions. First, **the joy of our hearts has ceased**. Internal joy of the heart had ceased. The cessation of joy can include the idea of exterminating or destroying. While our hearts desire to be filled with joy, circumstances may wring happiness from our lives as one would squeeze liquid from a sponge (see 2:15; Is. 24:6–12). The people's joyful lifestyle had been lost, and their current thoughts were of shame and slaughter. The landscape was a scene of destruction and desolation. Their immediate future was designed to make them miserable. Therefore, the joy in their hearts had been replaced with pressure and pain.

Second, **our dancing has been turned into mourning**. External circumstances offered no occasion for joyful jumping or dancing in praise (see Ps. 149:1–6; 150:1–6). The only favorable activity was projected as a divine promise that applied to some distant

---

[8]Ibid., 1:503.

[9]This has also been seen as a reference to the cessation of temple worship. (Adele Berlin, *Lamentations*, Old Testament Library [Louisville, Ky.: Westminster John Knox Press, 2004], 124.)

tomorrow (Jer. 31:4, 13). At this moment, their merriment gave way to "mourning" (אֵבֶל, 'ebel), as in a funeral ceremony.[10] This "mourning" can be a response to death (Gen. 37:34), the loss of a son (2 Sam. 13:37), or calamity (Neh. 1:4; Esther 4:1–3). Most of all, it is related to God's judgments because of sin (Jer. 4:27, 28; Lam. 1:4, 5; 2:5, 8). This last meaning certainly fits these lamentations and the circumstances which confronted God's people.

Verse 16a. Third, **the crown has fallen from our head**. The dignity had been replaced by disgrace. The fallen crown is a figurative expression of the loss of position, power, honor, beauty, and propriety. All of this had been taken from the kings, princes, and elders. Citizens were subjected to the hands of slaves (5:8). This whole survey in chapter 5 is a sordid story of subjection and humiliation. The next expression is an agonizing cry explaining why these tragedies had happened.

"WOE TO US, FOR WE HAVE SINNED" (5:16b–18)

¹⁶ᵇWoe to us, for we have sinned!
¹⁷Because of this our heart is faint,
Because of these things our eyes are dim;
¹⁸Because of Mount Zion which lies desolate,
Foxes prowl in it.

Verse 16b. This confession now referred to accounts for all the calamity covered in verses 1 through 16a. Jeremiah's impassioned cry of grief and despair, **Woe** [אוֹי, 'oy] **to us**, was a common expression for him (see Jer. 4:13, 31; 6:4; 10:19; 13:27; 15:10; 45:3; 48:46).[11] The word generally related to human failure, but here he used it as an open confession: **We have sinned!** (חָטָא, chata'). His phrasing acknowledged a variety of blunders: to "miss the mark," to "take a false step," to "stumble," to "wander from the way," to "take one's life into danger," incurring

---

[10]Ibid., 1:7.
[11]Brown, Driver, and Briggs, 17.

guilt and condemnation.[12] The fact that the people of Judah bore guilt and condemnation explains why the prophet shouted this woe and confession, rather than leveling charges against their adversaries. The mood and mindset in this confession included genuine penitence and acceptance of God's purpose for this painful punishment.

Verse 17. The conditions associated with that confession are covered by three expressions. First of all, the confession was surrounded by weariness. **Because of this our heart is faint** (דָּוֶה, *daweh*). Heartbreak for multiple sins and extended shameful conduct produced this sick, miserable feeling. Such a heart not only hurts, but it is also sapped of strength, leaving the person with weakened resolve, wavering before duty, and filled with doubt when sure steps ought to be taken.

The confession was gilded with confusion and humiliation. **Because of these things our eyes are dim.** The Hebrew term translated "dim," חָשַׁךְ (*chashak*), presents a sobering idea that includes fear and failure. Its basic meaning is to "be dark."[13] When associated with the eyes, it suggests blindness. For one with this condition, quick progress must be postponed; every step is restricted by concern and uncertainty. Lamentations 4:8 uses this word to describe the people's visage, or appearance, as "blacker than soot" or "a coal" (KJV). This expression, though difficult to translate, may be parallel to 4:14, 15, presenting a defiled and dirty reputation. These characteristics, as related to the eyes, would surely result in intimidation and humiliation. Guilt-ridden souls have no vision; they are unable to leave their darkness and doubt to grow up in God's perceptive powers (see Ps. 139:12). Job 38:2 also uses this term: "Who . . . darkens counsel by words without knowledge?" The reference there is to confused advice, limited insight, and unstable, unreliable speech. In this verse, then, these dim eyes were severely handicapped in knowing what direction to take or what to do.

Verse 18. His confession is made by a man who lives amidst geographical desolation. **Because of Mount Zion which lies**

---

[12]Ibid., 306–7.
[13]Ibid., 364–65.

desolate. "Desolate" has been used frequently in these lamentations (1:4, 13, 16; 3:11; 4:5). Solomon's temple had proudly stood as a bastion of spiritual stability (1 Kings 8:22–53), but that refuge was gone from its premises; carnage had taken its place. **Foxes prowl**[ed] among the burned and broken remains. Conditions internally, externally, and geographically declared the cost for sin by the calamity that had come upon Judah.

"YOU, O LORD, RULE FOREVER"
(5:19–22)

Through five chapters, we have observed multiple scenes of Judah's hurt and humiliation. The prophet lingered in the valley of devastation and destruction (3:47), but he closed his lamentations with his sight firmly fixed on the Almighty as the source of help for these sad scenes. It seemed that the throne of David had been vacated and destroyed, yet every expression in these closing verses presents a confident trust that God's rule and throne are able to endure. The writer here approached the Lord God with his questions, concern, and confidence.

> [19]You, O LORD, rule forever;
> Your throne is from generation to generation.
> [20]Why do You forget us forever?
> Why do You forsake us so long?
> [21]Restore us to You, O LORD, that we may be restored;
> Renew our days as of old,
> [22]Unless You have utterly rejected us
> And are exceedingly angry with us.

Verse 19. This chapter began with a plaintive cry to the Lord; and so it ends, acknowledging that the Lord's rulership will last "forever" (עוֹלָם, *'olam*, "age lasting"). (See comments on Jer. 49:33.) This term can relate to eternity, but it is often applied to an era of time (see Ex. 12:14, 24; 30:8; 31:17; 1 Chron. 15:1, 2). The classic proof is Jonah's being in the belly of the big fish "forever" (Jon. 2:6). Jonah was incarcerated for set period of time. He went into that fish with quite a different mindset from the one with he came out. When he emerged from the fish's stomach, he entered a new era in his life.

Verse 20. Two questions identify the plight of God's people before their Maker. The writer presented God's people as the forgotten ones: **Why do You forget us forever?** God had warned them that He would forget them, and He had told them why (see Jer. 23:39, 40). The problem was that His people had repeatedly forgotten Him (Deut. 8:19, 20; Ps. 50:22; Is. 17:10; Hos. 8:14; 13:6). Still, God assured them that—in spite of the charges they were making against Him—He would not forget them (Is. 49:14, 15). Jeremiah acknowledged this fact (Jer. 30:11).

Second, the prophet questioned God on behalf of these forsaken ones: **Why do You forsake us so long?** "Forsake" (עָזַב, 'azab) includes a variety of thoughts: "leaving behind" (Jer. 14:5), "having nothing to do with" (Prov. 9:6), and "abandoning" (Ps. 16:10; Jer. 4:29).[14] This question may have been based on the assumption that God did not see the evil that was being done because He had forsaken the land (Ezek. 8:12, 13; 9:9, 10). However, the all-knowing God is always aware when His people forsake Him (see Deut. 28:20; Jer. 2:17–19; 18:13–17). While God would keep His vow to forsake them, He informed them that the separation would be brief (see Is. 54:6–8). In His everlasting lovingkindness, He would have compassion on them (Jer. 29:1–14). For those who had endured the Babylonian siege and the early stages of servitude, the prospects of a return in seventy years offered no comfort (Jer. 25:12). They envisioned dying while subject to Babylon's vicious forces.

Verse 21. The captives cried out, **Restore us to You, O L**ORD. They longed to see the future, when their cry could be answered. The word "restore" (שׁוּב, shub) has tremendous hopes interwoven in it—hopes that were especially pertinent to the needs of Judah at that time. This Hebrew word is used extensively in the Old Testament with various nuances, including abandoning, paying back, and turning back to God.[15] The prophetic promise had been given, and it would be a happy day when God's polluted

---

[14]Ibid., 736–37.
[15]Koehler and Baumgartner, 2:1427–34.

people repented and cried to Him, "Bring me back that I may be restored, for You are the LORD my God" (Jer. 31:18). The divine plan told how the people would return (see Ezek. 11:14–20).

Verse 22. The expression regarding God's **utterly reject**[ing] them, or being **exceedingly angry** with them, appears to be incompatible with the divine promise of their return. God even supplied details of when that return would occur (see Jer. 25:8–12; 27). Theo. Laetsch saw this not as a cry of despair but a cry of trust:

> The same sense would be obtained if we translate: For if Thou wouldst utterly reject us, that would be excessive wrath, because it would not agree with Thy promise. The concluding verse, therefore, is not a lament nor a cry of despair, but rather the final fervent appeal of a soul that pins all its trust on God's promise and its fulfillment, guaranteed by the fact that He is the Lord Jehovah, the Covenant God.[16]

Therefore, a bright ray of hope appears beneath the burdened plea that closes the book. The prophet prayerfully offered his plea to the Lord, the one sure, forever-reigning God of heaven and earth. Jeremiah closed his laments by leaving the fate of the people to the infinite mercy of their Maker.

APPLICATION

"O Lord, Why . . . ?" (Ch. 5)

When a crisis or calamity comes, we must not forget to pray. The prophet, with better perception than many of us, devoted his entire fifth lament to the posture of prayer. At times "knee-ology" may be more practical than theology! The divine principle "You do not have because you do not ask" (Jas. 4:2) has too often reduced God's promises to dust and decay for the want of sincere, prevailing prayer (see Lk. 18:1–8).

---

[16]Theo. Laetsch, *Jeremiah*, Bible Commentary (St. Louis: Concordia Publishing House, 1965), 403.

Prayer is the bridge over which weeping and worry pass to action and devotion. This bridge can transport us across the canyon of despair and depression. One way to have less confusion and fewer conflicts with our fellow human beings is to wrestle more in prayer to God. Just as troubles and trials may drive us to prayer, prayer connects us to the Person who can drive away those troubles and trials.

The purpose of genuine prayer is not to inform God of our needs, which He already knows (see Mt. 6:24–33), but to team up with the One who rules and redeems our lives (1 Cor. 3:9; 2 Cor. 3:4–6). Therefore, we would do well to develop the disposition of William King: "O God, if in the day of battle I forget Thee, do not Thou forget me."[17] A person is never taller than when he humbly kneels before God. When a man prays properly, he can stand up to anything. With God to help us, we have nothing to fear (see Rom. 8:31–39; Heb. 13:5, 6).

"We Have Sinned" (5:1–16a)

Sin incurs punishment. Lamentations 5:1–16a is Jeremiah's discourse addressed to the Lord about disaster, explained in one poignant confession: "Woe to us, for we have sinned!" That context of hurt and horror, pain and pleading, is the awakening to the awful price we must pay for mistakes and misdeeds.

Admitting "I have sinned" is not easy for anyone (see Ps. 94:1–7; Prov. 30:20; Jer. 2:30–35; 1 Jn. 1:8, 10). However, God's response in Psalm 94:8–11 is that people are senseless to conclude that He does not hear or see sinners when they sin (see Num. 32:23; Eccles. 12:13, 14; Mt. 12:36, 37; Rom. 3:23; 6:23; 14:10–12; 2 Cor. 5:10). The Lord knows what we have done. These passages that assure us of a day of accounting for sin, and of the price to be paid for sin, show the wisdom of Proverbs 28:13: "He who conceals his transgressions will not prosper, but he who confesses and forsakes them will find compassion" (see Jer. 18:1–11; Jas. 5:16; 1 Jn. 1:9). Getting right with God is the only way to get better.

---

[17]Lewis C. Henry, *Best Quotations for All Occasions* (Greenwich, Conn.: Fawcett Publications, 1965), 183.

"Restore Us, O Lord" (5:21)

Restoration can be accomplished only in cooperation with God. When the prophet cried, "Restore us to You, O Lord" (5:21), he was recognizing the truthfulness of God's words in Jeremiah 30:17: "'For I will restore you to health, and I will heal you of your wounds,' declares the Lord" (see Is. 57:17–19). The psalmist was of a kindred spirit when he wrote, "Restore to me the joy of Your salvation and sustain me with a willing spirit" (Ps. 51:12). While we must repent, mend our ways, and seek God with our whole hearts (Jer. 29:10–14), our dependence on Him is declared by Christ: "For apart from Me you can do nothing" (Jn. 15:5).

Therefore, it should be no surprise that the prophet closed Lamentations with the prayerful appeal for the Lord to restore and renew His people. God is the eternal refuge of His children (see Ps. 46:1, 2, 10, 11; 62:7, 8). He will always welcome those who seek His grace and guidance, turning to Him in penitence and trust (2 Cor. 6:14–18).

Here, in this most melancholy message in the Bible—perhaps in all literature—we are able to see from eyes cleansed by tears that the grace of God is mightier than the sorrows of sin. Despite the disturbing deeds running rampant in the universe, may triumph from His throne and salvation in His Son lift us to confidence in Christ (Acts 4:12; Heb. 7:24, 25; 5:8, 9). One day, grief and destruction will give way to the glories of God's tomorrow, when even death will be swallowed up in victory through our Lord Jesus Christ (1 Cor. 15:50–58). Then all lamentations will surrender to the Lord of life and eternity.

Appendix
Maps and Charts

1. Jeremiah's World
2. The Assyrian Empire During Jeremiah's Early Prophecies
3. The Babylonian Empire During Jeremiah's Later Prophecies
4. Kings of Judah in the Book of Jeremiah
5. The House of Josiah
6. The Deaths of the Final Five Kings of Judah
7. Important Events During the Life of Jeremiah
8. Symbolic Actions & Object Lessons In the Book of Jeremiah
9. Parallels in the Book of Jeremiah Between Severe Treatment by Babylon & the Punishment of Babylon
10. Rulers of Egypt (664–525 B.C.)
11. The Deportations from Judah to Exile in Babylon
12. Corresponding Events in Jeremiah 52 (along with 39—41) & 2 Kings 24; 25
13. Parallel Phrases in Jeremiah & Lamentations Indicating the Same Author
14. Similar Struggles Described in Lamentations 3 & Jeremiah 1—20
15. The "Before" & "After" Pictures of God's People (Lam. 4:1–8)

APPENDIX: MAPS AND CHARTS

JEREMIAH'S WORLD

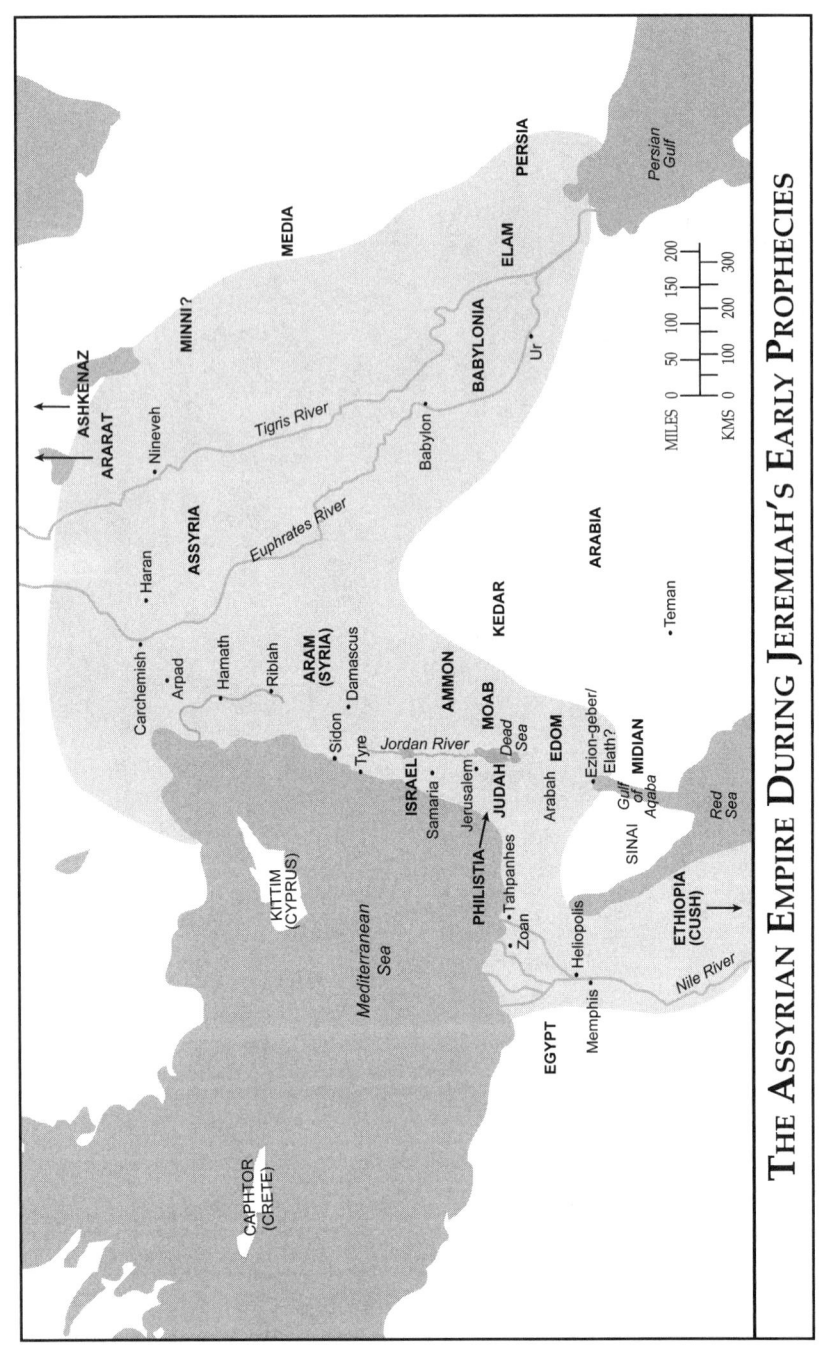

The Assyrian Empire During Jeremiah's Early Prophecies

APPENDIX: MAPS AND CHARTS

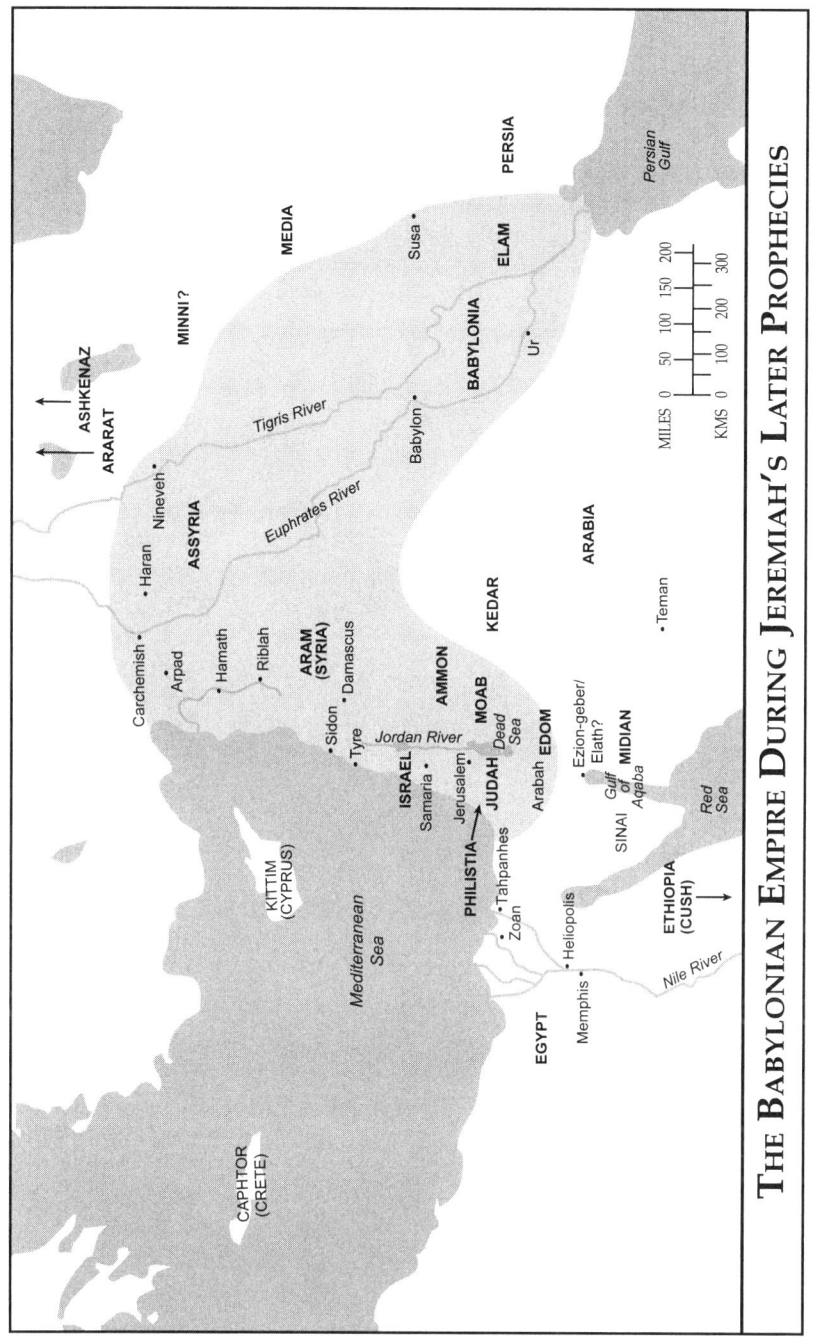

The Babylonian Empire During Jeremiah's Later Prophecies

KINGS OF JUDAH IN THE BOOK OF JEREMIAH

The following kings of Judah are listed in the order of their reign. The Scriptures make it evident that the Book of Jeremiah does not follow chronologial order.

King	Years of Reign	Length of Reign	Scripture References in Jeremiah Related to the Reign
JOSIAH	640–609 B.C.	31 years	1:2, 3; 3:6 22:11, 18; 25:3
JEHOAHAZ (Shallum, Joahaz)	609 B.C.	3 months	22:11
JEHOIAKIM (Eliakim)	609–598 B.C.	11 years	1:3; 22:13–19 25:1 (*4th year*) 26:1 (*beginning*) 35:1 36:1 (*4th year*) 36:9 (*5th year*) 45:1 (*4th year*) 46:2 (*4th year*)
JEHOIACHIN (Jeconiah, Coniah)	598–597 B.C.	3 months	22:24–30 27:20
ZEDEKIAH (Mattaniah)	597–586 B.C.	11 years	1:3; 21:1, 3, 7 24:1, 8 27:1 (*beginning*) 28:1; 29:1–3 32:1 (*10th year*) 34:2, 4, 6, 8 37:1, 3, 17, 18, 21 38:5, 14–19, 24 39:1 (*9th year*) 49:34 (*beginning*) 51:59 (*4th year*) 52:1 (*years 1–11*)

APPENDIX: MAPS AND CHARTS

THE HOUSE OF JOSIAH

Josiah and his descendants (except Johanan) were the kings during Jeremiah's lifetime:

JOSIAH
(1 Chron. 3:15, 16; Jer. 1:2, 3; Mt. 1:10, 11)

JOHANAN
(1 Chron. 3:15)

JEHOIAKIM
(2 Chron. 36:5; Jer. 25:1)
also called ELIAKIM
(2 Kings 23:34)

JEHOIACHIN
(2 Chron. 36:8, 9; Jer. 52:31)
also called JECONIAH
(Jer. 24:1; 27:20; 28:4)
also called CONIAH
(Jer. 22:24, 28; 37:1)

ZEDEKIAH
(2 Chron. 36:11;
Jer. 27:1; 28:1)
also called MATTANIAH
(2 Kings 24:17–20)

JEHOAHAZ
also called SHALLUM
(2 Kings 23:31; Jer. 22:11)
also called JOAHAZ
(2 Chron. 36:1, 2)

Note: The design of this chart is according to 1 Chronicles 3:15, 16 and not to the chronological order of Josiah's sons.

The Deaths of the Final Five Kings of Judah

JOSIAH	Judah was under Assyrian control, and Egypt was coming to the aid of Assyria in its war with Babylon. Josiah sided with Babylon and died in 609 B.C., after fighting against Pharoah Neco in the plain of Esdraelon, near Megiddo (2 Chron. 35:24). His body was buried in Jerusalem.
JEHOAHAZ	Pharoah Neco ruled over Palestine for several years. He took Jehoahaz as a captive to Egypt in 609 B.C., where he died in exile (2 Kings 23:30–34; 2 Chron. 36:1–4; see Jer. 22:10–12).
JEHOIAKIM	He died in Jerusalem, and his body was cast outside the city (Jer. 22:18, 19: 36:30).
JEHOIACHIN	He was exiled to Babylon in 597 B.C., along with many nobles, rulers, and artisans (including Mordecai; Esther 2:5, 6). Jehoiachin (Jeconiah) was allowed to leave prison and was given food, clothing, and palace favors for the rest of his life (2 Kings 25:27–30; Jer. 52:31–34).
ZEDEKIAH	In the fall of Jerusalem in 586 B.C. to the Babylonians, Zedekiah tried to escape but was captured and brought to Nebuchadnezzar, who killed Zedekiah's sons in front of him and then put out his eyes. He was exiled to Babylon along with many others. In fulfillment of the prophecy of Ezekiel 12:13, he did not see Babylon, but died there (Jer. 39:6–8; see 52:11; 2 Kings 24; 25; 1 Chron. 3:15; 2 Chron. 36:10, 11).

APPENDIX: MAPS AND CHARTS

Important Events During the Life of Jeremiah

640 B.C.	Josiah began to reign as king of Judah
627	Jeremiah began his ministry (in the 13th year of Josiah's reign; Jer. 1:2)
612	Babylon conquers Nineveh
609	Josiah died at Megiddo
	Jehoahaz (Shallum) became king and reigned for three months, then was carried to Egypt
	Jehoiakim became king
	Jeremiah delivered his Temple Sermon (Jer. 7:1—8:3)
605	Battle of Carchemish: Babylon crushed Egypt
598	Jehoiakim died
598–597	Jehoiachin became king and reigned for three months, then was carried to Babylon
597	Zedekiah was installed as king
586	Destruction of Jerusalem

Exact dating is impossible and therefore varies according to different scholars.

Symbolic Actions & Object Lessons In the Book of Jeremiah

Reference	Illustration	Lesson
1:11, 12	A rod of an almond tree (the Hebrew word for "almond" means "wakeful, vigilant")	God's alert watchfulness of His people.
1:13	A boiling pot, facing away from the north	God's destruction would come from the north, in the form of Babylonian conquest.
13:1–11	A linen waistband ruined and discarded by the Euphrates River	God's people would suffer captivity in Babylon.
13:12, 13	Every jug filled with wine	God would fill the land with drunkenness.
14:1, 14	A drought	False prophets who claimed there would be no danger would die by sword or famine.
18:3–6	A potter remade a spoiled pot	God's people would be reshaped.
19:1–13	The breaking of an earthenware jar	Judah would be broken.
24:1–10	Good figs and bad figs	God would bring the captives back to their land, but those in Jerusalem would be abandoned.
25:15–31	A cup of wine	The nations would drink of God's wrath.
27:1–12	Wearing a yoke	Judah and the nations should serve Babylon and live.

APPENDIX: MAPS AND CHARTS

Reference	Illustration	Lesson
32:6–15	Buying a plot of ground in Anathoth while the Babylonians controlled it	God's people would return to claim ownership of their conquered country.
35:1–19	The offering of wine to the Rechabites and obedience to an ancestor's command	Obedience to God's commands.
43:8–10	The placing of large stones in the clay before Pharaoh's palace in Tahpanhes, Egypt	Nebuchadnezzar's throne would be set on those stones as he established his sovereignty after invading Egypt.
51:61–64	Delivering a message of doom to Babylon, then casting the scroll into the river	Babylon would lose its splendor and sink from power, not to rise again.

Parallels in the Book of Jeremiah Between Severe Treatment by Babylon & The Punishment of Babylon

Severe Treatment by Babylon	The Parallel	Punishment for Babylon
1:11–16; 6:1–5, 22–24; 46:20, 24; 47:2–4	As Babylon had been a conquering force coming from the north, she would also be conquered by a nation from the north.	50:3, 9, 41, 42
20:5; 30:16	As Babylon had plundered nations, others would plunder her.	50:9, 10
25:9, 11, 18 (see 49:13, 17, 18)	As Babylon had left other nations desolate, she would be left desolate.	25:12; 50:10, 13, 40
46:2, 8–12	As Babylon had poured out God's vengeance on others, she would also feel His vengeance.	50:15
14:16–18; 48:31–34	As others had starved, fearing Babylon's army, she would fear other armies.	50:16
48:42–44	As Babylon had been a snare to others, she would be ensnared.	50:24
6:22, 23	As Babylon had drawn the bow against others, the bow would be drawn against her.	50:14, 29; 51:3
11:22; 18:21 (see 48:15; 49:26)	As Babylon had made young men fall in the streets, her young men would fall in the streets.	50:30; 51:3, 4

APPENDIX: MAPS AND CHARTS

Severe Treatment by Babylon	**The Parallel**	**Punishment for Babylon**
21:12, 14; 34:2, 22; 43:12, 13; 48:45; 49:2, 27	As Babylon had been a kindled fire to others, a kindled fire would rage in her.	50:32
6:24; 49:24 (see 4:31; 47:3)	As Babylon had made the hands of others "feeble" (KJV), she would be feeble.	50:43
4:7 (see 49:19)	As Babylon had come as a lion from the thicket of the Jordan River, another enemy would come on her in the same way.	50:44
4:8; 25:34; 48:20	As Babylon had caused others to wail, she would also wail.	51:8
48:15–18; 49:18–33	A general summary of conditions and causes of Babylon's downfall is given.	51:43, 53–58

Rulers of Egypt
(664–525 B.C.)

Psammetichus I	664–610 B.C.
Neco II	610–595 B.C.
Psammetichus II	595–589 B.C.
Apries (Hophra)	589–570 B.C.
Amasis II	570–526 B.C.
Psammetichus III	526–525 B.C.

The Deportations from Judah
To Exile in Babylon

605 B.C.	Nebuchadnezzar's victory over Egypt at Carchemish; 1st deportation, including Daniel (Dan. 1:1–6)
597 B.C.	2nd deportation, including Jehoiachin and Ezekiel; Zedekiah becomes king (2 Kings 24:8–17; Jer. 52:28; Ezek. 1:1–3)
586 B.C.	Fall of Jerusalem; 3rd deportation, including Zedekiah (2 Kings 25:1–21; Jer. 52:4–27, 29)
582 B.C.	4th deportation; after Gedaliah the governor was assassinated (2 Kings 25:22–26; Jer. 41:1–3; 52:30)

APPENDIX: MAPS AND CHARTS

CORRESPONDING EVENTS IN JEREMIAH 52 (ALONG WITH 39—41) & 2 KINGS 24; 25

Description/ Event	Jer. 52	Jer. 39—41	2 Kings 24; 25
Introduction of Zedekiah as king	52:1, 2		24:18, 19
Siege of Jerusalem	52:3–6	39:1	24:20—25:3
Fall of Jerusalem	52:7–16	39:2–10	25:4–12
Temple vessels taken	52:17–23		25:13–17
Leaders killed at Riblah	52:24–27		25:18–21
Numbers of exiles	52:28–30		24:14–16
Gedaliah assassinated		39:11—41:18	25:22–26
Release of Jehoiachin	52:31–34		25:27–30

This chart was adapted from Douglas Rawlinson Jones, *Jeremiah*, The New Century Bible Commentary (Grand Rapids, Mich.: Wm. B. Eerdmans Publishing Co., 1992), 547–48.

Parallel Phrases in Jeremiah & Lamentations Indicating the Same Author

Jeremiah	Similar Phrasing	Lamentations
3:1; 4:30; 30:14	Reference to allies as lovers	1:2, 19
30:14	Iniquity great/sins numerous	1:5, 8; 4:6
13:22, 26	Iniquity exposed/unclean skirts	1:8, 9
8:21	"Broken daughter of My people"	1:15
9:1, 18; 13:17	Eyes/weeping bitterly	1:16; 2:11
33:5; see 30:14	Slain as an enemy/"in My anger"	2:4
2:8; 5:31; 6:13	Sins of prophets/priests	2:14; 4:13
6:25; 20:10	Terror on every side	2:22
19:9	In hunger/mothers eat children	2:20; 4:10
8:11	"Daughter of My people"	2:11; 3:48; 4:10
20:7	Become a laughingstock	3:14
9:15; 23:15	Feed with wormwood	3:15
18:20; 37:16; 38:6	Cast into pit/dungeon/cistern	3:53, 55
11:20	Seek God's vengeance on them	3:60–66
18:6; 19:1–13	Figure of earthenware jars	4:2
4:13	Pursuers swifter than eagles	4:19
49:7, 12	Edom/cup (of wrath)	4:21, 22
13:18	Crown fallen from the head	5:16

Similar Struggles Described in Lamentations 3 & Jeremiah 1—20

Lamentations	Jeremiah
3:7—"He has walled me in so that I cannot go out. . . ."	15:17—". . . I sat alone. . . ."
3:8—". . . He shuts out my prayer."	7:16; 11:14; 14:11—". . . do not pray for this people. . . ."
3:14—"I have become a laughingstock. . . ."	20:7—"I have become a laughingstock. . . ."
3:18—"My strength has perished, and so has my hope from the Lord."	15:18—"Why has . . . my wound [been] incurable . . . ?"
3:27—"It is good for a man that he should bear the yoke in his youth."	1:6—"Behold, I do not know how to speak, because I am a youth."
3:30—"Let him give his cheek to the smiter. . . ."	20:2—"Pashhur had Jeremiah . . . beaten. . . ."
3:40—"Let us examine and probe our ways, and let us return to the Lord."	15:19—"Therefore, thus says the Lord, 'If you return, then I will restore you. . . .'"
3:49—"My eyes pour down unceasingly, without stopping."	9:1—"O that my head were waters and my eyes a fountain of tears, that I might weep day and night. . . ."
3:53, 55—"They have silenced me in the pit. . . ."	18:20—"For they have dug a pit for me. . . ." (see 37:16; 38:6)
3:64—"You will recompense them, O Lord, according to the work of their hands."	11:20—"But, O Lord of hosts . . . let me see Your vengeance on them. . . ."

The "Before" & "After" Pictures of God's People (Lam. 4:1–8)

How They Had Once Been	How They Had Become
Gold/sacred stones (4:1, 2)	Earthen jars (4:2)
Enjoyed delicacies (4:5)	Had no bread/great thirst (4:4)
Reared in purple (4:5)	Embracing ash pits (4:5)
Purer than snow (4:7)	Greater sin than Sodom (4:6)
White (like milk), delicate skin (4:7)	Blacker than soot (4:8)
Ruddy, handsome bodies (4:7)	Shriveled skin (4:8)
Polished people (4:7)	Skin withered like wood (4:8)

Selected Bibliography

GENERAL

Ash, Anthony L. *Jeremiah and Lamentations*. The Living Word Commentary. Abilene, Tex.: ACU Press, 1987.

Baxter, J. Sidlow. *Explore the Book*, vol. 3, *Poetical Books (Job to Song of Solomon), Isaiah, Jeremiah, Lamentations*. Grand Rapids, Mich.: Zondervan Publishing House, 1974.

Berlin, Adele. *Lamentations*. Old Testament Library. Louisville, Ky.: Westminster John Knox Press, 2004.

Bright, John. *Jeremiah*. The Anchor Bible. Garden City, N.Y.: Doubleday & Company, 1965.

Bromiley, Geoffrey W., ed. *The International Standard Bible Encyclopedia*, rev. ed. 4 vols. Grand Rapids, Mich.: Wm. B. Eerdmans Publishing Co., 1979, 1982, 1986, 1988.

Brown, Francis, S. R. Driver, and Charles A. Briggs. *A Hebrew and English Lexicon of the Old Testament*. Oxford: Clarendon Press, 1972.

Cawley, F. *Jeremiah*. The New Bible Commentary. Grand Rapids, Mich.: Wm. B. Eerdmans Publishing Co., 1954.

Cheyne, T. K. and W. F. Adeney. *The Pulpit Commentary*, vol. 11, *Jeremiah, Lamentations*. Grand Rapids, Mich.: Wm. B. Eerdmans Publishing Co., 1950.

Clarke, Adam. *The Holy Bible With a Commentary and Critical Notes*, vol. 4, *Isaiah to Malachi*. New York: Abingdon-Cokesbury Press, n.d.

Dobbs-Allsopp, F. W. *Lamentations*. Interpretation. Louisville, Ky.: John Knox Press, 2002.

Ellicott, Charles J. *Ellicott's Commentary on the Whole Bible*, vol. 5. Grand Rapids, Mich.: Zondervan Publishing House, 1959.

Feinburg, Charles L. "Jeremiah." In *The Expositor's Bible Commentary*, vol. 6, *Isaiah-Ezekiel*, ed. Frank E. Gaebelein. Grand Rapids, Mich.: Zondervan Publishing House, 1986.

Francisco, Clyde T. *Introducing the Old Testament*. Nashville: Broadman Press, 1950.

_____. *Studies in Jeremiah*. Nashville: Convention Press, 1961.

Gottwald, Norman K. *Studies in the Book of Lamentations*. Studies in Biblical Theology No. 14, rev. ed. London: SCM Press, 1962.

Graybill, John B. "Jeremiah." In *Zondervan Pictorial Bible Dictionary*, ed. Merrill C. Tenney. Grand Rapids, Mich.: Zondervan Publishing House, 1963.

Guest, John. *Jeremiah, Lamentations*. Communicator's Commentary. Waco, Tex.: Word Books, 1988.

Hallo, William W., ed. *The Context of Scripture*. 3 vols. Boston: Brill, 2003.

Harrell, Costen J. *The Prophets of Israel*. Nashville: Cokesbury Press, 1933.

Harrison, R. K. *Jeremiah and Lamentations: An Introduction and Commentary*. Tyndale Old Testament Commentaries. Downers Grove, Ill.: Inter-Varsity Press, 1973.

Hester, H. I. *The Heart of Hebrew History*. Liberty, Mo.: Quality Press, 1962.

Hoenig, Sidney B. and Samuel M. Rosenberg. *A Guide to the Prophets*. New York: Blick, 1942.

Hyatt, James Philip. "The Book of Jeremiah." In *The Interpreter's Bible*, vol. 5, ed. George Arthur Buttrick. New York: Abingdon, 1956.

Jellie, Harvey. "Jeremiah." In *Preacher's Homiletic Commentary*, vol. 17. Grand Rapids, Mich.: Baker Book House, 1974.

Jones, Douglas Rawlinson. *Jeremiah*. The New Century Bible Commentary. Grand Rapids, Mich.: Wm. B. Eerdmans Publishing Co., 1992.

Keil, C. F. and F. Delitzsch. *Commentary on the Old Testament*, vol. 8, *Jeremiah, Lamentations*. Grand Rapids, Mich.: Wm. B. Eerdmans Publishing Co., n.d.

King, Philip J. *Jeremiah: An Archaeological Companion*. Louisville, Ky.: Westminster/John Knox Press, 1993.

Koehler, Ludwig and Walter Baumgartner. *The Hebrew and Aramaic Lexicon of the Old Testament*. Study ed. Translated and edited by M. E. J. Richardson. 2 vols. Boston: Brill, 2001.

Laetsch, Theo. *Jeremiah*. Bible Commentary. St. Louis: Concordia Publishing House, 1965.

Leslie, Elmer A. *Jeremiah*. New York: Abingdon Press, 1954.

Lewis, Jack P. *The Major Prophets*. Henderson, Tenn.: Hester Publications, 1999.

Morgan, G. Campbell. *Studies in the Prophecy of Jeremiah*. Old Tappan, N. J.: Fleming H. Revell Co., 1969.

O'Connor, Kathleen M. *Lamentations and the Tears of the World*. Maryknoll, N.Y.: Orbis Books, 2002.

Pritchard, James B., ed. *Ancient Near Eastern Texts: Relating to the Old Testament*, 3d ed. Princeton, N.J.: Princeton University Press, 1969.

Provan, Iain. *Lamentations*. The New Century Bible Commentary. Grand Rapids, Mich.: Wm. B. Eerdmans Publishing Co., 1991.

Smith, James E. *Jeremiah and Lamentations*. Bible Study Textbook Series. Joplin, Mo.: College Press, 1972.

_____. *The Major Prophets*. Old Testament Survey Series. Joplin, Mo.: College Press Publishing Co., 1992.

Snaith, Norman. *The Distinctive Ideas of the Old Testament*. London: Epworth Press, 1945.

Thompson, J. A. *The Book of Jeremiah*. The New International Commentary on the Old Testament. Grand Rapids, Mich.: Wm. B. Eerdmans Publishing Co., 1980.

Voth, Steven. "Jeremiah." In *Zondervan's Illustrated Bible Backgrounds Commentary*, vol. 4, *Isaiah, Jeremiah, Lamentations, Ezekiel, Daniel*, ed. John H. Walton. Grand Rapids, Mich.: Zondervan, 2009.

Walton, John H. *Charts of the Old Testament*. Grand Rapids, Mich.: Zondervan Publishing House, 1994.

Willis, Timothy M. *Jeremiah-Lamentations*, The College Press NIV Commentary. Joplin, Mo.: College Press Publishing Co., 2002.

Young, Edward J. *An Introduction to the Old Testament*. London: The Tyndale Press, 1964.

SELECTED BIBLIOGRAPHY

BIBLE TRANSLATIONS

The Amplified Bible. Grand Rapids, Mich.: Zondervan Publishing House, 1987.

The Holy Bible; American Standard Version. Thomas Nelson & Sons, 1901.

The Holy Bible; Authorized King James Version. Colorado Springs, Co.: International Bible Society, 1987.

The Holy Bible; Contemporary English Version. New York: American Bible Society, 1995.

The Holy Bible; New Century Version. Dallas: Word Bibles, 1991.

The Holy Bible; New International Version. Grand Rapids, Mich.: Zondervan Publishing House, 1978.

The Holy Bible; New King James Version. New York: American Bible Society, 1990.

The Holy Bible; New Living Translation, 2d edition. Carol Steam, Ill.: Tyndale House Publishers, 2007.

The Holy Bible; New Revised Standard Version. Grand Rapids, Mich.: Zondervan Bible Publishers, 1989.

The Holy Bible; Revised Standard Version. Nashville: Thomas Nelson, Inc., 1972.

The Holy Bible; Today's English Version. New York: American Bible Society, 1976.

The Jerusalem Bible. Reader's Edition. Garden City, N.Y.: Doubleday & Company, Inc., 1966.

New American Standard Bible. Anaheim, Calif.: Foundation Publications, 1995.

The New English Bible. New York: Oxford University Press, 1971.

The New Jerusalem Bible. Reader's Edition. New York: Doubleday, 1990.

The Revised English Bible. New York: Oxford University Press, 1989.

Tanakh: The Holy Scriptures. Philadelphia: Jewish Publication Society, 1985.

From the Editor
Have You Heard...
About Truth for Today?

What are the big missionary needs of our time? Those who study missionary evangelism point to two paramount needs that are ever present in the mission field.

THE BIG NEEDS OF WORLD EVANGELISM

First, they tell us that educating and maturing the national Christian man so that he can preach to his own people in their own language is of supreme importance. Giving this type of assistance to the national man will help to make our missionary efforts more self-supporting and more enduring. We appreciate one of our own preaching to us, and so do other peoples of the world. When we consider the work "our work," we approach it with greater care and will sacrifice more for it. This principle holds true in all cultures.

Christianity can flourish in any nation and culture, in any time or circumstance, if we will let it. When it is established through national preachers, it is far more likely to grow and blossom in the lives of the national people and not become an effort that is totally dependent upon American support.

After the Restoration Movement began in America, it did not take the early preachers long to realize that they had to teach young men to preach if the movement was really to grow. Thus very early in the history of the Restoration Movement schools were established. Wisdom suggested that route.

Christians should be grateful for every mission effort that is going on, such as campaigns, medical missions, and television presentations. However, we must not overlook the surpassing value of providing educational opportunities overseas that will assist a man in becoming capable of preaching effectively to his own people. This approach is absolutely vital to the ongoing success of the overall missionary work of the church.

Second, those who have researched missionary evangelism tell us that we need to make available biblical literature that provides an understanding of the Bible on the level of the people. Those whom the missionary is seeking to teach need their own copies of the Bible and assistance in understanding the Scriptures. They require guidance so they can grow quickly and accurately in their comprehension of the Bible. (See Acts 8:30, 31.)

When Tex Williams, the former director of World Bible School, was on Harding University's campus sometime ago, he spoke to students about mission work. As a guest lecturer, he told one of the mission classes that the greatest need of Africa is Christian literature. "Without this literature," he said, "they simply cannot become Christians and grow into Christian maturity as they should." There is possibly one exception to this principle. The exception would be places where there is the presence of well-grounded men of faith continually teaching and preaching. This exception obviously applies to only a few places around the world. Even then, biblical literature is needed to support the teaching done.

Let us all consider carefully these two obvious missionary needs. Our efforts must be geared to meeting them. Not to address them is to ignore the clear results of the research that has been done in mission evangelism.

ADDRESSING THESE NEEDS

An effort is currently being made to address both of these big missionary needs. It has been designated the Truth for Today World Mission School (TFTWMS). Started in 1990 as a work under the oversight of the Champions church of Christ in Houston, Texas, it has proven to be a wonderful way to combine three methods of evangelism and thus minister to these supreme needs.

HAVE YOU HEARD... ABOUT TRUTH FOR TODAY?

First, TFTWMS is a unique preacher school. An education in the Scriptures is mailed to the national preacher. The work started with 1,460 native preachers enrolled from 110 nations. Now literature is mailed to 37,000 people in 145 nations. These preachers were recommended to the school by World Bible School teachers, missionaries, campaigners, and the national preachers themselves. The school has enjoyed amazing growth.

Second, it is a printed preacher school. Every three months, the men enrolled receive the equivalent of 450 pages of expository studies on the Scriptures. It is believed that the expository type of study crosses cultures better than other types of study. The materials sent give a thorough treatment of the New Testament book or Old Testament book being studied. It is designed to keep the national preacher enrolled in the school until he receives a study of each of the New Testament and Old Testament books, as well as several important special studies.

Picture three normal-sized books that are 150 pages in length, and you have the equivalent of the amount of material that is sent to these men every three months. The entire curriculum calls for these men to receive books that are 150 pages in size, that cover the entire Bible, and that include special studies on leadership, building sermons and Bible lessons, and soul-winning.

Third, in addition to sending expository studies to these men, a flexible, on-site preacher school is sometimes used as a follow-up to the printed material. This on-site school is literally taken to where the men are. Preachers and teachers go into a country and study with the national preachers in that location for two or three weeks. Students are provided with food and a syllabus for the classes they attend. They stay at that location day and night for the entire length of the school. They thus enjoy fellowship with other preaching brethren and are given opportunities to ask questions and receive feedback on problems they are facing.

The printed preacher school and the on-site school answer the big need of giving the national man an opportunity to prepare himself to preach to his own people in their own language. Since this work is accomplished to some extent through the printed page, it also answers the need of providing Christian literature for these teachers and preachers who are in desperate need of it.

THE STRONG POINTS

This unique missionary effort has strong points that should be immediately recognized. First, it provides an education to national men inexpensively. Expository materials can be sent to each of these men every two months in a cost-efficient way. Money for missions is hard to find or raise; what missionary money we have should be used to the maximum. TFTWMS sends an education to hundreds of national men with a small amount of money.

Second, the thrust of this work is to educate national men in their own land. Bringing these men to the United States for an education is very expensive. Often, when the national man tastes of the blessings of America, he does not want to return to his land. It is almost essential that a way be found through which the national preacher can receive an education in his own country.

Third, this effort can reach out to hundreds of national men quickly. All of these men are in need of assistance now! How can we get it to them? This method is one of the most practical ways of immediately getting materials to them.

Fourth, it allows the national man to receive an education over a period of time. Because the education comes in the form of printed matter, they have access to the material for months and even years. These men need time to comprehend and assimilate the studies. The printed page offers them that opportunity. They can read and re-read it. They can easily store it. They can share it with others. It can be retained in their possession for as long as ten to fifteen years.

PICTURING THE EFFECTIVENESS

Picture 37,000 men (and thousands more as the work grows) in 145 nations of the world, going out to preach in their own languages to their own people. They are committed to Christ but have had little teaching upon which to build. Furthermore, these men will never have the opportunity to study in the United States to enable them to preach more accurately and faithfully. They have few books, if any. Picture yourself in this type of situation. What would you need?

Can you imagine how these men would be assisted if they received materials on every Old Testament and New Testament book? Can you imagine how encouraging it would be to them to be able to attend a two- to three-week preacher school in their community? Can you picture them in a school, taking several courses in Bible studies, having fellowship with other preachers, having opportunities to have their questions answered, and getting assistance regarding the problems they are facing? Can you not see how these opportunities would increase their effectiveness in leading souls to Christ and in edifying those who have become Christians?

HELPING THOSE WHO HAVE NOT HEARD

In order to help those who have never heard the gospel to become Christians, a special book was designed in 1998 by TFTWMS. It contains three hundred plus pages on how to become a Christian. The reader of the book is introduced to God, Christ, the Holy Spirit, the Bible, the earthly life of Jesus, the death, burial, and resurrection of Jesus, the establishment of the church, and how one can live for Christ today as a member of His church. Then, in the last two hundred pages of the book, there is a complete copy of the New Testament (NASB).

Thousands of these books have been sent to Africa, the Eastern European countries, India, Latin America, and other areas. The success rate has been very high—almost amazing. The book, 512 pages in length, can be printed and sent to someone in another country for $1.50. It is an attempt to bring together the very message that any Christian would want to provide for someone who has not heard the gospel.

In 2005 a ten-year plan was made to cover a large area of the earth each year with these books. Before printing, the book is culturally adapted for the specific area into which it is being sent and translated into the most prevalent languages of that area.

HOW CAN YOU HELP?

Your help is needed to maintain this missionary effort that has become one of the largest, most cost-effective and productive efforts. Here is a two-part challenge for every Christian:

First, would you challenge the church where you worship and with whom you work to give a one-time contribution to this work? Even a small contribution will go a long way in providing teaching materials and on-site training for these national preachers.

Second, could you give a one-time contribution to this work? This contribution, of course, would have to be above and beyond your regular contribution to the local congregation of which you are a part. We are not asking anyone to interrupt his commitment to the work of the local congregation. The church needs more works, not fewer works. This effort is designed to strengthen every missionary activity and does not seek to detract from any one of them.

You would be surprised how much can be done if we all do a little extra. No one person has a lot of light, but if we put our lights together, we can have a big light that will reach out into all of the world. Would you decide today to dig a little deeper and give a little extra for this wonderful method of world evangelization?

CONTRIBUTIONS NEEDED

Contributions should be made out to Truth for Today World Mission School and sent to 2209 Benton, Searcy, AR 72143. Will you assist us in providing study materials for national preachers? This work is under the oversight of the Champions church of Christ in Houston, Texas.

Eddie Cloer